THE UNITED AMATEUR

SEPTEMBER 1915

HOWARD P. LOVECRAFT
First Vice-President U. A. P. A.

MISCELLANEOUS WRITINGS

H. P. Lovecraft

Edited by S. T. Joshi

Arkham House Publishers, Inc.

EDITORIAL NOTE

The compilation of this volume has understandably been a much more complicated matter than that of the previous Arkham House corrected editions of Lovecraft's work, in that this is an original selection of Lovecraft's nonfictional writing. From the start I was guided by a prospective table of contents prepared many years ago by Jim Turner, and I have done little save augment this list. The very division of Lovecraft's essays into discrete categories is occasionally problematical. Most of his essays were written during his amateur period, and most emerged in the course of discussions or controversies in the amateur press; in this sense, nearly the whole of Lovecraft's nonfiction can be thought of as "amateur journalism," not merely the few essays that have been placed in the section of that title. In particular, those essays under the heading "Literary Criticism" are very largely concerned with the state of amateur literature, but they touch upon broader and more general literary issues in such a way that their segregation into a separate section may be justified.

It would be cumbrous, in a volume containing so many items, to speak in detail of the textual history of each of these works. I trust that the bibliography I have appended to this volume may be sufficient for this purpose: there I tabulate the manuscript sources (if any), first publication, and important subsequent printings of each work. It can be readily seen that manuscripts exist for very few of these pieces. In some cases (notably "The Professional Incubus") the first publication is in places so garbled that certain passages are hopelessly corrupt. In a few instances, such as "The Challenge from Beyond," there exist errata sheets or other handwritten corrections by Lovecraft. Further notes on the textual status of some of these pieces can be found in the introductions to each section.

Throughout my work on this volume I have received invaluable advice from Jim Turner, who deserves credit as a virtual coeditor. Several of my other colleagues—among them Donald R. Burleson, Scott Connors, M. Eileen McNamara, Steven J. Mariconda, Marc A. Michaud, Will Murray, and David E. Schultz—have lent assistance in various ways. I am grateful to them and to my other colleagues for the support and encouragement they have provided over the past twenty years.—S. T. J.

The editor of Arkham House wishes to thank the following people for their assistance in assembling the very rare photographs and other illustrations that appear in this volume: Barbara Alley, April Derleth, Theodore Grieder, S. T. Joshi, Glenn Lord, John Meehan, Sam Moskowitz, Mildred Ellen Orton, David Rajchel, and Daniel Graham of The Fossils.

LIBRARY OF CONGRESS CATALOGING-IN-PUBLICATION DATA
Lovecraft, H. P. (Howard Phillips), 1890–1937.
[Selections]
Miscellaneous writings / H. P. Lovecraft ; edited by S. T. Joshi. – 1st ed.
p. cm.
Includes bibliographical references.
ISBN 0-87054-168-4 (alk. paper)
I. Joshi, S. T., 1958– II. Title.
PS3523.O833A6 1995
813′.52–dc20 94-27323

Printed in the United States of America

CONTENTS

II. The Weird Fantasist

III. Mechanistic Materialist

IV. Literary Critic

V. Political Theorist

VI. Antiquarian Travels

VII. Amateur Journalist

VIII. Epistolarian

IX. Personal

INTRODUCTION

Many things have been said about H. P. Lovecraft and his work, but there is one very prominent feature of his writing that receives surprisingly little attention: its rhetorical skill. The term *rhetoric* has long been viewed askance as something a little bogus and meretricious, but its root meaning is simply the artful manipulation of words for purposes of persuasion. In the midst of this postmodern age where the barrenness of Hemingway and Sherwood Anderson has given way to the convoluted esoterism of Thomas Pynchon and the rich lyricism of Gore Vidal, there will perhaps be fewer complaints about Lovecraft's "adjectivitis" and a better appreciation of the density of style and structure that makes the best of his stories something akin to hypnotic incantations. Rhetoric is no doubt present in them, but more in the sense of an all-pervading atmosphere that lightly erases the real and substitutes the fantastic in its place; for rhetoric in its purer form, we need look no further than Lovecraft's many essays, which make up the bulk of this volume.

Lovecraft's earliest writing appears to have been poetry, but stories and essays followed shortly thereafter. Of these juvenile essays not many remain, and we have lost such immortal masterpieces as "Mythology for the Young" (1899) and "An Historical Account of Last Year's War with SPAIN" (1899). But masses of Lovecraft's juvenile scientific journals, notably *The Scientific Gazette* (1899–1904) and *The Rhode Island Journal of Astronomy* (1903–07), survive, and their publication in facsimile would provide much edification and amusement. Science was at the foundation of Lovecraft's entire nonfictional writing—perhaps even his literary work as a whole—for a strain of scientific logic and reasoning is evident even in his literary essays. Part of the problem with his poetry, indeed, is that much of it is similarly intellectual in essence, creating the impression of a rhymed essay. Perhaps Lovecraft thought he was following the eighteenth century in this; perhaps he not only agreed with Matthew Arnold's dictum that Dryden and Pope were "classics of our *prose*" but also found a virtue therein.

The first thing Lovecraft did when he joined amateur journalism in 1914 was to flood amateur papers with poetry and essays; fiction would follow only in 1917, and even then in a trickle until about 1920 or so. This means that for at least six years the bulk of Lovecraft's literary work took the form of verse or of prose nonfiction; and that nonfiction spanned the full spectrum of subject matter, from literary criticism to philosophy to politics to amateur affairs. The majority of Lovecraft's essays—and, hence, the majority of works included here—were written before 1925, and in all charity must be called apprentice work. Their prime function was in letting Lovecraft flex his literary muscles, hone his style, and find out by experimentation how best to say what he wanted to say. In the end he determined, wisely, that fiction not only would allow him the greatest creative scope but could even subsume much of the essence of his nonfiction: his philosophy of cosmicism found no more potent expression than in "At the Mountains of Madness"; his late political thought was best encapsulated in "The Shadow Out of Time"; it could even be said that he wrote no finer travel essays than "The Colour Out of Space" and "The Whisperer in Darkness."

If, then, we must concede that Lovecraft's essays are by and large not intrinsically interesting, they nevertheless form invaluable adjuncts to his fiction. They state what the fiction implies; they clarify what the fiction masks in a haze of imagery and symbolism. Unlike his stories, most of his essays were written for a specific purpose or a specific market—usually the amateur press. It is, in fact, unfortunate and even a little strange that he never attempted to market the best of his later essays to a wider audience: the earnest political tract "Some Repetitions on the Times" (1933) could have found a place in the *Atlantic Monthly* or *Harper's*, while with very slight modification "Cats and Dogs" (1926) would not have been out of place in *The New Yorker*. J. Vernon Shea recommended that Lovecraft abstract some of the elaborate philosophical, political, or literary arguments in his letters and send them to professional magazines; Lovecraft claimed to be struck by the ingenuity of the idea, but never followed it up. Perhaps he feared rejection, or felt that he could never hope to secure even a small foothold in the mainstream of American literature and thought; whatever the reason, Lovecraft's diffidence relegated him and his oftentimes incisive nonfictional work to a position of self-imposed marginality, where its influence extended only to a small band of devoted followers. Lovecraft was a giant in the incredibly tiny realms of amateur journalism and weird fiction, but that is small comfort.

Let us return to the matter of rhetoric. Lovecraft's influences in his nonfiction were as diverse as Cicero, Addison, Johnson, and Macaulay, but this list alone suggests Lovecraft's adherence to the grand, lush "Asianic" style of composition in contrast to the restrained "Attic" style of Thucydides, Caesar, and Swift. The rhetorical flourish is something Lovecraft never abandoned. He was very fond of the epigrammatic opening that purported to utter some broad truth about human beings and the cosmos: "Endless is the credulity of the human mind"; "It is a particular weakness of the modern American press, that it seems unable to use advantageously the language of the nation"; "Extreme literary radicalism is always a rather amusing thing." The rhetorical purpose of this device is clear: it piques the reader's interest, either because such a resounding opening is rather transparently perceived to be a highly idiosyncratic opinion being passed off as an axiom or because the grandeur of it seems far out of keeping with the subject at hand. It allows Lovecraft an entry into his discussion; occasionally, indeed, an entire paragraph is spent in generalization before the actual topic is broached.

It is also clear that Lovecraft later transferred this device to his stories, so that they too open ponderously: "Life is a hideous thing"; "From even the greatest of horrors irony is seldom absent"; "Mystery attracts mystery." The influence of Poe is cited here (recall his "Misery is manifold. The wretchedness of earth is multiform" from "Berenice," the obvious ancestor to "Life is a hideous thing"), but Poe himself derived it from the eighteenth-century essayists and from the eighteenth and nineteenth century's perceived need to counteract the "lies" of fiction by a suitable dose of moralistic philosophizing. Lovecraft's early tales follow this tradition: the narrative itself becomes, formally, a mere instantiation of the generalized "truth" uttered at the outset.

The reason why rhetoric plays so central a role in Lovecraft's essays is that so many of them are polemics. In some cases they are aimed at specific individuals ("In a Major Key," "A Reply to *The Lingerer*"); more often they address general issues on which Lovecraft wishes to take a definite stand, usually in violent opposition to prevailing opinion ("Idealism and Materialism—A Reflection"; "The Vers Libre Epidemic"). Lovecraft felt embattled from many directions: a materialist in an age that was inclining toward idealism and mysticism; a traditionalist in poetry when poets were abandoning meter and rhyme; a militarist at a time when the world wished above all things to avoid another world war. Even when his attitudes modified with the passage of time, Lovecraft remained at loggerheads with his era: it is amusing to see him, as a Decadent, attacking those lingering old-timers who still saw Tennyson or Browning as the pinnacles of art, when a few years previous he might have been of their number. It is as if Lovecraft consciously wished not to fit into his age: even as a supporter of FDR he departed from him in recommending a limitation rather than an extension of the vote. Lovecraft throve by opposition: all his essays have a certain hectoring undertone, so as to make sure that even the most sympathetic reader is properly convinced of the incontrovertible truth of Lovecraft's position.

It is for this same reason, too, that satire—frequently of a vicious, biting, even malicious sort—so heavily enters these essays. Things that threaten the stability of civilization must be battled with the strongest tools available. Free verse is particularly hard hit. Practitioners of it reject the intellectual "(an element which they cannot possess to any great degree)"; and Lovecraft's "utterances prior to the summer of 1891 [i.e., prior to the age of one] betray a marked kinship to the vers libre of today." That this latter remark is really of the nature of an unprovoked attack—coming as it does suddenly in the midst of an autobiographical essay—shows Lovecraft's willingness to lash out at his opponents at every turn. Many of his satiric salvos are so effective, of course, because they are supported on the whole by a very keen exercise of logic that can demolish an opponent's argument if the least area of vulnerability is presented. Occasionally it backfires; and Lovecraft's sober statement that Charles D. Isaacson's lenient views on racial prejudice "are too subjective to be impartial" could be a textbook case of Freudian "projection." But generally the satire hits home precisely because it serves as a sort of knockout blow after a merciless logical dissection of the opposing view. In many cases, of course, we are lacking the actual words of the opponent (as with the Mr. Wickenden who receives the bulk of Lovecraft's unwontedly mild retorts in *In Defence of Dagon*), but they can usually be inferred well enough. And it has to be admitted, too, that Lovecraft wins the argument so often and so easily because he rarely meets an intellect equal to or surpassing his own.

The best of Lovecraft's essays are, on the whole, his later ones—such exceptions as *In Defence of Dagon* or "A Confession of Unfaith" are too few to make a difference. And we have already suggested the reasons why Lovecraft's essay production declined in his later years: correspondence had largely taken over this function, as had his fiction itself. Several of his better travel essays are, in fact, letters either sent to a single correspondent or typed up to distribute to many associates, so as to save the trouble of explaining the same things to different recipients. But even in his later years the amateur world served as the forum for most of his essays—that is, where the essays had a forum at all. We have already remarked that some of his essays never seem to have been submitted either to amateur or to professional markets; we do not even know why some pieces, like the curious "Some Causes of Self-Immolation," were even written, since they seem to have met no one's eye but their creator's, achieving instant oblivion as soon as the ink was dry.

The essays in this volume comprise examples of every subject Lovecraft chose to discuss: metaphysics, ethics, aesthetics, weird fiction, literary criticism, politics, travel, amateur journalism, and autobiography. More detailed information on the selections can be found in the introductory notes to each section. In their totality they reveal the breadth of Lovecraft's intellectual curiosity and the gradual expansion of his intellectual horizon with the passage of time. It cannot be repeated too often that most of these essays were written during a period when Lovecraft was still laboring under serious (and largely self-imposed) handicaps: the handicaps of sequestration, bookishness, dogmatism, self-centeredness, racism, and general intolerance and inflexibility. Lovecraft would not want to be judged or remembered by the great majority of works included here. The few later pieces, from "Cats and Dogs" (1926) to "Some Current Motives and Practices" (1936), provide glimpses—but no more—of a Lovecraft who has at last opened his eyes to the world around him and sloughed off many of the prejudices and affectations that limited his vision. This is the picture we come upon in his later fiction and letters, and it is that picture that Lovecraft would wish us to remember. Lovecraft has suffered by his own celebrity, which impels the discovery and dissemination of any work, however crude, embarrassing, or simply inferior, that came from his pen; but that celebrity rests upon strong foundations—the genuine merit of his later writing, which every fair-minded reader and critic will use as the yardstick of his achievement. His peripheral and incidental work, with its occasional brilliance of rhetoric, logic, and wit, can only augment, never compromise, that achievement.

S. T. Joshi

I

DREAMS AND FANCIES

"In my dreams I found a little of the beauty I had vainly sought in life": this line from "Ex Oblivione" could well serve as an emblem of Lovecraft's entire fictional oeuvre. The hard life of poverty Lovecraft led allowed few pleasures save those of his dreams and fancies; and, as he states repeatedly in letters, those dreams were frequently, perhaps invariably, the focus or nucleus of his tales of fantasy and horror.

The stories in this section have no overall unity save that they comprise the remaining scraps of Lovecraft's fictional output not included in the four previous Arkham House editions of his work. They are necessarily heterogeneous, and few are as memorable as the best of his other work, but they each add a little increment to the total picture of Lovecraft the man and writer. Few other writers' marginalia provides as much interest as do these items.

Of Lovecraft's juvenile tales little need be said. In a letter to J. Vernon Shea (July 19–30, 1931) Lovecraft states that his mother saved these earliest examples of his fictional art (although his very first tale, "The Noble Eavesdropper," has perished); it would not, however, have been a great tragedy had this material also been consigned to oblivion along with many other of his early works. What strikes us about these stories is how inferior they are to the verse he was writing at this time: such early poems as "The Poem of Ulysses" reveal a startlingly assured grasp of complex meters and rhyme-schemes, whereas his stories could have been the scribbling of any seven- or ten-year-old. "The Mysterious Ship" (1902) has the distinction of being Lovecraft's earliest surviving typescript; in fact, he has arranged this clipped little thriller into a miniature book, complete with illustrated cover. "The Mystery of the Grave-Yard" (1898) is an unusually elaborate detective story that clearly betrays Lovecraft's early reading of boys' adventure stories and dime novels.

Lovecraft may have claimed that he preferred not to mix humor and horror, but an unusual number of his minor stories are purely comic—at least seven in this section can be so considered. They are surprisingly effective. "A Reminiscence of Dr. Samuel Johnson" (1917) completely dynamites Lovecraft's pretensions of being an aged and archaic gentleman—or, rather, shows that that pose was adopted with tongue firmly in cheek. Most of the "reminiscences" of Johnson and his associates are pretty obviously derived from Boswell's *Life of Johnson* (one exceedingly clever stroke is Lovecraft's quoting of the quatrain, "When the Duke of *Leeds* shall marry'd be," directly from Boswell and supplying his own adept "revision" of it), but the exquisitely eighteenth-century tone of the piece makes it one of Lovecraft's little masterpieces. "Old Bugs" (1919), written to discourage his friend Alfred Galpin from delving too deeply into the forbidden pleasures of alcohol, manages to parody its own moralism and so becomes less heavy-handed than it might otherwise have been.

"Sweet Ermengarde" is the oddest specimen in this section, and not only because we have no clue whatever as to the date or the occasion of its composition. That it is designed to parody the Horatio Alger–type story is clear enough; and the handwriting of the manuscript indicates that it was written probably before 1925, perhaps as early as 1919. It too is highly successful as farce, and even anticipates in a bizarre way Nathanael West's *A Cool Million* (1934).

"History of the *Necronomicon*" must really be classified as a story: in spite of its ponderously essayistic tone, it is clearly a hoax or a spoof—unless, of course, one believes in the reality of the *Necronomicon*. Lovecraft records that he wrote it so as to be consistent in his references to the various editions and translations of the *Necronomicon* in his later fiction; but one gets the impression, from its deadpan sobriety and understated wit, that Lovecraft simply had fun composing this *jeu d'esprit*. "Ibid" (1928) was a product of the correspondence between Lovecraft and Maurice W. Moe. Lovecraft was assisting Moe extensively in tutoring his students in literature and composition; but the parody of the schoolboy's belief that *Ibid.* is a real author is only on the surface, and the real subject of attack is the pomposity of academic scholarship. In this sense "Ibid" is more vital today than when it was written.

Late in life Lovecraft was encouraged by his youthful friend R. H. Barlow in many frivolous literary efforts. "The Battle That Ended the Century" and "Collapsing Cosmoses" are two examples, written on Lovecraft's visits to Barlow's Florida home in 1934 and 1935, respectively. Barlow was the real initiator of these pieces: most of the prose of the former is his, although all the parodies of colleagues' names (Frank Chimesleep Short for Frank Belknap Long) are Lovecraft's; and Barlow wrote the bulk of "Collapsing Cosmoses," even though the putative point of this spoof was for each collaborator to write every other paragraph or so. Many of the better jokes are Barlow's. A more serious collaborative effort is the round-robin tale "The Challenge from Beyond" (1935), of which only Lovecraft's portion is here included. Lovecraft's correspondence records the somewhat silly wrangling among the five authors (C. L. Moore, A. Merritt, Lovecraft, Robert E. Howard, and Frank Belknap Long) as to who would write what in which order, and it is evident that Lovecraft's is the one segment that actually gets the plot going so that it can be brought to some sort of conclusion.

Probably Lovecraft's four prose poems are the most artistically finished items in this section, and each of them is a potent little vignette. It is here that the dream aspect of Lovecraft's work comes to the fore: it is well known that "Nyarlathotep" not only was inspired by a dream but that its first full paragraph was written while Lovecraft was still half-asleep. Each of the prose poems emphasizes some cardinal tenet of Lovecraft's outlook: "Memory" underscores the transience of mankind, "Nyarlathotep" is an apocalyptic vision of the collapse of civilization, "Ex Oblivione" speaks of the bliss to be found in extinction, and "What the Moon Brings," with its chiseled prose, hints of the nightmarish transformation of the world when it passes from day to night. These prose poems make us long for Lovecraft's one authentic "lost" story, "Life and Death" (c. 1920), which—if its description in Lovecraft's commonplace book is any indication—is probably also a prose poem.

Dream—in this case, a single, incredibly long and detailed dream—is at the heart of "The Very Old Folk" (1927), Lovecraft's account of his great "Roman dream" in a letter to Donald Wandrei. This dream was written up in three different letters by Lovecraft—this one to Wandrei (apparently the earliest), one to Frank Belknap Long (used almost verbatim in Long's novel *The Horror from the Hills*), and one to Bernard Austin Dwyer (November 1927), the most detailed of the three. The extent of Lovecraft's unconscious absorption of his early readings in Roman history is certainly remarkable, and one wishes Lovecraft himself had written this dream-fragment into a finished story.

Lovecraft's discarded draft of "The Shadow Over Innsmouth" may be his second or even third attempt at the story, since he announces in several letters that he is using the plot as "laboratory experimentation" by writing it out successively in different styles. This surviving draft exists only because it is found on the verso of pages of the final draft. It can be readily seen that this draft is written in a more compressed manner than the final version: the one-paragraph introduction to the story proper here becomes five paragraphs in the completed text. Lovecraft complained that in his later years he was unable to write a *short* story, but this became problematical only in terms of marketing that awkward amalgam known as the short novel; Lovecraft's later conceptions were such that he required the expansiveness of this length to realize all the implications of the idea. One has difficulty imagining what Lovecraft's first, sixteen-page draft of "The Shadow Out of Time" could possibly have been like.

Lovecraft, dogged by self-doubt and wounded by rejections and the tampering of his work by editors, felt in his later years that he was further from doing what he wished to do in fiction than when he began. He could not know that his friends would take the effort to rescue his work when major publishers refused to do so, and that he would eventually attract a worldwide following through the widespread dissemination and translation of his work. But all that has come about, and Lovecraft now occupies a small but unassailable niche in world literature. His fiction is known, but his other work—essays, letters, poetry—is less so, and only when the whole of his literary output is grasped can we recognize the greatness of the man whose every word can hold some meaning for us.

THE LITTLE GLASS BOTTLE

"Heave to, there's something floating to the leeward" the speaker was a short stockily built man whose name was William Jones. he was the captain of a small cat boat in which he & a party of men were sailing at the time the story opens.

"Aye aye sir" answered John Towers & the boat was brought to a stand still Captain Jones reached out his hand for the object which he now discerned to be a glass bottle "Nothing but a rum flask that the men on a passing boat threw over" he said but from an impulse of curiosity he reached out for it. it was a rum flask & he was about to throw it away when he noticed a piece of paper in it. He pulled it out & on it read the following

Jan 1 1864
I am John Jones who writes this letter my ship is fast sinking with a treasure on board I am where it is marked * on the enclosed chart

Captain Jones turned the sheet over & the other side was a chart

on the edge were written these words

dotted lines represent course we took

"Towers" Said Capt. Jones exitedly "read this" Towers did as he was directed "I think it would pay to go" said Capt. Jones "do you"? "Just as you say" replied Towers. "We'll charter a schooner this very day" said the exited captain "All right" said Towers so they hired a boat and started off govnd by the dotted lines of they chart in 4 weeks the reached the place where directed & the divers went down and came up with an iron bottle they found in it the following lines scribbled on a piece of brown paper

Dec 3 1880
Dear Searcher excuse me for the practical joke I have played on you but it serves you right to find nothing for your foolish act—

"Well it does" said Capt Jones "go on"

However I will defray your expenses to & from the place you found your bottle I think it will be $25.0.00 so that amount you will find in an Iron box I know where you found the bottle because I put this bottle here & the iron box & then found a good place to put the second bottle hoping the enclosed money will defray your expenses some I close—Anonymus"

"I'd like to kick his head off" said Capt Jones "Here diver go & get the $25.0.00 in a minute the diver came up bearing an iron box inside it was found $25.0.00 It defrayed their expenses but I hardly think that they will ever go to a mysterious place as directed by a mysterious bottle.

THE SECRET CAVE

or John Lees adventure

"Now be good children" Said Mrs. Lee "While I am away & dont get into mischief". Mr. & Mrs. Lee were going off for the day & To leave The Two children John 10 yrs old & Alice 2 yrs old "Yes" replied John

As Soon as The Elder Lees were away the younger Lees went down cellar & began to rummage among the rubbish little alice leaned against the wall watching John. As John was making a boat of barrel staves the Little girl gave a piercing cry as the bricks behind her crumbled away he rushed up to her & Lifted her out screaming loudly as soon as her screams subsided she said "the wall went away" John went up & saw that there was a passage he said to the little girl "lets come & see what this is" "Yes" she said the entered the place they could stand up it the passage was farther than they could see they John went back upstairs & went to the kitchen drawer & got 2 candles & some matches & then they went back to the cellar passage. the two once more entered there was plastering on the walls ceiling & floor nothing was visible but a box this was for a seat nevertheless they examined it & found it to contain nothing the walked on farther & pretty soon the plastering left off & they were in a cave Little alice was frightened at first but at her brothers assurance that it was "all right" she allayed her fears. soon they came to a small box which John took up & carried within pretty soon they came on a *boat* in it were two oars he dragged it with difficulty along with him soon they found the passage came to an abrupt stop he pulled the obstacle away & to his dismay water rushed in in torrents John was an expert swimmer & long breathede he had Just taken a breath so he tried to rise but with the box & his sister he found it quite impossible then he caught sight of the boat rising he grasped it – – – – – –

The next he knew he was on the surface clinging tightly to the body of his sister & the mysterious box he could not imagine how the water got in but a new peril menaced them if the water continued rising it would rise to the top suddenly a thought presented itself. he could shut off the water he speedily did this & lifting the now lifeless body of his sister into the boat he himself climed in & sailed down the passage it was gruesome & uncanny absolutely dark his candle being put out by the flood & a dead body lying near he did not gaze about him but rowed for his life when he did look up he was floating in his own cellar he quickly rushed up stairs with the body, to find his parents had come home He told them the story

* * * * *

The funeral of alice occupied so much time that John quite forgot about the box—but when they *did* open it they found it to be a *solid gold* chunk worth about $10,000 enough to pay for any thing but the death of his sister.

End

THE MYSTERY OF THE GRAVE-YARD

or "A Dead Man's Revenge"

A Detective Story,
by H. P. Lovecraft

Chapter I
The Burns's Tomb.

It was noon in the Little village of Mainville, and a sorrowful group of people were standing around the Burns's Tomb. Joseph Burns was dead. (when dying, he had given the following strange orders:—"Before you put my body in the tomb, drop this ball onto the floor, at a spot marked "A"." he then handed a small golden ball to the rector.) The people greatly regretted his death. After The funeral services were finished, Mr Dobson (the rector) said, "My friends, I will now gratify the last wishes of the deceased. So saying, he descended into the tomb. (to lay the ball on the spot marked "A") Soon the funeral party Began to be impatient, and after a time Mr. Cha's. Greene (the Lawyer) descended to make a search. Soon he came up with a frightened face, and said, "Mr Dobson is *not there*"!

Chapter II
Mysterious Mr. Bell.

It was 3.10 o'clock in ye afternoone whenne The door bell of the Dobson mansion rang loudly, and the servant on going to the door, found an elderly man, with black hair, and side whiskers. He asked to see Miss Dobson. Upon arriving in her presence he said, "Miss Dobson, I know where your father is, and for £10,000 I will restore him.

My name is Mr. Bell." "Mr Bell," said Miss Dobson, "will you excuse me from the room a moment?" "Certainly". replied Mr Bell. In a short time she returned, and said, "Mr. Bell, I understand you. You have abducted my father, and hold him for a ransom"

Chapter III
At The Police Station.

It was 3.20 o'clock in the afternoon when the telephone bell at the North End Police Station rang furiously, and Gibson, (the telephone Man) Inquired what was the matter,

"Have found out about fathers dissapearance"! a womans voice said. "Im Miss Dobson, and father has been abducted, "Send King John"! King John was a famous western detective. Just then a man rushed in, and shouted, "Oh! Terrors! Come To the Graveyard!"

Chapter IV
The West window.

Now let us return to the Dobson Mansion. Mr Bell was rather taken aback by Miss Dobson's plain speaking, but when he recovered his speech he said, "Don't put it quite so plain, Miss Dobson, for I–" He was interrupted by the entrance of King John, who with a brace of revolvers in his hands, barred all egress by the doorway. But quicker than thought Bell sprang to a west window,–and jumped.

Chapter V
The Secret of The grave.

Now let us return to the station house. After the exited visitor had calmed somewhat, he could tell his story straighter. He had seen three men in the graveyard shouting "Bell! Bell! where are you old man!?" and acting very suspiciously. He then followed them, and *they entered The Burns's Tomb!* He then followed them in and they touched a spring at a point marked "A" and then Dissapeared". "I wish king John were here", Said Gibson, "What's your name,"? "John Spratt". replied the visitor.

Chapter VI
The chase for Bell.

Now let us return To the Dobson Mansion again:–King John was utterly confounded at the Sudden movement of Bell, but when he recovered from his surprise, his first thought was of chase. Accordingly, he started in pursuit of the abductor. He tracked him down to the R. R. Station and found to his dismay that he had taken the train for Kent, a large city toward the south, and between which and Mainville there existed no telegraph or telephone. The train had Just Started!

Chapter VII
The Negro Hackman.

The Kent train started at 10.35, and about 10.36 an exited, dusty, and tired man* rushed into the Mainville hack. office and said to a negro hackman who was standing by the door—"If you can take me to Kent in 15 minutes I will give you a dollar". "I doan' see how I'm ter git there", said the negro "I hab'n't got a decent pair of hosses an' I hab—" "Two Dollars"! Shouted The Traveller, "all right" said the Hackman.

*King John.

Chapter VIII (*Long.*)
Bells Surprise.

It was 11 o'clock at Kent, all of the stores were closed but one, a dingy, dirty, little shop, down at the west end. It lay between Kent Harbour, & the Kent & Mainville R. R. In the Front room a shabbily dressed person of doubtful age was conversing with a middle aged woman with gray haire, "I have agreed to do the job, Lindy," he said, "Bell will arrive at 11.30 and the carraige is ready to take him down to the wharf, where a ship for Africa sails to-nighte".

"But If King John were to come?" queried "Lindy"

"Then we'd get nabbed, an' Bell would be hung" Replied The man.

Just then a rap sounded at the door "Are you Bell"? inquired Lindy "Yes" was the response, "And I caught the 10.35 and King John got Left, so we are all right". At 11.40 the party reached The Landing, and saw a ship Loom up in the darkness. "The Kehdive" "of Africa" was painted on the hull, and Just as they were to step on board, a man stepped forward in the darkness and said "John Bell, I arrest you in the Queen's name"!

It was King John.

Chapter IX
The Trial.

The daye of The Trial had arrived, and a crowd of people had gathered around the Little grove, (which served for a court house in summer) To hear the trial of John Bell on the charge of kid-napping.

"Mr Bell," said the judge "what is the secret of the Burns's tomb"

"I well tell you this much" said Bell, "If you go into the tomb and touch a certain spot marked "A" you will find out"

"Now where is Mr Dobson"? queried the judge, "Here"! said a voice behind them, and The *figure of Mr Dobson HIMSELF* loomed up in the doorway.

"How did you get here"!&c was chorused. "'Tis a long story," said Dobson.

Chapter X
Dobson's Story.

"When I went down into the tomb," Said Dobson, "Everything was darkness, I could see nothing. but Finally I discerned the letter "A" printed in white on the onyx floor, I dropped the ball on the Letter, and immediately a trap-door opened and a man sprang up. It was this man, here," (he said (pointing at Bell, who stood Trembling on the prisoner's docke) "and he pulled me down into a brilliantly lighted, and palatial apartment where I have Lived until to-day. One day a young man rushed in and exclaimed "The secret Is revealed!" and was gone. He did not see me. Once Bell left his key behind, and I took the impression in wax, and the next day was spent in filing keys to fit the Lock. The next day my key fitted. and the next day (which is to-day) I escaped."

Chapter XI
The Mystery unveiled.

"Why did the late J. Burns, ask you to put the ball there"? (at "A"?) queried the Judge? "To get me into trouble" replied Dobson "He, and Francis Burns, (his brother) have plotted against me for years, and I knew not, in what way they would harm me". "Sieze Francis Burns"! yelled the Judge.

Chapter XII
Conclusion.

Francis Burns, and John Bell, were sent to prison for life. Mr Dobson was cordially welcomed by his daughter, who, by the way had become Mrs King John. "Lindy" and her accomplice were sent to Newgate for 30 days as aidors and abbettors of a criminal escape.

The End.

Price 25¢

THE MYSTERIOVS SHIP

BY
HOWARD PHILLIPS LOVECRAFT.

THE ROYAL PRESS.
1902.

Chapter 1.

In the spring of 1847, the little village of Ruralville was thrown into a state of exitement by the arrival of a strange brig in the harbour. It carried no flag, & everything about it was such as would exite suspicion. It had no name. Its captain was named Manuel Ruello. The exitement increased however when John Griggs dissapeared from his home. This was Oct. 4. on Oct. 5 the brig was gone.

Chapter 2.

The brig, in leaving, was met by a U.S. Frigate and a sharp fight ensued. When over, they* missed a man. named Henry Johns.

*(The Frigate.)

Chapter 3.

The brig continued its course in the direction of Madagascar, upon its arrival, The natives fled in all directions. When they came together on the other side of the island, one was missing. His name was Dahabea.

Chapter 4.

At length it was decided that something must be done. A reward of £5,000 was offered for the capture of Manuel Ruello., When startling news came, a nameless brig was wrecked on the Florida Keys.

Chapter 5.

A ship was sent to Florida, and the mystery was solved. In the exitement of the fight they would launch a sub-marine boat and take what they wanted. there it lay, tranquilly rocking on the waters of the Atlantic when someone called out "John Brown has dissapeared." And sure enough John Brown was gone.

Chapter 6.

The finding of the sub-marine boat, and the dissapearance of John Brown, caused renewed exitement amongst the people, when a new discovery was made. In transcribing this discovery it is necessary to relate a geographical fact. At the N. Pole there exists a vast continent composed of volcanic soil, a portion of which is open to explorers. It is called "No-Mans Land."

Chapter 7.

In the extreme southern part of No-Mans Land, there was found a hvt, and several other signs of human habitation. they promptly entered, and, chained to the floor, lay Griggs, Johns, & Dahabea. They, upon arriving in London, separated, Griggs going to Ruralville, Johns to the Frigate, & Dahabea to Madagascar.

Chapter 8.

But the mystery of John Brown was still unsolved, so they kept strict watch over the port at No-Mans Land, and when the sub-marine boat arrived, and the pirates, one by one, and headed by Manuel Ruello, left the ship, they were met by a rapid fire. After the fight brown was recovered.

Chapter 9.

Griggs was royally recieved at Ruralville, & a dinner was given in honour of Henry Johns, Dahabea was made King of Madagascar., & Brown was made Captain of his ship.

THE END.

A REMINISCENCE OF DR. SAMUEL JOHNSON

The Privilege of Reminiscence, however rambling or tiresome, is one generally allow'd to the very aged; indeed, 'tis frequently by means of such Recollections that the obscure occurrences of History, and the lesser Anecdotes of the Great, are transmitted to Posterity.

Tho' many of my readers have at times observ'd and remark'd a Sort of antique Flow in my Stile of Writing, it hath pleased me to pass amongst the Members of this Generation as a young Man, giving out the Fiction that I was born in 1890, in *America.* I am now, however, resolv'd to unburthen myself of a Secret which I have hitherto kept thro' Dread of Incredulity; and to impart to the Publick a true knowledge of my long years, in order to gratifie their taste for authentick Information of an Age with whose famous Personages I was on familiar Terms. Be it then known that I was born on the family Estate in *Devonshire,* of the 10th day of August, 1690 (or in the new *Gregorian* Stile of Reckoning, the 20th of August), being therefore now in my 228th year. Coming early to *London,* I saw as a Child many of the celebrated Men of King *William's* Reign, including the lamented Mr. *Dryden,* who sat much at the Tables of *Will's* Coffee-House. With Mr. *Addison* and Dr. *Swift* I later became very well acquainted, and was an even more familiar Friend to Mr. *Pope,* whom I knew and respected till the Day of his Death. But since it is of my more recent Associate, the late Dr. *Johnson,* that I am at this time desir'd to write; I will pass over my Youth for the present.

I had first Knowledge of the Doctor in May of the year 1738, tho' I did not at that Time meet him. Mr. *Pope* had just compleated his Epilogue to his Satires (the Piece beginning: "Not twice a Twelvemonth you appear in Print."), and had arrang'd for its Publication. On the very Day it appear'd, there was also publish'd a Satire in Imitation of *Juvenal*, intitul'd "*London*", by the then unknown *Johnson;* and this so struck the Town, that many Gentlemen of Taste declared, it was the Work of a greater Poet than Mr. *Pope*. Notwithstanding what some Detractors have said of Mr. *Pope's* petty Jealousy, he gave the Verses of his new Rival no small Praise; and having learnt thro' Mr. *Richardson* who the Poet was, told me, 'that Mr. *Johnson* wou'd soon be *deterré*'.

I had no personal Acquaintance with the Doctor till 1763, when I was presented to him at the *Mitre* Tavern by Mr. *James Boswell*, a young *Scotchman* of excellent Family and great Learning, but small Wit, whose metrical Effusions I had sometimes revis'd.

Dr. *Johnson*, as I beheld him, was a full, pursy Man, very ill drest, and of slovenly Aspect. I recall him to have worn a bushy Bob-Wig, untyed and without Powder, and much too small for his Head. His cloaths were of rusty brown, much wrinkled, and with more than one Button missing. His Face, too full to be handsom, was likewise marred by the Effects of some scrofulous Disorder; and his Head was continually rolling about in a sort of convulsive way. Of this Infirmity, indeed, I had known before; having heard of it from Mr. *Pope*, who took the Trouble to make particular Inquiries.

Being nearly seventy-three, full nineteen Years older than Dr. *Johnson* (I say Doctor, tho' his Degree came not till two Years afterward), I naturally expected him to have some Regard for my Age; and was therefore not in that Fear of him, which others confess'd. On my asking him what he thought of my favourable Notice of his Dictionary in *The Londoner*, my periodical Paper, he said: Sir, I possess no Recollection of having perus'd your Paper, and have not a great Interest in the Opinions of the less thoughtful Part of Mankind." Being more than a little piqued at the Incivility of one whose Celebrity made me solicitous of his Approbation, I ventur'd to retaliate in kind, and told him, I was surpris'd that a Man of Sense shou'd judge the Thoughtfulness of one whose Productions he admitted never having read. "Why, Sir," reply'd *Johnson*, "I do not require to become familiar with a Man's Writings in order to estimate the Superficiality of his Attainments, when he plainly shews it by his Eagerness to mention his own Productions in the first Question he puts to me." Having thus become Friends, we convers'd on many Matters. When, to agree with him, I said I was distrustful of the Authenticity of *Ossian's* Poems, Mr. Johnson said: "That, Sir, does not do your Understanding particular Credit; for what all the Town is sensible of, is no great Discovery for a *Grub-Street* Critick to make. You might as well say, you have a strong Suspicion that *Milton* wrote *Paradise Lost!*"

Frontispiece and title page to a juvenile astronomy publication by Lovecraft

Plate I – Frontispiece

Jupiter, as seen near Opposition

THE

ANNUAL REPORT
ON THE
SCIENCE OF ASTRONOMY
1903

–⟨BY H. P. LOVECRAFT⟩–

PROVIDENCE;
1904

AN 1904

I thereafter saw *Johnson* very frequently, most often at Meetings of THE LITERARY CLUB, which was founded the next Year by the Doctor, together with Mr. *Burke,* the parliamentary Orator, Mr. *Beauclerk,* a Gentleman of Fashion, Mr. *Langton,* a pious Man and Captain of Militia, Sir J. *Reynolds,* the widely known Painter, Dr. *Goldsmith,* the prose and poetick Writer, Dr. *Nugent,* father-in-law to Mr. *Burke,* Sir *John Hawkins,* Mr. *Anthony Chamier,* and my self. We assembled generally at seven o'clock of an Evening, once a Week, at the *Turk's-Head,* in *Gerrard-Street, Soho,* till that Tavern was sold and made into a private Dwelling; after which Event we mov'd our Gatherings successively to *Prince's* in *Sackville-Street, Le Tellier's* in *Dover-Street,* and *Parsloe's* and *The Thatched House* in *St. James's-Street.* In these Meetings we preserv'd a remarkable Degree of Amity and Tranquillity, which contrasts very favourably with some of the Dissensions and Disruptions I observe in the literary and amateur Press Associations of today. This Tranquillity was the more remarkable, because we had amongst us Gentlemen of very opposed Opinions. Dr. *Johnson* and I, as well as many others, were high Tories; whilst Mr. *Burke* was a *Whig,* and against the *American* War, many of his Speeches on that Subject having been widely publish'd. The least congenial Member was one of the Founders, Sir *John Hawkins,* who hath since written many misrepresentations of our Society. Sir *John,* an eccentrick Fellow, once declin'd to pay his part of the Reckoning for Supper, because 'twas his Custom at Home to eat no Supper. Later he insulted Mr. *Burke* in so intolerable a Manner, that we all took Pains to shew our Disapproval; after which Incident he came no more to our Meetings. However, he never openly fell out with the Doctor, and was the Executor of his Will; tho' Mr. *Boswell* and others have Reason to question the genuineness of his Attachment. Other and later Members of the CLUB were Mr. *David Garrick,* the Actor and early Friend of Dr. *Johnson,* Messieurs *Tho.* and *Jos. Warton,* Dr. *Adam Smith,* Dr. *Percy,* Author of the *Reliques,* Mr. *Edw. Gibbon,* the Historian, Dr. *Burney,* the Musician, Mr. *Malone,* the Critick, and Mr. *Boswell.* Mr. *Garrick* obtain'd Admittance only with Difficulty; for the Doctor, notwithstanding his great Friendship, was for ever affecting to decry the Stage and all Things connected with it. *Johnson,* indeed, had a most singular Habit of speaking for *Davy* when others were against him, and of arguing against him, when others were for him. I have no Doubt that he sincerely lov'd Mr. *Garrick,* for he never alluded to him as he did to *Foote,* who was a very coarse Fellow despite his comick Genius. Mr. *Gibbon* was none too well lik'd, for he had an odious sneering Way which offended even those of us who most admir'd his historical Productions. Mr. *Goldsmith,* a little Man very vain of his Dress and very deficient in Brillian-

One of the 1936 "Shadow Over Innsmouth" drawings by Frank Utpatel *(see p. 65)*

cy of Conversation, was my particular Favourite; since I was equally unable to shine in the Discourse. He was vastly jealous of Dr. *Johnson,* tho' none the less liking and respecting him. I remember that once a Foreigner, a *German,* I think, was in our Company; and that whilst *Goldsmith* was speaking, he observ'd the Doctor preparing to utter something. Unconsciously looking upon *Goldsmith* as a meer Encumbrance when compar'd to the greater Man, the Foreigner bluntly interrupted him and incurr'd his lasting Hostility by crying, "Hush, Toctor *Shonson* iss going to speak!"

In this luminous Company I was tolerated more because of my Years than for my Wit or Learning; being no Match at all for the rest. My Friendship for the celebrated Monsieur *Voltaire* was ever a Cause of Annoyance to the Doctor; who was deeply orthodox, and who us'd to say of the *French* Philosopher: "Vir est acerrimi Ingenii et paucarum Literarum."

Mr. *Boswell,* a little teazing Fellow whom I had known for some Time previously, us'd to make Sport of my aukward Manners and old-fashion'd Wig and Cloaths. Once coming in a little the worse for Wine (to which he was addicted) he endeavour'd to lampoon me by means of an Impromptu in verse, writ on the Surface of the Table; but lacking the Aid he usually had in his Composition, he made a bad grammatical Blunder. I told him, he shou'd not try to pasquinade the Source of his Poesy. At another Time *Bozzy* (as we us'd to call him) complain'd of my Harshness toward new Writers in the Articles I prepar'd for *The Monthly Review.* He said, I push'd every Aspirant off the Slopes of Parnassus. "Sir," I reply'd, "you are mistaken. They who lose their Hold do so from their own Want of Strength; but desiring to conceal their Weakness, they attribute the Absence of Success to the first Critick that mentions them." I am glad to recall that Dr. *Johnson* upheld me in this Matter.

Dr. *Johnson* was second to no Man in the Pains he took to revise the bad Verses of others; indeed, 'tis said that in the book of poor blind old Mrs. Williams, there are scarce two lines which are not the Doctor's. At one Time *Johnson* recited to me some lines by a Servant to the Duke of *Leeds,* which had so amus'd him, that he had got them by Heart. They are on the Duke's Wedding, and so much resemble in Quality the Work of other and more recent poetick Dunces, that I cannot forbear copying them:

"When the Duke of *Leeds* shall marry'd be
To a fine young Lady of high Quality
How happy will that Gentlewoman be
In his Grace of *Leeds'* good Company."

I ask'd the Doctor, if he had ever try'd making Sense of this Piece; and upon his saying he had not, I amus'd myself with the following Amendment of it:

When Gallant LEEDS auspiciously shall wed
The virtuous Fair, of antient Lineage bred,
How must the Maid rejoice with conscious Pride
To win so great an Husband to her Side!

On shewing this to Dr. *Johnson,* he said, "Sir, you have straightened out the Feet, but you have put neither Wit nor Poetry into the Lines."

It wou'd afford me Gratification to tell more of my Experiences with Dr. *Johnson* and his circle of Wits; but I am an old Man, and easily fatigued. I seem to ramble along without much Logick or Continuity when I endeavour to recall the Past; and fear I light upon but few Incidents which others have not before discuss'd. Shou'd my present Recollections meet with Favour, I might later set down some further Anecdotes of old Times of which I am the only Survivor. I recall many things of *Sam Johnson* and his Club, having kept up my Membership in the Latter long after the Doctor's Death, at which I sincerely mourn'd. I remember how *John Burgoyne,* Esq., the General, whose Dramatick and Poetical Works were printed after his Death, was black-balled by three Votes; probably because of his unfortunate Defeat in the *American* War, at *Saratoga.* Poor *John!* His Son fared better, I think, and was made a Baronet. But I am very tired. I am old, very old, and it is Time for my Afternoon Nap.

OLD BUGS

An Extemporaneous Sob Story

by Marcus Lollius, Proconsul of Gaul

Sheehan's Pool Room, which adorns one of the lesser alleys in the heart of Chicago's stockyard district, is not a nice place. Its air, freighted with a thousand odours such as Coleridge may have found at Cologne, too seldom knows the purifying rays of the sun; but fights for space with the acrid fumes of unnumbered cheap cigars and cigarettes which dangle from the coarse lips of unnumbered human animals that haunt the place day and night. But the popularity of Sheehan's remains unimpaired; and for this there is a reason—a reason obvious to anyone who will take the trouble to analyse the mixed stenches prevailing there. Over and above the fumes and sickening closeness rises an aroma once familiar throughout the land, but now happily banished to the back streets of life by the edict of a benevolent government—the aroma of strong, wicked whiskey—a precious kind of forbidden fruit indeed in this year of grace 1950.

Sheehan's is the acknowledged centre to Chicago's subterranean traffic in liquor and narcotics, and as such has a certain dignity which extends even to the unkempt attachés of the place; but there was until lately one who lay outside the pale of that dignity—one who shared the squalor and filth, but not the importance, of Sheehan's. He was called "Old Bugs", and was the most disreputable object in a disreputable environment. What he had once been, many tried to guess; for his language and mode of utterance when intoxicated to a certain degree were such as to excite wonderment; but what he *was*, presented less difficulty—for "Old Bugs", in superlative degree, epitomised the pathetic species known as the "bum" or the "down-and-outer". Whence he had come, no one could tell. One night he had burst wildly into Sheehan's, foaming at the mouth and screaming for whiskey and hasheesh; and having been supplied in exchange for a promise to perform odd jobs, had hung about ever since, mopping floors, cleaning cuspidors and glasses, and attending to an hundred similar menial duties in exchange for the drink and drugs which were necessary to keep him alive and sane.

He talked but little, and usually in the common jargon of the underworld; but occasionally, when inflamed by an unusually generous dose of crude whiskey, would burst forth into strings of incomprehensible polysyllables and snatches of sonorous prose and verse which led certain habitués to conjecture that he had seen better days. One steady patron—a bank defaulter under cover—came to converse with him quite regularly, and from the tone of his discourse ventured the opinion that he had been a writer or professor in his day. But the only tangible clue to Old Bugs' past was a faded photograph which he constantly carried about with him—the photograph of a young woman of noble and beautiful features. This he would sometimes draw from his tattered pocket, carefully unwrap from its covering of tissue paper, and gaze upon for hours with an expression of ineffable sadness and tenderness. It was not the portrait of one whom an underworld denizen would be likely to know, but of a lady of breeding and quality, garbed in the quaint attire of thirty years before. Old Bugs himself seemed also to belong to the past, for his nondescript clothing bore every hallmark of antiquity. He was a man of immense height, probably more than six feet, though his stooping shoulders sometimes belied this fact. His hair, a dirty white and falling out in patches, was never combed; and over his lean face grew a mangy stubble of coarse beard which seemed always to remain at the bristling stage—never shaven—yet never long enough to form a respectable set of whiskers. His features had perhaps been noble once, but were now seamed with the ghastly effects of terrible dissipation. At one time—probably in middle life—he had evidently been grossly fat; but now he was horribly lean, the purple flesh hanging in loose pouches under his bleary eyes and upon his cheeks. Altogether, Old Bugs was not pleasing to look upon.

The disposition of Old Bugs was as odd as his aspect. Ordinarily he was true to the derelict type—ready to do anything for a nickel or a dose of whiskey or hasheesh—but at rare intervals he shewed the traits which earned him his name. Then he would try to straighten up, and a certain fire would creep into the sunken eyes. His demeanour would assume an unwonted grace and even dignity; and the sodden creatures around him would sense something of superiority—something which made them less ready to give the usual kicks and cuffs to the poor butt and drudge. At these times he would shew a sardonic humour and make remarks which the folk of Sheehan's deemed foolish and irrational. But the spells would soon pass, and once more Old Bugs would resume his eternal floor-scrubbing and cuspidor-cleaning. But for one thing Old Bugs would have been an ideal slave to the establishment—and that one thing was his conduct when young men were introduced for their first drink. The old man would then rise from the floor in anger and excitement, muttering threats and warnings, and seeking to dissuade the novices from embarking upon their course of "seeing life as it is." He would sputter and fume, exploding into sesquipedalian admonitions and strange oaths, and animated by a frightful earnestness which brought a shudder to more than one drug-racked mind in the crowded room. But after a time his alcohol-enfeebled brain would wander from the subject, and with a foolish grin he would turn once more to his mop or cleaning-rag.

I do not think that many of Sheehan's regular patrons will ever forget the day that young Alfred Trever came. He was rather a "find"—a rich and high-spirited youth who would "go the limit" in anything he undertook—at least, that was the verdict of Pete Schultz, Sheehan's "runner", who had come across the boy at Lawrence College, in the small town of Appleton, Wisconsin. Trever was the son of prominent parents in Appleton. His father, Karl Trever, was an attorney and citizen of distinction, whilst his mother had made an enviable reputation as a poetess under her maiden name of Eleanor Wing. Alfred was himself a scholar and poet of distinction, though cursed with a certain childish irresponsibility which made him an ideal prey for Sheehan's runner. He was blond, handsome, and spoiled; vivacious and eager to taste the several forms of dissipation about which he had read and heard. At Lawrence he had been prominent in the mock-fraternity of "Tappa Tappa Keg", where he was the wildest and merriest of the wild and merry young roysterers; but this immature, collegiate frivolity did not satisfy him. He knew deeper vices through books, and he now longed to know them at first hand. Perhaps this tendency toward wildness had been stimulated somewhat by the repression to which he had been subjected at home; for Mrs. Trever had particular reason for training her only child with rigid severity. She had, in her own youth, been deeply and permanently impressed with the horror of dissipation by the case of one to whom she had for a time been engaged.

Young Galpin, the fiancé in question, had been one of Appleton's most remarkable sons. Attaining distinction as a boy through his wonderful mentality, he won vast fame at the University of Wisconsin, and at the age of twenty-three returned to Appleton to take up a professorship at Lawrence and to slip a diamond upon the finger of Appleton's fairest and most brilliant daughter. For a season all went happily, till without warning the storm burst. Evil habits, dating from a first drink taken years before in woodland seclusion, made themselves manifest in the young professor; and only by a hurried resignation did he escape a nasty prosecution for injury to the habits and morals of the pupils under his charge. His engagement broken, Galpin moved east to begin life anew; but before long, Appletonians heard of his dismissal in disgrace from New York University, where he had obtained an instructorship in English. Galpin now devoted his time to the library and lecture platform, preparing volumes and speeches on various subjects connected with *belles lettres,* and always shewing a genius so remarkable that it seemed as if the public must sometime pardon him for his past mistakes. His impassioned lectures in defence of Villon, Poe, Verlaine, and Oscar Wilde were applied to himself as well, and in the short Indian summer of his glory there was talk of a renewed engagement at a certain cultured home on Park Avenue. But then the blow fell. A final disgrace, compared to which the others had been as nothing, shattered the illusions of those who had come to believe in Galpin's reform; and the young man abandoned his name and disappeared from public view. Rumour now and then associated him with a certain "Consul Hasting" whose work for the stage and for motion-picture companies attracted a certain degree of attention because of its scholarly breadth and depth; but Hasting soon disappeared from the public eye, and Galpin became only a name for parents to quote in warning accents. Eleanor Wing soon celebrated her marriage to Karl Trever, a rising young lawyer, and of her former admirer retained only enough memory to dictate the naming of her only son, and the moral guidance of that handsome and headstrong youth. Now, in spite of all that guidance, Alfred Trever was at Sheehan's and about to take his first drink.

"Boss," cried Schultz, as he entered the vile-smelling room with his young victim, "meet my friend Al Trever, bes' li'l' sport up at Lawrence—thas' 'n Appleton, Wis., y' know. Some swell guy, too—'s father's a big corp'ration lawyer up in his burg, 'n' 's mother's some lit'ry genius. He wants to see life as she is—wants to know what the real lightnin' juice tastes like—so jus' remember he's me friend an' treat 'im right."

As the names Trever, Lawrence, and Appleton fell on the air, the loafers seemed to sense something unusual. Perhaps it was only some sound connected with the clicking balls of the pool tables or the rattling glasses that were brought from the cryptic regions in the rear—perhaps only that, plus some strange rustling of the dirty draperies at the one dingy window—but many thought that someone in the room had gritted his teeth and drawn a very sharp breath.

"Glad to know you, Sheehan," said Trever in a quiet, well-bred tone.

"This is my first experience in a place like this, but I am a student of life, and don't want to miss any experience. There's poetry in this sort of thing, you know—or perhaps you don't know, but it's all the same."

"Young feller," responded the proprietor, "ya come tuh th' right place tuh see life. We got all kinds here—reel life an' a good time. The damn' government can try tuh make folks good ef it wants tuh, but it can't stop a feller from hittin' 'er up when he feels like it. Whaddya want, feller—booze, coke, or some other sorta dope? Yuh can't ask for nothin' we ain't got."

Habitués say that it was at this point they noticed a cessation in the regular, monotonous strokes of the mop.

"I want whiskey—good old-fashioned rye!" exclaimed Trever enthusiastically. "I'll tell you, I'm good and tired of water after reading of the merry bouts fellows used to have in the old days. I can't read an Anacreontic without watering at the mouth—and it's something a lot stronger than water that my mouth waters for!"

"Anacreontic—what 'n hell's that?" several hangers-on looked up as the young man went slightly beyond their depth. But the bank defaulter under cover explained to them that Anacreon was a gay old dog who lived many years ago and wrote about the fun he had when all the world was just like Sheehan's.

"Let me see, Trever," continued the defaulter, "didn't Schultz say your mother is a literary person, too?"

"Yes, damn it," replied Trever, "but nothing like the old Teian! She's one of those dull, eternal moralisers that try to take all the joy out of life. Namby-pamby sort—ever heard of her? She writes under her maiden name of Eleanor Wing."

Here it was that Old Bugs dropped his mop.

"Well, here's yer stuff," announced Sheehan jovially as a tray of bottles and glasses was wheeled into the room. "Good old rye, an' as fiery as ya kin find anyw'eres in Chi'."

The youth's eyes glistened and his nostrils curled at the fumes of the brownish fluid which an attendant was pouring out for him. It repelled him horribly, and revolted all his inherited delicacy; but his determination to taste life to the full remained with him, and he maintained a bold front. But before his resolution was put to the test, the unexpected intervened. Old Bugs, springing up from the crouching position in which he had hitherto been, leaped at the youth and dashed from his hands the uplifted glass, almost simultaneously attacking the tray of bottles and glasses with his mop, and scattering the contents upon the floor in a confusion of odoriferous fluid and broken bottles and tumblers. Numbers of men, or things which had been men, dropped to the floor and began lapping at the puddles of spilled liquor, but most remained immovable, watching the unprecedented actions of the barroom drudge and derelict. Old Bugs straightened up before the astonished Trever, and in a mild and cultivated voice said, "Do not do this thing. I was like you once, and I did it. Now I am like—this."

"What do you mean, you damned old fool?" shouted Trever. "What do you mean by interfering with a gentleman in his pleasures?"

Sheehan, now recovering from his astonishment, advanced and laid a heavy hand on the old waif's shoulder.

"This is the last time for you, old bird!" he exclaimed furiously. "When a gen'l'man wants tuh take a drink here, by God, he shall, without you interferin'. Now get th' hell outa here afore I kick hell outa ya."

But Sheehan had reckoned without scientific knowledge of abnormal psychology and the effects of nervous stimulus. Old Bugs, obtaining a firmer hold on his mop, began to wield it like the javelin of a Macedonian hoplite, and soon cleared a considerable space around himself, meanwhile shouting various disconnected bits of quotation, among which was prominently repeated, ". . . the sons of Belial, blown with insolence and wine."

The room became pandemonium, and men screamed and howled in fright at the sinister being they had aroused. Trever seemed dazed in the confusion, and shrank to the wall as the strife thickened. "He shall not drink! He shall not drink!" Thus roared Old Bugs as he seemed to run out of—or rise above—quotations. Policemen appeared at the door, attracted by the noise, but for a time they made no move to intervene. Trever, now thoroughly terrified and cured forever of his desire to see life via the vice route, edged closer to the blue-coated newcomers. Could he but escape and catch a train for Appleton, he reflected, he would consider his education in dissipation quite complete.

Then suddenly Old Bugs ceased to wield his javelin and stopped still—drawing himself up more erectly than any denizen of the place had ever seen him before. "*Ave, Caesar, moriturus te saluto!*" he shouted, and dropped to the whiskey-reeking floor, never to rise again.

Subsequent impressions will never leave the mind of young Trever. The picture is blurred, but ineradicable. Policemen ploughed a way through the crowd, questioning everyone closely both about the incident and about the dead figure on the floor. Sheehan especially did they ply with inquiries, yet without eliciting any information of value concerning Old Bugs. Then the bank defaulter remembered the picture, and suggested that it be viewed and filed for identification at police headquarters. An officer bent reluctantly over the loathsome glassy-eyed form and found the tissue-wrapped cardboard, which he passed around among the others.

"Some chicken!" leered a drunken man as he viewed the beautiful face, but those who were sober did not leer, looking with respect and abashment at the delicate and spiritual features. No one seemed able to place the subject, and all wondered that the drug-degraded derelict should have such a portrait in his possession—that is, all but the bank defaulter, who was meanwhile eyeing the intruding bluecoats rather uneasily. *He* had seen a little deeper beneath Old Bugs' mask of utter degradation.

Then the picture was passed to Trever, and a change came over the youth. After the first start, he replaced the tissue wrapping around the portrait, as if to shield it from the sordidness of the place. Then he gazed long and searchingly at the figure on the floor, noting its great height, and the aristocratic cast of features which seemed to appear now that the wretched flame of life had flickered out. No, he said hastily, as the question was put to him, he did not know the subject of the picture. It was so old, he added, that no one now could be expected to recognise it.

But Alfred Trever did not speak the truth, as many guessed when he offered to take charge of the body and secure its interment in Appleton. Over the library mantel in his home hung the exact replica of that picture, and all his life he had known and loved its original.

For the gentle and noble features were those of his own mother.

MEMORY

In the valley of Nis the accursed waning moon shines thinly, tearing a path for its light with feeble horns through the lethal foliage of a great upas-tree. And within the depths of the valley, where the light reaches not, move forms not meet to be beheld. Rank is the herbage on each slope, where evil vines and creeping plants crawl amidst the stones of ruined palaces, twining tightly about broken columns and strange monoliths, and heaving up marble pavements laid by forgotten hands. And in trees that grow gigantic in crumbling courtyards leap little apes, while in and out of deep treasure-vaults writhe poison serpents and scaly things without a name.

Vast are the stones which sleep beneath coverlets of dank moss, and mighty were the walls from which they fell. For all time did their builders erect them, and in sooth they yet serve nobly, for beneath them the grey toad makes his habitation.

At the very bottom of the valley lies the river Than, whose waters are slimy and filled with weeds. From hidden springs it rises, and to subterranean grottoes it flows, so that the Daemon of the Valley knows not why its waters are red, nor whither they are bound.

The Genie that haunts the moonbeams spake to the Daemon of the Valley, saying, "I am old, and forget much. Tell me the deeds and aspect and name of them who built these things of stone." And the Daemon replied, "I am Memory, and am wise in lore of the past, but I too am old. These beings were like the waters of the river Than, not to be understood. Their deeds I recall not, for they were but of the moment. Their aspect I recall dimly, for it was like to that of the little apes in the trees. Their name I recall clearly, for it rhymed with that of the river. These beings of yesterday were called Man."

So the Genie flew back to the thin horned moon, and the Daemon looked intently at a little ape in a tree that grew in a crumbling courtyard.

NYARLATHOTEP

Nyarlathotep . . . the crawling chaos . . . I am the last . . . I will tell the audient void. . . .

I do not recall distinctly when it began, but it was months ago. The general tension was horrible. To a season of political and social upheaval was added a strange and brooding apprehension of hideous physical danger; a danger widespread and all-embracing, such a danger as may be imagined only in the most terrible phantasms of the night. I recall that the people went about with pale and worried faces, and whispered warnings and prophecies which no one dared consciously repeat or acknowledge to himself that he had heard. A sense of monstrous guilt was upon the land, and out of the abysses between the stars swept chill currents that made men shiver in dark and lonely places. There was a daemoniac alteration in the sequence of the seasons—the autumn heat lingered fearsomely, and everyone felt that the world and perhaps the universe had passed from the control of known gods or forces to that of gods or forces which were unknown.

And it was then that Nyarlathotep came out of Egypt. Who he was, none could tell, but he was of the old native blood and looked like a Pharaoh. The fellahin knelt when they saw him, yet could not say why. He said he had risen up out of the blackness of twenty-seven centuries, and that he had heard messages from places not on this planet. Into the lands of civilisation came Nyarlathotep, swarthy, slender, and sinister, always buying strange instruments of glass and metal and combining them into instruments yet stranger. He spoke much of the sciences—of electricity and psychology—and gave exhibitions of power which sent his spectators away speechless, yet which swelled his fame to exceeding magnitude. Men advised one another to see Nyarlathotep, and shuddered. And where Nyarlathotep went, rest vanished; for the small hours were rent with the screams of nightmare. Never before had the screams of nightmare been such a public problem; now the wise men almost wished they could forbid sleep in the small hours, that the shrieks of cities might less horribly disturb the pale, pitying moon as it glimmered on green waters gliding under bridges, and old steeples crumbling against a sickly sky.

I remember when Nyarlathotep came to my city—the great, the old, the terrible city of unnumbered crimes. My friend had told me of him, and of the impelling fascination and allurement of his revelations, and I burned with eagerness to explore his uttermost mysteries. My friend said they were horrible and impressive beyond my most fevered imaginings; that what was thrown on a screen in the darkened room prophesied things none but Nyarlathotep dared prophesy, and that in the sputter of his sparks there was taken from men that which had never been taken before yet which shewed only in the eyes. And I heard it hinted abroad that those who knew Nyarlathotep looked on sights which others saw not.

It was in the hot autumn that I went through the night with the restless crowds to see Nyarlathotep; through the stifling night and up the endless stairs into the choking room. And shadowed on a screen, I saw hooded forms amidst ruins, and yellow evil faces peering from behind fallen monuments. And I saw the world battling against blackness; against the waves of destruction from ultimate space; whirling, churning; struggling around the dimming, cooling sun. Then the sparks played amazingly around the heads of the spectators, and hair stood up on end whilst shadows more grotesque than I can tell came out and squatted on the heads. And when I, who was colder and more scientific than the rest, mumbled a trembling protest about "imposture" and "static electricity", Nyarlathotep drave us all out, down the dizzy stairs into the damp, hot, deserted midnight streets. I screamed aloud that I was *not* afraid; that I never could be afraid; and others screamed with me for solace. We sware to one another that the city *was* exactly the same, and still alive; and when the electric lights began to fade we cursed the company over and over again, and laughed at the queer faces we made.

I believe we felt something coming down from the greenish moon, for when we began to depend on its light we drifted into curious involuntary formations and seemed to know our destinations though we dared not think of them. Once we looked at the pavement and found the blocks loose and displaced by grass, with scarce a line of rusted metal to shew where the tramways had run. And again we saw a tram-car, lone, windowless, dilapidated, and almost on its side. When we gazed around the horizon, we could not find the third tower by the river, and noticed that the silhouette of the second tower was ragged at the top. Then we split up into narrow columns, each of which seemed drawn in a different direction. One disappeared in a narrow alley to the left, leaving only the echo of a shocking moan. Another filed down a weed-choked subway entrance, howling with a laughter that was mad. My own column was sucked toward the open country, and presently felt a chill which was not of the hot autumn; for as we stalked out on the dark moor, we beheld around us the hellish moon-glitter of evil snows. Trackless, inexplicable snows, swept asunder in one direction only, where lay a gulf all the blacker for its glittering walls. The column seemed very thin indeed as it plodded dreamily into the gulf. I lingered behind, for the black rift in the green-litten snow was frightful, and I thought I had heard the reverberations of a disquieting wail as my companions vanished; but my power to linger was slight. As if beckoned by those who had gone before, I half floated between the titanic snowdrifts, quivering and afraid, into the sightless vortex of the unimaginable.

Screamingly sentient, dumbly delirious, only the gods that were can tell. A sickened, sensitive shadow writhing in hands that are not hands, and whirled blindly past ghastly midnights of rotting creation, corpses of dead worlds with sores that were cities, charnel winds that brush the pallid stars and make them flicker low. Beyond the worlds vague ghosts of monstrous things; half-seen columns of unsanctified temples that rest on nameless rocks beneath space and reach up to dizzy vacua above the spheres of light and darkness. And through this revolving graveyard of the universe the muffled, maddening beat of drums, and thin, monotonous whine of blasphemous flutes from inconceivable, unlighted chambers beyond Time; the detestable pounding and piping whereunto dance slowly, awkwardly, and absurdly the gigantic, tenebrous ultimate gods—the blind, voiceless, mindless gargoyles whose soul is Nyarlathotep.

EX OBLIVIONE

When the last days were upon me, and the ugly trifles of existence began to drive me to madness like the small drops of water that torturers let fall ceaselessly upon one spot of their victim's body, I loved the irradiate refuge of sleep. In my dreams I found a little of the beauty I had vainly sought in life, and wandered through old gardens and enchanted woods.

Once when the wind was soft and scented I heard the south calling, and sailed endlessly and languorously under strange stars.

Once when the gentle rain fell I glided in a barge down a sunless stream under the earth till I reached another world of purple twilight, iridescent arbours, and undying roses.

And once I walked through a golden valley that led to shadowy groves and ruins, and ended in a mighty wall green with antique vines, and pierced by a little gate of bronze.

Many times I walked through that valley, and longer and longer would I pause in the spectral half-light where the giant trees squirmed and twisted grotesquely, and the grey ground stretched damply from trunk to trunk, sometimes disclosing the mould-stained stones of buried temples. And always the goal of my fancies was the mighty vine-grown wall with the little gate of bronze therein.

After a while, as the days of waking became less and less bearable from their greyness and sameness, I would often drift in opiate peace through the valley and the shadowy groves, and wonder how I might seize them for my eternal dwelling-place, so that I need no more crawl back to a dull world stript of interest and new colours. And as I looked upon the little gate in the mighty wall, I felt that beyond it lay a dream-country from which, once it was entered, there would be no return.

So each night in sleep I strove to find the hidden latch of the gate in the ivied temple wall, though it was exceedingly well hidden. And I would tell myself that the realm beyond the wall was not more lasting merely, but more lovely and radiant as well.

Then one night in the dream-city of Zakarion I found a yellowed papyrus filled with the thoughts of dream-sages who dwelt of old in that city, and who were too wise ever to be born in the waking world. Therein were written many things concerning the world of dream, and among them was lore of a golden valley and a sacred grove with temples, and a high wall pierced by a little bronze gate. When I saw this lore, I knew that it touched on the scenes I had haunted, and I therefore read long in the yellowed papyrus.

Some of the dream-sages wrote gorgeously of the wonders beyond the irrepassable gate, but others told of horror and disappointment. I knew not which to believe, yet longed more and more to cross forever into the unknown land; for doubt and secrecy are the lure of lures, and no new horror can be more terrible than the daily torture of the commonplace. So when I learned of the drug which would unlock the gate and drive me through, I resolved to take it when next I awaked.

Last night I swallowed the drug and floated dreamily into the golden valley and the shadowy groves; and when I came this time to the antique wall, I saw that the small gate of bronze was ajar. From beyond came a glow that weirdly lit the giant twisted trees and the tops of the buried temples, and I drifted on songfully, expectant of the glories of the land from whence I should never return.

But as the gate swung wider and the sorcery of drug and dream pushed me through, I knew that all sights and glories were at an end; for in that new realm was neither land nor sea, but only the white void of unpeopled and illimitable space. So, happier than I had ever dared hope to be, I dissolved again into that native infinity of crystal oblivion from which the daemon Life had called me for one brief and desolate hour.

WHAT THE MOON BRINGS

I hate the moon—I am afraid of it—for when it shines on certain scenes familiar and loved it sometimes makes them unfamiliar and hideous.

It was in the spectral summer when the moon shone down on the old garden where I wandered; the spectral summer of narcotic flowers and humid seas of foliage that bring wild and many-coloured dreams. And as I walked by the shallow crystal stream I saw unwonted ripples tipped with yellow light, as if those placid waters were drawn on in resistless currents to strange oceans that are not in the world. Silent and sparkling, bright and baleful, those moon-cursed waters hurried I knew not whither; whilst from the embowered banks white lotos blossoms fluttered one by one in the opiate night-wind and dropped despairingly into the stream, swirling away horribly under the arched, carven bridge, and staring back with the sinister resignation of calm, dead forces.

And as I ran along the shore, crushing sleeping flowers with heedless feet and maddened ever by the fear of unknown things and the lure of the dead faces, I saw that the garden had no end under that moon; for where by day the walls were, there stretched now only new vistas of trees and paths, flowers and shrubs, stone idols and pagodas, and bendings of the yellow-litten stream past grassy banks and under grotesque bridges of marble. And the lips of the dead lotos-faces whispered sadly, and bade me follow, nor did I cease my steps till the stream became a river, and joined amidst marshes of swaying reeds and beaches of gleaming sand the shore of a vast and nameless sea.

Upon that sea the hateful moon shone, and over its unvocal waves weird perfumes brooded. And as I saw therein the lotos-faces vanish, I longed for nets that I might capture them and learn from them the secrets which the moon had brought upon the night. But when the moon went over to the west and the still tide ebbed from the sullen shore, I saw in that light old spires that the waves almost uncovered, and white columns gay with festoons of green seaweed. And knowing that to this sunken place all the dead had come, I trembled and did not wish again to speak with the lotos-faces.

Yet when I saw afar out in the sea a black condor descend from the sky to seek rest on a vast reef, I would fain have questioned him, and asked him of those whom I had known when they were alive. This I would have asked him had he not been so far away, but he was very far, and could not be seen at all when he drew nigh that gigantic reef.

So I watched the tide go out under that sinking moon, and saw gleaming the spires, the towers, and the roofs of that dead, dripping city. And as I watched, my nostrils tried to close against the perfume-conquering stench of the world's dead; for truly, in this unplaced and forgotten spot had all the flesh of the churchyards gathered for puffy sea-worms to gnaw and glut upon.

Over those horrors the evil moon now hung very low, but the puffy worms of the sea need no moon to feed by. And as I watched the ripples that told of the writhing of worms beneath, I felt a new chill from afar out whither the condor had flown, as if my flesh had caught a horror before my eyes had seen it.

Nor had my flesh trembled without cause, for when I raised my eyes I saw that the waters had ebbed very low, shewing much of the vast reef whose rim I had seen before. And when I saw that this reef was but the black basalt crown of a shocking eikon whose monstrous forehead now shone in the dim moonlight and whose vile hooves must paw the hellish ooze miles below, I shrieked and shrieked lest the hidden face rise above the waters, and lest the hidden eyes look at me after the slinking away of that leering and treacherous yellow moon.

And to escape this relentless thing I plunged gladly and unhesitatingly into the stinking shallows where amidst weedy walls and sunken streets fat sea-worms feast upon the world's dead.

SWEET ERMENGARDE;

OR, THE HEART OF A COUNTRY GIRL

by Percy Simple

Chapter I.
A Simple Rustic Maid

Ermengarde Stubbs was the beauteous blonde daughter of Hiram Stubbs, a poor but honest farmer-bootlegger of Hogton, Vt. Her name was originally Ethyl Ermengarde, but her father persuaded her to drop the praenomen after the passage of the 18th Amendment, averring that it made him thirsty by reminding him of ethyl alcohol, C_2H_5OH. His own products contained mostly methyl or wood alcohol, CH_3OH. Ermengarde confessed to sixteen summers, and branded as mendacious all reports to the effect that she was thirty. She had large black eyes, a prominent Roman nose, light hair which was never dark at the roots except when the local drug store was short on supplies, and a beautiful but inexpensive complexion. She was about 5^{ft} $5.33...^{in}$ tall, weighed 115.47 lbs. on her father's copy scales—also off them—and was adjudged most lovely by all the village swains who admired her father's farm and liked his liquid crops.

Ermengarde's hand was sought in matrimony by two ardent lovers. 'Squire Hardman, who had a mortgage on the old home, was very rich and elderly. He was dark and cruelly handsome, and always rode horseback and carried a riding-crop. Long had he sought the radiant Ermengarde, and now his ardour was fanned to fever heat by a secret known to him alone—for upon the humble acres of Farmer Stubbs he had discovered a vein of rich GOLD!! "Aha!" said he, "I will win the maiden ere her parent knows of his unsuspected wealth, and join to my fortune a greater fortune still!" And so he began to call twice a week instead of once as before.

But alas for the sinister designs of a villain—'Squire Hardman was not the only suitor for the fair one. Close by the village dwelt another—the handsome Jack Manly, whose curly yellow hair had won the sweet Ermengarde's affection when both were toddling youngsters at the village school. Jack had long been too bashful to declare his passion, but one day while strolling along a shady lane by the old mill with Ermengarde, he had found courage to utter that which was within his heart.

"O light of my life," said he, "my soul is so overburdened that I must speak! Ermengarde, my ideal [he pronounced it i-deel!], life has become an empty thing without you. Beloved of my spirit, behold a suppliant kneeling in the dust before thee. Ermengarde—oh, Ermengarde, raise me to an heaven of joy and say that you will some day be mine! It is true that I am poor, but have I not youth and strength to fight my way to fame? This I can do only for you, dear Ethyl—pardon me, Ermengarde—my only, my most precious—" but here he paused to wipe his eyes and mop his brow, and the fair responded:

"Jack—my angel—at last—I mean, this is so unexpected and quite unprecedented! I had never dreamed that you entertained sentiments of affection in connexion with one so lowly as Farmer Stubbs' child—for I am still but a child! Such is your natural nobility that I had feared—I mean thought—you would be blind to such slight charms as I possess, and that you would seek your fortune in the great city; there meeting and wedding one of those more comely damsels whose splendour we observe in fashion books.

"But, Jack, since it is really I whom you adore, let us waive all needless circumlocution. Jack—my darling—my heart has long been susceptible to your manly graces. I cherish an affection for thee—consider me thine own and be sure to buy the ring at Perkins' hardware store where they have such nice imitation diamonds in the window."

"Ermengarde, me love!"

"Jack—my precious!"

"My darling!"

"My own!"

"My Gawd!"

[Curtain]

Chapter II.
And the Villain Still Pursued Her

But these tender passages, sacred though their fervour, did not pass unobserved by profane eyes; for crouched in the bushes and gritting his teeth was the dastardly 'Squire Hardman! When the lovers had finally strolled away he leapt out into the lane, viciously twirling his moustache and riding-crop, and kicking an unquestionably innocent cat who was also out strolling.

"Curses!" he cried—Hardman, not the cat—"I am foiled in my plot to get the farm and the girl! But Jack Manly shall never succeed! I am a man of power—and we shall see!"

Thereupon he repaired to the humble Stubbs' cottage, where he found the fond father in the still-cellar washing bottles under the supervision of the gentle wife and mother, Hannah Stubbs. Coming directly to the point, the villain spoke:

"Farmer Stubbs, I cherish a tender affection of long standing for your lovely offspring, Ethyl Ermengarde. I am consumed with love, and wish her hand in matrimony. Always a man of few words, I will not descend to euphemism. Give me the girl or I will foreclose the mortgage and take the old home!"

"But, Sir," pleaded the distracted Stubbs while his stricken spouse merely glowered, "I am sure the child's affections are elsewhere placed."

"She must be mine!" sternly snapped the sinister 'squire. "I will make her love me—none shall resist my will! Either she becomes muh wife or the old homestead goes!"

And with a sneer and flick of his riding-crop 'Squire Hardman strode out into the night.

Scarce had he departed, when there entered by the back door the radiant lovers, eager to tell the senior Stubbses of their new-found happiness. Imagine the universal consternation which reigned when all was known! Tears flowed like white ale, till suddenly Jack remembered he was the hero and raised his head, declaiming in appropriately virile accents:

"Never shall the fair Ermengarde be offered up to this beast as a sacrifice while I live! I shall protect her—she is mine, mine, mine—and then some! Fear not, dear father and mother to be—I will defend you all! You shall have the old home still [adverb, not noun—although Jack was by no means out of sympathy with Stubbs' kind of farm produce] and I shall lead to the altar the beauteous Ermengarde, loveliest of her sex! To perdition with the crool 'squire and his ill-gotten gold—the right shall always win, and a hero is always in the right! I will go to the great city and there make a fortune to save you all ere the mortgage fall due! Farewell, my love—I leave you now in tears, but I shall return to pay off the mortgage and claim you as my bride!"

"Jack, my protector!"

"Ermie, my sweet roll!"

"Dearest!"

"Darling!—and don't forget that ring at Perkins'."

"Oh!"

"Ah!"

[Curtain]

Chapter III.
A Dastardly Act

But the resourceful 'Squire Hardman was not so easily to be foiled. Close by the village lay a disreputable settlement of unkempt shacks, populated by a shiftless scum who lived by thieving and other odd jobs. Here the devilish villain secured two accomplices—ill-favoured fellows who were very clearly no gentlemen. And in the night the evil three broke into the Stubbs cottage and abducted the fair Ermengarde, taking her to a wretched hovel in the settlement and placing her under the charge of Mother Maria, a hideous old hag. Farmer Stubbs was quite distracted, and would have advertised in the papers if the cost had been less than a cent a word for each insertion. Ermengarde was firm, and never wavered in her refusal to wed the villain.

"Aha, my proud beauty," quoth he, "I have ye in me power, and sooner or later I will break that will of thine! Meanwhile think of your poor old father and mother as turned out of hearth and home and wandering helpless through the meadows!"

"Oh, spare them, spare them!" said the maiden.

"Neverr . . . ha ha ha ha!" leered the brute.

And so the cruel days sped on, while all in ignorance young Jack Manly was seeking fame and fortune in the great city.

Chapter IV.
Subtle Villainy

One day as 'Squire Hardman sat in the front parlour of his expensive and palatial home, indulging in his favourite pastime of gnashing his teeth and swishing his riding-crop, a great thought came to him; and he cursed aloud at the statue of Satan on the onyx mantelpiece.

"Fool that I am!" he cried. "Why did I ever waste all this trouble on the girl when I can get the farm by simply foreclosing? I never thought of that! I will let the girl go, take the farm, and be free to wed some fair city maid like the leading lady of that burlesque troupe which played last week at the Town Hall!"

And so he went down to the settlement, apologised to Ermengarde, let her go home, and went home himself to plot new crimes and invent new modes of villainy.

The days wore on, and the Stubbses grew very sad over the coming loss of their home and still but nobody seemed able to do anything about it. One day a party of hunters from the city chanced to stray over the old farm, and one of them found the gold!! Hiding his discovery from his companions, he feigned rattlesnake-bite and went to the Stubbs' cottage for aid of the usual kind. Ermengarde opened the door and saw him. He also saw her, and in that moment resolved to win her and the gold. "For my old mother's sake I must"—he cried loudly to himself. "No sacrifice is too great!"

Chapter V.
The City Chap

Algernon Reginald Jones was a polished man of the world from the great city, and in his sophisticated hands our poor little Ermengarde was as a mere child. One could almost believe that sixteen-year-old stuff. Algy was a fast worker, but never crude. He could have taught Hardman a thing or two about finesse in sheiking. Thus only a week after his advent to the Stubbs family circle, where he lurked like the vile serpent that he was, he had persuaded the heroine to elope! It was in the night that she went leaving a note for her parents, sniffing the familiar mash for the last time, and kissing the cat goodbye—touching stuff! On the train Algernon became sleepy and slumped down in his seat, allowing a paper to fall out of his pocket by accident. Ermengarde, taking advantage of her supposed position as a bride-elect, picked up the folded sheet and read its perfumed expanse—when lo! she almost fainted! It was a love letter from another woman!!

"Perfidious deceiver!" she whispered at the sleeping Algernon, "so this is all that your boasted fidelity amounts to! I am done with you for all eternity!"

So saying, she pushed him out the window and settled down for a much needed rest.

Chapter VI.
Alone in the Great City

When the noisy train pulled into the dark station at the city, poor helpless Ermengarde was all alone without the money to get back to Hogton. "Oh why," she sighed in innocent regret, "didn't I take his pocketbook before I pushed him out? Oh well, I should worry! He told me all about the city so I can easily earn enough to get home if not to pay off the mortgage!"

But alas for our little heroine—work is not easy for a greenhorn to secure, so for a week she was forced to sleep on park benches and obtain food from the bread-line. Once a wily and wicked person, perceiving her helplessness, offered her a position as dish-washer in a fashionable and depraved cabaret; but our heroine was true to her rustic ideals and refused to work in such a gilded and glittering palace of frivolity—especially since she was offered only $3.00 per week with meals but no board. She tried to look up Jack Manly, her one-time lover, but he was nowhere to be found. Perchance, too, he would not have known her; for in her poverty she had perforce become a brunette again, and Jack had not beheld her in that state since school days. One day she found a neat but costly purse in the dark; and after seeing that there was not much in it, took it to the rich lady whose card proclaimed her ownership. Delighted beyond words at the honesty of this forlorn waif, the aristocratic Mrs. Van Itty adopted Ermengarde to replace the little one who had been stolen from her so many years ago. "How like my precious Maude," she sighed, as she watched the fair brunette return to blondeness. And so several weeks passed, with the old folks at home tearing their hair and the wicked 'Squire Hardman chuckling devilishly.

Chapter VII.
Happy Ever Afterward

One day the wealthy heiress Ermengarde S. Van Itty hired a new second assistant chauffeur. Struck by something familiar in his face, she looked again and gasped. Lo! it was none other than the perfidious Algernon Reginald Jones, whom she had pushed from a car window on that fateful day! He had survived—this much was almost immediately evident. Also, he had wed the other woman, who had run away with the milkman and all the money in the house. Now wholly humbled, he asked forgiveness of our heroine, and confided to her the whole tale of the gold on her father's farm. Moved beyond words, she raised his salary a dollar a month and resolved to gratify at last that always unquenchable anxiety to relieve the worry of the old folks. So one bright day Ermengarde motored back to Hogton and arrived at the farm just as 'Squire Hardman was foreclosing the mortgage and ordering the old folks out.

"Stay, villain!" she cried, flashing a colossal roll of bills. "You are foiled at last! Here is your money—now go, and never darken our humble door again!"

Then followed a joyous reunion, whilst the 'squire twisted his moustache and riding-crop in bafflement and dismay. But hark! What is this? Footsteps sound on the old gravel walk, and who should appear but our hero, Jack Manly—worn and seedy, but radiant of face. Seeking at once the downcast villain, he said:

" 'Squire—lend me a ten-spot, will you? I have just come back from the city with my beauteous bride, the fair Bridget Goldstein, and need something to start things on the old farm." Then turning to the Stubbses, he apologised for his inability to pay off the mortgage as agreed.

"Don't mention it," said Ermengarde, "prosperity has come to us, and I will consider it sufficient payment if you will forget forever the foolish fancies of our childhood."

All this time Mrs. Van Itty had been sitting in the motor waiting for Ermengarde; but as she lazily eyed the sharp-faced Hannah Stubbs a vague memory started from the back of her brain. Then it all came to her, and she shrieked accusingly at the agrestic matron.

"You—you—Hannah Smith—I know you now! Twenty-eight years ago you were my baby Maude's nurse and stole her from the cradle!! Where, oh, where is my child?" Then a thought came as the lightning in a murky sky. "*Ermengarde*—you say she is *your* daughter. . . . She is mine! Fate has restored to me my old chee-ild—my tiny Maudie!—Ermengarde—Maude—come to your mother's loving arms!!!"

But Ermengarde was doing some tall thinking. How could she get away with the sixteen-year-old stuff if she had been stolen twenty-eight years ago? And if she was not Stubbs' daughter the gold would never be hers. Mrs. Van Itty was rich, but 'Squire Hardman was richer. So, approaching the dejected villain, she inflicted upon him the last terrible punishment.

"'Squire, dear," she murmured, "I have reconsidered all. I love you and your naive strength. Marry me at once or I will have you prosecuted for that kidnapping last year. Foreclose your mortgage and enjoy with me the gold your cleverness discovered. Come, dear!" And the poor dub did.

THE END.

THE VERY OLD FOLK

Thursday
[November 3, 1927]

Dear Melmoth:—

. . . So you are busy delving into the shady past of that insufferable young Asiatic Varius Avitus Bassianus? Ugh! There are few persons I loathe more than that cursed little Syrian rat!

I have myself been carried back to Roman times by my recent perusal of James Rhoades' *AEneid*, a translation never before read by me, and more faithful to P. Maro than any other versified version I have ever seen—including that of my late uncle Dr. Clark, which did not attain publication. This Virgilian diversion, together with the spectral thoughts incident to All Hallows' Eve with its Witch-Sabbaths on the hills, produced in me last Monday night a Roman dream of such supernal clearness and vividness, and such titanic adumbrations of hidden horror, that I verily believe I shall some day employ it in fiction. Roman dreams were no uncommon features of my youth—I used to follow the Divine Julius all over Gallia as a Tribunus Militum o'nights—but I had so long ceased to experience them, that the present one impressed me with extraordinary force.

It was a flaming sunset or late afternoon in the tiny provincial town of Pompelo, at the foot of the Pyrenees in Hispania Citerior. The year must have been in the late republic, for the province was still ruled by a senatorial proconsul instead of a praetorian legate of Augustus, and the day was the first before the Kalends of November. The hills rose scarlet and gold to the north of the little town, and the westering sun shone ruddily and mystically on the crude new stone and plaster buildings of the dusty forum and the wooden walls of the circus some distance to the east. Groups of citizens—broad-browed Roman colonists and coarse-haired Romanised natives, together with obvious hybrids of the two strains, alike clad in cheap woollen togas—and sprinklings of helmeted legionaries and coarse-mantled, black-bearded tribesmen of the circumambient Vascones—all thronged the few paved streets and forum; moved by some vague and ill-defined uneasiness. I myself had just alighted from a litter, which the Illyrian bearers seemed to have brought in some haste from Calagurris, across the Iberus to the southward. It appeared that I was a provincial quaestor named L. Caelius Rufus, and that I had been summoned by the proconsul, P. Scribonius Libo, who had come from Tarraco some days before. The soldiers were the fifth cohort of the XIIth legion, under the military tribune Sex. Asellius; and the legatus of the whole region, Cn. Balbutius, had also come from Calagurris, where the permanent station was. The cause of the conference was a horror that brooded on the hills. All the townsfolk were frightened, and had begged the presence of a cohort from Calagurris. It was the Terrible Season of the autumn, and the wild people in the mountains were preparing for the frightful ceremonies which only rumour told of in the towns. They were the very old folk who dwelt higher up in the hills and spoke a choppy language which the Vascones could not understand. One seldom saw them; but a few times a year they sent down little yellow, squint-eyed messengers (who looked like Scythians) to trade with the merchants by means of gestures, and every spring and autumn they held the infamous rites on the peaks, their howlings and altar-fires throwing terror into the villages. Always the same—the night before the Kalends of Maius and the night before the Kalends of November. Townsfolk would disappear just before these nights, and would never be heard of again. And there were whispers that the native shepherds and farmers were not ill-disposed toward the very old folk—that more than one thatched hut was vacant before midnight on the two hideous Sabbaths. This year the horror was very great, for the people knew that the wrath of the very old folk was upon Pompelo. Three months previously five of the little squint-eyed traders had come down from the hills, and in a market brawl three of them had been killed. The remaining two had gone back wordlessly to their mountains—*and this autumn not a single villager had disappeared.* There was menace in this immunity. It was not like the very old folk to spare their victims at the Sabbath. It was too good to be normal, and the villagers were afraid. For many nights there had been a hollow drumming on the hills, and at last the aedile Tib. Annaeus Stilpo (half native in blood) had sent to Balbutius at Calagurris for a cohort to stamp out the Sabbath on the terrible night. Balbutius had carelessly refused, on the ground that the villagers' fears were empty, and that the loathsome rites of hill folk were of no concern to the Roman People unless our own citizens were menaced. I, however, who seemed to be a close friend of Balbutius, had disagreed with him; averring that I had studied deeply in the black forbidden lore, and that

I believed the very old folk capable of visiting almost any nameless doom upon the town, which after all was a Roman settlement and contained a great number of our citizens. The complaining aedile's own mother Helvia was a pure Roman, the daughter of M. Helvius Cinna, who had come over with Scipio's army. Accordingly I had sent a slave—a nimble little Greek called Antipater—to the proconsul with letters, and Scribonius had heeded my plea and ordered Balbutius to send his fifth cohort, under Asellius, to Pompelo; entering the hills at dusk on the eve of November's Kalends and stamping out whatever nameless orgies he might find—bringing such prisoners as he might take to Tarraco for the next propraetor's court. Balbutius, however, had protested, so that more correspondence had ensued. I had written so much to the proconsul that he had become gravely interested, and had resolved to make a personal inquiry into the horror. He had at length proceeded to Pompelo with his lictors and attendants; there hearing enough rumours to be greatly impressed and disturbed, and standing firmly by his order for the Sabbath's extirpation. Desirous of conferring with one who had studied the subject, he ordered me to accompany Asellius' cohort—and Balbutius had also come along to press his adverse advice, for he honestly believed that drastic military action would stir up a dangerous sentiment of unrest amongst the Vascones both tribal and settled. So here we all were in the mystic sunset of the autumn hills—old Scribonius Libo in his toga praetexta, the golden light glancing on his shiny bald head and wrinkled hawk face, Balbutius with his gleaming helmet and breastplate, blue-shaven lips compressed in conscientiously dogged opposition, young Asellius with his polished greaves and superior sneer, and the curious throng of townsfolk, legionaries, tribesmen, peasants, lictors, slaves, and attendants. I myself seemed to wear a common toga, and to have no especially distinguishing characteristic. And everywhere horror brooded. The town and country folk scarcely dared speak aloud, and the men of Libo's entourage, who had been there nearly a week, seemed to have caught something of the nameless dread. Old Scribonius himself looked very grave, and the sharp voices of us later comers seemed to hold something of curious inappropriateness, as in a place of death or the temple of some mystic god. We entered the praetorium and held grave converse. Balbutius pressed his objections, and was sustained by Asellius, who appeared to hold all the natives in extreme contempt while at the same time deeming it inadvisable to excite them. Both soldiers maintained that we could better afford to antagonise the minority of colonists and civilised natives by inaction, than to antagonise a probable majority of tribesmen and cottagers by stamping out the dread rites. I, on the other hand, renewed my demand for action, and offered to accompany the cohort on any expedition it might undertake. I pointed out that the barbarous Vascones were at best turbulent and uncertain, so that skirmishes with them were inevitable sooner or later whichever course we might take; that they had not in the past proved dangerous adversaries to our legions, and that it would ill become the representatives of the Roman People to suffer barbarians to interfere with a course which the justice and prestige of the Republic demanded. That, on the other hand, the successful administration of a province depended primarily upon the safety and good-will of the civilised element in whose hands the local machinery of commerce and prosperity reposed, and in whose veins a large mixture of our own Italian blood coursed. These, though in numbers they might form a minority, were the stable element whose constancy might be relied on, and whose coöperation would most firmly bind the province to the Imperium of the Senate and the Roman People. It was at once a duty and an advantage to afford them the protection due to Roman citizens; even (and here I shot a sarcastic look at Balbutius and Asellius) at the expense of a little trouble and activity, and of a slight interruption of the draught-playing and cock-fighting at the camp in Calagurris. That the danger to the town and inhabitants of Pompelo was a real one, I could not from my studies doubt. I had read many scrolls out of Syria and AEgyptus, and the cryptic towns of Etruria, and had talked at length with the bloodthirsty priest of Diana Aricina in his temple in the woods bordering Lacus Nemorensis. There were shocking dooms that might be called out of the hills on the Sabbaths; dooms which ought not to exist within the territories of the Roman People; and to permit orgies of the kind known to prevail at Sabbaths would be but little in consonance with the customs of those whose forefathers, A. Postumius being consul, had executed so many Roman citizens for the practice of the Bacchanalia—a matter kept ever in memory by the Senatus Consultum de Bacchanalibus, graven upon bronze and set open to every eye. Checked in time, before the progress of the rites might evoke anything with which the iron of a Roman pilum might not be able to deal, the Sabbath would not be too much for the powers of a single cohort. Only participants need be apprehended, and the sparing of a great number of mere spectators would considerably lessen the resentment which any of the sympathising country folk might feel. In short, both principle and policy demanded stern action; and I could not doubt but that Publius Scribonius, bearing in mind the dignity and obligations of the Roman People, would adhere to his plan of despatching the cohort, me accompanying, despite such objections as Balbutius and Asellius—speaking indeed more like provincials than Romans—might see fit to offer and multiply. The slanting sun was now very low, and the whole hushed town seemed draped in an unreal and malign glamour. Then P. Scribonius the proconsul signified his approval of my words, and stationed me with the cohort in the provisional capacity of a centurio primipilus; Balbutius and Asellius assenting, the former with better grace than the latter. As twilight fell on the wild autumnal slopes, a measured, hideous beating of strange drums floated down from afar in terrible rhythm. Some few of the legionarii shewed timidity, but sharp commands brought them into line, and the whole cohort was soon drawn up on the open plain east of the circus. Libo himself, as well as Balbutius, insisted on accompanying the cohort; but great difficulty was suffered in getting a native guide to point out the paths up the mountain. Finally a young man named Vercellius, the son of pure Roman parents, agreed to take us at least past the foothills. We began to march in the new dusk, with the thin silver sickle of a young moon trembling over the woods on our left. That which disquieted us most was *the fact that the Sabbath was to be held at all.* Reports of the coming cohort must have reached the hills, and even the lack of a final decision could not make the rumour less alarming—yet there were the sinister drums as of yore, as if the celebrants had some peculiar reason to be indifferent whether or not the forces of the Roman People marched against them. The sound grew louder as we entered a rising gap in the hills, steep wooded banks enclosing us narrowly on either side, and displaying curiously fantastic tree-trunks in the light of our bobbing torches. All were afoot save Libo, Balbutius, Asellius, two or three of the centuriones, and myself, and at length the way became so steep and narrow that those who had horses were forced to leave them; a squad of ten men being left to guard them, though robber bands were not likely to be abroad on such a night of terror. Once in a while it seemed as though we detected a skulking form in the woods nearby, and after a half-hour's climb the steepness and narrowness of the way made the advance of so great a body of men—over 300, all told—exceedingly cumbrous and difficult. Then with utter and horrifying suddenness we heard a frightful sound from below. It was from the tethered horses—they had *screamed* . . . not neighed, but *screamed* . . . and there was no light down there, nor the sound of any human thing, to shew why they had done so. At the same moment bonfires blazed out on all the peaks ahead, so that terror seemed to lurk equally well before and behind us. Looking for the youth Vercellius, our guide, we found only a crumpled heap weltering in a pool of blood. In his hand was a short sword snatched from the belt of D. Vibulanus, a subcenturio, and on his face was such a look of terror that the stoutest veterans turned pale at the sight. He had killed himself when the horses screamed . . . he, who had been born and lived all his life in that region, and knew what men whispered about the hills. All the torches now began to dim, and the cries of frightened legionaries mingled with the unceasing screams of the tethered horses. The air grew perceptibly colder, more suddenly so than is usual at November's brink, and seemed stirred by terrible undulations which I could not help connecting with the beating of huge wings. The whole cohort now remained at a standstill, and as the torches faded I watched what I thought were fantastic shadows outlined in the sky by the spectral luminosity of the Via Lactea as it flowed through Perseus, Cassiopeia, Cepheus, and Cygnus. Then suddenly all the stars were blotted from the sky—even bright Deneb and Vega ahead, and the lone Altair and Fomalhaut behind us. And as the torches died out altogether, there remained above the stricken and shrieking cohort only the noxious and horrible altar-flames on the towering peaks; hellish and red, and now silhouetting the mad, leaping, and colossal forms of such nameless beasts as had never a Phrygian priest or Campanian grandam whispered of in the wildest of furtive tales. And above the nighted screaming of men and horses that daemonic drumming rose to louder pitch, whilst an ice-cold wind of shocking sentience and deliberateness swept down from those forbidden heights and coiled about each man separately, till all the cohort was struggling and screaming in the dark, as if acting out the fate of Laocoön and his sons. Only old Scribonius Libo seemed resigned. He uttered words amidst the screaming, and they echo still in my ears. "*Malitia vetus—malitia vetus est . . . venit . . . tandem venit . . .*"

And then I waked. It was the most vivid dream in years, drawing upon wells of the subconscious long untouched and forgotten. Of the fate of that cohort no record exists, but the town at least was saved—for encyclopaedias tell of the survival of Pompelo to this day, under the modern Spanish name of Pompelona. . . .

Yrs for Gothick Supremacy—
C · IVLIVS · VERVS · MAXIMINVS.

HISTORY OF THE *NECRONOMICON*

Original title *Al Azif—azif* being the word used by the Arabs to designate that nocturnal sound (made by insects) suppos'd to be the howling of daemons.

Composed by Abdul Alhazred, a mad poet of Sanaá, in Yemen, who is said to have flourished during the period of the Ommiade caliphs, circa 700 A. D. He visited the ruins of Babylon and the subterranean secrets of Memphis and spent ten years alone in the great southern desert of Arabia—the Roba el Khaliyeh or "Empty Space" of the ancients—and "Dahna" or "Crimson" desert of the modern Arabs, which is held to be inhabited by protective evil spirits and monsters of death. Of this desert many strange and unbelievable marvels are told by those who pretend to have penetrated it. In his last years Alhazred dwelt in Damascus, where the *Necronomicon* (*Al Azif*) was written, and of his final death or disappearance (738 A. D.) many terrible and conflicting things are told. He is said by Ebn Khallikan (12th cent. biographer) to have been seized by an invisible monster in broad daylight and devoured horribly before a large number of fright-frozen witnesses. Of his madness many things are told. He claimed to have seen the fabulous Irem, or City of Pillars, and to have found beneath the ruins of a certain nameless desert town the shocking annals and secrets of a race older than mankind. He was only an indifferent Moslem, worshipping unknown entities whom he called Yog-Sothoth and Cthulhu.

In A. D. 950 the *Azif,* which had gained a considerable tho' surreptitious circulation amongst the philosophers of the age, was secretly translated into Greek by Theodorus Philetas of Constantinople under the title *Necronomicon.* For a century it impelled certain experimenters to terrible attempts, when it was suppressed and burnt by the patriarch

Michael. After this it is only heard of furtively, but (1228) Olaus Wormius made a Latin translation later in the Middle Ages, and the Latin text was printed twice—once in the fifteenth century in black-letter (evidently in Germany) and once in the seventeenth (prob. Spanish)—both editions being without identifying marks, and located as to time and place by internal typographical evidence only. The work both Latin and Greek was banned by Pope Gregory IX in 1232, shortly after its Latin translation, which called attention to it. The Arabic original was lost as early as Wormius' time, as indicated by his prefatory note; and no sight of the Greek copy—which was printed in Italy between 1500 and 1550—has been reported since the burning of a certain Salem man's library in 1692. An English translation made by Dr. Dee was never printed, and exists only in fragments recovered from the original manuscript. Of the Latin texts now existing one (15th cent.) is known to be in the British Museum under lock and key, while another (17th cent.) is in the Bibliothèque Nationale at Paris. A seventeenth-century edition is in the Widener Library at Harvard, and in the library of Miskatonic University at Arkham. Also in the library of the University of Buenos Ayres. Numerous other copies probably exist in secret, and a fifteenth-century one is persistently rumoured to form part of the collection of a celebrated American millionaire. A still vaguer rumour credits the preservation of a sixteenth-century Greek text in the Salem family of Pickman; but if it was so preserved, it vanished with the artist R. U. Pickman, who disappeared early in 1926. The book is rigidly suppressed by the authorities of most countries, and by all branches of organised ecclesiasticism. Reading leads to terrible consequences. It was from rumours of this book (of which relatively few of the general public know) that R. W. Chambers is said to have derived the idea of his early novel *The King in Yellow.*

Chronology

Al Azif written circa 730 A. D. at Damascus by Abdul Alhazred
Tr. to Greek 950 A. D. as *Necronomicon* by Theodorus Philetas
Burnt by Patriarch Michael 1050 (i.e., Greek text). Arabic text now lost.
Olaus translates Gr. to Latin 1228
1232 Latin ed. (and Gr.) suppr. by Pope Gregory IX
14... Black-letter printed edition (Germany)
15... Gr. text printed in Italy
16... Spanish reprint of Latin text

IBID

("... as Ibid says in his famous *Lives of the Poets.*"
—From a student theme.)

The erroneous idea that Ibid is the author of the *Lives* is so frequently met with, even among those pretending to a degree of culture, that it is worth correcting. It should be a matter of general knowledge that Cf. is responsible for this work. Ibid's masterpiece, on the other hand, was the famous *Op. Cit.* wherein all the significant undercurrents of Graeco-Roman expression were crystallised once for all—and with admirable acuteness, notwithstanding the surprisingly late date at which Ibid wrote. There is a false report—very commonly reproduced in modern books prior to Von Schweinkopf's monumental *Geschichte der Ostrogothen in Italien*—that Ibid was a Romanised Visigoth of Ataulf's horde who settled in Placentia about 410 A. D. The contrary cannot be too strongly emphasised; for Von Schweinkopf, and since his time Littlewit[1] and Bêtenoir,[2] have shewn with irrefutable force that this strikingly isolated figure was a genuine Roman—or at least as genuine a Roman as that degenerate and mongrelised age could produce—of whom one might well say what Gibbon said of Boethius, "that he was the last whom Cato or Tully could have acknowledged for their countryman." He was, like Boethius and nearly all the eminent men of his age, of the great Anician family, and traced his genealogy with much exactitude and self-satisfaction to all the heroes of the republic. His full name—long and pompous according to the custom of an age which had lost the trinomial simplicity of classic Roman nomenclature—is stated by Von Schweinkopf[3] to have been Caius Anicius Magnus Furius Camillus Aemilianus Cornelius Valerius Pompeius Julius Ibidus; though Littlewit[4] rejects *Aemilianus* and adds *Claudius Decius Junianus;* whilst Bêtenoir[5] differs radically, giving the full name as Magnus Furius Camillus Aurelius Antoninus Flavius Anicius Petronius Valentinianus Aegidus Ibidus.

The eminent critic and biographer was born in the year 486, shortly after the extinction of the Roman rule in Gaul by Clovis. Rome and Ravenna are rivals for the honour of his birth, though it is certain that he received his rhetorical and philosophical training in the schools of Athens—the extent of whose suppression by Theodosius a century before is grossly exaggerated by the superficial. In 512, under the benign rule of the Ostrogoth Theodoric, we behold him as a teacher of rhetoric at Rome, and in 516 he held the consulship together with Pompilius Numantius Bombastes Marcellinus Deodamnatus. Upon the death of Theodoric in 526, Ibidus retired from public life to compose his celebrated work (whose pure Ciceronian style is as remarkable a case of classic atavism as is the verse of Claudius Claudianus, who flourished a century before Ibidus); but he was later recalled to scenes of pomp to act as court rhetorician for Theodatus, nephew of Theodoric.

Upon the usurpation of Vitiges, Ibidus fell into disgrace and was for a time imprisoned; but the coming of the Byzantine-Roman army under Belisarius soon restored him to liberty and honours. Throughout the siege of Rome he served bravely in the army of the defenders, and afterward followed the eagles of Belisarius to Alba, Porto, and Centumcellae. After the Frankish siege of Milan, Ibidus was chosen to accompany the learned Bishop Datius to Greece, and resided with him at Corinth in the year 539. About 541 he removed to Constantinopolis, where he received every mark of imperial favour both from Justinianus and Justinus the Second. The Emperors Tiberius and Maurice did kindly honour to his old age, and contributed much to his immortality—especially Maurice, whose delight it was to trace his ancestry to old Rome notwithstanding his birth at Arabiscus, in Cappadocia. It was Maurice who, in the poet's 101st year, secured the adoption of his work as a textbook in the schools of the empire, an honour which proved a fatal tax on the aged rhetorician's emotions, since he passed away peacefully at his home near the church of St. Sophia on the sixth day before the Kalends of September, A. D. 587, in the 102nd year of his age.

His remains, notwithstanding the troubled state of Italy, were taken to Ravenna for interment; but being interred in the suburb of Classe, were exhumed and ridiculed by the Lombard Duke of Spoleto, who took his skull to King Autharis for use as a wassail-bowl. Ibid's skull was proudly handed down from king to king of the Lombard line. Upon the capture of Pavia by Charlemagne in 774, the skull was seized from the tottering Desiderius and carried in the train of the Frankish conqueror. It was from this vessel, indeed, that Pope Leo administered the royal unction which made of the hero-nomad a Holy Roman Emperor. Charlemagne took Ibid's skull to his capital at Aix, soon afterward presenting it to his Saxon teacher Alcuin, upon whose death in

804 it was sent to Alcuin's kinsfolk in England.

William the Conqueror, finding it in an abbey niche where the pious family of Alcuin had placed it (believing it to be the skull of a saint[6] who had miraculously annihilated the Lombards by his prayers), did reverence to its osseous antiquity; and even the rough soldiers of Cromwell, upon destroying Ballylough Abbey in Ireland in 1650 (it having been secretly transported thither by a devout Papist in 1539, upon Henry VIII's dissolution of the English monasteries), declined to offer violence to a relic so venerable.

It was captured by the private soldier Read-'em-and-Weep Hopkins, who not long after traded it to Rest-in-Jehovah Stubbs for a quid of new Virginia weed. Stubbs, upon sending forth his son Zerubbabel to seek his fortune in New England in 1661 (for he thought ill of the Restoration atmosphere for a pious young yeoman), gave him St. Ibid's—or rather Brother Ibid's, for he abhorred all that was Popish—skull as a talisman. Upon landing in Salem Zerubbabel set it up in his cupboard beside the chimney, he having built a modest house near the town pump. However, he had not been wholly unaffected by the Restoration influence; and having become addicted to gaming, lost the skull to one Epenetus Dexter, a visiting freeman of Providence.

It was in the house of Dexter, in the northern part of the town near the present intersection of North Main and Olney Streets, on the occasion of Canonchet's raid of March 30, 1676, during King Philip's War; and the astute sachem, recognising it at once as a thing of singular venerableness and dignity, sent it as a symbol of alliance to a faction of the Pequots in Connecticut with whom he was negotiating. On April 4 he was captured by the colonists and soon after executed, but the austere head of Ibid continued on its wanderings.

The Pequots, enfeebled by a previous war, could give the now stricken Narragansetts no assistance; and in 1680 a Dutch fur-trader of Albany, Petrus van Schaack, secured the distinguished cranium for the modest sum of two guilders, he having recognised its value from the half-effaced inscription carved in Lombardic minuscules (palaeography, it might be explained, was one of the leading accomplishments of New-Netherland fur-traders of the seventeenth century).

Ibidus rhetor romanus

From van Schaack, sad to say, the relic was stolen in 1683 by a French trader, Jean Grenier, whose Popish zeal recognised the features of one whom he had been taught at his mother's knee to revere as St. Ibide. Grenier, fired with virtuous rage at the possession of this holy symbol by a Protestant, crushed van Schaack's head one night with an axe and escaped to the north with his booty; soon, however, being robbed and slain by the half-breed voyageur Michel Savard, who took the skull—despite the illiteracy which prevented his recognising it—to add to a collection of similar but more recent material.

Upon his death in 1701 his half-breed son Pierre traded it among other things to some emissaries of the Sacs and Foxes, and it was found outside the chief's tepee a generation later by Charles de Langlade, founder of the trading post at Green Bay, Wisconsin. De Langlade regarded this sacred object with proper veneration and ransomed it at the expense of many glass beads; yet after his time it found itself in many other hands, being traded to settlements at the head of Lake Winnebago, to tribes around Lake Mendota, and finally, early in the nineteenth century, to one Solomon Juneau, a Frenchman, at the new trading post of Milwaukee on the Menominee River and the shore of Lake Michigan.

Later traded to Jacques Caboche, another settler, it was in 1850 lost in a game of chess or poker to a newcomer named Hans Zimmerman; being used by him as a beer-stein until one day, under the spell of its contents, he suffered it to roll from his front stoop to the prairie path before his home—where, falling into the burrow of a prairie-dog, it passed beyond his power of discovery or recovery upon his awaking.

So for generations did the sainted skull of Caius Anicius Magnus Furius Camillus Aemilianus Cornelius Valerius Pompeius Julius Ibidus, consul of Rome, favourite of emperors, and saint of the Romish church, lie hidden beneath the soil of a growing town. At first worshipped with dark rites by the prairie-dogs, who saw in it a deity sent from the upper world, it afterward fell into dire neglect as the race of simple, artless burrowers succumbed before the onslaught of the conquering Aryan. Sewers came, but they passed by it. Houses went up—2303 of them, and more—and at last one fateful night a titan thing occurred. Subtle Nature, convulsed with a spiritual ecstasy, like the froth of that region's quondam beverage, laid low the lofty and heaved high the humble—and behold! In the roseal dawn the burghers of Milwaukee rose to find a former prairie turned to a highland! Vast and far-reaching was the great upheaval. Subterrene arcana, hidden for years, came at last to the light. For there, full in the rifted roadway, lay bleached and tranquil in bland, saintly, and consular pomp the dome-like skull of Ibid!

[NOTES]

[1] *Rome and Byzantium: A Study in Survival* (Waukesha, 1869), Vol. XX, p. 598.

[2] *Influences Romains dans le Moyen Age* (Fond du Lac, 1877), Vol. XV, p. 720.

[3] Following Procopius, *Goth.* x.y.z.

[4] Following Jornandes, Codex Murat. xxj. 4144.

[5] After Pagi, 50–50.

[6] Not till the appearance of von Schweinkopf's work in 1797 were St. Ibid and the rhetorician properly re-identified.

DISCARDED DRAFT OF "THE SHADOW OVER INNSMOUTH"

[pp. 1–6:]
It was in the summer of 1927 that I suddenly cut short my sightseeing tour of New England and returned to Cleveland under a nervous strain. I have seldom mentioned the particulars of this trip, and hardly know why I do so now except that a recent newspaper cutting has somehow relieved the tension which formerly existed. A sweeping fire, it appears, has wiped out most of the empty ancient houses along the deserted Innsmouth waterfront as well as a certain number of buildings farther inland; while a singularly simultaneous explosion, heard for many miles around, has destroyed to a vast depth the great black reef a mile and a half out from shore where the sea-bottom abruptly falls to form an incalculable abyss. For certain reasons I take great satisfaction in these occurrences, even the first of which seems to me a blessing rather than a disaster. Especially am I glad that the old brick jewellery factory and the pillared Order of Dagon Hall have gone along with the rest. There is talk of incendiarism, and I suppose old Father Iwanicki could tell much if he chose; but what I know gives a very unusual angle to my opinion.

I never heard of Innsmouth till the day before I saw it for the first and last time. It does not seem to be mentioned on any modern map, and I was planning to go directly from Newburyport to Arkham, and thence to Gloucester, if I could find transportation. I had no car, but was travelling by motor coach, train, and trolley, always seeking the cheapest possible route. In Newburyport they told me that the steam train was the thing to take to Arkham; and it was only at the station ticket office, when I demurred at the high fare, that I heard about Innsmouth. The agent, whose speech shewed him to be no local man, seemed sympathetic toward my efforts at economy, and made a suggestion that none of my other informants had offered.

"You could take that old bus, I suppose," he said with a certain hesitation, "but it isn't thought much of hereabouts. It goes through Innsmouth—you may have heard about that—and so the people don't like it. Run by an Innsmouth man—Joe Sargent—but never gets any custom from here, or from Arkham either, I guess. Wonder it keeps running at all. I suppose it's cheap enough, but I never see more than two or three people in it—nobody but those Innsmouth folks. Leaves the Square—front of Hammond's Drug Store—at 10 a.m. and 7 p.m. unless they've changed lately. Looks like a terrible rattletrap—I've never been on it."

That was the first I ever heard of Innsmouth. Any reference to a town not listed in the guide-books would have interested me, and the agent's odd manner of allusion roused something like real curiosity. A town able to inspire such dislike in its neighbours, I thought, must be at least rather unusual, and worthy of a sightseer's attention. If it came before Arkham I would stop off there—and so I asked the agent to tell me something about it.

He was very deliberate, and spoke with an air of feeling somewhat superior to what he said.

"Innsmouth? Well, it's a queer kind of a town down at the south of the Manuxet. It used to be almost a city—quite a seaport before the War of 1812—but the place has all gone to pieces in the last hundred years or so. There's no railroad—the B & M never went through there, and the branch line from Rowley was given up years ago. More empty houses than there are people, I guess, and no business to speak of. Everybody trades either here or in Arkham or Ipswich. At one time they had quite a number of mills there, but nothing's left now but one jewellery refinery.

"That's a pretty prominent proposition, though—all the travelling salesmen seem to know about it. Makes a special kind of fancy jewellery out of a secret alloy that nobody can analyse very well. They say it's platinum, silver, and gold—but these people sell it so cheap that you can hardly believe it. Guess they have a corner on that kind of goods.

"Old Man Marsh, who owns the thing, must be richer than Croesus. Queer old duck, though, and sticks pretty close around the town. He's the grandson of Capt. Obed Marsh, who founded the business. His mother was some kind of foreigner—they say a South Sea native—so everybody raised Cain when he married an Ipswich girl fifty years ago. They always do that about Innsmouth people. But his children and grandchildren look just like anybody else so far as I can see. I've had 'em pointed out to me here. Never saw the old man.

"And why is everybody so down on Innsmouth? Well—you mustn't take too much stock in what people around here say. They're hard to get started, but once they do get started they never stop. They've been telling things about Innsmouth—whispering 'em, mostly—for the last hundred years, I guess, and I gather they're more scared than anything else. Some of the stories would make you laugh—about old Capt. Marsh driving bargains with the devil and bringing imps out of hell to live in Innsmouth, or about some kind of devil-worship and awful sacrifices in some place near the wharves that people stumbled on around 1850 or thereabouts—but I come from Panton, Vermont, and that kind of story doesn't go down with me.

"The real thing behind all this is simply race prejudice—and I don't say I'm blaming those that hold it. I hate those Innsmouth folks myself, and I wouldn't care to go to their town. I suppose you know—though I can see you're a Westerner by the way you talk—what a lot our New England ships used to have to do with queer ports in Asia, Africa, the South Seas, and everywhere else, and what queer kinds of people they sometimes brought back with them. You've probably heard about the Salem man that came back with a Chinese wife, and maybe you know there's still a colony of Fiji Islanders somewhere around Cape Cod.

"Well, there must be something like that back of the Innsmouth people. The place was always badly cut off from the rest of the country by salt marshes and inlets, and we can't be sure about the ins and outs of the matter, but it's pretty plain that old Capt. Marsh must have brought home some odd specimens when he had all three of his ships in commission back in the 1830's and 1840's. There certainly is a strange kind of a streak in the Innsmouth folks today—I don't know how to express it, but it sort of makes me crawl. You'll notice it a little in Joe Sargent if you take his bus. Some of them have flat noses, big mouths, weak retreating chins, and a funny kind of rough grey skin. The sides of their necks are sort of shrivelled or creased up, and they get bald very young. Nobody around here or in Arkham will have anything to do with them, and they act kind of offish themselves when they come to town. They used to ride on the railroad, walking and taking the train at Rowley or Ipswich, but now they use that bus.

"Yes, there's a hotel in Innsmouth—called the Gilman House—but I don't believe it can amount to much. I wouldn't advise you to try it. Better stay over here and take the ten o'clock bus tomorrow morning. Then you can get an evening bus there for Arkham at eight o'clock. There was a factory inspector who stopped at the Gilman a couple of years ago, and he had a lot of unpleasant hints about the place. It seems they get a queer crowd there, for this fellow heard voices in other rooms that gave him the shivers. It was foreign talk, but he said the bad thing about it was the kind of voice that sometimes spoke. It sounded so unnatural–slopping-like, he said–that he didn't dare go to sleep. Just kept dressed and lit out early in the morning. The talk went on most of the night.

"This man–Casey, his name was–had a lot to say about the old Marsh factory, and what he said fitted in very well with some of the wild stories. The books were in no kind of shape, and the machinery looked old and almost abandoned, as if it hadn't been run a great deal. The place still used water power from the Lower Falls of the Manuxet. There were only a few employees, and they didn't seem to be doing much. It made me think, when he told me, about the local rumours that Marsh doesn't actually make the stuff he sells. Many people say he doesn't get enough factory supplies to be really running the place, and that he must be importing those queer ornaments from somewhere–heaven knows where. I don't believe that, though. The Marshes have been selling those outlandish rings and armlets and tiaras and things for nearly a hundred years; and if there were anywhere else where they got 'em, the general public would have found out all about it by this time. Then, too, there's no shipping or in-bound trucking around Innsmouth that would account for such imports. What does get imported is the queerest sort of glass and rubber trinkets–makes you think of what they used to buy in the old days to trade with savages. But it's a straight fact that all inspectors run up against queer things at the plant. Twenty odd years ago one of them disappeared at Innsmouth–never heard of again–and I myself knew George Cole, who went insane down there one night, and had to be lugged away by two men from the Danvers asylum, where he is now. He talks of some kind of sound and shrieks things about 'scaly water-devils'.

"And that makes me think of another of the old stories–about the black reef off the coast. Devil's Reef, they call it. It's almost above water a good part of the time, but at that you could hardly call it a real island. The story is that there's a whole legion of devils seen sometimes on that reef–sprawled about, or darting in and out of some kind of caves near the top. It's a rugged, uneven thing, a good bit over a mile out, and sailors used to make great detours just to avoid it. One of the things they had against Capt. Marsh was that he used to land on it sometimes when it was fairly dry. Probably the rock formation interested him, but there was talk about his having dealings with daemons. That was before the big epidemic of 1846, when over half the people in Innsmouth were carried off. They never did quite figure out what the trouble was, but it was probably some foreign kind of disease brought from China or somewhere by the shipping.

"Maybe that plague took off the best blood in Innsmouth. Anyway, they're a doubtful lot now–and there can't be more than 500 or 600 of them. The rich Marshes are as bad as any. I guess they're all what people call 'white trash' down South—lawless and sly, and full of secret doings. Lobster fishermen, mostly—exporting by truck. Nobody can ever keep track of 'em, and state school officials and census people have a devil of a time. That's why I wouldn't go at night if I were you. I've never been there and have no wish to go; but I guess a daytime trip wouldn't hurt you—even though the people here will advise you not to take it. If you're just sightseeing, Innsmouth ought to be quite a place for you."

And so I spent that evening at the Newburyport Public Library looking up data about Innsmouth. When I had tried to question natives in the shops, the lunch room, and the fire station I had found them even harder to get started than the ticket agent had predicted, and realised that I could not spare the time to overcome their first instinctive reticence. They had a kind of obscure suspiciousness. At the YMCA the clerk merely discouraged my going to such a dismal, decadent place, and the people at the library shewed much the same attitude, holding Innsmouth to be merely an exaggerated case of civic degeneration.

The Essex County histories on the shelves had very little to say, except that the town was founded in 1643, noted for shipbuilding before the Revolution, a seat of great marine prosperity in the early nineteenth century, and later on a minor factory centre using the Manuxet as power. References to decline were very few, though the significance of the later records was unmistakable. After the Civil War all industrial life centred in the Marsh Refining Company at the Lower Falls, and the marketing of its products formed the only remaining bit of major commerce. There were very few foreigners; mostly Poles and Portuguese on the southern fringe of the town. Local finances were very bad, and but for the Marsh factory the place would have been bankrupt.

I saw a good many booklets and catalogues and advertising calendars of the Marsh Refining Company in the business department of the library, and began to realise what a striking thing that lone industry was. The jewels and ornaments it sold were of the finest possible artistry and the most extreme originality; so delicately wrought, indeed, that one could not doubt but that handicraft played a large part in at least their final stages of manufacture. Some of the half-tone pictures of them interested me profoundly, for the strangeness and beauty of the designs seemed to my eye indicative of a profound and exotic genius—a genius so spectacular and bizarre that one could not help wondering whence the inspiration had come. It was easy to credit the boast of one of the booklets that this jewellery was a favourite with persons of sophisticated taste, and that several specimens were exhibited in museums of modern craftsmanship.

Large pieces predominated—armlets, tiaras, and elaborate pendants

—but rings and lesser items were numerous. The raised or incised designs—partly conventional and partly with a curious marine motif—were wrought in a style of tremendous distinctiveness and of utter dissimilarity to the art traditions of any race or epoch I knew about. This other-worldly character was emphasised by the oddness of the precious alloy, whose general effect was suggested in several colour-plates. Something about these pictured things fascinated me intensely—almost disproportionately—and I resolved to see as many original specimens as possible both at Innsmouth and in shops and museums elsewhere. Yet there was a distinct element of repulsion mixed with the fascination; proceeding, perhaps, from the evil and silly old legends about the founder of the business which the ticket agent had told me.

[p. 17:]

The door of the Marsh retail office was open, and I walked in with considerable expectancy. The interior was shabby and ill-lighted, but contained a large number of display cases of solid and capable construction. A youngish man came forward to meet me, and as I studied his face a fresh wave of disturbance passed over me. He was not unhandsome, but there was something subtly bizarre and aberrant about his features and vocal timbre. I could not stifle a keen sudden aversion, and acquired an unexplained reluctance to seem like any sort of curious investigator. Before I knew it I found myself telling the fellow that I was a jewellery buyer for a Cleveland firm, and preparing myself to shew a merely professional interest in what I should see.

It was hard, though, to carry out this policy. The clerk switched on more lights and began to lead me from case to case, but when I beheld the glittering marvels before me I could scarcely walk steadily or talk coherently. It took no excessive sensitiveness to beauty to make one literally gasp at the strange, alien loveliness of these opulent objects, and as I gazed fascinatedly I saw how little justice even the colour-plates had done them. Even now I can hardly describe what I saw—though those who own such pieces or have seen them in shops and museums can supply the missing data. The massed effect of so many elaborate samples was what produced my especial feeling of awe and unrest. For somehow or other, these singular grotesques and arabesques did not seem to be the product of any earthly handiwork—least of all a factory only a stone's throw away. The patterns and traceries all hinted of remote spaces and unimaginable abysses, and the aquatic nature of the occasional pictorial items added to the general unearthliness. Some of the fabulous monsters filled me with an uncomfortable sense of dark pseudo-memory which I tried

[p. 21:]
the taint and blasphemy of furtive Innsmouth. He, like me, was a normal being outside the pall of decay and normally terrified by it. But because he was so inextricably close to the thing, he had been broken in a way that I was not yet broken.

Shaking off the hands of the firemen who sought to detain him, the ancient rose to his feet and greeted me as if I were an acquaintance. The grocery youth had told me where most of Uncle Zadok's liquor was obtained, and without a word I began leading him in that direction —through the Square and around into Eliot Street. His step was astonishingly brisk for one of his age and bibulousness, and I marvelled at the original strength of his constitution. My haste to leave Innsmouth had abated for the moment, and I felt instead a queer curiosity to dip into this mumbling patriarch's chaotic store of extravagant myth.

When we had bought a quart of whiskey in the rear of a dismal variety store, I led Uncle Zadok along South Street to the utterly abandoned section of the waterfront, and still farther southward to a point where even the fishermen on the distant breakwater could not see us, where I knew we could talk undisturbed. For some reason or other he seemed to dislike this arrangement—casting nervous glances out to sea in the direction of Devil Reef—but the lure of the whiskey was too strong for him to resist. After we had found a seat on the edge of a rotting wharf I gave him a pull at the bottle and waited for it to take effect. Naturally I graduated the doses very carefully, for I did not wish the old man's loquacity to turn into a stupor. As he grew more mellow, I began to venture some remarks and inquiries about Innsmouth, and was really startled by the terrible and sincere portentousness of his lowered voice. He did not seem as crazy as his wild tales would indicate, and I found myself shuddering even when I could not believe his fantastic inventions. I hardly wondered at the naive credulity of superstitious Father Iwanicki.

THE BATTLE THAT ENDED THE CENTURY
(MS. Found in a Time Machine)

[by H. P. Lovecraft and R. H. Barlow]

On the eve of the year 2001 a vast crowd of interested spectators were present amidst the romantic ruins of Cohen's Garage, on the former site of New York, to witness a fistic encounter between two renowned champions of the strange-story firmament–Two-Gun Bob, the Terror of the Plains, and Knockout Bernie, the Wild Wolf of West Shokan. Before the battle the auguries were determined by the venerated Thibetan Lama Bill Lum Li, who evoked the primal serpent-god of Valusia and found unmistakable signs of victory for both sides. Creampuffs were inattentively vended by Wladislaw Brenryk–the partakers being treated by the official surgeons, Drs. D. H. Killer and M. Gin Brewery.

The gong was sounded at 39 o'clock, after which the air grew red with the gore of battle, lavishly flung about by the mighty Texas slaughterer. Very shortly the first actual damage occurred–the loosening of several teeth in both participants. One, bouncing out from the Wolf's mouth after a casual tap from Two-Gun, described a parabola toward Yucatán; being retrieved in a hasty expedition by Messrs. A. Hijacked Barrell and G. A. Scotland. This incident was used by the eminent sociologist and ex-poet Frank Chimesleep Short, Jr., as the basis of a ballad of proletarian propaganda with three intentionally defective lines. Meanwhile a potentate from a neighbouring kingdom, the Effjay of Akkamin (also known to himself as an amateur critic), expressed his frenzied disgust at the technique of the combatants, at the same time peddling photographs of the fighters (with himself in the foreground) at five cents each.

Robert E. Howard,
aka "Two-Gun Bob"

In round two the Shokan Soaker's sturdy right crashed through the Texan's ribs and became entangled in sundry viscera; thereby enabling Two-Gun to get in several telling blows on his opponent's unprotected chin. Bob was greatly annoyed by the effeminate squeamishness shewn by several onlookers as muscles, glands, gore, and bits of flesh were spattered over the ringside. During this round the eminent magazine-cover anatomist Mrs. M. Blunderage portrayed the battlers as a pair of spirited nudes behind a thin veil of conveniently curling tobacco-smoke, while the late Mr. C. Half-Cent provided a sketch of three Chinamen clad in silk hats and galoshes—this being his own original conception of the affray. Among the amateur sketches made was one by Mr. Goofy Hooey, which later gained fame in the annual Cubist exhibit as "Abstraction of an Eradicated Pudding".

In the third round the fight grew really rough; several ears and other appurtenances being wholly or partially detached from the frontier battler by the Shokan Shocker. Somewhat irritated, Two-Gun countered with some exceptionally sharp blows; severing many fragments from his aggressor, who continued to fight with all his remaining members.

The entire affair was reported by Mr. W. Lablache Talcum, his copy being revised by Horse Power Hateart. Throughout the event notes were taken by M. le Comte d'Erlette for a 200-volume novel-cycle in the Proustian manner, to be entitled *Morning in September,* with illustrations by Mrs. Blunderage. Mr. J. Caesar Warts frequently interviewed both battlers and all the more important spectators; obtaining as souvenirs (after a spirited struggle with the Effjay) an autographed quarter-rib of Two-Gun's, in an excellent state of preservation, and three finger-nails from the Wild Wolf. Lighting effects were supplied by the Electrical Testing Laboratories under the supervision of H. Kanebrake. The fourth round was prolonged eight hours at the request of the official artist, Mr. H. Wanderer, who wished to put certain shadings of fantasy into his representation of the Wolf's depleted physiognomy, which included several supernumerary details supplied by the imagination.

The climax came in round five, when the Texas Tearer's left passed entirely through Battling Bernie's face and brought both sluggers to the mat. This was adjudged a finish by the referee—Robertieff Essovitch Karovsky, the Muscovite Ambassador—who, in view of the Shokan Shocker's gory state, declared the latter to be essentially liquidated according to the Marxian ideology. The Wild Wolf entered an official protest, which was promptly overruled on the ground that all the points necessary to technical death were theoretically present.

The gonfalons sounded a fanfare of triumph for the victor, while

Bernard Austin Dwyer,
aka "Knockout Bernie"

the technically vanquished was committed to the care of the official mortician, Mr. Teaberry Quince. During the ceremonies the theoretical corpse strolled away for a bite of bologna, but a tasteful cenotaph was supplied to furnish a focus for the rites. The funeral procession was headed by a gaily bedecked hearse driven by Malik Taus, the Peacock Sultan, who sat on the box in West Point uniform and turban, and steered an expert course over several formidable hedges and stone walls. About half way to the cemetery the cortège was rejoined by the corpse, who sat beside Sultan Malik on the box and finished his bologna sandwich—his ample girth having made it impossible to enter the hastily selected cenotaph. An appropriate dirge was rendered by Maestro Sing Lee Bawledout on the piccolo; Messrs. De Silva, Brown, and Henderson's celebrated aria, "Never Swat a Fly", from the old cantata *Just Imagine,* being chosen for the occasion. The only detail omitted from the funeral was the interment, which was interrupted by the disconcerting news that the official gate-taker—the celebrated financier and publisher Ivar K. Rodent, Esq.—had absconded with the entire proceeds.

Mr. Talcum's report of the event, illustrated by the well-known artist Klarkash-Ton (who esoterically depicted the fighters as boneless fungi), was printed—after repeated rejections by the discriminating editor of the *Windy City Grab-Bag*—as a broadside by W. Peter Chef. This, through the efforts of Otis Adelbert Kline, was finally placed on sale in the bookshop of Smearum & Weep, three and a half copies finally being disposed of through the alluring catalogue description supplied by Samuelus Philanthropus, Esq.

In response to this wide demand, the text was finally reprinted by Mr. De Merit in the polychromatic pages of Wurst's *Weakly Americana* under the title "Has Science Been Outmoded? or, The Millers in the Garage". No copies, however, remain in circulation; since all which were not snapped up by fanatical bibliophiles were seized by the police in connexion with the libel suit of the Wild Wolf, who was, after several appeals ending with the World Court, adjudged not only officially alive but the clear winner of the combat.

[*Glossary of Names*—Ed.

Two-Gun Bob—Robert E. Howard
Knockout Bernie, the Wild Wolf of West Shokan—Bernard Austin Dwyer, of West Shokan, New York
Bill Lum Li—William Lumley
Wladislaw Brenryk—H. Warner Munn
D. H. Killer—David H. Keller
M. Gin Brewery—Miles J. Breuer
A. Hijacked Barrell—A. Hyatt Verrill

G. A. Scotland–George Allan England
Frank Chimesleep Short, Jr.–Frank Belknap Long, Jr.
The Effjay of Akkamin–Forrest J. Ackerman
Mrs. M. Blunderage–Margaret Brundage (artist for *Weird Tales*)
Mr. C. Half-Cent–C. C. Senf (artist for *Weird Tales*)
Mr. Goofy Hooey–Guy L. Huey (artist for *Marvel Tales*)
W. Lablache Talcum–Wilfred Blanch Talman
Horse Power Hateart–Howard Phillips Lovecraft
M. le Comte d'Erlette–August Derleth (author of *Evening in Spring*)
J. Caesar Warts–Julius Schwartz
H. Kanebrake–H. C. Koenig (employed by the Electrical Testing Laboratories)
H. Wanderer–Howard Wandrei
Robertieff Essovitch Karovsky–Robert S. Carr
Teaberry Quince–Seabury Quinn
Malik Taus, the Peacock Sultan–E. Hoffmann Price
Sing Lee Bawledout–F. Lee Baldwin
Ivar K. Rodent–Hugo Gernsback
Klarkash-Ton–Clark Ashton Smith
Windy City Grab-Bag–*Weird Tales*
W. Peter Chef–W. Paul Cook
Smearum & Weep–Dauber & Pine
Samuelus Philanthropus–Samuel Loveman
Mr. De Merit–A. Merritt (author of *The Dwellers in the Mirage*)
Wurst's *Weakly Americana*–Hearst's *The American Weekly*]

COLLAPSING COSMOSES

by H. P. Lovecraft and R. H. Barlow

[Portions in brackets were written by R. H. Barlow.—Ed.]

Dam Bor glued each of his six eyes to the lenses of the cosmoscope. His nasal tentacles were orange with fear, and his antennae buzzed hoarsely as he dictated his report to the operator behind him. "It has come!" he cried. "That blur in the ether can be nothing less than a fleet from outside the space-time continuum we know. Nothing like this has ever appeared before. It must be an enemy. Give the alarm to the Inter-Cosmic Chamber of Commerce. There's no time to lose—at this rate they'll be upon us in less than six centuries. Hak Ni must have a chance to get the fleet in action at once."

[I glanced up from the *Windy City Grab-Bag*, which had beguiled my inactive peace-time days in the Super-Galactic Patrol. The handsome young vegetable, with whom I shared my bowl of caterpillar custard since earliest infancy, and with whom I had been thrown out of every joint in the intra-dimensional city of Kastor-Ya,] had really a worried look upon his lavender face. After he had given the alarm we jumped on our ether-bikes and hastened across to the outer planet on which the Chamber held its sessions.

[Within the Great Council Chamber, which measured twenty-eight square feet (with quite a high ceiling), were gathered delegates from all the thirty-seven galaxies of our immediate universe. Oll Stof, President of the Chamber and representative of the Milliner's Soviet, raised his eyeless snout with dignity] and prepared to address the assembled multitude. He was a highly developed protozoan organism from Nov-Kas, and spoke by emitting alternate waves of heat and cold.

["Gentlemen," he radiated, "a terrible peril has come upon us which I feel I must bring to your attention."

Everybody applauded riotously, as a wave of excitement rippled through the variegated audience; those who were handless slithering their tentacles together.

He continued: "Hak Ni, crawl upon the dais!"

There was a thunderous silence, during which a faint prompting was heard] from the dizzy summit of the platform. [Hak Ni, the yellow-furred and valorous commander of our ranks through numerous installments, ascended to the towering peak inches above the floor.

"My friends—" he began, with an eloquent scraping of his posterior limbs, "these treasured walls and pillars shall not mourn on my account. . . ." At this point, one of his numerous relatives cheered. "Well do I remember when . . ."

Oll Stof interrupted him.] "You have anticipated my thoughts and orders. Go forth and win for dear old Inter-Cosmic."

[Two paragraphs later found us soaring out past innumerable stars toward where a faint blur half a million light-years long marked the presence of the hated enemy, whom we had not seen. What monsters of malformed grotesqueness seethed out there among the moons of infinity, we really didn't know, but there was a malign menace in the glow that steadily increased until it spanned the entire heavens. Very soon we made out separate objects in the blur. Before all my horror-stricken vision-areas there spread an endless array of scissors-shaped space-ships of totally unfamiliar form.

Then from the direction of the enemy there came a terrifying sound, which I soon recognised as a hail and a challenge. An answering thrill crept through me as I met with uplifted antennae this threat of battle with a monstrous intrusion upon our fair system from unknown outside abysses.]

At the sound, [which was something like that of a rusty sewing-machine, only more horrible,] Hak Ni too raised his snout in defiance, radiating a masterful order to the captains of the fleet. Instantly the huge space-ships swung into battle formation, with only a hundred or two of them many light-years out of line.

THE CHALLENGE FROM BEYOND

[In the omitted introductory portions of this composite story, geologist George Campbell has encountered a curious crystalline cube while on vacation in the Canadian woods. Campbell examines the strange object, observes within a glimmering sapphire luminescence, and feels himself being drawn into the cube as Lovecraft's segment commences.—Ed.]

As the mist-blurred light of the sapphire suns grew more and more intense, the outlines of the globe ahead wavered and dissolved to a churning chaos. Its pallor and its motion and its music all blended themselves with the engulfing mist—bleaching it to a pale steel-colour and setting it undulantly and murmuringly in motion. And the sapphire suns, too, melted imperceptibly into the greying infinity of shapeless pulsation.

Meanwhile the sense of forward, outward motion grew intolerably, incredibly, cosmically swift. Every standard of speed known to earth seemed dwarfed, and Campbell knew that any such flight in physical reality would mean instant death to a human being. Even as it was—in this strange, hellish hypnosis or nightmare—the quasi-visual impression of meteor-like hurtling almost unhinged his mind. Though there were no real points of reference in the grey, pulsing, murmuring void, he felt that he was approaching and passing the speed of light itself. Finally his consciousness did go under—the merciful blackness swallowed everything.

It was very suddenly, and amidst the most impenetrable darkness, that thoughts and ideas again came to George Campbell. Of how many moments—or years—or eternities—had elapsed since his flight through the grey void, he could form no estimate. He knew only that he seemed to be at rest and without pain. Indeed, the absence of all physical sensation was the salient quality of his condition. It made even the blackness seem less solidly black—suggesting as it did that he was rather a disembodied intelligence in a state beyond physical senses, than a corporeal being with senses deprived of their accustomed objects of perception. He could think sharply and quickly—almost preternaturally so—yet could form no idea whatsoever of his situation.

Half by instinct, he realised that he was not in his own tent. True, he might have awaked there from a nightmare to a world equally black; yet he knew this was not so. There was no camp cot beneath him—he had no hands to feel the blankets and canvas surface and flashlight that ought to be around him—there was no sensation of cold in the air—no flap through which he could glimpse the pale night outside . . . something was wrong, dreadfully wrong.

He cast his mind backward and thought of the fluorescent cube which had hypnotised him—of that, and all which had followed. He had known that his mind was going, yet had been unable to draw back. At the last moment there had been a shocking, panic fear—a subconscious fear beyond even that caused by the sensation of daemoniac flight. It had come from some vague flash of remote recollection—just what, he could not at once tell. Some cell-group in the back of his head had seemed to find a cloudily familiar quality in the cube—and that familiarity was fraught with dim terror. Now he tried to remember what the familiarity and the terror were.

Little by little it came to him. Once—long ago, in connexion with his geological life-work—he had read of something like that cube. It had to do with those debatable and disquieting clay fragments called the Eltdown Shards, dug up from pre-carboniferous strata in southern England thirty years before. Their shape and markings were so queer that a few scholars hinted at artificiality, and made wild conjectures about them and their origin. They came, clearly, from a time when no human beings could exist on the globe—but their contours and figurings were damnably puzzling. They seemed to have been broken from some larger inscribed surface. That was how they got their name.

It was not, however, in the writings of any sober scientist that Campbell had seen that reference to a crystal, disc-holding globe. The source was far less reputable, and infinitely more vivid. About 1912 a deeply learned Sussex clergyman of occultist leanings—the Reverend Arthur Brooke Winters-Hall—had professed to identify the markings on the Eltdown Shards with some of the so-called "pre-human hieroglyphs" persistently cherished and esoterically handed down in certain mystical circles, and had published at his own expense what purported to be a "translation" of the primal and baffling "inscriptions"—a "translation" still quoted frequently and seriously by occult writers. In this "translation"—a surprisingly long brochure in view of the limited number of "shards" existing—had occurred the narrative, supposedly of pre-human authorship, containing the now-frightening reference.

As the story went, there dwelt on a world—and eventually on countless other worlds—of outer space a mighty race of worm-like beings whose attainments and whose control of natural forces surpassed anything within the range of terrestrial imagination. They had mastered the art of interstellar travel early in their career, and had peopled every habitable planet in their own galaxy—killing off the races they found.

Beyond the limits of their galaxy—which was not ours—they could not navigate in person; but in their quest for knowledge of all space and time they discovered a means of spanning certain trans-galactic gulfs with their minds. They devised peculiar objects—strangely energised cubes of a curious crystal containing hypnotic talismans and enclosed in space-resisting spherical envelopes of an unknown substance—which could be forcibly expelled beyond the limits of their universe, and which would respond to the attraction of cool solid matter only.

These, of which a few would necessarily land on various inhabited worlds in outside universes, formed the ether-bridges needed for mental communication. Atmospheric friction burned away the protecting envelope, leaving the cube exposed and subject to discovery by the intelligent minds of the world where it fell. By its very nature, the cube would attract and rivet attention. This, when coupled with the action of light, was sufficient to set its special properties working.

The mind that noticed the cube would be drawn into it by the power of the disc, and would be sent on a thread of obscure energy to the place whence the disc had come—the remote world of the worm-like space-explorers across stupendous galactic abysses. Received in one of the machines to which each cube was attuned, the captured mind would remain suspended without body or senses until examined by one of the dominant race. Then it would, by an obscure process of interchange, be pumped of all its contents. The investigator's mind would now occupy the strange machine while the captive mind occupied the interrogator's worm-like body. Then, in another interchange, the interrogator's mind would leap across boundless space to the captive's vacant and unconscious body on the trans-galactic world—animating the alien tenement as best it might, and exploring the alien world in the guise of one of its denizens.

When done with exploration, the adventurer would use the cube and its disc in accomplishing his return—and sometimes the captured mind would be restored safely to its own remote world. Not always, however, was the dominant race so kind. Sometimes, when a potentially important race capable of space travel was found, the worm-like folk would employ the cube to capture and annihilate minds by the thousands, and would extirpate the race for diplomatic reasons—using the exploring minds as agents of destruction.

In other cases sections of the worm-folk would permanently occupy a trans-galactic planet—destroying the captured minds and wiping out the remaining inhabitants preparatory to settling down in unfamiliar bodies. Never, however, could the parent civilisation be quite duplicated in such a case; since the new planet would not contain all the materials necessary for the worm-race's arts. The cubes, for example, could be made only on the home planet.

Only a few of the numberless cubes sent forth ever found a landing and response on an inhabited world—since there was no such thing as *aiming* them at goals beyond sight or knowledge. Only three, ran the story, had ever landed on peopled worlds in our particular universe. Of these one had struck a planet near the galactic rim two thousand billion years ago, whilst another had lodged three billion years ago on a world near the centre of the galaxy. The third—and the only one ever known to have invaded the solar system—had reached our own earth a hundred and fifty million years ago.

It was with this latter that Dr. Winters-Hall's "translation" chiefly dealt. When the cube struck the earth, he wrote, the ruling terrestrial species was a huge, cone-shaped race surpassing all others before or since in mentality and achievements. This race was so advanced that it had actually sent minds abroad in both space *and time* to explore the cosmos, hence recognised something of what had happened when the cube fell from the sky and certain individuals had suffered mental change after gazing at it.

Realising that the changed individuals represented invading minds, the race's leaders had them destroyed—even at the cost of leaving the displaced minds exiled in alien space. They had had experience with even stranger transitions. When, through a mental exploration of space and time, they formed a rough idea of what the cube was, they carefully hid the thing from light and sight, and guarded it as a menace. They did not wish to destroy a thing so rich in later experimental possibilities. Now and then some rash, unscrupulous adventurer would furtively gain access to it and sample its perilous powers despite the consequences—but all such cases were discovered, and safely and drastically dealt with.

Of this evil meddling the only bad result was that the worm-like outside race learned from the new exiles what had happened to their explorers on earth, and conceived a violent hatred of the planet and all its life-forms. They would have depopulated it if they could, and indeed sent additional cubes into space in the wild hope of striking it by accident in unguarded places—but that accident never came to pass.

The cone-shaped terrestrial beings kept the one existing cube in a special shrine as a relique and basis for experiments, till after aeons it was lost amidst the chaos of war and the destruction of the great polar city where it was guarded. When, fifty million years ago, the beings sent their minds ahead into the infinite future to avoid a nameless peril of inner earth, the whereabouts of the sinister cube from space were unknown.

This much, according to the learned occultist, the Eltdown Shards had said. What now made the account so obscurely frightful to Campbell was the minute accuracy with which the alien cube had been described. Every detail tallied—dimensions, consistency, hieroglyphed central disc, hypnotic effects. As he thought the matter over and over amidst the darkness of his strange situation, he began to wonder whether his whole experience with the crystal cube—indeed, its very existence—were not a nightmare brought on by some freakish subconscious memory of this old bit of extravagant, charlatanic reading. If so, though, the nightmare must still be in force; since his present apparently bodiless state had nothing of normality in it.

Of the time consumed by this puzzled memory and reflection, Campbell could form no estimate. Everything about his state was so unreal that ordinary dimensions and measurements became meaningless. It seemed an eternity, but perhaps it was not really long before the sudden interruption came. What happened was as strange and inexplicable as the blankness it succeeded. There was a sensation—of the mind rather than of the body—and all at once Campbell felt his thoughts swept or sucked beyond his control in tumultuous and chaotic fashion.

Memories arose irresponsibly and irrelevantly. All that he knew—all his personal background, traditions, experiences, scholarship, dreams, ideas, and inspirations—welled up abruptly and simultaneously, with a dizzying speed and abundance which soon made him unable to keep track of any separate concept. The parade of all his mental contents became an avalanche, a cascade, a vortex. It was as horrible and vertiginous as his hypnotic flight through space when the crystal cube pulled him. Finally it sapped his consciousness and brought on a fresh oblivion.

Another measureless blank—and then a slow trickle of sensations. This time it was physical, not mental. Sapphire light, and a low rumble of distant sound. There were vague tactile impressions—he could realise that he was lying at full length on something, though there was a baffling strangeness about the feel of his posture. He could not reconcile the pressure of the supporting surface with his own outlines—or with the outlines of the human form at all. He tried to move his arms, but found no definite response to the attempt. Instead, there were little ineffectual nervous twitches all over the area which seemed to mark his body.

He tried to open his eyes more widely, but found himself unable to control their mechanism. The sapphire light came in a vague, diffused, nebulous manner, and could nowhere be voluntarily focussed into definiteness. Gradually, though, visual images began to trickle in curiously and indecisively. The limits and qualities of vision were not those which he was used to, but he could roughly correlate the sensation with what he had known as sight. As this sensation gained some degree of stability, Campbell realised that he must still be in the throes of nightmare.

He seemed to be in a room of considerable extent—of medium height, but with a large proportionate area. On every side—and he could apparently see all four sides at once—were high, narrowish slits which seemed to serve as combined doors and windows. There were singular low tables or pedestals, but no furniture of normal nature and proportions. Through the slits streamed floods of sapphire light, and beyond them could be mistily seen the sides and roofs of fantastic buildings like clustered cubes. On the walls—in the vertical panels between the slits—were strange markings of an oddly disquieting character. It was some time before Campbell understood why they disturbed him so—then he saw that they were, in repeated instances, precisely like some of the hieroglyphs on the disc within the crystal cube.

The actual nightmare element, though, was something more than this. It began with the living thing which presently entered through one of the slits, advancing deliberately toward him and bearing a metal box of bizarre proportions and glassy, mirror-like surfaces. For this thing was nothing human—nothing of earth—nothing even of man's myths and dreams. It was a gigantic, pale-grey worm or centipede, as large around as a man and twice as long, with a disc-like, apparently eyeless, cilia-fringed head bearing a purple central orifice. It glided on its rear pairs of legs, with its fore part raised vertically—the legs, or at least two pairs of them, here serving as arms. Along its spinal ridge was a curious purple comb, and a fan-shaped tail of some grey membrane ended its grotesque bulk. There was a ring of flexible red spikes around its neck, and from the twistings of these came clicking, twanging sounds in measured, deliberate rhythms.

Here, indeed, was outré nightmare at its height—capricious fantasy at its apex. But even this vision of delirium was not what caused George Campbell to lapse a third time into unconsciousness. It took one more thing—one final, unbearable touch—to do that. As the nameless worm advanced with its glistening box, the reclining man caught in the mirror-like surface a glimpse of what should have been his own body. Yet—horribly verifying his disordered and unfamiliar sensations—it was not his own body at all that he saw reflected in the burnished metal. It was, instead, the loathsome, pale-grey bulk of one of the giant centipedes.

II

THE WEIRD FANTASIST

Lovecraft was distinctive in being both a powerful theoretician and practitioner of the weird tale. Some of his remarks—those, for example, found in his landmark critical essay "Supernatural Horror in Literature" (1925–27)—are nearly definitive and have influenced much subsequent work in the field. Of course, it could be said that his theory of weird fiction was largely an after-the-fact justification of his own brand of cosmic horror, but his pronouncements are no less suggestive for that.

Lovecraft's first utterance of his theory of the weird occurs in the *In Defence of Dagon* essays of 1921, which, because of their predominantly philosophical content, are included in the next section. There he makes a highly provocative division of fiction into three branches: romantic (this is "for those who value action and emotion for their own sake; who are interested in striking events which conform to a preconceived artificial pattern"); realistic (this is "for those who are intellectual and analytical rather than poetical or emotional"); and imaginative (this "groups isolated impressions into gorgeous patterns and finds strange relations and associations among the objects of visible and invisible Nature"). This tripartite division, unorthodox as it is, is vital to Lovecraft's purpose, for what he is really asserting is that imaginative fiction draws upon the best aspects of both realism and romanticism without the drawbacks of either. In later years Lovecraft was emphatic about the distinction between weird fiction and romanticism, probably because it was and continues to be an assumption of many readers, writers, and critics that the former grew out of the latter in the Gothic novels of the late eighteenth century and was therefore a part of the latter. In a letter to Clark Ashton Smith (November 16, 1926) Lovecraft rebuts this position with vigor: "As to romanticism and fantasy—I myself dislike the former except in the latter form. To me there is really something 'non-vital' about the overcoloured representation of *what purports to be real life*.... There is to me something puerile in devising a sort of conventionalised variant of life, with spurious and artificial thoughts and feelings, and then getting maudlin and excited and effusive over it. But *fantasy* is something altogether different. Here we have an art based on the imaginative life of the human mind, *frankly recognised as such;* and in its way as natural and scientific—as truly related to natural (even if uncommon and delicate) psychological processes as the starkest of photographic realism."

This passage is enormously significant because it underscores what Lovecraft has really been thinking all along but cannot quite bring himself to say: that weird fiction is almost indistinguishable from realism, and indeed *is* a sort of realism (as regards truth to human emotions and to the facts of science) except where the bizarre enters in. Lovecraft found actual realism—the realism, say, of Dreiser—wearisome and admitted to an inability to write it; but his type of weird fiction is realistic because, as he says in "Notes on Writing Weird Fiction," "Inconceivable events and conditions have a special handicap to overcome, and this can be accomplished only through the maintenance of a careful realism in every phase of the story *except* that touching on the one given marvel."

It is important to establish that the sort of "marvel" Lovecraft is conceiving here is not, strictly speaking, "supernatural." That word never appears in his later writing on the subject. When he says in "Notes on Writing Weird Fiction" that "I choose weird stories because they suit my inclination best—one of my strongest and most persistent wishes being to achieve, momentarily, the illusion of some strange suspension or violation of the galling limitations of time, space, and natural law which forever imprison us and frustrate our curiosity about the infinite cosmic spaces beyond the radius of our sight and analysis," he is careful to speak of the "illusion" of defying natural law; the "suspension or violation" pertains merely to the limitations of our own human conceptions of natural law. Lovecraft, I believe, came dimly to recognize that he was at a watershed in the history of weird fiction: gone was the time when even an aesthetic belief in such stereotyped creations as vampires, werewolves, and ghosts could be maintained for the duration of a tale; these creatures too obviously defy known and incontrovertible natural laws to be anything but preposterous. What remains? Chiefly it is the "great outside"—those vast untapped regions of space where man has not yet probed; as he wrote in a celebrated letter to Frank Belknap Long (February 27, 1931): "Reason as we may, we cannot destroy a normal perception of the highly limited and fragmentary nature of our visible world of perception and experience as scaled against the outside abyss of unthinkable galaxies and unplumbed dimensions. . . ." This leads to a momentous declaration: "The time has come when the normal revolt against time, space, and matter must assume a form not overtly incompatible with what is known of reality—when it must be gratified by images forming *supplements* rather than *contradictions* of the visible and mensurable universe. And what, if not a form of *non-supernatural cosmic art,* is to pacify this sense of revolt—as well as gratify the cognate sense of curiosity?"

It can be seen from all this that Lovecraft's mature weird writing is very close to science fiction, and it is not surprising that late in life Lovecraft seized the opportunity afforded by Hyman Bradofsky's *Californian* to write an essay (almost a polemic) about "interplanetary fiction," an essay that repeats many of the important theoretical statements of his piece on writing weird fiction. It is difficult to gauge the influence of Lovecraft's jeremiad, but shortly after his death the field certainly began to develop greater seriousness and substance, much along the lines Lovecraft here recommends. Fritz Leiber, himself one of the pioneers of literate and aesthetically refined science fiction, has aptly remarked that C. S. Lewis's *Out of the Silent Planet* (1938) seems almost to have been written with Lovecraft's stipulations in mind, especially as regards the sense of wonder attendant on leaving the earth and the nonanthropomorphism of alien entities.

The first item in this section, Lovecraft's commonplace book, relates not so much to his theory as to his practice of weird fiction. It is difficult to characterize this work: perhaps Lovecraft's own description, that it "consists of ideas, images, and quotations hastily jotted down for possible future use in weird fiction," is the best we can do. Much can be written on Lovecraft's use of this idea-book in his own fiction, and interested readers must consult David E. Schultz's definitive edition and commentary. Our text is a simplified one that strives to depart from the manuscript as little as possible; portions in brackets represent additions made by Lovecraft at a later time, many stemming from R. H. Barlow's request to date the entries and to indicate their use in Lovecraft's tales. The dates that Lovecraft has supplied are somewhat unreliable, and it is clear that he could not recall exactly when certain entries were made. Even the date of 1919, listed by Lovecraft as the commencement of the work, may be in doubt.

For our purposes we can remark on the "images" that the commonplace book contains in such abundance, for they relate to what Lovecraft says toward the end of "Notes on Writing Weird Fiction": ". . . all a wonder story can ever be is *a vivid picture of a certain type of human mood.*" That mood is to be evoked principally by the manipulation of images; and it becomes obvious upon reading the commonplace book that it was some focal image that gave birth to some of the best of Lovecraft's tales. In many cases, curiously, this image does not in the end occupy a central place in the finished story—the vignette of a man fashioning a bas-relief in his dreams is tossed almost haphazardly into "The Call of Cthulhu"—and yet that image nonetheless served as the nucleus around which the entire narrative was built. The commonplace book can tell us much about the psychology of Lovecraft's process of composition, but we remain bafflingly far from knowing how his mind absorbed the ideas, images, and moods he experienced and metamorphosed them into some of the finest weird fiction of the century. If we knew this, we could all be Lovecrafts.

COMMONPLACE BOOK

This book consists of ideas, images, and quotations hastily jotted down for possible future use in weird fiction. Very few are actually developed plots—for the most part they are merely suggestions or random impressions designed to set the memory or imagination working. Their sources are various—dreams, things read, casual incidents, idle conceptions, and so on.

H. P. Lovecraft

Presented to R. H. Barlow, Esq., on May 7, 1934—in exchange for an admirably neat typed copy from his skilled hand.

[1] *Demophon* shivered when the sun shone upon him. (Lover of darkness = ignorance.)

[2] Inhabitants of *Zinge*, over whom the star Canopus rises every night, are always gay and without sorrow.

[3] The shores of Attica respond in song to the waves of the Aegean.

[4] Horror Story—Man dreams of falling—found on floor mangled as tho' from falling from a vast height.

[5] Narrator walks along unfamiliar country road,—comes to strange region of the unreal.

[6] In Ld Dunsany's "Idle Days on the Yann": The inhabitants of the antient Astahahn, on the Yann, do all things according to antient ceremony. Nothing new is found. "Here we have fetter'd and manacled Time, who wou'd otherwise slay the Gods."

[7] *Horror Story:* The sculptured hand—or other artificial hand—which strangles its creator.

[8] Hor. Sto.: Man makes appt. with old enemy. Dies—body keeps appt.

[9] Dr. Eben Spencer plot.

[10] Dream of flying over city. [Celephaïs]

[11] Odd nocturnal ritual. Beasts dance and march to musick.

[12] Happenings in interval between preliminary sound and striking of clock—ending: "It was the tones of the clock striking three."

[13] House and garden–old–associations. Scene takes on strange aspect.
[14] Hideous sound in the dark.
[15] Bridge and slimy black waters. [Fungi–The Canal.]
[16] The walking dead–seemingly alive, but–
[17] Doors found mysteriously open and shut &c.–excite terror.
[18] Calamander-wood–a very valuable cabinet wood of Ceylon and S. India, resembling rosewood.
[19] Revise 1907 tale–painting of ultimate horror.
[20] Man journeys into the past–or imaginative realm–leaving bodily shell behind.
[21] A very ancient colossus in a very ancient desert. Face gone–no man hath seen it.
[22] Mermaid legend–*Encyc. Brit.* XVI–40.
[23] The man who would not sleep–dares not sleep–takes drugs to keep himself awake. Finally falls asleep–and *something* happens– Motto from Baudelaire p. 214. [Hypnos]
[24] Dunsany–"Go-By Street": Man stumbles on dream world–returns to earth–seeks to go back–succeeds, but finds dream world ancient and decayed as though by thousands of years.

[1919]

[25] Man visits museum of antiquities–asks that it accept a bas-relief *he has* just made–*old* and learned curator laughs and says he cannot accept anything so modern. Man says that 'dreams are older than brooding Egypt or the contemplative Sphinx or garden-girdled Babylonia' and that he had fashioned the sculpture in his dreams. Curator bids him shew his product, and when he does so curator shews horror, asks who the man may be. He tells modern name. "No–*before that*" says curator. Man does not remember except in dreams. Then curator offers high price, but man fears he means to destroy sculpture. Asks fabulous price–curator will consult directors.

Add good development and describe nature of bas-relief. [Cthulhu]

[26] Dream of ancient castle stairs–sleeping guards–narrow window–battle on plain between men of England and men of yellow tabards with red dragons. Leader of English challenges leader of foe to single combat. They fight. Foe unhelmeted, *but there is no head revealed.* Whole army of foe fades into mist, and watcher finds himself to be the English knight on the plain, mounted. Looks at castle, and sees a peculiar concentration of fantastic clouds over the highest battlements.

[27] *Life and Death:* Death—its desolation and horror—bleak spaces—sea-bottom—dead cities. But Life—the greater horror! Vast unheard-of reptiles and leviathans—hideous beasts of prehistoric jungle—rank slimy vegetation—evil instincts of primal man—Life is more horrible than death.

[28] *The Cats of Ulthar:* The cat is the soul of antique AEgyptus and bearer of tales from forgotten cities in Meroë and Ophir. He is the kin of the jungle's lords, and heir to the secrets of hoary and sinister Africa. The Sphinx is his cousin, and he speaks her language; but he is more ancient than the Sphinx, and remembers that which she hath forgotten. [used]

[29] Dream of Seekonk—ebbing tide—bolt from sky—exodus from Providence—fall of Congregational dome.

[30] Strange visit to a place at night—moonlight—castle of great magnificence &c. Daylight shews either abandonment or unrecognisable ruins—perhaps of vast antiquity.

[31] Prehistoric man preserved in Siberian ice. (See Winchell—*Walks and Talks in the Geological Field*—p. 156 et seq.)

[32] As dinosaurs were once surpassed by mammals, so will man-mammal be surpassed by insect or bird—fall of man before the new race.

[33] Determinism and prophecy.

[34] Moving away from earth more swiftly than light—past gradually unfolded—horrible revelation.

[35] Special beings with special senses from remote universes. Advent of an external universe to view.

[36] Disintegration of all matter to electrons and finally empty space assured, just as devolution of energy to radiant heat is known. Case of *acceleration*—man passes into space.

[37] Peculiar odour of a book of childhood induces repetition of childhood fancy.

[38] Drowning sensations—undersea—cities—ships—souls of the dead. Drowning is a horrible death.

[39] *Sounds*—possibly musical—heard in the night from other worlds or realms of being.

[40] Warning that certain ground is sacred or accursed; that a house or city must not be built upon it—or must be abandoned or destroyed if built, under penalty of catastrophe.

[41] The Italians call *Fear* La figlia della Morte—the daughter of Death.

[42] Fear of *mirrors*—memory of dream in which scene is altered and climax is hideous surprise at seeing oneself in the water or a mirror. (Identity?) [Outsider?]

[43] Monsters born living—burrow underground and multiply, form-

ing race of unsuspected daemons.

[44] Castle by pool or river—reflection fixed thro' centuries—castle destroyed, reflection lives to avenge destroyers weirdly.

[45] Race of immortal Pharaohs dwelling beneath pyramids in vast subterranean halls down black staircases.

[46] Hawthorne—unwritten plot: Visitor from tomb—stranger at some publick concourse followed at midnight to graveyard where he descends into the earth.

[47] From "Arabia" *Encyc. Britan.* II—255: Prehistoric fabulous tribes of Ad in the south, Thamood in the north, and Tasm and Jadis in the centre of the peninsula. "Very gorgeous are the descriptions given of Irem, the City of Pillars (as the Koran styles it) supposed to have been erected by Shedad, the latest despot of Ad, in the regions of Hudramaut, and which yet, after the annihilation of its tenants, remains entire, so Arabs say, invisible to ordinary eyes, but occasionally, and at rare intervals, revealed to some heaven-favoured traveller." Rock excavations in N. W. Hejaz ascribed to Thamood tribe.

[48] Cities wiped out by supernatural wrath.

[49] AZATHOTH—hideous name.

[50] *Phleg*'e-thon—a river of liquid fire in Hades.

[51] Enchanted garden where moon casts shadow of object or ghost invisible to the human eye.

[52] Calling on the dead—voice or familiar sound in adjacent room.

[53] Hand of dead man writes.

[54] Transposition of identity.

[55] Man followed by invisible *thing.*

[56] Book or MS. too horrible to read—warned against reading it—someone reads and is found dead. Haverhill incident.

[57] Sailing or rowing on lake in moonlight—sailing into invisibility.

[58] A queer village—in a valley, reached by a long road and visible from the crest of the hill from which that road descends—or close to a dense and antique forest.

[59] Man in strange subterranean chamber—seeks to force door of bronze—overwhelmed by influx of waters.

[60] Fisherman casts his net into the sea by moonlight—what he finds.

[61] A terrible pilgrimage to seek the nighted throne of the far daemon-sultan *Azathoth.*

[62] Live man buried in bridge masonry according to superstition—or black cat.

[63] Sinister names—Nasht—Kaman-Thah.

[64] Identity—reconstruction of personality—man makes duplicate of himself.

[65] Riley's fear of undertakers—a door locked on inside after death.
[66] Catacombs discovered beneath a city (in America?).
[67] An impression—a city in peril—dead city—equestrian statue—men in closed room—clattering of hooves heard from outside—marvel disclosed on looking out—*doubtful* ending.
[68] Murder discovered—body located—by psychological detective who pretends he has made walls of room transparent. Works on fear of murderer.
[69] Man with unnatural face—oddity of speaking—found to be a *mask*— Revelation.
[70] *Tone of extreme phantasy:* Man transformed to island or mountain.
[71] Man has sold his soul to devil—returns to family from trip—life afterward—fear—culminating horror—novel length.
[72] Hallowe'en incident—mirror in cellar—face seen therein—death (claw-mark?).
[73] Rats multiply and exterminate first a single city and then all mankind. Increased size and intelligence.
[74] Italian revenge—killing self in cell with enemy—under castle. [Used by FBL, Jr.]
[75] Black Mass under antique church.
[76] Ancient cathedral—hideous gargoyle—man seeks to rob—found dead—gargoyle's jaw bloody.
[77] Unspeakable dance of the gargoyles—in morning several gargoyles on old cathedral found transposed.
[78] Wandering thro' labyrinth of narrow slum streets—come on distant light—unheard-of rites of swarming beggars—like Court of Miracles in *Notre Dame de Paris.*
[79] Horrible secret in crypt of ancient castle—discovered by dweller.
[80] Shapeless living *thing* forming nucleus of ancient building.
[81] Marblehead—dream—burying hill—evening—unreality. [Festival?]
[82] Power of wizard to influence dreams of others.

[1920]

[83] Quotation: ". . . a defunct nightmare, which had perished in the midst of its wickedness, and left its flabby corpse on the breast of the tormented one, to be gotten rid of as it might." —Hawthorne.
[84] Hideous cracked discords of bass musick from (ruin'd) organ in (abandon'd) abbey or cathedral. [Red Hook]
[85] "For has not Nature, too, her grotesques—the rent rock, the distorting lights of evening on lonely roads, the unveiled struc-

ture of man in the embryo, or the skeleton?" Pater—*Renaissance* (da Vinci).

[86] To find something horrible in a (perhaps familiar) book, and not to be able to find it again.

[87] *Borellus* says, "that the Essential Salts of animals may be so prepared and preserved, that an ingenious man may have the whole ark of Noah in his own Study, and raise the fine shape of an animal out of its ashes at his pleasure; and that by the like method from the Essential Salts of humane dust, a Philosopher may, without any criminal necromancy, call up the shape of any dead ancestor from the dust whereinto his body has been incinerated." [Charles Dexter Ward]

[88] Lonely philosopher fond of cat. Hypnotises it—as it were—by repeatedly talking to it and looking at it. After his death the cat evinces signs of possessing his personality. N. B. He has trained cat, and leaves it to a friend, with instructions as to fitting a pen to its right fore paw by means of a harness. Later it writes with deceased's own handwriting.

[89] Lone lagoons and swamps of Louisiana—death daemon—ancient house and gardens—moss-grown trees—festoons of Spanish moss.

[1922?]

[90] *Anencephalous* or brainless monster who survives and attains prodigious size.

[91] Lost winter day—slept over—20 yrs. later. Sleep in chair on summer night—false dawn—old scenery and sensations—cold—old persons now dead—horror—frozen?

[1922?]

[92] Man's body dies—but corpse retains life. Stalks about—tries to conceal odour of decay—detained somewhere—hideous climax. [Cool Air]

[93] A place one has been—a beautiful view of a village or farm-dotted valley in the sunset—which one cannot find again or locate in memory.

[94] Change comes over the sun—shews objects in strange form, perhaps restoring landscape of the past.

[95] Horrible colonial farmhouse and overgrown garden on city hillside—overtaken by growth. Verse "The House" as basis of story. [Shunned House]

[96] Unknown fires seen across the hills at night.

[97] Blind fear of a certain woodland hollow where streams writhe among crooked roots, and where on a buried altar terrible sacrifices have occurr'd– Phosphorescence of dead trees. Ground bubbles.

[98] Hideous old house on steep city hillside–Bowen St.–beckons in the night–black windows–horror unnam'd–cold touch and voice–the welcome of the dead.

[1923]

[99] Salem story–the cottage of an aged witch–wherein after her death are found sundry terrible things.

[100] Subterranean region beneath placid New England village, inhabited by (living or extinct) creatures of prehistoric antiquity and strangeness.

[101] Hideous secret society–widespread–horrible rites in caverns under familiar scenes–one's own neighbour may belong.

[102] Corpse in room performs some act–prompted by discussion in its presence. Tears up or hides will, etc.

[103] Sealed room–or at least no lamp allowed there. Shadow on wall.

[104] Old sea-tavern now far inland from made land. Strange occurrences–sound of lapping of waves–

[105] Vampire visits man in ancestral abode–is his own father.

[106] A *thing* that sat on a sleeper's chest. Gone in morning, but something left behind.

[1923]

[107] Wall paper cracks off in sinister shape–man dies of fright. [Rats in Walls]

[108] Educated mulatto seeks to displace personality of white man and occupy his body.

[109] Ancient negro voodoo wizard in cabin in swamp–possesses white man.

[110] Antediluvian–Cyclopean ruins on lonely Pacific island. Centre of earthwide subterranean witch cult.

[111] Ancient ruin in Alabama swamp–voodoo.

[112] Man lives near graveyard–how does he live? Eats no food.

[113] Biological-hereditary memories of other worlds and universes. Butler–*God Known and Unk.* p. 59. [Belknap]

[114] Death lights dancing over a salt marsh.

[115] Ancient castle within sound of weird waterfall–sound ceases for a time under strange conditions.

[116] Prowling at night around an unlighted castle amidst strange scenery.

[117] A secret living thing kept and fed in an old house.

[1924]

[118] Something seen at oriel window of forbidden room in ancient manor house.

[119] Art note–fantastick daëmons of Salvator Rosa or Fuseli (trunk-proboscis).

[120] Talking bird of great longevity–tells secret long afterward.

[121] Photius tells of a (lost) writer named Damascius, who wrote *Incredible Fictions, Tales of Daemons, Marvellous Stories of Appearances from the Dead.*

[122] Horrible things whispered in the lines of Gauthier de Metz (13th cen.) *Image du Monde.*

[123] Dried-up man living for centuries in cataleptic state in ancient tomb.

[124] Hideous secret assemblage at night in antique alley–disperse furtively one by one–one seen to drop something–a human hand–

[125] Man abandon'd by ship–swimming in sea–pickt up hours later with strange story of undersea region he has visited–mad??

[126] Castaways on island eat unknown vegetation and become strangely transformed.

[127] Ancient and unknown ruins–strange and immortal bird who *speaks* in a language horrifying and revelatory to the explorers.

[128] Individual, by some strange process, retraces the path of evolution and becomes amphibious. ∴ Dr. insists that the particular amphibian from which *man* descends is not like any known to palaeontology. To prove it, indulges in (or relates) strange experiment.

[1925]

[129] *Marble Faun* p. 346–strange and prehistorick Italian city of stone.

[130] N. E. region call'd "Witches' Hollow"–along course of a river. Rumours of witches' sabbaths and Indian powwows on a broad mound rising out of the level where some old hemlocks and beeches formed a dark grove or daemon-temple. Legends hard to account for. Holmes–*Guardian Angel.*

[131] Phosphorescence of decaying wood–call'd in New England "fox-fire".

Virgil Finlay's "Shunned House" drawing (see entry 95)

MARGINALIA

By H. P. LOVECRAFT

Pickman's Model —
H.P. Lovecraft — July 28, 1934.

[132] Mad artist in ancient sinister house draws *things*. What were his models? Glimpse. [Pickman's Model]

[133] Man has miniature shapeless Siamese twin—exhib. in circus—twin surgically detached—disappears—does hideous things with malign life of its own. [HSW—Cassius]

[134] Witches' Hollow novel? Man hired as teacher in private school misses road on first trip—encounters dark hollow with unnaturally swollen trees and small cottage (light in window?). Reaches school and hears that boys are forbidden to visit hollow. One boy is strange—teacher sees him visit hollow—odd doings—mysterious disappearance or hideous fate.

[135] Hideous world superimposed on visible world—gate through—power guides narrator to ancient and forbidden book with directions for access.

[136] A secret language spoken by a very few old men in a wild country leads to hidden marvels and terrors still surviving.

[137] Strange man seen in lonely mountain place talking with great winged thing which flies away as others approach.

[138] Someone or something cries in fright at sight of the rising moon, as if it were something strange.

[139] DELRIO asks "An sint unquam daemones incubi et succubae, et an ex tali congressu proles nasci queat?" [Red Hook]

[140] Explorer enters strange land where some atmospheric quality darkens the sky to virtual blackness—marvels therein.

[1926]

[141] Footnote by Haggard or Lang in *The World's Desire:* "Probably the mysterious and indecipherable ancient books, which were occasionally excavated in old Egypt, were written in this dead language of a more ancient and now forgotten people. Such was the book discovered at Coptos, in the ancient sanctuary there, by a priest of the Goddess. 'The whole earth was dark, but the moon shone all about the Book.' A scribe of the period of the Ramessids mentions another indecipherable ancient writing. 'Thou tellest me thou understandest no word of it, good or bad. There is, as it were, a wall about it that none may climb. Thou art instructed, yet thou knowest it not; this makes me afraid.' Birch, *Zeitschrift,* 1871, pp. 61–64. *Papyrus Anastasi* I, pl. X. l. 8, pl. X. l. 4. Maspero, *Hist. Anc.,* pp. 66–67."

[142] Members of witch-cult were buried face downward. Man investigates ancestor in family tomb and finds disquieting condition.

Lovecraft's conception of "Pickman's Model" (see entry 132)

[143] Strange well in Arkham country—water gives out (or was never struck—hole kept tightly covered by a stone ever since dug)—no bottom—shunned and feared—what lay beneath (either unholy temple or other very ancient thing, or great cave-world). [Fungi—The Well]

[144] Hideous book glimpsed in ancient shop—never seen again.

[145] Horrible boarding house—closed door never opened.

[146] Ancient lamp found in tomb—when filled and used, its light reveals strange world. [Fungi]

[147] Any very ancient, unknown, or prehistoric object—its power of suggestion—forbidden memories.

[148] Vampire *dog*.

[149] Evil alley or enclosed court in ancient city—Union or Milligan Pl. [Fungi]

[150] Visit to someone in wild and remote house—ride from station through the night—into the haunted hills—house by forest or water—terrible things live there.

[151] Man forced to take shelter in strange house. Host has thick beard and dark glasses. Retires. In night guest rises and sees host's clothes about—also *mask* which was the apparent face of *whatever* the host was. Flight.

[152] Autonomic nervous system and subconscious mind *do not reside in the head.* Have mad physician decapitate a man but keep him alive and subconsciously controlled. Avoid copying tale by W. C. Morrow.

[1928]

[153] Black cat on a hill near dark gulf of ancient inn yard. Mews hoarsely—invites artist to nighted mysteries beyond. Finally dies at advanced age. Haunts dreams of artist—lures him to follow—strange outcome (never wakes up? or makes bizarre discovery of an elder world outside 3-dimensioned space?). [used by Dwyer]

[154] Trophonius—cave of. Vide Class. Dict. and *Atlantic* article.

[155] Steepled town seen from afar at sunset—*does not light up at night.* Sail has been seen putting out to sea. [Fungi]

[156] Adventures of a disembodied spirit—thro' dim, half-familiar cities and over strange moors—thro' space and time—other planets and universes in the end.

[157] Vague lights, geometrical figures, &c., seen on retina when eyes are closed. Caus'd by rays from *other dimensions* acting on optick nerve? From *other planets?* Connected with a life or phase of being in which person could live if he only knew how to

get there? *Man afraid to shut eyes*—he has been somewhere on a terrible pilgrimage and this fearsome seeing faculty remains.

[158] Man has terrible wizard friend who gains influence over him. Kills him in defence of his soul—walls body up in ancient cellar—BUT—the dead wizard (who has said strange things about soul lingering in body) *changes bodies with him* . . . leaving him a conscious corpse in cellar. [Thing on Doorstep]

[159] Certain kind of deep-toned stately music of the style of the 1870's or 1880's recalls certain visions of that period—gas-litten parlours of the dead, moonlight on old floors, decaying business streets with gas lamps, &c.—under terrible circumstances.

[160] Book which induces sleep on reading—cannot be read—determined man reads it—goes mad—precautions taken by aged initiate who knows—protection (as of author and translator) by incantation.

[161] Time and space—past event—150 years ago—unexplained. Modern period—person intensely homesick for past says or does something which is psychically transmitted back and *actually causes* the past event.

[162] Ultimate horror—grandfather returns from strange trip—mystery in house—wind and darkness—grandf. and mother engulfed—questions forbidden—somnolence—investigation—cataclysm—screams overheard—

[163] Man whose money was *obscurely* made loses it. Tells his family he must go *again* to THE PLACE (horrible and sinister and extra-dimensional) where he got his gold. Hints of possible pursuers—or of his possible non-return. He goes—record of what happens to him—or what happens at his home when he returns. Perhaps connect with preceding topic. Give fantastic, quasi-Dunsanian treatment.

[164] Man observed in a publick place with features (or ring or jewel) identified with those of man long (perhaps generations) buried.

[165] Terrible trip to an ancient and forgotten tomb.

[166] Hideous family living in shadow in ancient castle by edge of wood near black cliffs and monstrous waterfall.

[167] Boy rear'd in atmosphere of considerable mystery. Believes father dead. Suddenly is told that father is about to return. Strange preparations—consequences.

[168] Lonely bleak islands off N. E. coast. Horrors they harbour—outpost of cosmic influences.

[169] What hatches from primordial egg.

[170] Strange man in shadowy quarter of ancient city possesses something of immemorial archaic horror.

[171] Hideous old book discovered—directions for shocking evocation.

[1930]

[172] Pre-human idol found in desert.

[173] Idol in museum *moves* in a certain way.

[174] Migration of lemmings–Atlantis.

[175] Little green Celtic figures dug up in an ancient Irish bog.

[176] Man blindfolded and taken in closed cab or car to some very ancient and secret place.

[177] The *dreams* of one man actually *create* a strange half-mad world of quasi-material substance in *another dimension. Another man*, also a dreamer, blunders into this world in a dream. What he finds. Intelligence of denizens. Their dependence on the first dreamer. What happens at his death.

[178] A very ancient tomb in the deep woods near where a 17th century Virginia manor-house used to be. The undecayed, bloated thing found within.

[179] Appearance of an ancient god in a lonely and archaic place–prob. temple ruin. Atmosphere of beauty rather than horror. Subtle handling–presence revealed by faint sound or shadow. Landscape changes? Seen by child? Impossible to reach or identify locale again?

[180] A general house of horror–nameless crime–sounds–later tenants–(Flammarion) (novel length?).

[181] Inhabitant of another world–face masked perhaps with human skin or surgically alter'd to human shape, but body alien beneath robes. Having reached earth, tries to mix with mankind. Hideous revelation. [Suggested by CAS]

[182] In an ancient buried city a man finds a mouldering prehistoric document *in English and in his own handwriting*, telling an incredible tale. Voyage from present into past implied. Possible actualisation of this.

[183] Reference in Egyptian papyrus to a secret of secrets under tomb of high-priest Ka-Nefer. Tomb finally found and identified–trap-door in stone floor–staircase, and the illimitable black abyss.

[184] Expedition lost in Antarctic or other weird place. Skeletons and effects found years later. Camera films used but undeveloped. Finders develop–and find strange horror.

[185] Scene of an urban horror–Sous-le-Cap or Champlain Sts.–Quebec–rugged cliff-face–moss, mildew, dampness–houses half-burrowing into cliff.

[186] Thing from sea–in dark house, man finds doorknobs &c. *wet* as from touch of *something*. He has been a sea-captain, and once found a strange temple on a volcanically risen island.

[1931]

[187] Dream of awaking in vast hall of strange architecture, with sheet-covered forms on slabs—in positions similar to one's own. Suggestions of disturbingly non-human outlines under sheets. One of the objects moves and throws off sheet—non-terrestrial being revealed. Sugg. that *oneself* is also such a being—mind has become transferred to body on other planet.

[188] Desert of rock—prehistoric door in cliff in the valley around which lie the bones of uncounted billions of animals both modern and prehistoric—some of them puzzlingly gnawed.

[189] Ancient necropolis—bronze door in hillside which opens as the moonlight strikes it—focussed by ancient lens in pylon opposite?

[1932]

[190] Primal mummy in museum—awakes and changes place with visitor.

[191] An odd wound appears on a man's hand suddenly and without apparent cause. Spreads. Consequences.

[1933]

[192] Thibetan ROLANG—sorcerer (or NGAGSPA) reanimates a corpse by holding it in a dark room—lying on it mouth to mouth and repeating a magic formula with all else banished from his mind. Corpse slowly comes to life and stands up. Tries to escape—leaps, bounds, and struggles—but sorcerer holds it. Continues with magic formula. Corpse sticks out tongue and sorcerer bites it off. Corpse then collapses. Tongue becomes a valuable magic talisman. If corpse escapes—hideous results and death to sorcerer.

[193] Strange book of horror discovered in ancient library. Paragraphs of terrible significance copied. Later unable to find and verify text. Perhaps discover body or image or charm under floor, in secret cupboard, or elsewhere. Idea that book was merely hypnotic delusion induced by dead brain or ancient magic.

[194] Man enters (supposedly) own house in pitch dark. Feels way to room and shuts door behind him. Strange horrors—or turns on lights and finds alien place or presence. Or finds past restored or future indicated.

[195] Pane of peculiar-looking glass from a ruined monastery reputed to have harboured devil-worship set up in modern house at edge of wild country. Landscape looks vaguely and unplaceably *wrong* through it. It has some unknown time-distorting quality, and

comes from a primal, lost civilisation. Finally, hideous things in other world seen through it.

[196] Daemons, when desiring an human form for evil purposes, take to themselves the bodies of hanged men.

[197] Loss of memory and entry into a cloudy world of strange sights and experiences after shock, accident, reading of strange book, participation in strange rite, draught of strange brew, &c. Things seen have vague and disquieting familiarity. Emergence. Inability to retrace course.

[1934]

[198] Distant tower visible from hillside window. Bats cluster thickly around it at night. Observer fascinated. One night wakes to find self on unknown black circular staircase. In tower? Hideous goal.

[199] Black winged thing flies into one's house at night. Cannot be found or identified—but subtle developments ensue.

[200] Invisible Thing felt—or seen to make prints—on mountain top or other high, inaccessible place.

[201] Planets form'd of invisible matter.

[202] A monstrous derelict—found and boarded by a castaway or shipwreck survivor.

[203] A return to a place under dream-like, horrible, and only dimly comprehended circumstances. Death and decay reigning—town fails to light up at night— Revelation.

[204] Disturbing conviction that all life is only a deceptive dream with some dismal or sinister horror lurking behind.

[205] Person gazes out window and finds city and world dark and dead (or oddly changed) outside.

[206] Trying to identify and visit the distant scenes dimly seen from one's window—bizarre consequences.

[207] Something snatched away from one in the dark—in a lonely, ancient, and generally shunned place.

[208] (Dream of) some vehicle—railway train, coach, &c.—which is boarded in a stupor or fever, and which is a fragment of some past or ultra-dimensional world—taking the passenger out of reality—into vague, age-crumbled regions or unbelievable gulfs of marvel.

[209] Special Correspondence of *N.Y. Times*—March 3, 1935: "Halifax, N. S.—Etched deeply into the face of an island which rises from the Atlantic surges off the S. coast of Nova Scotia 20 m. from Halifax is the strangest rock phenomenon which Canada boasts. Storm, sea, and frost have graven into the solid cliff of what

has come to be known as Virgin's Island an almost perfect outline of the Madonna with the Christ Child in her arms.

"The island has sheer and wave-bound sides, is a danger to ships, and is absolutely uninhabited. *So far as is known, no human being has ever set foot on its shores.*"

[210] An ancient house with blackened pictures on the walls—so obscured that their subjects cannot be deciphered. Cleaning—and revelation. Cf. Hawthorne—"Edw. Rand. Port."

[211] Begin story with presence of narrator—inexplicable to himself—in utterly alien and terrifying scenes (dream?).

[212] Strange human being (or beings) living in some ancient house or ruins far from populous district (either old N. E. or far exotic land). Suspicion (based on shape and habits) that it is not *all* human.

[213] Ancient winter moods—moss—great boles—twisted branches—dark—ribbed roots—always dripping. . . .

[214] Talking rock of Africa—immemorially ancient oracle in desolate jungle ruins that *speaks* with a voice out of the aeons.

[215] Man with lost memory in strange, imperfectly comprehended environment. Fears to regain memory—a *glimpse*. . . .

[216] Man idly shapes a queer image—some power impels him to make it queerer than he understands. Throws it away in disgust—but something is abroad in the night.

[217] Ancient (Roman? prehistoric?) stone bridge washed away by a (sudden and curious?) storm. *Something* liberated which had been sealed up in the masonry thousands of years ago. Things happen.

[218] Mirage in *time*—image of long-vanish'd pre-human city.

[219] Fog or smoke—assumes shapes under incantations.

[220] Bell of some ancient church or castle rung by some unknown hand—a thing . . . or an invisible Presence.

[221] Insects or other entities from space attack and penetrate a man's head and cause him to *remember* alien and exotic things—possible displacement of personality.

[222] Quoted as motto by John Buchan: "The effect of night, of any flowing water, of lighted cities, of the peep of day, of ships, of the open ocean, calls up in the mind an army of anonymous desires and pleasures. Something, we feel, should happen; we know not what, yet we proceed in quest of it."—*R. L. Stevenson.*

LORD DUNSANY AND HIS WORK

The relatively slight recognition hitherto accorded Lord Dunsany, who is perhaps the most unique, original, and richly imaginative of living authors, forms an amusing commentary on the natural stupidity of mankind. Conservatives view him with patronage because he does not concern himself with the hoary fallacies and artificialities which constitute their supreme values. Radicals slight him because his work does not display that chaotic defiance of taste which to them is the sole identifying mark of authentic modern disillusion. And yet one might hardly err in claiming that he should have the homage of both rather than of neither; for surely if any man has extracted and combined the residue of true art in older and newer schools alike, it is this singular giant in whom the classic, the Hebraic, the Nordic, and the Irish aesthetic traditions are so curiously and admirably combined.

General knowledge of Dunsany seems to be limited to a vague impression that he is a member of the Celtic revival group who writes odd plays. Like most general knowledge, this is sadly fractional and incomplete; and in many ways somewhat misleading. Dunsany belongs, properly speaking, to no group whatsoever; while the mere authorship of dramatic phantasies is a small enough item in the personality of one whose poetic stories and plays reflect the sheer genius of a distinctive philosophy and aesthetic outlook. Dunsany is not a national but an universal artist; and his paramount quality is not simply weirdness, but a certain godlike and impersonal vision of cosmic scope and perspective, which comprehends the insignificance, cloudiness, futility, and tragic absurdity of all life and reality. His main work belongs to what modern critics have called the "literature of escape"; the literature of conscious unreality created out of an intelligent and sophisticated conviction that analysed reality has no heritage save of chaos, pain, and disappointment. He is in this way both a conservative and a modern; a conservative because he still believes that beauty is a thing of golden rememberings and simple patterns, and a modern because he perceives that only in arbitrarily selected fancy can we find fixed any of the patterns which fit our golden rememberings. He is the supreme poet of wonder, but of the intelligently assumed wonder to which one turns after experiencing the fullest disillusion of realism.

Edward John Moreton Drax Plunkett, Eighteenth Baron Dunsany, was born in 1878 at Dunsany Castle, County Meath, Ireland; and is a representative of the oldest and greatest blood in the British Empire. His race-stock is predominantly Teutonic and Scandinavian—Norman and Danish—a circumstance which gives to him the frosty heritage of Northern lore rather than the wilder and more mystical Celtic tradition. His family, however, is closely woven into the life of Ireland; and it is his uncle, the statesman Sir Horace Plunkett, who first proposed the Dominion idea now applied in the creation of the Irish Free State. Lord Dunsany himself is a loyal Imperialist in sympathies; a valiant officer in the British army, and veteran of both Boer and World wars.

Dunsany's earliest youth was spent at the ancestral estate of his mother, Dunstall Priory, Shoreham, Kent, England. He had a room whose windows faced the hills and the sunset, and to these vistas of golden earth and sky he attributes much of his poetic tendency. His unique manner of expression was promoted by his mother's careful choice of his reading; newspapers were wholly excluded, and the King James Bible made the principal article of literary diet. The effect of this reading on his style was permanent and marvellously beneficial. The simplicity and purity of archaic English, and the artistic repetitions of the Hebrew psalmists, all became his without conscious effort; so that to this day he has escaped the vitiation common to most modern prose-writers.

At his first public school, Cheam School, Dunsany received still more of the biblical influence, and obtained his first touch of an influence still more valuable; that of the Greek classics. In Homer he found a spirit of wonder akin to his own, and throughout his work one may trace the inspiration of the *Odyssey*—an epic, by the way, which is probably of much vaster genius than its more martial antecedent, the *Iliad*. The *Odyssey* teems with just that glamour of strange, far lands which is Dunsany's prime attribute.

After Cheam School came Eton, and after that Sandhurst, where the youthful Edward Plunkett was trained to that profession of arms which becomes a scion of nobility. In 1899 the Boer War broke out, and the youth fought with the Coldstream Guards through all its hardships. Also in 1899 he succeeded to his ancient title and his majority; the boy Edward Plunkett had become Lord Dunsany, man and soldier.

Dunsany first appears in literature shortly after the dawn of the new century, as a patron of the work of the Irish literary group. In 1905 he published his first book, *The Gods of Pegāna*, in which his original genius shines through the fantastic creation of a new and artificial Aryan mythology; a perfectly developed cycle of nature-allegories with all the infinite charm and shrewd philosophy of natural legendry. After that other books appeared in swift succession, all illustrated by the weird artistry of Sidney H. Sime. In *Time and the Gods* (1906), the mythic idea was extended with increasing vividness. *The Sword of Welleran* (1908) sings of a world of men and heroes ruled by Pegāna's gods, as does *A Dreamer's Tales* (1910). We here find the best Dunsanian forms fully developed; the Hellenic sense of conflict and fatality, the magnificently cosmic point of view, the superbly lyrical flow of language, the Oriental splendour of colouring and imagery, the titanic fertility and ingenuity of imagination, the mystical glamour of fabulous lands "beyond the East" or "at the edge of the world", and the amazing facility for devising musical, alluring, and wonder-making proper names, personal and geographical, on classical and Oriental models. Some of Dunsany's tales deal with the objective world we know, and of strange wonders therein; but the best of them are about lands conceivable only in purple dreams. These are fashioned in that purely decorative spirit which means the highest art, having no visible moral or didactic element save such quaint allegory as may inhere in the type of legendary lore to which they belong. Dunsany's only didactic idea is an artist's hatred of the ugly, the stupid, and the commonplace. We see it occasionally in touches of satire on social institutions, and bits of lamentation over the pollution of Nature by grimy cities and hideous advertising signs. Of all human institutions, the billboard is most violently abhorrent to Lord Dunsany.

In 1909 Dunsany wrote his first play, *The Glittering Gate,* at the request of W. B. Yeats, who desired something of his for the Abbey Theatre in Dublin. Despite the author's absolute previous inexperience, the result was highly successful; and turned Dunsany toward a steady career of dramatic composition. Though the present writer continues to prefer the stories, most critics unite in giving higher praise to the plays; and certainly the latter possess a brilliancy of dialogue and sureness of technique which place Dunsany among the greatest of dramatists. What simplicity! What fancy! What exalted speech! Like the stories, the best of the plays are of fantastic plot and setting. Most are very short, though at least two, *If* and *Alexander,* are of full length. The most esteemed is perhaps *The Gods of the Mountain,* which tells of the fate of seven beggars in the city of Kongros, who impersonated the seven green jade gods who sit on the mountain Marma. Green, by the way, is a favourite colour in Dunsany's work; and green jade its most frequent embodiment. In this play the Nietzschean figure of the chief beggar Agmar is drawn with a master's stroke, and is likely to live permanently among the vivid characters of the world's drama. Other marvellously powerful plays are *A Night at an Inn*—a bit worthy of the Parisian Grand Guignol—and *The Queen's Enemies*, an elaborated Egyptian incident from Herodotus. It is impossible to exaggerate the pure genius for dramatic utterance and situation which Dunsany shews in his best plays. They are thoroughly classical in every sense.

Dunsany's attitude of wonder is, as we have noted, a consciously cultivated one; overlying a keenly philosophical and sophisticated intelligence. It is therefore not remarkable that with the years an element of visible satire and acute humour began to appear in his work. There is, indeed, an interesting parallelism between him and that other great Irishman Oscar Wilde; whose fantastic and wittily worldly sides were so delightfully blended, and who had the same divine gift of gorgeous prose and exotic imagery. In 1912 appeared *The Book of Wonder*, whose brief fantastic tales all hold a certain humorous doubt of their own solemnity and truth. Soon afterward came *The Lost Silk Hat*, a one-act comedy of manners equalling in sheer sparkle and cleverness anything even Sheridan could devise; and since then the serious side of Dunsany has been steadily on the wane, despite occasional plays and tales which shew a survival of the absolute beauty-worshipper. *Fifty-one Tales*, published in 1915, have something of the urbane prose-poetic spirit of a philosophical Baudelaire, whilst *The Last Book of Wonder* (1916) is like the first volume of kindred title. Only in the scattered fragments forming *Tales of Three Hemispheres* (1919) do we find strong reminders of the older, simpler Dunsany. *If* (1921), the new long play, is mainly satirical comedy with one brief touch of exotic eloquence. *Don Rodriguez*, just announced by the publishers, has not been read by the present writer; but may have more of the old Dunsany. It is his first novel, and is highly regarded by those reviewers who have seen it. *Alexander*, a full-length play based on Plutarch, was written in 1912 and is considered by the author as his best work. It is to be regretted that this drama has been neither published nor acted. Dunsany's shorter plays are grouped in two volumes. *Five Plays*, containing *The Gods of the Mountain, The Golden Doom, King Argimēnēs and the Unknown Warrior, The Glittering Gate*, and *The Lost Silk Hat*, was published in 1914. In 1917 appeared *Plays of Gods and Men*, with *The Tents of the Arabs, The Laughter of the Gods, The Queen's Enemies*, and *A Night at an Inn*.

Dunsany has never forsaken his position as a patron of letters, and was the literary sponsor of the Irish peasant poet Ledwidge—that immortaliser of the blackbird, who fell in the Great War while serving in the Fifth Royal Inniskilling Fusiliers with Dunsany as his captain. The war engrossed much of Dunsany's imagination, since he saw active service in France and in the Dublin revolt of 1916, when he was badly wounded. This engrossment is shewn by a volume of charming and sometimes pathetic stories, *Tales of War* (1918), and a collection of reminiscent essays, *Unhappy Far-Off Things* (1919). His general view of war is the sane one; that conflict is a disaster as inevitable as the tides and the seasons.

America is highly regarded by Dunsany, since it has been readier than the mother country to give him what little appreciation he has. Most of his plays have been acted here by "Little Theatre" companies, especially that of Stuart Walker, and at times considerable enthusiasm has been developed. All such productions have been made with the careful supervision of the author, whose letters of directions are eminently interesting. Dunsany plays are favourites with many collegiate dramatic societies, and justly so. In 1919–20 Dunsany made a lecture tour of the United States, where he was generally well received.

The personality of Lord Dunsany is exceedingly attractive, as can be attested by the present writer, who sat in a front seat directly opposite him when he spoke in the Copley-Plaza ballroom in Boston in October 1919. On that occasion he outlined his literary theories with much charm, and read in full his playlet, *The Queen's Enemies.* He is a very tall man—six feet four—of medium breadth, with fair complexion, blue eyes, high forehead, abundant light brown hair, and a small moustache of the same colour. His face is wholesomely and delicately handsome, and his expression is one of charming and whimsical kindliness, with a certain boyish quality which no amount of worldly experience or his single eyeglass can efface. There is boyishness also in his walk and bearing; a trace of the stoop and the engaging awkwardness which one associates with adolescence. His voice is pleasant and mellow, and his accent the apex of British cultivation. His whole bearing is easy and familiar, so much so that the *Boston Transcript*'s reporter complained of his lack of unctuous platform presence. As a dramatic reader he undoubtedly lacks vividness and animation; obviously, he would be as poor as an actor as he is great as an author. He dresses with marked carelessness, and has been called the worst-dressed man in Ireland. Certainly, there was nothing impressive in the loosely draped evening attire which nebulously surrounded him during his American lectures. To Boston autograph seekers he proved very accommodating, refusing none despite a severe headache which forced his hand many times to his forehead. When he entered a cab his top hat was knocked off—thus do the small remember the mishaps of the great!

Lord Dunsany is married to a daughter of Lord Jersey, and has one son, the Hon. Randal Plunkett, born in 1906. His tastes, far from being the morbid predilections of the traditional cynic and fantaisiste, are distinctly outdoor and normal; savouring rather of his feudal and baronial side. He is the best pistol shot in Ireland, an ardent cricketer and horseman, a big game hunter, and a confirmed devotee of rural scenes. He has travelled extensively, especially in Africa; and lives alternately at his own Meath castle, at his mother's place in Kent, and at his London home at 55, Lowndes Square. That he has the truly romantic quality of modest heroism, is attested by an incident when he rescued a man from drowning, and refused to reveal his name to the admiring crowds.

Dunsany's writing is always very rapid, and is done mainly in the late afternoon and early evening, with tea as a mild stimulant. He almost invariably employs a quill pen, whose broad, brush-like strokes are unforgettable by those who have seen his letters and manuscripts. His individuality appears in every phase of his activity, and involves not only an utterly unique simplicity of style but an utterly unique scarcity of punctuation which readers occasionally regret. About his work Dunsany spreads a quaint atmosphere of cultivated naiveté and child-like ignorance, and likes to refer to historical and other data with a delightfully artless air of unfamiliarity. His consistent aim is to survey the world with the impressionable freshness of unspoiled youth—or with the closest approach to that quality which his experience will allow. This idea sometimes plays havock with his critical judgment, as was keenly realised in 1920, when he most considerately acted as Laureate Judge of Poetry for the United Amateur Press Association. Dunsany has the true aristocrat's attitude toward his work; and whilst he would welcome fame, he would never think of debasing his art either for the philistine rabble or for the reigning clique of literary chaoticists. He writes purely for self-expression, and is therefore the ideal amateur journalist type.

The ultimate position of Dunsany in literature depends largely on the future course of literature itself. Our age is one of curious transition and divergence, with an increasing separation of art from the past and from all common life as well. Modern science has, in the end, proved an enemy to art and pleasure; for by revealing to us the whole sordid and prosaic basis of our thoughts, motives, and acts, it has stripped the world of glamour, wonder, and all those illusions of heroism, nobility, and sacrifice which used to sound so impressive when romantically treated. Indeed, it is not too much to say that psychological discovery, and chemical, physical, and physiological research have largely destroyed the element of emotion among informed and sophisticated people by resolving it into its component parts—intellectual idea and animal impulse. The so-called "soul" with all its hectic and mawkish attributes of sentimentality, veneration, earnestness, devotion, and the like, has perished on analysis. Nietzsche brought a transvaluation of values, but Remy de Gourmont has brought a wholesale destruction of all values. We know now what a futile, aimless, and disconnected welter of mirages and hypocrisies life is; and from the first shock of that knowledge has sprung the bizarre, tasteless, defiant, and chaotic literature of that terrible newer generation which so shocks our grandmothers—the aesthetic generation of T. S. Eliot, D. H. Lawrence, James Joyce, Ben Hecht, Aldous Huxley, James Branch Cabell, and all the rest. These writers, knowing that life has no real pattern, either rave, or mock, or join in the cosmic chaos by exploiting a frank and conscious unintelligibility and confusion of values. To them it savours of the vulgar to adopt a pattern—for today only servants, churchgoers, and tired business men read things which mean anything or acknowledge any values. What chance, then, has an author who is neither stupid or common enough for the clientele of the *Cosmopolitan, Saturday Evening Post,* Harold Bell Wright, *Snappy Stories, Atlantic Monthly,* and *Home Brew;* nor confused, obscene, or hydrophobic enough for the readers of the *Dial, Freeman, Nation,* or *New Republic,* and the would-be readers of *Ulysses?* At present one tribe rejects him as "too highbrow", whilst the other ignores him as impossibly tame and childishly comprehensible.

Dunsany's hope of recognition lies with the literati and not with the crowd, for his charms are those of a supremely delicate art and a gentle disillusion and world-weariness which only the discriminating can ever enjoy. The necessary step toward such recognition is a rebound which is quite likely to come with a maturer understanding of modern disillusion and all its implications. Art has been wrecked by a complete consciousness of the universe which shews that the world is to each man only a rubbish-heap limned by his individual perception. It will be saved, if at all, by the next and last step of disillusion; the realisation that complete consciousness and truth are themselves valueless, and that to acquire any genuine artistic titillation we must artificially invent limitations of consciousness and feign a pattern of life common to all mankind—most naturally the simple old pattern which ancient and groping tradition first gave us. When we see that the source of all joy and enthusiasm is wonder and ignorance, we shall be ready to play the old game of blindman's buff with the mocking atoms and electrons of a purposeless infinity.

It is then that we shall worship afresh the music and colour of divine language, and take an Epicurean delight in those combinations of ideas and fancies which we know to be artificial. Not that we can resume a serious attitude toward emotion—there is too much intellect abroad for that—but that we can revel in the Dresden-china Arcadia of an author who will play with the old ideas, atmospheres, types, situations, and lighting effects in a deft pictorial way; a way tinged with affectionate reminiscence as for fallen gods, yet never departing from a cosmic and gently satirical realisation of the true microscopic insignificance of the man-puppets and their petty relations to one another. Such an author may well avoid flippancy or vulgarity, but he must keep the intellectual point of view paramount even when hidden, and beware of speaking seriously with the voice of passions proved by modern psychology to be either hypocritically hollow or absurdly animal.

And is not this a virtual description of Dunsany, a liquid prose-poet who writes classic hexameters by accident, with his stage set for relentless deities and their still more relentless conqueror Time; for cosmic chess-games of Fate and Chance; for the funerals of dead gods; for the birth and death of universes; and for the simple annals of that speck in space called the world, which with its poor denizens is but one of countless playthings of the little gods, who are in turn only the dreams of MĀNA-YOOD-SUSHĀI? The balance between conservatism and sophistication in Dunsany is perfect; he is whimsically traditional, but just as conscious of the chaotic nullity of values as any assertive modern. With the same voice that sings god-moving forces he mourns with a child's broken rocking-horse, and tells how a boy's wish for a hoop made a king sacrifice his crown to the stars; nor does he fail to chant of quiet villages, and the smoke of idyllic hearths, and the lights in cottage windows at evening. He creates a world which has never existed and never will exist, but which we have always known and longed for in dreams. This world he makes vivid not by pretending that it is real, but by exalting the quality of unreality and suffusing his whole dream-universe with a delicate pessimism drawn half from modern psychology and half from our ancestral Northern myths of Ragnarok, the Twilight of the Gods. He is at once modern and mythologist, viewing life correctly as a series of meaningless pictures, but investing it with all the ancient formulae and saws which like frozen metaphors in language have become an integral part of our cherished heritage of associations.

Dunsany is like nobody else. Wilde is his nearest congener, and there are points of kinship to Poe, De Quincey, Maeterlinck, and Yeats; but all comparisons are futile. His peculiar combination of matter and manner is unique in its imperious genius. He is not perfect, or not always perfect, but who indeed is continually so? Critics complain that he sometimes mixes satire with the atmosphere of tragedy; but this objection is a conventional one, and argues an unfamiliarity with the Irish tradition which has produced such perversely immortal classics as James Stephens' *Crock of Gold.* They cavil, too, at his introduction of walking stone gods and hideous Hindoo idols on the stage; but this cavilling is pitifully blind in its interpretation of apocalyptic visions in terms of theatrical mechanics. Any criticism by the present writer would be of the nature of a plea; urging a less complete metamorphosis of the old myth-making Dunsany into the newer and more sparklingly satirical Dunsany. A reincarnated Sheridan is precious indeed, but the Dunsany of *A Dreamer's Tales* is a wonder twice as precious because it cannot be duplicated or even approached. It is a wonder which has restored to us our childhood's dreams, as far as such things can ever be restored; and that is the most blessed happening which the earth may know.

The future is dark and dubious, and amidst its devastating introspection and analysis there may be no place for art as we know it. But if any existing art does belong to that future, it is the art of Lord Dunsany.

Dec. 14, 1922

NOTES ON WRITING WEIRD FICTION

My reason for writing stories is to give myself the satisfaction of visualising more clearly and detailedly and stably the vague, elusive, fragmentary impressions of wonder, beauty, and adventurous expectancy which are conveyed to me by certain sights (scenic, architectural, atmospheric, etc.), ideas, occurrences, and images encountered in art and literature. I choose weird stories because they suit my inclination best—one of my strongest and most persistent wishes being to achieve, momentarily, the illusion of some strange suspension or violation of the galling limitations of time, space, and natural law which forever imprison us and frustrate our curiosity about the infinite cosmic spaces beyond the radius of our sight and analysis. These stories frequently emphasise the element of horror because fear is our deepest and strongest emotion, and the one which best lends itself to the creation of Nature-defying illusions. Horror and the unknown or the strange are always closely connected, so that it is hard to create a convincing picture of shattered natural law or cosmic alienage or "outsideness" without laying stress on the emotion of fear. The reason why *time* plays a great part in so many of my tales is that this element looms up in my mind as the most profoundly dramatic and grimly terrible thing in the universe. *Conflict with time* seems to me the most potent and fruitful theme in all human expression.

While my chosen form of story-writing is obviously a special and perhaps a narrow one, it is none the less a persistent and permanent type of expression, as old as literature itself. There will always be a certain small percentage of persons who feel a burning curiosity about unknown outer space, and a burning desire to escape from the prison-house of the known and the real into those enchanted lands of incredible adventure and infinite possibilities which dreams open up to us, and which things like deep woods, fantastic urban towers, and flaming sunsets momentarily suggest. These persons include great authors as well as insignificant amateurs like myself—Dunsany, Poe, Arthur Machen, M. R. James, Algernon Blackwood, and Walter de la Mare being typical masters in this field.

As to how I write a story—there is no one way. Each one of my tales has a different history. Once or twice I have literally written out a dream; but usually I start with a mood or idea or image which I wish to express, and revolve it in my mind until I can think of a good way of embodying it in some chain of dramatic occurrences capable of being recorded in concrete terms. I tend to run through a mental list of the basic conditions or situations best adapted to such a mood or idea or image, and then begin to speculate on logical and naturally motivated explanations of the given mood or idea or image in terms of the basic condition or situation chosen.

The actual process of writing is of course as varied as the choice of theme and initial conception; but if the history of all my tales were analysed, it is just possible that the following set of rules might be deduced from the *average* procedure:

(1) Prepare a synopsis or scenario of events in the order of their absolute *occurrence*—not the order of their narration. Describe with enough fulness to cover all vital points and motivate all incidents planned. Details, comments, and estimates of consequences are sometimes desirable in this temporary framework.

(2) Prepare a second synopsis or scenario of events—this one in order of *narration* (not actual occurrence), with ample fulness and detail, and with notes as to changing perspective, stresses, and climax. Change the original synopsis to fit if such a change will increase the dramatic force or general effectiveness of the story. Interpolate or delete incidents at will—never being bound by the original conception even if the ultimate result be a tale wholly different from that first planned. Let additions and alterations be made whenever suggested by anything in the formulating process.

(3) Write out the story—rapidly, fluently, and not too critically—following the *second* or narrative-order synopsis. Change incidents and plot whenever the developing process seems to suggest such change, never being bound by any previous design. If the development suddenly reveals new opportunities for dramatic effect or vivid storytelling, add whatever is thought advantageous—going back and reconciling the early parts to the new plan. Insert and delete whole sections if necessary or desirable, trying different beginnings and endings until the best arrangement is found. But be sure that all references throughout the story are thoroughly reconciled with the final design. Remove all

possible superfluities—words, sentences, paragraphs, or whole episodes or elements—observing the usual precautions about the reconciling of all references.

(4) Revise the entire text, paying attention to vocabulary, syntax, rhythm of prose, proportioning of parts, niceties of tone, grace and convincingness of transitions (scene to scene, slow and detailed action to rapid and sketchy time-covering action and vice versa . . . etc., etc., etc.), effectiveness of beginning, ending, climaxes, etc., dramatic suspense and interest, plausibility and atmosphere, and various other elements.

(5) Prepare a neatly typed copy—not hesitating to add final revisory touches where they seem in order.

The first of these stages is often purely a mental one—a set of conditions and happenings being worked out in my head, and never set down until I am ready to prepare a detailed synopsis of events in order of narration. Then, too, I sometimes begin even the actual writing before I know how I shall develop the idea—this beginning forming a problem to be motivated and exploited.

There are, I think, four distinct types of weird story; one expressing a *mood or feeling*, another expressing a *pictorial conception*, a third expressing a *general situation, condition, legend, or intellectual conception*, and a fourth explaining a *definite tableau or specific dramatic situation or climax*. In another way, weird tales may be grouped into two rough categories—those in which the marvel or horror concerns some *condition* or *phenomenon*, and those in which it concerns some *action of persons* in connexion with a bizarre condition or phenomenon.

Each weird story—to speak more particularly of the horror type—seems to involve five definite elements: (a) some basic, underlying horror or abnormality—condition, entity, etc.—, (b) the general effects or bearings of the horror, (c) the mode of manifestation—object embodying the horror and phenomena observed—, (d) the types of fear-reaction pertaining to the horror, and (e) the specific effects of the horror in relation to the given set of conditions.

In writing a weird story I always try very carefully to achieve the right mood and atmosphere, and place the emphasis where it belongs. One cannot, except in immature pulp charlatan-fiction, present an account of impossible, improbable, or inconceivable phenomena as a commonplace narrative of objective acts and conventional emotions. Inconceivable events and conditions have a special handicap to overcome, and this can be accomplished only through the maintenance of a careful realism in every phase of the story *except* that touching on the one given marvel. This marvel must be treated very impressively and deliberately—with a careful emotional "build-up"—else it will seem flat and unconvincing. Being the principal thing in the story, its mere existence should overshadow the characters and events. But the characters and events must be consistent and natural except where they touch the single marvel. In relation to the central wonder, the characters should shew the same overwhelming emotion which similar characters would shew toward such a wonder in real life. Never have a wonder taken for granted. Even when the characters are supposed to be accustomed to the wonder I try to weave an air of awe and impressiveness corresponding to what the reader should feel. A casual style ruins any serious fantasy.

Atmosphere, not action, is the great desideratum of weird fiction. Indeed, all that a wonder story can ever be is *a vivid picture of a certain type of human mood.* The moment it tries to be anything else it becomes cheap, puerile, and unconvincing. Prime emphasis should be given to *subtle suggestion*–imperceptible hints and touches of selective associative detail which express shadings of moods and build up a vague illusion of the strange reality of the unreal. Avoid bald catalogues of incredible happenings which can have no substance or meaning apart from a sustaining cloud of colour and symbolism.

These are the rules or standards which I have followed–consciously or unconsciously–ever since I first attempted the serious writing of fantasy. That my results are successful may well be disputed–but I feel at least sure that, had I ignored the considerations mentioned in the last few paragraphs, they would have been much worse than they are.

SOME NOTES ON INTERPLANETARY FICTION

Despite the current flood of stories dealing with other worlds and universes, and with intrepid flights to and from them through cosmic space, it is probably no exaggeration to say that not more than a half-dozen of these things, including the novels of H. G. Wells, have even the slightest shadow of a claim to artistic seriousness or literary rank. Insincerity, conventionality, triteness, artificiality, false emotion, and puerile extravagance reign triumphant throughout this overcrowded genre, so that none but its rarest products can possibly claim a truly adult status. And the spectacle of such persistent hollowness has led many to ask whether, indeed, any fabric of real literature can ever grow out of the given subject-matter.

The present commentator does not believe that the idea of space-travel and other worlds is inherently unsuited to literary use. It is, rather, his opinion that the omnipresent cheapening and misuse of that idea is the result of a widespread misconception; a misconception which extends to other departments of weird and science fiction as well. This fallacy is the notion that any account of impossible, improbable, or inconceivable phenomena can be successfully presented as a commonplace narrative of objective acts and conventional emotions in the ordinary tone and manner of popular romance. Such a presentation will often "get by" with immature readers, but it will never approach even remotely the field of aesthetic merit.

Inconceivable events and conditions form a class apart from all other story elements, and cannot be made convincing by any mere process of casual narration. They have the handicap of incredibility to overcome; and this can be accomplished only through a careful realism in every *other* phase of the story, plus a gradual atmospheric or emotional building-up of the utmost subtlety. The emphasis, too, must be kept right—hovering always over *the wonder of the central abnormality itself.* It must be remembered that any violation of what we know as natural law is *in itself* a far more tremendous thing than any other event or feeling which could possibly affect a human being. Therefore in a story dealing with such a thing we cannot expect to create any sense of life or illusion of reality if we treat the wonder casually and have the characters moving about under ordinary motivations. The characters, though they must be natural, should be subordinated to the central marvel around which they are grouped. The true "hero" of a marvel tale is not any human being, but simply a *set of phenomena.*

Over and above everything else should tower the stark, outrageous monstrousness of the one chosen departure from Nature. The characters should react to it as real people would react to such a thing if it were suddenly to confront them in daily life; displaying the almost soul-shattering amazement which anyone would naturally display instead of the mild, tame, quickly-passed-over emotions prescribed by cheap popular convention. Even when the wonder is one to which the characters are assumed to be used, the sense of awe, marvel, and strangeness which the reader would feel in the presence of such a thing must somehow be suggested by the author. When an account of a marvellous trip is presented without the colouring of appropriate emotion, we never feel the least degree of vividness in it. We do not get the spine-tickling illusion that such a thing might possibly have happened, but merely feel that somebody has uttered some extravagant words. In general, we should forget all about the popular hack conventions of cheap writing and try to make our story a perfect slice of actual life except where the one chosen marvel is concerned. We should work as if we were staging a hoax and trying to get our extravagant lie accepted as literal truth.

Atmosphere, not action, is the thing to cultivate in the wonder story. We cannot put stress on the bare events, since the unnatural extravagance of these events makes them sound hollow and absurd when thrown into too high relief. Such events, even when theoretically possible or conceivable in the future, have no counterpart or basis in existing life and human experience, hence can never form the groundwork of an adult tale. All that a marvel story can ever be, in a serious way, is a *vivid picture of a certain type of human mood.* The moment it tries to be anything else it becomes cheap, puerile, and unconvincing. Therefore, a fantastic author should see that his prime emphasis goes into subtle suggestion—the imperceptible hints and touches of selective and associative detail which express shadings of moods and build up a vague illusion of the strange reality of the unreal—instead of into bald catalogues of incredible happenings which can have no substance or meaning apart from a sustaining cloud of colour and mood-symbolism. A serious adult story must be true to something in life. Since marvel tales cannot be true to the *events* of life, they must shift their emphasis toward something to which they *can* be true; namely, certain wistful or restless *moods* of the human spirit, wherein it seeks to weave gossamer ladders of escape from the galling tyranny of time, space, and natural law.

And how are these general principles of adult wonder fiction to be applied to the interplanetary tale in particular? That they *can* be applied, we have no reason to doubt; the important factors being here, as elsewhere, an adequate sense of wonder, adequate emotions in the characters, realism in the setting and supplementary incidents, care in the choice of significant detail, and a studious avoidance of the hackneyed artificial characters and stupid conventional events and situations which at once destroy a story's vitality by proclaiming it a product of weary mass mechanics. It is an ironic truth that no artistic story of this kind, honestly, sincerely, and unconventionally written, would be likely to have any chance of acceptance among professional editors of the common pulp school. This, however, will not influence the really determined artist bent on creating something of mature worth. Better to write honestly for a non-remunerative magazine than to concoct worthless tinsel and be paid for it. Some day, perhaps, the conventions of editors will be less flagrantly absurd in their anti-artistic rigidity.

The events of an interplanetary story—aside from such tales as involve sheer poetic fantasy—are best laid in the present, or represented as having occurred secretly or prehistorically in the past. The future is a ticklish period to deal with; since it is virtually impossible to escape grotesqueness and absurdity in depicting its mode of life, while there is always an immense emotional loss in representing characters as familiar with the marvels depicted. The characters of a story are essentially projections of ourselves; and unless they can share our own ignorance and wonder concerning what occurs, there is an inevitable handicap. This is not to say that tales of the future cannot be artistic, but merely that it is harder to make them so.

A good interplanetary story must have realistic human characters; not the stock scientists, villainous assistants, invincible heroes, and lovely scientist's-daughter heroines of the usual trash of this sort. Indeed, there is no reason why there should be any "villain", "hero", or "heroine" at all. These artificial character-types belong wholly to artificial plot-forms, and have no place in serious fiction of any kind. The function of the story is to express a certain human mood of wonder and liberation, and any tawdry dragging-in of dime-novel theatricalism is both out of place and injurious. No stock romance is wanted. We must select only such characters (not necessarily stalwart or picturesque characters) as would naturally be involved in the events to be depicted, and they must behave exactly as real persons would behave if confronted with the given marvels. The tone of the whole thing must be realism, not romance.

The crucial and delicate matter of getting the characters off the earth must be very carefully managed. Indeed, it probably forms the greatest single problem of the story. The departure must be plausibly accounted for and impressively described. If the period is not prehistoric, it is better to have the means of departure a secret invention. The characters must react to this invention with a proper sense of utter, almost paralysing wonder, avoiding the cheap fictional tendency of having such things half taken for granted. To avoid errors in complex problems of physics, it is well not to attempt too much detail in describing the invention.

Scarcely less delicate is the problem of describing the voyage through space and the landing on another world. Here we must lay primary stress on the stupendous emotions—the unconquerable sense of astonishment—felt by the voyagers as they realise they are *actually off their native earth,* in cosmic gulfs or on an alien world. Needless to say, a strict following of scientific fact in representing the mechanical, astronomical, and other aspects of the trip is absolutely essential. Not all readers are ignorant of the sciences, and a flagrant contravention of truth ruins a tale for anyone able to detect it.

Equal scientific care must be given to our representation of events on the alien planet. Everything must be in strict accord with the known or assumed nature of the orb in question—surface gravity, axial inclination, length of day and year, aspect of sky, etc.—and the atmosphere must be built up with significant details conducing to verisimilitude and realism. Hoary stock devices connected with the reception of the voyagers by the planet's inhabitants ought to be ruled rigidly out. Thus we should have no over-facile language-learning; no telepathic communication; no worship of the travellers as deities; no participation in the affairs of pseudo-human kingdoms, or in conventional wars between factions of inhabitants; no weddings with beautiful anthropomorphic princesses; no stereotyped Armageddons with ray-guns and space-ships; no court intrigues and jealous magicians; no peril from hairy ape-men of the polar caps; and so on, and so on. Social and political satire is always undesirable, since such intellectual and ulterior objects detract from the story's power as a crystallisation of a mood. What must always be present in superlative degree is a deep, pervasive sense of *strangeness*—the utter, incomprehensible *strangeness* of a world holding nothing in common with ours.

It is not necessary that the alien planet be inhabited—or inhabited at the period of the voyage—at all. If it is, the denizens must be definitely non-human in aspect, mentality, emotions, and nomenclature, unless they are assumed to be descendants of a prehistoric colonising expedition from our earth. The human-like aspect, psychology, and proper names commonly attributed to other-planetarians by the bulk of cheap authors is at once hilarious and pathetic. Another absurd habit of conventional hacks is having the major denizens of other planets always more advanced scientifically and mechanically than ourselves; always indulging in spectacular rites against a background of cubistic temples and palaces, and always menaced by some monstrous and dramatic peril. This kind of pap should be replaced by an adult realism, with the races of other-planetarians represented, according to the artistic demands of each separate case, as in every stage of development—sometimes high, sometimes low, and sometimes unpicturesquely middling. Royal and religious pageantry should not be conventionally overemphasised; indeed, it is not at all likely that more than a fraction of the exotic races would have lit upon the especial folk-customs of royalty and religion. It must be remembered that non-human beings would be wholly apart from human motives and perspectives.

But the real nucleus of the story ought to be something far removed from the specific aspect and customs of any hypothetical outside race—ought, indeed, to be nothing less than the *simple sensation of wonder at being off the earth.* Interest had better be sustained through accounts of bizarre and un-terrestrial natural conditions, rather than through any artificially dramatic actions of the characters, either human or exotic. Adventures may well be introduced, but they should be properly subordinated to realism—made inevitable outgrowths of the conditions instead of synthetic thrills concocted for their own sake.

The climax and ending must be managed very carefully to avoid extravagance or artificiality. It is preferable, in the interest of convincingness, to represent the fact of the voyage as remaining hidden from the public—or to have the voyage a prehistoric affair, forgotten by mankind and with its rediscovery remaining a secret. The idea of any general revelation implying a widespread change in human thoughts, history, or orientation tends to contradict surrounding events and clash with actual future probabilities too radically to give the reader a sense of naturalness. It is far more potent not to make the truth of the story dependent on any condition visibly contradicting what we know—for the reader may pleasantly toy with the notion that *perhaps* these marvels *may* have happened after all!

Meanwhile the deluge of inept interplanetary tosh continues. Whether a qualitative upturn will ever occur on anything like a large scale, this commentator cannot venture to prophesy; but at any rate, he has had his say regarding what he deems the main aspects of the problem. There are, without doubt, great possibilities in the serious exploitation of the astronomical tale; as a few semi-classics like *The War of the Worlds*, *Last and First Men*, *Station X*, "The Red Brain", and Clark Ashton Smith's best work prove. But the pioneers must be prepared to labour without financial return, professional recognition, or the encouragement of a reading majority whose taste has been seriously warped by the rubbish it has devoured. Fortunately sincere artistic creation is its own incentive and reward, so that despite all obstacles we need not despair of the future of a fresh literary form whose present lack of development leaves all the more room for brilliant and fruitful experimentation.

IN MEMORIAM: ROBERT ERVIN HOWARD

The sudden and unexpected death on June 11 [1936] of Robert Ervin Howard, author of fantastic tales of incomparable vividness, forms weird fiction's worst loss since the passing of Henry S. Whitehead four years ago.

Mr. Howard was born at Peaster, Texas, on January 22, 1906, and was old enough to have seen the last phase of southwestern pioneering —the settlement of the great plains and lower Rio Grande valley, and the spectacular rise of the oil industry with its raucous boom towns. His father, who survives him, was one of the pioneer physicians of the region. The family have lived in south, east, and west Texas, and western Oklahoma; for the last few years at Cross Plains, near Brownwood, Texas. Steeped in the frontier atmosphere, Mr. Howard early became a devotee of its virile Homeric traditions. His knowledge of its history and folkways was profound, and the descriptions and reminiscences contained in his private letters illustrate the eloquence and power with which he would have celebrated it in literature had he lived longer. Mr. Howard's family is of distinguished southern planter stock—of Scotch-Irish descent, with most ancestors settled in Georgia and North Carolina in the eighteenth century.

Beginning to write at fifteen, Mr. Howard placed his first story three years later while a student at Howard Payne College in Brownwood. This story, "Spear and Fang", was published in *Weird Tales* for July, 1925. Wider fame came with the appearance of the novelette "Wolfshead" in the same magazine in April, 1926. In August, 1928, began the tales dealing with "Solomon Kane", an English Puritan of relentless duelling and wrong-redressing proclivities whose adventures took him to strange parts of the world—including the shadow-haunted ruins of unknown and primordial cities in the African jungle. With these tales Mr. Howard struck what proved to be one of his most effective accomplishments—the description of vast megalithic cities of the elder world, around whose dark towers and labyrinthine nether vaults clings an aura of pre-human fear and necromancy which no other writer could duplicate. These tales also marked Mr. Howard's development of that skill and zest in depicting sanguinary conflict which became so typical of his work. "Solomon Kane", like several other heroes of the author, was conceived in boyhood long before incorporation in any story.

Always a keen student of Celtic antiquities and other phases of remote history, Mr. Howard began in 1929—with "The Shadow Kingdom", in the August *Weird Tales*—that succession of tales of the prehistoric world for which he soon grew so famous. The earlier specimens described a very distant age in man's history—when Atlantis, Lemuria, and Mu were above the waves, and when the shadows of pre-human reptile men rested upon the primal scene. Of these the central figure was King Kull of Valusia. In *Weird Tales* for December, 1932, appeared "The Phoenix on the Sword"—first of those tales of King Conan the Cimmerian which introduced a later prehistoric world; a world of perhaps 15,000 years ago, just before the first faint glimmerings of recorded history. The elaborate extent and accurate self-consistency with which Mr. Howard developed this world of Conan in his later stories is well known to all fantasy readers. For his own guidance he prepared a detailed quasi-historical sketch of infinite cleverness and imaginative fertility—now running in *The Phantagraph* as a serial under the title "The Hyborian Age".

Meanwhile Mr. Howard had written many tales of the early Picts and Celts, including a notable series revolving round the chieftain Bran Mak Morn. Few readers will ever forget the hideous and compelling power of that macabre masterpiece, "Worms of the Earth", in *Weird Tales* for November, 1932. Other powerful fantasies lay outside the connected series—these including the memorable serial "Skull-Face", and a few distinctive tales with a modern setting, such as the recent "Black Canaan" with its genuine regional background and its clutchingly compelling picture of the horror that stalks through the moss-hung, shadow-cursed, serpent-ridden swamps of the American far South.

Outside the fantasy field Mr. Howard was surprisingly prolific and versatile. His strong interest in sports—a thing perhaps connected with his love of primitive conflict and strength—led him to create the prize-fighting hero "Sailor Steve Costigan", whose adventures in distant and curious parts delighted the readers of many magazines. His novelettes of Oriental warfare displayed to the utmost his mastery of romantic swashbuckling, while his increasingly frequent tales of western life—such as the "Breckenridge Elkins" series—shewed his growing ability and inclination to reflect the backgrounds with which he was directly familiar.

Mr. Howard's poetry—weird, warlike, and adventurous—was no less notable than his prose. It had the true spirit of the ballad and the epic, and was marked by a pulsing rhythm and potent imagery of extremely distinctive cast. Much of it, in the form of supposed quotations from ancient writings, served to head the chapters of his novels. It is regrettable that no published collection has ever appeared, and one hopes that such a thing may be posthumously edited and issued.

The character and attainments of Mr. Howard were wholly unique. He was, above everything else, a lover of the simpler, older world of barbarian and pioneer days, when courage and strength took the place of subtlety and stratagem, and when a hardy, fearless race battled and bled and asked no quarter from hostile Nature. All his stories reflect this philosophy, and derive from it a vitality found in few of his contemporaries. No one could write more convincingly of violence and gore than he, and his battle passages reveal an instinctive aptitude for military tactics which would have brought him distinction in times of war. His real gifts were even higher than the readers of his published work could suspect, and had he lived would have helped him make his mark in serious literature with some folk-epic of his beloved Southwest.

It is hard to describe precisely what made Mr. Howard's stories stand out so sharply; but the real secret is that he himself was in every one of them, whether they were ostensibly commercial or not. He was greater than any profit-making policy he could adopt—for even when he outwardly made concessions to Mammon-guided editors and commercial critics he had an internal force and sincerity which broke through the surface and put the imprint of his personality on everything he wrote. Seldom if ever did he set down a lifeless stock character or situation and leave it as such. Before he concluded with it, it always took on some tinge of vitality and reality in spite of popular editorial policy—always drew something from his own experience and knowledge of life instead of from the sterile herbarium of desiccated pulpish standbys. Not only did he excel in pictures of strife and slaughter, but he was almost alone in his ability to create real emotions of spectral fear and dread suspense. No author—even in the humblest fields—can truly excel unless he takes his work very seriously; and Mr. Howard did just that, even in cases where he consciously thought he did not. That such a genuine artist should perish while hundreds of insincere hacks continue to concoct spurious ghosts and vampires and space-ships and occult detectives is indeed a sorry piece of cosmic irony.

Mr. Howard, familiar with many phases of southwestern life, lived with his parents in a semi-rural setting in the village of Cross Plains, Texas. Writing was his sole profession. His tastes in reading were wide, and included historical research of notable depth in fields as dissimilar as the American Southwest, prehistoric Great Britain and Ireland, and the prehistoric Oriental and African world. In literature he preferred the virile to the subtle, and repudiated modernism with sweeping completeness. The late Jack London was one of his idols. He was a liberal in politics, and a bitter foe of civic injustice in every form. His leading amusements were sports and travel—the latter always giving rise to delightful descriptive letters replete with historical reflections. Humour was not a specialty, though he had on the one hand a keen sense of irony, and on the other hand an abundant fund of heartiness, cordiality, and conviviality. Though having numerous friends, Mr. Howard belonged to no literary clique and abhorred all cults of "arty" affectation. His admirations ran toward strength of character and body rather than toward scholastic prowess. With his fellow-authors in the fantasy field he corresponded interestingly and voluminously, but never met more than one of them—the gifted E. Hoffmann Price, whose varied attainments impressed him profoundly—in person.

Mr. Howard was nearly six feet in height, with the massive build of a born fighter. He was, save for Celtic blue eyes, very dark; and in later years his weight averaged around 195. Always a disciple of hearty and strenuous living, he suggested more than casually his own most famous character—the intrepid warrior, adventurer, and seizer of thrones, Conan the Cimmerian. His loss at the age of thirty is a tragedy of the first magnitude, and a blow from which fantasy fiction will not soon recover. Mr. Howard's library has been presented to Howard Payne College, where it will form the nucleus of the Robert E. Howard Memorial Collection of books, manuscripts, and letters.

III

MECHANISTIC MATERIALIST

Philosophy traditionally contains five broad subdivisions—metaphysics, ethics, epistemology, politics, and aesthetics. Lovecraft dealt vigorously with each of these except epistemology (the theory of knowledge, or how we know what we know), an issue that never concerned him greatly even though it has become the dominant strain of twentieth-century philosophical thought in the work of Ludwig Wittgenstein, Bertrand Russell, Gilbert Ryle, and others. Aside from routine admissions of the fallibility of the senses, Lovecraft was confident that we could know enough about ourselves and the universe around us to take reasonably definite stands on the fundamental issues of philosophy. In this section we present a sampling of Lovecraft's opinions on these issues, chiefly metaphysics, ethics, and aesthetics; his political thought is reserved for a separate section, as is that branch of aesthetics that embraces literary criticism.

In this space we cannot hope to give anything like a full account of Lovecraft's philosophy, and perhaps there is no need, as his essays, a layman's views intended for other laymen, are largely self-explanatory. All we wish to do is to provide some background and context.

When Lovecraft declared himself a mechanistic materialist, he was asserting two related positions: first, the universe (and everything in it, including human beings) is a "mechanism," governed by fixed (if in some cases unknown) laws of causality, and is accordingly wholly deterministic (i.e., everything occurs through logical necessity, and there is no such thing as free will); second, there is no substance or essence in the universe not encompassed by the laws of physics, chemistry, and biology—in particular, there is no such thing as an immaterial "soul." Lovecraft was of course aware that the old-time atomistic materialism of Democritus had gone by the board with the division of the atom, and he states that the word *materialism* is now meant in a purely historical sense, not as implying that all entity is material. In effect, materialism is more important for what it denies than for what it affirms, since the denial of "soul" really means a discarding of the entire framework of religion. Lovecraft's is, indeed, one of the most purely secular philosophies ever envisaged.

Let us be clear that very little of Lovecraft's metaphysical thought is original. Most of it was derived from the great physicists and biologists of the later nineteenth century, and two works in particular—Ernst Haeckel's *The Riddle of the Universe* (1899) and Hugh Elliot's *Modern Science and Materialism* (1919)—supplied Lovecraft with nearly all the metaphysical tools he needed. Even his cosmicism—stressing the insignificance of humanity in an aimless and eternal cosmos—is implicit in these works, and Lovecraft simply laid greater emphasis on it. Similarly, Lovecraft's anthropological explanations of the natural origin of religious belief in primitive man—which he calls "the most important of all materialistic arguments"—were derived wholly from such works as E. B. Tylor's *Primitive Culture* (1871) and John Fiske's *Myths and Myth-Makers* (1872). Lovecraft also uses the theory of evolution to deny the existence of a human soul; for where along the course of our evolution from apes to human beings did we acquire this mysterious substance?

The affirmation of a mechanistic view of the universe necessitates the denial of *teleology*—the notion that the cosmos as a whole is evolving toward some goal or other, presumably (as in religious metaphysics) a superior state of existence. Lovecraft is tireless in refuting this point: it is as if he almost welcomes the prospect of the universe's purposelessness.

Conventional mechanistic materialism was dealt some serious blows by twentieth-century advances in astrophysics, notably Einstein's theory of relativity and Planck's quantum theory. Lovecraft's essays do not reveal his attempts to come to terms with these potentially devastating findings as well as his letters do, but it is evident that he grappled as best he could with these issues while still trying to maintain the essence of his creed. The matter is too complex for discussion here, but the interested reader should study two of Lovecraft's letters to Frank Belknap Long (February 20, 1929, and November 22, 1930) for his admirable attempt to harmonize mechanistic materialism with modern indeterminacy.

If Lovecraft's metaphysics is relatively unoriginal, his ethics is scarcely less so. The early influence of Schopenhauer and Epicurus can be felt throughout Lovecraft's thought: from Schopenhauer he derived the belief that pain is the predominant attribute of existence, while with Epicurus he maintained that the diminution of this pain is the highest pleasure human beings can achieve. (Lovecraft writes copiously and piquantly on the origin of his metaphysical and ethical views in "A Confession of Unfaith," but as that essay seems more autobiographical it has been placed in this volume's concluding section.) Lovecraft initially claimed to be a moral relativist (one man's meat is another man's poison), but gradually this view gave way to a belief in "tradition" as the "one anchor of fixity" (as he terms it in a letter to Elizabeth Toldridge of June 10, 1929) left to human beings in an aimless cosmos. This position is entirely indefensible philosophically, and is perhaps the most extreme example of what might be called Lovecraft's ethical fascism: what was suitable to *him* should, evidently, be suitable to all. Tradition meant much to Lovecraft, and he therefore finds convoluted sophistical arguments to erect it as the one bulwark against the meaninglessness of existence.

This emphasis on tradition is important, as it lays the groundwork for Lovecraft's entire aesthetic stance, represented here by "Heritage or Modernism: Common Sense in Art Forms" (1935). Art must, in Lovecraft's view, continue to build upon the past: modifications may be made because of evolving world-views, but a core of tradition must remain. From this perspective Lovecraft feels safe in demolishing the functionalists in architecture, and indeed many of his criticisms are telling. How Lovecraft's general aesthetic position comes into play in the realm of literary criticism is something we shall examine later.

Many of the essays in this section had a peculiar genesis, and there are unresolved questions concerning the composition of some of them. "Idealism and Materialism—A Reflection" appeared in the "July 1919" issue of *The National Amateur;* but this issue was much delayed, and in fact contained Lovecraft's story "The Picture in the House" (definitely dated to late 1920), so that the dating of the essay to 1919 is frankly tentative. The three *In Defence of Dagon* essays (the general title is R. H. Barlow's) were written for an Anglo-American correspondence group called the Transatlantic Circulator, where members exchanged stories, poems, and essays in manuscript. Without annotation it is sometimes difficult to follow Lovecraft's argument, as he is replying to comments made on his stories and his general philosophical position by other members; some of these comments still survive, while others (especially the philosophical remarks of the Mr. Wickenden Lovecraft so takes to task) have perished. Nonetheless, they remain some of Lovecraft's finest essays in their rhetorical brilliance, logical argumentation, and stylistic verve.

"Nietzscheism and Realism" is a series of extracts made by Sonia Greene from Lovecraft's letters to her, so that formal unity is not to be looked for; these extracts are, in fact, uncannily similar to Nietzsche's own aphorisms, although Schopenhauer also looms large as an influence. The title is almost certainly Sonia's. Then there is the bizarre piece called "Some Causes of Self-Immolation" (1931). There is no clue as to why Lovecraft wrote this essay or whether he attempted to secure its publication (it remained in manuscript until after his death); in spite of the flippancy of the title and the comical subtitle and pseudonym, it appears to be a seriously intended investigation of certain psychological phenomena.

It is in Lovecraft's letters that we may more readily and vividly discover the details of his philosophical thought; on the whole his essays are a little heavy and dogmatic, and do not quite display Lovecraft's ongoing quest to clarify and overhaul his philosophy as new evidence emerges or his attitudes change. If Lovecraft is by no stretch of the imagination a great philosopher, he is by all means an interesting one, and he made that philosophy the backbone of his entire literary work. That alone is sufficient reason for studying it.

IDEALISM AND MATERIALISM—A REFLECTION

Human thought, with its infinite varieties, intensities, aspects, and collisions, is perhaps the most amusing yet discouraging spectacle on our terraqueous globe. It is amusing because of its contradictions, and because of the pompousness with which its possessors try to analyse dogmatically an utterly unknown and unknowable cosmos in which all mankind forms but a transient, negligible atom; it is discouraging because it can never from its very nature attain that ideal degree of unanimity which would make its tremendous energy available for the improvement of the race. The thoughts of men, moulded by an innumerable diversity of circumstances, will always conflict. Groups may coincide in certain ideas long enough to found a few definite intellectual institutions; but men thinking together in one subject differ in others, so that even the strongest of such institutions carries within itself the seed of its ultimate downfall. Conflict is the one inescapable certainty of life; mental conflict which invariably becomes physical and martial when the intellectual breach attains sufficient width and the opposing minds are divided into factions of suitable proportions. Followers of the "world brotherhood" and "universal peace" delusion would do well to remember this scientific truth, grounded on the basic psychological nature of man, before deciding to continue in their always absurd and often disastrous course.

Most decided and obvious of all the eternal conflicts of human thought is that between the reason and the imagination; between the real and the material, and the ideal or spiritual. In every age each of these principles has had its champions; and so basic and vital are the problems involved, that the conflict has exceeded all others in bitterness and universality. Each side, having its own method of approach, is impervious to the attacks of the other; hence it is unlikely that anything resembling agreement will ever be reached. Only the impartial, objective, dispassionate observer can form a just verdict of the dispute; and so few are these observers, that their influence can never be great.

Man, slowly coming into existence as an efflorescence of some simian stock, originally knew nothing beyond the concrete and the immediate. Formerly guided by reflex action or instinct, his evolving brain was an absolute blank regarding everything beyond those simple matters of defence, shelter, and food-procuring whose exigencies had brought it into being. As this primal brain developed along the path of the original impelling force, its intrinsic strength and activity outstripped the material which it had to feed upon. Since no sources of information were in existence to supply it, its dawning curiosity perforce became inventive; and the phenomena of Nature began to be interpreted in such simple terms as a nascent race could devise and comprehend. The sun was good. Men were comfortable when it was present, uncomfortable when it was absent. Therefore men should act toward the sun as they might act toward a chieftain or pack-leader who was able to confer and withdraw favours. Leaders gave favours when people praise them or give them presents. Therefore the sun should be praised and propitiated with presents. And so were born the imaginative conceptions of deity, worship, and sacrifice. A new and wholly illusory system of thought had arisen—the spiritual.

The development of an ideal world of imagination, overlying and trying to explain the real world of Nature, was rapid. Since to the untutored mind the conception of impersonal action is impossible, every natural phenomenon was invested with purpose and personality. If lightning struck the earth, it was wilfully hurled by an unseen being in the sky. If a river flowed toward the sea, it was because some unseen being wilfully propelled it. And since men understood no sources of action but themselves, these unseen creatures of imagination were endowed with human forms, despite their more than human powers. So rose the awesome race of anthropomorphic gods, destined to exert so long a sway over their creators. Parallel illusions were almost innumerable. Observing that his welfare depended on conformity to that fixed course of atomic, molecular, and mass interaction which we now call the laws of Nature, primitive man devised the notion of divine government, with the qualities of spiritual right and wrong. Right and wrong indeed existed as actualities in the shape of conformity and nonconformity to Nature; but our first thinking ancestors could conceive of no law save personal will, so deemed themselves the slaves of some celestial tyrant or tyrants of human shape and unlimited authority. Phases of this idea originated the monotheistic religions. Then came the illusion of justice. Observing that exchange is the natural basis of human relations, and that favours are most frequently granted to those who give favours, man's imagination extended the local principle to the cosmos, and formed the sweeping conclusion that boons are always repaid by equal boons; that every human creature shall be rewarded by the powers of governing gods of Nature in proportion to his good deeds, or deeds of conformity. This conclusion was aided by the natural greed or desire of acquisition inherent in the species. All men want more than they have, and in order to explain the instinct they invoke an imaginary "right" to receive more. The idea of retribution and divine punishment was an inevitable concomitant of the idea of reward and divine favour.

This element of desire played a vast part in the extension of idealistic thought. Man's instincts, made more complex by the added impressions received through the nascent intellect, in many cases developed novel physical and mental reactions; and gave rise to the isolated phenomena of emotion. Emotion, working hand in hand with imagination, created such illusions as that of immortality; which is undoubtedly a compound of man's notions of "another world" as gained in dreams, and of the increasing horror of the idea of utter death as appreciated by a brain now able to comprehend as never before the fact that every man must sooner or later lose forever his accustomed pleasures of hunting, fighting, and lying before his favourite tree or cave in the sun. Man does not want to lose these pleasures, and his mind seeks an escape from the unknown and perhaps frightful abyss of death. It is doubtful if the savage, remembering nothing but life, can conceive of absolute non-existence. He finds false analogies like the vernal resurgence of plant life, and the beautiful world of dreams, and succeeds in persuading his half-formed intellect that his existence in the real world is but part of a larger existence; that he will either be re-born on earth or transplanted to some remote and eternal dream-world. Later on the illusion of justice plays a part in the comedy; and man, failing to find abstract equity in actual life, is glad to invent a future life of repayment and adjustment according to merit.

With such a beginning, we need not marvel at the development of an elaborate and highly cherished system of idealistic philosophy. The advance of the intellect without previous scientific knowledge to guide it had the effect of strengthening emotion and imagination without a corresponding strengthening of ratiocinative processes, and the immense residue of unchanged brute instinct fell in with the scheme. Desire and fancy dwarfed fact and observation altogether; and we find all thought based not on truth, but on what man wishes to be the truth. Lacking the power to conceive of a mighty interaction of cosmical forces without a man-like will and a man-like purpose, humanity forms its persistent conviction that all creation has some definite object; that everything tends upward toward some vast unknown purpose or perfection. Thus arise all manner of extravagant hopes which in time fasten themselves on mankind and enslave his intellect beyond easy redemption. Hope becomes a despot, and man comes at last to use it as a final argument against reason, telling the materialist that the truth cannot be true, *because it destroys hope.*

As the complexity of the mind increases, and reason, emotion, and imagination develop, we behold a great refinement, subtilisation, and systematisation of idealistic thought. In the interim aesthetic and intellectual interests have arisen, demanding improvements and concessions in the dominant religions or superstitions of man. Idealising must now be made to conform to the actual facts which have been unearthed, and to the quickened sense of beauty which has grown up. At this stage the great civilisations are forming, and each fashions one or more highly technical and artistic scheme of philosophy or theology. At first the advances tend to confirm the idealistic notion. Beauty breeds wonder and imagination, whilst partial comprehension of the magnitude and operation of Nature breeds awe. Men do not pause to question whether their gods could in truth create and manage an universe so vast and intricate, but merely marvel the more at gods who are able to perform such cosmic prodigies. Likewise, each thing on earth becomes merely the type of some imaginary better thing, or ideal, which is supposed to exist either in another world or in the future of this world. Out of the pleasantest phases of all objects and experiences imagination finds it easy to build illusory corresponding objects and experiences which are *all pleasant.* Whilst all mankind is more or less involved in this wholesale dreaming, particular nations develop particularly notable idealistic systems, based on their especial mental and aesthetic capacity. Here Greece, foremost of cultural centres, easily leads the rest. With a primitive mythology of unexcelled loveliness, she has likewise the foremost of later idealistic philosophies, that of Plato. It is this Platonic system, sometimes operating through the clumsy covering of an alien Hebraic theology, that forms the animating force in idealism today.

The idealists of today form two classes, theological and rationalistic. The former are frankly primitive, and use the crudest and least advanced methods of argument. The latter adopt an outwardly scientific attitude and honestly believe themselves to be working from facts alone, yet are overwhelmingly influenced by the illusions of human perfectibility and a better world. In clinging to these hoary fallacies, they generally seize upon the rather recently discovered and indubitably proven law of evolution to sustain them; forgetting the infinite slowness of the process, and overlooking the fact that when evolution shall have really affected our descendants to any appreciable degree, they will no longer belong to the human race, mentally or physically—any more than we belong to the simian race. Of the two idealistic types, the theological deserves respect for its accomplishments, the rationalistic for its intentions. Religion has undoubtedly been the dominant factor in facilitating human relations and enforcing a moral or ethical code of practical benefit in alleviating the sufferings of mankind. The human reason is weak in comparison to instinct and emotion, and up to the present these latter forces, in the guise of theology, have proved the only effective restraint from the disorders of utter licence and animalism. The percentage of men civilised and governed by reason is still relatively slight. True, certain religions have claimed exclusive credit. Christianity, for example, claims to have civilised Europeans; whereas in cold truth it is Europe which has civilised Christianity. The faith of Christus, adopted for political reasons by the Imperator Constantinus, was forcibly seated in power, whence it naturally assimilated to itself all the characteristics of the Graeco-Roman culture of the later Empire and of the European nations which rose from that Empire's ashes; a culture which would have elevated to supreme dignity any religion similarly linked with it. But despite such excessive claims, it remains fairly clear that some form of religion is at least highly desirable among the uneducated. Without it they are despondent and turbulent; miserable with unsatisfied and unsatisfiable aspirations which may yet lead the civilised world to chaos and destruction. The rationalistic idealist neglects this practical consideration, and denounces religion in terms of unmeasured scorn because he knows it to be untrue. Just as the theist forgets that his faith may be fallacious though its effects be good, so does the idealistic atheist forget that his doctrine may have ill effects though it be true. Both are governed by emotion rather than reason in their campaign of mutual destruction. Both cling to the primitive ideal of the ought-to-be. The rationalist is honest, and therefore to be admired. But when he allows his relentless and idealistic hostility to fallacy to lead him into a destructive course, he is to be censured. He should not pull down what he cannot replace; and since a preponderance of obvious evidence is against the possibility of rational self-government of the masses, he should obey the practical judgment which forbids a gardener to saw off the tree-limb on which he is sitting, even though it be dead and useless save as a support. In his passionately intense and narrowly single-minded public crusade against religion, the militant atheist shews himself as unbalanced an idealist as the Christian fanatic. Like the latter, he is following up one idea with febrile ardour and conviction; forgetting general conditions and the relative unimportance of truth to the world. Usually he acts in protest against the many undeniable evils of religion; evils which are outweighed by good effects, and which at worst are no graver than the evils inseparable from an atheistical code. It is this crusade against irremediable evils which stamps the idealist of every kind as childish. To fancy that age-old principles can be improved suddenly, or to fancy that the necessary little hypocrisies and injustices of ordinary life form a pretext for overturning the whole social structure, is in truth puerility of the most pitiful sort. The spectacle of Christians and idealistic atheists in mortal combat is indeed grotesque—one thinks of such things as the battles of the frogs and mice, or of the pygmies and the cranes.

The materialist is the only thinker who makes use of the knowledge and experience which ages have brought to the human race. He is the man who, putting aside the instincts and desires which he knows to be animal and primitive, and the fancies and emotions which he knows to be purely subjective and linked to the recognised delusions of dreams and madness, views the cosmos with a minimum of personal bias, as a detached spectator coming with open mind to a sight about which he claims no previous knowledge. He approaches the universe without prejudices or dogmata, intent not upon planning what should be, or of spreading any particular idea throughout the world, but devoted merely to the perception and as far as possible the analysis of whatever may exist. He sees the infinity, eternity, purposelessness, and automatic action of creation, and the utter, abysmal insignificance of man and the world therein. He sees that the world is but a grain of dust in existence for a moment, and that accordingly all the problems of man are as nothing—mere trifles without relation to the infinite, just as man himself is unrelated to the infinite. He sees through the feeble fallacy of justice, and perceives the absurdity of the doctrine of an immortal personality, when in truth personality and thought come only from highly organised matter. He recognises the impossibility of such things as vague, uncorporeal intelligences—"gaseous vertebrates", as Haeckel wittily called them. But while thus disillusioned, he does not fall into the rationalistic idealist's error of condemning as wicked and abnormal all religious and kindred benevolent fancies. Looking beyond the bald facts of atheism, he reconstructs the dawn of the human mind and perceives that its evolution absolutely necessitates a religious and idealistic period; that theism and idealism are perfectly natural, inevitable, and desirable concomitants of primitive thought, or thought without information. That they are still desirable for the many he accepts as a plain consequence of man's backward and atavistical nature. Actually, it can be shewn that man has made but little progress since the dawn of history save in facilities for physical comfort. What arouses the materialist to conflict is not the existence of idealism, but the extent to which idealists obtrude their illusions upon thinking men in an endeavour to befog the truth. Truth, be it pleasant or unpleasant, is the one object of the materialist's quest—for it is the only object worthy of the quest of an enlightened mind. He seeks it not to spread it and wreck happiness, but to satisfy the craving of his intelligence for it; to establish his right to the position of a rational man. When theists or atheistical idealists try to force their childish doctrines down the throat of realistic thinkers, the trouble begins. With the humble and unobtrusive church or the quiet and undemonstrative Utopian the materialist has no quarrel. But when either of these adopts arrogant tactics and seeks to discredit a philosophy which is honest, quiet, and sincere, the eternal enmity of dissimilar thought once more becomes manifest. No manly reasoner will tamely allow himself to be lulled into mental inactivity by the emotional soothing-syrup of faith, be it faith in a supernatural goodness, or a non-existent perfectibility of humanity.

Perhaps it is in the ethical field that materialists clash most decidedly with idealists; and curiously so, since in most cases the difference is one of approach rather than of actual code. Idealists believe in a right and wrong distinct from Nature, and therefore invent something they call "sin", building up a highly artificial system of mythology around it. They measure man's acts not by the standard of practical value in promoting the comfort and smooth existence of the race, but by imaginary ideals of their own construction. That materialists should not believe in this mythical system of ideals enrages idealists vastly, yet when both come to apply their codes of moral government, a surprising similarity is shewn. The fact is, that on the one hand ideals are largely formed with Nature as a pattern; whilst on the other hand, an efficient, practical code of ethics must always demand a bit more than it expects. An harmonious and workable moral system must satisfy as many aspects of Nature as possible, and accommodate itself to the peculiarities of the age and place. Where an idealistic code is well grounded, the materialist leaves it unaltered as a matter of sound common sense. Where it is not, he consults Nature, history, and good taste, and advocates a system most nearly in accord with these things. A study of history will shew that the basic moral ideals of the white race have been but little affected by its beliefs. Some systems bring out certain virtues more strongly than others, and some conceal vices more cleverly than others; but the general average is about the same. Of course, practical enforcement is another matter; and here the sincere materialist concedes the palm to religion. Superstition is stronger than reason, and a code will best touch the masses if sustained by supposed divine authority. In the case of our own Anglo-Saxon code, no honest materialist would wish to cause any marked alteration. With a little less Sabbatarianism and exaltation of meekness, the existing system would be admirably suited to natural wants and even these slight defects are now wearing rapidly away. If at the present time we complain at the tendency of the church to assume a position of ostentatious moral guardianship, it is because we perceive the signs of its decay, and wish to preserve its ethical legacy as best we can in a rationalistic manner. We do not wish to see faith and morals so inextricably intertwined that the latter will collapse with the former.

Beyond the sphere of simple conduct lies the question of one's attitude toward life as a whole. That the philosophy of materialism is pessimistic, none can deny; but much may be said in favour of a calm, courageous facing of the infinite by the resigned, disillusioned, unhoping, unemotional atom as contrasted with the feverish, pathological struggle and agony of the Christian mind, coping desperately with the mythical shadows and problems it has invented, and agitated by emotions which idealism has overstimulated instead of repressing as emotions should be repressed. The materialist has nothing to lose; the idealist is eternally suffering the pangs of disillusionment. And even the boasted theological "peace that passeth all understanding" is a weak, hollow thing as compared with the virtuous materialist's pride in an unshackled mind and an unsullied honour. If idealism really lived up to its promises, conditions might be otherwise; but no fallacy can wholly envelop the human mind, and there are terrible moments when even the unprepared intellect of the idealist is brought face to face with the truth about the cosmos and the lack of divine justice, purpose, and destiny.

Idealism as we know it today bases itself on the false premise that emotion forms under certain conditions a perfect substitute for reason in imparting positive knowledge. Mr. Dryden expressed this sentiment with great vividness at the beginning of his *Religio Laici:*

"And as those nightly tapers disappear
When day's bright lord ascends our hemisphere;
So pale grows Reason at Religion's sight,
So dies, and so dissolves in supernatural light."

Religious persons will assure you that they *know* their faith to be true by means of sensations or intuitions *too deep to be expressed.* The materialist cannot but smile at this readiness to accept hallucination as evidence. Those who make these assurances forget that *other* religions have undergone the same emotional experiences, and are equally certain that their respective faiths are the only true faiths; and they forget that many a man in bedlam has the certain belief that he is Alexander,

Caesar, or Napoleon. The subjective is always vague, variable, and visionary. It is based on false mental images like those of dreams, and can easily be proved to have no weight whatsoever in imparting facts, or distinguishing truth from error. The writer can cite a subjective childhood fancy of his own which well illustrates the false position of the intuitive theist. Though the son of an Anglican father and Baptist mother, and early accustomed to the usual pious tales of an orthodox household and Sunday-school, he was never a believer in the prevailing abstract and barren Christian mythology. Instead, he was a devotee of fairy tales and the Arabian Nights' Entertainments; none of which he believed, but which seemed to him fully as true as the Bible tales, and much more attractive. Then, at an age not much above six, he stumbled on the legends of Greece—and became a sincere and enthusiastic classical pagan. Unlearned in science, and reading all the Graeco-Roman lore at hand, he was until the age of eight a rapt devotee of the old gods; building altars to Pan and Apollo, Athena and Artemis, and benignant Saturnus, who ruled the world in the Golden Age. And at times this belief was very real indeed—there are vivid memories of fields and groves at twilight when the now materialistic mind that dictates these lines *knew absolutely that the ancient gods were true.* Did he not see with his own eyes, beyond the possibility of a doubt, the graceful forms of dryads half-mingled with the trunks of antique oaks, or spy with clearness and certainty the elusive little fauns and goat-footed old satyrs who leapt about so slyly from the shadow of one rock or thicket to that of another? He saw these things as plainly as he saw the antique oaks and the rocks and the thickets themselves, and laughed at unbelievers, *for he knew.* Now he realises that he saw these things with the eye of imagination only; that his devotion to the gods was but a passing phase of childish dreaming and emotionalism, to be dissipated with time and knowledge. But he has today every jot of evidence for Graeco-Roman paganism that any Christian has for Christianity, any Jew for Judaism, any Mahometan for Mahometanism, or any Lodge for Spiritualism. What mixture of crude instinct, desire, illusion, fancy, auto-hypnotism, delirium, and aesthetic fervour is the religious belief of the average theist! Much of the zeal he displays is undoubtedly derived from a perversion or modification of rather baser instincts, about which a psychologist of the Freudian type could speak more authoritatively than the writer. This very connexion betwixt religious and other emotion should be significant to the observer. It is the less thoughtful and more passionate man or race that possesses the deepest religious instincts, as we see in the case of the negro. The colder and more highly developed mind of the European is the birthplace of materialism.

Idealism and Materialism! Illusion and Truth! Together they will go down into the darkness when men shall have ceased to be; when beneath the last flickering beams of a dying sun shall perish utterly the last vestige of organic life on our tiny grain of cosmic dust. And upon the black planets that reel devilishly about a black sun shall the name of man be forgotten. Nor shall the stars sing his fame as they pierce the aether with cruel needles of pale light. But who shall be so heedless of analogy as to say that men, or things having faculties like men, do not dwell on uncounted myriads of unseen planets that whirl about the far stars? Greater or lesser than our own their minds may be —probably some worlds hold duller creatures, whilst some hold beings whom we would call gods for their wisdom. But be their inhabitants greater or lesser than we, none can doubt that on every world where thought exists, there exist also the systems of Idealism and Materialism, eternally and unalterably opposed.

Amateur journal containing Lovecraft's essay "Life for Humanity's Sake" (verso)

The American Amateur

A BI-MONTHLY MAGAZINE

FOR THE ADVANCEMENT
OF AMATEUR JOURNALISM

MARTHA WASHINGTON

Ridgefield Park, N. J., September 1920

Volume Two Number One

Life for Humanity's Sake

By H. P. LOVECRAFT

IT is with great interest that I have observed the widespread literary hostilities engendered by the publication of Miss Elsie A. Gidlow's article on "Life for Life's Sake" in the October, 1919, WOLVERINE. Its subject is one which has attracted my speculative attention since earliest youth; and which has, on account of my decided opinions, frequently drawn me into controversy. In offering additional comment my object is to touch upon the philosophical phase so promptly combated by Mr. Maurice Winter Moe, yet so oddly neglected by those who have held dispute on the artistic phase. Possibly my remarks will develop into a collective reply to Miss Gidlow and Mr. Moe, rather than a reply to the former alone; since despite their opposite views on theism, both seem curiously alike in their narrowly doctrinal as distinguished from generally philosophical attitude.

Miss Gidlow has discovered the fact that there is no vast supernatural intelligence governing the cosmos—a thing Democritus could have told her several centuries B. C.— and is amazingly disturbed thereat. Without stopping to consider the possibility of acquiescence in a purposeless, mechanical universe, she at once strives to invent a substitute for the mythology she has cast aside; and preaches as a new and surprising discovery the ancient selfish hedonism whose folly was manifest before the death of its founder Aristippus. There is something both amusing and pathetic about the promulgation of hedonism in this complex age of human interdependence. While of course the ultimate basis of every human act is selfishness, manifested as a craving for self-approval, it is easy to perceive the utter and destructive impracticability of any system exalting that crude and unmoral selfishness which has not been refined into a delicate altruism. Such a bestial relapse means the end of human harmony and co-operation, and therefore of civilisation.

Mr. Moe, fully alive to the absurdity of the Gidlovian philosophy, unfortunately chooses the most primitive, antiquated, and fallacious of methods to refute it. Rejecting the ready weapons supplied by sociology and common sense, he falls back upon the archaic notion that brutal selfishness can be fought only by belief in the supernatural; thus attacking hedonism purely as a theist, and actually strengthening Miss Gidlow's position by assuming that it is the one logical position of the rationalist. Mr. Moe, in his zeal for an outgrown faith, damages the cause of practical virtue by binding religion and morality so closely together that the precious verities of the latter must needs sink with the obsolete dogmata of the former.

How sickening is the eternal quest for "creeds" and "ideals" in which theists and atheists are alike engrossed! Why will not Miss Gidlow and Mr. Moe step down to earth for a while and face the problems of life as they are? We are all negligible, microscopic insects of a moment; waifs astray in infinity, born yesterday and doomed to perish tomorrow for all time. We have no reason to ask the trite questions of "whence, whither and why," for it is only our finite, subjective, rudimentary intellects which conjure up the notion of cosmic purpose. According to all the evidence we can command, we came from chaos and will return to chaos; drifting in a blind mechanical cycle devoid of anything like a goal or object. So much Miss Gidlow will perhaps concede, yet her rationalism seems to end at this point. Its futility having been demonstrated, mankind as a whole interests her no longer. She is joyously 'disburdened',

LIFE FOR HUMANITY'S SAKE

It is with great interest that I have observed the widespread literary hostilities engendered by the publication of Miss Elsie A. Gidlow's article on "Life for Life's Sake" in the October, 1919, *Wolverine.* Its subject is one which has attracted my speculative attention since earliest youth; and which has, on account of my decided opinions, frequently drawn me into controversy. In offering additional comment my object is to touch upon the philosophical phase so promptly combated by Mr. Maurice Winter Moe, yet so oddly neglected by those who have held dispute on the artistic phase. Possibly my remarks will develop into a collective reply to Miss Gidlow and Mr. Moe, rather than a reply to the former alone; since despite their opposite views on theism, both seem curiously alike in their narrowly doctrinal as distinguished from generally philosophical attitude.

Miss Gidlow has discovered the fact that there is no vast supernatural intelligence governing the cosmos—a thing Democritus could have told her several centuries B. C.—and is amazingly disturbed thereat. Without stopping to consider the possibility of acquiescence in a purposeless, mechanical universe, she at once strives to invent a substitute for the mythology she has cast aside; and preaches as a new and surprising discovery the ancient selfish hedonism whose folly was manifest before the death of its founder Aristippus. There is something both amusing and pathetic about the promulgation of hedonism in this complex age of human interdependence. While of course the ultimate basis of every human act is selfishness, manifested as a craving for self-approval, it is easy to perceive the utter and destructive impracticability of any system exalting that crude and unmoral selfishness which has not been refined into a delicate altruism. Such a bestial relapse means the end of human harmony and coöperation, and therefore of civilisation.

Mr. Moe, fully alive to the absurdity of the Gidlovian philosophy, unfortunately chooses the most primitive, antiquated, and fallacious of methods to refute it. Rejecting the ready weapons supplied by sociology and common sense, he falls back upon the archaic notion that brutal selfishness can be fought only by belief in the supernatural; thus attacking hedonism purely as a theist, and actually strengthening Miss Gidlow's position by assuming that it is the one logical position of the rationalist. Mr. Moe, in his zeal for an outgrown faith, damages the cause of practical virtue by binding religion and morality so closely together that the precious verities of the latter must needs sink with the obsolete dogmata of the former.

How sickening is the eternal quest for "creeds" and "ideals" in which theists and atheists are alike engrossed! Why will not Miss Gidlow and Mr. Moe step down to earth for a while and face the problems of life as they are? We are all negligible, microscopic insects of a moment; waifs astray in infinity, born yesterday and doomed to perish tomorrow for all time. We have no reason to ask the trite questions of "whence, whither, and why", for it is only our finite, subjective, rudimentary intellects which conjure up the notion of cosmic purpose. According to all the evidence we can command, we came from chaos and will return to chaos; drifting in a blind mechanical cycle devoid of anything like a goal or object. So much Miss Gidlow will perhaps concede, yet her rationalism seems to end at this point. Its futility having been demonstrated, mankind as a whole interests her no longer. She is joyously 'disburdened', and flies to individualistic gratifications.

A real ethical philosophy can be founded only on practicalities. We do not need to seek for a goal, since the goal of mental evolution and the subordination of pain stands so conspicuously before us. We can do nothing save try to make life tolerable for the greatest number of persons, and to do this we must supplant crude selfishness by that subtilised selfishness which is expressed in moral sacrifices of immediate pleasure for the common good and tranquillity. We need not look up to imaginary idols in the empty sky, but we must not relapse into the primitive selfish savagery from which we have evolved. Let us adopt the soundest motto of all—Life for Humanity's Sake!

IN DEFENCE OF DAGON

The Defence Reopens! Jany. 1921

In replying to the adverse criticisms of my weird tale "Dagon", I must begin by conceding that all such work is necessarily directed to a very limited section of the public. Fiction falls generally into three major divisions; romantic, realistic, and imaginative. The first is for those who value action and emotion for their own sake; who are interested in striking events which conform to a preconceived artificial pattern. These readers will accept psychological improbabilities and untruths, and even highly distorted objective happenings, but they demand a background of literalism. Romanticists are persons who on the one hand scorn the realist who says that moonlight is only reflected wave-motion in aether; but who on the other hand sit stolid and unmoved when a *fantaisiste* tells them that the moon is a hideous nightmare eye—watching . . . ever watching. . . . They will say to the realist that he forgets the emotional influence of moonlight; but they will not be able to follow up subjectively a fantastic conception involving myth-making, so will be equally opposed to the teller of strange legends.

The second fictional school—the realism which rules the public today—is for those who are intellectual and analytical rather than poetical or emotional. It is scientific and literal, and laughs both at the romanticist and the myth-maker. It has the virtue of being close to life, but has the disadvantage of sinking into the commonplace and the unpleasant at times. Both romanticism and realism have the common quality of dealing almost wholly with the objective world—with things rather than with what things suggest. The poetic element is wanting. Romanticism calls on emotion, realism on pure reason; both ignore the imagination, which groups isolated impressions into gorgeous patterns and finds strange relations and associations among the objects of visible and invisible Nature. Phantasy exists to fulfil the demands of the imagination; but since imagination is so much less widely diffused than are emotion and analytical reason, it follows that such a literary type must be relatively rare, and decidedly restricted in its appeal. Imaginative artists have been few, and always unappreciated. Blake is woefully undervalued. Poe would never have been understood had not the French taken the pains to exalt and interpret him. Dunsany has met with nothing but coldness or lukewarm praise. And nine persons out of ten *never heard of* Ambrose Bierce, the greatest story writer except Poe whom America ever produced. The imaginative writer devotes himself to art in its most essential sense. It is not his business to fashion a pretty trifle to please the children, to point a useful moral, to concoct superficial "uplift" stuff for the mid-Victorian hold-over, or to rehash insolvable human problems didactically. He is a painter of moods and mind-pictures—a capturer and amplifier of elusive dreams and fancies—a voyager into those unheard-of lands which are glimpsed through the veil of actuality but rarely, and only by the most sensitive. He is one who not only sees objects, but follows up all the bizarre trails of associated ideas which encompass and lead away from them. He is the poet of twilight visions and childhood memories, but sings only for the sensitive. All moods are his to reproduce, be they bright or dark. "Wholesomeness" and "utility" are to him unknown words. He mirrors the rays that fall upon him, and does not ask their source or effect. He is not practical, poor fellow, and sometimes dies in poverty; for his friends all live in the City of Never above the sunset, or in the antique rock temples of Mycenae, or the crypts and catacombs of Egypt and Meroë. Most persons do not understand what he says, and most of those who do understand object because his statements and pictures are not always pleasant and sometimes *quite impossible.* But he exists not for praise, nor thinks of his readers. His only [goal is] to paint the scenes that pass before his eyes.

Now far be it from me to claim the honour of being a real imaginative artist. It is my privilege only to admire from the abyss of mediocrity, and to copy in my feeble way. But what I have said of imaginative literature may help to explain what it is that I am feebly and unsuccessfully *trying to do.* It may explain why I do not tag my tales with copy-book morals or try to confine the events to cheerful, every-day happenings of unimpeachable probability. As to criticism—I ask only that my reviewers observe the basic law of their craft; a comparison between design and achievement. No one is more acutely conscious than I of the inadequacy of my work. Nothing exasperates me more than the failure of my written products to duplicate the visions and nightmares that lie behind them. I am a self-confessed amateur and bungler, and have not much hope of improvement—but the visions clamour for expression and preservation, so what is one to do?

To come to details—Miss Taylor says that "Dagon" 'does not awaken any responsive quiver of horror or repugnance' in her. A writer in the September *American Amateur,* referring to my efforts, said:

> "I recall that one night I let the moon shine in my eyes because I was afraid to get up and pull down the shade after reading one of his stories—'Dagon', I think it was."

"Who shall decide, when doctors disagree?" I paint what I dream, and will let the public settle the rest amongst themselves! About the bottom of the sea—one must use imagination in picturing the effect of an oceanic upheaval. The essence of the horrible is the *unnatural.* The thought of a *rock walking* is not necessarily repulsive, but in Dunsany's *Gods of the Mountain* a man says with a great deal of terror and repulsion, "Rock should not walk in the evening!" In estimating the effect of the sea-bottom on the man in "Dagon", we must remember that it has just been raised beneath his feet by some mysterious force—unnaturally raised from its age-long sleep in the darkness of ancient waters—and that it extends all around him as far as he can see. He does not know its extent—all is doubt, wonder, and unnatural mystery. This man might not be afraid to watch the tide go out on the beach at home; but under the circumstances of the tale, he is likely to be a rather badly scared sailor—or supercargo, to accept a Brunonian correction. Probably the worst thing is *solitude in barren immensity.* That has unhinged more than one mind. As to the fish—the assumption is correct. The earthquake killed some, and the rest died for want of water after the ocean bed rose to the air.

Mr. Brown is 'unimpressed as to the reality' of "Dagon", since to him it seems quite impossible. In reply I might say that realism was not the desired effect, although in past geological ages large bodies of land have both risen above and sunk beneath the waves. Does Mr. Brown recall the legend of "Atlantis"? I have written a long story on that theme. About the ocean bed—I shall have to disagree with Mr. Brown, summoning the facts of physical geography to my aid. The deep-sea bottom is smooth and monotonous—a rolling plain with few topographical features. There is no life—water-pressure is too great—but there is a deposit of "ooze" consisting of the tiny shells of simple marine organisms which live near the surface. One physiographer—to choose a book almost at random from my shelves—says:

> "The monotony, dreariness, and desolation of the deeper parts of this submarine scenery can scarcely be realised. The most barren terrestrial districts must seem diversified when compared with the vast expanse of ooze which covers the deeper parts of the ocean."

Shallow-water conditions are not true of the deep sea.

Why should the hero of "Dagon" wish to escape from the Germans if well-treated? For one thing, he might prefer the chances of rescue to the certainties of a Hun prison-camp at the end of the voyage.

Miss Fidlar's remark that war horrors have exhausted the capacity of the world for receiving new horrors may be answered in two ways—(1) I do not write for any particular age—I wrote as much before the war as after, and "Dagon" was written about the middle of it. (2) The physical horrors of war, no matter how extreme and unprecedented, hardly have a bearing on the entirely different realm of supernatural terror. Ghosts are still ghosts—the mind can get more thrills from unrealities than from realities!

Mr. Bullen's criticism is greatly appreciated, and I am glad that poor "Dagon" did not bore *everyone!* He overestimates the didactic element a trifle—like Dunsany I protest that except in a few cases I have no thought of teaching. The story is first, and if any philosophy creeps in it is by accident. "The White Ship" was an exception. As to the criticisms—the hero-victim *is* sucked half into the mire, yet he *does* crawl! He pulls himself along in the detestable ooze, tenaciously though it cling to him. I know, for I dreamed that whole hideous crawl, and can yet feel the ooze sucking me down! Possibly my description lacked clearness. As to the expression "completeness of the stillness"—I wish to emphasise a peculiar condition paralleled only by that in Poe's "Silence; a Fable", and also to *balance* the phrase "homogeneity of the landscape". "Certail" is a stenographic error—like the omission of "l" from *Piltdown,* which my critics overlooked. The suggestions anent the dubious word *scientist* and the phrase "whales and the like" are good, and will be acted on if the yarn is ever republished.

Mr. Munday asks the *raison d'être* of "Dagon"—I will give it—purely and simply to reproduce a mood. Its object is the simplest in all art—portrayal. (I must read *The Grim Thirteen.* Has Mr. Munday read *Can Such Things Be?*, by Ambrose Bierce?)

I am glad that several liked "Old Christmas". I would that Miss Taylor and Mr. Bullen were right about my being a poet, but must regretfully renounce the distinction. "Old Christmas" is a rhymed essay—light verse, verging on the whimsical. As to the poetic impossibility of such words as *gastronomic* and *patriarchal*—fully conceded! But investigation of Georgian and Queen-Anne verse will reveal the fountain-head of the venerable tradition I follow. I rejoice that Mr. Bullen, a native of the Mother Land, should find my pictures reasonably accurate. A comparative recluse, seeing little of any part of the world, is likely to take up his imaginative abode in whatever spot his main interest lies, unhampered by the conditions of actual geography. As a devotee of the past, I have naturally read more English than American books, and have felt profoundly the charm of those scenes and events amongst which my race-stock was moulded and developed; so that my conception of *home* and of natural beauty has come to centre in that soil around which so vast a majority of ancestral associations hover—

"This blessed plot, this earth, this realm, this England."

The scenes of my tales—or such of them as do not relate to imaginary regions—are laid in about equal proportion in England and America. Some day I will copy for the Circulator my various verses on America and England, as published in amateur journals on both sides of the water. One of them appeared in the (professional) *National Magazine* in Boston, and brought me an offer (albeit an impracticable one) from the book-publishing house of Sherman, French, & Co.

Last of all I will touch upon the allusions to me made in the Conductor's Notes. I trust that Mr. Bullen's flattering description will not lead the various members to expect from me more than I can furnish, for I am only too undeserving of such encomium. My imperfect productions speak louder than a charitable conductor's praise!

Regarding the Wickenden objections to my philosophical views, I am afraid I cannot be as much impressed as I should be, since most of the points on which I am attacked are really points of language rather than belief.* Mr. Wickenden jeers in a cocksure fashion at my use of the word *"know"*, when of course that word was employed with a full recognition of the metaphysical and epistemological difficulties involved. It is the only adequate word, though any philosophical user of it must concede that it is largely relative. And Mr. Wickenden forgets that the absence of certain knowledge militates as strongly against dogmatic theism as against dogmatic atheism; or rather, while not forgetting it, he uses it as propaganda for a set of opinions much less intrinsically probable than those he dismisses as unproven. One should not take too seriously a belittling of the scientific leaders who disposed of theism in the nineteenth century—but perhaps their overpraise by many justifies or explains an impulsive reaction against them. They were certainly not demigods, or even innovators in the ultimate sense. Materialism has represented man's most thoughtful attitude since the days of Leucippus and Democritus, and was the central phase of the Epicurean school. But Darwin, Huxley, Haeckel, and Spencer did perform a vast service in filling in details, systematising, and expounding.

*Mr. Bullen mentions my use of the phrase "vacuous and pompous idealists". This did not occur in the course of an argument, nor was it meant to apply to all idealists. It was designed to characterise a certain especially assertive school, to which Mr. Bayne's poem formed a delightful contrast.

Their results were not necessarily perfect, for inaccuracy enters all speculations, yet to say they are "superseded" or "overthrown" is sheer nonsense. It is impossible to produce any subsequent discoveries which controvert their main tenets. Modern science has probed deeper, but the probing has not disestablished the principles. There is a difference between a developed theory and an overturned theory. The atomic theory of Dalton, for example, is not disturbed by the recent subdivision of the atom. The *etymology* of the word is embarrassed, but so far as the reality of the "atom" as a chemical unit is concerned, very little has happened. "Atoms" exist and combine as Dalton discovered. It is only in the case of radio-activity that we encounter the results of the development.

In dealing with the relative values of reason and intuition Mr. Wickenden is equally sophistical. Common evidence shews him that intuition is as apt to be false as true—that it is [as] apt to lead to subsequently demonstrable errors as to facts, and that emotion is closely allied to it. He knows that both intuition and emotion are erratic, irregular, and frequently completely contradictory; that they depend upon individual wishes and hopes easily explainable on materialistic grounds, and that they inspire obvious hallucinations as often as they produce sensible convictions. Is a lunatic Caesar or Napoleon because his intuitions tell him so? Contrary to the cleverly introduced insinuation of Mr. Wickenden, emotion and intuition *do* "fit into my beautiful symmetrical pattern". It would be impossible to conceive of the development of the intellect from the primitive neural functions of low organisms without the existence of these intermediate stages. They are *not* to be ignored, for they furnish important light on biological and philosophical problems. The only rash thing is to accept their admittedly variable, contradictory, and nebulous evidence as a determinant of facts in opposition to genuine logic and reason, whose rigid consistency and reliability in every field cannot be disputed. A man may one day *feel* that there is a deity and another day *feel* that there is none. An Arab may *feel* that Mahomet is the only true prophet at the same time that an Englishman *feels* that Christ is. But none of these men can possibly differ as to the existence of land and water, or the sequence of the seasons. Reason has never yet failed. Intuition and emotion are constantly failing. Here is strong circumstantial evidence!

Mr. Wickenden asks how I "know" that oblivion awaits us. Again that needless objection to a word which *has* no *literal* meaning, and which is therefore permissible in this case. In reply, of course, I would have to say that while nothing in existence is certain, there is surely no ground for a notion as utterly extravagant and contrary to probability as that of immortality. We have no reason to think that the phenomena of consciousness and personality can arise from anything save complex organic evolution, or that they can exist apart from complex organic matter. All experience has taught us that consciousness and the organic brain are inseparable. A blow on the head can kill the qualities of consciousness and personality whilst the body and a few simple instincts vegetate on. The *person* is dead. Where is he—in heaven? And where were we before we existed—whence came the "immortal soul"? Likewise, since the notion of "soul" and immortality is so clearly akin to the conceptions of duality and eternity formed through dreams and dread of the unknown, what right have we to invent an artificial and less probable explanation, or to accept uncritically the animistic legends handed down from our savage and barbarian ancestors? In the face of such *probabilities*—all on the side of oblivion—it is rather disingenuous of Mr. Wickenden to call in the academic fact that nothing can be *known*. Still—that is true. We *know* nothing—surely nothing sufficient to justify the creation of a fanciful and elaborate eschatology! When we see a brain die and decay, is it more natural to assume that its functions have ceased, or to weave a story about the survival of the motions when the moving particles themselves are gone? Probability is not kind to Mr. Wickenden! But the question is open!!

As to the origin of a supposed deity—if one *always existed* and *always will exist,* how can he be developing creation from one definite state to another? Nothing but a *cycle* is in any case conceivable—a cycle or an infinite rearrangement, if that be a tenable thought. Nietzsche saw this when he spoke of the *ewige Wiederkunft.* In absolute eternity there is neither starting-point nor destination.

Mr. Wickenden frankly amuses me when he compares my rejection of teleology to a small boy's discarding and condemning a book he cannot understand—amuses me, because that is an excellent comparison for his own acceptance of teleology! He sees a process of evolution in operation at one particular cosmic moment in one particular point in space; and at once assumes gratuitously that *all the cosmos* is evolving steadily *in one direction* toward a fixed goal. Moreover, he *feels* that it all must amount to something—he calls it a thing of "heroism and splendour"! So when it is shewn that life on our world will (relatively) soon be extinct through the cooling of the sun; that space is full of such worlds which have died; that human life and the solar system itself are the merest *novelties* in an eternal cosmos; and that all indications point to a gradual breaking down of both matter and energy which will eventually nullify the results of evolution in any particular corner of space; when these things are shewn Mr. Wickenden recoils, and imitating the small boy of his own metaphor, cries out that it's all nonsense—it just *can't* be so!! But what of the actual probability, apart from man's futile wishes? If we cannot prove that the universe means *nothing*, how can we prove that it means *anything*—what right have we to invent a notion of purpose in the utter absence of evidence? Of course our savage forefathers could not conceive of a cosmos without a purpose any more than they could conceive of one without an anthropomorphic deity, but what place have their legends in 1921?

And then that Wickendenian sneer at my liking for Mark Twain's ethical precept—which was materialistic because it truly recognised no motive in man but basic selfishness. Mr. W. says or furnishes evidence that it is Christian. I can furnish evidence that it is rationalistic, pre-Christian, and Confucian. It is merely a truth based on expediency, free for any ethical teacher to seize and use, be he theistic or atheistic.

At the end of his discourse Mr. Wickenden professes himself the complete agnostic and relies on circumstantial evidence. I am content to follow his method, though such evidence as I behold leads me in the opposite direction.

Chesterton is hard to take seriously in the field of science. By manipulating the evidence—playing up trifles and minimising important facts—one may make a very brilliant case; but when a man soberly tries to dismiss the results of Darwin we need not give him too much of our valuable time. The exact details of organic progress as described in *The Origin of Species* and *The Descent of Man* may admit of correction or amplification; but to attack the essential principle, which alone is of universal importance, is pathetic. And so in a lesser degree with Freud. The doctrines which Mr. Chesterton so sweepingly sets aside are indeed radical, and decidedly repellent to the average thinker. Certainly, they reduce man's boasted nobility to a hollowness woeful to contemplate. But it is our business merely to observe impartially the extent to which the new views coincide with known phenomena, as compared with views hitherto held. When we do this we are forced to admit that the Freudians have in most respects excelled their predecessors, and that while many of Freud's most important details may be erroneous—one should not be too hasty in substituting any single or simple instinct for the complex and dominant *Wille zur Macht* as the explanation of man's motive force—he has nevertheless opened up a new path in psychology, devising a system whose doctrines more nearly approximate the real workings of the mind than any heretofore entertained. We may not like to accept Freud, but I fear we shall have to do so. It was only in the early seventeenth century that a Sizzi could refuse to look through Galileo's telescope for fear he would be convinced against his will of the existence of Jupiter's satellites!

And now let me insert my new contributions—three in number, a tale in prose, some weird stanzas, and a tale in rhyme. I regret sincerely that I have nothing "healthy" or "uplifting" to offer, but if I fall short of true artistic creation in those more "wholesome" fields, what am I to do? It is odd that my entire audience in the Circulator, save Mr. Bullen alone, should consist of realists and literalists. Perhaps in future I shall insert in this folio matter by other and more conventional members of my United Amateur Press Ass'n.

The Defence Remains Open! April 1921

I note with interest the various comments upon my latest round of literary attempts, and am grateful for the charity of judgment shewn. Mr. Brown is right in saying that tales of ordinary characters would appeal to a larger class, but I have no wish to make such an appeal. The opinions of the masses are of no interest to me, for praise can truly gratify only when it comes from a mind sharing the author's perspective. There are probably seven persons, in all, who really like my work; and they are enough. I should write even if I were the only patient reader, for my aim is merely self-expression. I could not write about "ordinary people" because I am not in the least interested in them. Without interest there can be no art. Man's relations to man do not captivate my fancy. It is man's relation to the cosmos—to the unknown—which alone arouses in me the spark of creative imagination. The humanocentric pose is impossible to me, for I cannot acquire the primitive myopia which magnifies the earth and ignores the background. Pleasure to me is wonder—the unexplored, the unexpected, the thing that is hidden and the changeless thing that lurks behind superficial mutability. To trace the remote in the immediate; the eternal in the ephemeral; the past in the present; the infinite in the finite; these are to me the springs of delight and beauty. Like the late Mr. Wilde, "I live in terror of not being misunderstood."

I note with interest the predilection of Miss Taylor for tales of a psycho-analytical, telepathic, and hypnotic order. Telepathy, the only mythical member of this triad, may some time furnish me with a plot; but the other two are likely to become systematised by science in the course of the next few decades, hence will pass out of the realm of wonder into that of realism. I prefer to stick to a more fantastic kind of explanation of the dream-world than that offered by Prof. Dr. Sigmund Freud—only illusions and insolvable mysteries are really fascinating to the imagination. I should not be surprised if hypnotism were to develop as an effective remedy for many disorders, since so many bodily functions are controlled wholly by cells of the brain. The only question, in my opinion, would be that of *permanence;* since the blind habits of cells are usually stronger in the end than the modes of motion set up by conscious thought or external forces. In some cases the new artificial habits might gain the ascendancy, but it would probably depend mainly on the temperament of the patient and previous duration of the malady.

Mr. Bullen's remarks are all of great interest to me, and I would appreciate it if he could later on send me his sheet of corrections—that I may act upon his suggestions when I have more leisure. At present I am about to investigate the status of *through* as used in "Psychopompos", pending which I have adopted the alternative ending:

> For Sieur De Blois (the old wife's tale is o'er)
> Was lost to mortal sight for evermore.

Regarding "The Tree"—Mr. Brown finds the climax insufficient, but I doubt if a tale of that type could possess a more obvious denouement. The climactic effect sought, is merely an emphasis—amounting to the first direct intimation—of the fact that there is something hidden behind the simple events of the tale; that the growing suspicion of Musides' crime and recognition of Kalos' posthumous vengeance is well founded. It is to proclaim what has hitherto been doubtful—to shew that the things of Nature see behind human hypocrisy and perceive the baseness at the heart of outward virtue. All the world deems Musides a model of fraternal piety and devotion although in truth he poisoned Kalos when he saw his laurels in peril. Did not the Tegeans build to Musides a temple? But against all these illusions the trees whisper—the wise trees sacred to the gods—and reveal the truth to the midnight searcher as they chaunt knowingly over and over again "Οἶδα! Οἶδα!" This, then, is all the climax so nebulous a legend can possess. Mr. Bullen, referring to the motto, asks what it is that the fates find a way to accomplish—to which the obvious reply is, that their aim is the avenging of murdered Kalos. This is an old tragic theme with the Greeks—does Mr. B. not recall Arion and the dolphins and Ibycus and the cranes?

I observe Mr. Bullen's complaint that no humour enters into my tales; which omission he deplores, assuming that these tales are designed to present a view of the universe. In reply, I would suggest that none of my narratives aims at scientific accuracy and inclusiveness, each being rather a mere transcript of an isolated mood or idea with its imaginative ramifications. Moreover, humour is itself but a superficial view of that which is in truth both tragic and terrible—the contrast between human pretence and cosmic mechanical reality. Humour is but the faint terrestrial echo of the hideous laughter of the blind mad gods that squat leeringly and sardonically in caverns beyond the Milky Way. It is a hollow thing, sweet on the outside, but filled with the pathos of fruitless aspiration. All great humorists are sad—Mark Twain was a cynic and agnostic, and wrote *The Mysterious Stranger* and *What Is Man?* When I was younger I wrote humorous matter—satire and light verse—and was known to many as a jester and parodist. I will enclose one of my old parodies, together with the piece I burlesqued, as an illustration of my comic side. But I cannot help seeing beyond the tinsel of humour, and recognising the pitiful basis of jest—the world is indeed comic, but the joke is on mankind. So when I delineate an intense mood I plough down to the subsoil and do not try to trifle with the layer of levity on top.* Humour is the whistling of man to keep up his courage as he travels the dark road. I once wrote:

> The wise to care a comic strain apply,
> And shake with laughter, that they may not cry.

Let it not be thought that I fail to appreciate humour—indeed, I employ it in discourse; being regarded as satirical and given to repartee. Lest my readers deem me a creature wholly without counterpart, I will enclose a cutting about an infinitely greater person—Charles Baudelaire—some of whose qualities may perhaps explain or illuminate the character of one with a (very roughly) similar outlook.

My contributions to this round of the Circulator will consist of a weird tale, "The Nameless City", some of my pseudonymous lines "On Religion"—an echo of the current controversy—a brief parody of some lines by the U.A.P.A. poet Rheinhart Kleiner, and a specimen of my older and more conventional work—"Quinsnicket Park", written in the Georgian manner in the year 1913, when I was 23 years of age. "Quinsnicket Park" has, of course, some of my pessimism; but there may be a youthful spirit and trace of "wholesomeness" lacking in the products of my riper years.

I perceive that Mr. Bullen and his lieutenants are anxious to carry on the controversy regarding materialism and idealism, which is surely agreeable enough to me, however ill it may conform to the rules of the Circulator. If the practice of drawing on "outside talent" be permitted to both sides, it is possible that I may later introduce the arguments of a very brilliant young materialist—Alfred Galpin, Jr., 536 College Ave., Appleton, Wisconsin, President of the United Amateur Press Association. Mr. Galpin is at present a student at Lawrence College, but in spite of his youth is a person of attainments little short of marvellous—a genuine "boy prodigy". He is now only 19, but I con-

* I have the sanction of the best models—Poe's intense tales are wholly humourless.

sider him already the most remarkable human being of my acquaintance, and believe he will become in time a critic and philosopher of international reputation. Mr. Galpin is a lineal descendant of Capt. James Cook, the celebrated explorer, who was killed by natives in the Sandwich Islands in 1776. His opinions are for the most part identical with my own.

That idealists should turn from the defensive to the offensive is something which cannot but benefit discussion. The tactics of the two attitudes differ, and a question cannot be displayed in its fulness till each antagonist has assumed both positions. Idealists were formerly on the defensive because, as the heirs of primitive tradition, they were first in the field and held all the territory. In their citadel of hereditary strength they were besieged by the materialists, a school of later growth whose doctrines sprang not from savage conjecture but from scientific observation. Now the citadel is captured, and the thinking world is materialistic. Realising that man possesses no innate knowledge, and that any claim regarding invisible and improbable phenomena must be supported by evidence, the victorious materialists hold the citadel and await the assaults of idealism, which now strikes back to regain the territory it has lost. But the strokes are strangely feeble, for the weapons of idealism melt in the sun of discovery.

Mr. Wickenden continues to attack *me* with more success than he attacks the ideas I utter, which are not of my creating. He points out some apparent ineptitude of rhetoric whereby I seem to arrogate to myself the title of "scientist"—which I certainly did not wish or intend to do—and thereupon fancies he has destroyed those other men's theories which I merely repeated. When he declares it more improbable for carbonates to change to protoplasm than for an organic substance to possess a "soul" and "immortality", he shews such an apparent misunderstanding of the principles involved that I despair of mutual comprehension. Perhaps a repetition of some basic facts might be clarifying—helping to define the conditions in each of the two cases. In the first place, no one assumes any *volition* on the part of a piece of chalk or other inorganic compound to change its mode of internal motion to the organic and vital type. The change, when it first occurred, must have been merely a rearrangement of moving particles incidental to the cooling and contraction of the whole planet; with no "volition" save the blind churning of electrons which constitutes all cosmic existence in the ultimate sense. Let Mr. Wickenden see very clearly that no radical change is involved—that nothing is either created or destroyed. The first appearance of life on any planet need be nothing more than a *change of motion* among certain molecules, atoms, and electrons. There is nothing new or occult. Since 1828 organic compounds have been synthesised, and he is indeed a bold speculator who will deny the possibility of actual abiogenesis as a future achievement of chemistry. Utterly different is the absurd conception of a "soul" or "immortality"—so different that Mr. Wickenden's description of it as "comparatively easy" reads more like jest than like sober discussion. Remember that in theorising on the origin of life we have not had to consider anything more than a shifting of material particles. How, then, may we call it "easier" to assume in one wild guess the existence of a whole world of entity, distinct from any provable substance, giving no evidence of itself, and independent of the known laws of matter? If it was hard to conceive of life as the product of lifeless matter, is it indeed easier to conceive of the existence of an airy nothing which can have no source at all, but which is claimed without proof or probability to hover around certain substances for certain periods, and subsequently to retain the personality of the substance around which it last hovers? Or perhaps Mr. Wickenden thinks that the material body creates the "soul"—in which case it would be interesting to discover how he thinks the emanation can be non-material, or how—if it be energy and not matter—it can retain the personality of the parent matter. I will not accuse Mr. Wickenden of being so naive as to perpetrate the blunder of the "Lieut.-Colonel" of Mr. Bullen's cutting—the assumption that the radiant heat emitted by a flame perpetuates in any way the flame itself. That betraying metaphor is ammunition for the materialist; for just as a candle burns itself out in smoke, vapour, and waves of thermal energy, leaving nothing to perpetuate its own individual qualities, so must a human brain burn itself out at last, after sending out irrecoverable ether-waves which disperse to the uttermost recesses of infinity. The tissues and cells which produced the motions of consciousness and personality—"the soul"—finally break down and dissociate, turning to liquid and gaseous decomposition-products and leaving nothing to mark their former temporary assemblage and motions. Can we imagine a continuance of motion when the moving particles are gone? Can we imagine a "soul" in existence after its parent body is dispersed—a candle-flame still burning after its energy and incandescent particles are dispersed? Nothing in human mythology is more patently unthinkable, and yet Mr. Wickenden would have us compare this crude and impossible bit of animism with the wholly commonplace hypothesis that one kind of material motion may at some period have been changed to another kind of material motion! In considering the matter of material change—either that of a fish to a crocodile or of limestone to protoplasm—Mr. Wickenden is handicapped by his belief that internal volition and "divine" guidance are the only two possible alternatives. With this dogma he can get nowhere.

He must recognise not only the element of chance in so-called natural selection, but also the fact that the initial change from inorganic to organic matter is probably accomplished by chemical and physical rather than biological laws. It is, in fact, only sensible to regard it as the transition from pure chemistry and physics to biology. Mr. Wickenden's difficulty in understanding why there should be any internal volition in organic types, such as that of a fish for dry land, would be removed if he would realise that all volition is merely a neural molecular process—a blind material instinct or impulse. The universal craving of the organic cell is for expansion of activity—an increase in those conditions which give it the most pleasurable excitation. This blind life-impulse is so clearly correlated with the general run of cosmic forces both organic and inorganic—gravitation, affinity, cohesion, etc.—that it needs no special explanation. There is no distinguishing feature in any of the various local modifications of the universal churning of matter through the endless cycles of the cosmos. An organic being blindly acts in whatever manner gives him the most satisfaction, and so the fish—vivified by the oxygen dissolved in its native waves—strains for as much oxygen as it can get, and eventually tends toward land and the free air. The previous environment and history of each group engaged in the automatic quest no doubt determines its degree of success. Likewise, to the impulse of the animal should be added the modification of the environment. Perhaps it is too hasty to attribute all evolutional changes to internal causes, since many may result from the animal's struggle to adapt itself to changing surroundings. The recession or evaporation of a body of water, giving rise to a swamp, may be the cause of changing fishes to amphibia in the course of generations; just as the subsequent drying of the swamp into solid land may transform the amphibia to land animals—first of the lizard kind, then mammals, including man, and no one knows what later on, if the planet lasts long enough. Changes are accomplished by all sorts of selective processes, largely choice of mates, dictated by the environment and blind impulses of countless generations. Definite intelligent volition is out of the question, Mr. Wickenden to the contrary.

When Mr. Wickenden jumps to the conclusion that divine guidance must exist simply because there is no readily visible reason why a fish should spontaneously seek land, he is certainly displaying a vast eagerness to accept the more superficial conclusion before analysing the apparent objections which he finds in the other. It would be possible to cite many reasons which would drive fish to land. Should it be demonstrated that the oxygen of the air is an insufficient bait, much might be said for the *light* of the upper regions, with its increased possibilities of pleasurably affecting the eye. Mr. Wickenden displays his weakness in the assumption that fish are "perfectly comfortable" in water—an absurd statement, in view of the obvious lack of continuous comfort in all beings with complex neural development. There is in every phase of vertebrate organic life a constant chafing and unrest, since adaptation to environment is never perfect. All life is struggle and combat—itself a disproof of divinity—and in this fray an organism fights both its fellows and its surroundings. When a certain act or change is of benefit in securing an advantage, and increasing the opportunities of pleasurable excitation, it is blindly persisted in through the universal tendency of following the line of least resistance. All organisms tend to do what secures them the most pleasure or best facilitates their continued existence; and in the end their course, determined by circumstance, produces various modifications of type. There is no conscious desire, no intelligent aspiration, no definite foreknowledge. It is all a process of stumbling in the dark—of recoiling from greater to lesser discomforts and dangers, and of groping for an increased amount of pleasures faintly tasted. To ignore this, and rush to the notion of divinity, is so rash that such a step may fairly be counted out of an argument. Mr. Wickenden depends on words rather than on facts and ideas, as witness his really delicious epigram about 'explaining evolution'.

I hardly know whether a reply is needed for the statement regarding the anomalous expansion of water just above the freezing-point. Certainly this is an unusual thing, but no more so than countless others having no possible purposive significance. It is not definitely explained —but neither are dozens of other phenomena of molecular physics. Why are all the anomalies of science? Why do the satellites of Uranus move in a plane nearly perpendicular to that of the planet's orbit, and why does Neptune's satellite move backward? Why does the moon appear larger to the naked eye when near the horizon when microscopic measurement and theory unite in shewing the apparent disc as smaller? But I need not make a catalogue—it is too childish. No one talks of "intelligence" in these cases of phenomena whose causes are at present obscure. Why, then, does Mr. Wickenden make such a vital argument of the anomalous expansion of water? Simply because water happens to contain a few organisms edible by man, which it could not contain if its physical properties were less unusual! On this one chance circumstance Mr. Wickenden founds a system of theology, singles out the case of water from that of all the other anomalies in creation, and assumes that the most stable and important of chemical compounds received its properties solely in order that fishes might inhabit brooks! How inconsiderate of Nature not to fashion water so that man might walk through it and build railways on the floor of the Atlantic! The same "intelligence" that created brooks for fishes neglected to make all parts of the land habitable by man—strange oversight! Why are not the Sahara and the Antarctic Continent habitable, if it is the "divine" purpose to adapt everything to the sustenance of life? Conversely, what calamity would result if fishes did *not* inhabit brooks—or if lakes were permanently semi-glacial?

Mr. Wickenden is right in declaring that "it is easy to scoff at any attempted explanation of life, but tremendously difficult to offer any explanation that other people cannot scoff at". In truth, knowledge has not yet extended very far below the surface, so that continual readjustments of thought are necessary. Beyond a certain limit knowledge may be impossible to acquire with man's present sensory and intellectual equipment, so that in all likelihood the universe will never be explained. Perhaps it were wiser not to try, but merely to take life as it comes, enjoying the pleasure and forgetting the pain as best we can. Since, however, our curiosity does prompt us to make inquiries; it is certainly more sensible to build up our speculations humbly, step by step from the known to the unknown, than to cast aside probability and experience altogether and accept dogmatically and uncritically the primitive legends of early man—legends based on transparent analogies and personifications, and professing to solve offhand those cosmic mysteries which offer the least real evidence and involve the most intricate and gradual kind of investigation. All theories may indeed be open to scoffing; but surely those are weakest which claim most and have least corroboration, while those are strongest which depend most on solid observation and make the fewest claims regarding matters beyond actual knowledge. In the absence of proof, the likeliest theory is that which conflicts least with the small amount of knowledge we already have.

"Lieut.-Colonel's" Open Letter contains one point so comic that I cannot forbear comment. After devoting several paragraphs to a vigorous condemnation of materialists who deny "spirit" because it cannot be seen and measured, he fails utterly to shew that Nature contains any phenomena establishing the existence of such an invisible and immensurable force! I might as easily assert the existence of a new ethereal entity called XYZABC, which makes the comets move; and defy any man to *disprove* it. Surely it could not be detected and measured by "calipers and balances"—therefore it is *above* truth!!!

Coming now to the old *Atlantic Monthly* article, "Whither" (in the General Discussion folio), I find much of genuine pathos. There is no real argument of importance in the harangue of the anonymous author, but the atmosphere of sorrow at the passing of the old illusions makes the whole complaint an absorbing human document. Certainly, there is much in the modern advance of knowledge which must of necessity shock and bewilder the mind accustomed to uncritical tradition. That the old illusions cheered and stimulated the average person to a more or less considerable degree cannot be denied—the dream-world of our grandsires was undoubtedly a sort of artificial paradise for mediocrity. To supply deficiencies in real life there was an imaginary "soul life" or "inner life" which probably seemed very vivid and actual to the subject of the delusion, and which must have helped to render him insensible to the manifold pains of genuine existence. The phenomenon can be duplicated on a small scale by any imaginative person, and those who have succeeded in thus creating for the nonce an unreal world can fully appreciate the sense of relative security and peace existing among those who accepted deity and immortality as actual facts. It is a general objection to Christianity, that it stifled artistic freedom, trampled on healthy instincts, and set up false and unjust standards. On this assumption a friend of mine, Samuel Loveman, Esq., has written a magnificent ode "To Satan". In truth, however, this stultifying effect injured only the most intelligent classes, who were capable of resisting it ultimately; so that we need not deny the narcotic comfort it brought to the less aspiring majority. The faith was, of course, in its details merely a symbol of that majority's own standards and hopes—for all religious systems are the outgrowths rather than rulers of the races which hold them. Just as paganism is the ideal aristocratic attitude—the cult of true strength and beauty—so was Christianity the bourgeois ideal; the *Sklavmoral* code of thrift and prudence. Its ultimate development was reached in the anaemic Massachusetts type of the nineteenth century—the Puritanical and Emersonian product which had so much "soul" that it mattered little. Nowadays these fellows, or their grandchildren, are amusing themselves with theosophy, "new thought", Christian Science, and Persian Bahaism. They cannot tell facts when they meet them! But most of the old Christians were less fanatical, and have developed less fantastically. They held their old faith simply from lack of the recent scientific information which most clearly proves it false, so when the information gradually reached them as a result of the unparalleled discoveries of the past century, they simply modified their views and accepted the inevitable. When they saw that their castles were of air—that there 'really is no Santa Claus'—they did not cry or cover up their eyes and ears, but bore the disillusionment like grown men. There had, indeed, been rare imaginative comfort in the old beliefs—but facts are facts! The withdrawal of the "spiritual" drug acted like the withdrawal of liquor from some topers—occasionally causing them to rise to greater mental heights by frankly facing things as they are. But as some lament prohibition, others lament philosophical disillusionment—in both cases a somewhat agreeable false stimulant has been withdrawn. The change has been very subtle; more often tacit than open, and affecting the all-important subconscious springs of thought and action rather than the outward qualities of apparent belief. Of the modern materialists a good majority probably attend some church and consider themselves Christians. That is because most persons never think accurately and searchingly. Their beliefs mean little—what matters is the deep inward disillusionment whereby they feel the change and dare not trust what they trusted before. Regrets are absolutely futile. The change is inevitable, because the last century has brought to light facts never suspected before; which not only upset all the old notions, but explain with considerable clearness the psychological and anthropological reasons those notions were held in the past. The suddenness of the change is not surprising—its seeds were sown in the splendour of the Renaissance, when thought was emancipated and scientific progress begun. New instruments, exciting new zeal and opening up new vistas, have appeared in logical succession; and minds formerly applied to other arts have joined in the quest for truth. The nineteenth and twentieth centuries mark the logical culmination of the advance of 500 years—the growth of philosophies on the new data—so that he who would order us back to superstition is like Canute commanding the waves. Unfortunately or not, the illusion of spirituality is dead among the thinking classes. A phase of primitive allegory has retreated into the past, and we must make the best of what we cannot help. If we tried to believe now we should feel the sham, and despise ourselves for it—we simply know better, like the small boy deprived of "Santa Claus". At the same time, we must not ignore the pathetic, sobbing intensity of the reaction among a certain emotionally delicate class. The wrench of disillusion is terrible for them, and according to their temperament they are driven either into blind occultism or passionate Christian apologetics. The author of "Whither" is of the latter type—seeking to stem the tide with sophistry, imperfect data, and weak logic. He weeps vainly for departed values, and pleads weakly for *continuity* in what he calls "spiritual evolution". Alas! he does not see that the "spiritual" is exploded, and that *continuity* is never possible in matters of *discovery*. Before America was discovered it was unknown—then suddenly it *was* known! And so with the facts overturning religion. Searching "Whither" for a real argument, the reader finds only one amidst the manifold question-beggings, sophistries, regrets, and gratuitous assumptions of values. And tragically enough that argument is so easily and fully answerable by natural science that it is no sooner uttered than nullified. "Why," asks the author, "may we not say, 'Here are certain persistent hopes, inner needs, longings, which we can explain only on the assumption that the universe is a universe of spirit'?" Because, the realist replies, all those hopes, longings, and alleged "needs" are natural attributes of a certain stage of primitive development, early implanted in man, and wholly explainable as products of his unfolding mind as it reacted to his surroundings and limited information. This matter of the explanation of "spiritual" feelings is really the most important of all materialistic arguments; since the explanations are not only overwhelmingly forcible, but so adequate as to shew that man could not possibly have developed without acquiring just such false impressions. The idea of deity is a logical and inevitable result of ignorance, since the savage can conceive of no action save by a volition and personality like his own. Animism could not be avoided by any ignorant mind familiar with dreams, and immortality is an easy step once a dual existence is admitted. The savage has always, so far as he can recall, lived—and he cannot picture a state of not living. In this matter of eternal life he is also guided by his dread of extinction—he has seen dead bodies, and cannot think that such will be the end of his consciousness. Desire becomes accomplished fact in his simple opinions. Then, seething through his crudely animal and emotional nature, are a thousand blind organic forces such as made his fish ancestors seek air and his amphibian ancestors seek the dry hills. His mind is not nearly so powerful as the primal, vestigial urges and currents that rack him, and when these are not drained by combative or other uses, they turn on the nervous system and produce the frenzies and wild hallucinations known as "religious experience". Freud has much to say of the share these primal urges play in forming thoughts when partly suppressed. As the savage progresses, he acquires experience and formulates codes of "right" and "wrong" from his memories of those courses which have helped or hurt him. His imagination becomes able to create pictures artificially, and as he dwells on the things he likes best he gradually comes to believe in a possible state of things where everything is homogeneously delightful. He usually places these ideal conditions in the past and future, where disproof is impossible—thus we have the "Golden Age" and "Elysium". The "Garden of Eden" and "Heaven". Then out of the principle of barter comes the illusion of "justice"—and so on, till at length we behold a whole system of theistic and idealistic legendry, developed gradually during man's susceptible childhood, and fastened on him as a second nature by countless generations of inherited belief. There is nothing to wonder at in the long survival and hard death of such a system. Its overthrow comes only as a result of the most conclusive and gigantic array of contrary evidence. The wonderful thing is that it should have been extensively challenged by an important section of Greek philosophers as far back as Democritus. However—perhaps one should not wonder at *anything* Greek; the race was a super-race. In one way religion probably helped to defeat itself. By dividing and subdividing, and developing subtle and scholastic systems of dogmata, it acquired a tinge of rationality fatal to belief. The Papists with their blind faith are the exception. Then man's whole trend has tended to refine him and tone down the brute impulses whose excess gave rise to extreme religious ecstasy. There is less primal vitality in modern civilisation—we fight less, seldom "run amok", and are generally more human and delicate. Greater delicacy means the subordination of simple protoplasmic cell-impulses to the more complex motions of cerebral tissue—the ascendancy of taste and reason over animal feeling—and as we thus grow away from the primitive, our chief urges toward religious grovelling are removed. All religious demonstrativeness and ceremony is basically orgiastic, as one may gather from the veiled or open symbolism of nearly every typical rite of every race.

But the survivors of Christianity take the whole question of modern change too seriously. Just how much of the possible decadence of this age may be traced to materialism it is impossible to say; at any rate, it cannot be helped. As a matter of fact, the connexion is probably other than causal. Progress and sophistication, arch-enemies of all illusion, have destroyed traditions of behaviour as well as of thought; and acting upon a sensitive and heterogeneous world have culminated in an inevitable bewilderment and realisation of futility. One cause may underlie decadence and materialism, but these two are sisters—not child and parent. No civilisation has lasted for ever, and perhaps our own is perishing of natural old age. If so, the end cannot well be deferred. On the other hand, we may be merely passing from youth to maturity—a period of more realistic and sophisticated life may lie ahead of us, filled with cynical resignation and dreams of languorous beauty rather than with the fire and faith of early life. We can neither predict nor determine, for we are but the creatures of blind destiny.

Materialism is not the tragedy—at least, not the utter tragedy—that idealists picture. It is grey rather than black, for even in the most idealistic ages a goodly share of the prevailing serenity came from physical and subconscious rather than conscious causes. No change of faith can dull the colours and magic of spring, or dampen the native exuberance of perfect health; and the consolations of taste and intellect are infinite. It is easy to remove the mind from harping on the lost illusion of immortality. The disciplined intellect fears nothing and craves no sugar-plum at the day's end, but is content to accept life and serve society as best it may. Personally I should not care for immortality in the least. There is nothing better than oblivion, since in oblivion there is no wish unfulfilled. We had it before we were born, yet did not complain. Shall we then whine because we know it will return?

It is Elysium enough for me, at any rate. Altogether, we have depended less than we think on Christian mythology. The French have done without it for a long time, yet their realistic culture maintains its brilliancy, and the national temperament has sunk to no perceptible degree. Our race is younger, but it is fast growing up—and I am confident that the Saxon can face maturity as bravely as the Gaul. If history teaches aright, he should do even better; for who were the victors at Agincourt, Crécy, Poictiers, and Trafalgar? Then, too, we overrate the religious influences we are losing. Stripping the past of its cloak of romantic rationalising and euphemism, we find that most human affairs have *always* been decided on wholly materialistic lines. Even the leading religious movements have their secret history—generally of a materialistic nature. The only human motive since the species has existed has been selfishness. If we are now less pious, we are also less hypocritical. One honest Nietzsche is worth a dozen mock-saints. And Greece, whose culture was the greatest of all, antedated Christianity and originated materialism.

Modern civilisation is the direct heir of Hellenic culture—all that we have is Greek. Since the transient Semitic importation of ascetic idealism has run its course, can we not recapture a trace of the old pagan light-heartedness that once sparkled by the AEgean? Surely we can think of life as having something of beauty, and only a glutton wants eternity.

Final Words September 1921

Unlimited apologies are due the members of the Circulator for the vast delay to which I have subjected it on this round, and for the inadequate contributions which I am making to it. All I may offer as an excuse, is that the pressure of other imperative matters, both in the field of associational amateur journalism and in that of professional revision, has rendered greater celerity quite impossible. Indeed, so manifold are the duties with which I find myself now enveloped, that I fear a relinquishment of Circulator membership will be inevitable after this round. By attempting too many things one becomes unable to do any of them justice; therefore it is most advisable to relinquish newer interests in order to fulfil faithfully one's older and accustomed pursuits. However, I am making a final contribution to the Circulator in the form of one more fantastic tale—"The Doom That Came to Sarnath"—which I insert not because of any particular merit, but because it has just won the Story Laureateship in the United Amateur Press Association; an honour which last year fell to my "White Ship", also exhibited in the Circulator.

To those of my readers who have disliked the fantastic and macabre tone of my work, I proffer the sincerest apologies; and would defend myself only by pointing out that there is an artistic ideal apart from the "wholesomeness" and "instructiveness" beloved by the worthy generality of citizens. For the endorsement and interest of the public I care not at all, writing solely for my own satisfaction. Writing for any other motive could not possibly be art—the professional author is the ultimate antithesis of the artist. My own failure to be an artist results from limited genius rather than mischosen object. In his preface to *The Picture of Dorian Gray* Oscar Wilde says many things which bourgeois critics should learn by heart—

> "No artist desires to prove anything. . . . No artist has ethical sympathies. An ethical sympathy in an artist is an unpardonable mannerism of style. No artist is ever morbid. The artist can express everything. . . . All art is at once surface and symbol. . . . Those who read the symbol do so at their peril. . . . It is the spectator, and not life, that art really mirrors. . . . All art is quite useless."

Elsewhere Wilde says:

> "A work of art is the unique result of a unique temperament. Its beauty comes from the fact that the author is what he is. It has nothing to do with the fact that other people want what they want. Indeed, the moment that an artist takes notice of what other people want, and tries to supply the demand, he ceases to be an artist and becomes a dull or an amusing craftsman, an honest or a dishonest tradesman. He has no further claim to be considered as an artist. Art is the most intense mode of individualism the world has ever known. . . .
>
> "From the point of view of style, a healthy work of art is one whose style recognises the beauty of the material it employs, be that material one of words or of bronze, of colour or of ivory, and uses that beauty as a factor in producing the aesthetic effect. From the point of view of subject, a healthy work of art is one the choice of whose subject is conditioned by the temperament of the artist, and comes directly out of it. . . . An unhealthy work of art, on the other hand, is a work whose style is obvious, old-fashioned, and common, and whose subject is deliberately chosen, not because the artist has any pleasure in it, but because he thinks that the public will pay him for it. In fact, the popular novel that the public calls healthy is always a thoroughly unhealthy production; and what the public calls an unhealthy novel is always a beautiful and healthy work of art."

For Mrs. Ashley's word in favour of the weird, I am very grateful. Under separate cover I am sending her some matter pertaining to the United Amateur Press Association; which I trust she will decide to join, and where may be found a variety of real artists of the most genuine kind. Some of my views on art will be found in my coming number of *The Conservative,* which I shall mail to the members of the Circulator. In bidding farewell to a discussion of the weird and the sombre, it may not be amiss to mention an excellent collection of tales to which my attention has just been drawn—*The Song of the Sirens and Other Stories,* by Edward Lucas White (Dutton, 1919)—which possesses considerable charm, artistry, and scholarship. Most of them have a very clever and accurate setting in classical antiquity, or in mediaeval Italy.

Mr. Wickenden's latest controversial assault is very interesting, and I accept with contrition the correction regarding "sneers". As to the "know" controversy—I will let the objectionable polysyllables rest, and merely state that in my opinion (an opinion shared by increasing multitudes) there is no evidence whatever concerning an object or meaning in life and the universe. And in the absence of evidence, all assumptions are totally baseless; the idea of an object or meaning becoming absurd.

Mr. Wickenden tries to demolish this important argument by denying the obvious absurdity and incredibility of the common myths of soul, immortality, and teleology. In support of his contention he cites the many persons who, drawing their ideas from their empirical racial heritage rather than from abstract scientific truths, find the conception of materialism, annihilation, and purposelessness "utterly extravagant and contrary to probability". This move is very clever, but its force dissolves upon analysis. Mr. Wickenden's appeals are all to impression and metaphor—he rejects the obvious *because it is obvious,* and actually presents the spectacle of one defending the grotesque idea that the more improbable and indirect of two theories is to be preferred! He goes back to the age of the disputatious church fathers with their "credo quia impossibile est". The phonograph metaphor is rhetorically brilliant—but that is all. Doubtless it could be "proved" in this way that Caruso himself was only a phonograph, and that we might still enjoy new songs from him if we could find the real singer behind his mortal form. But all this is futile. Metaphor and allegory are the smoke screen wherewith all mystics, theists, and obscurantists have shielded themselves from truth since the dawn of speculative thought. Materialism seems improbable only to those who think in terms of antique myths conceived in imperfect knowledge and utterly contrary to all the basic facts of science as subsequently discovered.

As to the matter of death and resuscitation—I had hardly expected this from Mr. Wickenden, who surely knows that many persons *have* been revived after a momentary cessation of heart-beats, and that true death is due either to a failure of the propelling energy or to a derangement of the organic mechanism. There *is*, most decidedly, something missing from a body dead half an hour or even much less. Decomposition always begins at once, and it takes very little to ruin hopelessly the complex and delicate machinery of vital action. When a man dies by accident, as in drowning, there is always a question (a) as to whether the vital momentum suddenly lost can be successfully restored by the crude processes of artificial respiration, and (b) as to whether there be any loss due to the chemical and physical deterioration of the bodily machine. The loss is one either of matter or of energy. If there were a question of another loss—the loss of "soul", as Mr. Wickenden hints—one might with equal ease ask where the "soul" originally came from—a matter which Haeckel treats very cleverly and amusingly.

To express incredulity that a chemical reaction could produce a Beethoven symphony proves absolutely nothing. In the first place, the reaction is probably more physical than chemical in its ultimate manifestation; but even assuming that it may all be chemical, we have before us merely a case of *complexity*. It seems to indicate a lack of constructive imagination when one cannot conceive of a material order involving all degrees of fineness in organisation, and rising eventually to the peak of what we know as psychic, intellectual, and aesthetic accomplishment. The steps between sounds and tears are more physical than chemical, and of course depend on the *working* of the vital cells. Why does not a dead man cry at sad music? . . . Why does not a still dynamo give current? To argue that one may prove the existence of the human "soul" from the fact that corpses do not weep when the orchestra plays "Hearts and Flowers", is something hardly calculated to disturb the assurance of the mechanistic materialist! Mr. Wickenden avoids the ticklish question of the lower animal world. Here we have organisms for which not even the boldest theist tries to claim "souls"—yet among them we find psychic phenomena of a very advanced order. Even a Beethoven symphony affects many animals strongly—a case where Mr. W. would find difficulty in tracing the physico-chemical action connecting the sounds and the manifestations. One might ask, to the confounding of those who aver that men have "souls" whilst beasts have not, just what the difference may be betwixt the effect of music on man and on beast; and also just how the evolving organism began to acquire "spirit" after it crossed the boundary betwixt advanced ape and primitive human? It is rather hard to believe in "soul" when one has not a jot of evidence for its existence; when all the psychic life of man is demonstrated to be precisely analogous to that of other animals—presumably "soulless". But all this is too childish. When we investigate both ontogeny and phylogeny we find that man has both individually and racially evolved from the unicellular condition. Every man living was at the beginning of his life a single protoplasmic cell, whose simple reflex sensitiveness is the source of all the neural and psychic activity which later develops through increasing complexity of organisation. We can easily trace the whole process of development from the irritability of the simple cell-wall through various intermediate stages of spinal and ganglial activity to the formation of a true brain and finally to the manifestation of those complex functions which we know as intellect and emotion. This development occurs both pre-natally and post-natally in the individual, and can be followed with much exactitude. In the species, we can follow it hardly less exactly by means of comparative anatomy and biology. Haeckel's *Evolution of Man,* in its final edition, leaves very little to be said.

When Mr. Wickenden objects to my assumption that he dislikes to face the possibility of a mechanistic cosmos, he is of course not to be disputed; and I ask his pardon for having misrepresented his former utterances. But he is exceeding fact when he calls materialists "strange people" for asserting that most theists are afraid of the truth. This matter of "aletheiophobia" (if I may coin an Hellenism) is something about which the theists themselves leave no doubt—it is they who loudly complain that the materialist is tearing away all the precious values and safeguards of life!

In conclusion, I would urge Mr. Wickenden not to feel that my necessitated withdrawal from active Circulatorship means a desire to terminate the present controversy. Like him, I can always find time to fight in retirement; so that philosophical epistles addressed to 598 Angell St., Providence, R.I., will be ever welcome and never neglected. I am not by any means such a "solemn cuss" as Mr. W. infers from my somewhat archaic prose style—in fact, I have an idea that my respected foe would find me almost human if dealing with me less indirectly! (As proof I will enclose a page from *The National Tribute,* which our conductor may send to Mr. W. if he chooses. Note that I am capable of even a *hearty laugh* at an amateur convention!)

And now I must bid the Circulator a reluctant farewell, trusting that at some future time a readjustment of activities will permit me to resume a connexion so pleasing; and that our novelists, Messrs. Munday and Bullen, will have the abounding charity to shew me the remainder of their respective novels, concerning whose terminations I am in a wholesome state of suspense.

AVE · ATQVE · VALE ·
IDIBVS · SEPTEMBRIBVS · MDCCCCXXI ·

NIETZSCHEISM AND REALISM

Concerning the quality of mastery, and of poise in trying situations, I believe that it arises more from hereditary than environmental considerations. Its possession cannot be acquired through the culture of the individual, although the systematic culture of a certain class during many generations undoubtedly tends to bring out such strength to a degree which will cause that class to produce a higher average of dominant individuals than an uncultivated class of equal numerical magnitude.

I doubt whether it would be possible to create any class strong enough to sway permanently a vast body of inferiors, hence I perceive the impracticability of Nietzscheism and the essential instability of even the strongest governments. There is no such thing—and there never will be such a thing—as good and permanent government among the crawling, miserable vermin called human beings. Aristocracy and monarchy are the most efficient in developing the best qualities of mankind as expressed in achievements of taste and intellect; but they lead to an unlimited arrogance. That arrogance in turn leads inevitably to their decline and overthrow. On the other hand, democracy and ochlocracy lead just as certainly to decline and collapse through their lack of any stimulus to individual achievement. They may perhaps last longer, but that is because they are closer to the primal animal or savage state from which civilised man is supposed to have partly evolved.

Communism is a characteristic of many savage tribes; whilst absolute anarchy is the rule amongst the majority of wild animals.

The brain of the white human animal has advanced to such a stage that the colourless equality of the lower animals is painful and unendurable to it; it demands an individual struggle for complex conditions and sensations which can only be achieved by a few at the expense of the many. This demand will always exist, and it will never be satisfied because it divides mankind into hostile groups constantly struggling for supremacy, and successively gaining and losing it.

When there is an autocracy, we may be sure that the masses will some day overthrow it; and when there is a democracy or ochlocracy, we may be sure that some group of mentally and physically superior individuals will some day overthrow it by establishing a more or less enduring (but never wholly permanent) supremacy, either through judgment in playing men against each other, or through patience and ability in concentrating power by taking advantage of the indolence of the majority. In a word, the social organisation of humanity is in a state of perpetually and incurably unstable equilibrium. The very notion of such things as perfection, justice, and improvement is an illusion based on vain hopes and overdrawn analogies.

It must be remembered that there is no real reason to expect anything in particular from mankind; good and evil are local expedients—or their lack—and not in any sense cosmic truths or laws. We call a thing "good" because it promotes certain petty human conditions that we happen to like—whereas it is just as sensible to assume that all humanity is a noxious pest which should be eradicated like rats or gnats for the good of the planet or of the universe. There are no absolute values in the whole blind tragedy of mechanistic Nature—nothing is either good or bad except as judged from an absurdly limited point of view.

The only cosmic reality is mindless, undeviating fate—automatic, unmoral, uncalculating inevitability.

As human beings, our only sensible scale of values is one based on the lessening of the agony of existence. That plan is most deserving of praise which most ably fosters the creation of the objects and conditions best adapted to diminish the pain of living for those most sensitive to its depressing ravages.

To expect perfect adjustment and happiness is absurdly unscientific and unphilosophical. We can seek only a more or less trivial mitigation of suffering.

I believe in an aristocracy, because I deem it the only agency for the creation of those refinements which make life endurable for the human animal of high organisation.

Since the only human motive is a craving for supremacy, we can expect nothing in the way of achievement unless achievement be rewarded by supremacy.

We cannot expect justice—justice is a mocking phantom—and we know that aristocracy has many undesirable features. But we also know—sadly enough—that we can never abolish the evils without abolishing everything of value to civilised man.

In an aristocracy some persons have a great deal to live for. In a democracy most persons have a little to live for. In an ochlocracy nobody has anything to live for.

Aristocracy alone is capable of creating thoughts and objects of value.

Everyone, I fancy, will admit that such a state must precede democracy or ochlocracy in order to build the original culture. Fewer are willing to admit the cognate truth that democracies and ochlocracies merely subsist parasitically on the aristocracies they overthrow, gradually using up the aesthetic and intellectual resources which autocracy bequeathed them and which they never could have created for themselves. The rate of squandering depends upon the completeness of the departure from aristocracy. Where the old spirit lingers, the process of deterioration may be very slow indeed—certain belated additions compensating for the decline. But where the rabble gain full sway taste is certain to vanish, and dulness reigns darkly triumphant over the ruins of culture.

Wealth and luxury are essential alike to the creation and the full appreciation of beauty and truth. Indeed, it is the existence of wealth and luxury, and of the standards which they establish, that gives most of the pleasure felt by the non-wealthy and non-luxurious. The masses would rob themselves by cutting off the real source of that slight enjoyment which they secure, as it were, by reflection.

When, however, I praise autocracy, I do not by any means refer to such absolute monarchies as czaristic Russia or kaiseristic Germany. Moderation is essential in all things, and overstressed political autocracy produces an infinity of stupid checks on art and intellect. A tolerable amount of political liberty is absolutely essential to the free development of the mind; so that, in speaking of the virtues of an aristocratic system, the philosopher has in view less a governmental despotism than an arrangement of well-defined traditional social classes, like those of England and France.

Governmental aristocracy need go no further than to safeguard an aristocratic class in its opulence and dignity so that it may be left free to create the ornaments of life and to attract the ambition of others who seek to rise to it.

The healthiest aristocracy is the most elastic—willing to beckon and receive as accessions all men of whatever antecedents who prove themselves aesthetically and intellectually fitted for membership. It gains, moreover, if its members can possess that natural nobility which is content with a recognition of its own worth, and which demonstrates its superiority in superior works and behaviour, rather than in snobbish and arrogant speech and attitude.

The real aristocrat is ever reasonable, kindly, and affable toward the masses—it is the incompletely cultured *novus homo* who makes ostentation of his power and position. Yet in the last analysis it is futile to pass judgment upon any type of social order, since all are but the blind result of uncontrollable fate and utterly beyond the power of any statesman or reformer to alter or amend.

All human life is weary, incomplete, unsatisfying, and sardonically purposeless. It always has been and always will be; so that he who looks for a paradise is merely a dupe of myths or of his own imagination.

The will and emotion of man crave conditions that do not and never will exist, so that the wise man is he who kills will and emotion to a degree enabling him to despise life and sneer at its puerile illusions and insubstantial goals. The wise man is a laughing cynic; he takes nothing seriously, ridicules earnestness and zeal, and wants nothing because he knows that the cosmos holds nothing worth wanting. And yet, being wise, he is not a tenth as happy as the dog or peasant that knows no life or aspiration above the simplest animal plane.

It is good to be a cynic—it is better to be a contented cat—and it is best not to exist at all.

Universal suicide is the most logical thing in the world—we reject it only because of our primitive cowardice and childish fear of the dark. If we were sensible we would seek death—the same blissful blank which we enjoyed before we existed.

It does not matter what happens to the race—in the cosmos the existence or non-existence of the earth and its miserable inhabitants is a thing of the most complete indifference. Arcturus would glow just as cheerfully if the whole solar system were wiped out.

The undesirability of any system of rule not tempered with the quality of kindness is obvious; for "kindness" is a complex collection of various impulses, reactions, and realisations highly necessary to the smooth adjustment of botched and freakish creatures like most human beings. It is a weakness basically—or, in some cases, an ostentation of secure superiority—but its net effect is desirable; hence it is, on the whole, praiseworthy.

Since all motives at bottom are selfish and ignoble, we may judge acts and qualities only by their effects.

Pessimism produces kindness. The disillusioned philosopher is even more tolerant than the priggish bourgeois idealist with his sentimental and extravagant notions of human dignity and destiny.

"The conviction that the world and man is something which had better not have been," says Schopenhauer, "is of a kind to fill us with indulgence toward one another. It reminds us of that which is after all the most necessary thing in life—the tolerance, patience, and regard and love of neighbour, of which everyone stands in need, and which, therefore, every man owes to his fellow."

THE MATERIALIST TODAY

Today a fresh wave of interest in philosophical speculation has arisen. The dissolution of old doctrines under the influence of science in the nineteenth century gave rise for a time to a rational materialism of which Huxley and Haeckel were conspicuous exemplars; but the later crumbling of moral standards, amidst the dizziness of mental liberation, has brought about a sense of restlessness and cerebral panic, and for the moment we witness the amusing spectacle of a reactionary scrambling for shelter beneath the wing of a supernatural belief either blindly conceived without intelligent reflection, or tenuously modified to accommodate as many angles of scientific truth as can be accommodated by a system of extra-rational origin.

Hence spring Fundamentalism and Modernism: both defensive emotional reactions against the ethical chaos of the present; and, as such, entitled to the sincere respect of all who realise that the sole beauty of life resides in its traditional patterns. It would not be the wish of any responsible materialist to destroy or combat the major social conditions at which these fervid believers are aiming; and the utmost attack of logic on faith serves only to replace an irrational with a rational reason for orderly life and thought.

The materialist denies that any standard is divine or absolute, and would free our conceptions of conduct from those supernatural fetters which impart a false perspective and cause the former believer to lose his moral sense as soon as he loses his faith. Conduct, of course, is only a side issue in the search for truth. But, so far as the modern materialist is interested in it at all, he merely recommends with gentle cynicism the adherence of each person to the ethical system in which he was reared, as constituting the only authentic source, in a purposeless cosmos without absolute standards, of those relative standards necessary to the orderly life and mental comfort of mankind.

Many specious arguments continue to be advanced by those labouring for a survival of religion. Fundamentalists, of course, do not argue; but the Modernists are very ingenious in adapting the language and conceptions of their ancient enemy, science, to their own uses, thus hoping to effect a reconciliation with that powerful adversary. Foremost among their contentions is that which affirms the existence of a "soul" and the truth of immortality by proclaiming mind a *thing* and thereupon invoking the scientific principle of the conservation of matter and energy to prove that it can never be destroyed—an argument, of course, which not only confuses the general mental principle with individual personality, but forgets that the law of conservation denies the fresh creation as well as the destruction of matter and energy, a point which would not allow for the birth of new souls! To the materialist, *mind* seems very clearly not a *thing*, but a *mode of motion* or *form of energy*.

Now, although the sum of energy in the universe is (speaking without reference to very recent discoveries in intra-atomic physics and chemistry) virtually indestructible, we see very clearly that it is most eminently subject to transformations from one form to another. Mechanical energy becomes electricity under the appropriate conditions, and, under other conditions, that electricity becomes light and heat. Nothing is *lost*, but all is *changed*.

Now I regard the vital principle as just such a form of energy—and *mind* is only one of the many complex manifestations of that principle. It is a product and attribute of certain forms and processes of matter; and when that matter is disintegrated, it ceases to exist—just as molecular heat ceases to exist upon the dispersal or disintegration of the material molecules which make it possible. Nothing is *lost*, any more than when electrical energy is transformed to luminous energy; but a complete metamorphosis occurs, and the identity of mind and life becomes effaced as the units of energy pass away in other forms—mostly radiant heat and other waves in the ether. Mind is no more immortal than a candle flame. The flame is just as *immortal*, if we wish to take a poetic view and reflect that the units of energy therein are never lost to the universe, but merely dissipated and incorporated into other forms and phenomena.

> "Imperious Caesar, dead and turn'd to clay,
> Might stop a hole to keep the wind away."

One might add, as noted above, that ultra-modern discovery, as based upon the phenomena of radio-activity, has opened wide and strange vistas, and perhaps defeated *in the last analysis* the idea of the indestructibility of matter and energy. Whilst matter and energy are clearly indestructible so far as any hitherto understood principles are concerned, it seems increasingly clear that cosmic force and substance have other and deeper relations and limitations—whose kinship to the phenomena we know is like that of an hour-hand to a minute- or second-hand on a clock.

It seems, in the light of recent discoveries, that all matter is in a state of balance betwixt formation and disintegration—evolution and de-volution—and that the infinite cosmos is like a vast patch of summer sky out of which little cirrus clouds gather here and there, presently to be dissolved into blankness again. The universes we know correspond to the little cirrus clouds of that summer sky, being merely transient aggregations of electrons condensed from that field of ungrouped electrons which we call space, and soon to be dissolved into that space again. This process of formation and destruction is the fundamental attribute of all entity—it is infinite Nature, and it always has been and always will be. The world, life, and universe we know, are only a passing cloud—yesterday in eternity it did not exist, and tomorrow its existence will be forgotten. Nothing matters—all that happens happens through the automatic and inflexible interacting of the electrons, atoms, and molecules of infinity according to patterns which are co-existent with basic entity itself. The general idea is that of a kaleidoscope with its endless rearrangements—there is no object or purpose in ultimate creation, since all is a ceaseless repetitive cycle of transitions from nothing back to nothing again.

However, all this need give worry to none. The aspirations of the human spirit, so movingly cited by theists, are pretty enough in themselves; and one need neither go to the trouble of breaking them up and finding their physiological components (although that is relatively easy to do) nor impute to them a cosmic significance which, though poetic to imagine, is certainly not logically deducible from their existence and characteristics. It is most sensible just to accept the universe as it is, and be done with it. All is illusion, hollowness, and nothingness—but what does that matter? Illusions are all we have, so let us pretend to cling to them; they lend dramatic values and comforting sensations of purpose to things which are really valueless and purposeless. All one can logically do is to jog placidly and cynically on, according to the artificial standards and traditions with which heredity and environment have endowed him. He will get most satisfaction in the end by keeping faithful to these things.

SOME CAUSES OF SELF-IMMOLATION

Motives for Voluntary Self-Subjugation to Unpleasant Conditions by Human Beings

by L. Theobald, Jun., N.G., A.S.S.,

Professor of Satanism and Applied Irreverence in Philistine University, Chorazin, Nebraska; Mencken Lecturer on Theology in Holy Roller College, Hoke's Four Corners, Tennessee.

Human action, diverse, complex, and contradictory, has always piqued the curiosity of thoughtful men. From the remotest times philosophers have searched for its basic source or sources; shewing little agreement until the last two generations, when scientific psychology has come to the rescue with considerable pertinent information.

Early interpretations depended almost wholly on the mental habits of their proponents. Many teachers proclaimed a diversity of prime motivations, whilst others sought to unify the various visible impulses and refer them to a common fountain-head. It was of course recognised by determinists that behind any proximate base must lie the general flux of the universe, be it simple or complex; that is, that in the last analysis each human act can be no less than the inevitable result of every antecedent and circumambient condition in an eternal cosmos. This recognition, however, did not prevent such thinkers from continuing to seek for the more proximate base or bases, and to speculate upon the immediate strings by which human puppets are moved.

In Grecian times, there persisted the very sound notion that the single dominant quest for life is some sort of happiness, or the harmonious exercise of the sum of man's various instincts and faculties;

though this central idea was conceived in various forms, and subjected to widely different interpretations. Plato imagined three principal springs of human action—physical appetite, pure emotion, and intellectual choice; though we may consider him to have regarded the latter two as outgrowths of the first. Aristotle, impressed by the complexity of man, is less clear-cut and consistent. Epicurus seems to have held the quest of rational pleasure—that is, the balanced exercise of the natural impulses—the mainspring of all sound action; regarding as abnormal or unsound such impulses as tend to disturb equilibrium and lead to misery. The Stoics, though differently conceiving the best interests of man, thought likewise that self-benefit was the ultimate goal of his quest; and pictured a definite principle which impelled his various actions toward that end. Any springs of action apart from that principle or impulse (which was suitably subdivided) were esteemed abnormal and diseased. All these Hellenic estimates had the vast advantage of being based upon a sane and inclusive survey of the various acts of men, and of the evident resemblances in the direction of those acts.

After Greece comes a period of confused and often irrelevant thought concerning human motives, owing to the wide supremacy of cosmic interpretations based on exotic and subjective supernaturalism. The first conspicuous return to honest thinking appears to be the system of Descartes, who referred human action to an exercise of natural instinct as guided by an ill-defined but separate "mind"—the two meeting in the pineal gland of the brain. This approach to modern endocrinology was, however, purely fortuitous. Descartes considered the springs of mental motivation to be six in number: admiration, love, hatred, desire, joy, and sadness; and described in some detail their mechanical operation in the brain as he conceived it. Spinoza far outstripped Descartes in depth and rationality of outlook, approaching the most modern conceptions in his estimate of human motivation. He saw that primitive instincts are desires to preserve and expand the individual, and traced the dependence of the more complex emotions upon them. Therefore, he inferred, action is inspired at third-hand (thought = emotion = instinct) by the natural impulse of man to survive, operating through varied and sometimes paradoxically opposed channels, and in turn derived through an infinite causal chain from the primary conditions of the cosmos. Spinoza, who returned to the sound Hellenic conception of happiness as the goal of mankind, may (despite a debt to Descartes) be viewed as the real father of modern ideas regarding human values and motives. In our own civilisation, Hobbes similarly emphasised the dominance of the survival-element, or self-interest, in human motivation; though he wholly lacked the subtlety and profundity of Spinoza. Hume is not fundamentally dissimilar, and in France La Mettrie and Helvétius likewise kept to a sound Hellenic concept based upon observation.

It was only in the nineteenth century, however, that the unity of human motivation was emphasised again by philosophers of the first rank. Schopenhauer placed the *will to live* at the bottom of all human action, while Nietzsche very acutely enlarged upon the idea through realisation of the essentially *expansive* quality of all human urges. For the mere *will to live* he substituted the more definite *will to power.* The positivists, such as Spencer, complicated the question by regarding all society as a quasi-biological organism—a concept still surviving in Oswald Spengler. In the twentieth century Bergson relapsed into misty metaphysics, but postulated a pervasive motivating force or *élan vital* as extending through the cosmos and determining our acts among other things. Bertrand Russell and Santayana favour a diversity of motivating forces, each based on a separate chemical reaction in the body; a mode of thought which behaviourists like Pavlov and Watson essentially pursue. All agree, however, that the single direction of these independent forces is toward the survival and well-being of the organism. As immediate sources of human motivation, the several endocrine glands—which act on the nervous system through the discharge of particles called *hormones* into the blood stream—are now considered paramount.

Freud largely returns to the concept of a single motivating force in a specific mechanical fashion, assuming the existence in man of a restless *libido* or impulse of ego-assertion equivalent to Bergson's *élan vital* and largely identifiable with erotic instinct. To diversions and modifications of this, induced by conscious or unconscious prudence, he attributes most human action; though he tends to admit sheer self-preservation as a parallel and somewhat differentiated force. It is with Freud that modern scientific psychology, with its recognition of the unconsciousness of our most salient motivating factors, largely begins; but Dr. Alfred Adler apparently clarifies it and carries it further by generalising the main ego-assertion urge beyond the boundaries of the merely sexual. His idea of a basically simple but diversely manifested ego-urge, at times frustrated by prudence or timidity, accounts with remarkable accuracy for the bulk of observed human motives.

Today, then, we may justly regard human action as resulting from a basic organic impulse of ego-assertion, manifested through several distinct physical instincts inherent in evolved nervous tissue, and operating—in connexion with the mentally associative outgrowths classed as *emotions*—through the system of ductless glands. That the ultimate manifestations are complex and often paradoxical need not be wondered at when we reflect on the complexity of the organism and the divided (and often accidentally conflicting) channels through which the ego-urge functions. For example, biological experience has fashioned, for survival-value under different circumstances, the *precisely opposite* instincts of overt assertion and defensive abasement. McDougall classifies the instincts and their derived simple emotions under twelve headings, though it is of course obvious that the number of additional emotions built up through combination and complex experience is vast indeed. The list follows. All simple instincts are normal in essence, though abnormal misproportionings, perversions, combinations, and inversions are commonly recognised and exhaustively studied.

Instinct	*Emotion*
Nutrition	Hunger
Flight	Fear
Repulsion	Disgust
Curiosity	Wonder
Assertion	Elation (= courage?)
Abasement	Subjection (= humility)
Acquisition	Love of possession
Constructiveness	Creative delight (phase of aestheticism)
Pugnacity	Anger
Sex	Love
Parentalism	Tenderness

The present writer feels convinced that one basic instinct plus its derivative emotion ought to be added to this list; namely, an instinct for *symmetry* in the abstract, based upon habituation to the ceaseless rhythms and regularities (astronomical and otherwise) of the terrestrial environment, which supplies many aesthetic feelings traceable neither to creativeness nor to any conceivable complex emotion or emotions.

When we come to correlate the human phenomena about us with the conclusions reached by modern observers, we find the majority of cases fitting in readily with the conception of a dominant ego-urge expressed first as physical impulse and additionally as a craving for ego-exaltation on the part of the imagination. We realise, naturally, that the associative and symbolising qualities of the mind will not always cause such an urge to manifest itself narrowly or directly. Frequently there will be imaginative transferences of the ego-image to objects, both concrete and abstract, outside the given organism; so that zeal for the promotion of certain apparently non-personal interests will be observed. This is not remarkable, and does not seem incompatible with the accepted concept of motivation. Occasionally, however, we behold individuals in the act of voluntarily choosing experiences which cannot be other than painful or unpleasant; hence are led to wonder how such choices can be accounted for in the light of our previous assumption.

It may be said, in general, that all cases of voluntary submission to hardship or pain involve the subordination of a lesser to a greater preference. In each case the individual is really doing, in the end, what most conduces to his own interest through the expansion of his subjective ego-image; and sometimes the case can be shewn to be a merely apparent one, since what seems outwardly unpleasant will not in fact be so to the given individual. At other times it can be shewn that the submission to hardship is not (at least wholly) truly voluntary. Seldom is the motivation simple or even nearly simple; so that it would be an infinitely cumbrous task to list and describe these cases under empirical headings—that is, to list specific cases of objective manifestation (as in the tentative synopsis suggested by Maurice Winter Moe, Esq.) instead of listing the relatively simple types of underlying motive whose combinations create the known array of vastly complex manifestations. In almost every specific manifestation, various distinct motives will be found—mixed in different portions, conscious or unconscious, and of varying degrees of recognisability. No layman is competent to determine the motive of any given course of human action, and there are cases where not even the most expert psychiatrist can speak with any real certainty.

Let us, then, try to enumerate the *motives* for self-immolation rather than any overt examples of that tendency; considering them in what may or may not be their approximate order of frequency, and mentioning the types of manifestation into which they enter—and which, of course, in a few cases some one of them may singly or at least preponderantly occasion. Upon mature reflection, we seem to recognise eight different species of motive leading toward the self-infliction of hardship or pain; seven reasonably normal, and the eighth technically abnormal although exceedingly common as an ingredient of complex motives.

The *Prudential Motive* is a name we may apply to that simple and universal policy of mankind whereby an immediate or lesser hardship is endured for the sake of future or greater personal pleasure or security. Of all the motives, it is the one most apt to be found in a relatively uncombined state; and is the least subtle and most direct in its operation. Many of the other motives may theoretically be regarded as subdivisions of it, but in practice we may limit the class to very literal cases, where the rewards are of a rather definite and tangible kind. Its operation can be direct, as in the habit of thrift, suffering experienced in social or political elevation, hard work performed to gratify intellectual curiosity or the ego-urge, hardship endured in mastering a pleasure-seeking accomplishment, asceticism suffered for the sake of keener later enjoyment, religious discipline endured for the sake of mythical celestial rewards, political sacrifices undertaken to effect later triumphs, prize-ring bruising in the hope of final victory with purse and honours, and so on; or it can be indirect, as in the observance of general civic or so-called moral inhibitions. It is also embodied in the gregarious subordination of personal tastes to the tastes of one's group, undertaken for the sake of the pleasure inherent in environmental harmony. A negative aspect of this motive is that in which fear of adverse consequences is a factor, as in old-time religion, some cases of civic and military obedience, and the like.

The *Inertia or Habit Motive* explains action or endurance undertaken because of the pressure of custom or precedent on pliant rather than vigorous intellects. The subject does not know how to avoid doing what the group recommends or has always recommended, or perhaps it does not occur to him that any alternative course is possible. This accounts for the tremendous number of instances where petty nuisances are needlessly endured from members of one's family or from others, where conventional and non-obligatory sacrifices are made, and where silly, meaningless, and oppressive customs or attitudes are kept up after all reason and compulsion for their maintenance has subsided. On a large scale it accounts for the endurance of grave and needless social and civic disadvantages by various elements of a community. This category may be largely an apparent rather than basic one, since its cases can be attributed to the fear-aspect of the prudential motive, or can be interpreted as being *not really voluntary* at all in the subtlest sense. But its empirical existence and vast extent are obvious.

The *Approval Motive,* whereby we obtain favourable distinction in the eyes of ourselves or of others by following a course regarded as difficult and admirable by the group to which we belong, is also exceedingly common. It is distinguished from a more profound quest for excellence, or a more spontaneous altruism, by its essential superficiality; and it dictates a large part of the social, religious, and civic behaviour of civilised man. It animates most reformers and puritanical prigs, and enters into most visible species of martyrdom, scholastic or other effort, marathon races, tree-sitting, military prowess, altruism, and so forth. A distinct variant is the *exhibitionist motive,* whereby one acquires distinction as an exceptional person by affecting to enjoy what most find unpleasant. We find this variant in such eccentrics as pretend to relish swimming in midwinter, and in analogous types.

The *Exterior-Gratification Motive,* though challenged by many, who refer its apparent phenomena to the prudential, approval, and perhaps other motives, probably has a distinct existence of its own; as attested by a definite though not very large minority of cases where the springs of certain acts not directly self-benefiting are found to be extremely powerful and at least consciously sincere. We may define this motive as that whereby a person endures hardship or pain—mental or physical—for the sake of some exterior or trans-personally expanded unit with which his ego has imaginatively (associatively or symbolically) identified itself. The existence of these imaginative transpositions or expansions of the ego-image has seldom been denied where self-immolation is not concerned, and there is no reason to limit the recognition to such an area. Primitive instinct—eroticism, parentalism, gregariousness, etc.—often temporarily transfers or extends the ego-concept without much loss of driving force; whilst associative emotion greatly enlarges an array of external or expanded ego-images. One's clan, race, country, or culture-group becomes an imaginative extension of oneself, as does also one's social system or body of opinion—political, scientific, philosophical, aesthetic, and so on. In theory, at least, many grandiloquent individuals have professed to identify themselves with the entire human species, the entire realm of organic life, or even the sum total of the cosmos or space-time continuum; but there is reason to think that most cases of this sort are hollow, charlatanic pretensions, and filled with self-deception. At best, most imaginative identifications beyond a roughly defined field approximately connected with racial, national, and cultural group limits are apt to be very tenuous, brief, fragmentary, and consciously or unconsciously insincere. There is, however, an auto-hypnotic and probably abnormal type of powerful cosmos-identification which we know as *mysticism,* and which figures in the operation of many Oriental religions. The exterior-gratification motive includes most sincere (i.e., not approval-seeking, prudential, etc.) cases of personal altruism, including those fear-cases where the subject symbolises disaster to himself in that of others, and feels impelled to relieve others at the cost of immediate pain. It also embraces many phases of genuine intellectual, religious, and aesthetic martyrdom, most sincere civic, patriotic, and humanitarian sacrifice and endeavour, and most real self-denial to promote intellectual, aesthetic, and moral objects. It motivates such asceticism as is undertaken for example's sake, and enters enormously into military courage.

The *Ego-Expansion Motive,* likewise challenged by critics, but presenting too many sound evidences of its existence to warrant a total denial, is that which causes us to endure hardship or pain for the sake of acquiring a genuinely higher intrinsic status in the environing pattern; a status either relative or—in the case of those still believing in absolute standards—absolute. This sincere motivation must be carefully distinguished from that deceptive form of the approval-motive in which the subject dramatises himself and plays rather cheaply and superficially for his own transient benefit. In the case of genuine ego-expansionism, the subject is relatively free from the habit of self-delusion and histrionics, and really wishes to attain an intrinsically increased development or more important essence in the fabrics to which he envisages himself as belonging. This motive includes most varieties of genuine religious and aesthetic asceticism, much of religious martyrdom (though not of other forms), and much hard work and study in intellectual, aesthetic, and social fields.

The *Emotional-Conflict Motive* consists of an overpowering or replacement of natural inhibitions or even of pain-consciousness by some powerfully driving urge, as of volition, love, fear, hatred, etc.—which causes the maintenance of accustomed safeguards or even the perception of pain to be temporarily forgotten. This is the cause of that Berserk mood whereby we "see red" and rush joyfully into any sort of danger and sanguinary suffering; and likewise of the "cornered rat" mood in which we defy any hazard in a final burst of fear-born action against the virtual certainty of a greater disaster. It figures greatly in many cases of altruism (combining with ego-expansionism, approval-seeking, exterior-gratificationalism, prudentialism, etc., in many sudden acts of so-called heroism), martyrdom, patriotism, military courage, etc.; as also in a wide variety of fear-moved actions and cases of endurance.

The *Craftsmanship Motive* is one of the rarest and subtlest of forces; causing certain sensitive persons to experience a positive pleasure, despite incidental hardship or pain, in shaping events, as well as tangible objects and media, in accordance with a subjectively envisaged rhythm-pattern. This motive, beside inciting the subject to direct aesthetic effort in the face of pain and difficulties, covers many phases of aesthetic and religious asceticism, in which the subject takes an abstract delight in having certain patterns of action followed or approached; a delight quite distinct from any improvement of his own status (as under the ego-expansion motive), since in his zeal for the abstraction which he calls "beauty", "virtue", or "piety", he is thinking of the pattern rather than of the performer, and is merely placing himself on a parity with others, for whose similar following of the pattern he is equally anxious. In practice, however, this motive is apt to occur as a concomitant of ego-expansionism rather than alone. In its least mixed form it is probably the chief ingredient of difficult mental, artistic, and kindred achievements. It is probably derived primarily from the basic instinct of constructiveness, plus the parallel motive of exterior-gratification, whereby the symbol of the ego has attached itself to the favoured pattern. Its ascetic aspects are distinguished from pure exterior-gratification phenomena because the safety and status of the favoured pattern are never at stake. The pattern's importance and security are taken for granted, so that there can be no idea of *assisting or benefiting* it. It is simply that the subject takes satisfaction in the performance of certain imaginatively related acts in a certain order. However—it is possible that the assignment of creative effort to the prudential class (hardship leading to reward), and the belief that the symbolic glorification of a favoured pattern inherent in its following places pure pattern-asceticism under the heading of exterior-gratification (with the ego transferred to the pattern), may be sufficient to eliminate this special category. Distinctions of this sort are necessarily highly nebulous.

The *Masochistic Motive,* involving the instinctive perversion known as masochism, whereby a sensuous delight is taken in the phenomenon of pain-perception, is comparatively rare as a pure source of action; though exceedingly common as a component in varying degree of various complex motivations. In its purest form it involves the usually fantastic and capricious self-infliction or induced affliction of pain, mental or physical. Usually, however, it is a fainter and more veiled auxiliary force. It dominates the mystical aspect of a majority of Oriental religions,* and incites many individuals to varying degrees of subtly titillating martyrdom, public or private. It can be found in the voluntarily endured domestic burdens and tyrannies of many households, and in many seemingly unhappy phases of erotic relationships. As an independent emotion it is undeniably abnormal, though most psychologists do not think it absent in small quantity from the average normal personality. Homely adage sums it up in describing the person who 'enjoys poor health'—though perhaps that person adds other motives, such as the ego-expanding gratifications of attention and sympathy, to the sheer masochism of his attitude. The possible connexion of masochism with the basic defensive abasement instinct is at least worth careful study.

Such are the eight well-defined motivational variants which appear, singly or in sundry combinations, to lie behind the whole wide array of self-immolatory acts. Attempts to evaluate such petty human motives, in an infinite and impersonal cosmos amidst which mankind is a negligible and microscopic accident, are at best rather naive; but we may, if we wish, seek to correlate them with this or that system of relative standards. Of such sets the least flimsy and empirical is that determined by organic evolution and aesthetic-intellectual development; which attributes may be said to measure the distance of an individual

* Some might attribute the Oriental's grovelling tendency to the basic instinct of defensive abasement, though that alone would not explain the religious devotee's delight in self-sought suffering of the Juggernaut type.

from the primal protoplasmic jelly. What balance of these motives, then, may we expect to find in the most preferred type of *homo sapiens?*

In general, we may say that in an evolved and cultivated man the intellect, imagination, and beauty-sense are developed prodigiously beyond their respective proportions in the primitive type. Accordingly, we may expect to find the powers of discrimination, association, symbolisation, and creativeness very strong. Motives dependent on animal instinct, insincerity, stupidity, or poor coördination—like the inertia, approval, emotional-conflict, and masochistic motives—may be expected to be relatively subordinate, hence may be classed as qualitatively inferior; whilst mental and imaginative motives—like exterior-gratificationalism, ego-expansionalism, and craftsmanship—will be very prominent, hence may receive a higher qualitative rank. The prudential motive is equally strong in developed and undeveloped personalities despite differences of application, hence may be regarded as essentially neutral qualitatively.

Another set of relative standards is that derived from the needs of human society as the present finds it to be most feasibly constituted; for naturally, a group of all-superior men could never arrive at a state of large-scale equilibrium and coördinated function. What self-immolatory motivations, then, are most socially serviceable in the masses of a people as opposed to its aristocracy? Naturally, the prudential motive must rate high; as must also the inertia and approval motives—since without these there can be no incentives to civil order amongst a herd deficient in the intellectual, associative, symbolic, and creative qualities. However, the exterior-gratification and ego-expansion motives are of equal value so far as they are operative at all on a large scale. We do often find certain of their manifestations in uncultivated though biologically evolved types. The emotional-conflict motive, though disastrous when employed against the social order, is infinitely valuable when employed in society's behalf; and indeed forms a sort of criterion of manly status among Aryan peoples. The craftsmanship motive is unqualifiedly good except when its ascetic aspect is turned to favour-patterns opposed to the social order, but on this latter account may be regarded as a less certain asset than some others. Masochism can conceivably work to advantage in maintaining order, but it has doubtful implications and is not to be encouraged. With this possible exception, we may say that virtually *all* the self-immolatory motives are of great value in the masses of society, since so much of social adjustment must necessarily consist of the renunciation of immediate advantages for the sake of a stable order productive of ultimately greater advantages.

That the nature and operation of these seemingly paradoxical impulses do indeed confirm our general belief in ego-assertion or ultimate self-interest as a supreme human motive, or principle underlying action, would appear to be too certain a thing for profitable challenging. As in many other philosophic spheres, the marvellous instinctive insight and subtle comprehension of the Greeks is vindicated after centuries of chaotic eclipse; while exact knowledge is rapidly filling up lacunae hitherto bridged over only by a bold exercise of the disciplined imagination.

Dec. 13, 1931

HERITAGE OR MODERNISM: COMMON SENSE IN ART FORMS

Aside from the morphological characteristics and neural, glandular, and organic reflexes determined by aeons of physical evolution, all that we are—all that we feel, think, say, do, hope, and dream—is the sole product of our environmental heritage. Allegedly "innate" tendencies in our mental and emotional life generally turn out to be mythical. We do, it is true, seem to have basic biological instincts of ego-assertion, manipulation, curiosity, and rhythm (each probably connected with self-defensive and other utilitarian reflexes) which lie at the base of thinking and feeling, but the part played by these in a full and satisfactory life is so small that we would be insane to attempt the establishment of a culture on them alone. The really supreme and determinant ingredient in everything which we consider "good", "beautiful", "significant", "normal", "appropriate", "agreeable", "comfortable", "important", and the like, is nothing more nor less than a certain kind of *familiarity;* a state involving some symbol or reminder of things we have known before. We have no ideas, standards, likes, dislikes, or interests except those which the accidents of personal and racial history have bequeathed to us; hence any new form or conception is, in our emotions, almost absolutely meaningless to us unless it can be associated with the chance background behind our individual lives—the background of usages, typical objects, habitual feelings, accustomed sights, ostensible goals, and quasi-instinctive criteria.

In an eternal and indifferent cosmos of which the galactic universe, the solar system, the earth, organic life, and the human race form only a momentary and negligible incident, there can be no such things as *value, purpose, direction,* or *meaning,* or even *interest,* except in a strictly local and relative sense. That is, nothing has value, direction, meaning, or relevance save in connexion with that fortuitous jumble of experiences, beliefs, and customs constituting each observer's local inheritance.

For example, the music of the Chinese is largely meaningless to Americans because the latter have not inherited the ideas and customs, nor shared the experiences of the Chinese people. Abstract harmony counts for little, since it is upon *association* that the primary appeal of anything depends. If we have no personal associations with a set of sounds, they will remain merely a set of sounds so far as we are concerned. They will not please us, nor become "music" to us, unless we are able to relate them to sound-combinations which we are accustomed to consider harmonious. What is music to one race is discord or irrelevant din to another—and so with all the arts and all phases of human feeling. Beliefs and standards which seem all-important to one culture-group may be either unimportant or antipathetic to another.

It all depends on what especial chaos of ideas and customs and habits the group in question may happen to inherit. (One says *inherit* because no other manner of acquisition—whatever be the mistaken beliefs of Russian bolsheviks—is sufficiently potent and pervasive to build up a quasi-instinctive pattern of standards and interests.) In some cases, it is true, different groups may share certain fields of experience and heritage to the extent of making a few isolated sections of their respective mental and artistic lives intelligible and significant to one another. Thus, although we cannot understand and appreciate Chinese music, we can keenly enter into the spirit of Chinese decorative and even pictorial art. But that is pure chance. Remove all sources of familiarity—all the subtle landmarks supplied by what we know of the past—and no phase of art or life can have more than the slenderest vestige of appeal, beauty, or meaning. Despite all careless talk of individuality and self-sufficiency, it is really only as *part of a pattern* that man can effectively envisage himself as a significant object. Take away all reference-points and he is lost. It is only against the background which stretches around and behind him that he is able to attain any sense of placedness, meaning, purpose, direction, or interest.

Hence the tragic fallacy of the "functional" and "modernistic" theories which in recent years have formed a serious threat to the artistic life of the western world. According to the pedlars of these theories, all art ought to be divorced completely from tradition and from earlier art-forms. Each age, they assert, ought to express itself in its own fashion and with its own materials; ignoring the modes of expression dictated in other ages by other modes of life, and existing only to fulfil an utilitarian function. If a chair or table or house is built, they would have us design it without any reference to the kind of chairs or tables or houses we have known; consulting only first-hand science, mathematics, and engineering to determine the most practical device as related to its use and to the materials and tools to be employed in its construction.

A literal following of this formula, they insist, will automatically result in something which we ought to recognise as "beauty" whether we like it or not. Materials, tools, and function are everything—the one must express the other, and nothing else must be expressed. The *associative* element in beauty is "false" even though it is obviously the most powerful of all elements. We must narrow our aesthetic feeling to the purely ego-assertive, constructive, and abstractly rhythmical aspects, even at the cost of stripping life and art of nine-tenths of the apparent significance and real value they possess. Nor do the modernists pause even here—for we find them arrayed against anything familiar or associatively beautiful *even when such familiarity or associative beauty does not conflict with the existing materials, tools, and function!* They hate the known and the home-like not merely on abstract grounds, but *intrinsically, for their own sakes.*

To cap the climax, these decadent madmen attempt to tell us that such a course of past-repudiation and scientific functionalism is merely a duplication in our own age, with our new materials, methods, and purposes, of what our predecessors did in their respective ages. They claim that the Athenians who conceived the Parthenon, the Choragic Monument of Lysicrates, and the Olympian Zeus, the mediaeval Nordics who conceived the cathedrals of Chartres and Lincoln, and the Georgian cabinet-makers who conceived the magnificent furniture of two centuries ago, were precisely on a par with the depression-age theorists who laboriously reared the steel-and-glass horrors of the late Chicago "Century of 'Progress' ", and who continue to plan and perpetrate nightmares in chromium, bakelite, glass, concrete, and other media—calling upon corkscrews, factory refuse, gas-tanks, oil derricks, chicken-coops, radio masts, and other "typical forms of our twentieth-century machine 'civilisation' " as models for what they ironically term chairs, tables, buildings, and the like. In the less utilitarian arts—where they declare that the only legitimate object is a scientific record of the images in the artist's subconscious—they affect to draw a parallel betwixt the ordered beauty of Theocritus and Vergil and Michelangelo and Shakespeare and Rembrandt and Keats in their ages, and the amorphous emanations of Gertrude Stein and Picasso and James Joyce and Modigliani in this age. In each case, they vow, the artist has merely embodied the feelings of his social-economic milieu in a piece of construction wholly conditioned by the materials, tools, and function of the moment. Backed by this specious theory, they shout warnings against "the sterile imitation of the past", and spout admonitions to us to "be creative and original in our own age, as the Greeks and the mediaevals and the Georgians were in their ages". Over and over we find such febrile propaganda in the books and articles of the "young intelligentsia".

This mess of theory and propaganda is dangerous because it brings in a vague general principle which really does have some truth in it. Otherwise it would have collapsed long ago. The principle in question is, of course, that of *basic appropriateness.* Certainly no work of art ought to be encumbered with excrescences wholly alien to its purpose, or to counterfeit—beyond certain bounds and without powerful and instinctive associative reasons—objects of alien function or alien workmanship. Fully half of the fatal weakness of Victorian "art" came from just this type of irrelevance and insincerity. But the existence of this shadowy and elastic principle is one thing, while its childishly literal interpretation and fanatical overapplication are another thing. Actually, we realise that the total function of art is by no means limited to the narrow image-catharsis, and mathematically rhythmical and practically efficient construction, beyond which the modernists refuse to look.

Art, to be real, must express all the overtones of our feelings—and among these the passionate quest for pattern-placement and continuity with known things is of course an overwhelming force. Our longing for familiar symbols—our homesickness, as it were, for the things we have known—is in reality the most authentic possible expression of the race's persistent life-force. It is the pitiful struggle of the ego against that ineluctable change which means decay and engulfment in the illimitable dark. Upon this struggle for survival and increased force depends the whole epic of organic life. It motivates all our acts, and gave rise to our ancestors' persistent illusion of personal immortality. How silly, then, to fancy that its most direct symbol—the protest against the loss of familiar things which appears alike in sorrow for deceased relatives and in yearning for old, familiar ways—can be deposed from its supremacy in aesthetics?

The "art" of the moderns is *not really functional* because what they conceive to be "function" is *not in truth fully or even approximately such.* A chair is *not,* in essence, simply a "sitting machine". A house is *not* merely a "living machine"—Frank Lloyd Wright and the late Raymond Mathewson Hood to the contrary notwithstanding. Both chairs and houses fail in their *true functions* unless they contribute to our emotional adjustment by corresponding in greater or lesser degree with our naturally ingrained and traditional images—based on our especial form of the past—of what a chair and a house ought to be. Thus certain lines or decorative elements in an object may not contribute to its direct material purpose, and may even suggest earlier and abandoned methods whereby similar objects were formerly made. The modernist condemns this, but the really reflective thinker is willing to accept the departures from practical function and constructive method *if they are sufficiently symbolic of deep and permanent human yearnings.* Victorian irrelevancies, excrescences, and insincerities were offensive and unjustified because they were *not* symbolic of such yearnings, being more often departures from tradition than adherences to it.

As for cases where material function neither demands nor contradicts traditional forms, there is of course no excuse whatever for a rejection of the traditional and all the enormous emotional force it involves. When a modernist, faced with a flat surface for treatment, deliberately chooses repulsive and meaningless stripes and conic sections in place of symmetrical classic patterns which soothe the eye and stimulate the emotions, he is committing an absolutely unjustified aesthetic crime. The fact is that the *real* emotion behind "functional" modernism is not by any means the undiluted scientific theory which its proponents so loudly mouth. Actually, modernism is very largely a mere decadent dissatisfaction with existing things—an hysterical emotional extravagance *precisely akin to the very Victorianism it condemns.* The absurdities of 1935 and those of 1885 are all of a piece. Both represent decadent emotion justifying itself with an imposing facade of overdrawn theory and mistaken originality-worship. 1885, like 1935, sought to "express the age in the age's own way"—but its copyrighted catchwords happened to be "romanticism" and "eclecticism" instead of "functionalism". Both ages produced and are producing a melancholy amount of junk which the future will be anxious to sweep out of sight. They have failed because they have disregarded tradition.

The claim that older art forms were purely functional and untraditional, each in its age, is nonsense which any unbiassed survey of aesthetic expression from Egypt and Chaldaea down ought to knock on the head. The truth is that every civilised art stream has been a natural and continuous development from some previous stream or streams, with holdovers of innumerable familiar phases. Even Greek art was no momentary, autochthonous, and artificial growth. As every informed person knows, it possesses roots in Cretan, Egyptian, Persian, and Mesopotamian art, and represents simply the gradual fusion and modification of earlier ideas and methods by a new people on a new soil. And as for "functional sincerity"—it is no secret that this was not pushed to extremes. The Doric triglyphs, for example, were symbols of the beams used in earlier and bygone modes of construction. Mediaeval pointed architecture, too, had a long and gradual history including debased Roman and Saracenic sources. It did not spring up overnight in response to some theorist's conception of what ought to express the economics and technology of the period, nor did it overthrow any deeply seated and sharply differentiated school. Instead, it developed spontaneously amidst a sterile chaos of crudity, seven hundred years after the decay of the last well-defined preceding school of architecture. The modernists might as well realise that no successful aesthetic forms were ever created to order through the repudiation of all the influences extending behind them. Although Renaissance art may have *seemed* revolutionary, it was tremendously spontaneous, and was indeed merely a return to earlier forms which had never been wholly forgotten or absent from sight and tradition.

If the moderns were *truly* scientific, they would realise that their own attitude of *self-conscious theory* removes them absolutely from all kinship with the creators of genuine artistic advances. Real art must be, above all else, *unconscious and spontaneous*—and this is precisely what modern functionalism is *not.* No age was ever truly "expressed" by theorists who sat down and deliberately mapped out a technique for "expressing" it. What actually "expresses" an age is the perfectly unhampered and untheorising creativeness of artists who simply do what they feel like doing—who fashion what they conceive to be beautiful, without reflecting on *why* it is beautiful or whether it mathematically symbolises the politics, economics, raw materials, engineering methods, and tools of the existing civilisation. Who is so silly as to fancy that Wren, Gibbs, Hawksmoor, or the brothers Adam fashioned their exquisite buildings in accordance with some theory of engineering, carpentry, masonry, or contemporary sociology?

Nor is this all. It is not enough to shew that the attitude of the modernists prevents their achieving any real art. We may further demonstrate that their grotesque nightmares do not in any way truly express the period they are claimed to express. Would any reasonable psychologist justify "The Waste Land" as typifying 1922 as "Endymion" justified the early nineteenth century? How characteristic or universal is the mood expressed? And as regards the motifs of modernistic furniture and architecture—visible marks of materials, machine design, and scientific adaptation of form to function—who is so naive as to fancy *that these obscure technical elements enter into the popular conception of the given products sufficiently to form valid symbols of those products and of the milieu behind them?* The moderns hold that an architectural outline like a steam-boiler or a fertiliser-grinder is a poignant and proper symbol of steel-and-aluminum construction and therefore the only suitable design for a building with a steel or aluminum frame! The real truth is that nobody except a few theorists and technicians knows anything about construction details—or would attach the least aesthetic significance to such matters even if he did know! To the normal man the natural emotional symbol of a house is not the machine that produced its girders, but simply the mental picture of what has always been recognised as a house—a visual image unmixed with thoughts of carpentry and engineering.

How, then, can the strained and artificial system of symbolism behind the moderns' position be anything but a sorry joke? They launch new decorative designs of cones and cubes and triangles and segments—wheels and belts, smokestacks and stream-lined sausage-moulders—problems in Euclid and nightmares from alcoholic orgies—and tell us that these things are the only authentic symbols of the age in which we live. But who on earth really does, in his basic emotional life, ever think of these things as the motive forces of his environment? Common sense sweeps the whole preposterous fakery out of court in three seconds. We have not even the brains to conceive of external forms, deeply and continuously, in terms of their concealed components and processes of construction!

Regarding the question of *changed function*—the claim that the present generation does not really want the traditional objects which it accepts through tradition, and that it would prefer objects radically untraditional to fulfil its new wants with mechanical directness—one concrete instance will dispel such nonsense. We are told that modern hygiene demands a life of increased sunlight, while modern domestic needs call for large, non-private rooms of adjustable size. Therefore, say the moderns, let us dwell in houses of aluminum with great glass sides instead of windows, and with interiors having light movable partitions. We do not need small individual rooms now that the technique of heating is perfected. Such is the picture—but what do common sense and a knowledge of human psychology say of such a scheme? Is homesickness for every vestige of accustomed living conditions to be wholly discounted? Is the natural instinct for individual privacy to be ignored? Are the requirements of different climates to be overlooked? Have the disposition of furniture and the conservation of wall-space been investigated? The real truth is that the doctrine of changed function is in this case, as in most others, a sheer myth. A nightmare dwelling of the modernists' type is *not truly functional* because *it is not what people want.* Actually, the traditional type of house with normal windows and partitions is exactly what the modern man, like his ancestors, requires for the fulfilment of his real wants. It is therefore just as appropriate as ever—as a study of contemporary building projects will shew in the most practical fashion.

It would seem, then, that we are justified in regarding radical aesthetic modernism as in the main a somewhat annoying and potentially harmful false alarm. Good sense dictates a gradual growth from our normal and familiar antecedents—holding fast to whatever elements we still deem beautiful and useful, and attempting no theory-born outrage upon our natural craving for the familiar. Science and philosophy unite in testifying how anchorless and emotionally impoverished we should be if all the long-recognised externals of life were stripped away—and reason assures us that nothing has happened to make such a tragedy needful.

Nor need we worry with the modernists over the fact that the last few decades—or centuries, for that matter—have produced no wholly [original] set of artistic forms. Why should they, when the previous forms are still valid? Do we really think in cones and square roots and dynamos to such an extent that Shelley and Praxiteles and Balzac are obsolete, whilst the dwellings and public halls and furniture around us are no longer appropriate for our bodies and activities? Is it indeed usual for radical new schools to arise every century? How about the life-spans of Egyptian, Greek, Roman, Gothic, and Chinese art? When a given age has no new *natural* impulse toward change, is it not better to continue building on the established forms than to concoct grotesque and meaningless novelties out of thin academic theory?

Indeed, under certain conditions is not a policy of frank and virile antiquarianism—a healthy, vigorous revival of old forms still justified by their relation to life—infinitely sounder than a feverish mania for the destruction of familiar things and the laboured, freakish, uninspired search for strange shapes which nobody wants and which really mean nothing? Who can say that the Egyptian art of the eighteenth dynasty—a revival of eleventh-dynasty forms—was less vigorous and genuine than that of any other period? This was the age of Tut-ankh-Amen and his splendours. Or that the revived Memphian art of the twenty-sixth dynasty (though admittedly inferior to the eighteenth dynasty's revival) was feebler than any new experiments in which that late and basically uncreative age might have indulged?

Naturally, every new age has additions, subtractions, and modifications to make to its inherited art traditions. No one argues in behalf of a rigidly static art. As man adds to his knowledge of the cosmos and his own relation to it, the new light on his mental and emotional processes is certain to produce moods requiring new tones in literature, music, and painting. New objects are invented and old ones are altered, thus providing constant opportunities for reworking and expanding our familiar structural forms. The point is that there is no need to destroy and replace accustomed aesthetic fundamentals when they can so much more advantageously be retained and developed as reason and conditions dictate. The basic elements of design and expression around which all our memories, traditions, affections, sense of normality, and feelings of cosmic placedness, direction, and purpose are intertwined, are just as effective and susceptible of expansion and recombination today as in the past; and there is absolutely no excuse for their arbitrary radical destruction. New elements may indeed be introduced with proper caution if they are capable of harmonious assimilation to the main fabric. But such novelties must not be antagonistic nor destructive; neither must they seek a supremacy which they have not rightly earned. They must blend with what we already possess and cherish.

Whether the radicals admit it or not, our genuine stream of art and civilisation is still the ancient western one which took its general form in Greece and Rome. Pretending to repudiate it does not give us any other real stream in its place. Let us therefore accept it as our fathers did, and rejoice in possessing so great a tradition. We shall not find it inadequate to the demands of either the present or the future.

IV
LITERARY CRITIC

Lovecraft's literary criticism outside the domain of weird fiction is disappointing at best, and of interest only for the light it sheds on other aspects of his work and thought. Most of his pure literary criticism was written during his amateur period, and includes such things as a basic guide to prose grammar and syntax ("Literary Composition"), a skeletonic outline of the principles of verse ("What Belongs in Verse"), and windy "puffs" of leading amateur writers ("The Poetry of Lilian Middleton"), which sound like nothing so much as Poe's effusive reviews of women poets. All this is routine, but other pieces help to trace the surprisingly radical evolution of Lovecraft's critical thought during the last two decades of his life.

In an unpublished letter to August Derleth (c. 1929) Lovecraft made a very important assessment of his aesthetic development: "I can look back . . . at two distinct periods of opinion whose foundations I have successively come to distrust—a period before 1919 or so, when the weight of classic authority unduly influenced me, and another period from 1919 to about 1925, when I placed too high a value on the elements of revolt, florid colour, and emotional extravagance or intensity." Classicism and Decadence: these are the two successive phases of Lovecraft's early critical theory. We hardly need evidence of his classicist tendencies; a passage from "The Case for Classicism" (1919) is both a summation and a swan song for this view: "The literary genius of Greece and Rome, developed under peculiarly favourable circumstances, may fairly be said to have completed the art and science of expression. Unhurried and profound, the classical author achieved a standard of simplicity, moderation, and elegance of taste, which all succeeding time has been powerless to excel or even to equal." But if the ancients have said everything worth saying, all the moderns can (and should) do is to imitate them; and Lovecraft, faithful to his principles, did just that, writing masses of poetry under the dominant influence of Dryden and

Pope and composing prose derived from the periodical essays of Addison and Johnson. But a classicist in the early part of this century might well have felt embattled; and such things as free verse, simple spelling, and other evils of the day had to be vigorously combated. It is no surprise that the sixth word of "Metrical Regularity" (1915) is "decadence": Lovecraft saw decadence everywhere—in art and architecture as well as in literature—and up to 1919 he was conducting a heroic rearguard battle against it.

Then something strange happens: Lovecraft begins to embrace the "Decadents." These Decadents are, of course, not the ones who practice free verse or simple spelling, but those later nineteenth-century French writers such as Verlaine and Huysmans, along with such of their English disciples as Pater and Wilde, who are rebelling at the limitations of bourgeois aesthetics and seeking to go beyond them. What seems to have happened to Lovecraft is that during the period 1919–21 he read a number of writers and thinkers who influenced him profoundly—Haeckel, Wilde, Freud—and so belatedly entered the twentieth century. He began to see that his old-time classicism was no longer viable; as he writes in "Rudis Indigestaque Moles" (1923): "Do our members realise that the progress of science within the last half-century has introduced conceptions of man, the world, and the universe which make hollow and ridiculous an appreciable proportion of all the great literature of the past? Art, to be great, must be founded on human emotions of much strength; such as come from warm instincts and firm beliefs. Science having so greatly altered our view of the universe and the beliefs attendant upon that view, we are now confronted by an important shifting of values in every branch of art where belief is concerned." The advances of modern science (notably psychology, physics, and biology) have made many older aesthetic attitudes untenable; and a selective adoption of Decadence was, for Lovecraft, actually a means for *preserving* (or, as he might have said, conserving) as much of the past as possible. Some things, of course, would have to go: the didactic principle, so essential to classical aesthetics, was in truth never espoused by Lovecraft and, under the influence of Wilde (see "Ars Gratia Artis"), definitively dispensed with. Even such things as unity and restraint would require modification: "What is art but a matter of impressions, of pictures, emotions, and symmetrical sensations? It must have poignancy and beauty, but nothing else counts. It may or may not have coherence" ("In the Editor's Study"). But note how quickly Lovecraft points out that he "is no convert to Dadaism." Lovecraft's Decadence, in effect, was his way of showing his scorn for the outmoded aesthetics of the Victorians while at the same time maintaining a distance from the extreme radicals in prose (Joyce, Stein) and verse (Eliot, cummings) whose work he always considered beyond the pale.

Lovecraft's later literary theory is on the whole found in his letters and so is difficult to represent here. Lovecraft in fact ceases to be interested in literary criticism as such and instead turns his attention to broader questions of aesthetics: How to distinguish good art from bad? What is the purpose of art? What is art's relation to human psychology? Lovecraft's answers to these questions take us beyond the scope of this note, but "What Belongs in Verse" (1935) is worth considering in that it provides a hint of the spectacular metamorphosis in Lovecraft's attitude to poetry. It did not, in fact, take long for Lovecraft to recognize that his early verse was shallow and insincere; as he writes to Elizabeth Toldridge (March 8, 1929): "In my metrical novitiate I was, alas, a chronic and inveterate mimic; allowing my antiquarian tendencies to get the better of my abstract poetic feeling. . . . Self-expression as such sank out of sight, and my sole test of excellence was the degree with which I approached the style of Mr. Pope, Dr. Young, Mr. Thomson, Mr. Addison, Mr. Tickell, Mr. Parnell, Dr. Goldsmith, Dr. Johnson, and so on." His verse writing, in other words, was an extension of his antiquarianism. As Lovecraft sloughed off his exclusively classicist mode, he began to realize that the verse of today must be expressed in the language of today; more, that certain issues and subjects "belong essentially to the domains of science, history, administration, and philosophy," so that a poet must decide not only *how* to say what he has to say but *whether* what he has to say is even amenable to verse treatment. Lovecraft practiced what he preached, and his later verse deals with ethereal images and moods whose embodiment could only be poetry, not the philosophical essay or the short story. "Fungi from Yuggoth" redeems all the "eighteenth-century rubbish" he ever wrote.

It is safe to say that Lovecraft's literary criticism will never gain much recognition in its own right. Its value lies rather in helping to chart the wide-ranging evolution of his critical theory and to provide clues as to how that changing critical theory found expression in his creative work. It is hard to imagine the author of "Metrical Regularity" and "The Vers Libre Epidemic" referring in later years to Cabell's *Jurgen* and Joyce's *Ulysses* as "significant contributions to contemporary art," but that he did so is, once again, a tribute to the unflagging flexibility and openness of his mind. That Lovecraft could continue to evolve—intellectually, aesthetically, and personally—at an age when most are settling into fossilized complacency is the most admirable thing about him.

METRICAL REGULARITY

"Deteriores omnes sumus licentia."
—Terence.

Of the various forms of decadence manifest in the poetical art of the present age, none strikes more harshly on our sensibilities than the alarming decline in that harmonious regularity of metre which adorned the poetry of our immediate ancestors.

That metre itself forms an essential part of all true poetry is a principle which not even the assertions of an Aristotle or the pronouncements of a Plato can disestablish. As old a critic as Dionysius of Halicarnassus and as modern a philosopher as Hegel have each affirmed that versification in poetry is not alone a necessary attribute, but the very foundation as well; Hegel, indeed, placing metre above metaphorical imagination as the essence of all poetic creation.

Science can likewise trace the metrical instinct from the very infancy of mankind, or even beyond, to the pre-human age of the apes. Nature is in itself an unending succession of regular impulses. The steady recurrence of the seasons and of the moonlight, the coming and going of the day, the ebb and flow of the tides, the beating of the heart and pulses, the tread of the feet in walking, and countless other phenomena of like regularity, have all combined to inculcate in the human brain a rhythmic sense which is manifest in the most uncultivated, as in the most polished of peoples. Metre, therefore, is no such false artifice as most exponents of radicalism would have us believe, but is instead a natural and inevitable embellishment to poesy, which succeeding ages should develop and refine, rather than maim or destroy.

Like other instincts, the metric sense has taken on different aspects among different races. Savages shew it in its simplest form while dancing to the sound of primitive drums; barbarians display it in their religious and other chantings; civilised peoples utilise it for their formal poetry, either as measured quantity, like that of Greek and Roman verse, or as measured accentual stress, like that of our own English verse. Precision of metre is thus no mere display of meretricious ornament, but a logical evolution from eminently natural sources.

It is the contention of the ultra-modern poet, as enunciated by Mrs. J. W. Renshaw in her recent article on "The Autocracy of Art" (*The Looking Glass* for May), that the truly inspired bard must chant forth his feelings independently of form or language, permitting each changing impulse to alter the rhythm of his lay, and blindly resigning his reason to the "fine frenzy" of his mood. This contention is of course founded upon the assumption that poetry is super-intellectual; the expression of a "soul" which outranks the mind and its precepts. Now while avoiding the impeachment of this dubious theory, we must needs remark, that the laws of Nature cannot so easily be outdistanced. However much true poesy may overtop the produce of the brain, it must still be affected by natural laws, which are universal and inevitable. Wherefore it is possible for the critic to assume the attitude of the scientist, and to perceive the various clearly defined natural forms through which the emotions seek expression. Indeed, we feel even unconsciously the fitness of certain types of metre for certain types of thought, and in perusing a crude or irregular poem are often abruptly repelled by the unwarranted variations made by the bard, either through his ignorance or his perverted taste. We are naturally shocked at the clothing of a grave subject in anapaestic metre, or the treatment of a long and lofty theme in short, choppy lines. This latter defect is what repels us so much from Conington's really scholarly translation of the *Aeneid.*

What the radicals so wantonly disregard in their eccentric performance is unity of thought. Amidst their wildly repeated leaps from one rough metre to another, they ignore the underlying uniformity of each of their poems. Scene may change; atmosphere may vary; yet one poem cannot but carry one definite message, and to suit this ultimate and fundamental message must one metre be selected and sustained. To accommodate the minor inequalities of tone in a poem, one regular metre will amply lend itself to diversity. Our chief, but now annoyingly neglected measure, the heroic couplet, is capable of taking on infinite shades of expression by the right selection and sequence of words, and by the proper placing of the caesura or pause in each line. Dr. Blair, in his 38th lecture, explains and illustrates with admirable perspicuity the importance of the caesura's location in varying the flow of heroic verse. It is also possible to lend variety to a poem by using very judiciously occasional feet of a metre different from that of the body of the work. This is generally done without disturbing the syllabification, and it in no way impairs or obscures the dominant measure.

Most amusing of all the claims of the radical is the assertion that true poetic fervour can never be confined to regular metre; that the wild-eyed, long-haired rider of Pegasus must inflict upon a suffering public in unaltered form the vague conceptions which flit in noble chaos through his exalted soul. While it is perfectly obvious that the hour of rare inspiration must be improved without the hindrance of grammars or rhyming dictionaries, it is no less obvious that the succeeding hour of calmer contemplation may very profitably be devoted to amendment and polishing. The "language of the heart" must be clarified and made intelligible to other hearts, else its purport will forever be confined to its creator. If natural laws of metrical construction be wilfully set aside, the reader's attention will be distracted from the soul of the poem to its uncouth and ill-fitting dress. The more nearly perfect the metre, the less conspicuous its presence; hence if the poet desires supreme consideration for his matter, he should make his verses so smooth that the sense may never be interrupted.

The ill effect of metrical laxity on the younger generation of poets is enormous. These latest suitors of the Muse, not yet sufficiently trained to distinguish between their own artless crudities and the cultivated monstrosities of the educated but radical bard, come to regard with distrust the orthodox critics, and to believe that no grammatical, rhetorical, or metrical skill is necessary to their own development. The result cannot but be a race of churlish, cacophonous hybrids, whose amorphous outcries will waver uncertainly betwixt prose and verse, absorbing the vices of both and the virtues of neither.

When proper consideration shall be taken of the perfect naturalness of polished metre, a wholesome reaction against the present chaos must inevitably occur; so that the few remaining disciples of conservatism and good taste may justly entertain one last, lingering hope of hearing from modern lyres the stately heroics of Pope, the majestic blank verse of Thomson, the terse octosyllabics of Swift, the sonorous quatrains of Gray, and the lively anapaests of Sheridan and Moore.

THE VERS LIBRE EPIDEMIC

The alarming prevalence in contemporary periodicals of "poetry" without shape, wit, or artistic beauty, has caused no little alarm amongst the true friends of verse, and has given rise to the apprehension that the Aonian art has entered upon a definite phase of decadence. It is the belief of *The Conservative,* however, that the situation is more complex and less basically menacing than it appears from superficial indications.

It must be remembered that despite the kinship between human fancy and its mode of expression, there is a sharp distinction betwixt radicalism of thought and ideals, and mere radicalism of form; and that while the most notorious specimens of free verse represent complete chaos both of sense and of structure, the majority of that which gains admission to reputable magazines is decadent only in technique. The poetical fraternity have a new plaything, and all must needs have their hour of sport with it; but the better sort of bards possess too much inherent good taste and sanity to wander too far afield. They will soon be writing real verse by accident, in spite of themselves, for they cannot defeat the natural laws of rhythm in poetical expression. Even now, the work of these poets is replete with occasional reactions to normal rhyme and rational metre. Our fellow-amateur Mrs. Renshaw, a superlatively good poet despite radical theories, has recently composed a piece of apparent vers libre which is really a well-defined iambic composition with variation in the length of the lines. The innate poet has unwittingly triumphed over the radical theorist! We may, then, safely trust to time to bring the really gifted experimenters within the fold again.

The second or wholly erratic school of free poets is that represented by Amy Lowell at her worst; a motley horde of hysterical and half-witted rhapsodists whose basic principle is the recording of their momentary moods and psychopathic phenomena in whatever amorphous and meaningless phrases may come to their tongues or pens at the moment of inspirational (or epileptic) seizure. These pitiful creatures are naturally subdivided into various types and schools, each professing certain "artistic" principles based on the analogy of poetic thought to other aesthetic sources such as form, sound, motion, and colour; but they are fundamentally similar in their utter want of a sense of proportion and of proportionate values. Their complete rejection of the intellectual (an element which they cannot possess to any great extent) is their undoing. Each writes down the sounds or symbols of sounds which drift through his head without the slightest care or knowledge that they may be understood by any other head. The type of impression they receive and record is abnormal, and cannot be transmitted to persons of normal psychology; wherefore there is no true art or even the rudiments of artistic impulse in their effusions. These radicals are animated by mental and emotional processes other than poetic. They are not in any sense poets, and their work, being wholly alien to poetry, cannot be cited as an indication of poetical decadence. It is rather a type of intellectual and aesthetic decadence of which vers libre is only one manifestation. It is the decadence which produces "futurist" music and "cubist" painting and sculpture.

If concrete examples of the two sorts of unmetrical verse—the really poetical and the distinctly abnormal—be needed to illustrate their difference, the reader may compare Richard Aldington's "Inarticulate Grief" (*The Poetry Review*, August, 1916) with the following bit of sober nonsense, written by one of the so-called "Spectrists" without any idea of humour, but found by *The Conservative* in one of the whimsical paragraphs of a New York "colyum conductor"; where its complete ridiculousness and irrationality recommended it for citation. Mr. Aldington is a poet of genuine depth and feeling despite his awkward medium; the reader may judge of the following without aid of critic or commentator:

Her soul was freckled
Like the bald head
Of a jaundiced Jewish banker.
Her fair and featurous face
Writhed like
An Albino boa-constrictor.
She thought she resembled the Mona Lisa.
This demonstrates the futility of thinking.

And the futility of accepting the chronic free "poets" as serious factors in the literary situation today!

THE CASE FOR CLASSICISM

A Reply to Prof. Philip B. McDonald

In another part of this issue Prof. Philip B. McDonald, Chairman of the Department of Private Criticism, presents some views on amateur journalism which well exhibit his firm belief and constructive interest in our modest institution. At the same time, however, he criticises the United's present literary policy in a manner which calls for immediate reply on the part of those who have laboured to establish existing standards.

Prof. McDonald believes, if we are to accept his verdict literally, that amateurdom's attempts to attain a classical level of expression are the result of a misconception of our province. Averse to the thought that we should perfect ourselves in those tasteful modes of utterance which are eternal and universal in the conservative world outside, he urges that our papers descend to a realm of more intimate subjectivity and personality; including, to quote his own words, "more of the human and American".

Not for a moment can this plea be permitted to pass unchallenged, since it is so likely to affect the multitude of crude and youthful writers who need little to discourage them from the pursuit of urbane scholarship. But in challenging it, one need not impugn in any way the contention that informal and subjective expression is desirable or even necessary in amateurdom. It will be sufficient to insist that such expression belongs solely to the epistolary branch of our activities, leaving our printed publications free for more ambitious experiments in the formation of a real style and a real kinship with standard literature.

The local, intimate, and subjective phase of amateurdom is without a doubt far greater than a member so recent as Prof. McDonald can realise. The correspondence of amateurs, including both personal and circulating letters, is prodigious; and the ever-multiplying array of manuscript magazines and epistolary groups is increasing this informal contact immensely. Members with similar interests or intellectual processes are being banded together in circles like the "Kleicomolo" described in the March *United Amateur;* and it may be safely said that our thoughts, feelings, and individual reactions to literature and events are pretty generally shared without the necessity of dragging them into print.

Turning now to our regular publications, it must be emphasised that their purpose is not to replace chit-chat or correspondence, but to give publicity to our finished literary products. In our cultural development we must differentiate betwixt processes and results. The subjectivity of our correspondence rightly exemplifies our processes of digesting literature; but the objectivity of our published work exemplifies, also rightly, our results in producing literature of our own, be it ever so humble. In that literature we have not only the right but the obligation to strive for the best style, and emulate the best authors, within our scope of reading; even though our work must necessarily resemble more or less that of professionals. And why, indeed, should Prof. McDonald deem it so vast a crime for us to parallel standard books and periodicals? Are we, as he fancies, trying to compete with them, merely because we employ them as models? We must needs wonder whether Prof. McDonald realises the immeasurably closer sympathy one can attain with the standard authors and their thoughts, by sedulously following in their footsteps. This keener comprehension of good literature is alone sufficient to justify the experiments of the tyro in conventional expression. Our avowed object is to give the novice training and experience in authorship. Is it not then an occasion for satisfaction rather than for sorrow, that our members should adopt the style of the best authors? Any other course would inevitably result in the acquisition of a vague, objectionable, and irremediably vicious style. By training the novice exclusively in informal subjectivity, we should ruin his ability to write with force, correctness, and dignity. There are many living examples, surviving from cruder ages of amateurdom, to prove this contention.

Another aspect of Prof. McDonald's scholastic thought is revealed in a more incidental way by his article. This is his attitude toward general literature; as evinced by his cautious disparagement of mellowed, broadly representative books, in favour of modern, locally American, and potentially ephemeral writings. He seems to typify the spirit recently referred to by President Faunce of Brown University, who declared that most of us are "too desperately contemporary".

It is not my purpose here to engage in any extensive battle of ancient and modern books, such as that fought in Saint-James's Library and veraciously chronicled by Dean Swift; but I cannot refrain from insisting on the permanent paramountcy of classical literature as opposed to the superficial productions of this disturbed and degenerate age. The literary genius of Greece and Rome, developed under peculiarly favourable circumstances, may fairly be said to have completed the art and science of expression. Unhurried and profound, the classical author achieved a standard of simplicity, moderation, and elegance of taste, which all succeeding time has been powerless to excel or even to equal. Indeed, those modern periods have been most cultivated, in which the models of antiquity have been most faithfully followed. When Prof. McDonald rather proudly points to certain recent great rhetoricians as apparently uninfluenced by the classics, he forgets that the models which they did adopt were indeed strongly influenced by those selfsame classics. Be it directly, as in the case of Mr. Burke, or indirectly, as in the case of Mr. Wilson, classicism is ever the moulder of effective rhetoric.

Prof. McDonald's plea for a more local American flavour in amateur writing, though sustained by an utterance of the eternally quoted Emerson, is in reality an appeal for a rather pernicious provincialism. Not that it is less the patriotic duty of the local writer to immortalise his native place in literature; but that it is undesirable to encourage the growth of dialectic and stylistic variants from the general type which possesses so long and so illustrious an ancestry. Breadth, not narrowness, is the great cultural desideratum. Prof. McDonald's view reminds me of that of a young amateur journalist of five years ago; who complained because two of our members, one in Massachusetts and the other in California, wrote alike—thus disregarding possible opportunities for "local colour" in expression.

As to the applicability of a classical style to present needs, I think no branch of thought today would be the worse for expression in the clear rhetoric of better times. In fact, I cannot but believe that such a course would help greatly to weed out unworthy and unsubstantial things in contemporary life. We moderns have overreached ourselves, and are blundering along with a dislocated sense of values amidst a bustle of heavy trivialities and false emotions which find reflection in the vague, hectic, hurried, and impressionistic language of decadence. Translation of our thoughts into the clear-cut, rational phrases of classicism might help to reveal the flimsy fatuity of most of the innovations we so blindly worship.

The assertion of Prof. McDonald that the classical style is too restrained, and lacking in humanity, seems to me scarcely supported by evidence. The vital eloquence of the classics cannot be disputed; and if there be any restraint in their language, it is but for the purpose of strengthening their ultimate effect. Compare, for example, the simple force of Graeco-Roman writing, with the florid emptiness of Oriental effusions. So far as restraint goes, a malicious commentator might easily use Prof. McDonald's own bare and staccato prose style as an illustration of inconsistency betwixt precept and practice. The first thing one remarks on reading his frigid "Engineering English" is its laconic atmosphere of aloofness from vivid feeling and from love of pure harmonic beauty. Noting the rhetorical correctness and literary background possessed by Prof. McDonald, one cannot but wish that he might add to his work the crowning graces of classical fluency and moderate ornamentation.

In conclusion, let me express my position in the matter unequivocally. I am an advocate of the highest classical standard in amateur journalism, and shall continue to bend all my energies toward its maintenance. Printed papers are not suitable repositories for loose informality, nor are the hasty and ill-formed writings of today models for emulation. Should the subject receive further discussion in the amateur press, I should be gratified. Meanwhile I may humbly say to my learned adversary,

"Maxime, si tu vis, cupio contendere tecum."

LITERARY COMPOSITION

In a former article our readers have been shewn the fundamental sources of literary inspiration, and the leading prerequisites to expression. It remains to furnish hints concerning expression itself—its forms, customs, and technicalities—in order that the young writer may lose nothing of force or charm in presenting his ideas to the public.

Grammar

A review of the elements of English grammar would be foreign to the purpose of this department. The subject is one taught in all common schools, and may be presumed to be understood by every aspirant to authorship. It is necessary, however, to caution the beginner to keep a reliable grammar and dictionary always beside him, that he may avoid in his compositions the frequent errors which imperceptibly corrupt even the purest ordinary speech. As a general rule, it is well to give close critical scrutiny to all colloquial phrases and expressions of doubtful parsing, as well as to all words and usages which have a strained or unfamiliar sound. The human memory is not to be trusted too far, and most minds harbour a considerable number of slight linguistic faults and inelegancies picked up from random discourse or from the pages of newspapers, magazines, and popular modern books.

Types of Mistakes

Most of the mistakes of young authors, aside from those gross violations of syntax which ordinary education corrects, may perhaps be enumerated as follows.

(1) Erroneous plurals of nouns, as *vallies* or *echos.*
(2) Barbarous compound nouns, as *viewpoint* or *upkeep.*
(3) Want of correspondence in number between noun and verb where the two are widely separated or the construction involved.
(4) Ambiguous use of pronouns.

(5) Erroneous case of pronouns, as *whom* for *who,* and vice versa, or phrases like "between you and *I*", or "Let *we* who are loyal, act promptly".
(6) Erroneous use of *shall* and *will,* and of other auxiliary verbs.
(7) Use of intransitive for transitive verbs, as "he *was graduated* from college", or vice versa, as "he *ingratiated* with the tyrant".
(8) Use of nouns for verbs, as "he *motored* to Boston", or "he *voiced* a protest".
(9) Errors in moods and tenses of verbs, as "If I *was* he, I should do otherwise", or "He said the earth *was* round".
(10) The split infinitive, as "*to* calmly *glide*".
(11) The erroneous perfect infinitive, as "Last week I expected *to have met* you".
(12) False verb-forms, as "I *pled* with him".
(13) Use of *like* for *as,* as "I strive to write *like* Pope writes".
(14) Misuse of prepositions, as "The gift was bestowed *to* an unworthy object", or "The gold was divided *between* the five men".
(15) The superfluous conjunction, as "I wish *for* you to do this".
(16) Use of words in wrong senses, as "The book greatly *intrigued* me", "*Leave* me take this", "He was *obsessed* with the idea", or "He is a *meticulous* writer".
(17) Erroneous use of non-Anglicised foreign terms, as "a strange *phenomena*", or "two *stratas* of clouds".
(18) Use of false or unauthorised words, as *burglarise* or *supremest.*
(19) Errors of taste, including vulgarisms, pompousness, repetition, vagueness, ambiguousness, colloquialism, bathos, bombast, pleonasm, tautology, harshness, mixed metaphor, and every sort of rhetorical awkwardness.
(20) Errors of spelling and punctuation, and confusion of forms such as that which leads many to place an apostrophe in the possessive pronoun *its.*

Of all blunders, there is hardly one which might not be avoided through diligent study of simple textbooks on grammar and rhetoric, intelligent perusal of the best authors, and care and forethought in composition. Almost no excuse exists for their persistent occurrence, since the sources of correction are so numerous and so available. Many of the popular manuals of good English are extremely useful, especially to persons whose reading is not as yet extensive; but such works sometimes err in being too pedantically precise and formal. For correct writing, the cultivation of patience and mental accuracy is essential. Throughout the young author's period of apprenticeship, he must keep reliable dictionaries and text-books at his elbow, eschewing as far as possible that hasty extemporaneous manner of writing which is the privilege of more advanced students. He must take no popular usage for granted, nor must he ever hesitate, in case of doubt, to fall back on the authority of his books.

Reading

No aspiring author should content himself with a mere acquisition of technical details. As Mrs. Renshaw remarked in the preceding article, "Impression should ever precede and be stronger than expression." All attempts at gaining literary polish must begin with judicious *reading*, and the learner must never cease to hold this phase uppermost. In many cases, the usage of good authors will be found a more effective guide than any amount of precept. A page of Addison or of Irving will teach more of style than a whole manual of rules, whilst a story of Poe's will impress upon the mind a more vivid notion of powerful and correct description and narration than will ten dry chapters of a bulky text-book. Let every student read unceasingly the best writers, guided by the admirable Reading Table which has adorned the *United Amateur* during the past two years.

It is also important that cheaper types of reading, if hitherto followed, be dropped. Popular magazines inculcate a careless and deplorable style which is hard to unlearn, and which impedes the acquisition of a purer style. If such things must be read, let them be skimmed over as lightly as possible. An excellent habit to cultivate is the analytical study of the King James Bible. For simple yet rich and forceful English, this masterly production is hard to equal; and even though its Saxon vocabulary and poetic rhythm be unsuited to general composition, it is an invaluable model for writers on quaint or imaginative themes. Lord Dunsany, perhaps the greatest living prose artist, derived nearly all of his stylistic tendencies from the Scriptures; and the contemporary critic Boyd points out very acutely the loss sustained by most Catholic Irish writers through their unfamiliarity with the historic volume and its traditions.

Vocabulary

One superlatively important effect of wide reading is the enlargement of vocabulary which always accompanies it. The average student is gravely impeded by the narrow range of words from which he must choose, and he soon discovers that in long compositions he cannot avoid monotony. In reading, the novice should note the varied mode of expression practiced by good authors, and should keep in his mind for future use the many appropriate synonyms he encounters. Never should an unfamiliar word be passed over without elucidation; for with a little conscientious research we may each day add to our conquests in the realm of philology, and become more and more ready for graceful independent expression.

But in enlarging the vocabulary, we must beware lest we misuse our new possessions. We must remember that there are fine distinctions betwixt apparently similar words, and that language must ever be selected with intelligent care. As the learned Dr. Blair points out in his Lectures, "Hardly in any language are there two words that convey precisely the same idea; a person thoroughly conversant in the propriety of language will always be able to observe something that distinguishes them."

Elemental Phases

Before considering the various formal classes of composition, it is well to note certain elements common to them all. Upon analysis, every piece of writing will be found to contain one or more of the following basic principles: *Description,* or an account of the appearance of things; *Narration,* or an account of the actions of things; *Exposition,* which defines and explains with precision and lucidity; *Argument,* which discovers truth and rejects error; and *Persuasion,* which urges to certain thoughts or acts. The first two are the bases of fiction; the third didactic, scientific, historical, and editorial writings. The fourth and fifth are mostly employed in conjunction with the third, in scientific, philosophical, and partisan literature. All these principles, however, are usually mingled with one another. The work of fiction may have its scientific, historical, or argumentative side; whilst the text-book or treatise may be embellished with descriptions and anecdotes.

Description

Description, in order to be effective, calls upon two mental qualities; observation and discrimination. Many descriptions depend for their vividness upon the accurate reproduction of details; others upon the judicious selection of salient, typical, or significant points.

One cannot be too careful in the selection of adjectives for descriptions. Words or compounds which describe precisely, and which convey exactly the right suggestions to the mind of the reader, are essential. As an example, let us consider the following list of epithets applicable to a *fountain,* taken from Richard Green Parker's admirable work on composition.

> Crystal, gushing, rustling, silver, gently-gliding, parting, pearly, weeping, bubbling, gurgling, chiding, clear, grass-fringed, moss-fringed, pebble-paved, verdant, sacred, grass-margined, moss-margined, trickling, soft, dew-sprinkled, fast-flowing, delicate, delicious, clean, straggling, dancing, vaulting, deep-embosomed, leaping, murmuring, muttering, whispering, prattling, twaddling, swelling, sweet-rolling, gently-flowing, rising, sparkling, flowing, frothy, dew-distilling, dew-born, exhaustless, inexhaustible, never-

decreasing, never-falling, heaven-born, earth-born, deep-divulging, drought-dispelling, thirst-allaying, refreshing, soul-refreshing, earth-refreshing, laving, lavish, plant-nourishing.

For the purposes of securing epithets at once accurate and felicitous, the young author should familiarise himself thoroughly with the general aspect and phenomena of Nature, as well as with the ideas and associations which these things produce in the human mind.

Descriptions may be of objects, of places, of animals, and of persons. The complete description of an object may be said to consist of the following elements:

1. When, where, and how seen; when made or found; how affected by time.
2. History and traditional associations.
3. Substance and manner of origin.
4. Size, shape, and appearance.
5. Analogies with similar objects.
6. Sensations produced by contemplating it.
7. Its purpose or function.
8. Its effects—the results of its existence.

Descriptions of places must of course vary with the type of the place. Of natural scenery, the following elements are notable:

1. How beheld—at dawn, noon, evening, or night; by starlight or moonlight.
2. Natural features—flat or hilly; barren or thickly grown; kind of vegetation; trees, mountains, and rivers.
3. Works of man—cultivation, edifices, bridges, modifications of scenery produced by man.
4. Inhabitants and other forms of animal life.
5. Local customs and traditions.
6. Sounds—of water; forest; leaves; birds; barnyards; human beings; machinery.
7. View—prospect on every side, and the place itself as seen from afar.
8. Analogies to other scenes, especially famous scenes.
9. History and associations.
10. Sensations produced by contemplating it.

Descriptions of animals may be analysed thus:

1. Species and size.
2. Covering.
3. Parts.

4. Abode.
5. Characteristics and habits.
6. Food.
7. Utility or harmfulness.
8. History and associations.

Descriptions of persons can be infinitely varied. Sometimes a single felicitous touch brings out the whole type and character, as when the modern author Leonard Merrick hints at shabby gentility by mentioning the combination of a frock coat with the trousers of a tweed suit. Suggestion is very powerful in this field, especially when mental qualities are to be delineated. Treatment should vary with the author's object; whether to portray a mere personified idea, or to give a quasi-photographic view, mental and physical, of some vividly living character. In a general description, the following elements may be found:

1. Appearance, stature, complexion, proportions, features.
2. Most conspicuous feature.
3. Expression.
4. Grace or ugliness.
5. Attire—nature, taste, quality.
6. Habits, attainments, graces, or awkwardnesses.
7. Character—moral and intellectual; place in the community.
8. Notable special qualities.

In considering the preceding synopses, the reader must remember that they are only suggestions, and not for *literal* use. The extent of any description is to be determined by its place in the composition; by taste and fitness. It should be added, that in fiction description must not be carried to excess. A plethora of it leads to dulness, so that it must ever be balanced by a brisk flow of *Narration*, which we are about to consider.

Narration

Narration is an account of action, or of successive events, either real or imagined; and is therefore the basis both of history and of fiction. To be felicitous and successful, it demands an intelligent exercise of taste and discrimination; salient points must be selected, and the order of time and of circumstances must be well maintained. It is deemed wisest in most cases to give narratives a climactic form; leading from lesser to greater events, and culminating in that chief incident upon which the story is primarily founded, or which makes the other parts important through its own importance. This principle, of course, cannot be literally followed in all historical and biographical narratives.

Fictional Narration

The essential point of fictional narration is *plot*, which may be defined as a *sequence of incidents designed to awaken the reader's interest and curiosity as to the result.* Plots may be simple or complex; but suspense, and climactic progress from one incident to another, are essential. Every incident in a fictional work should have some bearing on the climax or denouement, and any denouement which is not the inevitable result of the preceding incidents is awkward and unliterary. No formal course in fiction-writing can equal a close and observant perusal of the stories of Edgar Allan Poe or Ambrose Bierce. In these masterpieces one may find that unbroken sequence and linkage of incident and result which mark the ideal tale. Observe how, in "The Fall of the House of Usher", each separate event foreshadows and leads up to the tremendous catastrophe and its hideous suggestion. Poe was an absolute master of the mechanics of his craft. Observe also how Bierce can attain the most stirring denouements from a few simple happenings; denouements which develop purely from these preceding circumstances.

In fictional narration, verisimilitude is absolutely essential. A story must be consistent and must contain no event glaringly removed from the usual order of things, unless that event is the main incident, and is approached with the most careful preparation. In real life, odd and erratic things do occasionally happen; but they are out of place in an ordinary story, since fiction is a sort of idealisation of the average. Development should be as life-like as possible, and a weak, trickling conclusion should be assiduously avoided. The end of a story must be stronger rather than weaker than the beginning; since it is the end which contains the denouement or culmination, and which will leave the strongest impression upon the reader. It would not be amiss for the novice to write the last paragraph of his story first, once a synopsis of the plot has been carefully prepared—as it always should be. In this way he will be able to concentrate his freshest mental vigour upon the most important part of his narrative; and if any changes are later found needful, they can easily be made. In no part of a narrative should a grand or emphatic thought or passage be followed by one of tame or prosaic quality. This is *anticlimax*, and exposes a writer to much ridicule. Notice the absurd effect of the following couplet—which was, however, written by no less a person than Waller:

> "Under the tropic is our language spoke,
> *And part of Flanders hath receiv'd our yoke.*"

Unity, Mass, Coherence

In developing a theme, whether descriptive or narrative, it is necessary that three structural qualities be present: Unity, Mass, and Coherence. Unity is that principle whereby every part of a composition must have some bearing on the central theme. It is the principle which excludes all extraneous matter, and demands that all threads converge toward the climax. Classical violations of Unity may be found in the *episodes* of Homer and other epic poets of antiquity, as well as in the digressions of Fielding and other celebrated novelists; but no beginner should venture to emulate such liberties. Unity is the quality we have lately noted and praised in Poe and Bierce.

Mass is that principle which requires the more important parts of a composition to occupy correspondingly important places in the whole composition, the paragraph, and the sentence. It is that law of taste which insists that emphasis be placed where emphasis is due, and is most strikingly embodied in the previously mentioned necessity for an emphatic ending. According to this law, the end of a composition is its most important part, with the beginning next in importance.

Coherence is that principle which groups related parts together and keeps unrelated parts removed from one another. It applies, like Mass, to the whole composition, the paragraph, or the sentence. It demands that kindred events be narrated without interruption, effect following cause in a steady flow.

Forms of Composition

Few writers succeed equally in all the various branches of literature. Each type of thought has its own particular form of expression, based on natural appropriateness; and the average author tends to settle into that form which best fits his particular personality. Many, however, follow more than one form; and some writers change from one form to another as advancing years produce alterations in their mental processes or points of view.

It is well, in the interests of breadth and discipline, for the beginner to exercise himself to some degree in every form of literary art. He may thus discover that which best fits his mind, and develop hitherto unsuspected potentialities.

We have so far surveyed only those simpler phases of writing which centre in prose fiction and descriptive essays. Hereafter we hope to touch upon didactic, argumentative, and persuasive writing; to investigate to some extent the sources of rhetorical strength and elegance; and to consider a few major aspects of versification.

ARS GRATIA ARTIS

Amongst the lessons which *The Conservative* has learnt since his advent to the United, is the folly of judging an artist by his subject-matter and spirit. To maintain at all times the proper distinction betwixt art and the field of philosophy and ethics is an accomplishment to be acquired only by degrees, but one which stamps its possessor as having passed a definite milestone on the road to a truly civilised attitude. It is not the sluggish bourgeois mind which can endorse sincerely the dictum of Oscar Wilde, that "No artist is ever morbid. The artist can express everything."

That many of our members have so far failed to reach this important milestone is unfortunately demonstrated by a multitude of stupid moralisings on the part of amateur critics; moralisings almost as stupid as those of *The Conservative* himself in other days. Sometimes they rise to heights of absurdity which almost redeem them as pieces of unconscious burlesque, as when a certain gentleman lectured Mr. Samuel Loveman on his sombre poetry. At other times, when their object is less brilliant, they are themselves merely dull; as when a well-meaning reformer lectures *The Conservative* on some weird stories, which were declared to "pollute the pages on which they appear". But always they are discouraging in the mental immaturity they imply, and ominous in their revelation of the natural narrowness of mankind.

Until the progress of civilisation shall have become impossibly complete, we shall never fail to be bored by Boeotian condemnations of sincere art as "gloomy", "morbid", or "unhealthy", as the case may be. The epithets will continue to be hurled about with zeal and blindness as long as sleepy critics persist in judging art as something made to order on a false and conventional pattern for the uplift and amusement of the rabble, instead of something purely in the nature of portrayal and self-expression. Would that the proper teacher might inculcate in the minds of such critics some sentences of Wilde on the subject of "healthiness":

> "From the point of view of style a healthy work of art is one whose style recognises the beauty of the material it employs, be that material one of words or of bronze, of colour or of ivory; and uses that beauty as a factor in producing the aesthetic effect. From the point of view of subject, a healthy work of art is one the choice of whose subject is conditioned by the temperament of the artist, and comes directly out of it. . . . An unhealthy work of art, on the other hand, is a work whose style is obvious, old-fashioned, and common; and whose subject is deliberately chosen not because the artist has any pleasure in it, but because he thinks that the public will pay him for it."

THE POETRY OF LILIAN MIDDLETON

Assuming that conditions in amateur journalism duplicate in miniature those of the general literary world, there is significance in the consistent conservatism of its foremost figures. Art, after all, is founded on the unchanging qualities and fundamental experiences of mankind; and despite the occasional adoption of novel phases is always most genuine when it adheres most closely to the normal tradition. Nowhere is this truer than in the poetic field, where we find normality and rational aesthetic proportion in almost every truly dominant artist. Of amateurdom's three preëminently notable poets of the last decade, Samuel Loveman, Winifred Virginia Jackson, and "Lilian Middleton", not one is lacking in that sense of symmetry, relativity, fulness, and structural harmony which constitutes true conservatism. Impressionism, if ever occurring in these bards, is present only so far as it is an accurate reflection of Nature. Of "imagism", the abnormal expression of partial and non-rational perception, there is hardly a trace.

Samuel Loveman has for nearly twenty years symbolised the high-water mark of amateur art. Winifred V. Jackson, entering amateurdom in 1915, has recently received the acclamation of the larger literary sphere as one of America's new poets of genius. This article will attempt to survey the merits of "Lilian Middleton", former United Laureate, whose increasing array of excellent verse has assured her a place of eminence beside the two just mentioned.

S. Lilian Middleton-McMullen, whose works are now distinguished by publication in poetry magazines all over the country, is a discovery of Winifred V. Jackson's, and an added plume in the cap of that noted poetess. She is a native of Ireland, of a loyal British Unionist family, and inherits a trace of French blood through a great-grandmother. In her heredity there is a definitely artistic element, as shewn by the fact that both her mother and sister are poets of no mean skill.

Mrs. McMullen was educated in English private schools, and originally specialised in music; being a violoncellist and pianiste of great ability, and to some extent a composer. At an early age she was given to the writing of verse, but these older specimens are notable only for grace and correctness. Amateurdom has seen two of them—"Late Autumn" in *The Tryout*, and "The 'Cellist" in *The United Co-operative*. They are, quite obviously, *juvenilia;* though of unusual merit for such work.

Not until after Mrs. McMullen's removal to the United States and acquaintance with Miss Jackson was her later and richer poetic vein uncovered. In 1918, at Miss Jackson's suggestion, she wrote as a credential to the United the poem "My Mistress—Music", which excited such favourable notice in manuscript that it was at once featured in *The United Amateur*. Critical comment was unanimously approving, for it was clear that amateurdom had at last acquired another real singer—one with that distinct individuality and felicity which make true art. The rest we know, for the partial pseudonym of "Lilian Middleton" has since become associated with one of the most poignant and beautiful elements in our literature.

The poetry of Mrs. McMullen, like all authentic art, possesses qualities of individuality which can be isolated and defined only by close analysis. Lesser writers may have *mannerisms*—affectations of form put on or put off at will—but only real artists can have *style;* that subtle and unmistakable uniqueness of expression which never comes save as the result of an absolute originality of perception, appraisal, and comparison. Style Mrs. McMullen has in abundance, and style of so piquant and truly lyrical a nature that a foreigner might derive pleasure from the cadence of her verses without understanding their purport. Much of this lyrism is certainly due to her intelligent musical education, but that factor is not enough to account for the *curiosa felicitas* whereby all harsh effects are instinctively rejected, and all lines modulated with a Tennysonian liquidity quite uncommon in amateurdom. To achieve such results one must have an innate lyrical genius; a sensitiveness to beauty of spoken sound as connected with beauty of imagery which a purely musical training can hardly supply in full.

Mrs. McMullen's inspiration is gratifyingly free from the taint of modernism, whether in the sense of imagistic affiliations, unpoetic realism, or sloppy emotional waste. Her lyrics, perhaps influenced by some Celtic heritage, are things of infinite daintiness and witchery; often homely and familiar in theme, but invariably raised above the commonplace by the piquant originality of treatment and masterly refinement of rhythm. Original genius, it may incidentally be remarked, is found quite as often in method as in subject-matter; so that in judging a simple *genre* poem one must not cavil till he has investigated the kind of fancy animating the various images. Only if this fancy be commonplace, will condemnation be justified. Mrs. McMullen gives to a simple scene or sentiment that indefinable charm and faery glamour which belong to genius, as the moonlight gives charm and glamour to a landscape which by day is prosaic and undistinguished.

With literary sources as varied as Chaucer, Browning, Tennyson, and Austin Dobson—to name a few—Mrs. McMullen has evolved an original style whose keynotes are exquisite lightness and buoyancy, quaint delicacy, and gentle pathos. She has, perhaps unconsciously as yet, a daintily coloured vision of life in its true proportions; for even in writing from the conventional point of view she glimpses the world's absence of substance—the need to retreat into the more tenuous upper regions of the fancy to escape pain and sordidness, and the underlying sadness which pursues one even to that ethereal haven. This apparent preoccupation with externals should not be judged as shallowness, but rather as a mark of aesthetic soundness in conformity with the truth emphasised by Schopenhauer, that the world is *beautiful as an object but ugly as a source of experience.*

The variety of Mrs. McMullen's work is considerable; ranging from Dresden-china bits of *vers de société* and Gallic ballades, triolets and villanelles about Watteau shepherdesses, to serious pieces of greater length, imagination, and wistfulness. Her song-poetry, which includes some delectable child verse, has already found favour with composers and publishers; while her occasional departures into the realm of the sombre are, though not equal to her lighter productions, by no means infelicitous. Mrs. McMullen's Muse is still in a state of active growth, so that it will not do to impose too rigid a classification upon her art at this juncture.

It is illuminating to glance at some typical McMullen poems with an eye for their peculiar beauties. In sheer exuberance of sprightly melody and whimsicality, the Parisian trifle "Dans la Rue" is rich. A stanza or two illustrates how much piquancy can be extracted from the sheerest material:

How I love you, Petite,
  With your gay little air,
As you pass down the street!

I shall hasten!—*toute suite*
  You will hear me declare
How I love you, Petite,
As you pass down the street!

France is in Mrs. McMullen's blood, and appears deliciously in occasional French phrases and subjects. Note such vivacious stanzas as the following, taken from the poem "Petit à Petit, L'Oiseau Fait Son Nid":

Specimen page from Lovecraft's UAPA journal, The Conservative

THE CONSERVATIVE

Edited by H. P. Lovecraft

Vol. II. PROVIDENCE, R. I., OCTOBER, 1916. No. III.

THE MOCKING BIRD

When Southern moonlight softly falls,
  When Day has died and stars unfold,
From jasmine-scented groves—Oh, Love!
  A Mocking-bird with Lyre of Gold!

All of your tears, all of your sighs;
  All of Life's joys that thrill you through;
God's benediction and His love—
  Are speaking in those notes to you.

All that you long'd and meant to be;
  Your pray'rs, your dreams—(Oh, earthly bars!)
Are mounting, mounting, with that voice,
  Straight up God's stairway to the stars!

—OLIVE G. OWEN

OLD ENGLAND AND THE "HYPHEN"

By H. P. LOVECRAFT

Of the various intentional fallacies exhaled like miasmic vapours from the rotting cosmopolitanism of vitiated American politics, and doubly rife during these days of European conflict, none is more disgusting than that contemptible subterfuge of certain foreign elements whereby the legitimate zeal of the genuine native stock for England's cause is denounced and compared to the unpatriotic disaffection of those working in behalf of England's enemies. The Prussian propagandists and Irish irresponsibles, failing in their clumsy efforts to use the United States as a tool of vengeance upon the Mistress of the Seas, have seized with ingenious and unexpected eagerness on a current slogan coined to counteract their own traitorous machinations, and have begun to fling the trite demand "America first" in the face of every American who is unable to share their puerile hatred of the British Empire. In demanding that American citizens impartially withhold love and allegiance from any government save their own, thereby binding themselves to a policy of rigid coldness in considering the fortunes of their Mother Country, the Prusso-Hibernian herd have the sole apparent advantage of outward technical justification. If the United States were truly the radical, aloof, mongrelised nation into which they idealise it, their plea might possibly be more appropriate. But in comparing the lingering loyalty of a German-American for Germany, or of an Irish-American for Ireland, with that of a native American for England, these politicians make their fundamental psychological error.

England, despite the contentions of trifling theorists, is not and never will be a really foreign country; nor is a true love of America possible without a corresponding love for the British race and ideals that created America. The difficulties which caused the severance of the American Colonies from the rest of the Empire were essentially internal ones, and have no moral bearing on this country's attitude toward the parent land in its relations with alien civilisations. Just as Robert Edward Lee chose to follow the government of Virginia rather than that of the Federal Union in 1861, so did the Anglo-American Revolutionary leaders choose local to central allegiance in 1775. Their rebellion was in itself a characteristically English act, and could in no manner annul the purely English origin and nature of the new republic. American history before the conflict of 1775-1783 is English history, and we are lawful heirs of the unnumbered glories of the Saxon line. Shakespeare and Milton, Dryden and Pope, Young and Thomson, Johnson and Goldsmith, are our own poets; William the Conqueror, Edward the Black Prince, Elizabeth, and William of Nassau are our own royalty; Crecy, Poictiers, and Agincourt are our own victories; Lord Bacon, Sir Isaac Newton, Hobbes, Locke, Sir Robert Boyle, and Sir William Herschel are our own philosophers and scientists; what true American lives, who would wish, by rejecting an Englishman's heritage, to despoil his country of such racial laurels? Let those men be silent, who would, in envy, deny to the

The United Co-operative

Vol. 1 April 1921 No. 3

"PETIT A PETIT, L'OISEAU FAIT SON NID!"

By Lillian Middleton

My Breton maid that dwells beside the Rance,
Your snowy breast contains a heart e'en colder
Than any snow that ever fell o'er France!
Altho' I grow each day a trifle bolder,
You smile secure! But listen, hark to me,
"*Petit a petit, l'oiseau fait son nid!*"

'Tis many months since first I saw you smile,
(The dullest day your sunny smile would hallow!)
Tout transporte, I stood and watched you, while
Vite comme le vent, you pass'd me at St. Malo;
One flashing glance from sloe-black eyes, *Petite*,
And, *tout a coup*, my heart was at your feet!

Each day I come with burning words of love,
You listen to me, yes, yet scarcely heeding
You reach where honey-suckle hangs above
Our heads, and turn a deaf ear to my pleading!
But some day you will listen, *ma cherie*,
"*Petit a petit, l'oiseau fait son nid!*"

But still, methinks, last eve ere set of sun
A flush o'erspread your brow; the faintest flutter
Disturbed the kerchief at your breast. Did one
Of all the pleading words you heard me utter,
Shake for one instant that *air nonchalant*
And leave you less serene, perhaps?—less strong?

And now 'tis morn, and all your winsome grace
Is gliding slowly o'er the grass to meet me,
But why this new demureness in your face?
And why so tremulous a smile to greet me?
One glance 'neath quiv'ring lids! *Ah! c'est ma vie!*
"*Petit a petit, l'oiseau a fait son nid!*"

The Crawling Chaos

By Elizabeth Berkeley and Lewis Theobald, Jun.

Of the pleasures and pains of opium much has been written. The ecstasies and horrors of De Quincey and the *paradis artificiels* of Baudelaire are preserved and interpreted with an art which makes them immortal, and the world knows well the beauty, the terror and the mystery of those obscure realms into which the inspired dreamer is transported. But much as has been told, no man has yet dared intimate the *nature* of the phantasms thus unfolded to the mind, or hint at the *direction* of the unheard-of roads along whose ornate and exotic course the par-

'Tis many months since first I saw you smile,
  (The dullest day your sunny smile would hallow!)
Tout transporte, I stood and watch'd you, while
  Vite comme le vent, you pass'd me at St. Malo;
One flashing glance from sloe-black eyes, *Petite,*
  And, *tout à coup,* my heart was at your feet!

But it is in other poems—poems with the element of pathos more emphasised—that one finds Mrs. McMullen's fancy at its best. In such verse there is all the distinctiveness which results from viewing the eternal human tragedy through the diminishing-glass of romantic selection, and transfiguring it with the gentle glow of music, restraint, and a singularly original quaintness. "The Token" is a good sample—telling of how a dweller in "a little house of stone" received a loved one's messages from the evening star that shone in the west across the fields, and how sadness came when a mansion was built and shut out the light of the star. "In My Wee Room" is perhaps even better, giving a picture of a transition from joy to sadness with a few deft touches describing articles of furniture and decoration. "Desirée Logier" is a masterpiece—extremely simple in plot, relating only an idyllic courtship in war-torn France which ended in the weeping of Desirée by the poppied grave of the young Fusilier Dennis O'Toole, it derives from its skilfully breathed atmosphere and inherent music a charm and brooding sadness which scores of more hectic and apparently intense emotional outbursts fail to exhibit. Later fragments of McMullen verse shew the same qualities in even more mature form—the following stanzas are from different poems:

But oh! my meadows are so sweet
  That I must sing when grasses sway—
What matters *now,* that soon my feet
  Shall not pass here on any day?

Out to the west with a full sail
  Eagerly fare the ships,
And into the crest of the white foam
  Lightly the sea-gull dips.
But I would plunge to the gray deeps
  In search of a dead man's lips.

But they say that on the mountain where I've lain among the heather,
  With the plover's note a-mourning thro' the haze of blue,
That the cold and dead are lying in the soft-cheek'd Irish weather,
  And oh! my heart is breaking for the mountain that I knew.

Original appearance of a poem
by Lilian Middleton

The same musical and atmospheric qualities can be found in documents of other moods, among which the gentle domestic affections, sometimes associated with picturesque Irish scenes, hold a large place. "When I Am a Lady, Old and Gray" has won a Laureateship—and deserved it. A few lines will suggest its magic:

I shall smile at things the young folks do,
  And shall counsel give, so kind and wise!
All dress'd in a gown of soft old blue,
  Old blue to match my faded eyes!

"The Fairy-Maiden" has an elfin, elusive quality:

Ah! yes; you may woo me—and win me—enfold me
  But when the dew glistens, and starlight is falling,
  And all the night-voices are whisp'ring—are calling,
Then you never can keep me—you never can hold me!

Childhood has a charm for Mrs. McMullen, as shewn in the quaintly grave long narrative poem "Understanding", the haunting lyric "In the Far Field", and others as yet unpublished. For this subject her lightness of touch fits her preëminently. Of plain amatory verse the bard does not produce a great quantity, but what she does write is of inimitable grace and musical tenderness, as we may see by pieces like "Eventide", whose final stanza reads as follows:

Now up a pathway steep
  Moon mounts the skies—
Dear, let me long and deep
  Drink of your eyes.
Ah! what the bliss to know
Your sweet head pillow'd, so!

The poetry of spiritual revolt—the eternal cry of man at the limitations of Nature—is another phase of the McMullen genius. "In Rein" is familiar to all amateurs. Less so, perhaps, is "The Prisoner", which begins:

My soul would be for ever free
  Of this dull body where it hides!
My body wanders stumblingly
  While light as air my spirit rides!

With these varied samples, it will perhaps be needless to speak in detail of Mrs. McMullen's especial gift for vivid metrical effects. Her mastery of quaint and captivating metres is notable, irregular anapaests being perhaps her favourite form. We see this skill illustrated in many unusual compositions, among them "My Mistress—Music", which is the author's first poem of maturity:

I have a Mistress fair to see,
  But oh! she's fickle as she is fair.
What would you do if you were me?
  Let my passion seem
  But a cherish'd dream
That fades away into thinnest air?

The following is very recent—from a lyric entitled "On the Heart of the Spring":

O! Birdie a-swing
On the heart of the spring,
As you lightsomely hover
And skim o'er the clover,
What a torrent of rapturous, lyrical madness
In a frenzy of turbulent spring-blossom gladness
  You fling!

The individuality of Mrs. McMullen's subtler metrical qualities is infinite—one might point out a delightfully quaint habit of accenting adjectives instead of the nouns they modify, as, for example,

And a *white* bird mounts on a *strong* wing.

That the growth of this unique genius will be eminently interesting to watch, none may dispute. Mrs. McMullen is already a lyrist of the first order—second to none in amateurdom so far as music of phrase, magic of metre, and buoyancy of fancy are concerned—and from the advances she has already made we may predict much. Young in years, replete with studious energy, and having a background of exceptional cultivation, her expanding special reading and increasing experience promise notable results. Philosophy may temper the serenity of her work with a more poignant note of despair, while sophistication may emphasise the hollowness of sentiments now treated as at least presumable actualities. But always there will be an airy and exquisite soaring above the commonplace—a lyrical freshness of mood and repudiation of prosaic, unsubtilised realism.

Mrs. McMullen is fortunate in having an appeal which is popular as well as classical. The professional success of her work, while not affecting her pure artistry of method, will serve as an added assurance of excellence and encouragement to progress. She is, it seems quite certain, among the very few amateurs who are destined for an early and cordial recognition by the general literary world.

RUDIS INDIGESTAQUE MOLES

The Conservative, observing the complacent indifference of most amateurs toward the present state of literature and general aesthetics, hath frequently wondered how acute be their realisation of just what is taking place. The average amateur paper, when it can spare the space from subjects so titanic as politics, conventions, and personalities, is unique in its allegiance to the accepted art and literature of the past; and in its happy oblivion regarding the menaces offered by the present and future. To read such a paper one would gather that Tennyson and Longfellow are still taken seriously as poets, and that the sentiments and sentimentalities of our fathers are still capable of awakening the Muse and forming the basis of future works of art. A protest against this species of myopia was some time ago uttered by one of our ultra-radicals; but lost force because of its origin and form. Perhaps it would not be improper for a *Conservative,* whose sympathy with extreme manifestations is little enough, to call renewed attention to the situation.

Do our members realise that the progress of science within the last half-century has introduced conceptions of man, the world, and the universe which make hollow and ridiculous an appreciable proportion of all the great literature of the past? Art, to be great, must be founded on human emotions of much strength; such as come from warm instincts and firm beliefs. Science having so greatly altered our view of the universe and the beliefs attendant upon that view, we are now confronted by an important shifting of values in every branch of art where belief is concerned. The old heroics, pieties, and sentimentalities are dead amongst the sophisticated; and even some of our appreciations of natural beauty are threatened. Just how expansive is this threat, we do not know, and *The Conservative* hopes fervently that the final devastated area will be comparatively narrow; but in any case startling developments are inevitable.

A glance at the serious magazine discussion of Mr. T. S. Eliot's disjointed and incoherent "poem" called "The Waste Land", in the November *Dial*, should be enough to convince the most unimpressionable of the true state of affairs. We here behold a practically meaningless collection of phrases, learned allusions, quotations, slang, and scraps in general; offered to the public (whether or not as a hoax) as something justified by our modern mind with its recent comprehension of its own chaotic triviality and disorganisation. And we behold that public, or a considerable part of it, receiving this hilarious mélange as something vital and typical; as "a poem of profound significance", to quote its sponsors.

To reduce the situation to its baldest terms, man has suddenly discovered that all his high sentiments, values, and aspirations are mere illusions caused by physiological processes within himself, and of no significance whatsoever in an infinite and purposeless cosmos. He has discovered that most of his acts spring from hidden causes remote from the ones hitherto honoured by tradition, and that his so-called "soul" is merely (as one critic puts it) a rag-bag of unrelated odds and ends. And having made these discoveries, he does not know what to do about it; but compromises on a literature of analysis, chaos, and ironic contrast.

What will come of it? This we cannot say; but certainly, great alterations are due amongst the informed. European culture has reached the Alexandrian stage of effeteness, and we probably cannot hope for anything better than diverging streams of barren intellectualism and of an amorphous, passionate art founded on primal instincts rather than delicate emotions. The emotions will be minutely analysed and laughed at; the instincts will be glorified and wallowed in. The hope of art, paradoxically enough, lies in the ability of future generations not to be too well informed; to be able, at least, to create certain artificial limitations of consciousness and enjoy a gently whimsical repetition and variation of the traditional images and themes, whose decorative beauty and quaintness can never be wholly negligible to the sensitive taste. It is, for example, hardly possible that moonlight on a marble temple, or twilight in an old garden in spring, can ever be other than beautiful in our eyes. Bourgeois and plebeian literature, of course, will undoubtedly go on without change; for the thoughts of the great majority are rarely affected by the subtleties of progress. The Edgar A. Guests are secure in their unassuming niches. But it is only by the higher strata that we can judge a literature in its historic perspective, so that the permanent residuum of folk or ballad aesthetics does not figure in the problem. Never before, it is interesting to note, have the popular and the sophisticated types of literature been so widely divergent as at the present.

Meanwhile it is singular that so few echoes of the prevailing turbulence should have reached our amateur press. Shall we remain comfortably cloistered with our Milton and Wordsworth, never again to know the amusing buzzing of such quaint irritants as *Les Mouches Fantastiques*? *The Conservative* confesses himself curious to know what other amateur authors and editors think of "The Waste Land" and its bizarre analogues!

IN THE EDITOR'S STUDY

A desperate need of amateurdom today is an enlightened critical standard which shall save us from devotion to false, conventional, and superficial values, and blindness to all that is sincere, vital, penetrating, or genuinely ecstatic in art. The relative rarity of young blood has begun to give us a perilously Philistine bias, so that the path of the uncompromising artist in our midst is much thornier than it should be. These are times when a flash of subtle emotion or a colourful appeal to obscure and fantastic recesses of the imagination is likely to evoke a superior titter if the words sound in the least extravagant or unfamiliar to a mind bred on Dickens or the *Saturday Evening Post.* Good homely common sense, no doubt, but sadly disastrous to amateur literature.

It is time, *The Conservative* believes, definitely to challenge the sterile and exhausted Victorian ideal which blighted Anglo-Saxon culture for three quarters of a century and produced a milky "poetry" of shop-worn sentimentalities and puffy platitudes; a dull-grey prose fiction of misplaced didacticism and insipid artificiality; an appallingly hideous system of formal manners, costume, and decoration; and worst of all, an artistically blasphemous architecture whose uninspired nondescriptness transcends tolerance, comprehension, and profanity alike.

These reflections are elicited by the urbane warfare of Philistine and Grecian so opportunely precipitated by Mr. Michael White's critique of Mr. Samuel Loveman's poetry. Mr. White, taking his stand with the hard-headed and condemning an artist who employs such strange materials as ecstasy or imagination, has naturally aroused the opposition of certain ardent fantaisistes like Mr. Frank Belknap Long, Jun.; whose impressionistic reply appeared in these columns. And now we find Mr. Long the recipient of some priceless comic-supplement sarcasm from the admirers of Mr. White, a typical Boston group to whom New England's Puritan heritage has denied that touch of ethereal madness which makes for the creation and appreciation of universal, fundamental art.

Just what do these mild hostilities signify? Should we after all denounce our Eminent Victorians merely because of their support of the critic who classifies Macaulay, Carlisle (sic), Emerson, and Shaw as "great poets", attributes unique limitations to the word *chorus*, and sits stolid in the beams of imaginative art? Is this protest of humorous, sensible clearness against symbolic, colourful intensity indeed a mark of Victorian obtuseness instead of a sane defence of tradition in the face of chaotic innovation? Certainly the position of Mr. White's circle is flawless if we are to accept art as an affair of the external intellect and commonplace, unanalysed emotions alone. *The Conservative* dissents only because he believes with most of the contemporary world that the actual foundations of art differ widely from those which the prim nineteenth century took for granted.

What is art but a matter of impressions, of pictures, emotions, and symmetrical sensations? It must have poignancy and beauty, but nothing else counts. It may or may not have coherence. If concerned with large externals or simple fancies, or produced in a simple age, it is likely to be of a clear and continuous pattern; but if concerned with individual reactions to life in a complex and analytical age, as most modern art is, it tends to break up into detached transcripts of hidden sensation and offer a loosely joined fabric which demands from the spectator a discriminating duplication of the artist's mood. The Philistine clamour for a literature of plain statement and superficial theme loses force when we assign to literature—especially poetry—its proper place in aesthetics, and compare it to such modes of expression as music and architecture, which do not speak in the language of primers.

The Conservative is no convert to Dadaism. Nothing, on the contrary, seems more certain to him than that the bulk of radical prose and verse represents merely the extravagant extreme of a tendency whose truly artistic application is vastly more limited. Traces of this tendency, whereby pictorial methods are used, and words and images employed without conventional connexions to excite sensations, may be found throughout literature; especially in Keats, William Blake, and the French symbolists. This broader conception of art does not outrage any eternal tradition, but honours all creations of the past or present which can shew genuine ecstatic fire and a glamour not tawdrily founded on utterly commonplace emotions.

Thus the shrill laughter of the thin-blooded literalist at the ecstatic artist is founded mainly on one-sidedness and conventionality of background; the scoffer being nearly always a follower of an obsolete tradition, steeped in the orthodox English literature of the middle nineteenth century rather than immersed in the universal stream which knows neither time nor country. Such a sage, like the proverbial *homo unius libri,* may prove a formidable and witty antagonist; but his parochial limitations obviously unfit him for anything like an authoritative pronouncement on laws touching the entire human spirit. *"Les esprits médiocres,"* says La Rochefoucauld, *"condamnent d'ordinaire tout ce qui passe leur portée."* Before intelligently approaching a work of art a critic must absorb at least the rudiments of the background from which it was developed—which takes us back to the problem of dealing with the Victorian scolding and giggling which bid fair to discourage sincere aesthetic endeavour in amateur journalism.

The Conservative would unassumingly urge a slight course of literary research upon those critics who are hurling the English nineteenth century in our faces with so much gusto, finality, and drollery. Without wishing to emulate their own fetching pageantry of mighty names across the learned page, he would bid them consider such titans as Walter Pater, Lafcadio Hearn, Arthur Symons, Arthur Machen, Wilde, Gautier, Flaubert, Baudelaire, Verlaine, Rimbaud, Mallarmé, Laforgue, D'Annunzio, or Croce—titans about whom much may be learnt even through reviews. Once really aware of the existence of this wider field, and of the extent to which it has influenced contemporary ideas of art, our conscientious Philistines could not but enlarge their horizons of tolerance. How much they might actually understand or sympathise, is a temperamental matter alien to the problem.

THE PROFESSIONAL INCUBUS

It has often been remarked that fiction is the weakest point in amateur literature, and I do not think the belief is a mistaken one. None can deny that we have nothing in the field of the story which may be compared with the poetry of Samuel Loveman, the essays of James F. Morton, Jr., the critical analyses of Edward H. Cole, or the phantasies of Frank Belknap Long, Jr. True, Mrs. Edith Miniter produces work of the highest quality—but unfortunately only the most infinitesimal fraction of this appears in the amateur press. Our loss is the outside world's gain.

The generally assigned cause for our fictional debility is lack of space, and this factor is certainly a potent one. For the adequate development of a story idea, ample room is an absolute essential; and this we are unable to provide for under present financial conditions. But of late I have come to believe that there is another cause; a cause extending very deeply into the composition of the American scene, and affecting us because of our slowness in making a certain distinction. This cause is the hopeless inferiority and inartistry of the entire standard of American bourgeois fiction, and the neglected distinction is that between successful professional fiction and honestly artistic attempts at self-expression in the narrative.

If the object of amateur journalism were to train likely young plodders in the skilled manual labour of professional fiction carpentry, no one might justly protest at the existing condition. But the idea has been held by some that amateurdom is synonymous with aesthetic sincerity, and with the loving craftsmanship for its own sake which is art. If this is so, we are on the wrong track; for there is nothing of art or true merit in the "salable short story" which too often forms the model of our efforts. I do not think any meritorious short story could be sold to an average professional magazine of the popular class except by accident. He who strives to produce salable fiction is lost as an artist, for the conditions of American life have made art impossible in the popular professional field.

Editors and publishers are not to blame. They cater to their public, and would suffer shipwreck if they did not. And even when one transfers the blame to this larger unit, one cannot justly be very savage in his blaming; for analysis shews that most of the trouble is absolutely inevitable—as incapable of human remedy as the fate of any protagonist in the Greek drama. Here in America we have a very conventional and half-educated public—a public trained under one phase or another of the Puritan tradition, and also dulled to aesthetic sensitiveness because of the monotonous and omnipresent overstressing of the ethical element. We have millions who lack intellectual independence, courage, and flexibility to get an artistic thrill out of an original and realistic situation, or to enter sympathetically into a story unless it ignores the colour and vividness of actual human emotion and [. . .] conventionality presents a simple plot based on artificial, ethically sugar-coated values and leading to a flat denouement which vindicates every current platitude and leaves no mystery unexplained by the shallow comprehension of the most mediocre reader.

That is why our professional fiction is unworthy of the emulation of any literary artist. Editors, however, cannot logically be blamed. If any magazine sought and used artistically original types of fiction, it would lose its readers almost to a man. Half the people wouldn't understand what the tales were about, and the other half would find the characters unsympathetic—because these characters would think and act like real persons instead of like the dummies which the American middle classes have been taught and persuaded to consider and accept as human beings. Such is the inevitable condition regarding the enormous bulk of fiction which sets the national standard and determines the type of technical training given all fictional students even in our best universities.

But even this is not all. Added to this, as if by the perversity of a malign fate, is the demand of an overspeeding public for excessive quantity production. Simply put, the American people demand more stories per year than the really artistic authors of America could possibly write. A real artist never works fast except by mood, and never turns out large quantities except by rare chance. He cannot contract to deliver so many words in such and such a time, but must work naturally, gradually, sometimes very slowly, and always as his psychological state determines; utilising favourable states of mind and refraining from putting down the stuff his brain turns out when it is tired or disciplined to such effort. Now this, of course, will not do when there are hundreds of magazines to fill at regular intervals. So many pages per month or week must be filled; and if the artistic writers lag behind, the publishers must find the next-best thing—persons of mere talent, who can learn certain mechanical rules and technical twists, and put forth stuff of external smoothness, whose sole merit is in conforming to patterns and rehashing the situations and reactions which have been found interesting to the people by previous experience. In many cases these writers achieve popularity—because the public recognises the elements that pleased it before, and is satisfied to receive them again in dexterously transposed form. Actually, the typical reader has very little true taste, and judges by absurd freaks, sentimentalities, and analogies. So it has come to be an accepted tradition that American fiction is not an art but a trade—a thing to be learnt by rule by almost anybody, and demanding above all else a complete submergence of one's own personality and thought in the general stream of conventional patterns which correspond to the bleakly uniform view of life forced on us by mediocre leadership. Success therefore comes not to the man of genius, but to the clever fellow who knows how to catch the public point of view and play up to it. Glittering tinsel reputations are built up, and †dumb driven† [. . .] hundreds of otherwise honest and respectable plumbers take correspondence courses to crush their individuality and try to be like these scintillant "great ones" whose achievements are really no more than mere charlatanry.

Such is our fictional situation—indiscriminate hordes of writers, mostly without genius, striving by erroneous methods toward a goal which is erroneous to start with! One sees the thing at its zenith in periodicals like the *Saturday Evening Post*, where men of more or less real talent are weighed down with the freely flung gold which forms the price of their originality and artistic conscience. A fearful incubus—which only a few adroit or daring souls ever shake off. But here in amateurdom there is no gold to weigh us down or buy our conscience. Here, if anywhere, we ought to be able to write for the love of writing and the thrill of aesthetic conquest. Shall we not at least strive to do this, in order that our institution may be a thing of real dignity and value instead of a rather ridiculous caricature of the tawdry professional sphere?

THE OMNIPRESENT PHILISTINE

Amateurdom's progress toward a civilised condition is halting and devious. No sooner do we advance a step, than some obstacle in the shape of glorified mediocrity or aesthetic and philosophical reaction appears to block the path; so that half our energy is spent in brushing away false ideas rather than increasing our store of genuine ideas. It is so in most departments of life, hence need call for no especial resentment among us—but it is none the less provoking.

The past official year has witnessed a depressing revival of obsolete notions and parading of outworn theories of art, as conspicuously exemplified by the anti-Loveman criticisms of last December. We were then informed in the best mid-Victorian manner that classical themes are obsolete, that Poe is reprehensibly "morbid", that Swinburnian paganism is too "blasphemous" for proper use in a decorous Christian country, that verse must not be above the interests and understanding of the "folksy" throng, that poets must protest against the evils of the age—and much more of the same. This precipitated a controversy yet in its prime, and now there dawns a new effulgence of pale-pink primness and propriety in the shape of *Pauke's Quill*, edited and published by the diverse avatars, aboriginal and otherwise, of that spirited adolescent Paul Livingston Keil, Esq.

Far be it from the undersigned to discourage young Mr. Keil. Indeed, it is our sincere opinion that his vigorous personality will ultimately be of immense benefit in revivifying Amateur Journalism. But certain qualities of his present offering move us to protest in the name of rational thought and artistic progress against a renewed wave of unthinking reaction and emotional Puritanism which cannot but hurt the advance of amateur culture.

Mr. Keil's cry for literary censorship is something particularly dangerous because it excites our sympathy before we fully realise all its implications. Not many of us, even in this age, have any marked leaning toward public pornography; so that we would generally welcome any agency calculated to banish offences against good taste. But when we come to reflect on the problem of enforcement, and perceive how absurdly any censorship places us in the hands of dogmatic and arbitrary officials with Puritan illusions and no true knowledge of life or literary values, we have to acknowledge that absolute liberty is the lesser evil. The literature of today, with its conscientious striving toward sincerity, must necessarily contain large amounts of matter repugnant to those who hold the hypocritical nineteenth-century view of the world. It need not be vulgarly presented, but it cannot be excluded if art is to express life. That censors actually do seek to remove this legitimate and essential matter, and that they would if given greater power do even greater harm, is plainly shewn by the futile action against *Jurgen,* and the present ban on *Ulysses,* both significant contributions to contemporary art. And, ironically enough, this same censorship blandly tolerates, through legal technicalities, infinite sewers full of frankly and frivolously nasty drivel without the least pretence of aesthetic or intellectual significance.

But Mr. Keil's major contribution to obscurantism is to be found under the heading "Opinion vs. Fact", where he assiduously strives to prove that the merit of an author's work depends absolutely on the philosophical views he happens to hold. According to our editor-sage, beauty is not beauty if created by a gentleman who does not belong to our church or bet on our favourite racehorse. No matter how masterful the limning of a picture, it must not hang on our wall unless the painter is endorsed by the Ku Klux Klan, the Y.M.C.A., and the Epworth League. This is quite entertaining, even if not much more luminous than Mr. Keil's masterpiece of meaningless metaphor—the quart of black paint as a tavern night scene. Can it be that people ever believed this sort of thing? It may be so, for anything was possible in Victorian times. There was a tenebrous period, if our grandsires speak truth, when Shelley was banished from the best parlour bookcase because his social and religious principles "weren't quite correct".

But this is 1923—an adult age—and we can ill afford to waste time on chimaeras which perished with Rogers groups and haircloth. Accordingly it is not encouraging to see these periodic recrudescences. Mr. Keil's final air-rifle shot at philosophy is an offhand distinction between "fact" and "opinion" which makes us wonder what supernal wisdom has decided for him a question which yet baffles the eminent of the earth. We would certainly like to discover that solid and irrefutable body of fact, opinions contrary to which are absolutely and irredeemably worthless. Somehow, though, we fear that a voyage of discovery would only bring us once more against the age-old question-mark, and explain away Mr. Keil's boyish certitudes in a manner already made common property by Herr Nietzsche's *Genealogy of Morals.*

Pauke's Quill is a welcome arrival—let us not undervalue it—but it is a pity that its effervescent influence should be lent to the side of obstruction and reaction. It will doubtless mature as Mr. Keil himself matures, and some day we hope to praise it for its virile support of that sounder civilisation which it now opposes with such sprightly ardour.

WHAT BELONGS IN VERSE

In reading over a large part of the current amateur verse—as well as many of the ephemeral rhymes in newspapers and minor professional magazines—one is led to wonder just why the writers ever chose a metrical medium for what they had to say. We glance at these more or less measured lines and behold an unlimited number of statements, opinions, and admonitions on a few extremely familiar subjects, each phrased in the literal narrative manner of prose, and reflecting some conventional point of view made popular by copy-book repetition. There may or may not be some valid reason for the writer's wishing to say something. But is there any valid reason why he should depart from unrhymed, continuous prose text when he wishes to state facts, register beliefs and predilections, and make ethical or prudential recommendations?

These processes, notwithstanding the custom of many old-time versifiers of wide household fame, belong essentially to the domains of science, history, administration, and philosophy, and rest basically on intellectual explanation and clear definition. From their very nature they demand embodiment in forms suited to accurate exposition, rather than in those suited to emotional catharsis and imaginative symbolism. Why, then, do so many offerers of statements, doctrines, and sermons persist in assuming the ill-fitting cloak of rhyme and metre which was designed for the poet?

It would be well if every metrical aspirant would pause and reflect on the question of just what, out of the various things he wants to utter, ought indeed to be expressed in verse. The experiences of the ages have pretty well taught us that the heightened rhythms and unified patterns of verse are primarily adapted to *poetry*—which consists of strong feelings sharply, simply, and non-intellectually presented through indirect, figurative, and pictorial images. Therefore it is scarcely wise to choose these rhythms and patterns when we wish merely to tell something or claim something or preach something.

The time to use verse is when some mood or feeling about something becomes so strong and insistent that it calls up various concrete pictures and resemblances and symbols in our minds, and makes us long to shout it or put it on record vividly in terms of these images and symbols. If the sight of the white clouds arouses in us only a wish to point a moral based on their insubstantiality and deceptive aspect, then the best thing for us to do is either to preserve silence or write a sermon, preferably the former. If, on the other hand, such a sight makes us think of things like ships or swans or fleecy flocks or ethereal castles, then we may properly begin to consider whether the feeling is strong enough, and the especial image fresh and original enough, to warrant our breaking into metre.

Poetry, the normal subject-matter of verse, never defines or analyses or asserts or urges or proves anything. It merely depicts, emphasises, symbolises, illuminates, or otherwise expresses some mood or strongly felt object. Therefore when we try to write it we must not state and describe and argue in direct, literal fashion, but must instead convey our meaning through suggested comparisons, elusively symbolic visual images, and—in general—*concrete* associative pictures of some sort.

As a recent specimen of the amateur didactic utterance which could obviously find a more appropriate channel than rhyme, one might cite the following:

"Gossip sometimes does some good
While other times does not but should.
Thus, when it's said with words unkind,
Consider it with a just mind."

Contrasting with this is the following quatrain of real poetry from the same magazine—a sample of the kind of emotional utterance which does indeed call for metrical dress:

TO MOTHER
By Albert Chapin

I saw your loving eyes—yet mine were closed;
  I heard your tender voice—though stilled in death;
I felt your gentle touch, and as I dozed
  There came a summer breeze—your sweet, warm breath.

The question of *light verse,* involving some apparent contradictions of the principles here suggested, forms a wholly separate subject, and one which merits subsequent treatment in these columns. Meanwhile it is in any case wise to pause carefully before beginning a piece of rhyme—asking oneself whether the subject is indeed fitted for such a vehicle, or whether a prose conveyance could better accommodate its particular bulk and contours.

V
POLITICAL THEORIST

Lovecraft would probably be embarrassed at the reprinting of most of the essays in this section: it is well known that his political philosophy experienced—outwardly, at any rate—the most spectacular revolution of any aspect of his thought, and late in life he was fond of berating himself for the lack of true insight into political matters he had displayed in youth. In a letter to Jennie K. Plaisier (July 8, 1936) he writes: "I used to be a hide-bound Tory simply for traditional and antiquarian reasons—and because I had never done any real *thinking* on civics and industry and the future. The depression—and its concomitant publicisation of industrial, financial, and governmental problems—jolted me out of my lethargy and led me to reëxamine the facts of history in the light of unsentimental scientific analysis; and it was not long before I realised what an ass I had been. The liberals at whom I used to laugh were the ones who were right—for they were living in the present while I had been living in the past. They had been using science whilst I had been using romantic antiquarianism." Bearing in mind, then, that all the essays in this section except the last represent this earlier, unthinking attitude, let us see what can be made of them.

The cardinal tenet of Lovecraft's early political thought is aristocracy in all its forms—political, social, racial, and intellectual—and he stresses one or the other aspect of it as it suits his purpose. In truth, aristocracy is a tenet he retained, with considerable modifications, throughout his life, so that it is misleading to speak of his progress *from* aristocracy *to* socialism; it would be more accurate to say that he arrived at socialism *through* aristocracy. We have already read Lovecraft's paean to aristocracy in "Nietzscheism and Realism" (1921): "I believe in an aristocracy, because I deem it the only agency for the creation of those refinements which make life endurable for the human animal of high organisation." No doubt Lovecraft considered himself such an animal, and his ideal governmental system would be designed to foster the comfort of himself and people like him. Self-serving as this appears to be, it is entirely understandable and requires no especial comment. In his earlier years he felt that a frank hereditary or culturally recognized aristocracy would be the only way to ensure such comfort; and it was, ironically, his upper-class disdain of money-grubbing capitalism (something he himself could never adopt, as is seen in his humiliating attempts to take on various commercial occupations in his New York period) that turned him from a pure aristocrat into a socialist aristocrat. Capitalism is the foe to both aristocracy and socialism, and Lovecraft's gradual shift only occurred because of his grudging admission that the old-time aristocracy he longed for—and had actually experienced in his early youth as a member of Providence's social elite—was dead in the mechanized world of the 1920s and 1930s.

There are those who find Lovecraft's whole concept of "fascistic socialism" paradoxical: many political theorists maintain that participatory democracy is an essential component of the sort of moderate socialism Lovecraft was proposing. Lovecraft thought differently, and his socialism would, while distributing economic wealth more equitably to all, restrict political power to the few—that "oligarchy of intelligence" (as he terms it in "Some Repetitions on the Times") that alone, in Lovecraft's mind, is capable of deciding on the highly complex political and economic issues of a mechanized world. Whether this is any different from a sort of old-world benevolent aristocracy is something Lovecraft never addresses.

Lovecraft's early political essays are not quite as embarrassing as some of his contemporaneous letters, and a few of them actually utter truths that were valid enough in their day. Lovecraft is right to criticize naive American patriotism in "Revolutionary Mythology" (1918); his hard-headed realism regarding the inevitability of war led him to condemn the League of Nations in "The League" (1919); and Lovecraft even has some justification for attacking German- and Irish-Americans in "Old England and the 'Hyphen'" (1916), for this essay was written not long after actual plots against the government by these groups were discovered. And Lovecraft is within his rights to denounce alcohol and the hypocrisy of advertising in "More *Chain Lightning*," even though he ultimately came to realize the unworkability of Prohibition. And yet, it is still enormously refreshing to come to "Some Repetitions on the Times" (1933). (This essay was written shortly before the inauguration of Roosevelt, but Lovecraft never seems to have made any effort to prepare it for publication.) It is not simply that this piece states political positions more in line with our own: this would be a superficial, if not contemptible, reason for praising it. Rather, it finally reveals some of the flexibility and insight that Lovecraft was showing in all phases of his thought at this time: Lovecraft seems at last to know what he is talking about, instead of rattling off dogmatic opinions spawned in the cloistered confines of his reclusive youth.

"The Crime of the Century" (1915), however, raises one issue we have hitherto ignored: racism. I am no longer convinced that we can be very lenient on Lovecraft on this matter. Yes, it is true that many of his time and class thought as he did; but it is also true that the foremost thinkers of his day were shedding these beliefs in light of evidence amassed by biologists, anthropologists, and psychologists. Lovecraft maintained the error of the black's biological and cultural inferiority to the end of his life, even though studies by Franz Boas and W. E. B. Du Bois at the turn of the century had destroyed such a contention; he was always a segregationist, claiming that assimilation of aliens could only occur with racially homogeneous groups and only if the aliens shed the entirety of their heritage and culture and adopted those of the dominant group. And it is a sad fact that Lovecraft's views did not change nearly as much toward the end of his life as some apologists wish us to believe. This is the tragedy of Lovecraft's racism: in this one regard he failed to exhibit that openness to new evidence that he displayed in every other facet of his thought. The mere fact that he was forced to debate the issue so vehemently with his younger correspondents, who had not received the upbringing he had, should have urged him to give his views a careful scrutiny; but nothing of the sort happened.

Lovecraft's entire political thought is only a sort of adjunct to his aesthetics: what he wished was a political system that could ensure the maintenance of a high cultural standard, and it hardly mattered which system it was so long as the desired result was accomplished. That he finally woke up from his dream of hereditary aristocracy and embraced a socialism that could deal with the problems of the modern world is a tribute to his clear-headedness, and that he could infuse such narratives as "At the Mountains of Madness" and "The Shadow Out of Time" with such searching political speculations shows how politics had risen to the forefront of his attention in his later years. In this sense, these two works are at once his most cosmic and his most human stories.

THE CRIME OF THE CENTURY

The present European war, occurring as it does in an age of hysterical sentimentality and unsound political doctrines, has called forth from the sympathisers of each set of belligerents an unexampled torrent of indiscriminate denunciation.

The effeminate idealist, half awaked from his roseate vision of universal brotherhood, shrieks at the mutual slaughter of his fellow-men, or singles out individual acts of cruelty or treachery as the objects of his well-meaning rage; while the erratic socialist, saturated with false notions of equality and democracy, raves unendingly against cruel systems of government which sacrifice a peaceful peasantry to the greed and ambition of their warlike masters.

But though the sober philosopher perceives in war a phenomenon eminently natural and absolutely inevitable; though he realises that the masses of mankind must remain subject to the will of a dominant aristocracy so long as the present structure of the human brain endures; he can none the less find in the colossal conflict an ample cause for the deepest regret and the gravest apprehension. High above such national crimes as the Servian plots against Austria or the German disregard of Belgian neutrality, high above such sad matters as the destruction of innocent lives and property, looms the supremest of all crimes, an offence not only against conventional morality but against Nature itself; the violation of race.

In the unnatural racial alignment of the various warring powers we behold a defiance of anthropological principles that cannot but bode ill for the future of the world.

That the maintenance of civilisation rests today with that magnificent Teutonic stock which is represented alike by the two hotly contending rivals, England and Germany, as well as by Austria, Scandinavia, Switzerland, Holland, and Belgium, is as undeniably true as it is vigorously disputed. The Teuton is the summit of evolution. That we may consider intelligently his place in history we must cast aside the popular nomenclature which would confuse the names "Teuton" and "German", and view him not nationally but racially, identifying his fundamental stock with the tall, pale, blue-eyed, yellow-haired, long-headed "Xanthochroi" as described by Huxley, amongst whom the class of languages we call "Teutonic" arose, and who today constitute the majority of the Teutonic-speaking population of our globe.

Though some ethnologists have declared that the Teuton is the only true Aryan, and that the languages and institutions of the other nominally Aryan races were derived alone from his superior speech and customs; it is nevertheless not necessary for us to accept this daring theory in order to appreciate his vast superiority to the rest of mankind.

Tracing the career of the Teuton through mediaeval and modern history, we can find no possible excuse for denying his actual biological supremacy. In widely separated localities and under widely diverse conditions, his innate racial qualities have raised him to preëminence. There is no branch of modern civilisation that is not of his making. As the power of the Roman Empire declined, the Teuton sent down into Italy, Gaul, and Spain the re-vivifying elements which saved those countries from complete destruction. Though now largely lost in the mixed population, the Teutons are the true founders of all the so-called Latin states. Political and social vitality had fled from the old inhabitants; the Teuton only was creative and constructive. After the native elements absorbed the Teutonic invaders, the Latin civilisations declined tremendously, so that the France, Italy, and Spain of today bear every mark of national degeneracy.

In the lands whose population is mainly Teutonic, we behold a striking proof of the qualities of the race. England and Germany are the supreme empires of the world, whilst the virile virtues of the Belgians have lately been demonstrated in a manner which will live forever in song and story. Switzerland and Holland are veritable synonyms for Liberty. The Scandinavians are immortalised by the exploits of the Vikings and Normans, whose conquests over man and Nature extended from the sun-baked shores of Sicily to the glacial wastes of Greenland, even attaining our own distant Vineland across the sea. United States history is one long panegyric of the Teuton, and will continue to be such if degenerate immigration can be checked in time to preserve the primitive character of the population.

The Teutonic mind is masterful, temperate, and just. No other race has shewn an equal capability for self-government. It is a significant fact that not one square inch of Teutonic territory is governed save by its own inhabitants.

The division of such a splendid stock against itself, each representative faction allying itself with alien inferiors, is a crime so monstrous that the world may well stand aghast. Germany, it is true, has some appreciation of the civilising mission of the Teuton, but has allowed her jealousy of England to conquer her intellectual zeal, and to disrupt the race in an infamous and unnecessary war.

Englishmen and Germans are blood brothers, descended from the same stern Woden-worshipping ancestors, blessed with the same rugged virtues, and fired with the same noble ambitions. In a world of diverse and hostile races the joint mission of these virile men is one of union and coöperation with their fellow-Teutons in defence of civilisation against the onslaughts of all others. There is work to be done by the Teuton. As a unit he must in times to come crush successively the rising power of Slav and Mongolian, preserving for Europe and America the glorious culture that he has evolved.

Wherefore we have reason to weep less at the existence or causes of this stupendous fray, than at its unnatural and fratricidal character; at the self-decimation of the one mighty branch of humanity on which the future welfare of the world depends.

MORE *CHAIN LIGHTNING*

Of the various outside activities of our United members, none is more deserving of sincere commendation and respect than the campaign for temperance and reform now being conducted by Mr. Andrew Francis Lockhart of Milbank, S.D. His little professional magazine, *Chain Lightning,* last April succeeded in ridding the city of Milbank of its licenced saloons, and in securing the conviction of illicit retailers and resort proprietors. Not even a dastardly and cowardly physical assault from behind his back, committed in the office of *The Milbank News* by a disreputable fellow whom Mr. Lockhart had exposed, has deterred our fearless amateur associate from his noble and necessary work. Since most United members have probably seen *Chain Lightning,* it appears rather extraordinary that the amateur papers have made so little endeavour to assist in combating the menace of strong drink and kindred evils; wherefore the writer feels constrained to urge some concerted action by our publishers in supporting Mr. Lockhart's campaign for decency, and in attacking any remaining phases of the liquor problem which *Chain Lightning* has not yet struck.

Chief among these hitherto neglected phases is one for which the *professional* press is largely to blame, and which, therefore, the *amateur* press can oppose with a particularly poetic justice; the advertising of beer and whiskey, and especially that disgustingly insidious type of advertising which deliberately seeks to create a false *moral sentiment* in favour of drink, at the same time placing the prohibitionists in the light of tyrannical meddlers.

A notorious beer-brewing corporation of St. Louis, sustained by an enormous capital which extends high into the millions, and therefore capable of buying the servile sentiment of the prostituted press, has during the past few months been issuing a series of infamous advertisements which constitute an insult to the greatest men this nation ever produced, and which for its pernicious tendencies should have been suppressed at its very inception. The general plan of this contemptible series is to present a brief biography of some eminent American statesman such as Washington, Jefferson, Carroll, or Morris, who lived before science had demonstrated the overwhelmingly deleterious properties of alcoholic beverages, and therefore before the moral necessity of total abstinence was emphasised. After justly lauding the virtues of each statesman, the scheming biographer mentions the fact, of course inevitable on account of the early period, that the subject of the essay was a moderate drinker of liquor, and, now departing utterly from reasonable probability, asserts that "if the great man were living today, he would be opposed to Prohibition, which limits the rights of the individual" (etc., etc., ad nauseam). What comment is necessary upon such a flagrant abuse of the liberty of the press? This series, entitled "Framers of the Constitution", is published in practically every current American daily, reaching and tainting the primitive mind of the labourer, and perverting the impressionable intellect of the child. It is poison of the vilest kind, distributed for hire by supposedly respectable newspapers, including those of the very highest class, such as the Providence *Daily Journal* and *Evening Bulletin.* The intelligent reader can discern with ease the despicable hypocrisy and falsity of these miserable advertisements. He realises keenly the fact that our serious, virtuous forefathers would have been not only participators, but active leaders in the temperance movement, had it existed in their time. As to the "personal liberty", "rights of man", and other popular phrases similarly misused, there are few indeed who can fail to perceive that the "liberty" and "right" of a man voluntarily to transform himself to a beast, and in the end to degrade himself and his descendants permanently in the scale of evolution, is equivalent to his "liberty" and "right" to rob and murder at will. If the law may justly suppress theft and homicide, it may certainly with equal justice suppress the manufacture, sale, and consumption of that liquid evil which incites most of the world's theft and homicide. As to "moderate drinking", we might on similar ethics condone "moderate larceny" or "moderate manslaughter". Human nature admits of no exact middle course in drinking. He who usually drinks "a little", will always on occasion drink "a little too much", wherefore the only sane course is absolutely total abstinence. The practical difficulty in enforcing Prohibition is admittedly great, but no man of virtue can do otherwise than work toward the final downfall of Rum. To distinguish between beer and ardent spirits is to quibble. The poison is different only in degree, and the use of the one inevitably encourages the use of the other.

But though these facts are perfectly evident to the enlightened reader, they are but vaguely comprehended by the masses, who therefore fall an easy prey to the alluring advertisements of the brewer and distiller. Such evil propaganda deserves no place in modern civilisation, though it perhaps reveals to the prohibitionist the essential unnaturalness of the craving for drink, and the increasing power of reform; the advertisements are obviously designed both to arouse the liquorish desires of the public, and to nullify the good effect of Prohibition work.

As Mr. Lockhart has regretfully asserted in a letter to the writer, a moral or legal appeal to the brewing class would be fruitless. Dulled in the first place to ethical impressions, their tainted money protects them from the law. The professional press, therefore, is the vulnerable spot, and the logical point for our attacks. No method should be spared to decrease the circulation and popularity of every journal, high or low in its cultural appeal, which sells itself and its pages to the daemon Rum. Remonstrant letters to some of the less offensive of these papers might well serve as a beginning, whilst every amateur publisher should be willing to give space to the intelligent denunciation of the liquor interests. Extra copies of these amateur journals, judiciously distributed to professional editors who tolerate advertisements of whiskey and beer, might do more good than the majority now believe.

Print and publicity, declares Mr. Lockhart, are the only effective weapons against corruption, wherefore the members of the United may find in temperance work a splendid opportunity to demonstrate their energy and ability.

OLD ENGLAND AND THE "HYPHEN"

Of the various intentional fallacies exhaled like miasmic vapours from the rotting cosmopolitanism of vitiated American politics, and doubly rife during these days of European conflict, none is more disgusting than that contemptible subterfuge of certain foreign elements whereby the legitimate zeal of the genuine native stock for England's cause is denounced and compared to the unpatriotic disaffection of those working in behalf of England's enemies. The Prussian propagandists and Irish irresponsibles, failing in their clumsy efforts to use the United States as a tool of vengeance upon the Mistress of the Seas, have seized with ingenious and unexpected eagerness on a current slogan coined to counteract their own traitorous machinations, and have begun to fling the trite demand "America first" in the face of every American who is unable to share their puerile hatred of the British Empire. In demanding that American citizens impartially withhold love and allegiance from any government save their own, thereby binding themselves to a policy of rigid coldness in considering the fortunes of their Mother Country, the Prusso-Hibernian herd have the sole apparent advantage of outward technical justification. If the United States were truly the radical, aloof, mongrelised nation into which they idealise it, their plea might possibly be more appropriate. But in comparing the lingering loyalty of a German-American for Germany, or of an Irish-American for Ireland, with that of a native American for England, these politicians make their fundamental psychological error.

England, despite the contentions of trifling theorists, is not and never will be a really foreign country; nor is a true love of America possible without a corresponding love for the British race and ideals that created America. The difficulties which caused the severance of the American Colonies from the rest of the Empire were essentially internal ones, and have no moral bearing on this country's attitude toward the parent land in its relations with alien civilisations. Just as Robert Edward Lee chose to follow the government of Virginia rather than that of the Federal Union in 1861, so did the Anglo-American Revolutionary leaders choose local to central allegiance in 1775. Their rebellion was in itself a characteristically English act, and could in no manner annul the purely English origin and nature of the new republic. American history before the conflict of 1775–1783 is English history, and we are lawful heirs of the unnumbered glories of the Saxon line. Shakespeare and Milton, Dryden and Pope, Young and Thomson, Johnson and Goldsmith, are our own poets; William the Conqueror, Edward the Black Prince, Elizabeth, and William of Nassau are our own royalty; Crécy, Poictiers, and Agincourt are our own victories; Lord Bacon, Sir Isaac Newton, Hobbes, Locke, Sir Robert Boyle, and Sir William Herschel are our own philosophers and scientists; what true American lives, who would wish, by rejecting an Englishman's heritage, to despoil his country of such racial laurels? Let those men be silent, who would, in envy, deny to the citizens of the United States the right to cherish and revere the ancestral honours that are theirs, and to remain faithful to the Anglo-Saxon ideals of their English forefathers!

Since the establishment of a republic by the Englishmen of the American Colonies, millions of non-British persons have been admitted to share the liberty which English hands created. In many cases, these immigrants have proved valuable accessions, and when accepting fully the ideals of the Anglo-American culture, those of them who are of North European blood have become completely amalgamated with the American people. Germans, in particular, being of identical racial stock, are able to fuse quickly and wholly into the colonial population. But as they become Americans, so must they also, in a sense, become Englishmen. When the Elector of Hanover, a thorough German, acceded to the English throne, it was his duty to become an English monarch; and in a similar way it is an obligation of all other non-English individuals, princes or peasants, to adopt Anglo-Saxon ideals when they come to reap the advantages of an Anglo-Saxon nation. That millions of virile Germans have done so, is a gratifying fact to consider.

But since alien immigration has far exceeded normal proportions, it is but natural that we have among us an alarmingly vast body of foreigners from various countries who are totally unable to appreciate Anglo-American traditions. If not still attached to their respective nations, they are at least prone to regard the United States as a sort of spontaneously evolved territory without previous history or ancestry. Forgetting the Saxon inheritance that gave us language, laws, and liberty, they speak of America as a composite nation whose civilisation is a compound of all existing cultures; a melting-pot of mongrelism wherein it is a crime for a man to know his own grandfather's name. They prate of Americanism as something of autochthonous growth, neglecting or unwilling to assign England the credit for its origin; and presuming to blame any citizen who is more just than they in his appreciation of the Mother Land.

More guileful immigrants use their "Americanism" as a blind for treason. Leaving their own countries in dissatisfaction, they assume the cloak of American citizenship; organise and finance conspiracies with American money; and finally, with an audacity almost ironical, call upon the United States for help when overtaken by justice! Half the detestable violence of the Irish "Fenians" and "Sinn Fein" ruffians was hatched in America by those who dare drivel about such a thing as "neutrality"! Others continue to serve their own countries under the all-enveloping American mantle. Prussian-American patriots deep in the sanctimonious circles of "Americanism" and "pacifism" are at the same time secretly destroying American property for the benefit of the Prussian cause. And these are the sort of worthies who compare their treacherous and anti-American acts with the traditional affection of a real American for the land which gave birth to the American nation!

The very small surviving flock of native Fourth-of-July England-haters must not be charged with that moral delinquency which attaches to the foreign agitators. These belated Revolutionists mean well, and are to be tolerated with kindness. They head that amusing element which applauds every Englishman who becomes naturalised in the United States, but which denounces with unmerciful inconsistency every American who, like the late Henry James, renews ancestral ties with Great Britain.

Summing up, we may well declare it folly to taunt the American lover of Old England with the cry of "Hyphenate!" His passion is not, like that of the Prussian or Irish "hyphenate", based exclusively on personal ancestry; in his affection for the parent Kingdom he is but reiterating his devotion to the ideals of the daughter Republic; he is giving to his country a double loyalty!

REVOLUTIONARY MYTHOLOGY

Events in our little sphere of amateurdom sometimes coincide remarkably with those of the world outside. The announcement in United circles of Mr. Henry Clapham McGavack's forthcoming essay on "Preliminaries of the American Revolution", wherein some hoary Yankee myths will be dissected, comes almost simultaneously with the storm of resentment awaked among professional American patriots by the lamentable faux pas of Prof. Wilson's pacifistical Secretary of War; who asserted in a campaign speech on October 16 that the Mexican banditti of today are comparable to the American revolutionists of Gen. Washington's army.

Secretary Baker has undoubtedly perpetrated another characteristically Wilsonian blunder in drawing a parallel between the pure-blooded Anglo-Saxon rebels of 1775 and the herd of half-breed swine, bent only on plunder, who are grunting, shooting, cavorting, and misbehaving generally below our southern border; but the loud denunciation comes rather from the truth he has let slip than from the erroneous inference he has drawn.

The American Revolution has created a more marvellous fund of genuine legendary lore than any other event in modern history. Not only to the proletariat, but to the bulk of our intelligent countrymen, the colonists who caused the withdrawal of America from the British Empire stand forth as heroes unsullied; as veritable Galahads, Bayards, and Sidneys. It is soberly believed by grown men that the defiers of George III were a host of terrestrial Seraphim, the like of whom have never been known before or since. Willingly enough do we confess weaknesses on both sides of other intestine struggles through which our race has passed. In reflecting upon the Civil Wars which culminated in Cromwell's usurpation, we all acknowledge on the one hand that King Charles I was weak, that his promises were not inviolable, and that many of his adherents were luxurious and dissipated men; and on the other hand that the rebels were hasty, cruel, coarse, hypocritical, and animated by many absurdly false notions. Neither Charles nor Cromwell is to the descendants of his followers a supernal being "sans peur et sans reproche". But in mentioning the Continental army of 1775–1783, the average American assumes an unconscious accent of prayer, and damns any possible blasphemer with the true fervour of the fanatic. That the band of American colonists who seceded from the authority of Great Britain in 1775 contained at least several human beings, is well proven by careful students. That these beings possessed their full share of what we call "human nature", is likewise not unknown. Which compels *The Conservative* to smile a trifle at the legends of Revolutionary Gods and Heroes preserved by each Yankee fireside, and transmitted both orally and verbally to each succeeding generation.

The American Revolution arose from a fatal misunderstanding between the Englishmen at home and those upon this continent. Neither side can claim the exclusive sanction of Heaven, nor must either side be blackened with the imputation of infamy. Saxon fought Saxon as men always fight men. The record of each army is as clean, or as soiled, as that of any other body of embattled human creatures who contend under the best traditions of civilised warfare. That a certain amount of looting, burning, and other irregularities existed on both sides, is no cause for surprise or indignation in the mind of the student or historian, for these things are inseparable from armed conflict of any sort, though training may modify them. Even the sainted Crusaders of old were less Christian toward the Saracens than we would like to imagine.

If the time has come when Revolutionary mythology may be placed in honoured banishment beside the similar lore of infant Rome; if men may at last be suffered openly to speak the truth about those brave Britons and Colonials of yesterday, it is to be hoped that justice may be done that most maligned class in all America—the loyalists, or "Tories". In the year 1775 this country was a legitimate part of the British domain, under the rightful authority of the King and his Parliament. The rebellious decision of a majority of the people can certainly form no ground for complaint against those Americans who felt that their duty lay with the existing government, and who upheld their Sovereign's rule with valour and distinction. That selfish interest dwelt beneath the acts of the "Tories" is often asserted, and may in some instances be true; but it is only the most crass ignorance or most malicious prejudice which can thus defame the multitude of patriotic American Royalists who willingly suffered or died in the service of the third George.

AMERICANISM

It is easy to sentimentalise on the subject of "the American spirit"—what it is, may be, or should be. Exponents of various novel political and social theories are particularly given to this practice, nearly always concluding that "true Americanism" is nothing more or less than a national application of their respective individual doctrines.

Slightly less superficial observers hit upon the abstract principle of "Liberty" as the keynote of Americanism, interpreting this justly esteemed principle as anything from Bolshevism to the right to drink 2.75 per cent. beer. "Opportunity" is another favourite byword, and one which is certainly not without real significance. The synonymousness of "America" and "opportunity" has been inculcated into many a young head of the present generation by Emerson via Montgomery's *Leading Facts of American History*. But it is worthy of note that nearly all would-be definers of "Americanism" fail through their prejudiced unwillingness to trace the quality to its European source. They cannot bring themselves to see that abiogenesis is as rare in the realm of ideas as it is in the kingdom of organic life; and consequently waste their efforts in trying to treat America as if it were an isolated phenomenon without ancestry.

"Americanism" is expanded Anglo-Saxonism. It is the spirit of England, transplanted to a soil of vast extent and diversity, and nourished for a time under pioneer conditions calculated to increase its democratic aspects without impairing its fundamental virtues. It is the spirit of truth, honour, justice, morality, moderation, individualism, conservative liberty, magnanimity, toleration, enterprise, industriousness, and progress—which is England—plus the element of equality and opportunity caused by pioneer settlement. It is the expression of the world's highest race under the most favourable social, political, and geographical conditions. Those who endeavour to belittle the importance of our British ancestry, are invited to consider the other nations of this continent. All these are equally "American" in every particular, differing only in race-stock and heritage; yet of them all, none save British Canada will even bear comparison with us. We are great because we are a part of the great Anglo-Saxon cultural sphere; a section detached only after a century and a half of heavy colonisation and English rule, which gave to our land the ineradicable stamp of British civilisation.

Most dangerous and fallacious of the several misconceptions of Americanism is that of the so-called "melting-pot" of races and traditions. It is true that this country has received a vast influx of non-English immigrants who come hither to enjoy without hardship the liberties which our British ancestors carved out in toil and bloodshed. It is also true that such of them as belong to the Teutonic and Celtic races are capable of assimilation to our English types and of becoming valuable acquisitions to the population. But from this it does not follow that a mixture of really alien blood or ideas has accomplished or can accomplish anything but harm. Observation of Europe shews us the relative status and capability of the several races, and we see that the melting together of English gold and alien brass is not very likely to produce any alloy superior or even equal to the original gold. Immigration cannot, perhaps, be cut off altogether, but it should be understood that aliens who choose America as their residence must accept the prevailing language and culture as their own; and neither try to modify our institutions, nor to keep alive their own in our midst. We must not, as the greatest man of our age declared, suffer this nation to become a "polyglot boarding-house".

The greatest foe to rational Americanism is that dislike for our parent nation which holds sway amongst the ignorant and bigoted, and which is kept alive largely by certain elements of the population who seem to consider the sentiments of Southern and Western Ireland more important than those of the United States. In spite of the plain fact that a separate Ireland would weaken civilisation and menace the world's peace by introducing a hostile and undependable wedge betwixt the two major parts of Saxondom, these irresponsible elements continue to encourage rebellion in the Green Isle; and in so doing tend to place this nation in a distressingly anomalous position as an abettor of crime and sedition against the Mother Land. Disgusting beyond words are the public honours paid to political criminals like Edward, alias Eamonn, de Valera, whose very presence at large among us is an affront to our dignity and heritage. Never may we appreciate or even fully comprehend our own place and mission in the world, till we can banish those clouds of misunderstanding which float between us and the source of our culture.

But the features of Americanism peculiar to this continent must not be belittled. In the abolition of fixed and rigid class lines a distinct sociological advance is made, permitting a steady and progressive recruiting of the upper levels from the fresh and vigorous body of the people beneath. Thus opportunities of the choicest sort await every citizen alike, whilst the biological quality of the cultivated classes is improved by the cessation of that narrow in-breeding which characterises European aristocracy.

Total separation of civil and religious affairs, the greatest political and intellectual advance since the Renaissance, is also a local American—and more particularly a Rhode Island—triumph. Agencies are today subtly at work to undermine this principle, and to impose upon us through devious political influences the Papal chains which Henry VIII first struck from our limbs; chains unfelt since the bloody reign of Mary, and infinitely worse than the ecclesiastical machinery which Roger Williams rejected. But when the vital relation of intellectual freedom to genuine Americanism shall be fully impressed upon the people, it is likely that such sinister undercurrents will subside.

The main struggle which awaits Americanism is not with reaction, but with radicalism. Our age is one of restless and unintelligent iconoclasm, and abounds with shrewd sophists who use the name "Americanism" to cover attacks on that institution itself. Such familiar terms and phrases as "democracy", "liberty", or "freedom of speech" are being distorted to cover the wildest forms of anarchy, whilst our old representative institutions are being attacked as "un-American" by foreign immigrants who are incapable both of understanding them or of devising anything better.

This country would benefit from a wider practice of sound Americanism, with its accompanying recognition of an Anglo-Saxon source. Americanism implies freedom, progress, and independence; but it does not imply a rejection of the past, nor a renunciation of traditions and experience. Let us view the term in its real, practical, and unsentimental meaning.

THE LEAGUE

Endless is the credulity of the human mind. Having just passed through a period of indescribable devastation caused by the rapacity and treachery of an unwisely trusted nation which caught civilisation unarmed and unawares, the world purposes once more to adopt a policy of sweet trustfulness, and to place its faith again in those imposing 'scraps of paper' known as treaties and covenants; this time setting up as its bulwark against barbaric inroads a prettily and abstractly conceived 'parliament of man and federation of the world' popularly and semi-officially labelled as "The League of Nations". It is to be a very nice and attractive League, we are told; brimful of safeguards against ordinary war, even though somewhat deficient in safeguards against Bolshevism. War, in fact, is to be formally and distinctly prohibited, or at least discouraged; which is of course an absolute guarantee of an immediate millennium of universal peace! Ultimately, as the grave proponents of the scheme condescend to inform us, all nations are to be included in this Utopian circle of friendship and confidence; thus giving us the valued collaboration of our highly honourable German, Turkish, and Bulgarian brothers in the momentous task of governing the future earth-wide Elysium. Verily, it is a pleasing vision.

But visions generally become dangerous when mistaken for practical policies, and the present case is not likely to prove an exception. Since a war-weary and mentally fatigued world is really listening soberly to the vague theorising of league-advocates, it behooves us to awake to full consciousness and examine this roseate rhetoric in the white light of reason, history, and science. To sign any hastily drawn and clumsily patched league covenant without such an examination would be contrary to the traditions of a free and enlightened people.

Is it indeed true that man has suddenly discovered an infallible panacea for all political ills? Is it indeed certain that a general entanglement of diverse and in many cases opposed countries offers a solution of all national difficulties? Have we indeed exchanged the natural laws of mankind and this earth for those of fairyland? To all these queries *The Conservative* is inclined to venture a negative reply.

Warfare, whose minimising is the avowed object of the proposed league, is something which can never be abolished altogether. As the natural expression of such inherent human instincts as hate, greed, and combativeness, it must always be reckoned with in some degree. Men will submit to argument only up to a certain point, beyond which they invariably resort to force, however great the odds against them. Would the league reduce warfare? On the contrary, it would probably have a precisely opposite effect. By multiplying international contacts, it would multiply international animosities; and upon each outbreak of trouble the indirectly involved powers would be less likely to act constitutionally as suppressors, than to divide according to sympathy and previous alignment, and to participate as combatants. Oaths and treaties are worth no more than the honour of those who make them. Set up one league, and it will soon be undermined by a score of clandestine inner leagues.

What we need as an international safeguard is not a cumbrous and futile federation of miscellaneous nations good and bad, with the independence of each one virtually destroyed; but a simple and practical alliance betwixt those powers such as the United States, Great Britain, France, and Italy, which inherit in common the highest ideals, and which possess almost no conflicting interests. Those who hold up our Federal Union as an example of a "League" in working order would do well to mark the fact that the component states are all of one general type, and not in any way comparable to the widely diverse nations of the globe. Such an alliance, properly armed, would constitute an almost resistless and stable force in world-politics; affording the best defence possible for our civilisation, and providing the best possible guarantee against needless wars.

Let us cease to think in unrealities, or to mouth such benevolent but empty catchwords as "disarmament" and "universal brotherhood". We are living not in Paradise but on Earth; and will fare best if we marshal the harmonious forces of civilisation in a sensible way for an attainable object, rather than rashly yoke together opposed and dissimilar cultures in the vain hope of realising a fantastic and impossible ideal.

BOLSHEVISM

The most alarming tendency observable in this age is a growing disregard for the established forces of law and order. Whether or not stimulated by the noxious example of the almost sub-human Russian rabble, the less intelligent element throughout the world seems animated by a singular viciousness, and exhibits symptoms like those of a herd on the verge of stampeding. Whilst long-winded politicians preach universal peace, long-haired anarchists are preaching a social upheaval which means nothing more or less than a reversion to savagery or mediaeval barbarism. Even in this traditionally orderly nation the number of Bolsheviki, both open and veiled, is considerable enough to require remedial measures. The repeated and unreasonable strikes of important workers, seemingly with the object of indiscriminate extortion rather than rational wage increase, constitute a menace which should be checked.

To a certain extent, our government will probably meet these conditions with legislation affecting seditious speech and treasonable acts; but if a permanent cure is to be accomplished, something deeper and more educational will be needed. It will require propaganda to combat propaganda. The present agitation undoubtedly arises from false belief in the possibility of a radically altered social order. The workers who strike, and the shouters who incite to crime, are obviously possessed of the notion that the property of the wealthy could practicably be shared with them; that even if they were to seize the things they covet, they could continue the enjoyment of civilised existence and of protection against violence.

We need a new Menenius Agrippa to proclaim and demonstrate widely the total fallacy of such an illusion. Our present social order, whilst capable of some degree of liberalisation, is the product of the natural development of human relations. It is not ideal, nor could anything on earth be ideal—but it is inevitable. Just as long as some men are more intelligent than others, so long will there be inequality of wealth. The type of persons who indulge in strikes and socialism seem never to realise how much they depend on the brains of their hated "economic masters". They do not reflect that if they were to seize the factories and governments as they desire, they would be totally powerless to run them. The lawless I. W. W. sometimes boasts of its prospective ability to overthrow orderly government and substitute a sanguinary reign of the so-called "proletariat". Perhaps such a catastrophe will come, just as the Russian catastrophe came; but how little will the blind anarchists gain therefrom! With the intelligent element removed, the rabble will use up the resources of civilisation without being able to produce more; cities and public works will fall into decay, and a new barbarism arise, out of which will spring in time the natural chieftains who will constitute the "masters" of another era of capitalism. Far better that the impressionable and inflammable masses be taught these things before they embark upon a futile revolution which will ruin all civilisation, themselves included, without helping anyone.

SOME REPETITIONS ON THE TIMES

This is to be a blunt endeavour to emphasise some basic and desperate truths about the present economic impasse—swelling ever so little the chorus now besieging the ears of our incoming legislators. It will be remarked that nothing in these paragraphs has not been suggested several hundred times before, but such a remark can hardly be taken as a proper objection. In social and political crises no idea or perspective can gain an adequate hearing except through insistent echoes, and today there cannot be too many voices raised in exactly similar outlines of our civilisation's real plight, and exactly similar demands for a brushing aside of irrelevant precedents and preconceptions in facing that plight.

Only reiteration will help. The realities have been starkly and powerfully stated by competent individuals again and again, yet official thought and legislation very largely continue in their sluggish, superficial course, motivated by catchwords and conceptions left from former ages whose basic industrial and financial conditions no longer exist. For several generations the man-displacing effect of the machine has been realised by a few, yet the momentary ability of new industries to absorb displaced labour was enough to blind nearly everyone to the consequences inevitable after the end of this plainly temporary absorption. Even when the end did come, the majority refused to realise it. It took the repetitions and inculcations of the "technocracy" survey—a tremendously valuable and significant movement despite its handicaps of poor leadership and extravagant conclusions—to give the general public a really vivid glimpse of the permanently altered set of conditions around us.

Thus we may see the need for a repeated presentation of the whole dismal picture in all its familiar outlines and implications. Its desperateness—and the probably dire results of its neglect or subordination—must be literally hammered into the popular consciousness until increasing clamour reaches the legislator and forces him to face the facts and take drastic action concerning them. Our governing body must be brought to understand that the time is past for cherishing abstract institutions and deferring to purely theoretical ideals such as "rugged individualism", "unregulated private property", "sound money", "free initiative", "legitimate profits", "economic laws", "balanced budgets", and so on. These institutions and ideals have to do with *methods*, but not with the realities underlying them—and today it is with the naked realities that we are having to deal.

The *real* problem is to accomplish certain ends *irrespective of methods*, as is done in such other emergencies as warfare and pioneering. A certain morale is to be preserved, and certain resources are to be distributed where they will do the most good. During the late war there was no talk of theoretical technicalities (or if so, it was justly reprehended) when a definite thing was to be done. If a certain number of men in a certain military area needed a certain amount of food, clothing, or other supplies, that amount was produced somehow—by drastic commandeering if necessary—and delivered where it was required. Still farther back in history, the rigid apportionment of labour and resources in the Plymouth colony—and traces of it in later American colonies—shews again that drastic and concrete action is not (despite the perfervid rhetoric of certain distinguished and plutocratic Elder Statesmen) incompatible with the real American tradition as distinguished from the artificial finance-and-business tradition built up during the myopic nineteenth century.

Today the country has plenty of resources and productive facilities, so that enough exists to support the entire population very comfortably —and without any of the destructive absolute equalisation demanded by ruthless communists. The problem is to get the existing material to those who need it—and the obstacles in the way are the theories which protect mere *methods* and abstract institutions and ideals.

We all realise that the existing equilibrium must not be disrupted by a violent overthrow of all the safeguards of property in moderate quantities. It is only increasing an evil if those who have a few resources left are to be shorn of their pittance and thrown into the plight of the destitute. But we also realise that a prodigious amount of concrete rectification can be accomplished by arbitrarily distributive methods productive of no physical or cultural hardship to anyone—measures which are really *very moderate and conservative when judged in relation not to abstract theory but to human needs and cultural standards.*

This is what the controllers of our political destiny must be made by popular clamour to see—that what is to be sought is not the preservation of a parcel of commercial methods and economic ideals, but a rational apportionment of resources and a continuation of our hereditary way of life as regards art, ethics, intellectual perspective, and the niceties of personal existence. We must stop thinking primarily in terms of "money" and "business"—both artificial things—and begin to think increasingly in terms of the actual resources and products on which "money" and "business" are based. In terms of these, of the human beings to whom they are to be distributed, and of the cognate human values which make the accidents of life and consciousness worth enduring.

Part of the task of our repetitions must be to convince the holders of power of something which the farther-sighted philosopher long ago realised—namely, that the present collapse is not merely a transient depression from which automatic recovery is possible. This, we hope, may be accomplished through the soberly disinterested efforts of that Columbia group of energy-surveyors under Prof. Rautenstrauch from whom the more sensational Scott "technocrats" have now been weeded. It is by this time virtually clear to everyone save self-blinded capitalists and politicians that the old relation of the individual to the needs of the community has utterly broken down under the impact of intensively productive machinery. Baldly stated—in a highly mechanised nation there is no longer enough work to be done, under any conceivable circumstances, to require the services of the entire capable population if each individual is worked to his maximum (even an humane and rational maximum) capacity.

This is an unbeatable truth around which no amount of sophistry can get. It means that from now on no person of average ability and willingness can be given a guarantee of food, clothing, and shelter in exchange for work performed. There is not enough, under a laissez-faire system, for all to do; hence a residue of the permanently unemployable, increasing as mechanical ingenuity increases, must always be with us. We have the three alternatives of feeding this residue charitably, starving it into a civilisation-ending revolt, or restoring it to self-respecting effectiveness by artificially spreading work. Of these alternatives the third is the obvious choice—but, since it involves a regulation or minimisation of private profit, it can be adopted only through a facing of realities and a wholesome repudiation of empty political and economic theories. To make the moulders of policy realise this, our repetitions must be insistent, sober, and well-informed.

We must also repeat endlessly the very real danger of annihilative revolution which, in case of indefinitely delayed relief, lurks in the offing despite the truly astonishing degree of popular patience exhibited thus far. Men cannot be starved or buffeted about perpetually without protest—and when a person has nothing to gain from an existing social order, he feels free to act against it. If a sufficiently large minority become convinced that an honest willingness to work under the present system will no longer gain them a living, they cannot be expected to do otherwise than strike out for another system. Even now the anti-legal acts of the Iowa farmers—who prevent mortgage foreclosures through mob intimidation—are highly significant.

It is of course true—despite the bolshevistic howlings in foreign centres like New York City—that what the overwhelming bulk of discontented Americans would aim for in a revolution would not be Bolshevism, but merely a new system of state control of property ensuring a decent apportionment of resources within the existing civilisation. It is not, however, equally certain that that is what they would get if they were actually stirred up to decisive and successful action.

Americans know little of the technique of social revolt, hence administrative leadership would inevitably fall into the hands of aliens already highly trained in that respect, and harbouring altogether different ideas regarding proper objects. Once the avalanche was started, it would be difficult for the conservative but untrained revolutionists to preserve their rational programme against the astute machinations of the imported leaders with their utterly repulsive ideas derived from the slave-heritage of Continental Europe's under-men.

As the rational Russian revolution of Kerensky, Kornilov, and Miliukov became at last the tragic cataclysm of Lenin, Trotsky, and Stalin, so might a well-meant farmer's and mechanic's uprising in America become an orgy of slaughter and cultural destruction. It must not be forgotten, in this connexion, that the alien leaders of such an orgy would have powerful support from a superficially impressive and dangerously articulate American element in sympathy with them; the neurotic "intelligentsia" which includes persons of substantial achievement in non-political fields—authors, critics, and scientists like Dreiser, Anderson, Edmund Wilson, and V. F. Calverton. Clearly, it would pay to go to almost any length to avoid even the start of an upheaval of any sort—and repetition must not fail to emphasise this.

Nor should we neglect to repeat the details of the dark picture presented by this age. To use a very conservative estimate, about 12,000,000 people in the United States are unemployed, while a much larger number—perhaps half the entire population—are suffering hardship to a greater or less degree as a result of reduced income, unsatisfactory employment, or the burden of assisting unemployed relatives. Of the unemployed, an undoubted majority are persons of ample skill, experience, and capacity, prepared to offer in exchange for decent wages certain definite services which have hitherto been useful and necessary. They are not less capable than the average run of persons still employed, but are merely the unlucky ones in the constant competition for the insufficient number of positions now available. A natural upturn in the current of business would restore work to many, but not to a great remaining bulk. Mechanical and commercial efficiency has arranged more and more methods—many of them devised since the dawn of the depression as aids in saving private profit—whereby all the needs of an unlimited consuming public can be supplied through the services of fewer and fewer human workers.

These unemployed persons are for the most part still comparatively young and in reasonable health. They have diligently sought for work not only in their own respective lines but in all other lines which they feel they have any chance at all of competently following; and in general tend to be the sincere, industrious, and persevering type usually regarded as assets to the country and to their local communities. Being accustomed to consider themselves necessary parts of the industrial system, whose labour has a real and definite value, they have developed a high degree of self-respect; while the assurance of at least a modest income has given them a wholesome, comfortable, and in many cases tasteful standard of living. This standard of living is now so deeply ingrained that it cannot be lightly abandoned—indeed, it would be a calamity if it were abandoned, since its good effect on the tone of the whole nation's civilisation is so ample.

Its holders expect certain normal rewards from life, and in return are staunch sustainers of the peaceful system of law and order which has until lately made such rewards possible. They feel that their contributions to society ought to earn for them, and for the young, aged, and infirm persons dependent upon them, a definite material security and spiritual dignity. When, through no fault or diminished capacity of theirs, the assurance of that security and dignity seems about to be withdrawn, they have a right to demand that vigorous steps be taken to restore it. They believe that it is a duty of government to try to establish—by any means whatever—a degree of balance which will once more make the normal prizes guaranteed results of industrial willingness and ability.

The psychological effect of the present catastrophe on these sturdy and competent unemployed—for whom the securing of money has suddenly become an impossibility—is disastrous and far-reaching. Faced in most cases with actual and unaccustomed hardships, and in any case with a preying anxiety about the future, they have on their hands an aimless idleness (for only the topmost strata are trained to the intellectually and aesthetically profitable use of leisure) which vastly aggregates their mounting worry about food, clothing, shelter, and the maintenance of decent standards.

The higher in the cultural scale the victim is, the more heavily does his new destitution press upon him and bewilder him—and many of great refinement and cultivated mode of life have been engulfed. The anguish attendant upon the loss of cherished possessions and habits which have become dominant landmarks of existence is probably the most thoroughly poignant which any human being can endure, and it is not alone the former possessor of luxuries who suffers through the present debacle. As previously mentioned, a large majority of the unemployed possess deeply seated standards which, though far from sybaritic, nevertheless indicate self-respect and well-regulated social experience—and which must be almost wholly relinquished amidst the universal discomfort and distress of today. Many accustomed to the social amenities are now obliged to live in unutterably depressing and dispiriting quarters—with an insufficient and unpalatable food-supply, and with eviction and unthinkable horrors of starvation and exposure staring them in the face. Desperation or deterioration of morale are under such circumstances almost inevitable. With nothing to enjoy or hope for, the victims are confronted by a choice between suicide and beggary—the proudest and most potentially valuable individuals often choosing the former.

That this condition harms the national tradition as well as the individuals concerned can hardly be disputed. The dominantly commercial civilisation of boom times was itself an anti-cultural influence, and this addition of a materially degrading element greatly abets the decline. When families of taste are no longer able to maintain the dignified and independent form of life which has hitherto distinguished them, and when even the essentials of a neat personal appearance are made impossible for formerly fastidious multitudes, the general standard is bound to suffer. High levels of living are hard-won enough in any case, and tend to disintegrate alarmingly when existence becomes a sordid, aimless, and apparently helpless struggle. Ethics perish along with good manners when people begin to feel that there is nothing to live or fight for any more.

Naturally, some steps have been taken toward the relief of the people's more elemental woes; but their ironic inadequacy is easy to see. In many cities the artificial work created for the jobless is wholly unsuited to most of the victims concerned, and far too fragmentary to give any of its recipients a genuine living. Usually, too, the process of application for such work is rendered infinitely painful and humiliating by the personal catechisms imposed, and by the general sense of defeat and insignificance inculcated through the harsh and individuality-crushing red tape made necessary by the very nature of the enterprise. The abnormal, artificial, and essentially charitable character of the alleged "work"—haphazardly created as an excuse for giving out monetary driblets—is almost always manifest to a devitalising and spirit-dampening extent. It is so clearly a disguised "dole" that it lacks all the stimulus of that genuine work which supplies the actual needs of the community. Moreover, it is usually so repugnant in nature, and so ill-adapted to the capacities and temperaments of its performers (ditch-digging and brush-clearing for soft-handed, short-winded office clerks, and so on), that it tends all too often to become a stultifying and sullenness-breeding nightmare.

The tactics of profit-seeking private employers in the crisis are about what might be expected. In the city of New York many commercial and industrial enterprises have taken advantage of the tragic labour surplus by discharging their normally paid help and hiring new staffs from the ranks of the unemployed at the same pitifully small wage—$12.00 per week—which is usually offered by the local Emergency Work Bureau for the Unemployed.

One result of these palliatives and piracies is to give the much-buffeted victim a disconcerting and conceivably dangerous feeling of his precarious, puppet-like position and constant instability under the existing system. Another result is the total or partial alienation of skilled workers from their normal occupations, so that they will be clumsy and rusty if ever called back to these pursuits. It is of course needless to remark on the obvious problem of the young, who are now growing into adulthood without any chance to learn and practice a regular occupation.

For the southern and western farmer the outlook is as dire as for the eastern labourer or urban clerk. Agricultural products bring no appreciable money, and foreclosed mortgages are rapidly transforming self-respecting freeholders into peasant-like and increasingly penniless tenants. Vigorous and progressive Westerners cannot look with equanimity upon a system which bids fair to reduce them to the servile state of the deep South's poor-white cotton "croppers".

With large sections of the population in this hopeless and torturesome state of dispossessedness—Yankee and Southerner, Easterner and Westerner, rustic and urbanite, Republican and Democrat, patrician and plebeian, wet and dry, old-American and assimilated immigrant for once united in a desperate common cause—it would be idle and frivolous to minimise the danger of a spread of revolutionary sentiment from the old "red" class of chronic incompetents, malcontents, fanatics, and foreigners to those responsible elements of the people who have so far been our chief bulwarks against social explosion. Of course it would not be a communistic revolution that these elements would desire, but as pointed out before, a revolution is a much easier thing to start than to control. We cannot well starve and goad the people into an uprising, and at the same time expect to be guaranteed immunity from those extreme lengths to which uprisings are fatally apt to go.

If a revolt comes, it is likely to mean Bolshevism in the end—hence it behoves us to look closely at that article as now practiced in Russia and see if it be not a thing worth going to any length to escape.

In considering Soviet Russia we do not need to consult the reports of its impassioned enemies. The plainest proofs of the unfitness of its methods for nations of Western-European traditions and race-stock are to be found in the preachments of its own leaders. Certainly, many individual details of its programme—such as the coördination of industries—are of admitted ingenuity and worthy of possible adoption in modified form by the Western countries; but the merest glance at the whole underlying fabric is enough to demonstrate its unsuitability.

What the Soviets have done is to ensure a meagre livelihood to the least competent classes by destroying the whole background of tradition which made life endurable for persons of a higher degree of imagination and richer store of cultivation. It is their claim that they could not have guaranteed security to the humble without this wholesale destruction of accustomed ideas, but we may easily see that this is but a thin veil for a purely theoretical fanaticism bearing all the earmarks of a new religion—a fetichistic cult woven around the under-man's notion of transvaluated social values and around a fantastically literal application and extension of the groping theories and idealistic extravagances of the late Karl Marx.

While of course the backward production-capacity of Russia creates problems unknown in America, it is none the less clear that quasi-religious zeal for a "new order" with unaccustomed values—born of the present leaders' hatred for the old culture which gave them a subordinate place—lies behind the wanton destruction by the Soviets of all the refinements, cherished memories, familiar customs, artistic traditions, and historic associations which gave the civilised Russian his primary reasons for existence. To claim that a production and distribution system including the humblest elements could not have been devised and eventually made effective without this cultural vandalism is the sheerest nonsense—a form of nonsense arising from the Marxians' hoary fallacy that economics and the arts are inextricably connected. The Bolsheviki's real objects are not primarily to feed the starving and give decent jobs to those willing to work, but to disrupt the whole system of privilege-tenure in accordance with an elegance-hating theory of abstract justice. As between this theoretical ideal and the preservation of a real civilisation of natural growth, they chose the former. They have made it possible for everyone to live—but have deprived life of all that makes it worth living. Such is the system which communists would like to see forced upon the United States.

It is needless to rehearse the utter and degrading loss of individual liberty which results from the orthodox communistic theory that society is itself an organism in which each person is merely an insignificant cell. It is not in anti-Soviet libels, but in the proud reports of Soviet leaders, that we read of the forcible transfer of whole village populations from their ancestral abodes to new locations in the Arctic, and of the arbitrary ordering of Moscow clerks to tasks of manual labour in the farms and forests of Siberia. All these things are logical outgrowths of what the Bolsheviks call their "collectivistic ideology", and typical examples of the horrors which might fall upon us if communism were to gain a foothold here.

The irreparable destruction on the purely cultural side is equally flagrant. The identification of all art (or what passes for it) with political and economic propaganda, and the virtual outlawry of the artist whose work is sincere and non-propagandist, are things too well known to need emphasis. What they have produced is a vast desert of dry and immaturely conceived social tracts, redeemed only by a few promising (and generally disapproved) experiments. This in the country which produced Turgeniev, Dostoievsky, and Tschaikovsky, and whose pre-revolutionary traditions are still a powerful influence in the Western world! Of the Soviets' architectural vandalism, which destroys beauty right and left in the interest of "practical efficiency" or anti-religious fanaticism, the less said the better. Even pure science is belittled in favour of applied technology, and of the pseudo-science which can be made to serve as communistic propaganda.

While the meddling of the Bolsheviks with matters of personal identity and family life is perhaps exaggerated by some, it remains a fact that the hereditary traditions of honour and human relationships which mean so much in Western-European life would be seriously imperilled wherever communism might secure a foothold. Likewise, our deepest racial instincts would be outraged by attempts to enforce negro social equality. Cherished landmarks and background details—the small things which give us a sense of placement, direction, and purpose in life—would be snatched away by the dozen. Our calendar, for example, would probably be butchered almost beyond recognition, with numbers substituted for the names of the months and days as frequently in seventeenth-century New England and among the Quakers.

The squalor and lack of privacy in living conditions imposed upon the Russian population is a portent of what would follow in communism's wake. It is, of course, clear that no nation with a fully representative population would for a moment tolerate such a chaos—Russia having succumbed only after her better elements were murdered or exiled. That such murder and exile would be the lot of the best American elements in case of a communistic revolt is virtually self-evident—and it might be added that the exiles would probably find much difficulty in gaining a permanent haven elsewhere, since all the European and colonial nations are too racked with unemployment problems of their own to welcome any large body of newcomers, no matter how high in quality. Probably Canada—climatically unsuited for a large number of us—would form the principal refuge, unless parts of the United States (such as the loyal, conservative, and overwhelmingly native-American South) remained free from Bolshevik control.

If it be fancied that a realisation of these perils will be enough to deter the desperate and dispossessed American unemployed from any rash move, we must remember that on the other hand provocations are rapidly and unbearably increasing. Each year the situation grows worse, and relief money comes harder and harder. When all charities and appropriations trickle down to nothingness, and actual starving looms close at hand, how likely are the victims to employ the finer gradations of reason? Clearly, a change must come somehow—and the earnest wish of the good citizen is that it may come through the intelligent action of properly seated legislators and lead to something like a remedy, rather than through a general tumult and chaos leading in all probability to destruction. The cultural fruits of 1500 years of continuous Anglo-Saxon life, 300 of them amidst the moulding influences of this continent, are too precious to be risked in the arena of savage strife.

What, then, is to be done? Certainly no one is naive enough to fancy that a casual edict or two from congress, even in the most approved direction, will be sufficient to produce an overbrimming Utopia on twenty-four hours' notice! At the moment it is unlikely that anyone could outline the long series of gradual steps and legislative experiments which will be needed to bring our political institutions into accord with changed realities, facilitate the wider distribution of resources, and restore to the willing workman the certainty of receiving a good living in exchange for his labour. All we can expect at first is that the legislators will slowly begin—through popular clamour and repetitions of the obvious—to shed the almost insane cowl of blindness, indifference, evasion, and self-deception which the mixed forces of inertia, reckless plutocratic pressure, and obsolete, preconceived doctrines have drawn so tightly over their eyes. A genuine readiness to abandon the worship of methods, abstract formulae, and catchwords, to think in terms of the entire population rather than of the larger business interests, and to face the realities of the present industrial muddle with an open willingness to use unorthodox methods in achieving specific ends, is the most one may ask of the government at present, except perhaps a few immediate and temporary palliatives such as domestic debt cancellation and an increase in public relief through the heavy taxation of very large accumulations of private capital.

It would be absurd for a layman, ignorant of the complex links of cause and effect involved in the regulation of production and distribution, and in the readjustment of resources, to do more than guess vaguely at any of the elements of possible recovery. Probably a bald assertion of governmental control over large accumulations of resources—a potential limitation of private property beyond certain liberal limits—would form one of the salient features. This would involve the state coördination and operation of the wider fundamental industries on a basis of service rather than profit, and would enable the hours and conditions of labour to be artificially regulated with a view to distributing work among the whole population, no matter how little is left by machinery to be done, or how little profit could be obtained from the employment of many persons at a really living wage for only a few hours per week.

It will probably be thought advisable to guarantee decently appropriate work to every citizen of the state, with a really substantial unemployment insurance to allow for the natural imperfections in this universal allotment. Reciprocally, however, the state will probably reserve the right to make work compulsory upon everyone when circumstances demand it—though refraining from forcing persons into remote and inappropriate industries as the Soviets do. Liberal old-age pensions, beginning early enough to help in cutting down the permanent labour surplus, are virtually a foregone conclusion.

Whether independent agriculture can be preserved, no one can properly predict. If this, and independent merchandising, survive, certain complex price-fixing and other auxiliary measures will probably be necessary. Otherwise the growth of governmentally controlled farms and chain selling establishments seems likely, the operators of these things receiving the customary guarantees of employed persons. There would seem to be no barrier against such an universal condition of working for the government; nor would such an arrangement, in a country of unlimited resources and production, necessitate any of the restrictions on the individual which the Soviets ruthlessly impose.

Levels of salary in every branch of activity would be determined by the complexity and difficulty of the work performed, so that high-grade executives would receive as much more than common labourers as is now the custom. The continued protection of limited private property would of course enable persons of the executive class to retain their present type of existence—minus some of the extravagances—and to retire on the modest scale without calling on the pension funds except in case of necessity.

The state control of industry would naturally introduce new factors into the matter of foreign commerce, and one cannot well predict the future of tariff and free trade. Large investments in foreign countries —and especially the wholesale exploitation of economically backward countries—would almost certainly be discouraged as a leading provocative in war-breeding. For defensive purposes, of course, an army and navy of great strength would be rigorously maintained—perhaps through universal training.

On the cultural side the existing tradition need not be menaced. Education, however, will require amplification in order to meet the needs of a radically increased leisure among all classes of society. It is probable that the number of persons possessing a sound general culture will be greatly increased, with correspondingly good results to the civilisation. On the other hand, it would be foolish to assume that the more mentally sluggish types will ever lose their present cultural inferiority. Curricula will naturally be shaped to fit existing conditions; and in view of the now complex nature of government and industry, civics and economics will receive enhanced attention.

If anything approaching the Soviets' re-shaping of popular conceptions is attempted, it will probably be in the direction of removing the old tendency to judge the individual by his industrial status—a step made necessary by the extension of much potentially cultivated leisure to persons of varying occupation. Naturally this leisure, plus education, will bring many of the skilled labouring class into fields of intellectual and aesthetic activity, removing them altogether from the traditional cultural state of the "workman"; and this removal must be recognised.

Where the course of good sense will have to differ most widely from the plans of old-time idealistic socialism is in the matter of political organisation. Nowadays we realise that no layman, no matter how generally cultivated, is in any way capable of passing on any average point of governmental policy. National affairs, in an age of intensive mechanisation and widespread organisation, have become so involved and technical that only an administrative and economic expert or a trained engineer can form any genuinely clear idea of how certain broadly desirable results can be secured, or what the ultimate consequences of any proposed measure will really be. All the factors of cause and effect in political action, and in the problems of production, distribution, and national maintenance, have become so infinitely complex that the ordinary individual can no longer hope to trace them. Today the "man in the street" casts his vote for things he actually knows nothing about, and nothing but the subterranean control of large industrial interests (now a menace because of our changing economy) has so far saved the nation from general incompetence and irresponsible chaos in government.

Obviously government *by* the people is now a joke or a tragedy, although government *for* them remains as the most logical goal. Though the wider distribution of *resources* must be accepted as a cardinal policy, the narrower restriction of *power* will be a necessary corollary. No bungling democratic government could even begin to accomplish the delicate adjustments which loom ahead. Laymen of slight education and low intelligence are wholly useless and potentially harmful as determiners of the national course, and even laymen of wide education and high intelligence can do no more than roughly (and often erroneously) judge the general executive calibre of certain administrators from watching their performances in a few fields which may happen to be familiar. No non-technician, be he artist, philosopher, or scientist, can even begin to judge the labyrinthine governmental problems with which these administrators must deal.

Accordingly we must expect any adequate government to be of the sort now generally called "fascistic"—forming, as it were, an oligarchy of intelligence and education. Office-holding must be limited to men of high technical training, and the franchise which elects them must be granted only to those able to pass rigorous educational examinations (emphasising civic and economic subjects) and scientific intelligence tests. Elective offices ought to be very few—perhaps no more than a single dictator—in order to ensure harmony and speed in the execution of necessary measures. What would make such a system perfectly fair and representative would be, of course, the equal availability of franchise-earning education to all—an effective reality in view of the leisure of the future. Corruption, naturally, could not be entirely abolished; but there would undoubtedly be far less of it in a government of the educated and the intelligent than in the haphazard governments of today.

The difficulties in getting such a government established, like those in getting any useful measure enacted, need be underestimated by none. Therein lies the tenuous uncertainty of all predictions. However, it is noteworthy that in times of national peril the bulk of the people—holding the balance of physical power—are often willing to support policies which, although beyond their understanding and tending to curtail their power, seem to them honestly designed for their benefit. Thus, despite minority grumblings, Mussolini was borne to office by the genuine will of the Italian people.

Such are the prophetic guesses of a layman—self-disqualified, as just noted, from any pretence to authoritativeness. It must be understood that the real developments of the future are utterly beyond prediction, since wholly unseen or wrongly appraised factors may swing matters in totally unexpected directions. Even without these factors many conceivable alternative courses, some not vastly removed from ordinary capitalism, exist; the preceding guesses including perhaps the extremes of departure from present conditions which could reasonably be called for, according to our present idea of the possibilities. All that seems certain is that the general problem must very soon be squarely and scientifically faced by the government without regard for political and economic orthodoxies, if the peril of an unfathomed revolutionary abyss is to be averted.

Hence these repetitions of things which thousands have been thinking, saying, writing, and publishing in the last few years. They are things which must be repeated more and more widely—publicised as "technocracy" was publicised—if the slow and dim-eyed forces at the helm are to be impressed in time to take preservative action. We must cease to fear being trite.

Here are the facts:

> Millions are unemployed, probably permanently under the present system, and existing in increasing misery and fear.
>
> It is no longer possible for ability and willingness to work to guarantee a man a decent living, and the widespread conviction of this is undermining public morale.
>
> There are plenty of resources in the country, *withheld* by artificial *methods* from those who need them.
>
> Attempts at relief have so far been irregular, inadequate, unscientific, and painful to the recipients; producing a dangerous popular psychology.
>
> When men feel that an existing system has nothing to give them, they will strike out for another system. Insecurity for half the nation means disaster for the whole.
>
> If the people are starved into revolution, the worst excesses of communism are very likely to occur.
>
> Precedent makes it certain that, given the will, brains, independence, and determination of high-grade men, the forces of government can accomplish a recuperative redistribution of resources through emergency measures ignoring the absolute orthodoxies of politics and economics.
>
> What is needed is a restoration of the power of normal work to ensure each individual a self-respecting status and a modest quota of food, clothing, shelter, freedom, and recreation; enough rewards, that is, to make life under the existing civilisation worth enduring.

These matters cannot be dodged, and every moment of delay in facing them increases the nation's peril. We have plenty of thoughtful and liberal men who cannot or do not act, and plenty of strong men of action who cannot or will not think in a far-sighted or liberal way. Are there not a few in the seats of power who have both the minds to think and the strength and opportunity to act?

Feby. 22, 1933

VI
ANTIQUARIAN TRAVELS

When we read in a 1915 letter that "I have never been outside the three states of Rhode Island, Massachusetts, and Connecticut!" we sense behind the feigned humility a disingenuous smugness at having led so circumscribed an existence; by contrast, a 1931 letter listing nineteen states visited suggests not merely greater mobility but a firmer grasp of political, social, and cultural reality through the abandonment of self-conscious sequestration. If anyone still believes the hoary myth of Lovecraft's reclusiveness, the travelogues in this section will certainly be a powerful antidote; but we should beware of falling into the opposite fallacy of assuming that Lovecraft's extensive travels along the eastern seaboard during the last decade of his life suddenly show him to be a worldly-wise, cosmopolitan sophisticate of the Henry James sort. The continuing provinciality of much of Lovecraft's outlook can, if in no other way, be detected by the frequency with which, in these essays, he compares so many different architectural, scenic, and historical features of the lands he is visiting with the corresponding features in New England. It is as if New England in general, and Providence in particular, were the eternal standard or touchstone by which everything else is judged; and, for all the cosmicism of his metaphysics, he knew that his emotional ties were deeply rooted in the soil and culture of New England. Lovecraft may have traveled far, but he always came home.

In those travelogues not designed for publication—represented here by "Observations on Several Parts of America" (1928) and the hitherto unpublished "Travels in the Provinces of America" (1929) and "An Account of Charleston" (1930)—Lovecraft was free to indulge his every whim. The antiquated style of these pieces is the first thing that strikes us; and yet, they provide emphatic evidence to demolish another silly myth, that of Lovecraft's archaistic "pose." What this position claims is that Lovecraft's archaism was an affectation intended with naive seriousness; and what these travelogues reveal is the tongue-in-cheek humor indicative of Lovecraft's complete awareness of his "affectation" and his adoption of it very largely with playful intent. Lovecraft's general adherence to the standards of the past is not in question; but surely such a sentence as "The chasmal majesty of the enormous gulph was such as to suggest the monstrous scenery of other planets" is meant to dynamite its own ponderousness.

Less attractive idiosyncrasies of Lovecraft find their way into these travelogues, notably racism and even occasional snobbery. In so late a work as his Charleston travelogue of 1930 he writes, with evidently a straight face: "Gentlefolk in Charleston still pursue their ways for pleasure and not for show or profit, and are still decently anxious to keep their names and personal affairs *out* of the papers. . . . The Charleston dailies are the only ones without a vulgar 'society column' to spy upon the comings and goings of important people." This was written at about the same time Lovecraft was violently attacking these same "important people" for their hopelessly reactionary political and social ideals: "God! The utter ignorance and sappiness of the snivelling, myth-swallowing, church-going stuffed shirts who go about cackling dead slogans and spreading the heraldic tail-feathers that proclaim them self-conscious members of a close corporation of 'best people'!" In charity to Lovecraft one can suppose that he feels the Charleston "important people" are actual upholders of an enlightened cultural tradition while the "best people" are not; but all this is really another example of Lovecraft's inability to shed the aristocracy of his upbringing even in his socialist period.

Other portions of these travelogues are more amusing. In speaking of the early colonization of Virginia Lovecraft writes: "In 1619 wives were sent out for the colonists, and in the same year the first cargo of African blacks arriv'd—proving that troubles never come singly." Yes, this is sexist and racist, but it is also funny. More genuinely mirthsome is the hilarious vignette of the slightly crazed German ("No doubt he was a leader in some modern religious or ethical cult") whom Lovecraft encountered on his train ride to the South in 1929; it is still more amusing to reflect that this figure was transmogrified into the mad villain of Lovecraft's revision of Adolphe de Castro's "The Electric Executioner."

A more important relation between Lovecraft's travelogues and his fiction occurs in "Vermont—A First Impression" (1927). It is readily apparent that Lovecraft used whole passages of this essay in the latter portion of "The Whisperer in Darkness" (1930); but a close comparison shows that the wistful nostalgia of the travelogue becomes in the story something darker and more sinister, as if Nature and antiquity have themselves become an emblem for the transience of man. This is one very obvious way in which Lovecraft's travelogues nurtured his creative imagination; indeed, the travelogues themselves approach fictional technique in their careful selectivity of detail, the narrative drive of their historical disquisitions (how can we not think of "The Shunned House" or "The Case of Charles Dexter Ward"?), and their carefully crafted structure behind a mere appearance of rambling spontaneity.

Two of the travelogues were written to order: "Some Dutch Footprints in New England" (1933) was commissioned by Wilfred B. Talman for *De Halve Maen*, the journal of the Holland Society of New York, and "Homes and Shrines of Poe" (1934) was written for Hyman Bradofsky's *Californian*. "An Account of Charleston" was completed shortly after Lovecraft's first visit to Charleston in 1930; and the wealth of historical, architectural, and topographical detail it contains, as well as its exquisite eighteenth-century prose, is a testimonial to the profound impression Charleston made upon him. Lovecraft frequently averred that the city was second only to Providence in his esteem, and that he would willingly move there were it not for the many ties he had to his native city. In 1936 H. C. Koenig was planning to visit Charleston and asked Lovecraft for a brief guide; Lovecraft unearthed his unpublished essay—written solely for his own satisfaction—and truncated it significantly, watering down the eighteenth-century English and also removing some of the more piquant portions. Koenig published this letter as *Charleston*, but a comparison of the two travelogues reveals the earlier one to be far superior both intrinsically and as a key to Lovecraft's own predilections.

Lovecraft's travels played a significant role in his later life, for aside from stimulating his creativity they provided what joy and expansiveness there was in his restricted and penurious existence. There are those who say he "wasted" much of his life in correspondence and in travels that habitually consumed the entire summer: why could he not have written more fiction? There are many fallacies and injustices in this position, but the worst is the tacit assumption that Lovecraft should have lived his life for our, not his own, benefit. If Lovecraft had never written any fiction, it would be our loss but his prerogative; if he wished to while away the time writing postcards on a park bench in Charleston, that was entirely his right. Lovecraft in fact led very much the life he wished to lead; and the vitality of his travelogues bespeaks the pleasure he derived from absorbing the antiquities of an entire continent. To have squeezed so much enjoyment from such limited means is something we might all emulate.

VERMONT—A FIRST IMPRESSION

To the southern New-Englander entering Vermont for the first time there is a sense of mystic revivification. On the towns of the lower coast the blight of mutation and modernity has descended. Weird metamorphoses and excrescences, architectural and topographical, mark a menacing tyranny of mechanism and viceroyalty of engineering which are fast hurrying the present scene out of all linkage with its historic antecedents and setting it adrift anchorless and all but traditionless in alien oceans. Swart foreign forms, heirs to moods and impulses antipodal to those which moulded our heritage, surge in endless streams along smoke-clouded and lamp-dazzled streets; moving to strange measures and inculcating strange customs. All through the nearer countryside the stigmata of change are spreading. Reservoirs, billboards, and concrete roads, power lines, garages, and flamboyant inns, squalid immigrant nests and grimy mill villages; these things and things like them have brought ugliness, tawdriness, and commonplaceness to the urban penumbra. Only in the remoter backwoods can one find the pristine and ancestral beauty which was southern New-England's, or the unmixed signs of that continuous native life whose deep roots make it the one authentic outgrowth of the landscape. There are traces enough to allure and tantalise, but not enough to satisfy. With our keenest pleasure and satisfaction is mixed a certain melancholy; for it is upon the ghost of something beloved and departed, rather than upon the thing itself, that we gaze. Our own country and history seem subtly dissolving away from us, and we clutch frantically at the straws and symbols through which our imaginations may momentarily recall and recapture a past which is really our own.

With such a mood, softened perhaps by the beauty of the hills and river-bends which flank the gateway, the southern New-Englander enters Vermont. He has seen its hills for some time across the Connecticut, domed and undulant, and shining with a clear emerald light unmarred by vapour or defacement. Then comes a sweeping downward curve, and beyond limpid water the climbing terraces of an old town loom into sight, as a loved, remembered picture might appear when the leaves of a childhood volume are slowly turned. It is plain from the first that this town is not quite like those one has left behind. Roofs and steeples and chimneys, prosaic enough in the telling, here cluster together on the green river-bluff in some magical collocation that stirs dim memories. Something in the contours, something in the setting, has power to touch deep viol-strings of feeling which are ancestral if one be young and personal if one be old. The whole scene vaguely brings us a fleeting quality we have known before. We have seen such towns long ago, climbing above deep river-valleys and rearing their old brick walls beside sloping, cobbled streets. Grandeur may be wanting, but the marvel of rekindled vision is there. Something is alive that is dead elsewhere; something that we, or the blood that is in us, can recognise as more closely akin to ourselves than anything in the busy cosmopolis to the southward. This, in fine, is a surviving fragment of the old America; it is what our other towns used to be in the days when they were most themselves, the days when they housed their own people and gave birth to all the little legends and bits of lore which make them glamorous and significant in the eyes of their children.

By an ancient covered bridge we ride back through decades and enter the enchanted city of our fathers' world. We had not thought such bridges still existed, for southward the last of them was demolished years ago. The river-valley is deep, and as we come from the wooden tunnel we feel the kind guardianship of the ancient hills and the eternal streams from unknown fountains of the north. On past an island stepping-stone we go, and up the homely slopes of the dawn-fresh town. There is life here, and the clatter of modern industry; but somehow the life and industry are more our own than the febrile bustle to the southward. It is the fresher, more coherent vitality that springs from continuity with ancestral sources; the vitality our own coastal region might have had under different dispensations of history. This, then, is Brattleboro; the town where Kipling wrote and Royall Tyler rhymed. Say what you will of changing Vermont life, the outsider can still find in it far more of basic worth, far more of the unmixed primal fund of mood and fibre which was New-England's supreme heritage, than the commerce-plagued cities to the south can shew. Into this hive of half-concealed glamour we ascend, stirred and rejuvenated by memories and influences too ethereal to define. The kinship and hospitality of the Main Street spread over us, and encourage us to climb higher into the charmed sea of westerly greenness to which these atavistic bricks form pylon and peristyle. The wild hills are before us, where song and witchery lurk.

And now we cast off all allegiance to modern things; to change, and the rule of steel and steam, and the crumbling of ancient visions and simple impulses. The tar and concrete roads, and the vulgar world that bred them, have ended; and we wind rapt and wondering over elder and familiar ribbons of rutted whiteness which curl past alluring valleys and traverse old wooden bridges in the lee of green slopes. The nearness and intimacy of the little domed hills have become almost breath-taking. Their steepness and abruptness hold nothing in common with the humdrum, standardised world we know, and we cannot help feeling that their outlines have some strange and almost-forgotten meaning, like vast hieroglyphs left by a rumoured titan race whose glories live only in rare, deep dreams. We climb and plunge fantastically as we thread this hypnotic landscape. Time has lost itself in the labyrinths behind, and around us stretch only the flowering waves of faery. Tawdriness is not there, but instead, the recaptured beauty of vanished centuries—the hoary groves, the untainted pastures hedged with gay blossoms, and the small brown farmsteads nestling amidst huge trees beneath vertical precipices of fragrant brier and meadow-grass. Even the sunlight assumes a supernal glamour, as if some special atmosphere or exaltation mantled the whole region. There is nothing like it save in the magic vistas that sometimes form the backgrounds of Italian primitives. Sodoma and Leonardo saw such expanses, but only in the distance, and through the vaultings of Renaissance arcades. We rove at will through the midst of the picture; and find in its necromancy a thing we have known or inherited, and for which we have always been vainly searching.

At the heart of this weirdly beautiful Arcadia Vermont's gentle poet dwells. One with his hereditary hills and groves, with the spreading, venerable trees and the ancient peaked roofs of the vine-banked cottages, lives Arthur Goodenough; singer of the olden strain and last of the long line of New-England's Puritan oracles. Tilling ancestral acres in the good old way, and keeping alive beside his daily hearth the well-loved thoughts and customs of our Golden Age, he is vastly more than a retrospective teller of bygone tales. Alone amongst the surviving choir he truly leads the pastoral life he breathes; so that we need not wonder at the flawless authenticity of his message. He has prolonged our old New-England in himself, and his stately charm and genial hospitality are as truly poems as anything the pen could write. Lovely beyond words is the realm over which the poet holds agrestic sway. The ancient house on the hillside, embowered in greenery and shadowed by a lone leafy monarch; the dream-stirring slope to the westward, where earth's beauty melts into the cosmic glory of sunset; the narrow, beckoning road, the outspread, dew-glistening meadows, and the hint of spectral woodlands and valleys in the background—all these mark out a perfect poet's seat, and cause us to thank Fate that for once in history a man and his setting are well matched.

Northward from Brattleboro the charm still holds. There are glorious sweeps of vivid valley where great cliffs rise, New-England's virgin granite shewing grey and austere through the verdure that scales the crests. There are gorges where untamed streams leap, bearing down toward the river the unimagined secrets of a thousand pathless peaks. Narrow, half-hidden roads bore their way through solid, luxuriant masses of forest, among whose primal trees whole armies of elemental spirits lurk. Archaic covered bridges linger fearsomely out of the past in pockets of the hills, and here and there a summit bears a tiny hamlet of trim, clean old houses and steeples that Time has never been able to sully.

Now to the right the river shimmers mystically around its bends, while New-Hampshire's granite vistas stretch panoramically toward the unknown East, whence far birds bring legends of the sea's wonder. Putney, East Putney, Grout, Westminster—one by one new piquancies unfold and retire as the traveller fares northward. The steep river-bank quaintness and ancient Yankeedom of Bellows Falls appears, a bridge is crossed, and suddenly one realises that Vermont has been left behind.

But it is still visible for leagues across the river, veiled in distance and golden with elfin light. The spell of the past has not departed, for Vermont has given us something that we have always sought, and that can never be effaced from our spirit. Dim on the horizon the purpling hills rise, Ascutney towering in lordship above its neighbours. A bend shuts it from sight, and we are alone with our meditations.

OBSERVATIONS ON SEVERAL PARTS OF AMERICA;

Being the Journey of H. Lovecraft, Gent., into His Majesty's Colonies of New-York and the Massachusetts-Bay; the New-Hampshire Grants; the Towns of Philadelphia and Baltimore; Annapolis, Georgetown, Alexandria, and the rebel Federal City call'd Washington; and certain Parts of Virginia, westward to the Endless Caverns.

PROVIDENCE, RHODE-ISLAND

Printed and Sold by John Carter, at Shakespear's-Head in King-Street, over-against the Court House, and Sold by Merchants generally.

1728

Being oblig'd by circumstances to spend above a month and a half, last spring, in the town of Flatbush, near New-York, in the province of that name, I resolv'd to make my sojourn pleasant by means of such observations of good scenery and historick monuments as the nature of the region permitted. By good fortune I came upon not a few things of lively interest and agreeableness; both close to the town, and on short coach journeys out of it. These things, however, turn'd out to be no more than a prologue to the wider travels and sprightlier sights that follow'd them; so that a compleat record of my late wanderings must embrace near three months of time, and a territory of extream bigness, extending from His Majesty's New-Hampshire Grants (lately known to the rebels as the Federal State of Ver-mont) to the antient and civilised Province of Virginia.

My stay in Flatbush was chiefly notable for my discovery, thro' diligent searching of many books, of several objects of much antiquity which I had never discover'd before. The western end of Long-Island, in which the village is situate, was settled by Hollanders at a very early date; and so widely scatter'd were their architectural constructions, that a surprising number have surviv'd to the present time amidst surroundings more and more incongruous. On this occasion it may be imagin'd that I did not neglect the old church whose steeple, put up in 1796, still dominates the village so agreeably. It is to be lamented, that a recent sprucing-up of the churchyard hath deprived the place of some of that air of picturesque neglect which so much captivated me six years ago; but despite all changes there remains an air of loveliness and mellow repose which nothing can take away. To behold this venerable fane in the golden light of a setting sun is an experience not to be scoff'd at; and having once done this, the visitor is dispos'd to forget the constant decay which is debasing a quiet and beautiful village little by little to the state of a crowded mongrel suburb.

But most of my late explorations dealt with those parts of the country south of the village; once very open and sparsely settled, but now fast spoilt by cheap streets and the cottages of an hybrid foreign rabble. On the 19th of May I made a trip to that part of Jamaica Bay call'd the Mill Basin, there seeing for the first time the Jan Schenck house, built in 1656 from the timbers of a privateer, and reputed to be the oldest house in the entire province of New-York. This house, an old Dutch cottage with steep peaked roof, is situate on a flat tidal marsh near the shoar, and is now being crowded by the growth of an ugly manufactory district. Its condition is still very good, and the trees and buildings immediately around it help to save it from the squalor so close upon it. It is very little alter'd from its original state, and such alterations as have been made, are all of the eighteenth century. Many newspaper articles attribute a very romantick history to the house, but I do not find these tales sustain'd by such guide-books as I deem responsible. The Schencks, in general, came from Holland in 1650 and establisht many homesteads near the south shoar of western Long-Island, where the numerous creeks and salt marshes gave the country something of the home-like aspect of the Netherlands. On another trip I beheld the Nicholas Schenck house in Canarsie, only second to the Jan Schenck house in age, but sunk into a frightful state of disrepair. On still another occasion I visited the old Gerritsen Tide Mill on a creek south of Flatbush. This was built in 1688, and a dam made at the same time still confines the rising waters of the sea. The wheel is in a good state, though the building itself hath suffer'd considerably since its abandonment near forty years ago.

I vary'd these excursions into Hollandish history by a trip to a forgotten village which, tho' close at hand, is of as truly ENGLISH an origin as any town on the sacred soil of my own NEW-ENGLAND. This is the hamlet of Gravesend, south of Flatbush on the road to Coney-Island, and at no great distance from that plebeian watering-place. Gravesend was settled in 1643 by an English gentlewoman of non-conformist persuasion, one Lady Moody, who like the people of New-England, dislik'd the usages of the establisht church and sought a retreat therefrom. Tho' her settlement was within the domain of the Holland States-General, she was allow'd perfect freedom to live in the English way, and gather around her a British population; so that the region was fully prepar'd for the change which came in 1664, when Col. Nicholls and His Majesty's fleet took over the province to add to our empire. There were, of course, a sensible number of Dutch residents, as is manifest to this day in many family names. I had never seen Gravesend before, but came upon it without difficulty. Its present situation is very unfavourable, insomuch as the thickest part of it is buried beneath the trestles of an elevated rail-road; but the number of buildings still standing is singularly large. Near on a dozen cottages in plain sight date from before 1700, and not even the spreading of a vast colony of Italians can destroy the air of antiquity that hangs over the place. The Hicks-Platt house, a low cottage cover'd with thick ivy, was built in the time of Lady Moody; and within its walls the Holland governors, Willem Kieft and Petrus Stuyvesant, are known to have been entertain'd.

Further explorations in Flatbush, Flatlands, New Utrecht, and related regions yielded many highly picturesque glimpses of old farm-houses, churches, churchyards, and other reliques of better days. In some cases these were wholly surrounded by the incursions of decadent modernity, whilst in other cases small bits of contiguous farmyard or boskage lent a touch of redeeming congruity to the background. The region, as a whole, is doomed; for it is slowly being bought out by oily Jews fat with ill-got money, who are flocking out from the New-York Ghetto. Only certain parts in Flatbush proper, now zoned with fanatical strictness and held by families who have long liv'd there, will remain as a civilised oasis amidst this flood of ethnick and social putrefaction.

More striking, perhaps, than these Flatbush excursions, were those long coach journeys made once or twice each week with the family of my small foster-grandchild Frank Belknap Long, Jun. I was by this means made familiar with the pleasing rolling country north of New-York, wherein are many attractive farmsteads and villages not greatly inferior to those of New-England. The Croton reservoir region on the east side of the Hudson is mark'd by many noble hills and valleys, and I can still recall a multitude of vivid prospects very like those to be had from the hills of the Connecticut Valley. Our trips on this side of the river extended as far north as Peekskill and Lake Mahopac, and as far east as Stamford and Ridgefield, in His Majesty's Colony of Connecticut, in New-England. It was an almost unbearably tantalising experience to dip within the edge of my native country of New-England, only to emerge again into the desart of New-York. We also crossed the Bear Mountain Bridge, and enjoy'd the truly magnificent spectacle of the domed hills along the Hudson's margin. On one occasion we visited the fortress and school of West-Point, witnessing a highly impressive dress-parade from a bench beside an elderly gentleman in uniform who turn'd out to be the commandant of the Academy. Another trip on the west shoar extended to that impressive hill country wherein Tuxedo is situate, and where the Ramapaugh mountains assume an agreeable diversity of aspects. We return'd across the hills, by a winding road which travers'd the so-call'd Seven Lakes country; emerging on the shoar of the Hudson at Haverstraw.

Naturally I did not omit the town of Paterson from my itinerary, but was very congenially entertain'd by the head of the local Musaeum there; a fat, shock-headed gentleman named Morton, with whom I had had considerable previous acquaintance. James Ferdinand, I may remark, is an ideal host; and his establishment is a marvel of accomplishment and effective administration. A building all too small is utilis'd with the greatest ingenuity conceivable, and the system of arrangement and labelling wou'd do credit to the most veteran practitioner of the curatorial art. The mineral collection, which covers the entire exhibition part of the second floor, is one of the most ample and well-classify'd in these colonies; and is due entirely to the keen skill and unremitting vigilance and activity of our genial colleague. Mortonius also shew'd me as much of the local scenery as limited time wou'd permit; taking me to the top of Garrett Mountain, whence is observable as fine a prospect of Paterson on one cou'd ask—a prospect which removes much of the grimy sordidness habitual to the town as seen closely.

Another trip of interest was with our young fellow-amateur Wilfred B. Talman, Esq., to his ancestral region of Spring Valley, on the west of the river. I here beheld an unspoilt Dutch countryside still in the hands of its original families, of whom young Talman is an unmixt descendant. Tho' the village is ugly, the farm lands adjacent are very fine; and the number of old Dutch houses and burying places is almost past counting. We concluded the day with a full survey of the village of Tappan, where the unfortunate Major André was confin'd, try'd, and put to death by the rebel army in 1780. The tavern which form'd his prison (in 1780 kept by an ancestor of Talman's), and the headquarters of Genl. Washington (in which Talman's own mother was born), are still in unimpair'd condition; and the old church and churchyard (fill'd with Talman's forbears) form a spectacle worth a long journey to see. Sparkill, near by, is another antient village affording many fine specimens of Georgian architecture; but it is unfortunately given over altogether to Italians. Piermont, a river port adjacent to Sparkill, has a vast negro settlement; and affords a sinister study in decadence.

Not the least of my pleasures was a trip up the Hudson's east bank to Tarrytown, Sleepy Hollow, and the Washington Irving country in general. Tarrytown is an exquisite village perched on a cliff whose steepness and height make Providence's hill seem like a prairie. At Sleepy Hollow is an antient Dutch church built in 1685, which with the exception of the Old Ship Church at Hingham (1681) is the oldest house of publick worship, continuously us'd, in these colonies. It stands high on a terrace dominating the post road, and its churchyard has expanded into that enormous Sleepy Hollow Cemetery where the mortal remains of Mr. Irving repose. Sleepy Hollow itself, one of the finest wooded river gorges I have ever seen, is within the domain of the cemetery; no doubt forming a place of convocation for the numerous ghouls attendant upon the subterraneous population. I was every moment on the watch for the Headless Horseman, but was deny'd that sight by reason of the strength of the daylight. In returning to Flatbush, I stopt off the stage-coach at Irvington from a desire to visit Mr. Irving's country-seat of Sunnyside. Here, however, I met with disappointment; for though I descended the bank to the level of the grounds, I was inform'd by a lodge keeper that the present proprietors do not admit spectators.

Another field of exploration near New-York was the extensive county of Queens, now a borough of the greater city, and fast being ruin'd by cheap suburban villas. I made several trips thro' the still unspoilt parts of this territory, and found on its north shoar several old Dutch bouweries in much their original condition—pleasing reliques of healthier days, that will soon fall victims to the blight of vulgar land-agents. Some of the old Rapalye homesteads in this part of the county are among the best kept of all Dutch colonial specimens. In central Queens a sad transition is occurring; new rows of cheap houses being flung out across once lovely meadows where still an elder farmhouse may now and then be seen. I shall never forget my experience on the 31st day of May, when, at a point not far from Northern Boulevard, and at the very edge of a depressing line of flimsy stucco'd rookeries, I beheld a peaceful antient farmhouse with barns, byres, orchards, and plough'd fields about it; dreaming in compleat changelessness amidst so much of change. Westward, in fantastical outline against a glamorous sunset, tower'd the grotesque spires of Manhattan like a mirage of doom. Eastward the drab rows of sordid villas stretcht. But between the two the old farm still dream'd on, and the sturdy hind still bent behind the plough as the kine came in to rest at evening. It was of particular interest to me to learn, that this was not a Dutch place at all, but the farm of a New-England settler of early date, by the name of Hazard. Since all the colonial Hazards are descended from that Thomas Hazard or Hassard whose principal posterity settled in the Narragansett Country, and since I myself have a double line of Hazard ancestry in me, I felt that this place was indeed of a personal significance; and in truth it does very aptly typify the state of an archaick old gentleman left over from former times, and soon to be crowded into oblivion by the rise of a new aera to which he hath no resemblance, and with which he hath nothing in common. I need not say that my explorations of Queens included a revisiting of those spots formerly known to me; namely, the still pleasing old villages of Jamaica and Flushing. These towns were settled by gentlemen and yeomen from New-England, and were especial seats of the Quaker sect. Flushing contains the antient Bowne House, built in 1661, where George Fox once slept, and across the road from which he once preach'd. The meeting house of the Friends, built in 1694, has a very odd hay-cap roof, and is surrounded by a pleasing churchyard. I also explor'd antient Newtown, now call'd Elmhurst, with its quaint streets, old churches, and historick homesteads.

Nor must I overlook that one last bit of truly untainted countryside near New-York—the rolling agrestick reaches of Staten-Island. I saw much more of it than I ever had before, visiting in particular the tangled colonial alleys of Stapleton, the archaick lanes of New-Dorp, and the steep streets of Richmond, which rests in a picturesque valley. In New-Dorp is the antient Britton-Cubberly house, a hoary moss-grown pile now employ'd as a Musaeum; whilst at Richmond are the finest hilltop court-house and valley churchyard that the length and breadth of the island can afford. I shall never forget my sight of Richmond in a glorious sunset, when I stood on a neighbouring hill behind the churchyard and saw the spires and roofs of the drowsy village below tipp'd with a magick and trans-figuring flame.

I once remarked, that Flatbush forms the only habitable oasis in the immediate vicinity of New-York; and my late sojourn disclos'd to me but one exception. That exception is the strip of land just north of Manhattan Island, betwixt Van Cortlandt Park and the Hudson, and known by the name of Riverdale. It is here that the modern line of Broadway diverges from the course of the old Albany Post Road for a space, leaving the antient thoroughfare as a bend of hillside bye-street curving toward the bluffs above the river. Along this road many quaint houses of Georgian times still remain, whilst in the hills beyond it nestle the fine modern houses of such gentlemen of taste as appreciate the region and study to preserve its unspoil'd character. I spent a memorable day here, as a guest of my esteem'd friend, Vrest Orton, Esq., a gentleman of Vernon birth, rear'd in Athol, in the Massachusetts-Bay, and now enduring New-York from reasons of business necessity involving a connexion with the *Saturday Review of Literature.* Ortonius naturally took care not to settle in any but the least offensive parts of the metropolitan area, and he surely succeeded in choosing that section with the greatest number of mitigating points. I wander'd with pleasure over the quaint, shady roads, and lookt down with agreeable awe into the many pine ravines and graceful wooded gorges. Some of the antient houses were deserving of close study, whilst none of the newer ones was beneath contempt.

It was this same Vrest Orton, Esq., who was responsible for the first part of my subsequent wanderings. With the close of the Flatbush period I had design'd to go south at once, but by coincidence Ortonius also chose this precise season for a rural escape. Opprest by the noxious atmosphere of town, he had hired a delightful farm some miles out of Brattleboro, in Vermont, for the summer; and hither he insisted on my accompanying him for as long a period as I car'd to remain. It will be recall'd, how fervent was my admiration for Vermont when I beheld it so briefly last summer. This year my sentiments were in no wise chang'd, hence I did not waste time in hesitancy upon receiving this invitation. I had been away from my native New-England a month and a half. Now, in one glorious sweep of the rail-road coach, I left all decay behind me and was plung'd into an extatick delirium of familiar rolling hills, stone walls, embower'd white steeples, and slope-nestling farmhouse roofs. Home soil—antient New-England—loveliest land of all!

In one day I pass'd over the soil of no less than *four* of His Majesty's New-England Provinces—Connecticut, the Massachusetts-Bay, New-Hampshire, and that region of the New-Hampshire Grants which hath lately been given the name of "Vermont". New-Haven and Hartford were pass'd in the daylight. Springfield came at twilight. Greenfield was glimps'd in the dark, whilst Brattleboro came in the dead of midnight. The rail journey was at an end, and five miles of narrow hill road in a Detroit chaise brought me to the isolated Orton dwelling.

The history of the region whither I had come is known to most persons in rough outline. It is the last settled part of New-England, and remains the closest of any section to the ways of our ancestors. Before the period of its settlement it was but loosely allocated with respect to the other colonies, both New-Hampshire and New-York having vague claims of sovereignty. Colonisation began in 1724, and in times subsequent to that grants of land were made by His Majesty's Governor of New-Hampshire, the Honourable Benning Wentworth, Esq. (whose rambling country-seat near Portsmouth I saw a year ago), notwithstanding a verdict of the Crown in favour of the New-York claims. Until and during the late unfortunate revolution the region was subject to dispute, but generally known as the New-Hampshire Grants. The settlers themselves were inclin'd to oppose the New-York claims, by reason of the arbitrary acts of New-York agents who sought to invalidate the land titles obtain'd from New-Hampshire; and to resist these New-Yorkers was form'd the organisation call'd the Green Mountain Boys, who later turn'd arms against His Majesty's government as a whole. Upon the collapse of the lawful sovereignty in these parts, New-York still continued to assert her claim as a Federal State, as she had once asserted it as a British province. Vermont, resisting, maintained the status of an independent republick; disjoin'd from Great-Britain, but separate from the Federal union of the late colonies. This anomalous condition prevail'd until 1791, when after much debate Vermont was admitted to the new union—the first non-original State to be so included. The inhabitants of Vermont, of a hardier and more frugal sort than those of the rest of New-England, have never changed in character or habits to any large extent. They have stuck close to the soil, building but few large houses and founding but few large towns; and retain to this day the peculiar accents of other times, having a dialect of great singularity, unlike any to be found in other parts of New-England. Pleasingly few foreigners are amongst them, and the survival of old traditions is a common and gratifying spectacle. A few of the lower orders have fallen into a kind of gentle decay through poverty and isolation, relaxing those standards of enterprise and neat housekeeping which typified their ancestors. This decay, however, is very unlike the deep and insidious decay of central and western Massachusetts; where the moral and social order fall into odd perversions despite a maintenance of household neatness. The gentry, as in Massachusetts, maintain a very high level of life and thought; and indulge in a literary and aesthetick activity which is quite remarkable in view of their remote situation.

The country, as indeed my reports of last year attest, is of almost miraculous beauty and picturesqueness. It is a veritable fairyland of closely ranged green hillsides, multitudinous murmuring brooks, deep, wooded glens with many a cavern and waterfall, and steep, winding,

Lovecraft (right) in Brattleboro, Vermont, with Vrest Orton

rutted roads free from all trace of billboards and other defacements. Covered bridges of the antient sort abound, and the houses are old, simple, and ineffably lovely in their traditional hillside setting with rambling stone walls and gigantic elms in the background. The omnipresent vividness and poignancy of the landscape, in which every turn means a fresh hillside, glen, woodland rise, or steeple-filled valley vista, almost spoils one for any other kind of scenery; and gives a persistent impression of picturesque unreality. The mind vows that so much of breathless loveliness simply cannot be—and lays the sight to some subtle spell, emanating perhaps from the special aura or enveloping local atmosphere of the region. Hills and brooks—brooks and hills—these are the impressions that persist after all others become merged into the general background.

The farmhouse leased by Orton is of colonial date and idyllick setting; far from the nearest neighbour, and at the edge of an exquisite brook-filled ravine. It is of the familiar New-England story-and-a-half type, and is furnished entirely with eighteenth-century material, carefully selected by the antiquarian taste of the owner. There is no plumbing save a leaden pipe to lead in the spring water (a system which hath always serv'd the hilly Vermont to replace the wells common to flatter regions), and no illumination save oil lamps and candles. Orton is himself a stickler for the antient ways, and arranges all things with great care in the ancestral manner. The sitting-room of the house, with its great fireplace, crane, kettle, and andirons, is an object of admiration to all visitors; and the whole place form'd as appropriate a setting for an old country-gentleman like myself, as cou'd possibly be imagin'd.

In this elder paradise I remain'd two weeks, assisting in some of the rural activities of the locality—at least, to the extent of helping the neighbours' boys hunt stray kine, helping Orton dam up his brook to alter the channel, and looking on whilst Orton fished. I also took long solitary expeditions of scenick appreciation, ascending the highest peaks of the region, and exploring many a brook-murmurous ravine that led out to some open space where the setting sun lit up unexpected village spires or spread elfin glamour over some remote upper slope. I cou'd write a whole volume of verse about the vary'd prospects of ineffable loveliness which that region afforded me. Even a bald catalogue wou'd be a poem. The brook winding sinuously through the sunlit meadow—the great rock falls in the forest—the curve of great green terraces against the sky at Hinesburg—the hushed dip of the wood-bordered road beyond Watson's house—but Lud, Sir, this is prose! Be it sufficient to say, that I believe I did the region fair justice. The homely Yankee villages of Brattleboro and West Brattleboro I found very charming, and obtain'd what might be term'd the culminating view

Lovecraft (left) "helping the neighbours' boys hunt stray kine"

of both town and country from the top of wooded Mount Wantasiquet, across the river in New-Hampshire; whither I climb'd despite the grave warnings of villagers regarding rattlesnakes. From this eminence all of Brattleboro and West Brattleboro lie outspread—they, and the country and hills beyond them even unto the Green Mountains, and the curving reaches of the broad Connecticut that glimmer blue northward and southward as far as the eye can see.

Naturally enough, I saw considerable of the poet Goodenough, who dwells not much above a mile from Orton's; and again I took occasion to admire the exquisite scenick setting of his antient farmhouse with its giant elms and hillside vistas. On Sunday, June 17th, there was a literary assemblage of much interest at the poet's abode, to which came not only Orton and myself, but good old Cook from Athol, and the Vermont editor Walter J. Coates, all the vast way from the Montpelier region. Local literati, including a man from the Brattleboro paper, also attended; and the event received considerable publicity in the publick press. Orton and I were also the subject of newspaper articles, adulatory in the usual rural vein.

On Monday the 18th of June I took a trip south to the Province of the Massachusetts-Bay, visiting the drowsy and beautiful town of Greenfield, and the well-remember'd shades of hoary and portentous Deerfield. In the latter place I revived all my pleasing memories of last year; studying the century-lashed houses and living over again the frightful massacre of French-led Indians in 1704, which forms this town's chief claim to historick notice.

On June 24th the genial Cook, having come up in his coach, bore me away to Athol for another delectable sojourn. The ride was agreeable, and in the evening I was gratify'd to renew my acquaintance with that sightly town whence I deriv'd so much enjoyment last year. I visited the site of the original Pequoig settlement of 1735, and mark'd the older village common with its colonial houses and steeples, which towers so high on the bank above the river-valley in which the industrial and Victorian part of the town hath grown. My Athol days were spent in rural rambling, and in conversation with Cook and young Munn, the *Weird Tales* contributor. Munn took me out by coach to his residence, a farm some distance from town; and on another occasion shew'd me one of the finest woodland sights of my whole experience—a glen with high rock falls and a remarkable series of narrow caves or fissures. In Athol I was oblig'd to purchase a new suit of cloaths—a plain elderly outfit of blue serge—to replace one which wild Vermont had reduc'd beyond the limit of hasty repair.

Meanwhile I was receiving urgent invitations from the learned Mrs. Miniter, now residing with a cousin on her ancestral rural soil of

Wilbraham, to extend my round of visiting to her part of the Province; which is but a little south of Athol, across that lovely Swift River Valley now doom'd to extinction for reservoir purposes. Accepting without reluctance, I proceeded thither on Friday the 29th of June; going by rail-road and being met by the chaise of Mrs. Miniter's next-door neighbour. I found Mrs. Miniter not in the least aged by the five intervening years since I last beheld her; her defiance of time being somewhat akin to that of Tryout Smith, whom I last year found unchang'd after a similar stretch of time. Wilbraham is a very lovely country—in the rich, gentle way of Massachusetts as opposed to the bold, dramatick quality of Vermont scenery. The vegetation is thicker and greener; and the hills, tho' high and numerous, are more widely spread. Mrs. Miniter's cousin, a stout, important gentlewoman of 73, resides on an antient farm just across the marsh-meadows from Wilbraham Mountain; at a bend and dip of the road where giant maples form a green, mystical arcade. She is head of the local school committee, a member of the taown caouncil, and several other important official things; and is one of the Beebes ancestrally domiciled there. Curiously enough, she herself happened to be born in Wisconsin, during a pioneering venture which did not prove permanent in her family's case. Miss Beebe is one of the foremost private collectors of antiques in the country, and has her house packed with antient material of the most valuable sort; with only narrow lanes remaining to accommodate the seven cats, two dogs, and incidental human beings who sometimes traverse the rooms. Her farm also contains several poultry, two kine, two aged horses, and one hired boy. Her collection will be left to the museum in Springfield (the nearest city) upon her death.

I tarried eight days in Wilbraham, picking up many strange legends of great interest to me, since both Mrs. Miniter and Miss Beebe are expert in the curious folklore of that archaick region. I am at this very moment introducing one, as subsidiary colour, into a weird novelette I am writing. The peasantry hereabouts are somewhat decadent, and their odd beliefs and doings would fill volumes. Of the encroaching Polish element, Mrs. Miniter's novel of a decade ago treats very fully and cleverly. Old witchcraft whispers are remembered, and people nowadays wonder why so many people in a certain part of the neighbouring village of Monson go mad or kill themselves. I visited all the churchyards and burying places, and inspected the pleasing village of Wilbraham proper, where still flourishes the old academy founded in 1825. I was taken to Monson in a chaise, and walk'd myself to Hampden—a delightful old town at the bend of a stream, where all the houses are strung at length along a road winding up the side of a mountain from the valley. I also visited the other side of Wilbraham Mountain, where the vistas are vary'd and exquisite, and where a strangely blasted slope, supporting no living vegetation, is found.

On Sat'day, July 7th, I prepar'd to resume my journey, proceeding by chaise to the sizeable city of Springfield, which I had never seen before except from a train window. I found it not unbeautiful, tho' not sufficiently colonial to arrest my imagination. There is a pleasing old church on the green, and a museum of some interest; but it is not a place in which an antiquarian wou'd linger. Accordingly I started northward at once, with a design of ascending the Connecticut to Greenfield, and the next day going west to Albany over the famous Mohawk Trail. Towns along the coach route were Holyoke, a dingy mill city, Northampton, a pleasant, quiet town, and the residence of His Majesty's Viceroy, Sir Calvin Coolidge, and the antient Deerfield, already so favourably known to me. I arriv'd in Greenfield in the late afternoon, put up at a tavern, and saw the sunset from a neighbouring peak call'd the Poet's Seat, whence I obtain'd one of the most extensive prospects I have ever beheld. I also had my tye-wig put in shape by a good perruquier; it being very badly in need of such attention.

The following day dawn'd fair, and I embarkt upon the coach for Albany. To describe a route so well known as the Mohawk Trail wou'd savour of triteness; hence I can only say, that its marvels did not come below my expectations. The stupendous panorama of the Deerfield Valley from the eastern slope, and the dramatick vividness of such valley towns as Shelburne Falls, form a good preparation for the culminating sweep of limitless hill country to be seen from the very top, where tall observation towers have been erected. I ascended one of these, beholding at once I know not how many states. As one descends the western slope the scenery is even more wondrous. The rugged Berkshires here open out in all their majesty, and the precipitous descent into the valley town of North Adams, preceded by a distant view of it, is one of the experiences of a lifetime. North Adams itself is a place of great quaintness and attractiveness, wall'd in as it is on all sides by towering precipices of green. Beyond this point came the tranquil collegiate settlement of Williamstown, whose college edifices are all new Georgian structures of the greatest possible attractiveness. After this the coach cross'd a corner of Vermont, passing thro' the quaint town of Pownal, nam'd from Tho: Pownall, Esq., His Majesty's Governor of the Massachusetts-Bay from 1757 to 1759.

Now came the melancholy circumstance of quitting my native country of New-England once more; tho' I knew it wou'd be needful if I was to behold Philad'a, Baltimore, and the South. The scenery instantly became less attractive as the coach pass'd into the Province of New-York, tho' I was interested to reflect, that I was now in the general region inhabited by my good old friend Mr. Hoag, whose departure from earth scarce yet seems a reality. Troy is a detestably dingy place, but Albany is less repulsive. I did not relish Albany, since it is overwhelmingly Victorian; but I own'd a certain rococo glamour in the vast size and striking situation of the State House, which lyes at the head of a very broad uphill street, outlined boldly and picturesquely against the sunset sky. The bastard Renaissance architecture of Victorian times is in Albany carried out to greater extreams of size and grandeur than in any other place I have ever beheld; and for that reason it will be perniciously hard to get rid of. The older houses of Albany closely resemble those of a similar period in New-York, tho' the stoops tend uniformly to be lower. Albany, of course, is of Dutch settlement; though it is now wholly English'd. It appears commendably free from foreigners; most of these no doubt being the Manhattan delegates at the State House.

I stay'd in Albany only one night, embarking on a river packet the following morning and spending all that day amidst the imposing scenery of the hill-lined banks. Here again I will spare detail lest I be trite; for there is no one but knows of the great domed eminences and majestick bends which make the Hudson voyage one of the ultimate peaks of observational travel. The best part is that below Newburgh, along which I sail'd once before, in the year 1925.

Stopping in New-York only for brief calls on small Belknap and young Wandrei (who is now seeking his fortune there, having graduated from the U. of Minn. in June), I proceeded at once to the colonial shades of old Philadelphia, which I survey'd with undiminished affection. Since this town hath form'd the subject of two former treatises of mine, I will touch upon it but briefly; relating that I travers'd all my accustom'd routes in the city proper, and that I saw all the Georgian houses, churchyards, and lanes which have been wont to captivate me in the past. I spent the longest time in the churchyard of Gloria Dei Church, built in 1699 by the Swedes settled at the mouth of the Delaware.

That afternoon I took coach for Baltimore, finding the route sadly devoid of good scenery. The only spots I lik'd were a small village just beyond Wilmington, and the towns of Elkton and Havre-de-Grace, in Maryland. Baltimore was attain'd about sunset, and I had time only to survey its boldest central outlines before putting up at a tavern. The following day I survey'd the city in much detail, and receiv'd a very pleasing impression.

Baltimore, for a colonial town, is very new; having been founded in 1729, at a time when Annapolis was the metropolis of the province. Its original site was 60 acres of land on the north side of the Patapsco River—a stream which the present lower-class inhabitants insist on pronouncing "Pat-ap-si-co". Its growth was slow, and it did not outdistance Annapolis till just before the Revolution; this phenomenon of replacement being curiously like the passing of Newport by Providence, in my own colony, at about the same time. In 1776 the population was 6700. It is now about 750,000, including the niggers, who are segregated from the regular inhabitants in parks, schools, and places of publick conveyance or assemblage. It is one of the few really great seaports of the country, and has a very mature civilisation despite its loss of genuine southern quaintness. Its foreign population is unfortunately quite large, and not so well segregable as its niggers. The bulk of the town is unmistakably Victorian, though the slums near the Patapsco teem with brick colonial houses precisely like those of Philadelphia, after which they presumably pattern'd themselves. All the old houses have white marble steps, which are kept spotless by dint of constant labour.

The Popish cathedral, erected in 1808, is the most impressive of the edifices; crowning as it does the principal hill in a rather hilly town. The great column of 1815, with its surmounting statue of Gen. Washington, is another landmark of importance; and the source of the popular sobriquet "Monumental City", as apply'd to Baltimore. The country-seat of Charles Carroll, Esq., now in Carroll Park, is the oldest building in the city; dating from 1754. This and its congeners are not so much of the southern as of the middle-colonies type of architecture; favouring Philadelphian usage as do the town houses. Very interesting to behold was Fort McHenry, on a peninsula some distance from the centre of the town. This, as all are aware, was the fortress whose ensign mov'd Mr. Key to compose his spirited verses to the tune of "Anacreon in Heav'n" in 1814. The place is in excellent condition, with walls, gun emplacements, and soldiers' quarters precisely as they were at the beginning of the nineteenth century. It and the land around it form a publick government park, at whose entrance is an heroick bronze statue of Orpheus, dedicated to Mr. Key and set up only a few years ago. But to me the culminating thing in Baltimore was a dingy monument in a corner of Westminster Presbyterian Churchyard, which the slums have long overtaken. It is near a high wall, and a willow weeps over it. Melancholy broods around it, and black wings brush it in the night—for it is the grave of Edgar Allan Poe.

From Baltimore I took coach to Annapolis, that gorgeous centre of bygone taste and gaiety which still remains the capital of the province. It was founded in 1649 by Virginia Puritans who misliked the rule of the establisht church in that province, and was named at first PROVIDENCE, in view of the circumstances of its settlement. In 1694 it became the capital of Maryland in place of St. Mary's, and in 1708 it was incorporated as a city, having assum'd its present name in honour of Queen Anne. From 1694 on, its growth was very rapid; and it soon boasted one of the most brilliant and accomplisht societies of any town in the colonies. It fell within the truly southern area of the country, and follows the South rather than Philadelphia in architecture. This means that the country-seats have a large central portion flanked by two wings, and that the chimneys are wide and flat, and situate on the ends of the house. The street names well typify the conservatism of the South as oppos'd to the sadly seditious spirit of many parts of my own New-England. Here King St., Prince George St., Duke of Gloucester St., and so on, retain their original appellations despite disaster and rebellion. The naval academy is very pleasing, and I visited most parts of it; but to me it was not the really dominant feature of the place. The river Severn, on which the town is situate, shews a distinct yellowish tinge; which indeed is characteristick of all the southern streams I have seen.

The old houses and narrow streets are the real glory of Annapolis. At the centre of all is the fine old state house, built in 1772–74, but having a rather ugly dome added soon after the Revolution. As domes go, I prefer the modern Renaissance dome of gold surmounting the naval academy chapel. This dominates the skyline, and covers the ashes of that picaresque marine adventurer, John Paul Jones, whose elaborate bier is shewn in much detail to all visitors. The state house lyes atop an eminence near the centre of the town, all the streets tending to converge toward the circular street which wholly surrounds it. The building proper is in very good Georgian taste, and has an interior of singular grace and majesty. Not very far away is St. John's College, whose oldest building dates from 1789, and on whose campus is situate the great poplar tree under which the settlers treated with the friendly Susquehannock Indians in 1652. The tangle of ancient lanes down the hill east of the state house may be said to contain the greatest number of picturesque antiquarian effects. They make Annapolis the Marblehead of the South, and suggest an explanation for the old city by-law of Queen Anne's day:

> "Any person residing within this City or the Precincts thereof who shall by galloping or otherwise force any Horse, Mare, or Gelding through any of the Streets, Lanes, or Alleys of this City, or carry any Fire uncover'd through the same, shall if a Freeman forfeit and pay for every such Offence the sum of Ten Shillings Sterling to the use of this Corporation."

At least two houses in Annapolis, an official building on the state house grounds and a residence in Prince George Street nearby, date from the year of the transference of the capital–1694. They are both of brick, and marked by that peakedness typical of seventeenth-century architecture throughout the colonies. Fine houses of the eighteenth century, both late and early, are very common; both town houses and country-seats being represented. Houses of the rural type were built curiously close to the town, so that the two types are seen in rather singular juxtaposition. The Brice (1740), Paca (1763), Hammond (1750), Harwood (1770), Ogle (1742), and Randall (1730) houses are all worthy of detailed attention. A little out of the main section is a large colonial mansion said to have been used by Winston Churchill (who attended the naval academy and knew Annapolis well) as a prototype for his Carvel Hall. The application of the name "Carvel Hall" to the fashionable hotel housed in the old Paca mansion is purely fanciful.

The Stewart house (1763) in Hanover Street reminds one of a curious Revolutionary incident. During the tea agitation Mr. Anthony Stewart paid the duty on some tea which occurred in the mixt cargo of one of his brigs, the *Peggy Stewart;* thus antagonising the local rebels, who had resolv'd to exclude the commodity from the colony. Seeing that the popular hate was not to be appeas'd even by a burning of the offending cargo, Mr. Stewart was induc'd by the celebrated Charles Carroll (who was born in a mansion overlooking Spa Creek, which I beheld) to perform the still more dramatick gesture of burning the entire brig himself. This he carry'd out off Windmill Point, and was thereupon voted a "loyal" citizen by the rebels whom he had found it commercially and socially advantageous to please. Ever afterward the *Peggy Stewart* form'd a basis for local tradition.

Annapolis is one of those places which I surely must behold again. I left it with reluctance, but at last felt constrain'd to move onward to Washington. The coach was swift, and I arriv'd in the Federal capital late at night on July 12th; securing a cheap room recommended by the Y.M.C.A. and preparing to linger several days. The city itself I had seen, as former treatises attest; but I wish'd to make it a base for excursions into the surrounding territory.

On the 13th I revisited Alexandria, and renewed all the glowing colonial impressions describ'd in 1925. The town is much larger than Annapolis (25,000 as contrasted with 13,000), and is much less quaint owing to the regularity of the streets. It was lay'd out in 1749 under the name of Bellhaven, but soon changed its appellation to the present one. The oldest parts are those nearest the Potomac. Christ Church, which Gen. Washington attended, is undoubtedly the greatest single attraction of the place. It was built in the 1770's, and has one of the quaintest churchyards conceivable. But the whole town is fascinating, and abounds in brick Georgian houses of neat and tasteful outline. It calls up at once the picture of bygone times, and has much of the genial grace and well-bred somnolence of old Virginia life.

On the 14th I visited Gen. Washington's country-seat of Mt. Vernon, on the river below Alexandria, and left not a corner of house or grounds unexamin'd. It were trite to speak in detail of this well-known scene, but I may mention that the house was built in 1743 by Lawrence Washington, half-brother to the General, and that the latter inherited it in 1752, upon the death of Lawrence and his daughter. It was call'd Hunting Creek Estate till its builder renam'd it in honour of Admiral Vernon, the inventor of "grog", under whom he had serv'd against Spain. The house is low and spacious, most of the rooms being rather smaller than one wou'd expect in an edifice of such pretensions. The grounds, sloping down from a high bluff to the river with many a wooded ravine and willow-lin'd path, display the finest taste in selection. Stables and other outbuildings comport with the mansion house in style and beauty; the whole forming as sightly a plantation as any gentleman in Virginia cou'd reasonably demand. The elegance of the lower rooms, in point of architectural ornament, is carry'd almost to excess; but the upper rooms are singularly austere. I beheld the bed upon which the General dy'd, together with innumerable other objects connected with him. In walking thro' the grounds I came upon his tomb, and stood but a few feet from the body (in its sarcophagus beyond the grating) which even now must bear some resemblance to the living gentleman, so perfectly was it embalm'd. In the 1830's, when it was transferr'd from its original resting-place on the river bluff to this mausoleum, a person who gaz'd upon the features declar'd them but little impaired by the more than three decades of interment. I descended to the river, view'd all the buildings, and in general familiaris'd myself with the whole estate. I cannot praise it too highly, or hope too strongly that it may always be preserv'd with unremitting diligence as a specimen of good architecture and ideal type of a southern gentleman's seat.

Upon my return from Mt. Vernon I repair'd to Georgetown, the old city on the heights above Washington; far antedating the Federal City, but now included within it as Germantown is within Philadelphia. It was formerly part of Maryland, and has a pleasing irregularity lack'd by the too symmetrical artificial capital. I saw nothing I had not seen before, but upon re-crossing to Washington proper I visited the newer northwestern parts which I had never previously been over. Here I was arrested mainly by the great temple of the Scottish Rite Masons, whose striking architecture* lifts it out of the commonplace and mundane into the realm of the cosmick and mystical. Gazing upon it, I

*Modell'd upon that of the celebrated Mausoleum at Halicarnassus, which the Antients reckon'd amongst the Seven Wonders of the World.

could well believe all the vague legends connected with the Masonick order; for here surely dwelt arcana whose sources are not of this earth. I saw it first at night, when only the twin cryptick braziers beside the great bronze door lit up the grim guardian sphinxes and the huge windowless facade. Mystery dwelt there—and I departed full of vague thoughts hinging upon the obscurest of dream-memories.

Other Washington sights which I imbib'd at spare moments included the great new cathedral now building upon Mt. St. Alban. This gigantick fane, completed only at the apse end, is of the most exquisite Gothick beauty; and such is its design and setting, that I believe it will in time surpass its only American rival, St. John the Divine in New-York. I might likewise mention a brief pleasant trip to Falls Church, in Virginia, where I beheld a tasteful square edifice set in a grove, that once own'd Gen. Washington amongst its vestrymen. The village of Falls Church is in a beautiful valley, and is of extream quaintness. Virginia, in the direction of Fairfax Court House and Falls Church, has a scenick beauty comparable to that of New-England; and contrasting strongly with monotonous scenery higher up the Chesapeake coast.

On Sunday, June 15th, came the culminating event of the trip—the long railway excursion to the Endless Caverns, near New Market, in Virginia's exquisite Shenandoah Valley. The train pass'd thro' some of the most historick battlefields of the Civil War, beginning with Manassas and ending with the scenes of Sheridan's Ride; but the scenery did not become vivid till the latter half of the trip, when the mountains were reacht. Then I observ'd much the same kind of scenery that one finds around Athol, or the Connecticut Valley generally—bold ridges of hills, and splendid prospects of valleys and distant towns. The agricultural state of the country seems more prosperous than that of New-England, though none of the farms even begin to approach ours in neatness and beauty. Zigzag rail fences of the southern type serve generally, instead of stone walls, to divide the fields. A few stone walls, however, do exist; shewing the operations of New-England influences at a great distance. Foreigners seem altogether absent, an happy condition which I hope will be of permanent duration. Niggers are everywhere segregated, even in the smallest railway stations.

New Market was reacht after a four-hour ride, and a coach took the sightseers to the mouth of the actual caverns, some six miles away. These open from a pleasant spot just at the base of a great hill, where the owners have built an office and lay'd out grounds for the benefit of visitors. I purchas'd my ticket, enter'd the building covering the mouth, fell into a party, and was soon guided down steep stone steps into a region whose coolness contrasted oddly with the oven-hot day outside. I knew that I was at last in a real cavern—the first I had ever seen—and that I was about to sample in actuality those secrets of earth's ultimate abysses which heretofore I had traversed only in dreams and in literature. It was a great moment—and as the first of the wide gulfs opened out before me I felt that something out of fantasy had come earthward to meet me and give substance to my profoundest imaginings.

After the booklets to which I have given such wide circulation, I need say nothing in detail about the marvellous caves themselves. All I need do is to endorse with fervour each word of the printed text. There is no exaggeration! As deep gave place to deep, gallery to gallery, and chamber to chamber, I felt transported to the strangest regions of nocturnal fancy. Grotesque formations leer'd on every hand, and the ever-sinking level appris'd me of the stupendous depth I was attaining. Glimpses of far black vistas beyond the radius of the lights—sheer drops of incalculable depth to unknown chasms, or arcades beckoning laterally to mysteries yet untasted by human eye—brought my soul close to the frightful and obscure frontiers of the material world, and conjured up suspicions of vague and unhallowed dimensions whose formless beings lurk ever close to the visible world of man's five senses. Buried aeras—submerged civilisations—subterraneous universes and unsuspected orders of beings and influences that haunt the sightless depths—all these flitted thro' an imagination confronted by the actual presence of soundless and eternal night. I regretted the uniform illumination of the visited parts of the cave, and lagged behind the party as much as the rear guide would let me, in order to imbibe the stupendous spectacle without excessive human cluttering. I thought, above all else, of that strange old novel *Etidorhpa* once pass'd around our Kleicomolo circle and perus'd with such varying reactions. Dost recall it, O Sage? The Endless Caverns are amongst the best known in point of picturesque formations, though for great spaces they cannot compete with Kentucky's Mammoth Cave. I wished that I might visit the Luray and Shenandoah Caverns, not far from New Market; but the schedule of the excursion did not permit of it. Still—the sample I receiv'd was surely enough for a beginning. It was a glorious tangible introduction to that tenebrous nether world whereof I have scribbled so much, and I shall never forget the least particular of it. The crystal formations at several points were of a fantastick beauty so poignant that all sensations of horror were momentarily forgot. Words cannot describe the utter, supernal loveliness of those formations known as the Diamond Lake and Oriental Room. And at the bottom of all—far, far down, still trickles the water that carv'd the whole chain of gulfs out of the primal soluble limestone. Whence it comes and whither it trickles—to what awesome deeps of Tartarean nighted horror it bears the doom-fraught messages of the hoary hills—no being of human mould can say. Only They which gibber Down There can answer.

This was the climax of my spring and summer wanderings. After that, anything but a return home wou'd have been an anticlimax. The next day I took coach for Philadelphia, changed for New-York, and arrived in that pest spot in the dawn twilight of the 17th. Collecting mail from home, I learnt that my elder aunt was ill with lumbago and forc'd to employ a nurse; so that I gave over my design for a leisurely return by coach thro' rural Connecticut and at once hasten'd to Providence on the rail-road. On the morning of the 18th I saw in the distance the spires of my native town, and ere long I walked in the lee of the great green hill, crowned with its ancient domes and steeples, whereon I was born. The old village streets were quiet and mystical with dawn-haze and elder memories, and up the hill there beckoned long vistas of carven doorways and rayed fanlights, and iron-railed flights of steps such as I had not seen since I left there in the April before—things such as only Providence knows. A fresh salt wind came up from the harbour, over the roofs of the centuried warehouses and the Old Market House of 1773; and down the narrow, curving line of the old town street by the shoar I glimpsed the chimneys and gambrel roofs of mouldering houses known to ancient captains and tarry West Indian seamen. I was home again—in the old New-England seaport that is not quite like any other New-England seaport; in the old maritime New-England that is so different in its soul from even the inland New-England of Brattleboro or Athol or Wilbraham or Greenfield. Home—amongst the unnumber'd influences and sights and sounds which, operating through a full half of my heredity for three hundred years and through all my life from infant memories onward, has little by little moulded my germ-plasm and my spirit, and created out of formless protoplasm the individual entity that is I. For what is any man but the impress of his home and lineage? What is in us, that our pasts have not placed there? Truly, no man is himself save among the scenes that have shaped him and his fathers; nor cou'd I ever hope to find a lasting peace save close to the ancient monuments of green-leaved, hill-crowning Providence—Providence, of the old brick sidewalks and the Georgian spires and the curving lanes of the hill, and the salt winds from over mouldering wharves where strange-cargoed ships of eld have swung at anchor. Providence is I, and I am Providence. One and inseparable! So after all my wanderings I came back to a wonder and beauty greater and always stranger than any I sought in distant ports or found amidst the marvel of alien roofs and exotick mountains. GOD SAVE HIS MAJESTY'S COLONY OF RHODE-ISLAND AND PROVIDENCE-PLANTATIONS!

TRAVELS IN THE PROVINCES OF AMERICA;

Made in the Year 1929 by H. Lovecraft, Gent., and Extending from Jamestown, in Virginia, to the Southerly Part of His Majesty's New-Hampshire Grants, Latterly call'd Vermont. With observations upon the History, Scenery, and Antiquities of the Several Regions Travers'd.

PROVIDENCE, RHODE-ISLAND

Printed by John Carter, at Shakespear's-Head in King-street, over-against the Court House, and Sold by Merchants generally. 1929.

My travels for the year 1929 began at a somewhat earlier season than is customary with me, owing to an extreamly cordial invitation from Vrest Orton, Esq., of Yonkers, in the Province of New-York; that hospitable gentleman at whose estate in the New-Hampshire grants I spent so many pleasing days in 1928. I left Providence early on the 4th of April, arriving at my destination on the same day, and being much captivated by the charm of the Yonkers countryside, notwithstanding its close nearness to the ugly and foreign town of New-York. The section inhabited by Mr. Orton is not any meer suburban "development" of the kind often found on the rim of large cities, but a genuine open territory with wooded hills, lakes, farms, and glorious vistas. Houses are few, and no network of streets hath yet come to usurp supremacy from the winding hill roads, meadows, woods, and country-seats. The Orton house, a white gabled relique of Georgian times, is on a picturesque side-hill with grounds, fence, grape-arbour, and all the appurtenances of a real farm. A rushing, Vermont-like brook flows bubblingly beside the front gate, and the whole vicinity is antithetical to the ways and spirit of New-York. Nor does the house contain any jarring note. Flagstone walks, old white gate, low ceilings, small-paned windows, wide-boarded floors, white-manteled fireplace, cobwebb'd attick, rag carpets and hook'd rugs, old furniture, century'd Connecticut clock with wooden works—all things, in truth, bespeak an antient New-England hearthside. The guest-room to which I was assign'd is situate in the gabled second storey of the east wing, with windows on three sides—looking north over meadows and ponds to the hills, south across the flagstoned yard to the front gate and shady country road, and east to the deep forest that runs down a slope toward the great highway. Add to these advantages a gracious and congenial host, and a library almost unexcell'd amongst the members of our circle, and there will be form'd a picture of the pleasant environment in which I spent above two weeks. During this time I was oblig'd to visit New-York with frequency in order to look up old acquaintances, but I nevertheless contriv'd to indulge in many of my favourite antiquarian explorations. I need not speak of the antiquities of New-York proper, insomuch as I have describ'd them in so many previous volumes of travel; but will meerly mention that I visited most of them, such as the Van Cortlandt, Dyckman, and Gracie houses, the tangled Georgian streets of Greenwich, the antient waterfront of Brooklyn, and so on. I did not neglect the various museums and literary facilities of the metropolis, nor did I fail to pay a visit to Paterson, where my august and curatorial friend James Ferdinand Plantagenet-Morton was so good as to arrange for me a particularly fine display of the Great Falls of the Passaick River. On this occasion I beheld the stupendous torrent in all its force, forming a prodigiously impressive spectacle of roaring foam and rising mist, with a delicate rainbow arching over the whole band of scoriack crag and milk-white flood. The chasmal majesty of the enormous gulph was such as to suggest the monstrous scenery of other planets.

Of my New-York suburban trips to places I had never before seen, may be mention'd one to antient Eastchester, now included within the city of Mount-Vernon, where still remains one of the finest old churches in the Province. This archaick fane, known as St. Paul's, was built in 1761 upon the site of an edifice of 1699, and is surrounded by a churchyard with above six-thousand graves. It is of grey stone, with a rather low and unambitious belfry or steeple, and is of highly captivating aspect. During the late uprising of 1775–83 it was us'd as an hospital by His Majesty's forces; many soldiers both British and Hessian being here interr'd. Across the road is an old tavern frequented by His Majesty's officers; from whose signpost a deserter was once hang'd. As a village Eastchester is well-nigh obliterated; there being only one small stretch of rather quaint street some distance away from the church and tavern. Manufactories have brought that curse of smoke and decadence which invariably follows in the wake of machinery and excessive trade.

Another trip of uncommon interest was to the town of New-Rochelle, on whose outskirts is situate the cottage occupy'd by the eccentrick rebel philosopher and oeconomist Thomas Paine, author of *Common Sense, The Age of Reason,* and so on. The cottage, mov'd from its original site some years ago, stands on a picturesque slope in a highly pleasing small park, together with other antiquarian reliquiae brought from a distance—an old schoolhouse and a curious Indian idol-stone. The whole group, well arrang'd on a hillside with coursing stream and wooden foot-bridges, forms a landskip of the finest sort. The house, given to Mr. Paine by the grateful rebel nation at whose treasonable birth he so substantially assisted, was built in 1793 and 1794, upon his return from France, to replace an earlier gift-house which had been burnt. The interior is well furnisht with reliques by the New-Rochelle Historical Society, and possesses an admirably quaint and home-like aspect. Among the contents is a Franklin stove given to Mr. Paine by Dr. Franklin himself. New-Rochelle was founded in the seventeenth century by Huguenots from France, but retains lamentably little to remind the traveller of former times.

On the 21st of April I remov'd my visiting headquarters from Yonkers to New-York proper, where my host was my young adopted grandson, the eminent, sophisticated, and disillusion'd poet-critick Frank Belknap Long, Jun. Here, despite my dislike of the metropolis, congenial society serv'd to make my hours pleasant; and many trips on foot and by coach enliven'd a period of above a week. In this interval my host and I made many architectural excursions, surveying and studying the best Gothick edifices in the town, such as the churches of St. John the Divine (now well along toward completion), St. Thomas, the Heavenly Rest (with its barren modern use of Gothick design), and St. Patrick. Of rural trips, that to the town of Bedford was the most pleasing; for I am ever fond of this settled, reposeful old village, whose atmosphere is so greatly enhanc'd by its white church, hillside burying-ground, colonial houses, and triangular village green. On the road to New-England, it partakes not a little of the spirit and aspect of that idyllick region.

On the 1st of May I quitted the vicinity of New-York to begin the major part of my historick and antiquarian tour; whose earlier parts were schedul'd to lie in the southern colonies. Securing a stage-coach for Washington (the new Federal City put up by the rebels near Georgetown), I took a good seat and prepar'd to enjoy the archaick regions thro' which I was to pass. The journey was made amusing by the presence in the seat beside me of a slightly demented German—a well-drest and respectable-looking fellow whom I had observ'd at the tavern reading a German paper before the start of the coach. He shew'd no signs of his affliction till we reach'd a sort of stagnant mill-pond near Newark, in New-Jersey, when suddenly he burst forth with the question, "Iss diss der Greadt Zalt Lake?" Deeming the inquiry addrest to me, I reply'd that I scarcely thought his identification correct; whereupon he reliev'd me of all responsibility by remarking in a far-off, sententious voice—"I vassn't talkingk to you; I vass shoost leddingk my light shine!" Properly rebuk'd for my officious desire to give information, I held my peace and permitted my seatmate to illuminate without hindrance. After a time he became vocal again, confiding to the empty air ahead, "I'm radiatingk all der time, und nopotty knows it!" The passengers in general, to say nothing of the driver, were not insensible to the grotesqueness of the speech, but confin'd their comment to smiles. Apparently this was the proper course, insomuch as the thoughtful radiator shortly afterward signify'd his approval of the mundane scheme by beginning a series of impersonal ejaculations of the phrase, "Efferythingk iss luffly! Efferythingk iss luffly!" As the coach near'd Princeton, an exquisite colonial town which I must some day explore in detail, the mystical fellow-countryman of Kant and Hegel became concretely philosophical; evidently affected by the academick atmosphere of the old college village. "You make money your vay;" he volunteer'd to the circumambient air, "I make money my vay—diff'rent kinds of money!" After this supreme epitome of worldly wisdom, the philosopher attempted no further specific radiations. Thereafter his dicta, when articulate, were confin'd to reiterations of the genial "Efferythingk iss luffly!" He alighted at antient Philadelphia, and I saw him no more. No doubt he was a leader in some modern religious or ethical cult, for which post he appear'd especially fitted; or perhaps he was one of the traditional Quakers, Ephratans, Dunkards, or Moravians of the Teutonick and many-faith'd Pennsylvania Colony. I did not stop in Philadelphia on this southward trip, but kept on to Washington. The afternoon's ride was very beautiful, and I was glad to pay my respects to the South again as the coach enter'd the Colony of Maryland. Elkton, Havre-de-Grace, and other villages of this region are of extream quaintness and charm; and the whole landskip below Baltimore is of a marvellous glamour. I noted the yellowness of the streams—a leading characteristick of southern rivers, due to the soil thro' which they run—and was gratify'd by the increasing warmth of the air; the vernal scene having all the mildness and luxuriance of summer. The South is in some respects my favourite part of America; its climate, atmosphere, blood, traditions, and social-political views all being closer to my own liking than those of any other region. But for my ancestral attachment to the landskip, architecture, and geographick-historick memories of New-England, I wou'd certainly become an inhabitant of the sane, unhurried, racially pure, and perspective-blest southern colonies which I love so much to visit. Washington was reacht in the evening, and I took a pleasing twilight walk before putting up at a tavern near the starting-place of the Richmond coach. I did not design to stop long this time, deferring my Washington explorations till after my more southerly peregrination.

On the following morning I rose early and took the 6:45 Richmond coach; thereby embarking for a region I had never before seen. I had an excellent seat and an ideal day; and was glad to behold again the classick shoars of Virginia, and the ancient chimneys, gables, and steeples of Alexandria, whose colonial charm I have often describ'd in earlier books of travel. Old Virginia! Here, indeed, flower'd the earliest and the greatest Anglo-Saxon civilisation on this continent—and one which has perhaps left more tangible reliquiae in this decadent age than has my own almost equally antient New-England civilisation. I was glad to see old Pohick church, of which the late Gen. Washington was a parishioner, and enjoy'd such glimpses of great plantation-houses as I had. The dominant type hereabouts is the steep-roof'd brick manor with lateral connecting wings for kitchen and servants' quarters; a form found throughout the upper fringe of the South. I also observ'd with interest the smaller farm houses of the white freeholders and yeomen, and lesser gentry; narrow, two-storey edifices with chimneys on each end and steeply pitcht roof with dormers. This type is characteristically southern, scarce any example being found north of Maryland, where the Pennsylvania influence ends. In this Washington-Richmond interval agriculture is more abundant than in New-England, though the farmsteads are less picturesque. Blackamoors and mules are omnipresent, and the leisurely tempo of the prevailing life is refreshing to observe. All the natives are American, and now and then some very quaint and individualised specimens appear. Every rank of the community is markt with a kind of natural courtesy and good-will unknown to the decadent North; so that I verily believe I wou'd have less natural contempt and dislike for mankind if I were to live long in that district. These virtues proceed undoubtedly from the fact that the prevailing population *actually belongs here* by heredity and immemorial attachment. Race and landskip fit each other, and life has had an opportunity to crystallise into natural and beautiful forms. Only such an ancient seating of a race upon its terrestrial environment can produce a genuine and endurable civilisation—all other makeshifts and immigrant-huddles are vile and detestable parodies which are nothing and mean nothing. May Heaven preserve Old Virginia from the industrialisation and mongrelisation which have ruin'd New-England and virtually remov'd the city of New-York from the world of Western civilisation and Aryan thought and feeling! The Virginia soil is yellow and clayey, and colours all the numerous streams as in other parts of the South. Landskips are broad and rolling; and, until Richmond itself is reach'd, below those of New-England in beauty. High-roads are mostly of very recent construction, and lack the rambling charm which must have pervaded the famously bad clay roads that preceded them. Some of the rural crossroads or court-house villages are quaint beyond anything we have in New-England; being of great primitiveness in design, and great leisureliness in atmosphere. Points of historick interest along the route are carefully markt by the state, for the road traverses some of the most famous battlefields of the Civil War (including Fredericksburg and Spotsylvania) besides lying in a territory of the utmost colonial interest. The apex of charm along this route is the vicinity of the Rappahannock River, where Falmouth and Fredericksburg rear their ancient chimneys and gables. I had deferr'd my exploration of this region till my return trip, so on this occasion noted principally the charm of hilly Falmouth—a sleepy hamlet whose crumbling brick houses and general irregular plan make it a kind of Virginian Marblehead. Across the shallow, yellow Rappahannock is sedate and Georgian Fredericksburg—my glimpse of which made me eager for the exploration to come on the return trip. Toward Richmond the scenery became finer, till at length the world seem'd transform'd to a thing of unbelievable aestival beauty. At last the old Confederate capital began to make itself visible—tho' in a very modern way, since the newer boulevard section is thrust out in the general direction of the Washington road. The coach stopt at Murphy's antient tavern, near the old-time heart of things, and I there secur'd a room—determin'd to do the city justice, and to make it my headquarters whilst I visited still older and more historick parts of the great peninsula betwixt the James and York Rivers. Hail to Old Richmond! Opulent with memories of John Smith, William Byrd, Edgar Allan Poe, Robert Edward Lee, Jefferson Davis, and the Great Lost Cause! Repository of tradition and headquarters of reposefulness—closest approach to mine own psychological standpoint to be found amongst the sizeable cities of these colonies! I had dream'd of it for thirty years or more—now I was to behold and know it—to know it, and to know its venerable neighbours Williamsburg, Jamestown, and Yorktown! Even the prevailing speech of the town was delightful to me; for of all forms of American dialect, none is more pleasing and genuinely musical than the broad, drawling tones of the South, which here find full embodiment.

Richmond is a subtly delightful town of much poise and background, tho' a machine-age barbarian with false standards might complain that the languid negligence prevents its shops and restaurants from being numerous, sumptuous, and overflowingly stockt. The aristocratick residential districts are magnificent—mansions, broad boulevards, and park-like grounds in the full bloom of summer at May's beginning—but the business section has an air of shabbiness and Victorianism. There is no one vast colonial district, though colonial houses are likely to be found anywhere near the river. A diligent searcher can discover much to enthrall him architecturally, and of course a student of history could ask nothing more than this centre of Civil War operations. It is not as outwardly attractive a city as Washington or Alexandria, but is of the sort which grows on one. It is the most American city I have ever been in. Of a population of 200,000, about 30% are niggers and only 3% foreigners—the latter mostly Jews, who always swarm where money is to be had. The remaining 67%—forming indeed almost 97% of the white inhabitants—are pure-blooded English-Americans whose forbears have dwelt in Virginia from 300 to 325 years. It is this pure native stock which makes up all the crowds and controls all the functions of urban life. Everybody one speaks to is a regular American—hotel clerks, soda-fountain men, conductors, motormen, coach-drivers, and so on. And of course all the workmen and bootblacks and newsboys and lift-men are blacks. Blacks are not segregated as rigorously as in the farther South, because they are not as numerous. Indeed, one sees no more of them than in the upper part of New York City. Oddly enough, the much more northerly city of Baltimore (which is, incidentally, hideously foreignised) has strict segregatory ordinances which are unknown in Richmond.

Richmond lies along the northern bank of the yellow James River, at the falls forming the head of navigation; the oldest parts being naturally those nearest the water, where a bluff of varying steepness, at certain points rising into actual hills, ascends from the shore. Its ancient section was much decimated by the burning of the business district in 1865, to prevent valuable merchandise from falling into the hands of the Federal troops. The original town was built on seven hills like Providence and Rome—Church Hill (containing ancient St. John's), Smith's Hill, Libby Hill (now a park), Gamble's Hill (also a park), Oregon Hill, Hollywood Hill (site of the principal cemetery), and Capitol Hill (containing the fine old state capitol). It has tended, however, to shift westward—building up over the pleasant countryside and leaving the old eastern parts to a state of slumdom. The sections along the waterfront have long been given over to the tobacco industry, and possess at all times the pervasive odour of the weed. Richmond is the foremost tobacco town in the world. Parks are numerous and lovely—William Byrd Park on the western edge of the town being comparable to Providence's Roger Williams Park, tho' by no means rivalling it. Forest Hills Park across the river contains woodland ravines almost equal to New-England's. Richmond flora does not perceptibly differ from that of the North, though it perhaps grows in greater luxuriance. Several bridges connect Richmond with the opposite shore, using islands as stepping-stones. Across the river is the dingy district of South Richmond, formerly Manchester.

The colonial houses of Richmond are small and made of brick, having resemblances to those of Philadelphia and Alexandria. There is also a late-Georgian type quite peculiar to Richmond—square brick facade, and heavy Dorick porch like that on Providence's 1815-type houses. Peaked roofs with dormer windows seem to have been the rule—I have seen only *one* gambrel roof in all my Richmond wanderings! The oldest house—preserv'd as a Poe shrine though Poe never inhabited it—dates behind any of the others (estimates vary from 1685 to 1737!); it being a stone farmhouse preceding the urban settlement of the town.

Richmond—or the land it now covers—has been continuously known to the white man since the voyage of Captains Christopher Newport and John Smith in 1607—29 years before the founding of Providence, 23 before the settlement of Boston, and 13 before the Pilgrims landed on Plymouth Rock. It is thus the oldest civilised region I have ever seen in person so far. A cairn and cross on Gamble's Hill mark the spot where the voyagers debarked—their mission being to treat with the Indian Powhatan. The region, and the settlement founded there by Sir Thomas Dale, were at first call'd *Henricopolis*, in honour of King James the First's eldest son and heir-apparent Prince Henry (who dy'd, however, before succeeding to the throne, thus giving the Crown to his younger brother, the martyr'd Charles the First); a designation which still survives as *Henrico County*, in which Richmond is situate. Henricopolis lay some distance southeast of the present town, and was destroy'd by the Indians in 1622. In rebuilding, a safer site was naturally sought—hence the choice of the seven hills. Richmond proper was not establisht till 1737, when a settlement was made by the great landed proprietor, poet, and cavalier William Byrd, Gent., of Westover on the James—direct lineal ancestor of the present explorer Richard Byrd, and of his brother Harry Flood Byrd, now Governor of Virginia. Westover, a splendid Georgian manor-house built in 1737, lies some distance away; and I regret that I have not yet seen it. In the garden of this estate William Byrd lies buried; he having dy'd in 1744 at the age of seventy. In 1742 Richmond was incorporated as a town, and by 1779 it had so eclips'd the older town of Williamsburg (as Providence eclips'd Newport, and Baltimore eclips'd Annapolis) that it was made the capital of Virginia. In 1782 it was incorporated as a city, and it has since remain'd the metropolis of Virginia, having a population of 200,000 against Norfolk's 160,000. It is a seaport—lying at the James's head of navigation—though it is content to leave chief maritime honours to Norfolk. In the Revolution Richmond sided largely with the rebels, and was harass'd by Benedict Arnold after his transfer of allegiance to Great-Britain. Arnold burn'd dwellings and tobacco warehouses, displaying as savage a spirit as when he burnt New-London, in his own native Connecticut County. On June 16, 1781, the town was enter'd without opposition by Lord Cornwallis on his way to the York-James peninsula—the Virginia government having temporarily remov'd to Charlottesville, a great distance westward. The Civil War, however, brought Richmond its greatest and most tragick martial fame. As capital of the Confederate States its capture was always the prime objective of the Federal armies; and at two distinct periods it form'd the focus of some particularly desperate fighting. Constantly in a state of siege, it develop'd defensive fortifications of the utmost effectiveness—some of which may still be seen as grass-grown trenches and embankments. I saw some in the western part of the town, and believe a good number are always pointed out by the drivers of sightseeing coaches. It was around Richmond that the art of balloon observation first rose to prominence, this being the only method whereby the Federals cou'd ascertain the state of things within the Confederate redoubts. In this procedure the leaders were none other than James and Ezra Allen of Providence, with whom the young German attaché Graf von Zeppelin took that first flight which launch'd him upon his memorable career. The battles around Richmond are too well-known to old-timers to need description—Spotsylvania Court-House, the Wilderness, Cold Harbour, Yellow Tavern, Williamsburg, Seven Pines, Mechanicsville, Gaines' Mill, Savage's Station, Frazier's Farm, Malvern Hill, Sharpsburg, Drewry's Bluff, and so on. Grant's "hammering campaign" finally made the city's abandonment necessary, and on the morning of April 3, 1865 (six days before the surrender at Appomattox) the defenders mov'd out. It was decided to destroy all the tobacco and supplies in the warehouse district along the river at the foot of the hills lest it prove of value to the Federals, so sadly and reluctantly the whole section was put to the torch—just as the Yankee rebels in 1776 set fire to New-York when forc'd to surrender it to His Majesty's lawful troops. The fire proved more extensive than had been plann'd—destroying

Mayo's Bridge and obliterating nearly a thousand buildings. Reconstruction, however, was very rapid after the war; so that today all the structures in the burn'd district are old and dingy. Richmond will always remember the Civil War, and has erected some splendid monuments to Confederate heroes. Monument Avenue, a gorgeous boulevard with park centre strip and numerous landscape circles at intersections, contains many noble tributes to vanisht leaders—especially the great equestrian statues of Lee, Jackson, and Stuart, and the mighty Roman column, adorn'd by statuary and surrounded by a semicircular colonnade, sacred to President Jefferson Davis. In Hollywood Cemetery are bury'd Fitzhugh Lee, Stuart, Pickett, the oceanographer and naval officer Maury, and President Davis. On Libby Hill is another vast Roman column (modell'd after the pillar of Cn. Pompeius) dedicated to the Confederate dead.

Richmond's cultural life, like that of Providence, culminated in the 1830's and 1840's—the Poe period. It was then that the *Southern Literary Messenger* flourish'd, giving Philadelphia a close race for the cultural supremacy it was about to lose to Boston. Today the city has not a scholastick mood; at least, there are no museums, art galleries, or historical societies comparable to those of Worcester, Springfield, Providence, or other New-England cities of similar size. There are, however, signs of improvement in this direction—and a new publick library is under construction. There is one college—the University of Richmond.

As for specifick objects of interest—these are very numerous, tho' not beyond the compass of a single day's trip, especially if one avail himself of the excellent Grey Line sightseeing coaches. The splendid State Capitol, crowning a grassy Acropolis-like height whose slopes are a park, was design'd by the architecturally expert Mr. Tho: Jefferson, and forms perhaps the finest of early classick-revival specimens aside from Mr. Jefferson's products at Charlottesville. Its foundation was lay'd in 1785, and it was finish'd in 1792. The two wings—of congruous design—added in 1902 are regrettable, but not as bad as one might fear. Within is the famous Houdon statue of Genl. Washington and other matter of historical interest. The capitol grounds contain several noteworthy items—library and state office buildings, an old bell-tower used as a powder-magazine during the Civil War, a vast equestrian statue of Washington, and a fine Governor's mansion (now housing a true Virginia Byrd) built in 1811. Capitol Park is an ideal place to sit in the sun and read, for no barbarick spirit of haste or regularity obtrudes upon the omnipresent beauty and civilised reposefulness. Pres. Davis's executive mansion, not far away, is now a Confederate Museum. This is a fine old house built in 1819, with a splendid Georgian doorway on the street side, and a pillar'd portico on the garden side. Within, each of the Confederate States is represented by one room. In the yard is an anchor chain from the sunken *Merrimac.* The Valentine Museum, devoted to fine arts, archaeology, anthropology, and history, is noted as the repository of the Poe correspondence only recently made publick. It is housed in a fine mansion built in 1812 and containing notable interior woodwork. The Valentines are among the foremost families of Richmond. A third museum is the John Marshall house, residence of that famous Chief Justice of the U.S. Supreme Court from 1795 to his death in 1835. Most of the reliques are of Marshall himself, tho' there are a few of general nature. The town house of Genl. Robert E. Lee, occupied by the Virginia Historical Society, houses rare books, MSS., and reliques connected with the Old Dominion. Of supreme interest to me, however, was the ancient stone house and its adjuncts lying in the easterly slum reaches of Main Street and now serving as a "Poe Shrine". This house, a farmhouse built perhaps in 1685 (though some identify it with the Jacob Ege house, built in 1737) and overtaken by the growing town, is the oldest edifice in Richmond, and remains in a sound state of preservation. The space near it has been purchas'd by Poe-lovers and developed with great taste and ingenuity; an exquisite garden (suppos'd to represent symbolically that "enchanted garden" in Providence where Poe first glimps'd Mrs. Whitman and of which he wrote so movingly) lying in the rear, and the two adjacent houses on each side being annex'd as part of a three-building unit. Of these added houses that on the west is colonial, whilst that on the east is a fireproof museum in imitation of the Richmond residence of John Allan, Esq., where Poe was rear'd as an adopted son. I spent an hour in this fascinating place, and saw all manner of Poe reliques—far more than are stor'd in the Fordham cottage I know so well. Poe's chair, desk, and various personal belongings are there, as well as many architectural details (mantels, a staircase, etc.) from the two Allan houses and the *Southern Literary Messenger* building, all now demolish'd. One utterly magnificent feature is a gigantick model of the whole town of Richmond as it was during Poe's boyhood—about 1820—in a glass case occupying the entire ground floor space of the colonial house attached to the shrine. This model, made in natural colours and on a scale permitting even the smallest houses to be about an inch square, was constructed a few years ago with the utmost antiquarian accuracy and artistick skill; and is so vivid that one can almost imagine himself in a balloon looking down over the outspread Georgian city. Never have I seen an antient town so miraculously conjured out of the past—I wish someone wou'd do the same for Old Providence! It gave me a short cut to Richmond's topographical and architectural history which at once plac'd that venerable city amongst those I know best. What I had to worry out for myself in connexion with other colonial towns, was all done for me in the case of Richmond. I am convinc'd that models are the very best media for perpetuating the former appearance of old towns, and wou'd advise a widespread adoption of the Richmond idea were I a person of influence in historical circles.

It remains to describe the most historick churches of Richmond, of which antient St. John's, on Church Hill in the eastern part of the town, is easily the foremost. This is a lineal successor to the original Church of England of Henrico Parish—the parish surrounding the first settlement made by Sir Thomas Dale at Henricopolis. A building was under construction at Henricopolis when the Indians destroy'd it in 1622, and of this nothing remains but the baptismal font, which the salvages carry'd off, but which was recover'd from them in slightly damag'd condition. This font still remains in the present church. After the founding of Richmond in 1737 it was decided to rebuild the church there, and land was given by William Byrd for the purpose. The region —"Church Hill"—was then quite rural or suburban, on the eastern fringe of the town, tho' it is now of course urbanly ingulph'd. In 1741 a building was erected, part of which survives in the present edifice. The fane is very restful and captivating to the eye as it stands today in its antient churchyard—the whole rais'd above the street level on a gentle mound and surrounded by an iron railing. The stones in the churchyard date back to 1751; and among the interments is the unfortunate Mrs. Poe, actress-mother of the poet, who dy'd in destitution in 1811. A fine monument to Mrs. Poe was set up a year or two ago by admirers of her great son. During the course of time St. John's underwent such radical alterations and remodellings that almost nothing of the original church can be distinguisht. What was once the nave, running east and west, is now the transept of a new nave running north and south—tho' a few of the old pews, and the antient high pulpit and sounding-board, remain to this day. This church form'd the meeting-place of Virginia delegates on March 20, 1775, during the early stages of the treason against His Majesty's lawful government; among them being Genl. Washington, George Mason, of Gunston, Esqr., John Marshall, Tho: Jefferson, of Monticello, Esqr., Patrick Henry, and other celebrated figures. On this occasion Mr. Henry, standing up in his pew, utter'd those cheaply melodramaticall words which have become such a favourite saw of schoolboys—"Give me liberty, or give me death!" The pew from which he spoke is still preserv'd and markt with a tablet, but as a loyal subject of the King I refus'd to enter it. The whole ensemble of church and churchyard is marvellously fascinating, and I stroll'd thither more than once during my sojourn in the town. A pleasing mulatto sexton—very intelligent for his race—shews visitors around the building. Another celebrated fane is the Monumental Church in Broad St., on the site of the old Richmond Theatre where Mrs. Poe acted and where the Convention of 1788 met to ratify the U.S. Constitution. The theatre was burn'd for the second time on Decr. 26, 1811—during the performance of a weird-horror play, *The Bleeding Nun,* taken from Lewis's famous Gothic novel, *The Monk.* In this disaster, caus'd by the contact of an oil lamp with the scenery, 72 persons out of an audience of 643 lost their lives—among the victims being the Governor of Virginia, William Smith, Esq., who escap'd at the first alarum, but perisht when he reëntered the building in an effort to save his small son. The magnitude of this calamity was an occasion for general mourning, and for four months theatrical performances were forbidden in Richmond. Jany. 1, 1812 was sett aside as a day of fasting and prayer. At length it was decided to build a church on the site of the theatre, dedicated to the victims and forming a tomb for their mortal remains. The present edifice, finisht in 1814, is a sightly structure with low dome and portico of two Dorick columns *in antis.* Old St. Paul's church, near the capitol, has a belfry-tower and Ionick portico, and evidently belongs to the 1830–40 period, tho' I cannot ascertain the exact date. It was here that Genl. Lee and Pres. Davis both worshipp'd—and here that Pres. Davis receiv'd, on the morning of April 2, 1865, the fateful telegram from Lee warning him that Richmond must be evacuated. The Lee and Davis pews are markt by tablets, and the memorial windows to Lee are the finest things of their kind in the United States. In Franklin St. near 19th is an austere old structure which, tho' not a church, has an almost religious significance for many—being the oldest Masonick hall in the United States; i.e., the oldest edifice built as such and continuously used for the same purpose. The corner stone was lay'd in 1785 by the chief Masonick dignitaries of Virginia, and the building has been occupy'd since 1787 by Richmond-Randolph Lodge, No. 19. In the War of 1812 it form'd a military hospital, and Genl. La Fayette was here entertain'd in 1824.

Besides actual old buildings, I beheld many historick sites where famous structures have existed and pass'd away. Among these is the site of the dreaded Libby Prison, at Cary and 20th Streets near the waterfront. The building was originally a tobacco warehouse, and the hospital connected with it (probably a former dwelling-house) is still standing. The prison building existed until 1892, when it was taken down stone by stone to be reassembled and exhibited at the Chicago World's Fair. The intention was to return it later to Richmond, but for some reason this plan was never carry'd out. I do not know whether the building still exists in Chicago or not—but I am sure that Chicago cou'd use it, as well as many other extra gaols, to great advantage!

I quitted Richmond with the greatest reluctance, and only because my waning finances made a longer stay impossible. The place grows on one from day to day—and it gives one an amazing sensation to be in a *really American* city in the year 1929. After all, the old America is not yet truly *dead*, but simply *contracted in area*—confin'd to the South, and to isolated places like Vermont. This is the real old Richmond—real through the continuous habitancy and supremacy of the same kind of people—that William Byrd and Poe and Jefferson Davis knew. Its great charm is its utter lack of cheap "smartness" and senseless bustle. Like the old-time New-Englander, the Southerner has no false front. Life is divested of affected excrescences, stultifying routines, and meaningless speed, and kept to the significant essentials of the main Anglo-Saxon stream. I wish I liv'd there—tho' personal memories will always bind me to mine own antient town of Providence.

Prior to my departure from Richmond, I had the good fortune to behold the still older and richly historick towns of Williamsburg, Jamestown, and Yorktown in a single afternoon, thanks to the excellent sightseeing coaches of the Grey Line. The trip from Richmond to Williamsburg was made on the regular Norfolk coach—which was met by the sightseeing coach with able lecturer and full Williamsburg-Jamestown-Yorktown historick itinerary. Starting from Richmond, I pass'd over the old Williamsburg Road—or Nine-Mile Road, to use another antient name. This took me past some of the most celebrated battlefields of the Civil War, including Seven Pines and the Chickahominy Swamp. The Chickahominy River was cross'd on a new concrete bridge, and presented a weirdly fascinating swamp-like aspect with trees growing out of the water far back from the open channel. This is the most distinctively southern-looking landskip I have yet seen—for Virginia is not really a southern region except socially and politically. Climatically it is in the same approximate zone as New-England, as fauna, flora, and general atmosphere suggest. It is in the Carolinas and Georgia, I imagine, that the actual climatick South begins. As the coach near'd the drowsy and infinitesimal hamlet of *Providence Forge*, I lookt about with keen interest to see how well my own Providence might be echo'd. The place is too small for a post-office, and does not greatly suggest its Rhodinsular namesake—but I did experience one home touch when, by coincidence, there flasht by the coach a gentleman's private chaise bearing a Rhode-Island licence plate—"25.116—R.I.—29". It was my fortune to see many Rhode-Island and Massachusetts-Bay plates in the South—more, I think, than one commonly sees in New-York. After all, the real white men's parts of the colonies will hang together long after Manhattan is frankly recognis'd as an outpost of the Levant! Providence Forge was nam'd from an old forge used in the making of farm implements; sett up there in 1770 by three men, one of whom was a Presbyterian clergyman. It has given its name to the principal gentleman's seat near by—an eight-room colonial house of the farm type with dormer windows, and a pair of chimneys on each end. A stream, dam, and mill exist at Providence Forge, and remnants of the old forge itself were recently found. Some distance beyond this town I saw the small but famous old Hickory Neck Church, built in 1733 and serving as an academy for some time subsequent to 1825. It is a very small, plain brick structure—like an enlarged dog-kennel—of a type fairly frequent in Virginia. Toano next was reach'd—a straggling southern village without distinctive features.

At last came Williamsburg, where a change to the Grey Line sight-seeing coach was made. This is one of the best-preserv'd colonial towns in the country, and amply justifies the Rockefeller plan for restoring it to its pre-Revolutionary state. Much restoration has been accomplished even now, but most of it is still to come. Not only will decay'd and alter'd houses be put back into pristine shape, but intrusive modern buildings will be torn down, and vanisht colonial edifices reërected from old plans, prints, descriptions, and so forth—resting in many cases on their original foundation-walls as uncover'd by judicious excavations. In layout and atmosphere, Williamsburg resembles *Deerfield* more than any other New-England town; since it is largely concentrated along a broad main street, and consists of houses widely spaced amidst their grounds. The central thoroughfare, Duke of Gloucester Street, is well shaded with trees (including mulberry trees planted in a fruitless effort to establish the silk culture), and has a strip of park or turf down the centre. Houses vary from quaint peaked-roof affairs of early date (plus a few gambrel specimens) to fine Georgian mansions in the southern style. One by one the non-colonial intruders are coming down, whilst the Phoenix-like rise of the vanisht colonial buildings may soon be expected.

Williamsburg, the oldest incorporated town in Virginia, began in 1633 with a palisade built by Gov. Wyatt as a defence against the Indians. It grew very rapidly, and with the decline and burning of Jamestown (in Bacon's Rebellion of 1676) became the chief settlement in the Colony. It was made the Capital in 1699, after the burning of the Jamestown colony-house. During the eighteenth century it was the centre of a brilliant life, as is attested by its many noble mansions. It likewise became the seat of William and Mary College, founded in 1693. The name Williamsburg was first apply'd in 1699—the former designation having been "Middle Plantation". It was made a city in 1722, and has always remain'd such, tho' it is scarce more than a village in population. As Richmond rose, Williamsburg declin'd; till at length (1799) it gave place to its younger rival as capital. This stagnation, akin to that of Newport, in Rhode-Island, is what hath preserv'd its colonial reliquiae so marvellously.

I can describe but a few of the sights of Williamsburg, thro' which the Grey Line party was guided by a very bright young student from the college. Old Bruton Church, built 1710–15, is perhaps the most impressive object; and I was glad of a chance to explore it amply, crypt and all. It contains the antient silver communion service from the early church at Jamestown, as well as other colonial reliques of the highest value. The churchyard is, bar none, the most hauntingly picturesque I have ever seen; with curiously carv'd granite monuments bearing coats-of-arms. William and Mary College, at the west end of Duke of Gloucester Street, has for its original edifice (erected 1697) the only building in America design'd by Sir Christopher Wren. Newer buildings, including several still unfinish'd, all conform to the same type of design. The President's house, built in 1732, is of the steep-roof'd southern Georgian pattern. A chapel attach'd to the Wren building was erected in 1730, and another small building (presented by the eminent man of science Sir Robt. Boyle for use as an Indian school) was built in 1723. In front of the Wren building stands the marble statue of the colonial governor Lord Botetourt, originally set up near the colony-house, and remov'd hither in 1797. Ld. Botetourt himself lyes bury'd beneath the chapel. At the east or opposite end of Duke of Gloucester Street the foundations of the colonial capitol are still visible—or rather, visible again after excavation. This building will rise again from these foundations, a perfect copy of the one erected in 1705, rebuilt after burning in 1750, and abandon'd to decay in 1780. The white-belfried colonial court-house, built in 1769, is still in use as such; but will eventually become a publick library. The old "Powder Horn" is a typical colonial powder-house, like those at Marblehead and Somerville in the Province of the Massachusetts-Bay except that it is octagonal instead of cylindrical or conical. It was built in 1715, and hath been put to a curious variety of uses—market-house, Baptist church, dancing-school, Confederate arsenal, stable, and historical museum. Two interesting old gaols are shewn—the Debtors' Prison, built in 1748, and the Old Colony Prison built in 1705 with especially thick walls. In the latter were confin'd thirteen of the pirate Blackbeard's men—who were subsequently hang'd near by—as well as the royal governor of Detroit, Henry Hamilton, who was captur'd at Vincennes, Indiana, in 1779 by George Rogers Clark. Another interesting object is the pre-Revolutionary apothecary shop, now in process of restoration.

The private dwellings of interest are too numerous to catalogue.

Most famous perhaps is the George Wythe house in Palace Green,* built in 1755 and inhabited by the celebrated statesman from 1779 to 1789. It was the headquarters of Genl. Washington in 1781. In 1927 this fine middle-Georgian edifice became the Parish House of antient Bruton Church, and hath been restor'd as a museum. I was glad to be able to give it a thorough exploration. The Paradise house is a splendid Georgian mansion built in 1760 and inhabited in 1788–9 by John Paradise, at one time a member of Dr. Johnson's literary circle in London. The Gov. John Page house (1710), a smallish wooden structure, is the scene of Mary Johnston's novel *Audrey.* There are strange inscriptions scratch'd upon two of its window-panes—"S. B. 1796 Nov. 23 O fatal day." and "A. Boush 1734." The Vest house is the largest brick mansion in Williamsburg. The Galt house (1640) is the oldest in Williamsburg and probably the oldest private dwelling in Virginia. It is small, wooden, and steep-roof'd. Besides the existing houses, there are many sites where houses will be rebuilt from surviving foundations—among them the Governor's house, the Masonick Hall, and the famous Raleigh Tavern. I must revisit Williamsburg when the restorations are compleat, perhaps two to five years hence. It will then form, without doubt, one of the most impressive evocations of the colonial past that America can display. One curious fact emphasised by this restoring work is the manner in which Nature tends to give burial to the things which man hath forgotten—a slow, subtle burial inch by inch as the dust of decades drifts and accumulates. It is thus that half the steps of Notre Dame have been cover'd up, and thus that classick Rome lyes many feet below the level of the modern town. In Williamsburg the old foundation-walls of vanisht structures lye severall inches below the present surface; and I observ'd with interest the lost brick driveway of the Governor Dinwiddie house, rediscover'd only two or three weeks before my visit, which is fully a foot lower than the existing sidewalk.

From Williamsburg the coach drove over a lonely road to the island of Jamestown, birthplace of our British civilisation in America. On the way we pass'd several lakes of clear blue, exempt from the general yellow mud colour of southern waters. The reasons for this difference are intricately geologicall, so that only a Mortonius cou'd describe them; and I was soon to find that the great York River shares the happy exemption. The James is yellow, but the York is blue! Incidentally, the whole area travers'd in this town lyes betwixt the York and the James, being hence commonly known as "The Peninsula".

Jamestown is no longer a village, but simply a wind-swept grassy

*Which extends north of Duke of Gloucester St. So nam'd because the Governor's house or palace stood at the head of it.

expanse overlooking the river and strown with monuments and melancholy reliques. Yet it is here that our nation took its rise in 1607—thirteen years before the Plymouth landing of the Pilgrims. The fateful expedition sail'd from London on Dec. 30, 1606, in three ships—the *Sarah Constant* under Capt. Sir Chr: Newport, the *Goodspeed* under Capt. Bartholomew Gosnold (who also explor'd our New-England coast), and the *Discovery* under Capt. John Ratcliff. On May 13, 1607, the colonists landed at the spot which became Jamestown, naming their settlement from our Sovereign James the First. There were 105 settlers in all, all men, and mostly of good blood. First preparing a crude shelter for worship, they render'd thanks to Heaven according to the Church of England rite; and subsequently began building their primitive village. The first church was rough and ugly, but a finer brick Gothick specimen was put up in 1638 (not 1617 as often wrongly stated in guide-books), the tower of which yet remains in a ruin'd state, with a modern nave (1907) built on the excavated foundations of the old one. In 1608 Capt. John Smith became President of the Council, and used his distinguisht ability in furthering the fortunes of the settlement. He had sail'd up the James in 1607 with Capt. Newport and erected a cross at the falls and head of navigation where Richmond now stands. Indian troubles follow'd, as is well illustrated by the familiar incident of Pocahontas. In 1609 Capt. Smith was succeeded by Percy, and in that autumn came the great famine which left only sixty out of some 500 settlers. In 1610 the dissatisfy'd colonists all started back for England, but decided to stay when a fresh load of colonists (delay'd by shipwreck) arriv'd. Lord De La Warr now became Governor, and increas'd the general contentment; Sir Tho: Dale succeeding very ably to him. In 1619 wives were sent out for the colonists, and in the same year the first cargo of African blacks arriv'd—proving that troubles never come singly. This was under the governorship of Sir George Yeardley. Industry and agriculture grew, silk culture and glass-making being among the experiments. An Indian massacre in 1622 fail'd to kill off the settlement; and by the time of Bacon's Rebellion against Gov. Berkeley in 1676 the colony had so grown that Jamestown's burning meant only a local loss—Virginia's supremacy passing to Williamsburg, then call'd "Middle Plantation". Many buildings of brick and wood were put up in Jamestown, including several notable colony-houses, the last of which was burn'd in 1699. After 1700 the town was gradually abandon'd, so that fewer and fewer houses remain'd standing—the high winds destroying things rather readily. In the 1830's only one house—the brick Ambler house—existed on the island in addition to the ruin'd church tower; and today even this hath succumb'd save for part of the walls.

These reliquiae prove the house to have been of the Gothick design—for it must be remember'd that Jamestown was founded before the original Gothick period had wholly ended. The principal area of Jamestown is today own'd by the Association for the Preservation of Virginia Antiquities, and is strown with monuments and excavated foundation-walls. I cannot here attempt to describe these individually, save to say that the outlines of the old colony-house were unearth'd in 1903, together with those of four private dwellings in a solid block. The brick-pav'd cellar of one of the latter—Colonel Philip Ludwell's house—hath been carefully and compleatly excavated. The colony-house here unearth'd was that of 1686—whose burning led to the transfer of the capital to Williamsburg. There are two small museums in Jamestown, housing some minor excavated reliques and some historical pictures. A sea-wall hath been built around the island to check the constant encroachments of the wind-lash'd river. Part of Jamestown is privately own'd and not open to the publick—some day it will yield up rich archaeological material. The real focus of interest is the ruin'd and ivy'd church-tower of the 1638 edifice. Amidst its antient brick-wall'd churchyard, where curious giant roots weirdly creep and play havock with the slabs, and with its modern nave behind it, it well symbolises both the decay of the town and the permanence of the colony which sprang from it. Jamestown, despite its visual barrenness resulting from its desolation, is one of the most stimulating of all spots to the sensitive imagination. To stand upon the actual seed from which the Anglo-American provinces grew—to tread on soil once peopled by gallant gentlemen-adventurers of the Elizabethan generation—what more hath this continent to offer?

The coach now sett out for Yorktown, a quaint colonial city celebrated as the scene of Ld. Cornwallis's unfortunate surrender to the rebel armies of Genl. Washington and Marquess de La Fayette. This town, now sunk to a sleepy village, was once a port of very great wealth and standing, being a noted port of entry whose custom-house in 1749 recorded an annual trade of £32,000. It lyes on land first patented by one Nicholas Martiau, a Walloon, who came to Virginia in 1621. In 1691 Martiau's grandson Benj: Reade sold 50 acres of the tract to Messrs. Ring and Ballard to be settled as a town. The venture prosper'd, and in 1698 the new village became the seat of York county. In 1705 a brick custom-house, still standing, was built to accommodate its increasing trade. In 1781 the retreating troops of Ld. Cornwallis reach'd this place, establishing a final line of defence some distance east of the town and surrendering on the 19th of October. This event, deciding the colonial rebellion in favour of the rebels, mark'd the virtual close of hostilities and signalised the practical separation of the colonies from their rightful government; hence is widely celebrated throughout the present United States.

> "Treason doth never prosper, what's the reason?
> Why, if it prosper, none dare call it treason!"

Or as Seneca saith:

> "—Prosperum ac felix scelus
> Virtus vocatur."

The town and field are distinguisht by monuments, and the place much visited by travellers. Some events of the Civil War also took place here, Genl. McClellan employing Yorktown as a Federal base in 1862. There is a cemetery and a monument dedicated to the memory of Union soldiers kill'd in battel and in an accidental explosion.

Yorktown is situate on the south bank of the broad blue York River—a stream curiously exempt from the yellowness of most southern waters. A ferry connects it with Gloucester—which, together with another ferry across the James from Jamestown to Surry, forms a continuous route across the peninsula to the farther south. This is not, however, the main highway southward; the latter passing thro' Richmond and avoiding the peninsula altogether. Yorktown is twelve miles from the mouth of the York, eighteen from Jamestown, and twelve from Williamsburg. In proceeding from Jamestown, my coach re-pass'd thro' Williamsburg, which I was very glad to see again. On the highroad thence to Yorktown I beheld some Civil War and Revolutionary battlefields, and saw in the distance one or two famous colonial estates such as Carter's Grove, built in 1751 by Carter Burwell, Esq. The coach also pass'd thro' the shabby whitewash'd hamlet of Lackey, which is apparently inhabited wholly by blackamoors. It is notable that the blacks are much more numerous on the peninsula than in Richmond. The Richmond-Norfolk coaches require them to sit in the rear, and the stations around Williamsburg, Yorktown, and Lee Hall all have separate white and black waiting-rooms. In Norfolk, of course, the colour-line is necessarily very strictly drawn; for the place teems with niggers.

Yorktown proper is a kind of southern Marblehead, if I may overlook a designation I have worn trite by many applications, for most of the houses are of colonial date. There are no sidewalks, and the only pavement is the concrete of the state road. Its architecture is more typically southern than that of Richmond, steeply pitched roofs and end chimneys being everywhere seen. The Grey Line coach pass'd thro' it, view'd the battlefield, and then return'd to inspect the town at greater leisure. On the east edge of the compact part are the foundation-walls of the Nelson house, used by Ld. Cornwallis as his headquarters till its destruction by shell-fire on Octr. 11, 1781. These were excavated only a month before my visit, and will be very carefully preserv'd. The town as a whole is meerly a double line of straggling brick, stone, and wooden houses along the highway, and most of it can be seen from the coach. I was glad, however, when a stop was made which permitted me to indulge in some pedestrian exploration. The greatest mansion in Yorktown is the imposing Tho: Nelson house—York Hall—a middle-Georgian structure shewing the Pennsylvania-Welsh influence in its architecture. This was own'd by the nephew of Secretary Nelson, owner of the demolish'd house. During the Revolution it was held by His Majesty's officers, and to dislodge them the owner—himself serving as a rebel general under Washington—order'd his own mansion to be fir'd upon. Of this Spartan fusillade, which fortunately fail'd to destroy the splendid house, two cannon balls yet remain imbedded in the eastern gable end. A garden of particular beauty adjoins the edifice, and helps it to form one of the most pleasing gentleman's seats on the peninsula. The oldest house in Yorktown, built in 1690, stands next to York Hall, and is a modest brick dwelling with antient curb roof and colonial dormers. It was built by Tho: Sessions, and escap'd injury in the Revolution. Its present condition is excellent. Grace Church, built also in 1699 as York-Hampton Church, is of grey marl rock and having a modest white belfry. In the antient churchyard are some interesting slabs. The small brick custom-house put up in 1706 is the oldest custom-house in the U.S., and is now a publick museum operated by the D.A.R. The Yorktown Hotel, put up in 1725, is still in continuous use for its original purpose; rivalling in that respect the celebrated Red Horse Tavern in Sudbury, in the Massachusetts-Bay. It is a small, steep, southern-looking building with end chimneys and dormers, and has been enlarged by a long rear extension which does not mar the original street facade. Other noted old Yorktown houses are the Cole Digges (1705—small brick), the West (1706—small wooden), and the Moore, a farmhouse of early but uncertain date near the village. This latter was antiently the abode of Gov. Spottswood, and in 1781 form'd the scene of Ld. Cornwallis's conference with Genl. Washington as to terms of surrender. It is on that account highly esteem'd by those who sympathise with the revolt against our rightful sovereign.

I was very glad to have seen this village—and indeed, I reckon the whole itinerary of that day among the most pleasant and striking experiences I have ever had. From Yorktown the coach went to Lee Hall, a small town where it connected with the Richmond coach. The return trip to Richmond included one more welcome passage thro' Williamsburg, and a magnificently apocalyptick sunset seen over the Chickahominy Swamp. The scenery here has good isolated embodiments, but scarcely equals that of New-England as a whole.

It being now time to turn my course northward, I look'd forward with much eagerness to a detail'd exploration of that Fredericksburg-Falmouth region whose quaint and colonial picturesqueness I had glimps'd so tantalisingly on the southward trip. Taking an early stage-coach from Richmond, I was given some anxiety by the uncertainty of the weather; but fortunately the afternoon turn'd out clear when I reach'd Fredericksburg, so that I had quite perfect conditions for sightseeing. A very pleasant coach-driver supply'd me with information highly useful in getting about quickly and directly; and was so good as to furnish me with several guide booklets with maps, whereby I grew reasonably familiar with the plan of the town before attempting to wander through it.

Quaint and historick beyond my fondest expectations, Fredericksburg and environs kept me busy for all of the five hours at my disposal; and made me wish I had five more–or rather, five days more–in which to study its numberless antiquities and fascinating Old Virginia atmosphere. For here is a quiet village which has slept unchang'd thro' the centuries with its shady streets and colonial houses beside the green south bank of the yellow Rappahannock. The Civil War scarr'd it cruelly, but fail'd to impair its century'd charm and continuous tradition. There are very few foreigners, and very few persons of any kind whose ancestors have not dwelt there for centuries. Blacks are not numerous–indeed, they are by no means a conspicuous feature of the northern Virginia landskip. I was very fortunate in encountering a kindly, talkative, well-bred, and scholarly old gentleman who noticed my contemplative mien and frequent guide-book glances, and who volunteer'd to conduct me to the best uncharted colonial reliquiae. He was a connoisseur of Georgian architecture, inhabiting a colonial house himself and being no mean student of furniture, decorative detail, and early brick construction. Under his tutelage–and he tirelessly walkt me thro' street after street, lean and alert despite his years–I absorb'd dozens of sights and atmospherick touches which I wou'd otherwise have miss'd; and he offer'd to shew me interiors on some later visit when I might have more time. This good old man–a Mr. Alexander–is quite typical of nearly everyone I met in the South–including Mr. Strain, the genial coach-driver. Without question, I find southern people more congenial as a class than any other type I have so far seen–despite my devotion to New-England's landskip, architecture, and quiet ways. The Southerner reflects a civilisation of riper mellowness and higher graces than any other on this continent, and I wish this civilisation had a greater chance of spreading and leaving its impress on the culture of the nation as a whole—if indeed the nation as a whole may be said to possess any culture beyond a barbarick devotion to wealth, speed, glitter, and useless magnitude and activity.

Fredericksburg straggles sleepily along the southern bank of the shallow Rappahannock at the original head of navigation, with the green unspoil'd countryside (boasting the full luxuriance of summer early in May) drowsing exquisitely across the stream. Two bridges connect the town with the northern shoar—one from the "civick centre" to the roads of the open Stafford Heights country, and the other (the main Washington-Richmond highway bridge) from the extream westerly fringe to the quaint and somnolent hamlet of Falmouth, which is seven years older than Fredericksburg. The centre of the town before the Revolution lay farther west than at present, but a destructive fire during that period wiped out the business section and caus'd the residential streets farther east to turn to trade. The plan today is the same as in Civil War times. The town was named in honour of George the Third's father—Frederick, Prince of Wales, who dy'd before succeeding to the throne. All the principal streets are named from members of the royal family—Princess Anne St., Prince Edward St., Prince George St., William St., Sophia St., Amelia St., Caroline St., and so on. This is the kind of atmosphere in which my Tory soul revels—GOD SAVE THE KING!

The Fredericksburg region—to exclude all apocryphal tales—was first visited by Capt. John Smith with a crew of twelve men and Indian guide in 1608, on a trip during which he had a severe fight with a band of prowling Rappahannocks. Settlement—in the form of farms and gentlemen's plantations—was very gradual, but a fort was maintain'd near the falls of the river, and much sea-trade conducted; for the river was then broader and deeper than at present, and better adapted to navigation. In 1671 land patents were granted to Tho: Royston and John Buckner for the purpose of forming a settlement of forty persons, but this did not prove lasting. The tiny hamlet of Falmouth, on the north bank of the river near the falls, was founded in 1720, and is the earliest continuous settlement. Falmouth still contains many decrepit, steep-roof'd houses which must date back to almost the first decade of its colonisation. All these settlements reflect the desire of the neighbouring country-gentry for a town in their midst to serve as a trading-centre. Virginia was always rural by instinct, and even in 1700 Williamsburg was the only important town. Northern Virginians, wishing a more convenient centre of commerce, encourag'd the trading classes to settle around the Rappahannock region in urban fashion—then, realising the advantages of town houses for themselves, began to build mansions in the village and to develop a town social life in conjunction with their manorial existence. Fredericksburg, as a definite town, was incorporated and named in 1727. It was in this region that most of the Washingtons dwelt in the early eighteenth century; the "Cherry Tree" farm of Genl. Washington's father being just across the river from Fredericksburg. Young George and his brothers and sister went to school in Falmouth and Fredericksburg, and his mother always lived there. The sister, Betty, marry'd Col. Fielding Lewis, who built Kenmore mansion for her. In later years Madam Washington liv'd in a cottage near Kenmore to be close to her daughter, and there she dy'd in 1789. She is bury'd in the vicinity, and I beheld her tomb.

The early houses of Fredericksburg are small, steep-roof'd, wood and brick affairs with dormers and end chimneys—the regular southern type—built along the river-bank and sometimes forming solid blocks of four or five. Later and finer dwellings are on the higher parallel streets farther back from the stream. Kenmore—really a country-seat—is very far from the Rappahannock, in what were open fields at the time of its building. Madam Washington's cottage was connected with it by a flower-border'd path. Both are standing, and in excellent preservation—I gave them a close and appreciative survey. The oldest real mansion, the Charles Dick house, was built in 1745 and is still standing in good shape. I view'd it with much interest. Another thing which impress me greatly was the Rising Sun Tavern, built in the 1780's by Charles Washington, George's brother, and famous for having harbour'd most of the eminent southern statesmen of the eighteenth century. Still quainter is the little apothecary shop in Caroline Street kept by Col. Hugh Mercer, who was both a physician and a chemist, and who was kill'd in the Revolution. This has been fitted up exactly as it was in Mercer's day, with old-time jars, great brass scales, and all the appurtenances of a colonial pharmacy. Another cherisht sett of Fredericksburg associations is that connected with President James Monroe, who was born near by and who practis'd law there after the Revolution. His old law-office hath been refitted just as it was in his day, so that it forms an admirable companion-piece to the Mercer shop. Of great Masonick interest is the antient brick home of Lodge No. 4, where on Novr. 4, 1752, George Washington was initiated as a Mason. The Masonick order was very strong throughout colonial Virginia, and especially at Fredericksburg, where there is a special Masonick Cemetery.

But the chief charm of Fredericksburg is less in any one house than in its whole pervasive atmosphere of colonial Southernism—a culture which has certainly survived to a much greater extent than colonial New-Englandism. Fredericksburg doorways, whilst by no means equal to New-England specimens, are famous throughout the South. The doors are generally double—that is, *vertically* double like those of Philadelphia—and above them is generally a rectangular *transom* of the colonial New-York type rather than a *fanlight* in the New-England and Philadelphia manner. The traceries on these transoms are often exquisite in the extream, and are worthy of a special study. Only very late Georgian houses (circa 1825) have fanlights and sidelights. One or two of these have doorways very like those design'd by John Holden Greene of Providence for such Providence houses as the Beckwith, Allen, Halsey, Cooke, and Crawford mansions.

Kenmore deserves a chapter all to itself. This celebrated mansion was begun in 1752, on land survey'd on Feby. 20th of that year by young George Washington, brother-in-law of the builder. It is a splendid specimen of the plainer type of middle-Georgian architecture, and seems to follow northern or British models rather than the typical southern style. There is a portico and a garden in the rear, and the grounds are still spacious despite many ruthless subtractions from the original large estate. The doorways and panelling are very notable, and the great recess'd windows lend a charm of memorable poignancy. Massive locks and "Holy Lord" hinges form matters of importance to those interested in structural details. But the chief "show pieces" of Kenmore are, curiously enough, not parts of the original fabrick but additions made more than twenty years later—viz., the marvellous stucco'd ceilings and overmantels. Most of these were done in 1774 and 1775 by the same Frenchman who did the stucco work at Mount Vernon; and he hath left a monument to his national loyalty in the dining-room, the centre of whose ceiling is the head of King Louis XIV, surrounded by solar rays typifying the monarch's boasted function as the bright sun of civilisation. In the "great room" the stucco'd overmantel is of different and perhaps more interesting workmanship. This was done during the Revolution by two Hessian prisoners taken at the battle of Trenton and quarter'd at Falmouth. When Mrs. Lewis learn'd of these artisans and what they cou'd do, she decided to have them compleat the stucco work at Kenmore, and writ her brother Genl. Washington, asking for suggestions as to a good overmantel design. Aesopick fables being then of vast popularity as decorative themes, the General thought that the fable of the fox, the crow, and the piece of cheese would be a good thing to select for the place—both as an ornament and as a didactick lesson to his little nephews to beware of flatterers. Accordingly he sketcht out a rough design for the artists to follow—a design in which the landskip and buildings are typical of the homely rural Virginia scene. The suggestion was duly acted upon, and the result remains to this day in prime condition. Architects agree in praising it as a very fine specimen of its kind. Col. Lewis, his health and fortune wreckt by his unceasing expenditure of money and strength upon the rebel cause—for he was a leader in the intensive manufacture of muskets for the continental troops—dy'd penniless in January 1782, and his widow was forc'd to open a school and sell portions of the estate. Throughout her trials she was ably advised by her illustrious brother, and in 1786 she sold Kenmore and went to live with a marry'd daughter in Culpeper County, where she dy'd March 31st, 1797. She was greatly belov'd and mourn'd by Genl. Washington, who was of about the same age, and whom she so greatly resembled, that it was commonly said she cou'd well pass for him if drest in his cloaths. She had a sprightlier disposition, however, and a greater sense of humour than either her brother or mother. Temperamentally she seems to have been largely a Washington, whilst the General took after the Balls in his disposition. Kenmore remain'd in good hands after its sale, till in 1914 its use as a boarding-house was threaten'd. This peril gave rise to merited alarm, and an association was form'd to preserve it. Success happily crown'd the efforts of the association, and the house is today a publick museum of distinguisht excellence and wide repute. I thoroughly explor'd the house and grounds, and accounted my time well spent. Old Madam Washington's cottage is likewise safely preserv'd and open as a publick museum.

The Civil War history of Fredericksburg was of less interest to me, yet is dramatick in the extream. Its strategick position can be understood when we realise that the whole crux of the war was really the capture of Richmond, south of it. The great battel—a futile and wasteful affair—was precipitated by the rashness of our Rhode-Island Genl. Burnside and by the clamour of the northern press. The Yankees were encamp'd on Stafford Heights across the Rappahannock, and began on Dec. 13, 1862, with a cannonade almost unparallel'd in the annals of warfare prior to the Great War. The townspeople fled, and the Confederate defenders retir'd to Marye's Heights, which overlook the town on the south. Bridges having been burnt by the Confederates, Burnside's men crost the river on hastily lay'd pontoon-bridges, and for a few hours occupy'd the town—not without some vandalism. Notwithstanding the obviously impregnable defences of Lee and Longstreet on Marye's Heights, the brave and reckless Burnside determin'd to attack the Confederate position; and led his men to what was virtually a wholesale suicide. What happen'd to Genl. Meagher's Irish brigade is a sample of what the whole charge was like. Of that unit of 1200 men, *937* were left dead on the field—one officer's body being found within fifteen feet of the Confederate parapet. Utterly beaten, Burnside retir'd back across the river to Stafford Heights when night fell. He had kill'd the best part of his troops absolutely for nothing! Earlier in the war Fredericksburg had been the scene of a more peaceful Yankee occupation—in the spring of 1862, when Genl. McDowell controll'd the Rappahannock region. During that period Pres. Lincoln deliver'd an address from the steps of the (still standing) National Bank—fram'd in its exquisite colonial doorway. The Federal officer then in occupation was Genl. Marsena Patrick, whose kindliness and consideration won him many southern friends. His correspondence with Mayor Slaughter (for Fredericksburg, small as it is, is a real city) was of such courtliness that one historian hath said that the letters "read like the extracts from the correspondence of diplomats". Fredericksburg is also quite near to many other noted Civil War battlefields—such as Salem Church, Chancellorsville, Spotsylvania Court-House, and the Wilderness.

After a thorough survey of urban Fredericksburg, I walkt out along the high road to quaint Falmouth—about a mile and a half, and across the long Rappahannock bridge. This hamlet is ineffably archaick and half fallen to ruin, and evidently houses a rather poor class of whites in addition to its niggers. It lies picturesquely on a curving hill road which ascends the northerly slope of the river-valley, and most of its houses are of the early eighteenth century. A few late-Georgian houses lye on the lower level near the river-bank—one of them, with a splendid fanlighted doorway, being labell'd as the home of the "first millionaire in America". The interior woodwork of this fine house is announc'd as for sale—symbol of an increasing and very discouraging habit of stripping noble old buildings to enrich museums and the private houses of vulgar money'd parvenus. In returning to Fredericksburg I did not follow the main highway, but ambled along the leisurely, unfrequented old road that skirts the river's northern bank; crossing by the bridge from the foot of Stafford Heights to the centre of the town. I reacht the Princess Anne Tavern in time for the evening stage-coach to Washington, and after a pleasing drive in the twilight—during which I had a second glimpse of the old Pohick Church—was deposited in the Federal capital, where I found quarters at a good inn.

In Washington, owing to my now considerable familiarity with the local antiquities, I spent much time in museums and galleries; including the Smithsonian Institution and its striking collection in every field of learning and technology. Of everything I saw, nothing impress me more than the Cyclopean stone images from Easter Island in the Pacifick—last mute and terrible survivors of an unknown elder age when the towers of weird Lemurian cities clawed at the sky where now only the trackless waters roll. At the Library of Congress—whose overlavish building was design'd, by the way, by a remote blood-kinsman of mine—I beheld a wealth of interesting exhibits; including a sett of splendid colour'd photographs of the antient parish churches of Virginia. At the Corcoran Gallery I saw a sett of models illustrating coming architectural developments in Washington—developments, I am glad to say, which will involve no departure from classick and traditional designs. At the Freer Gallery the celebrated "Peacock Room" of Whistler was perhaps paramount in interest. On a side-trip I survey'd the results of the past year's progress toward compleating the magnificent Gothick cathedral atop Mount St. Alban. In many of my trips I was ably guided by my friend Edward Lloyd Sechrist, Esq., whose courtesy contributed so much to my Washington trip of 1925.

From Washington I took the coach for Philadelphia, and after a pleasing drive reacht that venerable and favourite town in the golden glamour of sunset. Here, besides renewing my acquaintance with the colonial streets and squares I know and love so well, I devoted some time to the museums—especially that marvellous new art museum near the Schuylkill at the end of the great Parkway. This latter is absolutely the most magnificent museum building in the world—the most exquisite, impressive, and imagination-stirring piece of contemporary architecture I have ever lay'd eyes on—the most gorgeously perfected and crystallised dream of beauty which the modern world hath to give. It is a vast Grecian temple group atop a high elevation (a former reservoir) which terminates the Parkway vista toward the Schuylkill; reacht by broad, spacious flights of steps, flankt by waterfalls, and with a gigantick fountain playing in the centre of the great tessellated courtyard. A veritable Acropolis—I had seen it before, but had never ascended the steps or enter'd the place. This time I did ascend and enter; and tho' the structure is not yet compleat or fully equipt, I found it no disappointment. Colonial and British Georgian rooms are there in infinite profusion; not so many American rooms as in the new decorative wing of the Boston museum or the American wing of the Metropolitan Museum of New-York, but much more British material than in either of those places. A very rare feature is a pair of rooms from an eighteenth-century Pennsylvania-German house—the only things of their kind in any museum I know of. The furniture and paintings occupying these rooms are as rare as the rooms themselves, and include the best work of the corresponding periods. The pictures have amongst them specimens by Reynolds, Gainsborough, Romney, Raeburn, Gilbert Stuart, and so on. The wide assortment of English rooms presented enables one to form a very good comparative estimate of English and American Georgian styles; and curiously enough, I think I prefer the American. The provincial interiors are less lavish in scale and decorative detail, and thereby gain a classick austerity of tone which wou'd be hard to surpass.

From Philadelphia I pass'd northward thro' New-York to a second phase of my travels which was to include the legend-haunted Hudson Valley as its chief seat; and owing to the kindness of my grandchild Belknap and his parents, I was provided with an instant up-river coach transportation which sav'd me from stopping in the metropolitan pest-zone. As the party fared northward, it was curious to reënter an early-spring environment whose delicate freshness contrasted so oddly with the lush summer luxuriance I had been enjoying in the South. This fragile exquisiteness of young foliage and apple-blossoms offers many compensations for the drowsy fulness, peace, and restfulness of my favourite aestival season, and I was well pleas'd to encounter it. It was curious, too, to pass from a purely English region into one where Dutch influences are ancestrally paramount. Crossing the ferry at Rhinebeck, we enter'd antient Kingston—which is truly one of the most delectable places I have ever seen; a sleepy, wide-spreading old city of about 30,000 population, with unbelievably antient stone houses and scores of old wooden buildings in the colonial tradition of northern New-York state. The old Dutch churchyard is ineffably fascinating—full of old red sand-stone markers, and redolent of fine traditions and civilised reposefulness. The church now standing is of Victorian date (1852), but in its facade are sett old Dutch Bible texts—stone slabs taken from an earlier church on the same site. Buildings as old as 1680 or so are fairly common, and the graceful court-house was built in 1818. The modern parts are surprisingly tasteful, and the whole town hath the atmosphere of a country village despite the phenomenally large area it covers. In many parts the open country is astonishingly near, and most of the street vistas west and northwest have dim tracings of the violet Catskill foot-hills at their far, mysterious ends. I can well imagine Rip Van Winkle as flourishing in such a place—in fact, it is still a perfect part of the old America; as authentick a survival as the story'd South which I left behind with so much regret. It has nothing to do with New-York City—all its affiliations being with the wholesome "York State" rustick region to the north. In this town I was the guest of Bernard Austin Dwyer, who is a product of the wild domed hills and hanging woods of the West Shokan hinterland. Most of my writing whilst there was done in a green and sunny country lane just around the corner from a fine residential street—a lane whose vistas are wholly rustick as far as the eye can reach, and from which can be obtain'd glimpses of a charming and mysterious gap in the far-off, vapour-wreath'd purple hills. There birds sang, and the sun filter'd down thro' delicate vernal foliage and trac'd strange faery patterns on the grass and sand of the lane. Near by I cou'd spy the picturesque, ivy-grown ruins of some great stone building as I sate on the tumbled rocks of a low wall evidently belonging to it. I was fortunate enough to be able to tarry long enough at Kingston to imbibe its atmosphere rather fully, besides visiting its two still more antient and glamorous neighbours, Hurley and New Paltz. It is a fine old place—the present city being a fusion of two once separate villages—*Kingston* proper, where my host dwells and which is about a mile inland, and the port of *Rondout* on the hilly Hudson bank where the ferry from Rhinebeck lands and where a somewhat picturesque slumdom now prevails.

The history of the region goes back to the decade of 1620–30, when the Dutch built a fort (*ronduit*) at the mouth of a creek on land call'd by the Indians *Ponckhockie.* The fort became the centre of a settlement call'd *Rondout,* and the creek receiv'd the name of Rondout Creek. About 1652 Kingston proper—the land then call'd *Atkarkton,* northwest of Rondout and inland along Esopus Creek—was settled by Dutchmen and Englishmen from Rensselaerwyck, farther up the river, after disputes regarding land titles had driven them from the latter place. In 1655 serious Indian wars convuls'd the locality, and in 1658 the Atkarkton settlers appeal'd to Gov. Petrus Stuyvesant for aid. "Old Silverleg" was dispos'd to grant the petition only on condition that the colonists form their holdings into a palisaded village, and this requirement was duly and immediately comply'd with. The resulting stockaded town, which was charter'd by Stuyvesant in 1661 under the name of *Wiltwyck,* was embraced in the area bounded by the present Main St., Clinton Ave., North Front St., and Green St. Streets were lay'd out, which correspond quite closely to the streets of today. After the transfer of New-Netherland to His Britannick Majesty's domain, the name of Wiltwyck was chang'd to *Kingston;* and the village prosper'd exceedingly. In 1695 the Revd. John Miller, Chaplain of His Majesty's forces and Aide to the Governor of New-York, publisht a book with maps descriptive of the Province, and therein spoke of Kingston as a town of the same area as Albany, but with half as many houses—i.e., as being six furlongs in circumference, and having an hundred buildings in its compass. Many of these buildings are still standing today. Severe Indian warfare harass'd the town throughout its early history—incidents not unprovok'd by the high-handed seizure of lands and cruel treatment of Indians by the Dutch settlers. When the unfortunate sedition against the lawful authority of Great-Britain occurr'd, Kingston had well-nigh 200 houses, a market and brew house, a church, an academy (still standing), a court-house, and two schools. As a storehouse and source of supply for the rebel armies operating in its vicinity, it was a highly dangerous menace to His Majesty's forces; so that in the autumn of 1777 its destruction by fire was found needful. Most of the rebel inhabitants, being forewarn'd, fled to the village of Hurley and other points, and our troops enter'd the place without opposition; setting fire to all the edifices save those inhabited by loyal subjects of His Majesty. This process consum'd only the wooden dwellings, leaving the walls and great beams of the much more numerous stone houses scarcely damag'd. Accordingly the returning rebels later rebuilt their homes, so that large numbers of the early structures still stand. At this time, Octr. 16, 1777, the rebel Senate of New-York was meeting at the Ten Broeck house in Kingston (now pointed out as the "Senate House" and forming a publick museum), and adjourn'd its sessions to the Van Deusen house in Hurley when our troops burn'd the former. The city of New-York was the legal capital of the Province; but it was not at that time in the hands of the rebels, hence their sessions at Kingston, which was the third town in importance in the colony, Albany being second. In the compact part of Kingston not above one or two houses were left undamag'd by flame. Today the Van Steenburgh house, in Wall St. at the head of Franklin (hardly in the village according to the limits of 1777), is pointed out as the only one which was not touch'd. For this exemption various reasons are assign'd—loyalty of the owner being the most probable one. The tenure of Kingston by His Majesty's forces was not of long duration, since powerful rebel detachments under Genl. George Clinton (a native of this Ulster County region, and later Governor of New-York for twenty-one years) were observ'd to be advancing toward the town. Having destroy'd all possible rebel supplies, the army evacuated without pursuit of the fleeing villagers; and did not again enter. The rebel army soon arriv'd, and with its aid the villagers quickly reëstablisht themselves in their accustom'd haunts. Local progress was by no means retarded, and in 1783 (being us'd to harbouring a legislative body) Kingston offer'd itself as a possible capital of the United States—which offer was declin'd, as the Federal City of Washington had been plann'd. After the Revolution Kingston remain'd a very important town, tho' it did not grow as rapidly as many—Albany and New-York City monopolising the activity along the Hudson. At the Bogardus Tavern, which stood at the corner of Fair St. and Maiden Lane, many persons of the first importance were entertain'd; and it was there that Aaron Burr, observing the clever chalk drawings of a stable-boy on a barn-door, resolv'd to send the lad to Europe for an art education, and thus produced the eminent painter John Vanderlyn. As the nineteenth century wore on, Kingston was more and more rivall'd commercially by the river settlement of Rondout, at the mouth of the creek, which habitually obtain'd a great share of the region's trade. By the 1840's Rondout was larger than Kingston in population, and was heavily built up along its narrow, hilly streets in contrast to Kingston's straggling houses, broad streets, and level terrain. At the same time it was less select in population and less rich in traditions—a hive of traders and bargemen rather than a settled domain of hereditary agricultural magnates. In the 'fifties Rondout apply'd for a city charter, and seem'd for a while likely to get it; but vested and dignify'd Kingston interven'd, and finally succeeded in disposing of its rival by ingulphing it—i.e., by securing a combin'd city charter for the two neighbouring villages of Kingston and Rondout, *under the name of Kingston.* Thus Kingston became, by one sudden act, a city and a Hudson River port, with two distinct settled areas separated by a sparsely populated zone. So it hath remain'd to this day; save that the sparse zone is gradually filling up with publick and private buildings including the railway station, post-office, publick library, city hall, hospital, and Y.M.C.A. Kingston proper (or "uptown") hath retain'd its social supremacy, and there may be found all the leading dwellings and shops. Hilly Rondout on the river hath become a sort of slum fringe—distinctly declassé, and largely given over to foreigners, from whom Kingston proper is almost wholly free. The city is distinguisht by a reposefulness highly pleasing to observe, and scarce changes in population—having linger'd betwixt 25,000 and 30,000 for the last thirty years. It has a single street-car line from the Hudson Day Line wharf at Kingston Point through Rondout to Kingston proper—which still remains wholly two-man, still uses little single-track cars, and still has open cars in season. I took several rides on the latter. Stage-coach service also exists; both local, and to other towns including New-York City. It must be a delightful place to reside, save for its coldness in winter, for it has all the freshness, charm, and simplicity of a small village.

Of the individual houses in Kingston, some of the most notable are the ancient Hoffmann house (just around the corner from where I slept in Green St.), built not long after 1660; the Ten Broeck or Senate House at North Front St. and Clinton Ave., built in 1676; the Elmendorf Tavern (1726), the Sleght or Capt. Tappan House (mid-Georgian), the Kingston Academy (1774—now housing a newspaper), the De Waal Tavern in N. Front St., and so on. The typical Kingston house is a seventeenth- or early eighteenth-century building of one or two storeys and attick, of solid drest stone, and early Dutch architectural lines. The style is predominantly rural and primitive until the Georgian period; no Dutch town-houses with stept gables, or cottages with curving gambrel roof, having been constructed in this northerly region. With this omnipresence of the plain, sloping roof, it may be seen that Dutch Wiltwyck (or *Esopus,* as it was likewise often call'd) must have been a very different-looking region from the Dutch areas nearer the mouth of the Hudson—New-Amsterdam, Long Island, and the adjacent parts of New-Jersey. I visited the Sleght house, a fine middle-Georgian mansion at the junction of Crown and Green Sts.; preserv'd by the D.A.R. and open as a publick museum. It has an excellent panell'd interior, and shews the spread of cultivated and British influences over the Dutch parts of the Province as the eighteenth century advanc'd. I also inspected the "Senate House"—the Ten Broeck homestead of 1676—which is likewise a museum. In this I was by no means disappointed; for the interior is of the greatest conceivable interest, with low ceilings, hand-hewn beams, Dutch doors with antient hinges, steps up and down caus'd by late seventeenth- and eighteenth-century additions to the original house, bullseyes in interior doors, and other typical earmarks of solid and conservative Dutch colonial craftsmanship. The Historical Society which controls it is building a splendid new museum—in the exact style of a typical Old Kingston stone house—on the grounds west of the antient edifice; into which the general historical collection will shortly be mov'd. When this transfer is effected, the Ten Broeck house will be furnisht as a colonial home; thus forming an analogue of the Pendleton house in Providence, or the Van Cortlandt house in New-York. In the historical collection are some prodigiously interesting items—including the wooden sides of the rural wain in which Genl. Burgoyne was convey'd from the battlefield of Saratoga as a prisoner.

There now remain'd to be cover'd the ineffably quaint and lovely neighbouring villages of Hurley and New Paltz—unspoil'd reliques of the earliest days—and of these I chose to see Old Hurley (as it is commonly known) first. I rose early on the designated day and caught the stage-coach at the ancient Van Ross Tavern, despite an unpleasant drizzle which persisted throughout the day. The road lay thro' an exceeding fine rolling countryside; with green cultivated fields in a very unspoil'd and un-modern state, and the foothills of the story'd Catskills as an eternal dominating background. In general, this territory is unchang'd since the colonial period; being still own'd and farm'd by the descendants of the original Dutch and Huguenot settlers. Hurley, some three miles northwest of Kingston, was not in any way a disappointment. It is a straggling village of antient stone houses stretcht along the high-road, with plenty of trees and diverging lanes, and with green fields and blossoming orchards stretching off on either side to where the purple mountains loom mystically. The houses are of Dutch masonry construction, some of them with wooden atticks and lean-to's, and a few with projecting porches. All have the horizontally divided Dutch door with iron knocker and hinges to match, and the average date is from about 1700 to 1730. It is noteworthy, as previously remarkt, that none of these Ulster County Dutch houses ever develop'd the gracefully curving roof-line or the gambrel arrangement so characteristick of the Dutch colonial architecture of southern New-York. Up here the plain peaked-roof tradition always persisted. The houses of Hurley have seen very little change in the more than two centuries of their existence, for the place is delectably slow and sleepy, with true Catskill conservatism. All the dwellings are tenanted by the same old families who built them—an Elmendorf still runs the single village store and post-office and the antient Dutch Reform'd Church still ends the vista at the bend of the road on the farther side from Kingston—the only church in the hamlet. The town is very famous among antiquarians, models of the houses being in the museum of the New-York Historical Society, and a large space being devoted to them in Eberlein's volume, *The Architecture of Colonial America.* A Dutch diplomat has call'd it "more Dutch than anything left in Holland".

Hurley, at first call'd merely "Nieuw Dorp" or the "New Village", was founded about 1660 by the overflow population of Wiltwyck, who desir'd to expand in the fertile untimber'd lowlands. A large proportion of the settlers were French Huguenots, tho' the Dutch element was very numerous. Land grants were made by Gov. Stuyvesant without consent of the Indians who form'd the original population; a circumstance which paved the way for considerable warfare and general harassment. On June 7, 1663, Hurley was burn'd to the ground by salvages, and all the women and children were carry'd away into captivity. It was not until September that the pursuing forces of the Dutch succeeded in discovering the unhappy prisoners—who had not been ill-treated, tho' they were seen to have been burn'd alive in revenge for certain Indians who had been captur'd by the whites and sold as slaves to traders from Curaçao. In the years that follow'd, Hurley prosper'd exceedingly; perhaps occupying a more important position in the life of the region than it does today. Its cheeses, milk, cakes, and other products were famous throughout the New-Netherlands, and became celebrated in more than one bit of Dutch doggerel folklore, of which the following is a typical specimen, literally translated:

"What shall we with the wheat-bread do?
Eat it with the cheese from Hurley!
What shall we with the pancakes do?
Dip them in the syrup of Hurley!
What shall we with the corn-meal do
That comes from round about Hurley?
Johnnycake bake, both sweet and brown,
With green cream cheese from Hurley!"

The resemblance betwixt the Dutch and English languages, both representatives of a Low-Germanick syntactical system, may be seen by citing the second distich of this piece with the original:

"Wat zullen wij met die pannekoeken doen?
Doop het met die stroop van Horley!"

It was from Hurley that the settlement of New Paltz was made by Huguenots in 1677; and to Hurley that the fleeing people of Kingston repair'd just a century later, when the torches of His Majesty's troops menaced their houses. On that latter occasion the rebel state senate also fled to Hurley, conducting its deliberations in the old Van Deusen house (1723), which is still standing and colonially furnisht with a view to antique-selling. I enter'd and thoroughly examin'd the Van Deusen house; noting in particular the graceful staircase and hall-panelling, and the marvellously quaint door-hardware. There has been little change in it since the eighteenth century, and one may recognise the atmosphere of the past on every hand. The oldest house in the village is the Elmendorf store, dating from about 1700—the proprietor of which gave me much valuable information.

On the afternoon of the same day I made the New Paltz trip, thus completing my long-plann'd circuit of the famous Ulster County triad of colonial survivals. New Paltz lyes about sixteen miles south of Kingston, by the Wallkill and Shawangunk Creeks, and in the eternal shadow of the lordly and lovely Shawangunk Hills. It is a thriving village with shops, hotels, banks, a normal-school, and a newspaper; but the modern (i.e., post-Revolutionary) town is at some distance from the heart of the antient settlement. This hath tended to preserve the original area in its pristine, Hurley-like state; so that we may still see the place as it was in the early eighteenth century. To reach the old town from the modern town one has to walk a considerable space, descending a steep hill and crossing the railway track. On this occasion the day was dismal, but I appreciated the splendid unspoil'd countryside none the less. Here is the old Hudson valley of Irving's day still flourishing and unalter'd; any of these villages being a suitable abode for the mellow Dutchmen of "Geoffrey Crayon's" fancy. Lovely valleys abound, and bends of streams in the lee of mountains produce a scenick effect hard to surpass. I saw at least one old-fashion'd cover'd bridge. Finally the coach ascended a hill and deliver'd me at the principal tavern of New Paltz—the "modern" part, tho' even that is as quaint as can be imagin'd, and marvellously native as to population. There are virtually no foreigners in this idyllick backwater, nearly all the population being descended from the original Huguenot settlers. Making judicious inquiries, I soon found my way down to the antient section—Huguenot Street—and there revell'd in the sparse line of old stone dwellings which hath given the town so great an historical and architectural fame. There are not many—perhaps half a dozen at best—but their fine preservation and isolation from modern influences give them a magnify'd charm. One of them is fitted up as a museum and open to the publick; others remain private dwellings, mostly in the hands of the families that built them more than two centuries ago. The museum—which is the old Jean Hasbrouck house built in 1712—is a large stone house of one full storey and two attick storeys under the immense sloping roof—an ideal storehouse for grain or other rural material. It is a fine type of early colonial construction under Dutch influence (tho' Frenchmen built it), and I examin'd it with the utmost thoroughness and interest; visiting the attick and noting the massive expos'd beams. It is call'd the "Memorial House", and a boulder monument to the town's founders stands on the small triangular green opposite it. Near by is the quaint burying-ground housing these 'rude forefathers of the hamlet'. The other houses—of vary'd types, and having features as unique as transoms with double rows of lights—stretch southward; the DuBois, Elting, Abraham Hasbrouck, Freer, etc. places. All are of about the 1700 period, as can be well seen from every detail of their construction. The interior of the Memorial House hath some highly primitive features such as the great plank doors—some unpanell'd, and some single-panell'd. Oddly enough, there is just one of the antient stone houses in the "modern" village—now us'd as a publick library. In the old times it must have been an isolated farmhouse on the hill.

New Paltz was settled by French Huguenots who had undergone a long and singular course of persecution and migration. Emigrating originally from France, they had settled at Pfalz or Paltz in the Protestant Rhineland; but had eventually been so harass'd by French troops from across the border in their Catholick homeland that they reëmigrated to Holland. There, affected by that longing for a new world which sent so many religious refugees overseas, they took part in the general Dutch migration to New-Netherland—tho' sedulously retaining their French language and customs; a Gallick characteristick which we see today exemplify'd in the French of Quebeck, and in those who have come thence to Rhode-Island. Preferring the rural reaches of the upper Hudson to the crouded and cosmopolitan New-Amsterdam, this band of Huguenots (led by one Louis DuBois, a Pioneer of the utmost solidity and ability) selected Wiltwyck—the Kingston of later times—as an abiding-place; but later transferr'd themselves to the New Village (Hurley), which they considered more favourable to their retention of French speech and ways than the rather uncongenial Dutch trading-post within the palisade. After the burning of Hurley in 1663, Louis DuBois was most impress by the lovely countryside south of Rondout Creek, which was made familiar to him during his participation in the search for the Indian captives—amongst whom were his own wife and three sons. Especially did he relish the idyllick valley of the Wallkill, nestling amidst the Shawangunks and cut off from the bustling world which had treated him and his kind so ill. During the next fourteen years—a span markt by the transfer of the region from the Holland States-General to the authority of His Britannick Majesty—DuBois interested many of his fellow-Frenchmen in a project for securing land patents and founding a new Huguenot village in the Shawangunk country; a project finally carry'd through with the aid of Abraham Hasbrouck, a young Huguenot having influence with His Majesty's Governor of the Province, Sir Edmund Andros—the same official whose arbitrary measures made him so much hated in New-England. Arrangements were also made to purchase the land lawfully from the Indians—a step which wou'd have delighted Mr. Roger Williams of Rhode-Island—for the patentees were not insensible of the hostility created by the high-handed seizures of the Dutch. In May, 1677, the Indians formally ceded the land in exchange for much assorted merchandise, and four months later His Majesty's Government granted the legal patent to the settlers—Louis, Abraham, and Isaac DuBois, Abraham and Jean Hasbrouck, Adries and Simon LeFevre, Pierre Deyo, Louis Bevier, Antoine Crispell, and Hugo Frere, ancestor of the Freer family. Homes were built the following spring—rude cabins on the site of the stone houses built during the next generation—and a few other settlers were admitted, including at least one Dutch family. A little stone Huguenot church, with services in French, soon adorn'd the village green; and the hamlet was nam'd *New Paltz* in honour of that place in Germany which had first given the wanderers a haven.

With the years New Paltz attain'd a very comfortably agricultural prosperity, tho' remaining in that unspoiled state which best suited its founders' wishes. Every effort was made to preserve the traditional piety and French ways of the forefathers, yet in the course of time the influence of the surrounding Dutch population cou'd not help being felt. It became harder and harder to secure French-speaking schoolmasters and clergymen, and after a while the younger generation fell into the habit of speaking Dutch. Naturally the elders protested, and there is a well-known tale of a child sent to a relative to borrow some household utility, and refus'd it because she cou'd not speak its name in French. This transition period was likewise markt by ecclesiastical schisms—some church members wishing to adhere to the Reform'd Dutch Church whilst others clung to a French Huguenot independence. By 1750 Dutch had definitely displac'd French as the language of New Paltz, and in 1752 the church commenc'd the use of that tongue. The village was now essentially a part of the Dutch Hudson Valley, tho' still remembering its different traditions. Some of the pathos of the linguistick change is reflected in the will of Monsieur Jean Tebenin, the local schoolmaster who flourisht in the early eighteenth century. He saw the gathering clouds; and when he left his French Bible to the church, provided for its sale for the benefit of the poor if the French language shou'd ever cease to be spoken thereabouts. New Paltz in its Dutch-speaking period enjoy'd a steady growth, and that happy immunity from striking incidents which marks a peaceful community. Branches of its Huguenot stock were represented in the late unfortunate rebellion against His Majesty's authority, yet the war itself left the town serene and unravag'd. As the eighteenth century drew to its close, time took its revenge upon the once conquering Dutch language by pressing it to extinction as French had formerly been prest—the latest conqueror being the all-ingulphing English. Signs of Yankee progress became manifest as an Anglo-Saxon population filter'd in, but the newer element built on the hill above old Huguenot Street; shifting the centre of gravity of the village and leaving the antient part undisturb'd to this day. In 1833 an academy was founded, which survives to the present as a state normal-school. Connected with these educational enterprises was the late Albert K. Smiley, once head of the Friends' School in Providence, Rhode-Island, who with his twin brother conceiv'd a vast liking for the region and develop'd a great estate at Lake Mohonk, in the neighbouring hills—where he founded a series of annual conferences on Indian affairs which endures to this day. New Paltz hath erected a memorial gateway at the entrance of the Smiley estate—thus linking the sleepy Shawangunk valley with the antient town of Providence, in His Majesty's Rhode-Island Colony!

Having completed the exploration of New Paltz, I return'd by stage-coach to Kingston and took the rail-road cars (new-fangled nuisance!) to Albany—my plan being to cross thence into New-England by way of the Berkshires, and pay a long-anticipated visit to the learned and congenial W. Paul Cook, Esq., at Athol, in the Province of the Massachusetts-Bay, before finally coming back to Providence. The ride to Albany was somewhat marr'd by misty weather, yet was not without picturesqueness; involving many weird glimpses of the vapour-cloakt Catskills. Reaching Albany—a town of no great attractiveness to which I had been before—I sought out but few sights; prominent amongst them being the graceful late-Georgian Albany Academy north of the massive and ugly Victorian state-house.

Having putt up at an inn, I the next day sett out in the rail-road cars (the stage line being out of operation at the time) for the Massachusetts-Bay. The day was good, and the trip pleasing—it being very agreeable to change at Troy into a train of the antient *Boston and Maine* railway; a system wholly bound up with New-England and its associations, and thus furnishing the first touch of concrete symbolism in my gradual homecoming. God Save His Majesty's New-England Colonies!

The ride thro' New-York State was not at all dull; for the landskip is very fine, and includes many sightly mountain vistas and delightful glimpses of river scenes. Then the hills grew wilder and greener and more beautiful—yet less luxuriant in foliage as we receded from the warmth of the south. Finally I saw a station-name which made my heart leap—North-Pownal, in His Majesty's New-Hampshire Grants, latterly call'd Vermont, in NEW-ENGLAND! God Save the King! A town nam'd for Tho: Pownall, Gent., Governor of the Province of the Massachusetts-Bay! Home at last! After all, there is nothing else like home-coming; and it was good to have the scene shift from the exotick to the accustom'd—no more unfamiliar names and sights, but the cherisht, familiar things I have always known. Vanisht were the pillar'd doorways of New-York, the steep roofs and dormers of the South, the marble steps and keystones of Philadelphia, and the old stone dwellings of the Esopus Valley—all these, and the century'd echoes of those who have known them. They were snapt off as by the turning of some new-fangled electrick switch, and thenceforward my eyes and talk were to be fill'd with known and neighbouring things—the eternal hills and stone walls of my native land, the oft-rehears'd legends of familiar tribes and settlements, the homely accents of Puritan speech, the white steeples and farmhouse gables of New-England's countryside, the lov'd, antient names of known places which look back only to English dreams and memories—Pownal, Vermont—Williamstown in the Massachusetts-Bay—North Adams—Zoar—Charlemont—Buckland—Shelburne-Falls—West Deerfield—Greenfield—Orange—and Athol!

A second thrill occurr'd when the cars enter'd the Massachusetts-Bay, for this region, close to Rhode-Island, hath ever been as a second home colony to me—my first conscious memories, indeed, dating from a summer's visit to Dudley in that province, in 1892, when I was one and three-quarters years old. Near North-Adams the Berkshires became highly impressive, and I regretted bitterly that I was to go under them instead of over them. Then came the Hoosack Tunnel, a long period of artificial night, and after that occasional exquisite glimpses of mountain and valley—Charlemont, Shelburne-Falls, and so on. The landskip grew best near the end of the Berkshire region, when the lovely valley of the Deerfield River open'd up in full sunny expansiveness. Then came the now-familiar Greenfield, and the picturesque run along Miller's River thro' Orange to Athol, where I once more, after near a month and a half, sett foot upon my native Novanglian soil! GOD SAVE THE KING!

My visit to Athol was of the most extream pleasantness; Mr. Cook being ever the most gracious of hosts, and the young weird author H. Warner Munn, Esq., being a companion of the greatest charm and congeniality. Mr. Cook's country-seat is in the township of Phillipston, adjoining Athol proper; a region whose beauty and atmosphere make it the very quintessence of traditional New-England. What a place to be in after a long voyage amongst alien scenes! Rolling stony hills, narrow, winding, rutted roads, stone walls, antient apple-orchards, sparsely scatter'd white farmhouses with trim gables peeping above the brier-bushes of wall-travers'd hill-crests—if this be not New-England, what is? My host's estate is a rural dwelling of the traditional kind, sett on high ground with one of the most magnificent agrestick landskip effects conceivable; as regards both foreground and far horizon of hills beyond hills. At one point a blue lakelet glistens among pines. No other estate is in sight—just stone walls, green fields, distant hills, and the rambling, scatter'd buildings of a typical New-England farm. It is a poem in real life—and the interior of the house prov'd quite compatible with the exterior scene; low ceilings, glamorous atticks, and other suitable appurtenances leaving nothing to be desir'd by the lover of century'd beauty and background.

The town of Athol itself I have describ'd many times before, so I need not here dwell upon its pleasing qualities. It remains to be said, that my stay in this region was enliven'd by many coach trips provided by Messrs. Cook and Munn, amongst them being one of the scene of my sojourn of the previous year—the exquisite and magical hills of Brattleboro, in Vermont. The day of this trip was ideal in its conditions, and I found Vermont fully as marvellous in its mystick grace as I found it in 1927 and 1928. We pay'd a call upon the gentle bucolick poet Arthur Goodenough, whose lovely hillside seat I have so often and so rapturously describ'd; finding him at work upon his fences in the wooded hills behind his house, and enjoying the breathlessly marvellous panoramas afforded by every hilltop prospect. The sumptuous rustick fare offer'd us, and the ride back to Athol in the afternoon's golden light, are things not soon to be forgotten. Another trip lay through the Westminster region, where I was a summer visitor in the year 1899, and of which I retain'd many boyhood memories. The scene hath chang'd but little since then, and all the houses were familiar to me. Even the families are the same—tho' of course the old folks are no more.

At length the time arriv'd for me to return to my accustom'd Rhode-Island scenes, and my host very courteously gave me transportation thither in his coach. On a pleasant late-spring day we set out down the lovely Petersham-Barre road, enjoying the typical Massachusetts vistas, and the dense sylvan stretches belonging to the Harvard forestry department. Petersham is a delectable hilltop village abounding in fine old houses of the white-pillar'd classick-revival sort; and maintain'd in especially good state by wealthy persons dwelling there in the summer. It was here that Judge Royall Tyler, the celebrated Vermont statesman and man of letters, led the arm'd force which finally putt down "Shays' Rebellion" in 1786, when the debt-harass'd farmers of western Massachusetts rose to the number of two thousand in an effort to abolish all litigations for indebtedness. They had besieg'd the court-houses at Worcester and Springfield, and were not subdu'd without vast effort on the part of the military. A tablet at Petersham marks the scene of their final stand. Judge Tyler vainly pursu'd the instigator, Daniel Shays, into other states; but did not succeed in capturing him. Eventually Shays was not only pardon'd by the government, but even allow'd a pension for his services in the revolution. He dy'd at Sparta, in New-York State, on the 29th of September, 1825.

Barre is a sightly New-England town with a pleasing green, and the country south of it affords some extreamly imposing vistas. We later pass'd thro' Worcester, a very pleasant city of moderate size, whose inhabitants are noted for taste and scholarship. Then came the towns and terrain of the Blackstone Valley, and finally a crossing of the line into His Majesty's Colony of Rhode-Island and Providence-Plantations! A great moment, at which I remov'd my hat as a token of reverence for my native sod. Avoiding the centre of the border city of Woonsocket, an industrial town of French population, we hit upon the broad Louisquisset Turnpike and were soon spinning southward thro' the loveliest region in the colony. Old Rhode-Island! And where, after all, can greater charm be found? At Break-Neck Hill Road we diverg'd to the eastward and travers'd the winding roads thro' the exquisite sylvan stretches of Quinsnicket, or Lincoln-Woods, my favourite haunt on fine summer afternoons. It seem'd appropriate to return to my native scenes thro' this lovely and typical part of them—and this avenue of approach sett off very ably the occasional glimpses of the distant spires and domes of OLD PROVIDENCE which hilltop moments afforded. PROVIDENCE—my native land! No sensation at any stage of my travels equall'd that with which I was animated as we drew near the scene of my birth and lifelong memories. Pawtucket was a dingy interlude. Then the line of East Avenue and Hope Street—and the PROVIDENCE urban boundary at the end of Blackstone Boulevard, known to me for thirty years and more, and the scene of my choicest bicycle rides of boyhood! Again my three-corner'd hat was rais'd from the powder'd locks of my periwig. HOME! After that but a little space to Barnes Street, then a turn under shady trees, a square or two westward to where the road touches the brink of the antient hill and vanishes into the golden sunset sky betwixt old houses—and then Number Ten! My own hearthstone at last—and all the remember'd books and furniture of my youth! It was the eighteenth of May, and I had been abroad since the fourth of April! A marvellous, pleasing, and vary'd trip in all its parts, yet providing no sight more agreeable than Old Providence, or any moment so delightful as that of my return to my cherish'd doorstep.

GOD SAVE THE KING!

AN ACCOUNT OF CHARLESTON,

in His Maj[ty's] Province of *South-Carolina.*

Design'd for the Information of Travellers to that Place,
And for the Generall Instruction of the Curious.
By
H. Lovecraft, Gent.,
Of *Providence,* in *New-England*
MDCCCCXXX

I. The History and Civilisation of Charleston

In considering the town of Charleston, it is proper to take notice of the generall region to which it belongs, and to survey the events of history that extend behind it. The province of Carolina, lying just north of those parts of Florida settled by the earliest Spanish explorers, was first peopled by white men in the year 1562, when the French Huguenot Jean Ribaut establish'd a colony at Port-Royal, on the southerly part of the coast. The settlers number'd but thirty or less, and were confin'd in a miserable log fort; but great hopes were harbour'd for a vast French commonwealth, and the country was named *Carolina* in honour of King Charles the Ninth. Driven by hardship and homesickness, the Huguenots in the following year deserted their colony and sett out for Europe in a rudely built vessel; but in 1564 another colony was brought to America by Laudonnière, and establish'd at the mouth of the St. John's River in Florida. This being within the limits of Spanish settlement, it was mov'd against by Spain in the year 1565; the attack led by Pedro Menendez, who during his campaign built the fort of St. Augustine, destin'd to survive as the oldest continuous white settlement north of Mexico on this continent. Menendez surpris'd the French garrison and slew all the inhabitants of the St. John's colony, disregarding age and sex; later capturing the French arm'd forces under Ribaut and dedicating them to massacre and slavery. This ended the attempts of France to colonise the lower Atlantick seaboard, tho' shortly afterward the French Papist Dominic de Gourgues led an expedition of revenge which wiped out the Spanish garrison on the St. John's. When Menendez murther'd the French settlers, he had left a placard saying that he had slain them "not as Frenchmen, but as hereticks". De Gourgues, having hang'd the Spanish garrison, left a sinister retaliatory note declaring he had punished the men "not as Spaniards, but as assassins".

After this we behold the Spaniards in full possession of Florida, with Carolina largely uncolonis'd to the northward. The true history of the present province begins in the year 1663; when, claiming the region by right of exploration, our English monarch, Charles II, Whom God Save, granted the land betwixt Virginia and Florida to a company of gentlemen-proprietors compos'd of my Ld Clarendon, the High-Chancellor; Genl Monk, Duke of Albemarle; Anthony Ashley Cooper, First Earl of Shaftesbury; my Ld Craven; my Ld Berkeley; Sir J: Colleton; Sir Go Carteret; and Sir W: Berkeley, Governor of Virginia. From two of these gentlemen were nam'd *Albemarle* Sound, and the *Ashley* and *Cooper* Rivers. The name of the country was suffer'd to stand unchang'd, tho' now interpreted to honour the memory of His Martyr'd Britannick Majesty *Charles the First*, rather than the old French King. Vivat *Carolus Secundus*, Rex Britannorum!

At this time there were no white men in Carolina, except the few planters in the northern part who had straggled down from Virginia. These, in 1663, were made provisionally into a colony call'd *Albemarle*. In the year 1664 my Ld Clarendon's name was given to another small colony of gentlemen planters from the West Indies, some twenty-five miles up the Cape Fear River. All these settlements, of course, were within what is now North-Carolina.

The history of the present *South-Carolina* begins with the very settlement we are about to study, when in 1669 the proprietors sent out two shiploads of colonists to form a town on the Ashley River, near where it joins the sea in an excellent natural harbour. This group of 160, which included several women, were under the leadership of Col. William Sayle; and built their "Towne of Trade" on the Ashley's west bank, where two creeks (since call'd Orange Grove and Old Town Creeks) empty into the larger stream. At this time the two great neighbouring rivers were known by their Indian names of *Kiawah* (Ashley) and *Wando.* The new settlement was call'd at first Albemarle Point, and later Charles-Town, in His reigning Maj$^{ty's}$ honour.

The governance of the new colony was of a very philosophick sort, and may be taken to represent an application of theory to politicks such as Plato, or Sir T. More, wou'd have approved of. The plan of organisation and administration, called *The Grand Model,* was drawn up by My Ld Shaftesbury (then Lord Ashley), under the advice of the eminent philosopher Mr. John Locke, then resident with his L^{d}ship at Exeter House as private secretary; and was believed by its authors to be as perfect a scheme of rule as the human mind is capable of conceiving.

This enlighten'd constitution was of a wholesomely aristocraticall sort, and establish'd the Church of England throughout the Colony, whilst permitting other sects full liberty of worship. Carolina was made a *County Palatine,* wherein the Crown may delegate royall powers to one man for defence against enemies. Rank was apportion'd thro' the ownership of land; severall orders of nobility being fixt and endow'd with appropriate powers. A *landgrave* held 48,000 acres; a *cassique* (taken from ye Indian title *cacique*) 24,000; and a *baron* 12,000. These titles were not, however, commonly us'd as modes of address; the social ranks of the parent country being retain'd in ordinary as distinguisht from political usage. The lower orders, comprising those not granted land by the Lords Proprietors, had no political power, but were consider'd as attach'd to the soil. As years pass'd, and the influence of the non-landed classes increas'd, the provisions of the Grand Model were repeatedly attack'd, and finally fell into desuetude. It is probable that it had never been fully liv'd up to, and the government of proprietors was superseded by direct royall authority; the province being divided into North and South Carolina, and governors being appointed by the Crown. Black slaves were first brought in by the Governor Sir John Yeamans, who came from Barbadoes with his own niggers and sett the fashion for their ownership amongst others. Most of the large, negro-owning planters came from the West Indies and settled on plantations along Goose Creek, an affluent of the Cooper River somewhat above Charles-Town. Other immigrants were of humbler classes, largely dissenters, who arriv'd in large numbers from various places and settled in the town or elsewhere.

The Lords Proprietors were from the first sensible of the poor defencibleness of the original Town of Trade, and as early as 1671 took note of the superior strategick value of the neighbouring narrow peninsula betwixt the Ashley and Cooper Rivers. In that year a new town on this peninsula was propos'd, the site being thus describ'd by Mr. Dalton,

Secretary of the Grand Council of Carolina, in a letter to my L[d] Ashley (Shaftesbury):

> "It must of necessity be very healthy, being free from any noxious vapours, and all the summer long being refresh'd with continual cool breathings from the sea, which up in the country men are not soe fully sensible of."

This site, already thinly inhabited since 1672, was then call'd Oyster Point, and in 1679 my L[d] Ashley order'd Governor West to build and settle on it according to a very fixt and ambitious plan; it being clearly his design to make it the chief town of the colony. In the following year the orders were acted on, and after that the old town fell largely into disuse; being formally abandon'd in 1682, and sinking finally to a meer plantation. It is this founding of the *new town* which, in the eyes of recent historians, forms the true birth of *Charleston* (for the name *Charles-Town* became quickly transferr'd to it); and which is now receiving special celebration upon its 250th anniversary.

In order to secure perfect defence against the Spaniards and Indians, the new Charles-Town of 1680 was very strongly fortify'd by means of breastworks, which soon develop'd into a full line of city walls, with bastions, salients, and guard posts at the gates. According to the plan of the Lords Proprietors, put into effect by Surveyors-General Culpepper and Bull to as great an extent as possible (for the original design was too ambitious for use), the town was to have regular streets; a great street 100 to 120 feet wide, lesser streets not under 60 feet wide, and alleys 8 or 10 feet wide—the whole protected by a palisado and ditch against the Indians. Around the town for half a mile outside the walls was to extend a common without any buildings whatsoever. As it turned out, the town became a narrow parallelogram 4 squares long and 3 wide, fronting on the Cooper River and bounded on the south by Vanderhorst's Creek—now fill'd in and forming the line of Water St. The western boundary corresponded to the present Meeting St., having here a wall, gate, and drawbridge. Places were reserv'd for a church, a town hall, and a parade-ground. The north-and-south streets, from the river-front inward, were Bay, Church, and Meeting; whilst the east-and-west ones, from the south boundary upward, were Tradd (nam'd from the first white child born in the town), Elliott, Broad, and Dock (afterward Queen).

The town very soon outgrew its original wall'd space, and by 1700 had spread desultorily westward to the Ashley River. Many liv'd outside the walls on small farms, and the peninsula was order'd cleared of heavy vegetation to destroy Indian ambushes. The decade 1679–1689 brought heavy immigration, especially after the accession of James II promoted the exodus of dissenters from England. One dissenting colony of 500 was brought over in a single month by Morton and Axtell, who were made landgraves for their services. Gentlemen planters also flock'd in from Barbadoes and other West-Indian places, together with large numbers of men of every sort from England. Typical surnames, persisting to this day because of Charleston's happy immunity from value-destroying change, were Blake, Drayton, Middleton, Daniel, Moore, Ladson, Grimball, Carter, Boone, Smith, Schenking, and Izard. Lands granted to these gentlemen are still held by their descendants in the year 1930, when the world outside is sunk in chaos and decay. The first settlers were planters and merchants, trading in many cases full 1000 miles inland with the redskin salvages. In 1693 the culture of *rice* was experimentally introduc'd, and so well succeeded, that rice-planting soon became the chief pursuit of the inhabitants. The later introduction of *indigo* (1741) provided another major industry which remain'd dominant till the nineteenth-century age of cotton.

Churches very early appear'd; the Establish'd Church, the Baptists, and the Presbyterians or Congregationalists soon having houses of worship. Not long after came the French Huguenots and the Quakers, both building suitable edifices. All of these sects save the Quakers (who are extinct in Charleston, but whose adherents elsewhere maintain the antient burying-ground in King St.) still worship on their original sites; the Huguenot church being the last of its kind in America.

The Huguenots, who form'd so important an element in Charles-Town's population despite their gradual assimilation into the dominant British fabrick, came mostly betwixt 1680 and 1688, the greatest influx stimulated by the revocation of the Edict of Nantes. About 450 in all arriv'd, coming to a community of some 2500 souls. Some Dutch from New-Netherland likewise appeared, whilst in 1695 there came a body of Puritan Yankees from Dorchester, in the Province of the Massachusetts-Bay. These latter settled twenty miles from town in a place which they call'd "Dorchester"; building a meeting-house and dwelling there for half a century, but finally moving en masse into Central Georgia, whose climate they preferr'd. A small minority of them remain'd and mixt with the general population of the region. At a later date many Germans and Swiss came to Carolina, probably establishing the wrought-iron industry whose products have so added to Charles-Town's beauty. Most of them, however, did not remain on the seabord. All elements got on rather well, and with a minimum of friction except in the case of some of the Huguenots in Craven County who were slow in becoming naturalised. An homogeneous English culture overshadow'd and absorb'd all other fabricks, and the protestant faith was everywhere paramount. The Church of England, proud, select, and officially establish'd, was not numerically strong; English, Scotch, and Irish dissenters claiming in 1706 to form $\frac{2}{3}$ of the whole population. Buildings of a good type were erected (tho' none survive from the seventeenth century), and the town began early to have the air of a cultivated metropolis; presaging that later day (1773) when Josiah Quincy of Boston was to say of Charles-Town, 'that in almost every thing it far surpass'd all he ever saw, or ever expected to see, in America'.

But the history of the place was not unmark'd by turbulence. In 1682 a colony of Scotch dissenters, whose position in Scotland was becoming increasingly precarious, was establish'd at Port-Royal, semi-independently of the authorities at Charles-Town, by Henry, L[d] Cardross. Disputes concerning power quickly arose with Gov. Joseph Morton of Carolina, and continu'd after Morton had been superseded by Quarry; Cardross finally resigning and returning to Scotland. In 1686 the Florida Spaniards raided the coast and burnt Port-Royal, torturing and killing its twenty-five inhabitants, robbing plantations, and carrying off prisoners to St. Augustine. Only two or three Scotchmen escaped to carry the news to Charles-Town, where it was receiv'd with varying sentiments. Most of the population wish'd to punish the Spaniards at once, but delay was caus'd by the new Governor, Sir Jas: Colleton, who sided with the papist King James II, and did not wish to attack the Spanish Catholicks on behalf of the murther'd dissenters. This difference led to an encreas'd friction betwixt the general inhabitants and the Lords Proprietors, which culminated in 1719 in the abolishment of the proprietors' government and the establishment of Carolina as a direct Royall province. The year 1699 was marked by an epidemick of yellow fever, and by a vast hurricane and flood. Fever, long the chief scourge of Charleston, has now been largely eradicated by medical science; tho' the gales of late August and September are still to be reckon'd with. Even these, however, are made less disastrous by stouter sea-walls and the better building construction of the eighteenth century.

It was in the eighteenth century that there finally flower'd and crystallis'd that perfect visual and social fabrick which is the Charleston of song and story—the ripe, compleat, and self-contain'd civilisation which has through some miracle been prolong'd to our day, and which is at present probably the only genuine civilisation surviving in the mechanised desert of decadence call'd North-America. The devastating effect of the floods of 1699 and 1700 must have been considerable; for we immediately afterward read of a great wave of building, this time of the type which has survived to the present. The oldest remaining edifice in Charleston is a bastion of the reinforced wall, built in 1703 and now known as "The Old Powder Magazine" in Cumberland St.

Of dwelling-houses, the oldest remaining are probably certain specimens in Hasell St. and in an alley off Tradd St., each dating from not much after 1720. Houses as early as the decade of the 1730's are still very numerous; and we still see the town, so far as general impressions go, as it was in the middle and later Georgian period. Block on block of the ancient houses may still be descried in the regions below Broad St.—to an extent not duplicated in any other American city.

In 1702 the Governor of Carolina, an ambitious Irishman nam'd Moore, conceiv'd the notion of developing mines in the western part of the province, and of marching against the Spaniards in Florida. The latter expedition was put into effect, and St. Augustine was for a time taken—though the inhabitants had all retired to the fortress and evaded capture. The expedition was on the whole an indecisive failure, and increas'd the dissatisfaction of the people with the government of the Lords Proprietors. Shortly afterward wars with France and Spain were threatened, and Indian menaces appeared on the horizon. Pirates likewise help'd to make the century's first quarter turbulent. At one time Colonel Rhett hang'd fifty-seven of them at once on a spot near the tip of the peninsula, betwixt the present Church and Meeting Sts., and in 1718 the notorious Capt. Teach, or Blackbeard, caus'd worry along the coast. This year also Colo. Rhett hang'd Capt. Stede Bonnet and forty men on the Battery near the foot of King St. To this day there are pointed out certain houses in Church St., near Queen, said to have been the rendezvous of pirates in the eighteenth century. Pirate lore is inherent in Charleston tradition, and is well reflected by Poe in "The Gold-Bug".

In 1719 the Province was taken from the Lords Proprietors and given directly (tho' unofficially) to the King, and a decade later—the Royal government being made official and definitive—it was divided into the present provinces of North and South Carolina. By 1720 Charles-Town had largely overflowed its walls, and these barriers now began to be demolish'd bit by bit. 1740 brought evangelical troubles due to the fanatical exhorting of the dissenter George Whitefield, but these were powerless to stay the tide of growing prosperity and culture.

We now see the city assuming very much of its present aspect. Roof-tiling—a rare thing in early American towns—was introduced about 1735, and gave to the steep gables of the houses their characteristick aspect. Early experiments with porches, occasion'd by the warm climate, must likewise have occurred about this time; for before the close of the century we behold Charleston as a town of outdoor living, with great verandahs on all three storeys of the south or west sides of the houses, opening on exquisite walled gardens which passers-by might glimpse through gates of magnificent wrought-iron grille-work. Little by little the inhabitants were achieving that settled and perfect adjustment to the climate and landskip which means a definite civilisation in its mellowest and most genuine sense. The brick and stucco houses generally follow'd the best Georgian models, but in an individual and localised way; so that no other colonial city looks just like Charleston. The climate, vegetation, and general natural conditions encouraged beauty and contentment to a singular degree. Palmettos, live-oaks with writhing branches, festoons of Spanish moss, fragrant magnolias, gorgeous azaleas, and an almost continental clearness of sky, brought out life at its best. At twilight—a very brief subtropical twilight—the birds sang in the gardens, and an insidious perfume of many blossoms floated cryptically over the whole city. Cool breezes sprang up, and those who disliked warmth would walk along the Battery, or White Point Gardens, at the very tip of the peninsula, which fronts the spacious harbour and receives a sweep of air from across the low islands dividing the harbour from the open Atlantick. It is no wonder that a great and gracious civilisation here flower'd, and it is pleasing to reflect that both the natural boons and the civilisation still remain as an oasis in this aera of social and physical ugliness.

We find the *gardens* of Charleston first mention'd about 1740. In 1748 the present proprietary library was founded, attesting to the good scholarship of a people more urban than the Virginians because of the heat and fever which drove them from their island plantations to their town houses during a great part of the summer. Theatres (the first in 1736) appear about the middle of the eighteenth century, the principal one being at the corner of Dock (Queen) and Church Sts. To these came the best companies of players, both British and provincial, presenting all the standard favourites of publick taste. In 1752 much damage was caus'd by a great hurricane, after which came the wave of rebuilding which gave the town—including the Battery—its exact present form. The present St. Michael's Church, whose lovely spire is the choicest object on the local skyline, was finish'd in 1761; and in 1774 receiv'd the famous set of chimes whose sweet musick has regaled the town ever since, save for intervals when the vicissitudes of war and accident made necessary their removal and re-casting.

Charles-Town encounter'd the unfortunate political difficulties of the 1770's with a remarkable amount of poise; tending to sympathise with the rebel cause more than did most towns of equal cultivation, such as Newport, New-York, and Philadelphia; yet preserving so rigidly aristocratick a personal tradition that this seditious radicalism occasion'd no loss of cultural tone. Boston and Newport were socially ruin'd by the disaster, but Charleston pass'd through it almost unscathed. Before the outbreak of overt treason, political debate was conducted in a more than commonly civil fashion; notwithstanding riots over the Stamp Act, and a very savage duel betwixt a loyalist visitor from New York—a Mr. Delancey, brother-in-law to a Charleston Izard—and the local rebel Dr. Haley, which took place at the South-Carolina Coffee-House, a highly genteel place of entertainment in St. Michael's Alley. Dr. Haley was arrested for Mr. Delancey's murther, but was acquitted at the next assizes. At this period many tea vessels enter'd Charleston Harbour, but for the most part the cargo was quietly stored in the vaults under the Exchange Building (built 1767—still standing in prime condition), awaiting some later adjustment of the question of duty. In a few later instances, however, seditious mobs dumped bales of tea into the harbour, much like the kindred rabbles of the North. By 1775 the disputes had grown to such an extent that cases of tarring and feathering became common; these indignities being always perpetrated by rebel bands. During the actual hostilities, Charleston was at first neither very strongly attack'd nor very strongly defended. The islands enclosing the harbour were fortify'd with breastworks of earth and palmetto logs, the main defence being old Fort Sullivan on Sullivan's Island, the logical key to the harbour and the city. His Majesty's vessels occasionally made casual attempts to take these fortresses, and on June 28, 1776, began that celebrated engagement with Fort Sullivan (then commanded by Col. William Moultrie and afterward call'd from him "Fort Moultrie") in which the rebel Sergeant Jasper leapt outside the breastworks and saved his colours under fire.

Charles-Town held out under the rebels until 1780, when the forces of Sir Henry Clinton and my Ld Rawdon mov'd in and took up headquarters at the splendid Brewton-Pringle mansion in lower King St.—a place still standing and open to the publick for a dollar admission fee. Some unpleasantness developed betwixt the troops and the populace, in which the blame seems pretty evenly divided. Charleston was us'd as a base of supplies by His Majesty's troops during most of the southern campaign; a campaign in which the chief obstacles were the Rhode-Island general Nathanael Greene, and the local South-Carolina guerrillas Francis Marion ("The Swamp Fox", at first scorn'd by his fellow-rebels for the rustick uncouthness of his band, but afterward the particular hero of Charleston), Sumter (after whom the celebrated fort in Charleston Harbour was named), and Pickens. After the disaster to Ld Cornwallis's army, the town was evacuated, the troops bearing away the chimes of St. Michael's to London, whence they were afterward regain'd by purchase. When the rebel army enter'd the town late in 1781, some unfortunate atrocities were committed against citizens who had been loyal to his Majesty's rightful cause.

In 1783 the name of the city was officially chang'd from *Charles-*

Town to its exact present form of *Charleston.* Its general culture had been very little impair'd by the upheavals of war; and despite the meaningless catchwords of impossible democracy mouthed by the vulgar orators of the day, the same old families continued to flourish and rule amidst an unbrokenly aristocratick social order. In 1792 the negro uprisings in St. Domingo sent to Charleston a great number of French gentlefolk; who were instantly made welcome, and who form'd a highly civilising influence at this stage of the city's growth. About this time Charleston was superseded by the inland town of Columbia as capital of South-Carolina—the new place being lay'd out for that purpose.

This age—the late eighteenth and early nineteenth century—marks the summit and heyday of Charleston's social glory and material prosperity. The local culture which had been crystallising for an hundred years had been singularly undisturbed by the war, and it was now to enjoy a similarly happy immunity from disturbance through mercantile, mechanical, and democratick contamination. For this immunity the depth and tenacity of the existing fabrick was in some degree responsible; but another contributing cause was the extream isolation of the city from the crude life of the commerce-minded colonies, coupled with its frequent marine intercourse with the most cultivated centres of the Old World. Charleston, situate at the coastal edge of a vast lowland plain of rural plantations, was (and still is) near no other town of any size, and did not lie along any trunk line of travel. It was a choice world in itself, and the logical focus of a stable social and intellectual life shared by planter families dwelling on hereditary estates under traditional conditions. The eldest sons of gentlemen went to Oxford and Cambridge for their education, and there was no such lapse of refinement as we find even in Virginia, where a negroid accent invaded common speech and became the typical dialect of the South. In Charleston the perverted accent never became deep or general; the standard of good English speech remaining permanent at all times.

When other regions, deprived of their wholesome linkage with the transatlantick source of culture, began to decline in civilisation and slip into the barbarities and extravagances of the 1830's and 1840's, Charleston remained as a solitary island of sound eighteenth-century taste. This is attested by all open-eyed analysts, and is mention'd with especial force by Samuel Gaillard Stoney, Esq., in his preface to the book on Charleston houses in the Octagon Series. He says:

> "A clue to the character of Charleston and her people is to remember that during this period of growth and greatest importance they were essentially of the eighteenth century. It was then that their culture crystallised; and their mode of thought, their

institutions, and their very pronunciation keep the flavour of the age. From that time they preserved the tradition of the classic; with its intellectual freedom, its moral tolerance, its discipline in matters of etiquette, its individualism, and the spirit of logic which elsewhere largely perished in the romantic movement."

One visible instance of this is shewn in the fine series of buildings erected from the decade of 1780 onward; buildings in which the Graeco-Roman tradition is employ'd in its happiest form, and in which an innate native taste crops out in all such adaptive details as wrought-iron work, curved flights of steps, railings, windows, and the like. Among these buildings—worthy successors to old St. Michael's of 1761 and the Exchange of 1767—are the Court-House (Broad and Meeting) (1788), the Orphan House (Calhoun St.—1792), the brick Vanderhorst Row (East Bay St.—1800), the City Hall (Broad and Meeting, 1801), the South Carolina Society's Hall (Broad below Meeting—1804), the Second Presbyterian Church (upper Meeting St. 1811), St. Paul's Church (Coming St.—1810–12), the First Presbyterian Church (Meeting St.—1814), St. John's Lutheran Church (Archdale St. 1817), the old Baptist Church (lower Church St. 1822), the Fireproof Record Building (Meeting and Chalmers 1826), the College of Charleston (George St. 1828), St. Philip's magnificent church and steeple (Church St. 1835), St. Mary's Catholick Church (Hasell St. 1838), Hibernian Hall (Meeting—1841), Charleston Market (Meeting and Market 1841), the Jews' Synagogue (Hasell St. 1841), Bethel M. E. Church (Pitt and Calhoun—1850–3), the splendid Custom House (E. Bay St.—1850 et seq.), the chapel of the Circular Congregational Church (Meeting St. 1867), and Trinity M. E. Church (upper Meeting 1875). This late persistence of good architecture is unique in the United States. Other fine buildings, of other schools, are the Gothick Unitarian Church in Archdale St., built in 1772 at a time when Gothick was almost unknown as a creative medium outside the realm of Strawberry-Hill, and the Gothick Huguenot Church at Church and Queen Sts., built in 1845 on the site of earlier fanes. Private houses, it may be added, bear out the picture suggested by the publick buildings. There was no such general lapse of taste in the Victorian age as we find elsewhere; tho' a few bad specimens were put up after the War between the States, on the northerly fringe of the town, and on the site of the burned district of 1861. Broadly speaking, the sound taste of the eighteenth century in architecture and other things has come down unbroken to this day; the Victorian years shewing merely a lessen'd deftness and coarsening of detail (due in part to the substitution of negro for white craftsmanship) instead of the total collapse elsewhere observable. The newest twentieth-century publick buildings are all in the old tradition—the Charleston Museum, Gibbes Art Gallery, and Publick Library being notable among them.

Light on Charleston's great days may be had by reading a few of the many works devoted to the subject, such as the volume by Mrs. St. Julien Ravenel (wife of the noted physician who eradicated yellow fever from the city), and the comprehensive guide-book by Mazÿck—a descendant of one of the old Huguenot families. In 1800 Charleston was the leading centre of culture on this continent, with graceful institutions and a high level of taste such as no other American region can ever parallel. The social season extended from May to November, when malaria drove the planters to town from their inland estates; and was supplemented by a shorter period around the end of January call'd the "Gay Season". The great social institution of the town, whose meetings and functions determined the recreative life of the greatest families, and whose judgments determin'd the status of every person of consequence, was (and *still is*) an organisation originally of musical purpose, call'd the St. Cecilia Society. The St. Cecilia's Day concerts and balls of this society, and its Thursday functions that began at 9 p.m., soon became bywords of exclusiveness; till at length its musical character was merged in its social dictatorship. Various other dancing assemblies were frequented by the gay, and the Philharmonick Concerts were also well thought of. Jockey balls attested the importance of the Sport of Kings, as did the Carnival Race Week, which form'd a sort of Charleston carnival. Business was likewise transacted during the "Gay Season", advantage being taken of the presence of many planters in town. Everyone was generally back in the country by the end of March, not to see Charleston again till May. Jedidiah Morse, in his *Geography* (1802), says: "In no part of America are the social blessings enjoy'd more rationally and liberally than in Charleston. Unaffected hospitality, affability, ease in manners and address, and a disposition to make their guests welcome, easy, and pleas'd with themselves, are characteristick of the respectable people of Charleston."

The gentlemen constituting this profound and permanent civilisation were almost without exception planters of rice and cotton—the latter having begun to replace indigo as a major staple. They were probably more maturely and mellowly cultivated than the corresponding class of fox-hunting squires in Virginia—the latter generally taking to civick and political pursuits rather than to the nicer elegancies of learning. This difference was doubtless largely due, as previously hinted, to the long urban season made necessary by the inland fever and malaria. Mercantile pursuits were abandon'd by good families after the Revolution, and left to new men from England and Scotland—a bourgeois class corresponding to that in Richmond which produced the Galts and Allans, amongst whom Poe's childhood was spent. These persons had a separate club and social life of their own, and have not much mixt with the planter class even to this day. Publick education was promoted about this time, tho' scholarship continu'd to have far more of aristocratick individuality than in Boston, New-York, Philadelphia, and other centres where insincere and conventionalised standards had begun to spring up. Favourite authors, besides the dominant Graeco-Roman classicks, were Shakespeare and Montaigne—an happy contrast to the sour-mouth'd and meaningless divines and quibblers pored over by the cramp'd neo-Puritans of the Massachusetts-Bay. Coaches now appear in frequent use, and on every hand we behold the ideal of gentlemanly carelessness (as oppos'd to peasant calculativeness, greed, shrewdness, and practicality) uppermost. No man of culture knew how much he was worth in cash, or indeed saw much actual currency. Trade and calculation were largely left to hirelings from the North, call'd "factors". It was a common jest, that a gentleman cou'd read Homer and explain the constitution, but cou'd not do a sum in vulgar fractions. Personal honour was very carefully guarded, and duelling was frequent despite much sentimental opposition.

In those days the factors' offices and merchants' warehouses form'd a distinct district along Bay St., which faces the Cooper River or principal waterfront. Popular shopping streets were the east ends of Broad, Tradd, and Elliott. General stores carrying all manner of goods were the rule, the jewellery shops forming the main exception. Country trade was conducted by long, white-topt waggons with 4 or 6 horses or mules, pil'd high with cotton-bales, high up in King St. near the present railway station. Most of the town was below, or only slightly above, Calhoun St. (then called Boundary St.); just as before the Revolution it had been mostly below Broad—or at most Queen or Cumberland—St. It shou'd be noted that Charleston is a narrow peninsula like the island of Manhattan, so that urban expansion is invariably northward. There was no one residence section, homes being scatter'd and surrounded by large gardens or tracts of land. The Battery, lower Meeting St., Legare St., and so on, were then as now favour'd for fine dwellings. Indeed, we may say that the social complexion of the town has chang'd but little since those gorgeous days of 1800. The Battery was, as it still is, a favourite place of resort and promenade, tho' the East Battery was not graded and built up till the 1830–1860 period. This sea-wall'd region at the tip of the peninsula was slow to develop because of the autumnal hurricanes. On a wharf from the South Battery was a popular tea-house, and near by was Watson's Botanick Garden.

About "Boundary St." (Calhoun) was the semi-rural region known as "The Neck", abounding in creeks and marshes. St. Paul's and the

Second Presbyterian were pioneer churches in this region. The neighbourhood of St. Paul's was known as Radcliffeborough; that below Calhoun, east of Meeting, as Ansonborough; and that around the corner of Meeting and Calhoun as Louisburgh. The western section of this district, along Calhoun and Bull Sts. to Rutledge Ave., was call'd Cannonsborough, and was partly given over to large rice and lumber mills on dammed-up creeks. Below it, along the line of the present Montague St., was the section called Harlestonborough. In this northerly region may be seen still some fine houses of the late eighteenth and early nineteenth century, spar'd by war and disaster; among them the splendid Manigault house (1790), whose unique circular gate lodge is now the ignominious adjunct of a gasoline filling station.

In 1822 the town was alarm'd by reports of a threaten'd insurrection of the numerous blacks, under the incitement of Boston abolitionists. The class affected were not the servants or rural workers, but that stratum of black artisans and mechanicks whose advent is to be traced in the declining level of craftsmanship. Their visible leaders were a free mulatto call'd Denmark Vesey, and an African-born conjurer or witch-doctor call'd Gullah Jack. Fortunately the plot came to nothing, but it put the people on their guard against the empty rantings of Northern abolitionists whose chief inspiration was a complete lack of first-hand knowledge of the negro. Shortly afterward tensity toward the North was increas'd by the tariff troubles culminating in the nullification agitation of 1832–3 et seq. South-Carolina, taking its cue from the rebellion of 1775–83, was ever a stronghold of local independence and separatist sentiment, and was not dispos'd to be trodden upon by Yankees who had set the example for secession in 1775 and had threaten'd to repeat it in 1809.

The more ordinary people of Charleston (and even many of the better class), no doubt influenced by the whispers of their black nurses and servants, were richly and picturesquely superstitious; and sponsor'd weird tales and beliefs which deserve the attention and literary treatment of the modern fantaisiste. Ghost legends multiply'd beyond all count, and anecdotes of second-sight and verify'd dreams grew common. Queer signs and omens were universally regarded with seriousness, and odd happenings always receiv'd the most mystical possible interpretation. Many of the popular tastes resemble the folklore of the picturesque Narragansett country, in southern Rhode-Island, whose close social resemblance to the South has often been pointed out. There was a belief in a great black dog which loped along a certain highway near the town in the morning and evening twilight; never harming anyone, and absolutely impervious to gunshot. Other suggestive narratives (to cite a late case) were developed from the case of an ancient house at Goose Creek, which upon being demolisht by the earthquake of 1886, was found to have a secret tunnel leading from the cellar to the interior of a tomb in a venerable neighbouring graveyard. Taste and literary life continued to flourish; producing such figures as the graceful poet Henry Timrod.

The Civil War naturally produc'd a great impression upon Charleston, tho' it was not the scene of any active land fighting, and was not laid waste by the Federal troops which finally pass'd through it. Secession began in South-Carolina, and the first shots of the war were fired at Fort Sumter in Charleston Harbour. Almost coincident with these events was the Great Fire of 1861, which created a vast burn'd district west of Meeting St. and along and below Broad, although it was of accidental origin and totally unconnected with the hostilities. This fire destroyed St. Andrew's Hall in Broad St., formerly the leading place of publick assemblage; and the site has never again been built upon. The whole burn'd district remain'd a desert throughout the war, and even afterward was a long time in getting built up once more. At the period of its greatest extent it virtually divided the city into two parts. Wartime hardships–blockade and siege and all their consequences–pressed heavily upon Charleston, but the population bore these afflictions with Spartan fortitude. St. Michael's chimes, sent inland to Columbia for safe-keeping, were destroy'd by the torch of Sherman's vandals; but were later recast in London to their pristine sweetness and purity of tone, the original moulds being still in existence. On account of the Federal gunfire in the harbour, the antient lower end of Charleston was left almost deserted during the war; the inhabitants congregating in those regions north of the burn'd district. Vegetation and solitude claim'd the most historick sections, tho' fortunately they came to no harm. At length the conflict ceas'd, Sherman came and went with less than his usual barbarousness, and the people normally redistributed themselves thro' Charleston's antient lanes. The material prosperity of the town had been destroy'd for ever; but despite external change, the basick civilisation proved too deep to eradicate. The old families still liv'd; and tho' without money, they still had their blood and standards. Good birth and taste depend not on riches; so that for all the visible decay, the ideals of beauty, discrimination, balance, and proud reticence did not depart from the gentlefolk of Charleston. Perspectives and institutions persisted, and the continuity which had withstood the successful rebellion of 1775 again withstood the unsuccessful one of 1861. Charleston endured the nightmare of carpet-baggery without flinching, and emerged with standards unimpaired. At length a limited prosperity began to dawn, and commerce surged back along the ancient ways. Broad St. again bristled with banks, brokers, and barristers, and King

St. became a fashionable shopping promenade of the elegant eighties. Meeting St. drove a thriving jobbing trade in dry-goods, clothing, shoes, and crockery, whilst the East Bay St. waterfront buzzed anew with the talk of grocers and ship-chandlers. The rice and cotton industries, however, never reached their former state of opulence.

In 1886 Charleston sustain'd the severest earthquake ever experienc'd on the Atlantick coast; a thing which demolisht many buildings and publick works, and severely injur'd many more—including the splendid old edifice of St. Michael's. Recuperation, however, was very swift; a circumstance testifying to the essential vitality of the antient town.

And so Charleston has come down to our own melancholy age of decay, to meet the greatest test of all as the engulphing barbarism of mechanised life, democratick madness, quantitative standards, and schedule-enslaved uniformity presses in upon it from every side and seeks to stifle whatever of self-respecting humanity and aristocratick individualism remains in the world. Against all the inherited folkways which alone give us enough of the illusion of interest and purpose to make life worth living for men of our civilisation, there now advances a juggernaut of alien and meaningless forms and feelings which cheapens and crushes everything fine and delicate and individual which may lie in its path. Noise—profit—publicity—speed—time-tabled convict regularity—equality—ostentation—size—standardisation—herding . . . The plague has swept all before it, saddling old New England with unassimilable and corrosive barnacles, extinguishing once-proud New York with a foetid flood of swart, cringing Semitism, and sapping even at Old Virginia and the Piedmont Carolinas with a tawdry industrial Babbittry all the more blasphemous because working through normal Anglo-Saxons. Values evaporate, perspectives flatten, and interests grow pale beneath the bleaching acid of ennui and meaninglessness. Emotions grow irrelevant, and art ceases to be vital except when functioning through strange forms which may be normal to the alien and recrystallised future, but are blank and void to us of the dying Western civilisation. James Joyce . . . *Erik Dorn* . . . Marcel Proust . . . Brancusi . . . Picasso . . . "The Waste Land" . . . Lenin . . . Frank Lloyd Wright . . . cubes and cogs and circles . . . segments and squares and shadows . . . wheels and whirring, whirring and wheels . . . purring of planes and click of chronographs . . . milling of the rabble of raucous yells of the exhibitionist . . . "comic" strips . . . Sunday feature headings . . . advertisements . . . sports . . . tabloids . . . luxury . . . Palm Beach . . . "sales talk" . . . rotogravures . . . radio . . . Babel . . . Bedlam. . . .

But Charleston is still Charleston, and the culture we know and respect is not dead there. Dilution there may be, but in the main there is more alive than in any other place in America. The original families still hold sway—Rhetts, Izards, Pringles, Bulls, Hugers, Ravenels, Manigaults, Draytons, Stoneys, Rutledges, and so on—and still uphold the basic truths and values of a civilisation which is genuine because it represents a settled adjustment betwixt people and landscape, old enough to have created the overtones needful to a sense of interest and significance. Here still dwell men who realise that quality is a matter of emotional adjustment to the external world; and that luxury, ostentation, visibility, and publicity are cheap tricks which a gentleman shuns as he would shun gaudy jewellery or pungent perfumes. Gentlefolk in Charleston still pursue their ways for pleasure and not for show or profit, and are still decently anxious to keep their names and personal affairs *out* of the papers, instead of vulgarly handing them over to low-bred "society editors" to be printed and mouthed over by the swinish herds of tradesfolk, Ford-owners, and bungalow-dwellers. The Charleston dailies are the only ones without a "society column" to spy upon the comings and goings of important people. Here, thank God, gentlemen still maintain a sense of proportion and individuality; and decline to let upstart curs snapshot them and their families for the greedy eyes of impertinent strangers! Testimony is united that Charlestonians are not yet ruin'd by the tendencies of the times. Business is not dehumanised by speed and time-tabling, or denuded of courtesy and leisureliness. Quality, not quantity, is the standard, and there is as yet scant use for the modern fetish of "maximum returns" to be obtain'd even at the sacrifice of everything which makes those returns worth having, or life itself worth preserving. Even the middle classes are not apt to make fools of themselves, for the whole community has a very deeply ingrained sense of real values—appreciating the fact that quiet and modesty and moderation and freedom and leisure and courage are excellent things, and that publicity and show and extravagance and megalomania and noisiness and pointless haste are cheap and inferior and irrelevant and contemptible things. The more one observes of Charleston, the more impress'd is he that he is looking upon the only thoroughly civilised city now remaining in the United States. The streets, of course, teem with blacks; but of the regular population all are hereditary Nordick-Americans of the English tradition. The foreigner, with his disruptive and disintegrative influence, has no place in the life of this genuine civick unit. In the magazine of the *New-York Times* for June 22, 1930, a correspondent writes:

> "Other towns have to make stoves or sell goods for a living; it is enough for Charleston only to be. The tourists who stop there sense at once, as one expressed it, that they are 'back in America'. They stop in increasing numbers and for longer intervals. Some of them stay. Have you noticed that when Americans

> are able to choose where they shall live they invariably select old places, calm and slow-paced, and when they settle there, as in Charleston, set themselves against change more implacably than the natives? Can it be that all of us in our hearts do not choose to run?"

Literary and artistic life remain in a healthy state, embracing both native aesthetes, and others who have come to enjoy the harmonious milieu. The local poetry society is one of the most important in the country, and has entertain'd the leading figures in contemporary letters. What the future holds, none may say; but one may feel confident that Charleston will stay longest above the flood of neo-American chaos and barbarism, just as Mt. Everest wou'd stay longest above a flood of water ingulphing the whole planet. Just now its prime menace is not so much the lowly immigrant as the wealthy settler from the North—whose coming in large numbers would introduce a jarring note and set up an alien atmosphere.

It remains to speak of the famous *street-cries* of Charleston; rare bits of folklore whose decline in the last twenty years is so great that old residents almost refuse to class the present remnants with the lusty rituals of the great old days. These cries were—and are—confin'd wholly to itinerant negro hucksters, and are most amply heard in the early morning. At their best they had a quality of joyousness and spontaneous balladry about them which prov'd that even the black of Charleston retains a large element of the personal and the decorative in his commercial transactions. Black or white, no human being is so barbarous as to harbour the ideal of "strictly business" in this antient and civilised town.

Typical cries are those of the dawnlight shrimp and crab sellers, who march through the cobbled streets and past the fanlighted doorways singing melodiously: "Swimy raw, raw!", and "She craib! She craib! She craib!"—the latter formula, however, being given something of a yelling, nasal intonation. In 1910 a negro did business in lower King St. under the sign of "Joe Cole and Wife". He look'd like an Indian, limp'd, and us'd his cane as a baton. Whilst selling porgy—a fish ally'd to the chub—he wou'd bellow the following elaborate refrain:

"Old Joe Cole—good ol' soul—
Porgy in the summer-time,
An e whiting in the spring,
Eight upon a string.
Don't be late, I'm waitin' at de gate,
Don't be mad,—here's your shad,
Old Joe Cole—good ol' soul!"

Another pedestrian merchant used to recite the following:

> "Here's your Little John, Ma'm. I got Hoppen John Peas, Ma'm! I got cabbage—I got yaller turnips, Ma'm, oh, yes, Ma'm!" [Variant: "I got sweet pertater—I got beets—I got spinach!"]

An older vendor used to cry:

> "Load my gun
> Wid Sweet Sugar Plum
> An' shoot dem nung gal
> One by one.
> Border lingo
> Water-million."

The ensuing cry of an aged negress becomes more explicable when we learn that the commodity named is really a very toothsome form of cocoanut and molasses candy:

> "Come on, chilluns, and get yer monkey meat!"

The ebon hind responsible for the following formula wished to call attention to his fresh "yard eggs"—i.e., eggs laid in his own farmyard: "Enny yad aigs terday, my Miss?"

Charleston chimney-sweeps all cultivated the refrain "Roo-roo", and were in consequence sometimes known as "Roo-roo[1] boys". The charcoal boy with his two-wheeled donkey-cart had a weird, melancholy way of chanting the unadorn'd word "char—coal". There was likewise a whole class of burly negresses known as "Vegetubble Mammas", who had cries such as "Red rose tomaytoes!", "Green Pease! Sugar Pease!", "Straw-*ber*-ry, an e fresh an e fine, an e just off the vine! Straw-*ber*ry!", and "Sweet Pete ate her!"

These street cries have received much serious study, and an excellent summary of them (with intonations reproduced as written musick) has been made in a small brochure available at the Charleston Publick Library.

II. The Architecture of Charleston

Architecturally Charleston is the most remarkable town in the United States; being built up differently from any other in colonial times, and having preserv'd a phenomenal proportion of its early construction. For this preservation three reasons may be assign'd: first, the decline in trade which discourag'd ambitious building projects after the War between the States; second, the native taste and conservatism of a civilised community, which appreciates existing beauty and avoids meaningless change; and third, the unusual excellence, spaciousness, and solidity of the colonial construction itself; this being far beyond the average level for American towns of the eighteenth century. Charleston, as the cultural centre of one of the richest planting districts in the world, was perhaps the foremost of all American cities in taste and civilisation before and just after the Revolution; and its architecture reflected the refinement and competence of its inhabitants.

Of the earliest wave of buildings in Charleston nothing at all survives; but we may conjecture that they were small, plain houses of brick design'd in an European manner (with perhaps more of the continental influence than the houses farther north) and without that system of piazzas typical of later Charleston dwellings. It was not to be expected that a northern European people, settling in this region, wou'd at once work out that rapprochement with their new southerly climate which ultimately gave rise to perfected Charleston architecture. The Charleston of the early eighteenth century, then, may be pictur'd as a compact town of European-like houses, built of brick and stucco in solid blocks, without porches or balconies, and with only the usual northern arrangement of doors and windows. This is borne out by a study of the oldest remaining houses, which date from about 1720, and whose original parts can be readily pick'd out by experts from amidst any such additions as may have cluster'd round them.

From the first, however, Charleston architecture seems to have been very distinctive. Styles were eclectick and vary'd, many experiments seeming to have been try'd and abandon'd before a widespread local type was finally hit upon. There is, for example, one surviving instance of the *gambrel roof* (the pink house in Chalmers St.) which became so universal in New-England, and which generally straggled down the coast as far as Virginia. Evidently the style was try'd, but found impracticable in the warm climate of Charleston and given early abandonment. If any kind of house seems typical of Charleston, it is a plain brick edifice cover'd with stucco, some three storeys tall, and with a fairly steep roof (with or without dormers) slanting up equally on all four sides and culminating in a single central peak. These houses were built both in blocks, directly on the street, and separately, with walled gardens around them—the latter fashion seeming to gain ground after 1740. Tiled roofs were introduced about 1735, and soon became very common and characteristick; the tiles often being given pronounc'd colours such as salmon pink or purple black. Concave curved tiles of local manufacture were most used. In early times shingle and slats were the rule. The stucco covering the brick walls was generally made of burnt oyster-shell lime, and was sometimes given a vivid and unusual colouring such as pink. Occasionally houses would be built of a brick-like composition call'd "Bermuda Stone", "horn-work", "coral-stone", or "tabby" [corrup. *tapia*], and made of lime, coral, and sea or oyster shells. Much of this material is found in old mills, and two finely preserv'd houses near St. Philip's Church are partly built of it. That Charleston has a more *continental* aspect than other colonial towns is universally conceded, and generally laid to the large Huguenot population. This continentalism, however, is distinctly more *Dutch* than *French;* perhaps owing to the long stay of many of the Huguenots in Holland before coming to Carolina. In France, *stone* is the great building medium; but here the Dutch custom of *brick* work holds universal sway. West-Indian influence was also very considerable. Expert architects point out many idiosyncratick features of Charleston building design, notably the tendency of the steep roof lines to flare up a trifle at the eaves. Many reasons have been assign'd for this; some postulating Dutch influence[2] and others adducing practical constructional considerations; but it must be admitted that the question is still unsettled. Walls were very thick, and windows often deeply recessed. Mediaeval features in gable and roof line are quite frequent, and include the so-call'd "jerkin head roof" found in seventeenth-century buildings elsewhere in the colonies. This quaint early diversity gives rise to some highly picturesque urban skyline effects; many artists delighting to study and record various groups of huddled roof lines as seen in perspective from sundry choice points of vantage. Chimneys were made very large to allow of frequent and easy sweeping by the "Ro-ro Boys", according to city ordinance. Many of the early houses bore the metal plaques of various insurance companies, as was the custom in Philadelphia. At some unplaced date, about midway in the eighteenth century, the famous and typical Charleston porches and balconies began to appear; marking the gradually perfected adaptation of a northern race to its present subtropical surroundings. Porches ran all the way up the houses, with levels for each storey, on the south or west sides to catch the prevailing winds. They faced at right angles to the street, and generally overlook'd a high-wall'd garden. On the end toward the street they generally had a wall, forming an extension of the wall of the house's lower storey, through which was cut a door giving directly on the street. This door, usually with all the typical adornments and accessories of a Georgian doorway, form'd the principal pedestrian entrance to the house and its premises; though the garden wall wou'd generally have a large gate at some other point (sometimes serving as a carriage entrance, as such gates did for large mansions set back from the street), closed by wrought-iron grille-work of the finest craftsmanship. Houses of this piazza'd type may be taken as the most typical form of Charleston domestick architecture; tho' it must be pointed out that all sorts of other designs were occasionally follow'd. After 1760 houses were commonly built higher than before—three storeys and attick at least, and with taller basements—in order to catch as much of the sea breeze as possible. French windows—especially where piazzas or balconies were involv'd—appeared at a date much earlier than in any other towns of America; and became highly characteristick of Charleston houses. All rooms were fully panell'd, and drawing-rooms were on the second storey overlooking the street.

One peculiarity of Charleston architecture in the eighteenth century was the whimsical use of *Gothick* design for casual, homely, or ignominious purposes—coach-houses, slave-quarters, gates, garden-walls, and the like. Such things frequently possess pointed windows or embrasures, and other elements of Gothic ornament, of a highly pleasing pattern; tho' the style was not seriously regarded, and was in no sense a precursor of the widespread revival of Gothick after 1830. Nor is it to be confus'd with the Strawberry-Hill spirit which prompted the construction of a large, fine, and compleatly Gothick church in Archdale St. in 1772. One favourite feature of Charleston architecture, launch'd before the Revolution but gaining greatest ascendancy afterward—and being a cardinal feature of many of Charleston's publick buildings of the 1800 period—was the double entrance flight of steps; railed, often gracefully curving, and having a long top platform under which in the centre an arched tunnel ran beneath the building and contain'd the doorways of the basement apartments. This arrangement has counterparts in the North, and is even remotely akin to the typical double flights of steps of colonial Providence; but nowhere save in Charleston did it receive its fullest development and most widespread use. Another typical Charleston feature is the parapet, or false attick front, extending a few feet above the roof line of many houses of a square, flat-roof'd type. In this are usually set two flattish rectangular horizontal embrasures, or false windows, symmetrical with the real windows below, and faced with iron grille-work.

Many of the architects of old Charleston are known by name, and venerated by the discriminating. The magnificent Brewton-Pringle mansion (1765) is the work of one Ezra Waite, "Civil Architect, House-Builder in General, and Carver, from London". Other local architects were the Horlbeck brothers, John, Adam, and Peter; masons from Plauen in Saxony, with much European experience, and especially skill'd in the execution of massive or monumental designs. In the late colonial period many British architects came to Charleston, and are responsible for an abundance of fine middle-Georgian and early-Adam-period architecture and decoration. A certain proportion of mansions in brick and wood, without stucco, and wholly transcending the local

Charleston type, may be traced with some certainty to them. After the Revolution a leading local architect was the gentleman-planter Gabriel Manigault (pronounc'd *Man-ĭ-go*), an Huguenot of independent means who had study'd in Europe and employ'd Adam designs with the utmost taste and skill. He is responsible for the splendid mansion of his brother Peter, built in 1790 and still to be seen, together with its unique circular gate lodge, at the corner of Ashmead and Meeting Sts. At this period we see panelling disappearing except as wainscots. Piazzas and open galleries multiply, and fix the permanent type of Charleston house which remains dominant till the Civil War. Architects working in Charleston from this period onward are the famous James Holme, and the local men Robert Mills, Col. E. Blake White, Jones and Lee, etc. To these are due that opulent wave of building-up which followed the first cotton prosperity after the invention of the cotton gin in 1793—the wave which produc'd such a wealth of classick publick buildings. Sheer hand *craftsmanship* had begun to decline, but these architects more than atoned for the slight falling-off by the artistick brilliancy of their *general designs.* These men likewise helped to conceal the menace of the nascent machine age by designing the steam rice mills which began to appear after 1817. Most if not all of such mill structures are really beautiful specimens of late Georgian architecture; their parts being functionally justify'd and admirably balanc'd.

It is also in this age that Charleston *wrought-iron work* becomes such an opulent and exquisite thing. Iron-working began before the Revolution with Tunis Tabaut and William Johnson, but it was later that its use became so universal. In 1820 the master craftsman Iusti came from Germany and fashion'd the magnificent gates of St. Michael's churchyard. Werner came, also from Germany, in 1828, and was still working in 1870. Ortmann, from Baden, came in 1847; and his descendants still conduct the exquisite and traditional industry.

We now face the advance of the nineteenth century, which brought so tragic a collapse to architecture throughout the United States. The general order of departure from the Georgian was through classicism to Gothicism and thence to utter disintegrative chaos—but in Charleston we find a marvellous and exceptional retention of sound elder standards. Classicism remained enthroned despite occasional Gothick churches, and in private houses the elements of late-Georgian design linger'd on miraculously into the thick of the Victorian age. Doorway-design, with fanlight and sidelights, remained the same in general essence; and the general house-plan did not greatly alter, notwithstanding a tendency toward the *colossal* and the *monumental,* perhaps induc'd by the expansive agricultural prosperity of the 1840's and 1850's. Houses began to have exaggeratedly lofty rooms, and winding staircases in hemicycles at the end of the hall, with niches at the landings and floor levels (cf. urban architecture elsewhere, especially Bulfinch's later houses on Beacon Hill, Boston). Heavy drapery became the mode, and Adam-period mantels gave place to mantels of dark vein'd marble shaped like Grecian temple-facades. Furniture of the heavy Empire type appear'd, but did not commonly degenerate into the most extream horrors of Victorian haircloth, marble-top, and jigsaw'd black-walnut. Architectural details became heavy and almost crude as negro craftsmen replaced skilled white carvers, though the good models of the eighteenth century were never wholly lost sight of.

Such was the Charleston—a Charleston still mainly Georgian in its visual as well as social-intellectual aspect—upon which the Civil War descended. Afterward a few ugly Victorian houses were erected in the newer sections and the burnt district; but these were very few indeed, relatively speaking. Cash for building was not plentiful, and local taste always tended to stay above the lower depths in which the rest of America was sunk. Charleston quickly responded to the architectural recuperation of the '90s and early twentieth century, and has recently built nothing in violation of the ancient Georgian tradition. Even the new Francis Marion Hotel is essentially conservative in pattern, and so far there would seem to be no danger of a lapse into the meaningless vortex of "modernistick" theory. Charleston is too profound a civilised entity to be swept off its feet by ephemeral abstraction, and is well aware of the authenticity with which the try'd, familiar forms express and symbolise its priceless history and heritage.

III. The Present State of Charleston, and Modes of Exploring It

Charleston occupies a flat—and originally marshy and creek-threaded—tongue of land betwixt the mouths of the rivers Ashley and Cooper, which here flow into one of the most spacious and notable harbours on the Atlantick coast; a harbour full seven miles across, and separated from the open sea by several islands, of which Sullivan's, containing Fort Moultrie, and the small isle holding Fort Sumter, are the most celebrated. The city is the natural port of a spacious lowland region of subtropical climate and fertility, cut by many rivers and once the seat of most extensive planting. Approaching the district by land from the ugly and barren uplands of Carolina, the traveller is imprest with the sensation of having enter'd an earthly paradise. All the way down from Camden, through Columbia and Orangeburg and Summerville, the genial and exotick character of the country is clearly manifest. Here are gardens of figs, pomegranates, peaches, oranges, oleanders, myrtles, azaleas, camellias, acacias, jujubes, and roses; and outside the towns one beholds the wild rose, the wild yellow jessamine, the magnolia, and the twisted and curious live-oak with festoons of Spanish moss hanging from spectral branches. Vast cathedral-like forests of pine and live-oak are common, and suggest the strange landskips pictur'd in Mons. Chateaubriand's romance of *Atala.* The resort town of Summerville, twenty-four miles from Charleston, lies imbedded in such a forest; and derives therefrom a curious picturesqueness. Amidst such natural beauty, we do not marvel at the fame of Charleston gardens, or at the circumstance that two of our most celebrated flowers, the *poinsettia* and the *gardenia,* were nam'd from gentlemen of Charleston, who cultivated them. The poignant and bristling *palmetto-tree* is very frequently met with, and more clearly than anything else proclaims the nearness of the region to the tropicks. Upon the sensitive imagination, accustom'd only to northern scenes, such sights cannot but produce an extreamly sharp effect; and it is universally allow'd that the literary genius of Mr. Poe, who spent a season at Fort Moultrie on Sullivan's Island, was very strongly influenc'd by this, his only glimpse of an environment other than northern.

Charleston itself lies in N. Latitude 32° 45′, and W. Longitude 79° 57′. Approach'd from the sea, its flatness gives it a very curious and engaging aspect; the many spires and roofs seeming to rise directly out of the water, as if forming the topmost pinnacles of a submerg'd Atlantis. St. Michael's and St. Philip's steeples are the dominant and traditional features of the skyline. Owing to the rigid plan of my L[d] Ashley, upon which the system of streets was first started, the town has not the maze of tangled lanes which we find in such other antient places as Boston, lower New-York, and Annapolis; yet the great age and diversity of the buildings cause the scene to lack nothing of quaintness. The generall arrangement of the town is much like that of New-York, with cross-streets, and long north and south streets ending in a battery with a sea-wall. The social topography, however, is very different; insomuch as the Battery is a fashionable place of residence and promenade (on account of the cool breezes), whilst business flourishes on the two great north-and-south streets, King and Meeting, about midway in their course. The principal cross-streets, from the Battery upward, are Tradd (a thoroughfare wholly colonial), Broad (the street of bankers and brokers), and Calhoun (which marks the focus of the modern business section, and crosses Meeting and King Sts. at an open park call'd Marion Square). The great north and south streets, from the Cooper River or principal waterfront westward, are East Bay, Church, Meeting, King, Legare (which runs north into Archdale and St. Philip, and which is pronounc'd *Le-gree'*). Rutledge Ave., and Ashley

Ave. The region below Broad St. is, except for the fringe along the Ashley River, almost wholly colonial. Along the line of Meeting St. and around the Battery it is exceedingly fashionable and beautiful; whilst east of this, along the line of Church St., it is quaint and homelike, and much given over to artists' studios. As one gets north of Stoll's Alley, a dismal slum district of abandon'd warehouses and negro tenements begins to develop along the Cooper waterfront; but this is well worth exploration because of the age and picturesqueness of the houses. One ought to study this section with a retentive memory, since it is likely to be swept away by a wave of hotel-building before many years have pass'd. Betwixt Broad and Calhoun lies a region which may be call'd *semi-colonial*, and which ought to be pretty thoroughly cover'd by the visitor, since it contains the leading publick edifices. The focal point of this and the older southerly region is the historic intersection of Broad and Meeting Sts., once the principal gate of the original wall'd town, and for two centuries the real civick centre. On the four corners of this intersection will be found antient St. Michael's (1761) (S.E.), the City Hall (1801) (N.E.), the Court House (1788) (N.W.), and the modern but sightly post-office (S.W.). Adjacent to it, and having gates on both Meeting and Broad Sts., is the old City Park or Washington-Square, which lies behind the City Hall and forms the principal down-town resting-place besides the Battery. Here we find an excellent statue of William Pitt, Esq., set up in 1770 and mov'd to the present site from elsewhere; also a monument to the graceful Charleston poet, Henry Timrod, Esq., and one to the Civil War general Pierre Gustave Toutant Beauregard. The park extends through to Chalmers St. on the north, and on the east is bounded by a very picturesque and antient Georgian wall. Encompass'd as it is by venerable publick structures, it forms a highly appropriate spot for the thoughtful visitor's repose and reflection.

In order to behold with intelligence the rich and vary'd antiquities of Charleston, it is advisable first to gain a good idea of the streets from the study of suitable maps. Of these there is no lack, the best available for distribution being those in the booklet issu'd by the street-car company, and in the guide brochure publish'd by W. W. De Renne of Savannah, Ga. Charleston's street plan ought to be master'd with some thoroughness, so that objects and places of interest may be quickly found and identify'd by their location as stated in guide-books or directions. Of course, everything cannot be carry'd in memory; so that it is well always to have a map (preferably that by A. T. S. Stoney in the De Renne booklet) in one's pocket.

Just what to see, if time be limited, must always be a question largely dependent on one's personal taste. To this end the consultation of a good array of guide-books is necessary. Of the free booklets distributed by various interests in Charleston, the following ought to be in the possession of the visitor:

(1) *Charleston, America's Most Historic City.*
Monthly magazine issued by Charleston Chamber of Commerce. Issue for Dec. 1929 contains the best short itinerary of sights, arranged in good walking order, but without map of city. Has map of Charleston environs, including harbour and islands. This is the most important of the free guide-books.

(2) *What to See–Where to Go–in Historic Charleston.*
Brochure published by W. W. De Renne, Box 481, Savannah, Ga., and sent free on request. Has excellent guide material, plus the best extant sightseeing map of Charleston. This book *and map* form almost an absolute necessity for the unguided sightseer.

(3) *The Lure of Charleston the Historic.*
Folder issued by Chamber of Commerce, with small map which points out historic spots by means of guide lines. Excellent, but requires a magnifying-glass for effective use.

(4) *See Charleston–Ride by Street Car.*
Brochure issued by S. C. Power Co., with excellent map of the city and complete information concerning street-car service. Ought to be carried by all sightseers.

But for the thorough student–or even for the casual visitor if he desires maximum pleasure and convenience–additional material is necessary. The one *indispensable* guide-book to obtain is:

Street Strolls
around
Charleston, South Carolina,
Giving the
History, Legends, and Traditions;
by
Miriam Bellangee Wilson[3]

This book is sold at all bookstalls for *75¢*, and ought to be obtain'd at the outset. In this book is told practically everything there is to tell about everything of interest in Charleston; walking itineraries being arranged, and every house or site or association along the way described in proper order and with adequate detail and background. The walks are arrang'd as conveniently as possible; with due regard for oeconomy of distance, and with a minimum of duplication. The whole city is cover'd; and he who has pursu'd the plan with fulness, may say very truthfully that he knows Charleston almost like a native. A good walker, persistent in his wish to master everything, might fully cover this itinerary in three or four days; tho' not less than a week ought to be given to it. The slower one goes, the better; so that the colour and atmosphere may be imbibed with an intelligent leisure permitting the fullest savouring, digestion, and correlation with one's historical, literary, and imaginative background. If a sort of preface, introduction, or orientation-tour is desired, it is pleasant to take the motor sightseeing trip of the Grey Line[4] before entering on detail'd pedestrian research. In the remarks to follow, it will be assum'd that the reader has the topography of the city at his disposal in the form of maps, and that he has access to suitable guide-book descriptions of the various objects of interest mention'd. Only the most salient things will be touch'd upon, tho' it is to be hoped that the visitor will not confine his inspection to these alone. No attempt will be made to describe the multiplicity of noble objects to be view'd in the rural regions around Charleston. These include many fine plantations, the ancient Goose Creek Church (1711), St. Andrew's Parish Church (1706), and the world-famous Magnolia and Middleton Gardens, which are open to the publick in the early spring. Objects like these deserve a special expedition devoted to them, a thing best accomplisht when one has a coach at his disposal; tho' there is a publick coach service to Magnolia and Middleton Gardens during the season (March and April) they are open.

Arriving in Charleston, the visitor beholds a city that is alive in the fullest sense despite its historick past. Tho' suggesting Salem and Newport in its physical aspect, it has not the languid deadness of those archaick towns; but is indeed the present metropolis of a vast and opulent region, in which it stands alone and unrivall'd. Accordingly, it will be found to possess a variety of urban refinements and facilities, and to harbour a metropolitan self-sufficiency, which wou'd not be found in a town of like size in the North. The population, including the blacks, of which there are a great number, does not much exceed 62,000; yet the general atmosphere is that of a large town of vast assurance and maturity. There are signs of a commercial revival in the near future, and an increasing flood of appreciative tourists heightens the aspect of liveliness during the early spring season. The vast new Cooper River Bridge (a marvellous feat of engineering worth the study of those interested in such matters) serves, in connexion with another bridge over the Ashley, to place Charleston on a new direct coastal route betwixt Florida and the North; a circumstance which may cause it to be more widely frequented by outsiders, yet which one hopes will not serve to destroy its individual and self-contain'd manner of life, or make it self-conscious and exhibitionistick like Cape Cod. Since the decline of rice and cotton prosperity, Charleston's chief industries have been the manufacture of phosphate fertilisers and asbestos products, and the export of vary'd agricultural products. The agricultural trade is very brisk, owing to the excellence and healthfulness of South-Carolina vegetable produce. The local farm products are phenomenally rich in the necessary *iodine* element; a circumstance deem'd so important by local oeconomists, that the word "IODINE" has (with somewhat doubtful taste) been plac'd upon the 1930 licence-plates of all South-Carolina motor vehicles.

Seeking a tavern to stop at, the stranger had better be guided by his personal taste and requirements. The ascetick antiquarian, to whom historick impressions are more important than ice-water and push-buttons, will do very well at the YMCA; whilst the man who demands an uniform environment of material luxury had better stop at the Francis Marion in Marion-Square, or the Fort-Sumter Hotel on the Battery. An ideal medium, perhaps, is the homelike and old-fashion'd *Timrod Inn,* a neat hostelry of reposeful pre–Civil-War design, with piazzas overhanging the street, which stands at the very centre of things in Meeting St. near Broad, on the eastern side of the street, facing Washington-Square. It is nam'd for the Charleston poet Henry Timrod, Esq., who dy'd in 1867, and is exceedingly well spoken of by a gentleman of the writer's acquaintance who lately stopt there. Its prices are moderate, even cheap—and it is very conveniently situated with respect to ordinaries and eating-saloons (an important matter with many), a good abundance of which are scatter'd along the west side of Meeting St. northward from its doors. These houses of refreshment are not of the one-arm'd sort now so universal in New-England; but remain (in accordance with Charleston conservatism) equipp'd with the old-fashion'd personal service so cherish'd by those accustom'd to Sybaritick refinements and Patersonian luxuries.

Sallying forth from his tavern with map and guide-book in hand, the stranger cannot but note the civilis'd and distinctive atmosphere of the antient city around him. The pace of life is sensible and leisurely, and there is no needless noise or bustle or excitement. Everything essential is accomplish'd without that needless parade of haste, and that criminal sacrifice of beauty and all that makes life worth enduring, which we find so universal amongst the foreign and barbarick industrial centres of the North. The abundance of negroes is picturesque, and now and then the sweet chimes of old St. Michael's can be heard striking the hours, halves, and quarters as they have done since 1774. Odd characters and quaint beggars abound to an extent unheard-of in the "efficient" and de-humanised North. Such misfits are view'd with kindly tolerance and even affection, and are assur'd of a livelihood thro' the bounty of the citizens. They include both white men and blacks, and are an integral part of the local folklore. Around Washington-Square a dreamy bearded man is often seen to loiter, and in the same region one may see Jimmy O'Brien, the idiot newsboy whose malform'd face and great teeth (either in laughter or in anger) are of so hideous a cast as to suggest the most nefandous daemons of the pit. Jimmy is of pure white Irish blood, but his form of physical atavism gives him a yellow Mongoloid cast which causes many to mistake him for a mulatto. His father, whom he resembles, was the town drunkard until delirium tremens removed him from the scene. Another local character is a slightly clouded little old gentleman of the antient planter stock, who dresses immaculately in a tight-fitting blue suit of elder pattern, clutches a neatly roll'd umbrella, and minces about to various shops in the business district asking pointless questions and ordering goods which he does not want and which everyone knows enough not to give him. A good central point to see local characters and hear local folklore is the photograph-shop of *George W. Johnson, 71 Hasell*[5] *St.,* where the best actual photographs of Charleston scenes (taken by Mr. Johnson personally, and retail'd at 5 cents each) may be obtain'd. Mr. Johnson is a man of venerable years, keen intelligence, and hospitable affability; very familiar with old times and old tales, and courteous and genial in his conversations with visitors. The best headquarters for penny postcards, quaint souvenirs, and guide-books of every description, is *Lighthart's Bookstore, 322 King St.,* on the east side of the street just below George. Here may be obtain'd, likewise, the New-York papers; or if Lighthart is out of them, they can generally be had from a smaller place a few doors down on the same side of the street. Lighthart is open daily till 9 p.m., tho' Mr. Johnson keeps the usual hours.

The stranger cannot but find the climate of Charleston much to his taste; it being mild in winter, and in summer cool'd by the breezes of the neighbouring ocean. The annual mean temperature is 67° Fahrenheit, and there are on the average only six freezing days in a year. The Battery is never warm, and the writer cou'd never endure the cold of it any evening in the early part of May. The sun in Charleston shines more continuously than in any other American city except Los Angeles; and in the writer's sojourn of eleven days there was not a single rainfall or long cloudy period. The one drawback is the tendency toward gales and hurricanes in late August and September; a thing largely offset by stout building construction and massive sea-walls. The beaches of Charleston—Folly Beach, Sullivan's Island, and Isle of Palms—are among the finest in the South; and being directly on the open ocean, ought to be a good source of deep-sea shells and marine vegetation for those who collect such material. Sullivan's Island, with Fort Moultrie (pronounc'd *Moo-'try*), ought in particular to be visited because of its association with Mr. Poe, its part in his celebrated tale, "The Gold-Bug", and its possession of the grave of the unfortunate Seminole chieftain *Osceola*, who was there confin'd. Happily, one of the sightseeing excursions of the Grey Line (offices in Marion Sq.) include all the features of this island. General information about anything in Charleston can be obtain'd from the Chamber of Commerce at the corner of Broad and Church Sts. Its address is 50 Broad St., and its telephone numbers are 440, 240, and 4160. (No local exchange names in Charleston.) Research at the publick library is also desirable, nor should one omit visits to the Museum and the Gibbes Art Gallery.

The best way to see Charleston is first to drift aimlessly about the ancient streets below Broad, picking up random impressions of centuried charm and exotic tradition without the psychological hindrance of a preconceiv'd or systematick plan, and then—having reach'd the palmetto-fring'd and live-oak-dotted Battery with its numerous monuments—to begin the regular following up of some stated sightseeing route; preferably the compleat series given in the Wilson guide-book *Street Strolls Around Charleston* (75¢ at Lighthart's or any bookstall), or if this is impossible, one of the briefer schedules outlined in the Chamber of Commerce's magazine, the De Renne brochure, or the ensuing pages of this description. In the random Batteryward stroll a very good notion of Old Charleston may be secur'd. One will stumble on the quaintest conceivable streets, alleys, squares, and hidden churchyards, and will encounter the most sumptuous mansions imbedded in wall'd tropical gardens. Along the principal waterfront, that on the Cooper side, he will discern the myriad abandon'd and ruin'd brick warehouses which speak so eloquently of former shipping prosperity. As in Newport and Salem, relatively few of the antient houses are ever demolish'd; tho' there are threats of a vast hotel development amidst the curious old slums of lower East Bay St. The exoticism of the old tiled and stucco'd houses, with their occasionally bright hues, will engage the eye from the outset; suggesting something oddly French, or Latin, or foreign in some obscure way. The great blackness of the numerous negroes will also be remark'd; it being evidently the custom for mulattoes to keep to themselves in the newer far-northern part of the town. Foreign faces are almost wholly absent except in the small Italian quarter around State St.; though there are some Jew merchants and Greek keepers of ordinaries. For the most part Charleston is strictly a Nordick-American town. Here and there a classick, old-fashion'd publick building or church will attract notice; and at all times one is looking for glimpses of the two dominant landmarks, St. Michael's and St. Philip's spires. *Wrought-iron work* produces a deep impression because of its universal profusion—gates, balconies, window grilles, railings, and the like; all of the finest craftsmanship. The gates are especially numerous because of the prevalence of high-wall'd gardens in this land of luxurious flowers, rambling vines, and opulent trees that weave an omnipresent green twilight redolent of perfume and musical with bird-song when the sun goes down. Charlestonians endeavour to secure privacy and the open air at the same time. One tasteful feature of this antient part of the town is the absence of obtrusive street signs; the names of the streets being on bronze plates sett in the sidewalks at the street corners. This custom is becoming universal throughout Charleston.

Having thus absorb'd the general colour of the town, and having form'd a good idea of the general street system—an idea buttress'd by an adequate map in one's pocket—one shou'd next proceed to make a tour of the principal sights[6] according to a regular plan. The following brief itinerary, beginning at the Battery, is design'd to cover the whole city in a single route with as few repetitions as possible; but is of course merely fragmentary as compar'd with all the sights to be seen. It may be follow'd in one long walk—a full day's pedestrian quota—or taken in sections; and in any order whatsoever. It is not meant to include everything in Old Charleston, and it wou'd be a pity if any reader were to follow it blindly without consulting the guide-books and ascertaining what else is to be seen. Likewise, it leaves to these fuller guide-books the task of supplying ampler descriptions of the few things which are touch'd upon. A map with the course outlined in blue is appended to this itinerary.

Beginning at the *Battery,* the visitor shou'd observe the semi-tropical scenery of that pleasing area, and pay good attention to the mansions fronting on it. Looking down the harbour somewhat eastward, he may behold historick *Fort-Sumter* upon its small island in the distance, and see to the left of it *Fort-Moultrie,* occupying a point of land on *Sullivan's Island.* Turning inland, there is to be seen at No. 8, South-Battery (on the left-hand corner of Church-Street), the elegant private mansion built in 1768 by Tho: Savage, Gent., and in 1785 built by *Col. Wm Washington* of the celebrated Virginia family. If any one now chuse to go up King-St. to N° 27 and explore the antient *Brewton-Pringle house* (hdqtrs. of H.M. arm'd forces 1780–81), he may well do so; tho' this dwelling will be later encounter'd along the bending line of exploration. If not, it is proper to begin the tour by turning up *Church-Street;* tho' not without carefully looking up *Meeting-Street,* and observing the

Charleston map showing sightseeing routes prescribed by Lovecraft

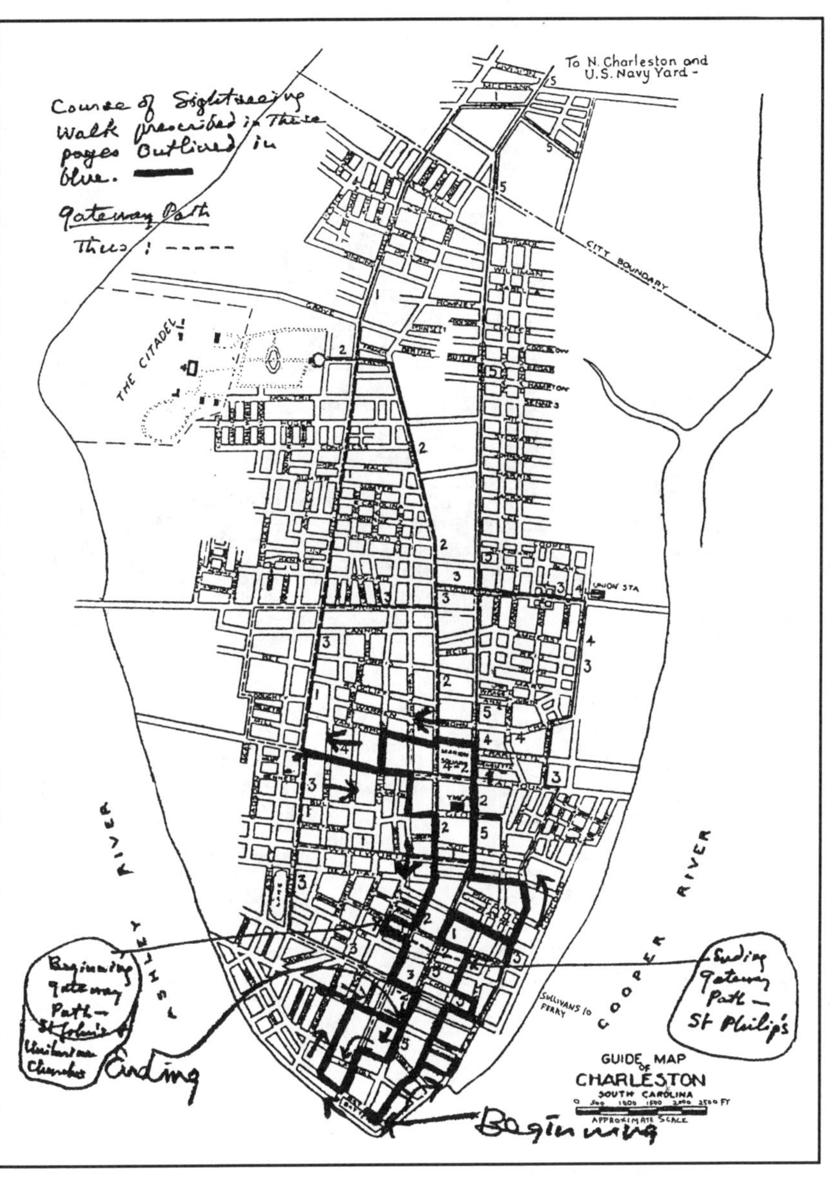

Course of Sightseeing Walk prescribed in these pages Outlined in blue.
Gateway Path Thus: -----
To N. Charleston and U.S. Navy Yard -
THE CITADEL
CITY BOUNDARY
UNION STA
ASHLEY RIVER
COOPER RIVER
SULLIVANS IO FERRY
Beginning Gateway Path — St John's Unitarian Churches
Ending
Ending Gateway Path — St Philip's
Beginning
GUIDE MAP OF CHARLESTON SOUTH CAROLINA
0 500 1000 1500 2000 2500 FT
APPROXIMATE SCALE

Typical Charleston gable of old brick house (stuccoed). Probably French influence.
Typical curved eaves of old Charleston house.
Typical Square Charleston house (mostly in business district) with parapet or false attic front having imitation windows & grille-work.
Mediaeval gable & roof line in Charleston
Typical Charleston street view — early type house.
Charleston street view, showing old house with porch — late 18th century. Typical of its period & later. Note grille-work balcony overhanging the street.
Charleston — Typical urban group, showing porch on lower storey — door opening from street on verandah, which fronts a walled garden with iron grille-work gates.
Typical neo-classical edifice in Charleston, showing common form of steps in railed double flight.

spacious mansions and estates lining both its sides. Advancing along Church-St., which is here very narrow, we pass by quaint antient houses and stables, and notice the trim dwellings of artists as well across Atlantick-Street. After this we encounter a bend, on the left-hand side of which are some very antient houses. No. 35, once inhabited by the learned author of Johnson's *Traditions of the American Revolution,* was built in 1745. No. 37 was built before 1733. No. 39, the well-known *George Eveleigh house,* was built in the decade 1743–53, and had a secret stairway to the second floor. All three of these houses once had a secret passage to Vanderhorst Creek, which follow' d the line of the present *Water St.* We now come to Water St., which in its aqueous days was here crost by a bridge. That part of Church St. we have just been traversing, was antiently call'd Fort-Street. The large round object which we see in the sidewalk at this intersection is a *tidal drain,* made necessary by the low and watery nature of the region. Somewhat west of this is the spot where Col. Rhett caused fifty-seven pirates to be hang'd in a single afternoon. Advancing around the bend, we now encounter on our right the entrance to *Stoll's Alley,* lately a slum, but now splendidly restor'd as an habitation for artists. It is to be hop'd, that this colony will remain sacred to the genuine followers of the arts, and not sink to the state of a Greenwich-Village. An exploration of this alley is well worth one's while, nor is it a vain digression to go all the way through the narrow part to *East-Bay St.* In the wider part the Georgian restorations are of the most tasteful and agreeable sort. At East-Bay St. we turn to the left, noting the abandon'd and ruin'd warehouses along the waterfront. We soon come to *Longitude-Lane,* leading back to Church-Street, opposite which, on the water side of the street, is an exceeding sightly edifice of brick, of Adam-period design, and in a pathetick state of desertion and decrepitude. This is *Vanderhorst Row,* put up in the year 1800 and said to be the oldest apartment house in America. Now turning into Longitude-Lane, we pass by the moss-grown brick walls of abandon'd cotton warehouses; noting the cobblestones set for mules' feet, the flagstones for the dray-wheels, and the snubbing-posts at the warehouse doors. One of these posts is an old ship's cannon. To the writer this place has a melancholy charm of a very acute sort. Once back in Church-Street, we look to the left and digress backward a bit to see the entrance of an old warehouse on the eastern side, and the classick facade of the *First Baptist Church* (1822) opposite it. Next the church, and opposite the mouth of Longitude-Lane, is (#69) the *Jacob Motte house,* built in 1760 and having a pink colour which it has borne from the earliest times. Next door—at #71—is the *Robert Brewton house* built in 1721 and forming a fine example of the smaller single houses of early Charleston. Still

Drawings by Lovecraft to illustrate Charleston antiquities

further along—at #73—is the *Miles Brewton house* (a typical old-Charleston double house) built in 1733. Across the street from it, at #78, is an old house with a fine wrought-iron balcony from which Genl. Washington is reputed to have deliver'd an address. A study of this balcony tends to disprove the tradition, since (although the house itself is antient) the craftsmanship points to a later date than 1791, the period of the General's visit. One singular feature of the house is the symmetrical central position of the doorway; a thing universally met with in Georgian New-England, but very uncommon in the South. We come now to quaint and antient *Tradd St.,* which is so picturesque that it will pay us to stroll down it to the river and return. On both sides we may see very antient houses, built flush with the street and with walls adjoyning, as a protection against the raids of pirates, Spaniards, and Indians. *Bedon's Alley,* a very old and curious byway containing a large three-storey brick house which may possibly be the oldest in Charleston, extends northward from a point half-way to the river; on its western corner being the site once housing the *Carolina Coffee-House.* There, in 1790, the St. Cecilia Society held one of its concerts; and in 1793 the Ugly-Club us'd it as a dining place. At East Bay St. we again behold Vanderhorst Row, and note on the northern corner of Tradd the site of the birthplace of the first white child of the town; Robert Tradd, from whom the street was nam'd. Looking out over the river past *Adger's Wharf,* we behold the island call'd *Castle-Pinckney;* and farther off, the opposite shoar of Mt. Pleasant, and part of Sullivan's Island. Returning now to Church St. and resuming a northerly course, we behold on the left at #87 the *Heyward house,* a fine Georgian mansion of generalised rather than Charlestonian architecture, now under careful restoration by the Society for the Preservation of Old Dwellings and the Charleston Museum. This house was built in the 1770's or before, and was us'd by Genl. Washington during his Charleston visit of May 1791. Adjoining this structure is an old house which in 1791–1810 was the *French Theatre,* afterward the *City Theatre.* The auditorium was in the rear, reach'd by crossing thro' an archway and traversing an inner court. In more recent times, the place was sunk to a slum and used by negroes as a vending-place of vegetables, being commonly known as *"Cabbage Row"*, and presented in the novel *Porgy,* by DuBose Heyward, Esq., as *"Catfish Row"*. Very lately it has been reclaim'd to its original elegance and neatness, and is now the abode of art shops. Proceeding onward, we shou'd note the quaint alleys on either side of the street—*St. Michael's Place* to the left, and *Elliott St.* to the right. We now come to *Broad St.,* the leading transverse thoroughfare of the town, and an abode of bankers and brokers. On the northeast corner is the new bank building which has most unfortunately displac'd the old and historic Shepheard's Tavern, where the first Masonick Lodge in America was organised in 1736. On the northwest corner the *Chamber of Commerce* occupies the brick structure erected in 1784 for the Bank of South-Carolina, and used from 1835 to 1914 as a publick library. It will be worth our while to walk down Broad St. to the river and study the antient and remarkable publick building which squarely faces the end of the street. This is the *Old Exchange*, built in 1767 on the site of the old guard post call'd "Half-Moon Bastion", and used as executive headquarters by His Majesty's Forces in 1780–81. It was later a post-office, and is now an headquarters of the D.A.R.—also housing certain clerical federal activities. During the Revolution prisoners were confin'd in the basement of this building; and on the northern end, close to the ground, can still be seen the small square holes, with heavy grating, which afforded scanty light and air to some of the dungeons. The architecture of the building in general is very fine. To the right of the Old Exchange, across a seaward lane and on the water side of East Bay St. at *Nos. 114–116*, will be found a *group of very antient buildings*, two of which have cupolas, or observation-towers. These towers were us'd by observers to watch the incoming shipping and transmit the news to the publick. Ships were first sighted from a tower on Sullivan's Island, whose watchman relay'd the news to these Charleston towers by raising ball signals on a pole—a black ball for a square-rigger, and a white one for a schooner-rigg'd vessel. These signals were repeated by the Charleston watchers, the signal-balls being left up until the ships they represented came to anchor. The small building on the corner (later the British consulate) next the tallest cupola'd building is the old *French Coffee-House or Harris's Tavern*. Beneath this structure may still be found the antient wine-cellars, which form a tunnel extending far out under East Bay St., and then turning toward the Battery in an arm reaching half a block. We now, after a glance at the classick bank facade on the landward side of E. Bay above Broad, turn back along Broad St. for one block; then turning northward into *State St.*, originally call'd *Union St.* Following this to the first intersection, we there turn to the left into antient and picturesque *Chalmers St.*, a broad cobbled thoroughfare, at whose farther end can be seen in the distance the splendid classick pillars of *Hibernian-Hall* (1841) in Meeting St. Almost all the houses along Chalmers St. are colonial. At No. 8, the small, low archway adjoining a pretentiously turreted building, is the *Old Slave Market* at which train'd servants and skill'd artisans were sold—the common field niggers being procurable at "Vendue Range", the foot of Queen St. where the Clyde Line wharves now extend. Nearly opposite the "Slave Mart" is that curious pink-colour'd building which possesses the *only gam-*

brel roof in Charleston. This is a very old house, and was a tavern before the Revolution. It has three storeys, but only one room to a floor. We are now back at Church St., tho' it wou'd do no harm to walk along Chalmers to Meeting and back in order to observe the antient houses. Turning up Church, we next come to *Queen St.* (formerly Dock St.), at whose southeast corner is the sightly Gothick church (1845) and churchyard of the Huguenots. This is today the only Huguenot church in the country, and deserves the support (which it sorely needs) of every surviving group of Huguenot descendants. Money may be subscrib'd in the name of some bygone Huguenot leader, to whom a memorial tablet will be erected within the edifice. Many such are already in position. Across the street from the church is the deserted and dilapidated ruin of the *Planters' Hotel,* built about 1805, and famous in the great cotton aera as a rendezvous of neighbouring planters and their families. On the northwest corner, and extending a considerable space along Church St., is a group of five small houses built of brick and Bermuda coral-stone, and known to have been standing prior to 1742. These are the so-called *Pirate Houses;* reputed to have received visits at a later date from Mr. Poe. Of the truth of these traditions the writer has no opinion to offer. They are now all converted into fashionable shops, and the courtyard betwixt them has been developed as a highly fascinating byway. Beyond these comes the bend in the street, with the fine porticoes and steeple of *St. Philip's* Episcopal Church looming up in the foreground, and sections of the churchyard stretching off on both sides of the way. St. Philip's present edifice does not antedate 1835, but it is a fine late-Georgian specimen whose steeple shares honours with St. Michael's as a landmark of the city, and a welcoming symbol to the mariner approaching the port. The tower, with its triple portico, is very notable. When this fane was built, Church St. did not extend in front of it; the bend being made to accommodate it. The present street cuts the old churchyard in two, separating the larger part (which contains the last mortal resting place of the Hon. John C. Calhoun) from the edifice itself. We now push on to *Cumberland St.,* chusing whether or not we shall stroll down toward the waterfront to see the old house (on the N. side) with the elaborate ironwork, and the wrought-iron emblem of the Iron Workers' Guild—which was probably the residence and shop of a master craftsman. With this side-trip made or omitted, we follow Cumberland west of Church toward Meeting, noting on the left-hand side the *Old Powder Magazine* in its limited but pleasing grounds. This squat, peaked-gabled bit of Cyclopean vaulted masonry is the oldest structure in Charleston, dating from 1703 and having form'd a bastion of the city wall. It is the only surviving fragment of that wall. The Colonial Dames are in charge of it, and visitors are admitted to the heavily vaulted interior for a shilling. We now follow Cumberland to Meeting and turn northward to *Market St.*, beholding in the middle of that thoroughfare the high classick facade of the *Old Market House*, whose upper part is now a Confederate Museum. This edifice, built in 1841, is typical of Old Charleston publick architecture; having the characteristick double flight of steps with the mouth of an arched tunnel beneath. Behind the building the low-roofed shed of the Market (erected in 1800) extends all the way to the river, along the line of what was once Fish Market Creek. In earlier times the refuse of this market attracted a famous array of buzzards, which became incredibly tame. Following the market shed to East Bay St., after a glance upward along Meeting at the classick facade of the old *Charleston Hotel*, we behold somewhat to the right, and set near the water, the massive and splendid *Custom-House* with its classick architecture, begun in 1850 and finish'd after the Civil War. From the seaward side of this building an impressive view of the harbour may be obtain'd. We now proceed three squares up East Bay to *Hasell St.*, here turning to the left and proceeding again toward Meeting St. On the north or right-hand side, at #54, is what is probably (the claim of the Bedon's Alley house notwithstanding) the *oldest dwelling in Charleston*, built in 1722 or before by the old pirate-fighter William Rhett, and later forming the birthplace of the eminent soldier and statesman, Genl. Wade Hampton. Reaching Meeting St., we may if we wish make a side-trip beyond to see the venerable classick facade of the *Jews' Synagogue* (1841) on the right, and *St. Mary's Romish Church* (1838) on the left. We then turn northward along Meeting toward George, noting on the left the stately columns of *Trinity M. E. Church* (1875), call'd "the youngest church below Calhoun St." At George St. we note on the N.W. corner the fine but dilapidated *King mansion* with its wall'd grounds, built in 1806 and later used as a high-school. Making a side-trip eastward along George, we see on the north side the grounds and building of the local water-works—which is the old *Elliott-Pinckney-Middleton house*, finished in 1797 and forming one of the finest possible specimens of Adam-period architecture. The interior of this mansion, defac'd tho' it is by industrial uses, still retains much fine woodwork and proportioning—especially the circular stairway and the oval room upstairs. Travellers shou'd explore the interior, insomuch as opportunities for seeing Charleston interiors are somewhat limited for strangers without local introductions. The region around this place was once called Ansonborough. Returning now to Meeting St., we follow it northward again till we come to *Calhoun St.* and the easterly end of the open park or parade-ground known successively as *Inspection Square, Citadel Green*, and *Marion Square*. This was formerly the line of the city's northernmost defences, and in the midst of the park may be seen a single remaining bit of the old *"Horn Wall"*—made of a mixture of lime and sea shells—which form'd the fortifications of 1780. On the north side of the green is the long, battlemented line of *The Old Citadel* (1822), which form'd the home of the Military College of S.C. from its foundation in 1842 to its recent removal (1924) to new quarters in the extream northwestern part of the city. The King St. side of the green is the focus of modern business life and the seat of the leading new hotel. The Meeting St. side marks the local district once known as Louisburgh. Continuing along Meeting beyond the Square, we see above Charlotte St. the splendid avenue of approach to the *Second Presbyterian Church,* which was built in 1811. Just beyond this, at the corner of Ashmead St. and much defac'd by an encroaching petrol station, is the fine old *Peter Manigault mansion,* with its striking circular gate lodge (a typical Old Charleston feature, though only two now survive), built in 1790. At times this house is open as a publick museum, tho' it is too often found clos'd. The interior contains a splendid curved staircase, as well as an interesting secret stairway.

We have now reached a logical northerly limit of travel, tho' many may wish to proceed westward thro' Hudson and Vanderhorst Sts. to *Coming St.,* up which, on the right-hand side, is *St. Paul's Episcopal Church,* a spacious fane built in 1810–12. This district was once known as Radcliffeborough. Proceeding south to *Calhoun St.* we may, if we desire, go westward several blocks to *Rutledge Ave.,* in the old Cannonsborough section (south of which lay Harlestonborough), where we will find the *Charleston Museum* with its many antiquarian and other exhibits. Typical Old Charleston rooms and apothecary shops are shewn in the gallery of this celebrated institution. The museum is the oldest in America, having been founded in 1773. Returning along Calhoun to *St. Philip St.,* we see in the next block, on the north side of Calhoun and extending to the new hotel fronting Marion Sq., the spacious grounds and venerable building (1792) of the *Charleston Orphan House.* The early prevalence of cholera, fever, and smallpox in the district left so many orphans that this institution was deem'd a necessity. It still serves its original purpose—tho' the inroads of disease have long since been reduc'd to normal thro' the progress of medical science. Descending St. Philip St. we come, at George St., upon the grounds, edifices, and lodge-gate of the stately and reposeful *College of Charleston,* whose oldest structure was erected in 1828. Proceeding eastward thro' George to King St., we turn to the right and descend that business thoroughfare for many blocks. In the course of our walk we shall see two surviving instances of antient *shop signs;* the *drum clock* over the jewellery shop at #285, betwixt Society and Wentworth Sts.

on the western side, and the *plough* over McIntosh's Seed Store next the Masonick Temple on the eastern side betwixt Wentworth and Hasell. At *Clifford St.* we turn to the right, proceeding through to *Archdale St.* (a thoroughfare known for a time, and so designated on signs and maps, as *Charles St.*, which causes considerable confusion). On the southeast corner we behold the ancient edifice and picturesque churchyard of *St. John's Lutheran Church;* which is directly adjoin'd on the south—in Archdale St.—by the Gothick precincts of the famous *Unitarian Church,* where for forty years preach'd the Rev[d] Sam[l] Gilman, of the Province of the Massachusetts-Bay, author of the widely known college hymn, "Fair Harvard". In the tower of this church a Memorial Room has been dedicated to D[r] Gilman by Harvard alumni. The edifice is very remarkable as being one of the very few *Gothick* specimens erected in the eighteenth century. It was built in 1772; and tho' badly damag'd by the earthquake of 1886, has been carefully restor'd to pristine strength. Its churchyard, together with the neighbouring churchyard of St. John's, which is virtually one with it, is the supreme epitome of exotick glamorousness; a perfum'd green tropick twilight of twisted-branch'd, overarching live-oaks and hanging vines, with antient slabs and altar-stones peeping thro' a vivid, verdurous undergrowth threaded by curious winding walks. It is truly something out of a dream—such things do not belong to the waking world! Recognising this quality of fascination in the old Archdale St. churchyards, as well as in other churchyards and garden plots to the east, the President of the Charleston Garden Club some time ago form'd the notion of mapping out an idyllic cross-town walk which might include as many as possible of these with a fair degree of continuity. The Unitarian churchyard had already establish'd a walk thro' to King St. opposite the publick library, with a fine wrought-iron gate on the latter thoroughfare; and now a similar walk with gates was provided in the garden area just across the way—extending from the publick library grounds in King St. to the yard of the *Gibbes Art Gallery* in Meeting St. Still further coöperating, the *Circular Congregational Church* in Meeting St. opposite the Gibbes Art Gallery (an ugly Victorian church, but having a delightful Old-Charleston chapel [1867], with classick facade and double entrance flights, in its grounds) open'd its spacious churchyard as a continuation of the garden stroll; being seconded by St. Philip's Church, whose westerly churchyard spreads from Church St. to meet the rear of the Congregational churchyard. Thus the walk is made continuous from Archdale St. across King and Meeting to Church St.; and now there is talk of continuing it through St. Philip's *easterly* churchyard—behind the church, and emerging in Cumberland St. thro' a future gate. Such is the *Gateway Path,* so-call'd; and every visitor to

Charleston ought at some time or other to thread its entire length from St. John's to St. Philip's. For our *present* tour, we follow it from the Unitarian churchyard out to King St. and the library; there turning to the right and following King St. southward. On the easterly side of King below Queen, at #138, is the *site of the old Quaker Meeting-House,* enclos'd by a tall iron fence. The first meeting house was built in 1694, but there has been no edifice on the site since the fire of 1861; the Quakers being now extinct in Charleston. The churchyard, however, is own'd and maintain'd in good condition by the central organisation of Quakers in Philadelphia; and two of the central antient graves may yet be seen. Having seen this, we advance down to *Broad St.,* making a short side-trip along this thoroughfare to the right to see the *Ralph Izard house* at #110 (1750), *the later Izard house* (#114) (1827) now occupy'd by the Catholick Bishop, *the Rutledge house* (1760), and the still *intact site (#118) of St. Andrew's Hall,* built in 1814 and burn'd in the fire of 1861. It is melancholy to observe the decaying garden walls and the mossy bricks of the long-disused walks. This was, in its day, the principal auditorium of the town, a distinction now falling to Hibernian Hall in Meeting St. The St. Andrew's Society, which built it, was organised in 1729, and is alive in a flourishing state, having celebrated its 200th anniversary in 1929. Genl. Lafayette was entertain'd in the vanisht building in 1825. Beyond this site may be seen the modern *Cathedral of St. John the Divine,* but we must now return eastward; retracing our steps to King St., and proceeding beyond to the important Meeting St. intersection. On the left-hand side of Broad, just back of the Court-House, is a small street known as *Court-House Square.* The large Georgian double house visible at its end, with a peculiarly Charlestonian arrangement of steps, and twin colonial doorways with transoms having double rows of lights, is the house exploited in the novel *Lady Baltimore,* by Owen Wister. Approaching this house and proceeding thro' the *green gateway on the left,* we encounter a quasi-rustick lane which leads to a hidden group of idyllically embower'd houses—a sylvan oasis not a stone's throw from the town's civick centre. This is the champion "and where" of all time! Emerging thence to the intersection of Broad and Meeting, we are indeed at the civick heart of things. On the N.W. corner is the *Court-House,* built in 1788 on the site of a burn'd down State House in the days of Charleston State Capitalship. Across on the N.E. corner is the *City Hall,* built in 1801 as the United States Bank, and used as a City Hall since 1818. On the S.E. corner is ancient *St. Michael's* (1761) with its glorious steeple, exquisite chimes, and quaint old churchyards with wrought-iron gates by Iusti. And on the S.W. corner is the modern but by no means unsightly *Post-Office.* Back of the City Hall is *Washington-Square,* with its walks, benches, Pitt, Timrod, and Beauregard Monuments, and ancient rear wall with arch'd embrasures. In the N.W. corner of the park, on the S.E. corner of Meeting and Chalmers Sts., stands the classick hall of records put up in 1826 and call'd the *Fireproof Building* because it was the first of that type erected in America. It prov'd its worth in the earthquake of 1886, when alone of all the structures in this region it remained uninjur'd. Opposite the park in Meeting St. is the old *Timrod Inn* with its archaick portico extending over the sidewalk. On the same western side of the street opposite the end of Chalmers is the stately classick facade of *Hibernian Hall* (1841), the city's principal auditorium and the home of a society of gentlemen of Irish descent, who alternately elect a Protestant and a Catholick as their president in their annual elections. Hence proceeding south down Meeting St., we behold on our left, below St. Michael's Place, the splendid edifice of the *South Carolina Society,* built in 1804 and design'd by Gabriel Manigault, Esq. This is a masterpiece in the true Charleston tradition, with double steps flankt by wrought-iron lamps. The colonial portico over the sidewalk is very justly esteem'd, and is of a somewhat later date than the building proper. The society which this building houses, was form'd for charitable purposes in 1736, and is still vigorously flourishing. Descending to Tradd St., we behold on the N.W. corner an antient mansion with a two-storey'd porch (probably of much later date) overshadowing the street. This is the *Governor Branford or Horry House,* built in 1751–57. On the S.W. corner is the old *Scotch or First Presbyterian Church* and churchyard, the present sightly edifice dating from 1814. Just below this, on the same side of the street (#51), is the splendid *Nathaniel Russell mansion* built in 1811 and following general Adam-period designs in its exterior, which is of un-stucco'd brick. Over the doorway the initials "N.R." are woven into the wrought-iron balcony. The interior is very celebrated, and includes a magnificent circular stairway lighted by two vast and unusual windows. Descending Meeting St. still farther, we must not omit to glance down any quaint alleys we may pass. At Water St. we are near the spot where Rhett hanged fifty-seven pirates. Here were antiently the sources of Vanderhorst Creek. All along the street, on both sides, are now seen residences of the greatest beauty and antiquity. *No. 39,* on the right-hand side, was built in 1767. *No. 35* was the residence of Mr. Bull, a Charleston gentleman who was Lieutenant-Governor at the time of the Revolution. Just across the street, at *No. 34,* resided the last lawful Governor of the Province, appointed by the Crown; *Ld William Campbell,* who at length was so threaten'd by seditious mobs that he withdrew secretly, thro' an hidden passage, to a small boat in Vanderhorst Creek, by which he was convey'd to His Maj^ty's^ vessel *Tamar,* then lying in the harbour. We now turn to the right thro' *Ladson St.,* tho' not without a glance down Meeting (to meet the upward glance we made when starting from the Battery) at the many fine mansions and gardens. Proceeding thro' Ladson to its end in King St., we find ourselves at the splendid *Miles Brewton or Pringle house* (#27), a spacious brick mansion with wall'd garden, coach-house, and slave-quarters, built in 1765, and displaying the best British architecture modified for Charleston needs with a two-storey'd portico. It was us'd as an headquarters for His Majesty's officers in 1780–81, and is open to the publick at the rather high admission-fee of one dollar. The interior, from vaulted basement to rafter'd attick, is well worth inspection. All the great rooms are finely decorated and panell'd, and shew early phases of the Adam influence—rare in the colonies as early as 1765. There are some notably fine mantels, and much good furniture is present. The gardens and outbuildings are all highly interesting—especially the *coach-house* fronting on the street just above this house, which displays very fully the whimsical use of Gothick as practic'd in Georgian Charleston. We now proceed southward along King St.; noting, as we cross it, the extream narrowness (on the left-hand side) of *Lamboll-St.;* which despite its alley-like dimensions betwixt Meeting and King, is a residential thoroughfare of the first order. As we approach the Battery, we may well pause to observe *#3 King St.* on our right; this antient house being call'd by guide-books the *narrowest* residence in Charleston, and perhaps in the whole South. Arriv'd at the *Battery,* we turn to the right, or westward; pausing as we do so to reflect that on this spot in 1718 were hang'd the celebrated pirate captain *Stede Bonnet,* and some forty of his men. It is said, that Colo. Rhett compell'd these malefactors to dig their own graves, so that upon being cut down their bodies fell into them, where they still lye. Another account has it that they were hang'd above the water, and cut down so that the ebb of the tide might carry them away. At all events, it is known that the efforts of Rhett made Charleston reasonably safe from pirates. There is much doubt, confusion, and hear-say in all these tales; and this hanging on the Battery is often mixt up with that other hanging of the fifty-seven over-against Vanderhorst Creek about the same period. Several guide-books declare, that it was *Bonnet's* hanging which took place on the creek; appearing to joyn the facts of two events in one. It is not well to place too much reliance on any statement made concerning these nebulous and traditional matters. We now proceed westward, or toward the Ashley River, for a single square; then turning to the right up *Legare St.* This is equal to lower Meeting St. in the taste and elegance of its dwellings, and is altogether inhabited by families of consequence. Like all places long tenanted by a vivid gentlefolk, it is full of old legends which guide-books still relate; amongst them being that of a duel fought with pistols from opposite upper windows across the street. On every hand are exquisite specimens of wrought-iron work, old granite and cypress hitching-posts (very typical of Charleston), fine polisht knockers, graceful gates and doorways, pleasing house-facades, and wall'd gardens of unutterable charm. At the head of *Gibbes St.* we observe in a wall one of the most famous pairs of *wrought-iron gates* in Charleston. At #14, on the eastern or right-hand side of the street, we come to the *George Edwards* house in its wall'd grounds, noticing the famous *gates* with their pineapple-topt posts, which were erected in 1820. Into the iron-work around the doorway are woven the script initials "G" and "E". The iron-work of the gates is piec'd out with cypress-wood, but so cunningly that the difference cannot be told. Cypress was at one time a great medium of construction in Charleston, many entire houses being built of it. Such an one is now seen, on the left, at *#15 Legare St.;* this being one of the houses from whose upper windows the celebrated duel of tradition was fought. On the right, the *knockers* of the Edwards house and of its neighbour at #16 are deserving of especial notice. We ought also to observe the antient iron lanthorns over the entrance gates, the finest of which will be found at #18. Approaching *Tradd St.,* we see in the brick wall on our right, at #32, the famous *Simonton Sword Gates,* which are perhaps the most beautiful specimens of their kind in Charleston, or in the country. They derive their name from the central horizontal bars of their design, which are in the form of Roman short swords, on which impinge vertical supports in the form of Roman javelins. The scroll-work supplementing these is of the most graceful description, and the whole is topt by a fine lanthorn. Behind the gates are spacious and well-order'd grounds and an old flagston'd avenue of magnolias leading to a mansion built before 1776. The gates are reckon'd of more recent date than this. In the late eighteenth century this estate became a fashionable girls' school conducted by a French gentlewoman, Madame Talvande, who fled hither from the San Domingo massacre. Later the place was own'd by a young gentleman from England, whose revelry and gaming made it a scene of nightly resort for the gayest of Charleston's young bloods. We now reach the corner of *Tradd St.,* and may if we wish digress westward toward the Ashley River to observe some of the old houses and gateways. At *#127,* on the left, is a fine recess'd gate with a curving wall on each side. Next it, at *#131,* is another excellent specimen. Across the street at *#128* is a fine old house built in 1760 and reached by curv'd steps climbing to a high porch. Around the corner, to the right, in *Logan St.* is the antient churchyard of a vanish'd church, old *St. Peter's.* This is in the burn'd district of 1861, hence beyond it most of the houses are new. At *#141 Tradd St.,* however, is a fine old recess'd fence with a splendid gate of cluster-and-arrow ironwork at the inner bend of the curve. Behind it is a deep garden with trees, at the end of which the mansion may be seen at a distance. Now retracing our steps toward Meeting, we re-cross Legare and note some more objects of interest. On our left *Orange St.* runs up to Broad, and we may behold at its end the younger Izard house now occupy'd by the Catholick Bishop. On the N.W. corner, at *#104 Tradd,* is the *Stuart house,* built in 1772 and own'd by a loyalist. At *King St.* we note the fine tiling of the three-storey edifice on the N.W. corner. Beyond this, on our left, we see at *#72–4 Tradd St.* a fine old English double house with steps, built in 1734. Next door, at *#70,* is the Robert Pringle house, built in 1774 and since defaced by the addition of a bay-window. The next corner is *Meeting St.,* with the *Branford-Horry house* on our left and the *South or First Presbyterian Church* on our right. Those we beheld before, when descending Meeting St., and we are at last aware that we have come upon the end of our sightseeing route.

The End

July 17, 1930

1. Or "Ro-ro", as others interpreted the sound.
2. Quebec resemblances suggest French influence.
3. A flat, grey-cover'd pamphlet; which, once folded, will neatly fit the pocket. It is #2 of a series of Charleston guide-books and maps, later items of which will describe the churches and publick buildings in some detail.
4. Offices in Marion-Square, King and Calhoun Sts.
5. Pronounc'd *Ha'zel.*
6. Many of the more important houses and sites are mark'd by very convenient historical placards.

SOME DUTCH FOOTPRINTS IN NEW ENGLAND

Devotees of the Dutch colonial tradition do not commonly look upon New England as within their field. If they think of it at all, it is largely as the foe whose outposts on the Connecticut River called forth certain steps from the mountainous Wouter van Twiller—the building of an armed fort on the site of Hartford in 1633, and the fruitless despatch of a force of seventy soldiers in the following year. The Dutch, it will be remembered, claimed all the territory up to the Connecticut's west bank (notwithstanding the counter-claim of England to all the Atlantic coast region); and it is by no means certain that they were not the discoverers of that river. Vaguer Dutch claims extended all the way to Cape Cod.

It is not true, however, that this boundary dispute formed the sole link of Holland with Novanglian history; for a fairly close survey reveals a multitude of Dutch footprints in New England. The record begins in 1614 with Adriaen Block, whose expedition in the New Netherland-built ship *Onrust* explored the New England coast as far as Cape Cod; charting the principal features and applying a nomenclature which includes several still-surviving names. Not only does Block Island preserve his memory, but he is probably responsible (notwithstanding contrary hypotheses) for the name of the distinguished State of Rhode Island; since his account of a small reddish island *(een rodtlich Eylandken)* in Narragansett Bay seems to have caused later settlers to apply that designation by mistake to the larger island of Aquidneck, on which Newport stands, and thence to the colony established there. It is a little-known fact that the Dutch nomenclature of Block persisted quite generally on charts of Narragansett Bay until the very close of the seventeenth century.

Rhode Island has another Dutch link on its southern coast; where a ruinous old fortification, long attributed to the Indians and known as Fort Ninigret, is now quite generally considered of Dutch origin. Dutch artifacts including Delft ware, clay pipes, and items for Indian trade have been found on this site; and it seems highly probable that the fort was one of several along the New England coast, with which the Dutch sought to establish a title to the region. Its probable date is 1627, a conjecture supported by a letter of the Dutch ambassador to England in 1631. In 1637 the Dutch acquired an island in that western part of Narragansett Bay which Block had named "Sloop Bay", and built a trading post upon it; causing it to become known to later generations as "Dutch Island".

Still another Dutch–Rhode Island link is afforded by Roger Williams, who had studied the Dutch language at Cambridge through his belief in Holland's importance as a factor in religious freedom. He had long associated with Anabaptists and Mennonites of Dutch origin in England, and in the new world his relations with New Netherland were especially cordial. In June, 1643, when in New Amsterdam for the purpose of embarking for England, Mr. Williams was able to perform notable service in mediating between the Dutch and the warring Indians of Long Island. Later, on his second visit to England in 1652 and 1653, occurred his well-known service of instructing Milton in Dutch.

Rhode Islanders, whose long-standing differences with the Massachusetts Bay Colony made Boston an uncongenial port for them, employed New Amsterdam more than once as a place of embarkation for the old world. It was from there that Samuel Gorton, second only to Williams as a champion of liberty, sailed for Holland and thence for England in 1645. A further Netherlandish link with Rhode Island is afforded by the Holland education of Dr. John Clark, the eminent physician and clergyman who founded the Baptist church in Newport and secured for the colony its charter of 1663.

More surprising to the layman than the connexion of southern New England with the Dutch is the fact that a part of Maine's rocky coast has known the rule of the States-General. Such, however, is the case; for the ancient fortress and trading post of Pentagoët at Castine (founded by the French in 1613, and by some claimed to be the oldest permanent settlement in New England) was held by the Dutch from 1674 to 1676. On August 10, 1674, the French garrison under Captain de Chambly was overcome after an hour's hot fighting by a force from the Dutch privateer the *Flying Horse,* commanded by Captain Jurriaen Aernouts and piloted by an Englishman from Boston. The visitors disarmed the fort and removed the cannon, taking Captain de Chambly to Boston, whence he was later ransomed for a thousand beaver-skins.

The bulk of the French colonists, who had settled there in 1671, submitted to the invaders. In November, 1676, two years after the second and peaceable transfer of New Netherland to the English by the Treaty of Westminster (October 31, 1674), a French force under Baron de St. Castin recaptured the stronghold, expelling the settlers because of their readily granted allegiance to the Dutch. Thus for more than twenty-four months after the treaty with England by which the Netherlands nominally resigned all claim to North American soil in exchange for a recognition of their rights in the West Indies and in Surinam, an actual Dutch hold on this continent existed.

Certain older historians have tended to dismiss this capture of Pentagoët as a mere buccaneering incident, though the old Jesuit chronicler Charlevoix speaks of Captain Aernouts as having a commission from the Prince of Orange. Others, however, have always recognised the official nature of the Dutch hold on Pentagoët; and in recent years this recognition has become quite general. On the site of Fort Pentagoët—in Perkins Street, Castine—there is now a tablet whose inscription relates, among other things, that the post "became the seat of government . . . of the Province of New Holland, the capture of which by Baron de St. Castin—November, 1676—ended the Dutch authority in America".

That Plymouth should possess many Dutch connexions is only natural in view of the long sojourn of the Pilgrims in Holland. Correspondence between Pieter Minuit and Governor Bradford was courteous and friendly; and in 1627 Minuit's secretary Isaac de Rasieres spent some time in Plymouth, being very cordially received and establishing fruitful and long-enduring trade relations between that colony and New Netherland. It is from a letter of de Rasieres that we derive the best of all descriptions of early Plymouth. Less generally known is the fact that the Pilgrims picked up several Dutch expressions during their stay in Leyden, several of which retained currency in the new colony. Chief among these is "meerstead", applied to the plots of land assigned to each member of the colony.

That the Dutch gave New England several of its choicest strains of blood is no news to those who recall the famous name of Wendell. Another noted line of this sort is that of the Rhode Island Updikes, planters and gentry in the old Narragansett country, and derived from a New Netherland ancestor, Dr. Gysbert op Dyck.

It would be hard to catalogue the various Dutch influences manifest to a greater or less extent in New England folkways. There is considerable evidence that the gambrel roof is of New Netherland origin, despite the different form which it took throughout the Yankee countryside; while the popularity of Dutch scriptural titles around New

England fireplaces speaks for itself. Dutch culinary and linguistic influences certainly filtered eastward from the Hudson Valley at a very early date; as attested on the one hand by the doughnut, and on the other hand by such words as cookie, stoop (small porch), span (of horses), pit (stone of fruit), boss, scow, waffle, and hook (point of land).

The currency of Dutch coins—along with those of other nations—in colonial New England is of course a matter of common knowledge; this circumstance oddly surviving in the name Guilder Street, applied to a quaint alley along the ancient waterfront of Providence.

Thus we realise that the old New Netherland civilisation is one which the seemingly alien Yankee cannot look upon as wholly detached from his own background. Between New England and its Dutch neighbour were all the ties of proximity, and of kindred settlement, purpose, and modes of life; hence today their respective sons cannot but look back together upon a substantial fund of common memories, prides, and institutions.

HOMES AND SHRINES OF POE

When amateurs visit the Fossil Library in its new Philadelphia home, it is to be hoped that they will not overlook another literary landmark of the colonial metropolis, also opened during the past few months. This is the neat brick cottage at North Seventh and Spring Garden Streets, where from 1842 to 1844 lived Edgar Allan Poe, the greatest author our country has so far produced.

Because of Poe's migratory life, the number of houses and sites associated with him is very great. Many are known, but only a few are properly marked or restored as shrines. The site of the cheap boarding-house in Boston's South End, where in 1809 he was born to a pair of strolling players, bears a bronze tablet with the simple facts; and at one time the junction near it—Broadway and Carver Street—was named "Edgar Allan Poe Square".

In 1811 Poe's mother, then acting in Richmond, died and left him to be adopted by the wealthy local merchant John Allan. She was then stopping at a small brick cottage in the rear of the theatrical boarding-house on the northwest corner of Main and 23rd Streets. This cottage (and the boarding-house as well) is still standing though unmarked. The district, inhabited by negroes, is very squalid. Mrs. Poe was buried in St. John's churchyard at Broad and 24th Streets, and her grave was suitably marked in 1928.

The Allan home into which the child was taken, a three-story brick house at 14th Street and Tobacco Alley, is still standing, though long ago converted into a shop and now deserted and unmarked.

The Poe sites in England and Scotland, where young Edgar was taken by his foster-parents and where he remained from 1815 to 1820, are not marked or generally known. The school at Stoke-Newington, so vividly described in the story "William Wilson", has long been demolished.

When the Allans returned to Richmond their first permanent home

—after a summer at the bygone and uncommemorated house of Mr. Allan's partner at Franklin and Second Streets—was at Clay and Fifth Streets. This house has vanished, and the site is unmarked. In 1825 Mr. Allan purchased the mansion called "Moldavia" at Main and Fifth Streets, and it is there that the most important crisis in Poe's life occurred. This house also is demolished without the marking of the site.

Poe's brief period at the University of Virginia in Charlottesville is, fortunately, well commemorated. His room at 13 West Range is fitted up as it was during his tenancy, and above the door is a plaque reading "EDGAR ALLAN POE—MDCCCXXVI—DOMUS PARVA MAGNI POETAE".

After Poe's breach with his guardian he entered the army as a common soldier; and many of the military landmarks connected with him—Fort Independence in Boston Harbour, Fort Moultrie on Sullivan's Island in Charleston Harbour, and Fortress Monroe, Virginia—survive, though without Poe tablets.

Discharged from the army, Poe stayed for a time with his blood-relatives in Baltimore. The house was in Mechanics Row, Milk Street, and has vanished without commemoration. In 1830, after a brief reinstatement in the Allan home, Poe went to West Point; but no marker remains to record his sojourn in Room 28, South Barracks. After he prematurely left the Academy he returned to the Milk Street house in Baltimore. Thence, in the autumn of 1832, he removed with his relatives to a dormer-windowed brick house at 3 Amity Street, which is still standing though unmarked.

In 1835 Poe went to Richmond with his aunt Mrs. Clemm and her daughter Virginia, having married the latter. The family lived at a boarding-house in Bank Street, Capitol Square, which has disappeared and whose site is unmarked.

Early in 1837 Poe and his family migrated to New York City, living at the corner of Sixth Avenue and Waverly Place in Greenwich Village, where no trace of his tenancy remains. In the spring he moved to 13½ Carmine Street, a site still commonly associated with him, though neither house nor marker exists.

In August, 1838, the family began its six years' residence in Philadelphia. The first two stopping-places were boarding-houses situated respectively at Twelfth Street above Arch, and on the northeast corner of Fourth and Arch; neither site now possessing the original house or any tablet. In September they moved to a small house—also gone and uncommemorated—in 16th Street near Locust. Late in 1839 or early in 1840 another move was made—to a brick house of three stories at the junction of Coates Street and Fairmount Drive, overlooking the Schuylkill. Though without a marker, this building is still standing unless very recently destroyed.

Some time before the end of May, 1842, Poe transferred his household to the cottage now restored and opened as a shrine. Here, amidst an environment then village-like and semi-rural, he performed considerable work of importance. When he left it in the spring of 1844, it was to go to New York once more for the final phase of his tragically brief career.

The first haven in Poe's second New York period was Morrison's boarding-house on the northwest corner of Greenwich and Albany Streets; an ancient brick building which had once been the Planter's Hotel, favoured by Southern visitors. This structure still exists in good condition as a restaurant; though there is no tablet to indicate Poe's connexion with it. The poet himself soon resigned the Greenwich Street quarters exclusively to his wife and aunt; taking a room of his own at 4 Ann Street, where all traces of his presence are swept away.

When summer came the family was reunited in the rustic Bloomingdale region then far north of the compact town; boarding at a farmhouse which stood on a knoll near what is now the busy intersection of Broadway and 84th Street. The house has of course long vanished, nor does any marker amidst the babel of shops and apartments attest the fact that "The Raven" was completed on that spot.

In November Poe left the country and took quarters in a Greenwich Village rooming-house at 15 Amity Street. Neither the house nor any marker exists at present. In May, 1845, a removal to 195 Broadway was effected. Here the whole family lived in extreme poverty, sharing a single back room in a run-down tenement long ago destroyed and forgotten. By midsummer a change for the better was made—a return to Amity Street, this time to No. 85, which like so many other Poe abodes has sunk without a trace. In the spring of 1846 the family returned briefly to the Bloomingdale farmhouse, moving later to another rural boarding-house at Turtle Bay, where the present 47th Street meets the East River. This was a large farmhouse, of which no vestige or memorial now survives.

The next and final move—near the end of May, 1846—was to the famous Fordham cottage. This small but shapely farmhouse, of an early nineteenth-century type common in the region, was in Poe's time situated amidst a countryside of the greatest possible beauty. Here, early in 1847, Poe's wife died; and it was still the family home when the poet himself expired in 1849. In time the expanding metropolis engulfed the district, and the cottage was hemmed in by new buildings. In 1913 the city purchased the edifice as a public museum and moved it northward about 450 feet to the crossing of the Grand Concourse and Kingsbridge Road, in a small park named for Poe. By 1921 its restoration was complete, and the surrounding landscape was made to resemble its original setting as closely as possible. It is furnished just as it was in Poe's time; three articles—a rocking-chair, a bedstead, and a mirror—being actually the ones he owned and used. Various relics of Poe are present, and there is a notable collection of different editions of his works.

Poe died in Baltimore October 7, 1849, and two days later was buried among his relatives there in a corner of Westminster Presbyterian Churchyard. A stone prepared by a cousin was accidentally destroyed before being set in place; so that for twenty-five years the poet's grave remained unmarked. In November, 1875, a marble monument was placed beside the grave by admirers; this forming the first of Poe's public shrines. Today the churchyard is in a decaying section, but within its walls dignity still reigns. The grave is adorned with green vines, and those who come to pay tribute feel that this last of the weary, wayworn wanderer's many homes is not the least appropriate.

In Richmond, which he always regarded as his real home, Poe's memory is perpetuated through a shrine unconnected with any actual dwelling of his, though not far from where his mother died. The nucleus of this shrine is a venerable stone house on Main Street near 19th, undoubtedly the oldest building in Richmond. Just east of it is a fireproof structure in the ancient manner, having built into it two architectural features—the staircase and the mantel of Poe's room—from the old Allan home at 14th Street and Tobacco Alley. Behind the house is an exquisite garden with a loggie built of bricks from the demolished magazine office where Poe worked. The shrine as a whole—which was dedicated in the early 1920's—contains one of the best Poe collections in existence.

The newly opened Philadelphia house is unique in being the only Poe dwelling on its original site to become a memorial museum. It is a pleasant brick cottage of three stories in the rear of a larger house at 530 North Seventh Street; evidently built early in the nineteenth century and perhaps originally forming servants' quarters. Around it is a small and tasteful garden, now restored as in Poe's time except that a great pear tree which he loved is missing. The front yard opens on an alley extending in from Seventh Street, with the dreary width of Spring Garden Street just beyond. It is hard to visualise the secluded, almost rustic neighbourhood that the poet knew.

Once in the garden or house, however, we step out of the present. The cottage has lasted well, and no structural alterations have ever been made. The small-paned windows, harmonious mantels, and panelled doors all bespeak the quiet grace of Georgian architecture. There are only two rooms to a floor, and all are furnished just as during Poe's tenancy; though only a desk and a chair are actual Poe relics. Eastward on the ground floor is the parlour with its attractive fireplace, pianoforte, sofa, and book-closet. Across a narrow hall is the kitchen, where the family also ate. On the second floor is Poe's bedroom, with a neat black slate mantel; while across the hall is a smaller study. Here can be found his desk, with appropriate books of the period along the top. On the low-ceiled third floor are the rooms of Poe's wife and aunt, with modest fireplaces and small casement windows. Everything is neatly kept—curtains, flowers, plants, pictures, china, and linen—just as it was in Poe's time.

In the large adjoining house, which has a connecting door, is a notable Poe collection. Here are copies of magazines containing the first appearance of most of the tales and poems, and other associative items too numerous to record.

Of the Poe houses still standing, none comes to life more vividly as a typical home than this unpretentious cottage. Its recent restoration and opening to the public, made possible through the generosity of the Philadelphia merchant Richard Gimbel, form an event at which devotees of Poe and of American letters cannot sufficiently rejoice. Though heretofore surprisingly little known, this shrine is likely to become, as time passes, a leading place of pilgrimage for those who revere genius and admire one of the greatest and unhappiest of its exemplars.

VII
AMATEUR JOURNALIST

The circumstances that led to Lovecraft's entry into amateur journalism in 1914, after six years of virtual hermitry, are now well-known: his letters to the editor of the *Argosy* criticizing the romantic stories of Fred Jackson; the development of a lively feud, conducted in both prose and verse, between those who sided with Lovecraft and those who opposed him; the invitation by Edward F. Daas to join the United Amateur Press Association (UAPA), and Lovecraft's alacrity in doing so. What is less understood is Lovecraft's abiding fascination with and devotion to the amateur cause: why, in spite of the bitter rivalries, pettinesses, and controversies in which he was involved, in spite of the utter and hopeless mediocrity of most of the writers in the amateur world, did Lovecraft never relinquish his association with amateur journalism even after the full-fledged commencement of his career as a professional weird fictionist? Many of the essays in this section provide an answer; and few passages in Lovecraft are more poignant than that in "What Amateurdom and I Have Done for Each Other" (1921), where he reveals the invaluable psychological aid amateurdom provided: "In 1914, when the kindly hand of amateurdom was first extended to me, I was as close to the state of vegetation as any animal well can be. . . . With the advent of the United I obtained a renewed will to live; a renewed sense of existence as other than a superfluous weight; and found a sphere in which I could feel that my efforts were not wholly futile. For the first time I could imagine that my clumsy gropings after art were a little more than faint cries lost in the unlistening void."

There is more to it than this, however. Let us consider another passage, this one from "For What Does the United Stand?" (1920): ". . . the United now aims at the development of its adherents in the direction of purely artistic literary perception and expression. . . . It aims at the revival of the uncommercial spirit; the real creative thought which modern conditions have done their worst to suppress and eradicate.

It seeks to banish mediocrity as a goal and standard; to place before its members the classical and the universal and to draw their minds from the commonplace to the beautiful." Are these not Lovecraft's own literary and political tenets? The repudiation of commercialism and the maintenance of classicism are the cornerstones of Lovecraft's own aesthetic; and it was the nucleus of these values that he claimed to find in amateur letters and strove to foster as best he could. Amateurdom also allowed Lovecraft to fall into his natural role of tutor: when, in "Amateur Journalism: Its Possible Needs and Betterment" (1920), he speaks of the need for the "raising of standards," he takes it as axiomatic that he would be one of those who—by reason of his clear eminence in this tiny realm—would lead the way both by example and by precept. There is, accordingly, no need to wonder why Lovecraft so readily accepted so many different official functions in the amateur world: President, Vice-President (in which capacity he wrote the promotional flyer *United Amateur Press Association: Exponent of Amateur Journalism*), Official Editor, and, perhaps most important, Chairman of the Department of Public Criticism, which supplied a forum for the expression of his views on the current state of amateur literature.

The Lovecraft we encounter in his earliest amateur years is not an attractive one. It is not so much the substance of his views—racism, political and literary conservatism, militarism—as the dogmatism, inflexibility, and self-righteous pomposity of their expression that is to be regretted. Amateurdom ultimately freed him from the worst of these traits, but the process was more gradual than we might like to believe: as late as "Lucubrations Lovecraftian" (1921) he is seen still cloaking himself with the aura of infallibility and striking out with astonishing viciousness at his opponents.

Perhaps what amazes us most of all about some of these essays is the seriousness with which Lovecraft takes the petty disputes arising in amateurdom. It is one thing to debate politics and literature with Charles D. Isaacson in "In a Major Key" or ethics with the editors of *The Symphony* in "Symphony and Stress"; but Lovecraft devotes just as much energy refuting Graeme Davis's attacks on the UAPA in "A Reply to *The Lingerer*" or arguing the role of amateur criticism in "Lucubrations Lovecraftian." One of Lovecraft's first goals upon entering amateur journalism was to attempt to reunite the UAPA after it split into two rival factions in 1912 ("A Matter of Uniteds" [1927] is a eulogy to this hopeless effort); and in many early essays on the subject Lovecraft seems to have regarded it as tantamount to a civil war. The UAPA essentially collapsed in the mid-1920s, and Lovecraft thereafter turned full attention to the other amateur organization, the National Amateur Press Association (NAPA), although he had been a member of it since 1917; and as late as 1936, in the broadside *Some Current Motives and Practices,* Lovecraft is attempting to heal rifts and fend off attacks on the NAPA's president, Hyman Bradofsky. Amateur journalism, like fandom, is never-changing, and the puerility of most of its members (a product not merely of youth but of the temperament of those who are a part of it) makes one realize why the word *amateur* has gained such overtones of immaturity, incompetence, and triviality. Lovecraft eventually became aware of all this, but his allegiance to both amateurdom and fandom remained.

But if *Some Current Motives and Practices* at least reveals a more mature Lovecraft in his ability to steer clear of savage retort and in his stalwart defense of a beleaguered associate (and Bradofsky, let us recall, was a Jew), then "Mrs. Miniter—Estimates and Recollections" (1934) shows Lovecraft at his most mellow. It is one of his finest efforts. In truth, the essay says as much about Lovecraft as about Miniter: we not merely learn valuable details of his travels to western Massachusetts and the bits of weird folklore Miniter supplied him, but we see a Lovecraft deeply touched by the loss of an old friend, a Lovecraft who has put aside the silly polemics of prior days to write a tribute that reveals his own humanity and sensitivity. If amateurdom had any role in effecting this monumental change—and clearly it did—then it deserves all the encomia Lovecraft gave to it in the course of a lifetime.

IN A MAJOR KEY

It was lately the good fortune of *The Conservative* to receive from The Blue Pencil Club a pamphlet entitled *In a Minor Key,* whose phenomenal excellence furnishes emphatic evidence that the old National still retains some members who would have done it credit even in its palmiest days. But great as may be the literary merit of the publication, its astonishing radicalism of thought cannot but arouse an overwhelming chorus of opposition from the saner elements in amateur journalism.

Charles D. Isaacson, the animating essence of the publication, is a character of remarkable quality. Descended from the race that produced a Mendelssohn, he is himself a musician of no ordinary talent, whilst as a man of literature he is worthy of comparison with his co-religionists Moses Mendez and Isaac D'Israeli. But the very spirituality which gives elevation to the Semitic mind partially unfits it for the consideration of tastes and trends in Aryan thought and writings; hence it is not surprising that he is a radical of the extremest sort.

From an ordinary man, the acclamation of degraded Walt Whitman as the "Greatest American Thinker" would come as an insult to the American mind, yet with Mr. Isaacson one may but respectfully dissent. Penetrating and forgetting the unspeakable grossness and wildness of the erratic bard, our author seizes on the one spark of truth within, and magnifies it till it becomes for him the whole Whitman. *The Conservative,* in speaking for the sounder faction of American taste, is impelled to give here his own lines on Whitman, written several years ago as part of an essay on the modern poets:

> Behold great *Whitman,* whose licentious line
> Delights the rake, and warms the souls of swine;
> Whose fever'd fancy shuns the measur'd pace,
> And copies Ovid's filth without his grace.

In his rough brain a genius might have grown,
Had he not sought to play the brute alone;
But void of shame, he let his wit run wild,
And liv'd and wrote as Adam's bestial child.
Averse to culture, strange to humankind,
He never knew the pleasures of the mind.
Scorning the pure, the delicate, the clean,
His joys were sordid, and his morals mean.
Thro' his gross thoughts a native vigour ran,
From which he deem'd himself the perfect man:
But want of decency his rank decreas'd,
And sunk him to the level of the beast.
Would that his Muse had dy'd before her birth,
Nor spread such foul corruption o'er the earth.

Mr. Isaacson's views on racial prejudice, as outlined in his *Minor Key*, are too subjective to be impartial. He has perhaps resented the more or less open aversion to the children of Israel which has ever pervaded Christendom; yet a man of his perspicuity should be able to distinguish this illiberal feeling, a religious and social animosity of one white race toward another white and equally intellectual race, from the natural and scientifically just sentiment which keeps the African black from contaminating the Caucasian population of the United States. The negro is fundamentally the biological inferior of all White and even Mongolian races, and the Northern people must occasionally be reminded of the danger which they incur in admitting him too freely to the privileges of society and government.

Mr. Isaacson's protest is directed specifically against a widely advertised motion picture, *The Birth of a Nation,* which is said to furnish a remarkable insight into the methods of the Ku-Klux-Klan, that noble but much maligned band of Southerners who saved half of our country from destruction at the close of the Civil War. *The Conservative* has not yet witnessed the picture in question, but he has seen both in literary and dramatic form *The Clansman,* that stirring, though crude and melodramatic story by Rev. Thomas Dixon, Jr., on which *The Birth of a Nation* is based, and has likewise made a close historical study of the Ku-Klux-Klan, finding as a result of his research nothing but Honour, Chivalry, and Patriotism in the activities of the Invisible Empire. The Klan merely did for the people what the law refused to do, removing the ballot from unfit hands and restoring to the victims of political vindictiveness their natural rights. The alleged lawbreaking of the Klan was committed only by irresponsible miscreants who, after the dissolution of the Order by its Grand Wizard, Gen. Nathan Bedford Forrest, used its weird masks and terrifying costumes to veil their unorganised villainies.

Race prejudice is a gift of Nature, intended to preserve in purity the various divisions of mankind which the ages have evolved. In comparing this essential instinct of man with political, religious, and national prejudices, Mr. Isaacson commits a serious error of logic.

The Conservative dislikes strong language, but he feels that he is not exceeding the bounds of propriety in asserting that the publication of the article entitled "The Greater Courage" is a crime which in a native American of Aryan blood would be deserving of severe legal punishment. This appeal to the people to refuse military service when summoned to their flag is an outrageous attack on the lofty principles of patriotism which have turned this country from a savage wilderness to a mighty band of states; a slur on the honour of our countrymen, who from the time of King Philip's War to the present have been willing to sacrifice their lives for the preservation of their families, their nation, and their institutions. Mr. Isaacson, however, must be excused for his words, since some of his phrases shew quite clearly that he is only following the common anarchical fallacy, believing that wars are forced upon the masses by tyrannical rulers. This belief, extremely popular a few months ago, has received a rude blow through the acts of the Italian people in forcing their reluctant government to join the Allies. The socialistic delusion becomes ridiculous when its precepts are thus boldly reversed by facts. Bryan is out of the way at last, and in spite of Mr. Isaacson and his hyphenated fellow-pacifists, the real American people, the descendants of Virginian and New England Christian Protestant colonists, will remain ever faithful to the Stars and Stripes, even though forced to meet enemies at home as well as abroad.

THE DIGNITY OF JOURNALISM

It is a particular weakness of the modern American press, that it seems unable to use advantageously the language of the nation. While our speech is probably the most forceful and expressive of modern tongues, combining as it does the vigour of the Teutonic with the precision of the Latin elements, the journalistic fraternity have apparently lost completely the art of employing its admirable words and phrases in their compositions. In lieu of correct English, these careless scribes have found it necessary to resort to the jargon of the street, the prize ring, and the bar room, whence they have imported a select assortment of idioms, generically known as "slang"; which, construed in sentences of rustic and plebeian mould, they are endeavouring to foist upon us as a language.

That corrupt forms of speech have existed in all ages and in all countries we cannot doubt. Plautus gives us hints of the idiomatic vagaries of the Roman republic, whilst Petronius Arbiter shews effectively the vulgar patois of imperial Rome. Indeed, the extinction of culture by the Gothic invaders ultimately brought Latin slang to the surface, creating the modern Romance languages. But the plight of America is very different. Here we find no such contempt for the common tongue as existed among the scholars and writers of the Roman period; instead, the pernicious vulgarisms of the rabble are creeping upward into the speech of the most cultured, where they are received with a dangerously increasing favour.

For the use of this barbaric caricature of English, two principal theories have been advanced; first, that it is more conducive to forcible expression and ready comprehension than is correct language; and second, that it lends to reading and discourse an animation otherwise unattainable.

The reason first assigned is, if true, a shameful confession of clownishness on our part. Our language is above all others direct and clear, with the straightforwardness of its Teutonic skeleton and the exactness of its Latin vocabulary. No person in the least familiar with the English classics can justly complain that the language wants force and perspicuity. Nor is the use and appreciation of this excellence necessarily the result of long study. The average man's stock of words includes all that are needed for pure and emphatic expression, were the possessor but free from contaminating familiarity with corrupt diction. There is nothing which cannot be better said or written in good English than in slang, save among the lowest and most vicious classes, which latter scarcely constitute the general reading public.

The idea that slang-infested literature is more readable and pleasing than that which conforms to refined taste is nearly parallel to that of the Italian peasant immigrant, who fondly considers his soiled but flaming kerchief and other greasy but gaudy apparel far more beautiful than the spotless white linen and plain, neat suit of the American for whom he works. While good English may in unskilful hands sometimes become monotonous, this defect cannot justify the introduction of a dialect gathered from thieves, ploughboys, and chimney sweeps. The reader, if disgusted with a dull author's use of the language, should turn to the masters of literature, with whose grace, animation, and general excellence no fault can be found. If any user of slang can excel in fluent ease the sentences of an Addison or a Steele, he does well indeed. As in the matter of clearness, this seeming ease of slang is merely a sign of poor culture. If the public could abandon its indolence long enough to appreciate the artistic possibilities of well-used English, slang would retreat to the slums and low dens whence first it emanated.

The pernicious platitude, 'that the slang of today is the classic tongue of tomorrow', is best refuted by a perusal of any one of the numerous dictionaries of slang and Americanisms. Therein will be found thousands of colloquial words and phrases, which, though on the tip of the vulgar tongue of yesterday, are today absolutely unintelligible. Many of the old terms and constructions which have been retained are at this moment no nearer adoption than when in their infancy; those which have actually entered the language are few indeed as compared with the whole.

In the United Amateur Press Association the effects of colloquial composition are beheld at their worst. Three-quarters of our writers possess styles so contaminated with deliberate violations of journalistic dignity, that their works send a shudder through the sensitive system. This tendency extends not alone through the domain of lighter literature, but reaches to the serious editorial and even to the weighty official report.

That something must be done to correct the increasing evil is obvious. Amateur authors and editors guilty of consciously bad English must be brought to a realisation of their dereliction, and to an understanding of the vulgar example which they are setting for younger recruits. In *The Olympian* may be found a model of pure English which ought to be followed with the greatest assiduity. This magazine, apart from its own literary worth, is valuable as a perpetual refutation of the fallacy that amateur papers cannot be made interesting without slang. Not so long as Edward Cole remains in the field of amateur journalism have we the right to plead the necessity, or the expediency, of debasing the dignity of our art.

SYMPHONY AND STRESS

A recent article in *The Symphony*, entitled "Buzzards", condemns the man of "negative" characteristics, incidentally denouncing the critic and the reformer. The psychological characteristics thus revealed in the anonymous author are of even greater interest than the unusual theories displayed. *The Symphony* is the product of a small circle of cultured ladies, most of them United members, exempt from contact with the world and its sordidness. They agree with the utterance of the author, that in promoting virtue it is best for each person to make himself virtuous, letting his brothers, under the stimulus of mutual encouragement and inspiration, do likewise, rather than to interfere with the habits of others from the outside. As they say, "it's better to begin on the inside and work out!" But have the Family of Symphonics ever pondered on the condition of their inferiors; the sluggish-brained, morally weak lower classes of drunkards and degenerates? Symphonics may undoubtedly keep themselves on a high plane through their exalted system of Positive Ideals, but are they satisfied to look down upon a population steeped in vice, and lacking the intellect to raise itself? Before condemning the reformer, they might well look upon the clean, virile personality of Andrew Francis Lockhart of Milbank, South Dakota, who has succeeded in driving the evils of Rum from his native city. This man has Positive Ideals, ideals as positive in their righteousness as those of any Symphonic, but he has the negative element as well. He not only preaches and practices virtue; he is actively engaged in its extension through the destruction of vice. Threats of death and murderous assaults upon his person are as nothing to him. He sees the duty, and follows it as best he understands it. He has made South Dakota a better state wherein to live; indeed, where could pure-minded idealists live in security, were there not a few vigorous, negative souls who dare to attack corruption and clear the way for decency? No, Andrew Francis Lockhart is a reformer, but he is not a "buzzard".

The Symphony is one of the most beautiful of all the semi-professional papers issued by United members. Each issue is perused with the keenest interest and delight by *The Conservative,* who feels strongly its uplifting influence, and appreciates the uniformly delicate artistry of its tone. But *The Conservative* also reads another semi-professional journal issued by a United member; Lockhart's *Chain Lightning.* Here all is different. We read not of happy souls re-purified through wholesome thought; but of drugged, soulless bodies depraved through drink and debauchery, of law bought by depraved criminals, of vice made a municipal institution, of all that fills the mind with aversion and disgust. No elaborate, musical sentences here delight the ear; instead, a fierce, tense colloquialism drives home the ugly truths which we are reluctant to hear, but which, without hearing, we may never comprehend or remedy. Most of these horrors are utterly beyond the realisation of the sheltered Symphonics, many of them are beyond the realisation of the secluded *Conservative;* but that they exist, the burning indignation and sincerity of Mr. Lockhart forbid us to doubt. This is a world of wonderful good and unspeakable evil. Let the Family of Symphonics extend throughout the upper realm which gave it birth, but let it forbear too hastily to frown on those noble reforming souls who are willing to imperil their lives, sacrifice their illusions, abandon their happiness, and walk among the vicious and the lowly, even as did one Man nineteen hundred years ago.

UNITED AMATEUR PRESS ASSOCIATION: EXPONENT OF AMATEUR JOURNALISM

ITS OBJECT

The desire to write for publication is one which inheres strongly in every human breast. From the proficient college graduate, storming the gates of the high-grade literary magazines, to the raw schoolboy, vainly endeavouring to place his first crude compositions in the local newspapers, the whole intelligent public are today seeking expression through the printed page, and yearning to behold their thoughts and ideals permanently crystallised in the magic medium of type. But while a few persons of exceptional talent manage eventually to gain a foothold in the professional world of letters, rising to celebrity through the wide diffusion of their art, ideals, or opinions; the vast majority, unless aided in their education by certain especial advantages, are doomed to confine their expression to the necessarily restricted sphere of ordinary conversation. To supply those especial educational advantages which may enable the general public to achieve the distinction of print, and which may prevent the talented but unknown author from remaining forever in obscurity, has risen that largest and foremost of societies for literary education—*The United Amateur Press Association.*

ITS ORIGIN

Amateur journalism, or the composition and circulation of small, privately printed magazines, is an instructive diversion which has existed in the United States for over half a century. In the decade of 1866–1876 this practice first became an organised institution; a short-lived society of amateur journalists, including the now famous publisher, Charles Scribner, having existed from 1869 to 1874. In 1876 a more lasting society was formed, which exists to this day as an exponent of light dilettantism. Not until 1895, however, was amateur journalism established as a serious branch of educational endeavour. On September 2nd of that year, Mr. William H. Greenfield, a gifted professional author, of Philadelphia, founded *The United Amateur Press Association*, which has grown to be the leader of its kind, and the representative of amateur journalism in its best phases throughout the English-speaking world.

ITS NATURE

In many respects the word "amateur" fails to do full credit to amateur journalism and the association which best represents it. To some minds the term conveys an idea of crudity and immaturity, yet the *United* can boast of members and publications whose polish and scholarship are well-nigh impeccable. In considering the adjective "amateur" as applied to the press association, we must adhere to the more basic interpretation, regarding the word as indicating the non-mercenary nature of the membership. Our amateurs write purely for love of their art, without the stultifying influence of commercialism. Many of them are prominent professional authors in the outside world, but their professionalism never creeps into their association work. The atmosphere is wholly fraternal, and courtesy takes the place of currency.

The real essential of amateur journalism and *The United Amateur Press Association* is the amateur paper or magazine, which somewhat resembles the average high-school or college publication. These journals, varying greatly in size and character, are issued by various members at their own expense; and contain, besides the literary work of their several editors or publishers, contributions from all the many members who do not publish papers of their own. Their columns are open to every person in the association, and it may be said with justice that no one will find it impossible to secure the publication of any literary composition of reasonable brevity. The papers thus published are sent free to all our many members, who constitute a select and highly appreciative reading public. Since each member receives the published work of every other member, many active and brilliant minds are brought into close contact, and questions of every sort—literary, historical, and scientific—are debated both in the press and in personal correspondence. The correspondence of members is one of the most valuable features of the *United*, for through this medium a great intellectual stimulus, friendly and informal in nature, is afforded. Congenial members are in this way brought together in a lettered companionship, which often grows into life-long friendship; while persons of opposed ideas may mutually gain much breadth of mind by hearing the other side of their respective opinions discussed in a genial manner. In short, the *United* offers an exceptionally well-proportioned mixture of instruction and fraternal cheer. There are no limits of age, sex, education, position, or locality in this most complete of democracies. Boys and girls of twelve and men and women of sixty, parents and their sons and daughters, college professors and grammar-school pupils, aristocrats and intelligent labourers, Easterners and Westerners, are here given equal advantages; those of greater education helping their cruder brethren until the common fund of culture is as nearly level as it can be in any human organisation. Members are classified according to age; "A" meaning under sixteen, "B" from 16 to 21, and "C" over 21. The advantages offered to those of limited acquirements are immense; many persons having gained practically all their literary polish through membership in the *United.* A much cherished goal is professional authorship or editorship, and numerous indeed are the *United* members who have now become recognised authors, poets, editors, and publishers. True, though trite, is the saying that amateur journalism is an actual training school for professional journalism.

ITS PUBLISHING ACTIVITIES

Members of the *United* may or may not publish little papers of their own. This is a matter of choice, for there are always enough journals to print the work of the non-publishing members. Youths who possess printing-presses will find in publishing an immense but inexpensive pleasure, whilst other publishers may have their printing done at very reasonable rates by those who do own presses. The favourite size for amateur papers is 5 x 7 inches, which can be printed at 55 or 60 cents per page, each page containing about 250 words. Thus a four-page issue containing 1000 words can be published for less than $2.50, if arrangements are made, as is often the case, for its free mailing with any other paper. Certain of the more pretentious journals affect the 7 × 10 size, which costs about $1.60 for each page of 700 words. These figures allow for 250 copies, the most usual number to be mailed. Mr. E. E. Ericson of Elroy, Wisconsin, is our Official Printer, and his work is all that the most fastidious could demand. Other printers may be found amongst the young men who print their own papers. In many cases they can quote very satisfactory prices. Two or more members may issue a paper coöperatively, the individual expense then being very slight.

ITS CONTRIBUTED LITERATURE

The *United* welcomes all literary contributions—poems, stories, and essays—which the various members may submit. However, contribution is by no means compulsory; and in case a member finds himself too busy for activity, he may merely enjoy the free papers which reach him, without taxing himself with literary labour. For those anxious to contribute, every facility is provided. In some cases negotiations are made directly between publisher and contributor, but the majority are accommodated by the two Manuscript Bureaux, Eastern and Western, which receive contributions in any quantity from the non-publishing members, and are drawn upon for material by those who issue papers. These bureaux practically guarantee on the one hand to find a place for each member's manuscript, and on the other hand to keep each publisher well supplied with matter for his journal.

ITS CRITICAL DEPARTMENTS

The two critical departments of the *United* are at present the most substantial of the various educational advantages. The Department of Private Criticism is composed exclusively of highly cultured members, usually professors or teachers of English, who practically mould the taste of the whole association; receiving and revising before publication the work of all who choose to submit it to them. The service furnished by this department is in every way equal to that for which professional critical bureaux charge about two dollars. Manuscripts are carefully corrected and criticised in every detail, and authors are given comprehensive advice designed to elevate their taste, style, and grammar. Many a crude but naturally gifted writer has been developed to polished fluency and set on the road to professional authorship through the *United*'s Department of Private Criticism.

The Department of Public Criticism reviews thoroughly and impartially the various printed papers and their contents, offering precepts and suggestions for improvement. Its reports are printed in the official organ of the association, and serve as a record of our literary achievement.

ITS LITERARY AWARDS

To encourage excellence amongst the members of the *United*, annual honours or "laureateships" are awarded the authors of the best poems, stories, essays, or editorials. Participation in these competitions is not compulsory, since they apply only to pieces which have been especially "entered for laureateship". The entries are judged not by the members of the association, but by highly distinguished litterateurs of the professional world, selected particularly for the occasion. Our latest innovation is a laureateship for the best home-printed paper, which will excite keen rivalry among our younger members, and bring out some careful specimens of the typographical art. Besides the laureateships there are other honours and prizes awarded by individual publishers within the *United;* many of the amateur journals offering excellent books for the best stories, reviews, or reports submitted to them.

ITS OFFICIAL ORGAN

The association, as a whole, publishes a voluminous 7 x 10 monthly magazine called *The United Amateur,* which serves as the official organ. In this magazine may be found the complete revised list of members, the reports of officers and committees, the ample reviews issued by the Department of Public Criticism, a selection of the best contemporary amateur literature, together with the latest news of amateur journalists and their local clubs from all over the Anglo-Saxon world. *The United Amateur* is published by an annually elected Official Editor, and printed by the Official Publisher. It is sent free to all members of the association.

ITS GOVERNMENT

The United Amateur Press Association is governed by a board of officers elected by popular vote. The elections take place at the annual conventions, where amateurs from all sections meet and fraternise. Those who attend vote in person, whilst all others send in proxy ballots. There is much friendly rivalry between cities concerning the selection of the convention seat each year. The principal elective offices of the United are the President, two Vice Presidents, the Treasurer, the Official Editor, and the three members of the Board of Directors. There are also an Historian, a Laureate Recorder, and two Manuscript Managers. Appointed by the President are the members of the two Departments of Criticism, the Supervisor of Amendments, the Official Publisher, and the Secretary of the association. All save Secretary and Official Publisher serve without remuneration. The basic law of the *United* comprises an excellent Constitution and By-Laws.

ITS LOCAL CLUBS

The *United* encourages the formation of local literary or press clubs in cities or towns containing several members. These clubs generally publish papers, and hold meetings wherein the pleasures of literature are enlivened by those of the society. The most desirable form of club activity is that in which a high-school instructor forms a literary society of the more enthusiastic members of his class.

ITS PLACE IN EDUCATION

During the past two years, as it has approached and passed its twentieth birthday, the *United* has been endeavouring more strongly than ever to find and occupy its true place amongst the many and varied phases of education. That it discharges an unique function in literary culture is certain, and its members have of late been trying very actively to establish and define its relation to the high-school and the university. Mr. Maurice Winter Moe, Instructor of English at the Appleton High School, Appleton, Wisconsin, and one of our very ablest members, took the first decisive step by organising his pupils into an amateur press club, using the *United* to supplement his regular classroom work. The scholars were delighted, and many have acquired a love of good literature which will never leave them. Three or four, in particular, have become prominent in the affairs of the *United.* After demonstrating the success of his innovation, Mr. Moe described it in *The English Journal;* his article arousing much interest in educational circles, and being widely reprinted by other papers. In November, 1914, Mr. Moe addressed an assemblage of English teachers in Chicago, and there created so much enthusiasm for the *United,* that scores of instructors have subsequently joined our ranks, many of them forming school clubs on the model of the original club at Appleton. Here, then, is one definite destiny for our association; to assist the teaching of advanced English in the high-school. We are especially eager for high-school material, teachers and pupils alike.

But there still remain a numerous class, who, though not connected with school or college, have none the less sincere literary aspirations. At present they are benefited immensely through mental contact with our more polished members, yet for the future we plan still greater aids for their development, by the creation of a systematic "Department of Instruction", which will, if successfully established, amount practically to a free correspondence school, and an "Authors' Placing Bureau", which will help amateurs in entering the professional field. Our prime endeavour is at present to secure members of high mental and scholastic quality, in order that the *United* may be strengthened for its increasing responsibility. Professors, teachers, clergymen, and authors have already responded in gratifying numbers to our wholly altruistic plea for their presence among us. The reason for the *United*'s success as an educational factor seems to lie principally in the splendid loyalty and enthusiasm which all the members somehow acquire upon joining. Every individual is alert for the welfare of the association, and its activities form the subject of many of the current essays and editorials. The ceaseless writing in which most of the members indulge, is in itself an aid to fluency, while the mutual examples and criticisms help instill further the pleasantly unconscious acquisition of a good literary style. When regular courses of instruction shall have been superimposed upon these things, the association can indeed afford to claim a place of honour in the world of education.

ITS ENTRANCE CONDITIONS

The only requirement for admission to the *United* is earnest literary aspiration. Any member will furnish the candidate for admission with an application blank, signed in recommendation. This application, filled out and forwarded to the Secretary of the association with the sum of fifty cents as dues for the first year, and accompanied by a "credential", or sample of the candidate's original literary work, will be acted upon with due consideration by the proper official. No candidate of real sincerity will be denied admittance, and the applicant will generally be soon rewarded by his certificate of membership, signed by the President and Secretary. Papers, letters, and postal cards of welcome will almost immediately pour in upon him, and he will in due time behold his credential in print. (Unless it be something already printed.) Once a member, his dues will be one dollar yearly; and if he should ever leave the *United*, later desiring to join again, his reinstatement fee will be one dollar.

ITS REPRESENTATIVES

The United Amateur Press Association is anything but local in its personnel. Its active American membership extends from Boston to Los Angeles, and from Milwaukee to Tampa; thus bringing all sections in contact, and representing every phase of American thought. Its English membership extends as far north as Newcastle-on-Tyne. Typical papers are published in England, California, Kansas, Wisconsin, Ohio, Illinois, Alabama, Mississippi, North Carolina, District of Columbia, New York, and Rhode Island.

In writing for entrance blanks or for future information concerning the *United*, the applicant may address any one of the following officers, who will gladly give details, and samples of amateur papers:

Leo Fritter, President, 503 Central National Bank Bldg., Columbus, Ohio; H. P. Lovecraft, Vice President, 598 Angell St., Providence, R.I.; Mrs. J. W. Renshaw, Second Vice President, Coffeeville, Miss.; William J. Dowdell, Secretary, 2428 East 66th St., Cleveland, Ohio; or Edward F. Daas, Official Editor, 1717 Cherry St., Milwaukee, Wis. Professional authors interested in our work are recommended to communicate with the Second Vice President, while English teachers may derive expert information from Maurice W. Moe, 658 Atlantic St., Appleton, Wis. Youths who possess printing-presses are referred to the Secretary, who is himself a young typographer.

ITS PROVINCE SUMMARISED

If you are a student of elementary English desirous of attaining literary polish in an enjoyable manner,

If you are an ordinary citizen, burning with the ambition to become an author,

If you are a solitary individual wishing for a better chance to express yourself,

If you own a printing-press and would like to learn how to issue a high-grade paper,

If you are a mature person eager to make up for a youthful lack of culture,

If you are a professor or teacher seeking a new method of interesting your English class, or

If you are an author or person of ripe scholarship, anxious to aid your cruder brothers on their way, then,

YOU ARE CORDIALLY INVITED TO BECOME A MEMBER OF THE UNITED AMATEUR PRESS ASSOCIATION.

A REPLY TO *THE LINGERER*

Editor *Tryout:*

It was with no little interest that I perused the recent attack on the United Amateur Press Association made by the Rev. Graeme Davis in his excellent publication *The Lingerer.* Since the culture and intellectual quality of Mr. Davis forbid one to charge him with the trivial and illiberal prejudices of association politics, it is an inevitable deduction that his anti-United attitude arises from lack of recent information concerning the two major societies and their places in the amateur world today.

It is entirely true that much puerility and much immaturity does exist within the United. The discovery of this condition requires no considerable acumen, nor does its mention in an United paper constitute either a treasonable revelation or a naive admission. The *Conservative* editorial from which Mr. Davis derives such unholy glee was a frank criticism of a remediable fault; and was directed against a small clique, also active in the National, whose maleficent energy seems now quite spent. For evidence of a puerility that is permanent or an immaturity that is immutable, our critic should look elsewhere; nor should he close his eyes to his own association whilst sifting out the flaws of another.

To speak brutally and impartially, all amateurdom is more or less homogeneously tinctured with a certain delicious callowness. To confound this callowness with downright density would be most unjust, for it is merely a healthy adolescence which results from the continual infusion of young blood. But why exclude the United from this charitable interpretation? Is the ancient and honourable lineage of the National a fetish so potent that what passes for budding genius within its fold, must in the United be branded with alliterative ingenuity as "permanent puerility and immutable immaturity"? I would admonish Mr. Davis that it ill becomes the pot to call the kettle black.

When Mr. Davis essays a direct comparison between the United and the National, he exhibits most clearly the effects of his long absence from amateurdom. Proud of the justly famous personages in the old association, he is entirely ignorant of the new and commanding figures in the literary life of the United; men and women of ideals and scholarship who have appeared above the horizon during his seven years of retirement.

Perhaps it is the dormant state of the amateur press which has kept many of these gifted recruits from his notice, but he at least owes it to the United to withhold invidious comparisons before acquainting himself with our present personnel.

To refute Mr. Davis' none too generous suggestion that my own loyalty to the United is caused by a conceited desire to stand out against a background even more mediocre than myself, I need only mention the names of a score of fellow members, to each of whom I can justly and gladly concede the palm of vastly superior genius, scholarship, and expression. Were I desirous of shining at the expense of youth and crudity, I am sure that my search for suitable "foils" would lead me through pastures much closer to Mr. Davis than the United.

If in the preceding paragraphs I have seemed to bear criticism with less than Christian meekness and acquiescence, it is because of the peculiarly unprovoked and uncalled-for nature of Mr. Davis' attack on the United. It would perhaps have been more seemly and logical to explain to *The Lingerer* some of the ceaseless and laborious enterprises undertaken by the United in the ill-rewarded cause of serious educational service; enterprises whose very spirit and essence are unknown to the basically dilettante mind of the typical Nationalite; but I feel that he should have known of these before seizing upon an exceptional case of criticism as grounds for a polite sneer. The standards of a decade ago are no longer to be applied to amateurdom, for the United has left the beaten path and is pioneering in fields to which the National does not aspire. Each association has now its separate niche, and the need for mutual rivalry, jealousy, and hostility is past.

Rev. Graeme Davis is deservedly classed as one of the elect in our miniature world. His *Lingerer* is one of the few papers of which no recipient will ever throw away a copy. Must he not, considering the intellectual height from which he views the panorama of amateurdom, soon grasp the scene as a whole, without the prejudices common to less disciplined mentalities?

LES MOUCHES FANTASTIQUES

Extreme literary radicalism is always a rather amusing thing, involving as it does a grotesque display of egotism and affectation. Added to this comic quality, however, there is a distinct pathos which arises from reflection on the amount of real suffering which the radical must, if serious, endure through his alienation from the majority.

Both of these aspects lately impressed *The Conservative* with much force, as he glanced over a new and most extraordinary amateur publication entitled *Les Mouches Fantastiques*, published by Miss Elsie Alice Gidlow and Mr. Roswell George Mills of Montreal. Miss Gidlow and Mr. Mills are sincere and solemn super-aesthetes, fired with the worthy ambition of elevating dense and callous mankind to their own exalted spiritual plane, and as such present vast possibilities to the humourist; but it is also possible to view their efforts in another light, and to lament the imperfect artistic vision which imparts to their utterances so outré an atmosphere.

The Gidlow-Mills creed, so far as may be discovered from their writings, is that Life is a compulsory quest of beauty and emotional excitement; these goals being so important that man must discard everything else in pursuing them. Particularly, we fancy, must he discard his sense of humour and proportion. The sceptical bulk of humanity, who cannot or do not enter upon this feverish quest, are (as Miss Gidlow tactfully tells us) "unnecessary".

And of what do these great objects of Life, as revealed in the pages of *Les Mouches*, consist? The reader may, up to date, unearth nothing save a concentrated series of more or less primitive and wholly unintellectual sense-impressions; instinct, form, colour, odour, and the like, grouped in all the artistic chaos characteristic of the late Oscar Wilde of none too fragrant memory. Much of this matter is, as might be expected, in execrable taste. Now is this Life? Is human aspiration indeed to be circumscribed by the walls of some garishly bejewelled temple of the Dionaean Eros; its air oppressive with the exotic fumes of strange incense, and its altar lit with weirdly coloured radiance from mystical braziers? Must we forever shut ourselves in such an artificial shrine, away from the pure light of sun and stars, and the natural currents of normal existence?

It seems to *The Conservative* that Miss Gidlow and Mr. Mills, instead of being divinely endowed seers in sole possession of all Life's truths, are a pair of rather youthful persons suffering from a sadly distorted philosophical perspective. Instead of seeing Life in its entirety, they see but one tiny phase, which they mistake for the whole. What worlds of beauty–pure Uranian beauty–are utterly denied them on account of their bondage to the lower regions of the senses! It is almost pitiful to hear superficial allusions to "Truth" from the lips of those whose eyes are sealed to the Intellectual Absolute; who know not the upper altitudes of pure thought, in which empirical forms and material aspects are as nothing.

The editors of *Les Mouches* complain very bitterly of the inartistic quality of amateur journalism; a complaint half just and half otherwise. The very nature of our institution necessitates a modicum of crudity, but if Miss Gidlow and Mr. Mills were more analytical, they could see beauty in much which appears ugly to their rather astigmatic vision.

FOR WHAT DOES THE UNITED STAND?

It is easy to comply in 500 words with a request for an article on what the United represents. An amateur journalistic association is generally too democratic to have any one object for long; it is rather a battleground between the proponents of ideas. I think, however, that since the dawn of the Hoffman administration, when the best elements were automatically sifted out through the secession of most of the confirmed politicians, we have been gradually acquiring a policy and a tradition which will endure. The printing-press, political, and frivolous phases have been passed through; and our aspirations seem to be crystallising into a form more worthy than any of our past aspirations.

Judging from the majority of our truly active members, the United now aims at the development of its adherents in the direction of purely artistic literary perception and expression; to be effected by the encouragement of writing, the giving of constructive criticism, and the cultivation of correspondence friendships among scholars and aspirants capable of stimulating and aiding one another's efforts. It aims at the revival of the uncommercial spirit; the real creative thought which modern conditions have done their worst to suppress and eradicate. It seeks to banish mediocrity as a goal and standard; to place before its members the classical and the universal and to draw their minds from the commonplace to the beautiful.

The United aims to assist those whom other forms of literary influence cannot reach. The non-university man, the dwellers in distant places, the recluse, the invalid, the very young, the elderly; all these are included within our scope. And beside our novices stand persons of mature cultivation and experience, ready to assist for the sheer joy of assisting. In no other society does wealth or previous learning count for so little. Merit and aspiration form the only criteria we apply to our members, nor has poverty or primitive crudity ever retarded the steady progress of any determined aspirant among us. We ask only that the goal be high; that the souls of our band be seeking the antique legacy of verdant Helicon.

Practically, we are aware of many obstacles; yet we think we are in the main fulfilling our functions. Naturally, we do not expect to make a Shelley or Swinburne of every rhymer who joins us, or a Poe or Dunsany of every teller of tales; but if we enable these persons to appreciate Shelley and Swinburne and Poe and Dunsany, and teach them how to shed their dominant faults and use words correctly and expressively, we cannot call ourselves unsuccessful. Only genius can lead to the heights; it is our province merely to point the way and assist on the gentler, lower slopes.

The United, then, stands for education in the eternal truths of literary art, and for personal aid in the realisation of its members' literary potentialities. It is an university, stripped of every artificiality and conventionality, and thrown open to all without distinction. Here may every man shine according to his genius, and here may the small as well as the great writer know the bliss of appreciation and the glory of recognised achievement.

AMATEUR JOURNALISM: ITS POSSIBLE NEEDS AND BETTERMENT

It is with great humility that I respond to an invitation to speak on Amateur Journalism: Its Possible Needs and Betterment, to an audience most of whose members are far better equipped to speak than am I. In the presence of our cause's most honoured and able veterans, the remarks of one active for only six years must necessarily lack authority. However, in case the opinions of a relative novice may possess some slight spark of value, I will not decline the proffered opportunity for discussion.

Had I devised the title of this address myself, I should have introduced a transposition, saying "amateurdom's *needs* and *possible betterment*". For our needs are certainties, while it is our betterment which contains the element of doubt. That we are imperfect, we know well; that we can find a mode of improvement, is problematical in view of the long existence of our hobby at practically the same level. There is less progress in the world than idealists affect to believe. It is, nevertheless, our duty to give constant attention to the state of amateur journalism; that its best traditions may not be obliterated, nor its literary quality impaired by carelessness or the dominance of unworthy political groups. Symposia like the present gathering are invaluable in their tendency to renew interest and permit of an exchange of views and plans for resisting decadence.

The present needs—or I might say the perpetual needs—of amateurdom are naturally divisible into two classes; qualitative and quantitative. The first class may be exemplified by many conspicuous phenomena, such as crude, flamboyant, and inartistic papers, papers of lax literary standards, and official criticism so puerile that its appearance in an official organ is almost an insult to amateur letters. All these qualitative evils are traceable to the lack of some centralised authority capable of exerting a kindly, reliable, and more or less invisible guidance in matters aesthetic and artistic. Such an authority must obviously be unofficial, since official recognition of literary capability is impossible, and should preferably consist of a small group of members representing various phases and ideals. It can never be created by any formal process, but must be born spontaneously out of the aspiration of amateurs in general; existing through tradition and tacit recognition by the majority. The important thing is to have such a group enthroned apart from the political processes of the various associations, like the learned academies of the Latin countries, surviving all changes of official boards and exerting its sway in a spirit of coöperation rather than of dictatorship. Lest I seem to deal in vague abstractions, let me suggest how such an academic authority might be composed, and how it might discharge its functions. Its beginning must be purely voluntary—an offer of services on the part of those qualified to render them. Certain qualified members must undertake the entirely new burden of offering help to both writers and publishers. They must approach crude authors whose work shews promise, and crude publishers whose papers appear to possess the spark of aspiration; offering a revision and censorship which shall ensure the publication of the articles or journals in question, free from all the main errors in taste and technique. That a majority of the crude authors and publishers will accept this aid has already been proved by concrete instances; so we can state with safety that if literary leaders can be found, a fairly high standard can be established at once, and maintained in a majority of the current amateur publications. In brief, it is possible to create a standard of correct writing and editing by forming a voluntary board of censorship and revising practically all the products of the cruder amateurs. The good effects of such a standard are not far to seek. When a majority of the amateur journals shew a proper degree of polish, whether natural or artificial, writers and editors will no longer be content with crudeness. The pitiful self-complacency of the inveterate dunce will necessarily vanish, so that his kind will be forced either to improve or to quit organised amateurdom; whilst the worthy ambition of the real aspirant will be encouraged by the aid extended, and the recipients of revision and censorship will learn correctness from their unofficial preceptors. One consequence of this policy would be the raising of standards on the part of careless editors. Many good papers are at present hampered by certain crude contributions which appear interspersed among the meritorious matter. These contributions should be either revised or eliminated, for they furnish a discouraging setting for the better work; and they would be attended to if amateurdom demanded it. The paramount object should be to outlaw the imperfect. Not to discourage the aspirant in his first stages, but to give nothing but the best the stamp of final approval; to fix the goal unalterably high. It is the creation of a sentiment which we need; a sentiment of endeavour which shall spurn conscious laxity and satisfied mediocrity. Here the question of official criticism enters. I do not think that it is my own United affiliation which impels me to say that much of the criticism in the National is not only worthless but harmful. The inability of the best qualified critics has left the field open to others, and a majority of the current reviews in *The National Amateur* have become highly reprehensible in their failure to point out flaws and recommend improvements. Such laxity is harmful because it is a tacit endorsement of crudity. If faults be left uncensured, there will be no spur to set the novice onward toward his goal. With an unofficial "little senate" to determine literary standards and revise amateur matter adequately, such feeble reviews would not be tolerated. Authors and editors who failed to conform to the standard would be given the impetus needed—their deficiencies would be noted and singled out. Of course, no unofficial authority could remedy poor criticism without coöperation from the official board. Only a higher sense of discrimination and responsibility on the part of those who appoint critics could prevent the publication of such humiliatingly inane things as the recent attack on Samuel Loveman's exquisite lyrics on the ground that they do not belong to the "cheer-up" penny-a-line school. To recapitulate on the subject of qualitative improvement and centralised authority, let me say that in my opinion there should be correspondence between the literary leaders of amateurdom on the subject of wholesale revision and censorship. The few who start the movement should strive to interest other capable leaders, with the purpose of creating a board of practical service to offer aid to all writers and publishers willing to accept it. This board should work unselfishly, unceasingly, and almost unrecognised, for the good of amateurdom; until very soon it would be recognised as a permanent arbiter of taste, above and apart from the political machinery of any association. If any idealistic and ultra-conscientious person object to the plan on account of its possible oligarchical tendencies, let him consider the lessons of history. All brilliant periods of literature have corresponded with the existence of dominant coteries, from Pericles to Augustus, and down through the ages to the coffee-house circles of Dryden and Addison and the literary club of Dr. Johnson. In truth, the ideal of utter democracy in the arts is a false and misleading one; which though zealously cherished by many persons, ought to be discarded in the interest of truth and progress. Centralised authority has existed for many years and with marked success in the United Association, raising that organisation to a literary supremacy which even its worst enemies hesitate to challenge. That the principle should be more widely extended, is both logical and desirable.

I fear I have not left myself space to speak at length regarding quantitative improvement, but I will make the most of my limited opportunities. This problem is both psychological and financial, involving the enthusiasm of the membership on the one hand, and the difficulties of printing on the other hand. The first phase, I confess, baffles me somewhat. The public mind seems to have been adversely affected by the force of the present crisis in world affairs, so that a dampening spirit of lassitude and futility envelops everything. Spontaneity and buoyancy such as we knew before 1914 are impossible to achieve nowadays, when the very foundations of society and government seem in jeopardy. That cannot be improved. If I knew how to remedy world psychology I should not be speaking before amateurs, but in the councils of state and the parliaments of the powers. However, I can at least suggest that the more ardent few do what they can to arouse greater interest by pointing out the advantages of amateurdom over other hobbies and diversions. I would especially recommend the deliberate creation of interesting controversies, either on subjects of worldwide general interest, or on purely literary topics; avoiding only amateur politics, which presents unsuspected potentialities of evil. Above all, let mutual comment be encouraged. We should make it virtually a rule to see that as many articles as possible receive printed replies. The controversies and comments in Master John Milton Heins's *American Amateur* furnish an ideal example of what is needed.

The financial problems are, when one comes to consider them at close range, almost as baffling as the psychological problems. That the increase in printers' rates must greatly curtail the volume of published matter is a foregone conclusion, and we may only urge with redoubled force that every owner of a home press publish to the very extent of his capacity—as a duty to the institution which has given him so much of pleasure and profit in the past. C. W. Smith is a model whom every press-owner should keep constantly in mind—that is, as regards intent and volume, not typographical accuracy. Then we must investigate to the full the possibilities of the mimeograph. John Clinton Pryor and Horace L. Lawson have shewn us what can be done without a printing press, and we must encourage the extension of this kind of activity by ceasing to harbour any prejudices in favour of printing. Let us remember that print is only a form—only a medium. The important thing in literature is the transmission of thoughts, so that no writer should hesitate to send his best work to the non-printed magazines.

If these periodicals cannot command the coöperation of our authors, they can never flourish. Manuscript magazines, while manifestly far behind printed and duplicated magazines in utility, should be encouraged in every known way. Of these, Mrs. Eleanor B. Campbell's *Corona* is the logical model. This paper was circulated by typing as many carbon copies as possible and setting each of them along a designated route to be passed around. None of the circulation lists was unwieldy, yet a large territory was covered. The fatal obstacle to success in this field is the negligence of those who receive magazines. I myself attempted to circulate one two years ago, yet it disappeared before it could leave New England. Another magazine, which I circulated for the editors, started on its rounds in April, 1919; and has only just reached New York State! The only remedy for this reprehensible state of things is increased conscientiousness, which I hope the pressure of hard times will develop in most of us. In leaving the subject of papers, I will again repeat what I have so often said elsewhere—that coöperative publishing should be encouraged as widely as possible. It may soon be the only feasible method of issuing a printed journal, and all objections against it should be overruled in the shortest possible order.

Increase in revenue in all associations is now practically a necessity, and should be adopted as quickly as possible. That we should still charge only pre-war dues is manifestly absurd. But even these increases can hardly ensure suitable official organs. Both associations have kept their official organs alive only through individual philanthropy, and for this unorganised charity some more equitable system of endowment should be substituted. Finally, we must reflect upon the waste of dual organisation. The separateness of the United and National is regrettable, and if consolidation could be effected according to the Morton plan we would be amply repaid for laying aside small prejudices and subordinating minor differences.

So, to my mind, stands the present situation. Roseate dreams are futile, yet our institution cannot but benefit from intelligent and concerted endeavour.

WHAT AMATEURDOM AND I HAVE DONE FOR EACH OTHER

I entered Amateur Journalism late in life—at the age of nearly twenty-four—so that I cannot justly attribute all my education to its influence. This lateness was, however, most emphatically not of my choosing. The instant I heard of amateurdom's existence I became a part of it, and count among my deepest regrets the fact that I did not discover it some seventeen years earlier, when as a youth of seven I put forth my first immortal literary product, "The Adventures of Ulysses; or, The New Odyssey".

Upon joining the United Amateur Press Association I spent the first few months in an attempt to discover just what Amateur Journalism is and just what it is not. My notions had been rather nebulous, and I was not sure whether delight or disillusion awaited me. Actually, I found both; but delight was so much in the majority that I soon realised I was a permanent amateur. That was in 1914. In 1921 I can report unchanged sentiments.

What I have done for Amateur Journalism is probably very slight, but I can at least declare that it represents my best efforts toward coöperating in a cause exceedingly precious to me. As I began to perceive the various elements in the associational sphere, I saw that heterogeneity and conflict were, as in all spheres, the rule. Trying to judge impartially, I concluded that at that particular time the purely literary element stood most in need of support. Fraternalism and good cheer are largely self-sustaining. Politics, in my honest individual opinion, is an evil. What required fostering was the very object which amateurdom professes to hold supreme—aid to the aspiring writer. Accordingly I decided that while sharing in all the general responsibilities of active membership, I would chiefly lend whatever small influence I might have toward the encouraging of mutual literary help.

My chance to do something tangible came sooner than I expected.

In the fall of 1914 I was appointed chairman of the Department of Public Criticism in the United, and was thus provided with a bimonthly medium of expression, together with a certain seal of officialdom on my utterances. What I did was to commence a definite campaign for the elevation of the literary standard—a campaign attempting on the one hand a candid and analytical demonstration of prevailing crudities, and on the other hand a tireless flow of suggestions for improvement. I abandoned altogether the policy of praising crude papers and articles because of obscure considerations connected with their standing in amateurdom, and insisted that writers and editors at least choose a goal of urbane correctness. Knowing that such a demand entailed an obligation to help personally, I undertook a fairly extensive amount of private criticism, and offered my services to any person wishing the revision of manuscripts or magazine copy. There were many responses to this offer, and I immediately found myself very busy reconstructing prose and verse and preparing copy for various amateur journals. I met with a certain amount of opposition and made many enemies, but believe that on the whole I may have accomplished some good. The standard of correctness in the United certainly rose, and most of the writers and editors I helped soon began to take pains on their own account; so that my aid became less and less necessary. This, however, is due only in part to my efforts. My successors in the critical bureau have been decidedly better, and the work was at the outset facilitated by a change in recruiting policy, established by others, whereby our new members were drawn from sources involving more extensive previous education.

In other fields I fear I have done all too little for amateur journalism. From 1915 to 1919 I issued an individual paper called *The Conservative*, but circumstances have since forced me to suspend its publication. I have helped in coöperative publishing enterprises, though never with very brilliant results. As official editor of the United this year I am trying to issue a paper of the best quality, but am able to make little headway against the quantitative limitations. I have, I hope, done my share of administrative drudgery both official and unofficial. Despite a distaste for office holding I have accepted various posts in the United whenever my services seemed desirable, and have tried to be useful in substituting for incapacitated officials.

As a writer, the field in which I should like to serve most, I seem to have served least. When I entered amateurdom, I unfortunately possessed the delusion that I could write verse; a delusion which caused me to alienate my readers by means of many long and execrably dull metrical inflictions. An old-fashioned style at present out of favour added to the completeness of my failure. Since emerging from the poetical delusion I have been almost equally unfortunate, for in following my natural inclination toward fantastic and imaginative fiction I have again stumbled upon a thing for which the majority care little. My attempts appear to be received for the most part with either coolness or distaste, though the encouragement of a few critics like W. Paul Cook, James F. Morton, Jr., and Samuel Loveman has more than compensated for the hostility of others. The Cleveland-Chico clique, seeking by ridicule to drive me from the amateur press, is well offset by any one of the gentlemen just named. Only time, however, will shew whether or not my effusions possess any value.

Happily, I can be less reserved in stating what amateurdom has done for me. This is a case in which overstatement would be impossible, for Amateur Journalism has provided me with the very world in which I live. Of a nervous and reserved temperament, and cursed with an aspiration which far exceeds my endowments, I am a typical misfit in the larger world of endeavour, and singularly unable to derive enjoyment from ordinary miscellaneous activities. In 1914, when the kindly hand of amateurdom was first extended to me, I was as close to the state of vegetation as any animal well can be—perhaps I might best have been compared to the lowly potato in its secluded and subterranean quiescence. With the advent of the United I obtained a renewed will to live; a renewed sense of existence as other than a superfluous weight; and found a sphere in which I could feel that my efforts were not wholly futile. For the first time I could imagine that my clumsy gropings after art were a little more than faint cries lost in the unlistening void.

What Amateur Journalism has brought me is a circle of persons among whom I am not altogether an alien—persons who possess scholastic leanings, yet who are not as a body so arrogant with achievement that a struggler is frowned upon. In daily life one meets few of these—one's accidental friends are either frankly unliterary or hopelessly "arrived" and academic. The more completely one is absorbed in his aspirations, the more one needs a circle of intellectual kin; so that amateurdom has an unique and perpetual function to fulfil. Today, whatever genuine friends I have are amateur journalists, sympathetic scholars, and writers I should never have known but for the United Amateur Press Association. They alone have furnished me with the incentive to explore broader and newer fields of thought, to ascertain what particular labours are best suited to me, and to give to my writings the care and finish demanded of all work destined for perusal by others than the author.

After all, these remarks form a confession rather than a statement, for they are the record of a most unequal exchange whereby I am the gainer. What I have given Amateur Journalism is regrettably little; what Amateur Journalism has given me is—life itself.

LUCUBRATIONS LOVECRAFTIAN

The Loyal Coalition

Of the various unsolved mysteries of the American public mind, none is more baffling than the persistent failure of the people to awaken to the menace of Irish rebel propaganda. Proud as this nation seems to be in most matters respecting its independence, it has again and again suffered seditious minorities of Hibernian malcontents to affront its dignity and imperil its tranquillity through their criminal attempts to use it as a tool in effecting their own selfish ends. We have condemned in terms of unmeasured scorn the Germans, both citizens and non-citizens, who abused our hospitality by plotting in our midst and seeking to exploit us to Germany's advantage. These vipers we called "hyphenates", and denounced as un-American; justly abhorring their service of a foreign master whilst enjoying the advantages of residence here. We said much, in fact, concerning the impossibility of divided allegiance. Yet through it all we have supinely tolerated a serpent a thousandfold more hateful than the Prussian hydra; a monster which owes us more loyalty because of longer American heritage, yet which gives us, if anything, less—the odious dragon of Fenianism and its successors; which has for over sixty years crouched in the United States, never accepting Americanism or placing our interests first, but working stealthily and unceasingly to employ our giant strength in fomenting rebellion in that alien and distant Ireland which it values so much more than the America which has given its adherents protection and prosperity for so long.

The bare facts of the case hardly need re-stating in these columns. We have all viewed with disgust the tactics of the Fenian organisation and of the more recently formed Sinn Fein; the subtle campaigns of hatred against our Mother Nation, whose friendship is so important to us and to the world's equilibrium; the creation of a solid and unscrupulous "Irish Vote" to intimidate our weaker politicians into passing legislation favouring Irish rebellion and endangering Anglo-American harmony; the open and unashamed employment of every sort of power, civil and ecclesiastical, to fill our public offices with disloyal Irishmen; the aid, both tacit and unconcealed, given to Germany at a time when war with that country was a duty of honour on our part; and the open insults to a friendly power which have compelled our Secretary of State to tender needed apologies to its ambassador. Such things cannot be endured forever, for they are increasingly dangerous. If our personal pride of Anglo-Saxon blood and American nationality is not enough to stir us to resentment against the trouble-makers who defame the one and seek to use the other as a lever for foreign political manoeuvres, we must at least concede that action is necessary when these malefactors approach the point of actually embroiling us in a nefarious war with our British kinsfolk over a question which concerns us not at all. Let us not be deceived. A small but darkly potent Sinn Fein minority in America is striving day and night to commit America to an endorsement or recognition of the mythical "Irish Republic" which cannot but strain Anglo-American friendship to the utmost. It is striving to place America in the anomalous position which England would have occupied had it recognised the Confederate States over half a century ago. Is America ready to be plunged into a new war; a war in which she will be in the wrong, and which her decent inhabitants will loathe and will wage only with the leaden heart and consciousness of error which spell defeat? If not, let her crush with iron heel the noxious head of the thing that has crawled upon her soil since 1858, and dismiss in everlasting disgrace the political forces whose eyes, focussed on Ireland, see the United States only as a pawn.

Who shall awake us? Around what standard shall we rally in our combat against the foe within our gates? An answer to these questions, so long wanting, has at last been supplied by an organisation formed at Boston a year ago, and known as *The Loyal Coalition.* Growing out of the Boston committee formed to receive the Ulster clergymen who lectured on the truth about Ireland in 1919–20, the Coalition has crystallised into permanent form and national scope; conducting an educational campaign both through printed matter and public speakers, and seeking to found branches in every part of the United States. Sponsored by patriotic men and supported by voluntary contributions from loyal American citizens of every kind and belief, it is giving organised utterance to the hitherto inarticulate majority who demand that foreign agitators—foreign by allegiance if not by birth—keep their hands off the American government. In supporting the Loyal Coalition, the members of the United Amateur Press Association should take a prominent part. As beneficiaries of an undivided Anglo-Saxon civilisation, it is our particular duty to advance its interests and oppose its enemies; and we should not regard contributions to the Coalition's treasury as any less important than the contributions which we made so cheerfully to the various war activities three or four years ago. Our enemies are contributing freely to the "bond issue" of the scoundrel De Valera; shall we be less loyal to the right, than they are to the wrong? The address of the Loyal Coalition is 24 Mount Vernon St., Boston 9, Massachusetts. Membership may be secured by any contribution of a dollar or more, and this dollar entitles the donor to a goodly amount of Coalition literature for distribution. Several of the best-known members of the United are already active Coalitionists, and it is to be hoped that the majority will emulate their example; joining the new society, spreading its doctrines, and if possible forming local branches. Let us play our part in this silent war—a war in many ways as significant in its potentialities as the horrible cataclysm from which we are just emerging.

Though the facts of the Irish problem do not concern us as Americans, and could not, even if justifying rebellion in Ireland, justify interference by our country, it may be well for us to glance at the situation and appreciate the utter emptiness of the Sinn Fein's claims. Ireland, never a separate nation, has been a part of the British dominions since 1172; prior to which time it was merely a battle-ground of half-barbarian chiefs. It is as integral a part of our Mother Land as Texas is of our own land. The early "English oppression" over which Sinn Feiners wax so eloquent and incoherent was never as severe as is popularly stated, and was not so much an isolated case as a type of all provincial government in the somewhat distant past. Ireland suffered no more "wrongs" than dozens of provinces which are today staunchly loyal to their respective governments, and in modern times there has been nothing even remotely resembling oppression. Ireland is today the spoiled child of the British Empire, and the political repressions now practiced by the government are merely temporary emergency measures designed to meet a sedition indescribably flagrant. The Sinn Feiners in Ireland are criminals of nearly the lowest type—traitors, slackers, pro-Germans, murderers, maimers, rioters, and cattle-thieves—and in dealing with them the British authorities are as lenient as they can be. Here in America such creatures would be lynched by an indignant citizenry. These are the folk who talk of their legendary "republic", and make themselves absurd by comparing their island to the various subject nationalities of the Continent which are now undergoing repatriation. Ethnically and linguistically Ireland is not a separate unit, but a part of the British fabric. Its race-stock in the East and North is as Teutonic as that of England and Scotland, and its only real language is English. The effort of the Sinn Fein leaders to learn and speak the nearly obsolete Gaelic jargon of the ancient tribes adds a comical touch to a grave situation. And when the spectre of "self-determination" is brought up, we are forced to smile again; for perhaps the most complete conceivable negation of this much-discussed principle is that contained in the secessionist Sinn Fein's attitude toward loyal British Ulster. Ulster, says the Sinn Fein, must secede whether it wants to or not! Ireland is not a separate nation, and could not exist apart from the Empire. Only a fatal defect in the reasoning powers of some of its people keeps alive the tradition of Anglophobia and secession. Sooner or later the Sinn Fein must calm down and accept the advantages afforded by a section of the British Empire which is not only free from all persecution, but especially blessed with favours.

Perhaps a final word on Ireland as a world problem may not be amiss, as a hint why this troubled region can never safely be set adrift as a separate "nation". To approach this matter, we must brush aside the deliberately and maliciously circulated lies of William R. Hearst and other poisonous publicists concerning England's alleged acquisitiveness, and recognise frankly that the whole maintenance of the far-flung civilisation we know depends absolutely on the power and integrity of the British Empire, sustained by the strength of our own kindred nation. We Anglo-Saxons have founded a civilisation undoubtedly greater than any other in existence. In justice, morality, progressiveness, and general effectiveness, that civilisation leads all others so conspicuously that comparison is useless. Only a keen imagination can picture the deplorable state of the world if such an immense and beneficent influence were to weaken, be dethroned from world-wide supremacy, and suffer replacement by another culture. It is a calamity which we cannot really visualise, since we instinctively accept Anglo-Saxonism as something to be taken for granted; something natural and eternal. Yet the secession of Ireland would in an instant enfeeble the whole body of Anglo-American power by placing at England's very gate a separate and dangerous enemy; one which has by past actions proved itself ready to intrigue and ally itself with the worst foes of civilisation. Given complete independence, a Sinn Fein republic would prove the ready weapon and strategic base of any alien power operating against Great Britain, America, or both. The safety of our enlightened ideals and institutions, the safety of the civilised world itself, depends upon the retention of Ireland within the British Empire. The Sinn Fein seeks to use America as a tool toward the destruction of the widespread cultural edifice of which America is itself a part; seeks to use the great national exponent of law and order as an abettor of chaos and disintegration. Let its answer come in unmistakable accents from the Loyal Coalition!

Criticism Again!

It would be futile for the United's Department of Public Criticism to reply to most of the querulous complaints levelled against it. In nine cases out of ten the circumstances are very simple—one mediocre and egotistical author plus one honest review equals one plaintive plea that the bureau, or part of it, is engaged in a diabolical plot to suppress incipient genius. The complainer, as a type, is one who candidly opposes any attempt at genuine constructive criticism, but who expects the department to mince along as a medium of flattery. He feels that his dollar dues entitle him to a certain amount of praise irrespective of merit.

But there is another sort of complaint which must be received very differently—a calm, balanced sort prompted by intelligent difference in opinion, and connected only subconsciously with personal feelings anent reviews. This sort of censure comes from cultivated scholars with fixed and rigid theories regarding the province and limitations of literary criticism. As a rule, they have never been adversely criticised by the bureau they attack; and therefore make their objections with unquestionably detached and disinterested intent, in the name of abstract justice and conventional art. Only close analysis would reveal the slight personal animus—perhaps some trifling instances wherein the bureau's evident prejudices clashed with the complainants' equally cherished prejudices. This is pardonable, because it is human—but it explains why many deem it their duty to attack the relatively inoffensive critics whilst permitting real associational menaces to flourish unrebuked. Lest my observation seem to carry a hidden sting, let me hasten to say that I do not speak as one holier than the majority. I felt it a "sacred and impersonal obligation" in 1919 (although my plaint never saw the light) to express my disapprobation when the National's reviewer made some hasty remarks on my "Earth and Sky"; chiding me for emphasising man's insignificance in the *infinite universe* when he is so clearly the supreme being of *this one tiny globe* (reward for discovery of critic's logic!) and stumbling over my use of the intransitive verb *to south,* which he could have found with ease in the Farmer's Almanack or Webster's Unabridged. No, the writing public cannot be blamed for keeping a sharp lookout for the sins and blunders of the critic—but the critic himself must not be left undefended.

As an ex-critic in the United, and one of those who stand in the path of the darts which Messrs. J. Clinton Pryor and W. Paul Cook are hurling from the pages of *The United Co-operative* and *The Vagrant,* respectively, I will venture to speak a word in behalf of myself and my former colleagues. It is with reluctance that one opposes two amateurs of such sterling quality as those just named, especially since one must deeply respect their attitudes whilst refuting their conclusions; but such opposition is necessary if the board of critics is to work unhampered. Man is an imitative animal, and the regrettable concentration of hostile attention on the critical bureau will cause a legion of dunces to emulate irresponsibly what Messrs. Cook and Pryor have done responsibly; the result being a pandemonium which these gentlemen will relish as little as will any other serious scholars.

The one leading protest of Messrs. Pryor and Cook is that personal opinions on various subjects have been expressed in the official critical reviews. They argue that such a practice is harmful, in that it causes the views of individuals to be published as the official views of the United as a body. This contention, forming indeed the whole crux of Mr. Cook's elaborate indictment in *The Vagrant*, surely sounds weighty and plausible enough when carelessly stated; yet may be thoroughly exploded almost at the very outset.

Official criticism is "official" only so far as it concerns the relation of the work criticised to the artistic standards recognised as universal. This may be accepted as axiomatic, since the official functions of the board cannot be held to extend beyond the province assigned to it; and by Messrs. Cook and Pryor's own admission, that province is art only. Most critics are far from stolid and unimaginative, and naturally tend to view a theme humanly rather than mechanically. They behold a subject in all its lights and relations, and in many cases round out their reviews by including trains of suggested thoughts and opinions which are decidedly individual. It may be that this habit is sometimes carried to excess—our critics are not unearthly paragons—but whatever one may think about it, this fact remains: *no personal opinions are given the stamp of officialdom, because officialdom does not extend beyond art.* Suppose, to quote an instance brought up by Mr. Pryor a year ago, a critic is reviewing an amatory poem. He points out its excellence of rhythm, its beauty of sound, and its cleverness of conception—then adds that in his opinion amatory verse is "old stuff" at best, and hardly worthy of the poet's powers. Has he exceeded his province? Not in the least. He has, if anything, made himself clearer by honestly stating his own position instead of concealing it—for all critics really have views of their own—and in adding this personal touch he has in no way involved the United officially. Seldom have our critics failed to separate general and personal views. The expressions of political and philosophical opinion to which Messrs. Pryor and Cook object so violently, are of course entirely outside the question. Such expressions, from their very nature, cannot possess official authority; so that the Association is well aware that the critics speak individually. When a critic adds to his conventional dictum a view of his own, he does not impair the force of the dictum in the least. The addition is often necessary to produce a human and interesting review, and its worst possible fault is space consumption. It may be taken for granted that the average critic will neither usurp large amounts of space for his views, nor air opinions subversive of the public interest. A survey of *The United Amateur* fails to disclose anything alarming, and often reveals that both sides of a question are espoused with equal vigour by different critics.

Often the objectors reveal distinct and amusing prejudices of their own. Mr. Pryor—a clergyman—complains of the uttered views of a rationalist reviewing an orthodox essay, yet passes over in significant silence an equally polemical review of a rationalist essay by an orthodox critic! In passing, it may be remarked that in this particular case both critics were not altogether outside the field of their duty. They were analysing the reasoning of the essays they were dissecting, and proving rather well that the essayists were not grappling with the cores of their respective problems at all.

In the present *Co-operative* Mr. Pryor repeats his error. Disliking a plainly worded criticism of *The Lingerer,* he forgets to note the critic's admiring concessions and distinctions. Even more strongly disliking the utterly impersonal *Clarion* review, a review far milder than many unofficial critiques of the same paper, he condemns the critic for merely repeating the ordinary rules of taste prevailing in the cultivated world—presumably because they conflict with the obsolete theories of Puritan theocracy. Mr. Pryor also—curiously enough—objects to a comment on one of his own articles which was actually made in his defence! When a man writes seriously of having an open mind toward spiritualism, most hard-headed readers will tend to smile; but the abused critic took pains to emphasise the real truth that the author expressed—that spiritualism must not be condemned dogmatically *by those who believe in immortality.* Surely, the critic remarked, the one idea is no more absurd than the other.

Mr. Cook's encyclopaedic article in *The Vagrant,* aside from the fundamental fallacy previously noted, contains more than one vulnerable spot. In his anthology of critically uttered opinions, the compiler sets down many things which could be culled from almost any series of reviews extending over a space of two and a half years; besides calling up as questionable at least two points about which nobody concedes room for debate at all. He indicates, accusingly enough, that one critic "believes in the principles of heredity". Really! We know a critic who believes that the earth is round! He also shews that a critic "does not believe any of the tales of supernatural phenomena told by soldiers on the European battlefields". How strange! It is also rumoured that there were really no witches in Salem! There is not a single view cited by Mr. Cook which is not held by millions of intelligent average citizens. The Association as a whole, despite the complainant's gratuitous assumption, stands behind none of the extraneous topics; though the questions of Greenwich Village decadence and vers libre, being wholly artistic, do border on the critic's legitimate province and involve our aesthetic policy more or less. But in these matters the majority are not powerless. Just as soon as they wish to favour modern corruption, they may elect a President pledged to appoint a sympathetic Critical Chairman. Which leads one to inquire why more elections are not conducted on literary issues?

From Mr. Cook's really wild condemnation of anti-Wilson matter, one would hardly be surprised to discover that he is or has been rather a Wilson partisan. Surely he seems more spontaneously indignant at anti-Wilson than at pro-Wilson utterances—a strange attitude indeed for an absolutely dispassionate observer! As a matter of fact, he has declared that his Wilson idolatry ceased in that fateful spring of 1917, *for reasons just opposite to those which cause the average patriot to oppose the arrogant theorist.* I hesitate to suggest the two or three more obvious interpretations, for I hardly think them true. Mr. Cook likes subtlety, mystery, and "diplomacy", and one may read his preferences in several ways. At any rate, I know that he has never been pro-German. But it remains a fact that he passionately hates the point of view of the ordinary Wilson critic, who opposes that politician on conservative patriotic grounds. One may wager safely that our gifted *Vagrant* is no Republican! I freely affirm that I am the anti-Wilsonite whose sins Mr. Cook deems "more than unpardonable"—to quote the least hectic of his fervid expressions—yet I must plead, with many others, that *facit indignatio versum.* History will rightly adjudicate the question. Since I am the "offender", I cannot but smile at my opponent's too great readiness to read a subtle anti-Wilsonism into the casual critical reference to Colonel Roosevelt, before his decease, as "America's greatest man". True, the anti-Wilsonism might have been there; yet when I wrote that passage I was thinking not of the smallness of any man, but of the greatness of Theodore Roosevelt—and what American of the present age can be classed with him? Does Mr. Cook fancy that the title of President necessarily raises a man to supreme greatness, and that to call anyone but the President our "greatest man" is *lèse majesté?* Was it considered an insult to President Adams in 1798 to call George Washington our "greatest man"? Of course, Colonel Roosevelt was against the late Wilson administration—as the truest patriots were—but general praise of an anti-administrationist does not necessarily imply a special condemnation of the opposite party.

In censuring the critic who congratulated the United on its escape from the Dowdell menace of 1919, Mr. Cook is ostentatiously combating a shadow. It is true that this congratulation might be rather out of place if coming from the pen of any person connected with the campaign; but as it happens, *every* reference to the Cleveland ring was left to other hands. The criticism in question was the work of a young man totally inactive during the first half of 1919—who, although a candidate for office, took no part in the real campaign, and had scarcely any communication with the campaigners prior to the election. Mr. Cook knew this—which makes one doubly sorry. In commenting on the whole unfortunate political contretemps, Mr. Cook somewhat surprises his readers by his cold reference to the work of those who have striven to advance the United's cause. It is to be hoped that his own truly titanic efforts and almost incredible generosity will not be similarly unappreciated by others—as they certainly are not by those whom he seems in this reference to slight ever so subtly.

Mr. Cook, I have not a doubt, honestly considers himself absolutely impersonal—a superman, as it were. Surely he *is* a superman in his services to the amateur cause! But why can he not perceive the plain truth that any assumption of godlike impersonality is for the most part a species of unconscious egotism and petty vanity?

Summing up the entire criticism situation, I cannot repress a certain discouragement at the trend of affairs. The recent labours of our reviewers have with few exceptions been ungratefully minimised and subjected to withering and injudicious tirades which devitalise the whole critical fabric. As objectors multiply the restrictions with which they would fain fetter the bureau members, all the usual incentives for service gradually disappear, and it becomes increasingly difficult to induce really qualified persons to serve. These self-constituted reformers are really doing an irreparable damage to the public criticism of the United.

It seems to be the duty of both critics and objectors to exercise forbearance. Realising the prevalent prejudice against frankness, the reviewer must unselfishly strive to adopt an artificially opinionless style as completely as possible. He must not hesitate to acknowledge occasional past instances of extremism and intolerance, or fail to sympathise as best he can with his opponents' point of view. And upon the thoughtful objector rests a reciprocal obligation. He must not expect more than mortal perfection from the critic, or seek to hamper him by the imposition of too many arbitrary limitations. He must observe closely before drawing conclusions. Frequent informal exchanges of ideas between the critics and those who have suggestions to make, would be of great mutual aid.

So great is my confidence in the lofty motives of Messrs. Cook and

Pryor, that I should like nothing better than to see them appointed to the bureau at some future time; with one of them as Chairman. Mr. Cook, at least, has had much experience in this field; and I trust that he and Mr. Pryor may seriously consider such an arrangement. To the amateur public it would bring two valuable reviewers in an age when good critics are scarce. To Messrs. Cook and Pryor it would bring a chance to develop their original theories, and to obtain a full idea of the contemporary critic's province "from the inside", as it were.

The experiment is worth trying.

Lest We Forget

Mr. Gibson's brief article in this issue of the *Co-operative* affords an excellent example of the idealistic reaction to the recent war. Sickened with blood, injustice, and cruelty, the sensitive soul recoils from the thought of another conflict, and preaches a peace based on rational remembrance of what has been.

And yet how futile is every aspiration of mankind! The same causes which have made men forget the lessons of past wars, will make them forget the lessons of this war; and none can tell how soon another menace may rise from the lands beyond the Rhine, where power is held more precious than life. When that menace takes bodily form, what remembrance of ours will defend us from its aggressions? So to our list of things not to be forgotten we must add one more item—vigilant strength! Let us indeed remember the horrors of war, but let us remember that those horrors are greatest for the nation least prepared. Let us seek no conflict, but let no conflict find us weak and unready. The hand which rises forbiddingly, or the voice which cries "No!" to war, must have the physical force to master those who do not acknowledge its authority.

A Conjecture

In the July *American Amateur,* the precocious Miss Elsie (alias Elsa) A. Gidlow of *Les Mouches* fame refers with admirable courtesy to "Mr. Lovecraft with his morbid imitations of artists he seems not even able to understand". Possibly Mistress Elsie-Elsa would prefer that the amateurs follow her own example, and perpetrate morbid imitations of morbid artists whom nobody outside the asylum is able to understand.

A MATTER OF UNITEDS

There has recently been pointed out to me in an issue of Mr. Erford's *United Amateur* an editorial note concerning the other branch of the United and its Official Editor which really requires a word of rectification among the few who have received the paper. It seems impossible that Mr. Erford's information can be as meagre as would appear from his remarks, so I can only conjecture that his attitude is one of shrewd effect, as frequently practiced in the legalistic pleading of special causes.

The existence of two Uniteds since 1912 has been so well known a phenomenon that only the very newest members can be deluded by statements such as Mr. Erford makes in his excessive though well-intentioned zeal; but for the sake of those novices it ought to be pointed out that the United duplication is the result of no deliberate creation or imposture on either side. In 1912, at which time the United was living up to its name in spite of more than one previous division, a very hotly contested election took place at the annual convention; the final vote being so close and so dependent on a technically accurate interpretation of the voting status of many members that no one can say even now with absolute finality which side gained the legal victory. Unfortunately, much recalcitrance was displayed in both camps; and in the end each group of adherents claimed the shade of preference necessary to a decision. Since both parties considered their respective candidates elected as President, each naturally viewed the candidate of the other in the light of an usurper; and in the end a general cleavage occurred, each division realigning its membership and official board in conformity with its conception of who was President, and regarding itself as the authentic continuation of the original society.

Now although I did not join amateurdom until two years after these events, they were still recent enough in my time to make it very plain to me that both sides were equally sincere in their conflicting positions. The branch which I happened to join was that opposed to Mr.

Erford's, and I naturally have a bias in its favour; but at no time have I been disposed to brand the other branch as illegal or unjustified, or to do other than regret that continuance of ill-feeling on both sides which makes recombination impossible. Opinionated "die-hards" in either faction are really playing with amusing unconsciousness into the hands of the National when they perpetuate this United division; for with a friendly and coöperative use of half the energy which they spend in calling each other "rebels" and "pro-National traitors" they could undoubtedly reorganise a solid and compact body of literary aspirants which, because of its essential difference of aim from the fraternal National's, would need to fear no competition from that august and archaic body.

The question of United-National relations has always been obscured by error—though probably through misconception rather than through deliberate misstatement. Neither branch of the United owes anything to the National, and all attempts to make the non-Erford branch appear an ally of the older body are fallacies—probably based on the purely accidental circumstance that its President at the time of the "split" was in social touch with some National members through membership in the Blue Pencil Club of Brooklyn. At the present time, of course, when the very existence of all amateurdom is menaced by indifference and decadence, the subject of consolidation for mutual strengthening has been freely broached; but never except on terms of the most unquestioned equality. The very notion that either United could ever form a National tributary of any sort is so amusing that only ignorance or deliberate obscurantism could ever cause it to be suggested. The National has no more interest in one of our branches than in the other—and if it has ever contributed toward the creation or support of any volume of the *United Amateur*, I am in a position to know that the volume in question is not one published by the non-Erford branch.

Both Uniteds have existed continuously though with varying fortunes since the time of their "split", each developing certain individual characteristics peculiar to itself. My own branch—the non-Erford one—has specialised in serious literary upbuilding more than in social or fraternal features, and has consequently sacrificed some of the fanatical esprit de corps which makes its rival so violently and picturesquely in evidence at times; but I can give assurance that its continuity through various ups and downs is no less absolute. We have not taken gaps in the visibility of Mr. Erford's society as evidence of its final cessation, and we doubt very much the seriousness of Mr. Erford when he so blithely interprets similar gaps of our own as evidence of our definite death and burial. Only the extreme novice, as we have said, can possibly be deceived by rhetorical efforts such as this.

Mr. Victor E. Bacon, the object of Mr. Erford's ill-considered and ill-informed attack, was Official Editor of the United before he ever heard of the existence of the Erford branch. He was persuaded to assume this responsibility, much against his own inclinations, by those anxious to bring about a revival of literary amateur journalism; taking office at a time when scant funds and adverse conditions had limited *The United Amateur* to a single annual number for the two years preceding. His sole object was a renaissance and maintenance of the United's best traditions, and he has continued to discharge his duties with the highest credit; slighting no task because of the National office thrust upon him by those who had watched his valiant fight in the United. His policy has been in no way affected by his discovery that Mr. Erford's United exists, and he has indeed exchanged many friendly letters with Erfordites since coming in contact with the rival branch.

It is quite time that vestigial feuds and naive poses of assumed ignorance be dropped on both sides of the United controversy. Years enough have elapsed since 1912 to make United members realise the smallness of the original difference; and to cause all sensible partisans to wish for a concerted drive toward a greater strength, rather than for a perpetuated squabbling over issues which less than a hundredth of the present personnel of either branch knows or cares anything about. Both Uniteds are a fact, and both will continue to be such until someone has the breadth, courage, and diplomacy to effect a reunion. Neither has enough in common with the National, as a careful survey has developed, to make consolidation with that body practicable; so that good sense and a liberal desire for amateurdom's general welfare would seem to dictate an amicable and tolerant reunion as the only decently rational course to follow in a depressed period when every waste of energy in duplicated organisation and internecine strife is a direct blow at the existence of the amateur institution itself.

The thing about the United which distinguishes it from the National is the fact that for a majority of its members in both branches the art of writing itself, as distinguished from social and fraternal features only loosely connected with writing, forms the dominating interest. This is a characteristic which ought to override all inherited acrimonies and bring about a coalescence of forces in which both branches might recombine on equal terms; each recognising the claims of the other, and frankly admitting the ambiguous nature of the 1912 election, where the possibilities of error in either direction were so great. Both branches carry an alert and interested membership of considerable size, none of whose individuals is deriving the fullest benefits of his affiliation so long as this mutually exclusive division continues. In the Erford society localisation produces a very unfortunate twist, and in the other there is a diffuseness forming an almost equal evil. It is time to pool strengths and weaknesses, welding all elements into one compact body in which a sane and effective average can be struck between the narrow and literalistic chauvinism on one side, and the loose organisation and apathy-breeding anti-politicalism on the other. With a nation full of young and active persons anxious to write and still unable to find a place in the larger literary world, it is absurd that no adequate society should exist at this moment for their coördination and arrangement in channels of mutual helpfulness. To this purpose the United was originally dedicated; and that the energy which ought to go toward its realisation should be squandered in vapid personal prides and meaningless rivalries, is an eternal reflection on the cultural quality and administrative competency of amateur journalism.

Let there be no more cheap abuse, then, in an age when more worthy tasks demand performance. Leaders of both Uniteds ought to confer as soon and as seriously as possible on a recombining move whereby the dual membership can expend its energies toward one object instead of two; and this would indeed be no difficult task in the eyes of anyone whose vision is not clouded by obsolete and irrelevant issues. The recognition of both official boards on equal terms between 1912 and the date of reunion would involve no prohibitive sacrifice for any rational partisan, and would solve a problem whose continued existence saps wickedly and inexcusably at the vitality of an institution which all factions equally cherish. Of course, the appropriate leaders for such a conference are the younger rather than the older members. Veterans long identified with arbitrary bitternesses are no persons to inaugurate a forward-looking policy of concession and compromise, but they can shew their breadth of vision by abstaining from obstructionist tactics. Slander leads nowhere save backward, and if both sides are wise there will come in the near future a very alert and determined analysis of the situation by amateurs of the present generation—not by the bygone period, to various phases of which both Mr. Erford and I belong—whereby there may be born again a United Amateur Press Association justifying every word and syllable of its long-belied yet well-beloved title.

MRS. MINITER—ESTIMATES AND RECOLLECTIONS

I.

It would be an interesting if invidious task to attempt a classification of amateur journalists past and present on a basis of sheer quality. The process would not be simple; for to be a "great amateur" one must not only possess absolute intellectual or aesthetic talent, and excellence in scholarship and letters, but must successfully devote a substantial part of his energies to the furtherance of what is really best in the amateur cause. Fame founded on political prowess and purely social activity in amateurdom, or on triumphs—literary or otherwise—in the outside world, would not count. Only high-grade thinkers and creators serving amateurdom in a high-grade way would be eligible for exaltation. The number of the "great" as reckoned by such a standard would probably be smaller than we like to think—but in their very front rank, acclaimed without a dissenting voice, would undoubtedly be placed the late Edith Miniter.

Mrs. Miniter was the daughter of a poetess and a mathematician, and in her own personality and work as a fiction-writer the diverse strains clearly shewed. She had, while disavowing poetry as a major interest, a sense of the soil, and of the pageantry of life and visible forms, which amounted to a poet's symbolism. Yet at the same time her keen faculty for observation, analysis, and comparison forbade her to view mankind and the world through a poet's sentimental haze. Her eye for the minutiae of human conduct, speech, and manners was almost preternaturally sharp; and this, coupled with her extreme sensitiveness to incongruities and comic contrasts, marked her out early as a natural humourist and ironist. She was a sworn and consistent foe of the pompous, the extravagant, and the romantic. A born deflater, she scorned the stupid optimisms, violent, overcoloured situations, false emotions and motivations, and artificial "happy endings" which cluttered up the dominant fiction of her earlier years.

In short stories and novels alike she chose to draw the ordinary people she knew in the ordinary situations most common to them. With her tremendous command of detail, she built up characters so life-like that our memories confuse them with persons we have met. All their traits and foibles stand out before us, and we watch their groping progress through the familiar every-day world toward that impasse of unsatisfying inconclusiveness which forms the goal of most human pilgrimages. We see their fatuous, practical, or greedy springs of action without the varnish of conventional sentiment and mendacious melodrama; we follow their gestures, idioms, accents, and typical absurdities, till each figure becomes utterly individualised and unforgettable. The satire is never heavy or violent. Always subtle, it peeps forth slyly as an integral part of the description and perspective. Addison and Jane Austen, especially the latter, are comparisons which naturally occur to one. And yet there is at times a certain grim realism which vaguely suggests something more—perhaps the objective school of Flaubert and de Maupassant, despite Mrs. Miniter's conscious rejection of all influences and subjects outside her own ancestral stream.

For above all things, Mrs. Miniter was an unalloyed outgrowth of her hereditary soil. It was supremely appropriate that, though her childhood home was in Worcester and the scene of her mature activities as writer and newspaper woman was Boston, she chanced to be born in her grandfather's farmhouse on Wilbraham Mountain in Central Massachusetts, amidst fields and groves that her forbears had known for generations. New England's rock-strown countryside, its great elms, its stone walls and winding roads, its white-steepled villages, and its curious moods, phrases, and folkways formed the core of her inheritance; and upon this most of her interests and art was built.

The books, records, and tangible objects connected with the long continuous stream of local life fascinated her profoundly, so that eventually her antiquarianism reached a professional status. As a collector of old china she was notable, and readers of the *Boston Transcript* and *Springfield Republican* will not soon forget her articles on antiques, old schoolbooks, local history, and bygone customs of which she was almost the last first-hand reporter. Her zeal in research and her memory for ancient things were fully as sharp as her observation of details around her. No more indefatigable collector of quaint epitaphs ever lived.

Nor was she ever long out of touch with the ancestral scene. Nearly every summer or autumn found her in the shadow of Wilbraham

Mountain—while, with a symbolic aptness rivalling that of her birth, the last nine years of her life were spent on the ancient soil, in the rambling, antique-filled farmhouse of a close friend and extremely distant cousin. With such a programme, her detailed, coördinated knowledge and basic, sympathetic comprehension of Central New England character, speech, legends, manners, and customs became those of a profound specialist. The field was worthy of her devotion, for the Connecticut Valley's backwaters present typical and tenacious phases of life not to be found elsewhere; phases contrasting sharply with the brisk, well-ordered, seaward-gazing, and often adventurous life of coastal New England and its vivid old ports.

In the first Puritan days this region was a trackless wilderness covered with black woods whose depths the settlers' fancy peopled with unknown horrors and evil shadows. Then the Bay Path was hewn through to the settlements on the Connecticut, and after King Philip's War thin streams of pioneers began to trickle along it and branch off from it; cutting faint roadways and clearing meagre farmsteads on the silent rocky hillsides. Grim, low-pitched, unpainted farmhouses sprang up in the lee of craggy slopes, their dim, small-paned windows looking secretively off across leagues of loneliness. Life was hard and practical, and contact with the world very slight. Old tales and thoughts and words and ways persisted, and people remembered odd fancies which others had forgotten. There was less breadth and changing of ideas—less response to new times—than on the coast, where links with Europe were many, and where prosperity and "book-l'arnin'" had fostered a more flexible mentality.

The years passed, and modern influences stole into the Wilbraham country. Springfield's proximity began to be felt, and a stately brick academy arose in the village on fields above the sleepy, elm-shaded street. Farmers throve in a modest way, and took on a literacy and taste clearly reflected in the general life. Finer houses were built. But always the undercurrent of isolation and ancient whispers persisted. One of Mrs. Miniter's ancestresses in the early nineteenth century was a suspected witch; and people talked about the queer sounds in the air each evening at the pasture bars where the road bends north of the mountain.

Then the cityward tide set in, and some of the most vigorous stock vanished—to return only for burial in the spectral cemeteries near the village. Funerals, Mrs. Miniter once wrote, came to form Wilbraham's chief industry. Deserted houses grew common, and some of the humbler farmers began to shew queer softenings of morale and queer vagaries in their standards. Foreigners appeared—the typical Connecticut Valley Poles whom the keen realist so faithfully depicted in her novel *Our Natupski Neighbors.* A new element of sombreness was added to the old background of persistent legend—the sombreness of decay, desolation, and impending change. Even in its late phases the ancient land cannot lose its distinctiveness! All this Mrs. Miniter caught as clearly as she caught the ancestral heritage. She was, from first to last, a realist; and in her the brooding countryside had a voice and an historian.

But in no sense was Mrs. Miniter a rustic, provincial, or one-sided artist. Side by side with her reflection of old backgrounds was a mature, cosmopolitan scholarship and general culture which always made her see her chosen field in its true perspective. Her interests were as wide as those of any other urban litterateur, as all who knew her stories, book-reviews, and brilliant conversation can well attest. In taste she followed the nineteenth-century main stream, though constantly transcending it in unexpected ways. None excelled her in social accomplishments and organising genius; qualities which made her for over thirty years the natural leader of Boston amateurdom and the originator of the most typical touches of wit and distinctiveness in the Hub Club's programmes and publications. No mere coincidence caused the death of the club only a few months after her final departure from Boston.

II.

The details of Mrs. Miniter's long career—a career inseparable from amateur journalism after her sixteenth year—will doubtless be covered by writers well qualified to treat of them. Reared in Worcester, taught by her poet-mother and at a private school, and given to solid reading and literary attempts from early childhood onward, the erstwhile Edith May Dowe entered amateurdom in 1883 and was almost immediately famous in our small world as a fictional realist. Controversies raged over her stories—so different from the saccharine froth of the period—but very few failed to recognise her importance. After 1890 she was engaged in newspaper and magazine work in the larger outside world, though her interest in amateur matters increased rather than diminished.

From 1894 onward she dominated the historic Hub Club of Boston, and was foremost in ensuring the success of amateur conventions in her city. In 1895 she was official editor of the National, and in 1909 she became its president. Her occasional editorship of *The Hub Club Quill,* and of various individual papers, gave repeated proof of her peculiar charm as a humorous commentator, and of her skill and effectiveness in meeting amateurdom's diverse issues. Especially famous was her *Aftermath,* published after the conventions she attended and touching on their salient features with inimitable humour and acuteness.

The same qualities of wit and observation animated all her letters, so that she was highly valued as a correspondent. Her home, whatever its location, was always a recognised headquarters of amateurs—its charm enhanced by the presence of her gifted mother, Mrs. Jennie E. T. Dowe, from 1896 until Mrs. Dowe's death in 1919.

In 1916 appeared Mrs. Miniter's novel *Our Natupski Neighbors*, the sequel to which has unfortunately never seen publication. Her short stories had meanwhile gained a substantial foothold in many standard magazines, while her reviews and antiquarian articles enjoyed more than a local fame. Actually, she deserved even more recognition than she received. It was her misfortune to follow a middle course in an age of abrupt transition—so that in youth her work was far in advance of its time, while in later life it failed to keep pace with the decadent and abnormal interests of modernism. It was in the *Natupski* period that she and her environment most closely coincided, and that she received the enthusiastic praise of William Lyon Phelps and other critics. At no time could she have been an idol of the masses, since her work was too honest for vitiated popular taste. Her integrity as an artist was absolute. She did not cater to the low-grade demands of the herd, and probably could not have done so had she wished.

My own direct acquaintance with Mrs. Miniter dates only from the summer of 1920, when I first attended gatherings of the Boston amateurs. She was then inhabiting the memorable halls of 20 Webster St. in Allston—"Epgephian Temple" of cryptic amateur lore—and was, as always, surrounded by a home-like array of antiques and family possessions, and attended by a faithful feline bearing the various names of "Grey Brother", "Grey Bother", and "Tat".

The festive July conclave marking my introduction is still fresh in memory. Though of diminutive stature, and given to choosing a low and inconspicuous seat amidst an assembly, Mrs. Miniter did not fail to dominate more or less imperceptibly every event at which she was present. Her piquant conversation and constant humour gave a vividness to the most ordinary happenings, and vastly enlivened an all-day trip to Castle Island. My own bias toward the archaic made me especially appreciative of her interests in that direction. Later I enjoyed the spirited and hilarious comments on the gathering which she published —both under her own name and as the amanuensis of "Tat"—in that short-lived but unforgettable journal *Epgephi*.

For the next few years I saw Mrs. Miniter quite often at meetings and festivals of the Hub Club, and always admired the effectiveness with which she devised entertainment and maintained interest. In April, 1921, her quaintly named and edited paper *The Muffin Man* contained a highly amusing parody of one of my weird fictional attempts . . .

"Falco Ossifracus, by Mr. Goodguile" . . . though it was not of a nature to arouse hostility. Notwithstanding her saturation with the spectral lore of the countryside, Mrs. Miniter did not care for stories of a macabre or supernatural cast; regarding them as hopelessly extravagant and unrepresentative of life. Perhaps that is one reason why, in the early Boston days, she had declined a chance to revise a manuscript of this sort which later met with much fame—the vampire-novel *Dracula*, whose author was then touring America as manager for Sir Henry Irving.

It was in September, 1921, that W. Paul Cook issued his ample brochure in memory of Mrs. Dowe, for which Mrs. Miniter furnished a magnificent tribute in the form of a biographical sketch of her mother. This sketch, in which the ancestral Wilbraham background is described with great piquancy and detail, and in whose later parts the fortunes of the household are traced with keen dramatic humour, contains not a little self-revelation, and forms one of the most adequate records of its writer's personality now available.

Throughout the N.A.P.A.'s Boston convention of 1921 Mrs. Miniter's guidance and inspiration were manifest. In the breezy *Aftermath* describing this event I was quite overwhelmed to find the chapter headings dedicated to me—each being a quotation from Dr. Samuel Johnson, as was fitting in commemorating an eighteenth-century devotee. Late in 1922 Mrs. Miniter was prominent in reorganising the Hub Club and broadening its personnel. Her abode was then the pleasant white house in Maplewood where the still-flourishing *L'Alouette* held forth. Here her library and her many antiques were displayed to especial advantage. Throughout 1923 she stood behind the club, aiding in its expansion campaign, and lending her wit to its banquet and convention programmes, and to its official organ.

At this period a heated controversy regarding schools of poetry was raging in amateurdom—the disciples of Victorian placidity being arrayed against the followers of Swinburne, Baudelaire, and the Symbolists. As an anti-Victorian, I published among other things an editorial with distinctly cool references to the soulful Messrs. Longfellow and Tennyson. Mrs. Miniter, on the other side, countered with a long column of comment whose paragraphs were separated by alternate quotations from the two gentlemanly versifiers in question.

This, too, was the time when explorers of the old Massachusetts coast towns had the benefit of Mrs. Miniter's antiquarian knowledge. I recall a trip to old Marblehead with its tangled ways and brooding gambrel roofs, in which Edward H. Cole also participated. Mrs. Miniter supplied many legends and particulars which no guide-book could furnish—and it was on this occasion that I first heard of the rustic super-

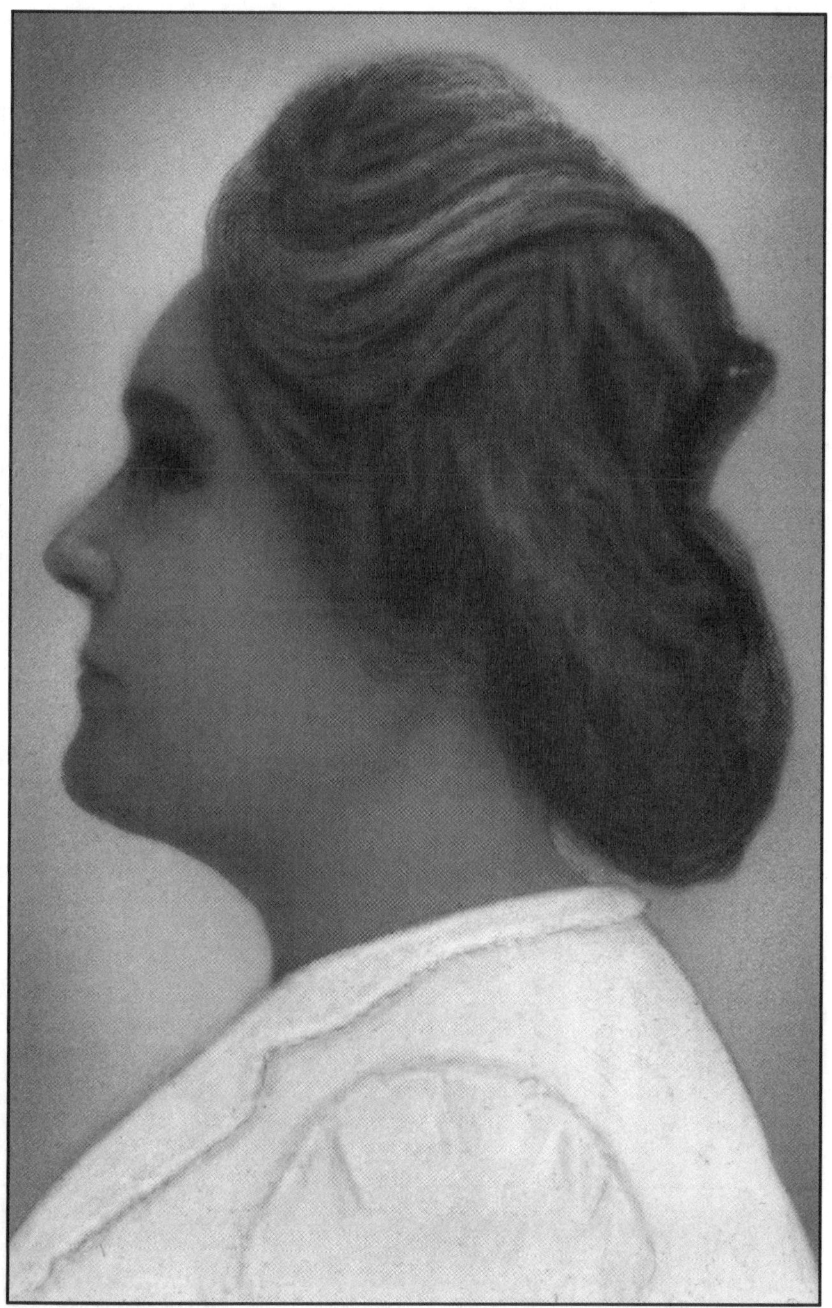

FALCO OSSIFRACUS.

-BY-

MR. GOODGUILE.

ANY form of inquisition into the meaning of this will be fruitless. Favour me, an' you will, with eternal confinement in a gaol, and everything that I now relate will be repeated with perfect candour.

Again I say I do not know anything at all about it, which is probably why I am making it the subject of this narrative. It is true that I have been for 18 years his closest friend and we had been seen by reputable witnesses near Greenwood, N.Y., Sleepy Hollow by the Hudson, Mt. Auburn, Cambridge, Mass., and Grant's Tomb, Manhattan, but that we possessed tastes mutually morbid or a predilection for graveyards I must strenuously deny.

I seem to remember a weird evening in November. The place was, of course, a cemetery; over the fence peered an inquisitive, waning, crescent moon, and on the fence a vulture and his vulturine a raven and a couple of comorants remained couchant. Behind the wall I discerned the loud moan of several man-eating sharks, from which I augured that the sea was not above a league distant. A few skulls and cross-bones lay in the foreground, while coffinplates, shreds

of shrouds, and mattocks which I instinctively knew appertained to gravediggers, scattered around loosely, completed the remarkable scene.

I had, for some time, missed my companion, but as he was most frequently absent when we were together I thought little of the occurrence. Indeed, the next moment, my attention was arrested by the hurried passing of a completely articulated skeleton, holding its nose, from whence the bright blue blood of a Colonial governor streamed. And this was rather unique, because it *had no nose!*

Meaning to employ a phraseology which my readers will at once recognize as the common and natural expression of frequenters of tombs, "How's his nibs?" I inquired. Unfortunately a slight nervousness changed the "n" to "r", and the offended object disappeared without replying. I succeeded better, however, with the next bag o' bones, which came forth applying a skeleton hand to the base of a spinal column and groaning frightfully, which was the more peculiar, as it had neither lungs nor windpipe.

"Your pal," came the response, "Iacchus Smithsonia," the name was originally John Smith, but it is always my will that my friends bear a name of my choosing and as cumbersome a one as possible, "is cleaning out Tomb 268."

It was indeed so. In the exact centre of the abode of corruption stood the self elected subsidiary of Perpetual Care. His shrunken eye sockets, his

stition which asserts that window-panes slowly absorb and retain the likeness of those who habitually sit by them, year after year. To Boston also Mrs. Miniter was an ideal guide. All the historic sites and literary landmarks were at her tongue's tip—including many which would otherwise have been very difficult to find. No one could surpass her in explaining the various minor domestic objects of the past—betty lamps, sausage-guns, potato-boilers, tinder-wheels, clock-jacks, plate-warmers, smoking-tongs, and the like—which are found in such abundance in antique collections, and around the kitchen fireplaces of old houses open as museums.

III.

1924 and 1925 brought many changes, and before the close of the latter year Mrs. Miniter's permanent return to her native countryside was effected. The seat of her residence was Maplehurst, "back of the mountain" in North Wilbraham; a large, rambling farmhouse, once an inn, which lies just across the marsh-meadows from Wilbraham Mountain, at a bend and dip of the road where giant maples form a green, mystical arcade. This is the ancestral domain of the Beebes—with whose surviving representative, the locally famous antiquarian and antique collector Miss Evanore Olds Beebe, Mrs. Miniter combined household forces.

Miss Beebe—now unfortunately an invalid—was then virtually the leading spirit of Wilbraham; a kind of feminine village Pooh-Bah who held, among numberless other offices, the posts of Superintendent of Schools and member of the town council. She was a stout, capable, kindly, and quietly humorous gentlewoman then about seventy years of age, and was looked up to as an oracle by all the surrounding population. Her telephone rang constantly with requests for information and advice—political, social, historical, domestic, or otherwise—from citizens and town officials, and her voice in civic affairs was one of almost supreme authority. Though of straitened finances, she was the owner of most of the land in sight, including a good part of Wilbraham Mountain. An old friend of the family, and a distant kinswoman of the Olds line, she had been Mrs. Miniter's hostess on many a summer sojourn; so that the returning native's immediate milieu was by no means a strange one.

The house, of early nineteenth-century date, was spacious and attractive; and was literally choked to repletion with the rare antiques inherited or assembled by its owner. The ancient tables, secretaries, and chests which crowded the large rooms were covered and piled high with lesser antiques of every conceivable sort—china, glassware, candle-

Opening pages from Mrs. Miniter's Lovecraft parody, "Falco Ossifracus"

sticks, snuffers, sand-boxes, whale-oil lamps, and all the other typical legacies of the past. Venerable paintings and samplers in close array all but hid the centuried paper of the walls, while the archaic fireplaces formed a setting for innumerable warming-pans, foot-stoves, sets of bellows and fire-irons, and less recognisable household appliances of yore. Amidst this antiquarian's paradise there moved—with a truly miraculous lack of evil consequences—a retinue of seven cats and two dogs, each with a distinct personality of his own.

"Printer" (whose name was a corruption of "Prince of Orange"—this in turn based on the colour of his eyes) was the dean of the felidae, and had seen nearly seventeen winters in this world. He was a tiger of friendly disposition, and last of the Beebe mousers to know or avail himself of the old-fashioned "cat-ladder"—a series of brick steps inside the great chimney—which led from the ground floor to the realms above. "Old Fats" was a bluff, brusque, plumpish outdoor cat of golden hue and great martial prowess, whose primary ambition seemed to be to become a dog. He would curl up beside the dogs as if one of their clan, and would follow his human friends all over the farm—trotting caninely at their heels. His three brothers "Tardee", "Pettie", and "Prince of Wails" (so named for his vocal attainments) were likewise of aureate colouring. Pettie was the most affectionate and gentlemanly of the household, while the Prince's chief fame arose from his ability to thread his way among and over the furniture without the least damage or even peril to the labyrinth of fragile antiques. Their sister "Little Bit" was a tiger, and fond of sleeping in a tripod-suspended kettle on the lawn. Her young daughter "Tiger Ann" (later renamed Marcelle) completed the feline roster at the period of the present writer's census. Of the two dogs "Stitchie" was an aged collie of aristocratic lineage and impeccable courtesy, beginning to suffer from deafness and dim sight, while "Donnie" was a boisterous and clumsy puppy in the process of growing to Gargantuan proportions.

The farm still existed as such, though operated on a reduced scale by the time of Mrs. Miniter's advent. Very little ground was really cultivated, but haying was conducted with local talent seasonally engaged—and with the more or less languid coöperation of the one hired boy, a sentimental vocalist whose melodic enthusiasm rivalled that of the Prince of Wails. Of livestock there remained some poultry, two lowing kine, and two patriarchal equines. The barn was a huge, spectral place with an immense hayloft. Picturesque sloping meadows stretched off in every direction, and just down hill at the road's bend there brooded the pasture bars where strange nocturnal influences were said to linger. Between the highway and the mountain the marsh spread out—half traversed by the grass-grown remnants of a never-finished road. On summer nights the throngs of dancing fireflies above the marsh—and above the pasture of the haunted bars—were of a strange multitudinousness and brilliancy which well justified the rustic whisperings attached to them.

Into this congenial environment Mrs. Miniter fitted admirably and instantaneously. It was her own country, and here she remained till the end; though a vague idea of a possible return to Boston caused her to keep some of her possessions stored there. More and more of her articles dealt with Wilbraham folklore—articles which she wrote at intervals between work on two still unpublished novels. Material was plentiful at hand, and not far away dwelt the colourful Polish family around which her *Natupski* novel had been written. Through her pen the reading public came to know of Lieut. Mirick, whose killing of a "pizen sarpient" in a hayfield on Wilbraham Mountain in 1761 gave rise to the name "Rattlesnake Peak" as applied to the principal summit. In other articles she told of the mysterious murders of travellers, of the man who moved a schoolhouse to his own neighbourhood to accommodate his children, of the inn whose floor shews the marks of stacked Revolutionary muskets, of the ensign who in 1744 could carry six bushels of salt on his back all at one time, and of kindred choice bits from Wilbraham's long annals.

An eight-day visit to the household at Maplehurst in July, 1928, formed my last personal glimpse of Mrs. Miniter. I had never seen the Wilbraham region before, and was charmed by the vivid vistas of hills and valleys, and the remote winding roads so redolent of other centuries. No better hierophants of the local arcana than Mrs. Miniter and Miss Beebe could possibly have been found, and my knowledge of Central New England lore was virtually trebled during my short stay.

I saw the ruinous, deserted old Randolph Beebe house where the whippoorwills cluster abnormally, and learned that these birds are feared by the rustics as evil psychopomps. It is whispered that they linger and flutter around houses where death is approaching, hoping to catch the soul of the departed as it leaves. If the soul eludes them, they disperse in quiet disappointment; but sometimes they set up a chorused clamour of excited, triumphant chattering which makes the watchers turn pale and mutter—with that air of hushed, awestruck portentousness which only a backwoods Yankee can assume—"They got 'im!" On another day I was taken to nearby Monson to see a dark, damp street in the shadow of a great hill, the houses on the hillward side of which are whispered about because of the number of their tenants who have gone mad or killed themselves.

I saw the haunted pasture bars in the spectral dusk, and one evening was thrilled and amazed by a monstrous saraband of fireflies over marsh and meadow. It was as if some strange, sinister constellation had taken on an uncanny life and descended to hang low above the lush grasses. And one day Mrs. Miniter shewed me a deep, mute ravine beyond the Randolph Beebe house, along whose far-off wooded floor an unseen stream trickles in eternal shadow. Here, I am told, the whip-poorwills gather on certain nights for no good purpose.

I was taken over the sightly Beebe acres by my hostess, Old Fats trotting dog-like at our heels; and beheld some of the silent, uncommunicative, slowly retrograding yeomanry of the region. Later the aged, courtly Stitchie and Mrs. Miniter were my joint guides to neighbouring Glendale and its ancient church and churchyard. Still another trip was up old Wilbra'm Mountain, where the road winds mystically aloft into a region of hushed skyey meadow-land seemingly half-apart from time and change, and abounding in breath-taking vistas. Through the haze of distance other mountains loom purple and mysterious. A line of fog marks the great Connecticut, and the smoke of Springfield clouds the southwestern horizon. Sometimes even the golden dome of the Hartford state house, far to the south, can be discerned. Though the slopes were much as Lieut. Mirick must have known them in his day, I saw no "pizen sarpients". On the way Mrs. Miniter pointed out the home of the "Natupskis" immortalised in her novel.

A subsequent day was devoted to a long walk around the mountain, over roads which included some of quite colonial primitiveness. On this occasion, for the only time in my life, I saw a wild deer in its native habitat. Wilbraham village, under the mountain's southern slope, is a drowsy, pleasant town with a quiet main street and giant elms. Mrs. Miniter displayed the moss-grown graveyards of the place—one of which, The Dell, includes a dank wooded declivity beside a stream that is said to wash away the earth and expose curious secrets at times. The old brick Academy, built in 1825 and still surviving after many vicissitudes, was another interesting sight. The return trip, beginning in the wild and picturesque woodlands behind the Academy, led over unspoiled colonial roads on the mountain's side, and revealed many of the brooding, unpainted houses of other generations. At one stage of the journey I saw the house where Mrs. Miniter was born—built in 1842 by her grandfather, Edwin Lombard Tupper, and still inhabited by his direct descendants. Among the varied and exquisite prospects along this route is one of a strangely blasted slope where grey, dead trees claw at the sky with leafless boughs amidst an abomination of desolation. Vegetation will grow here no longer—why, no one can tell.

Toward the end of my visit Mrs. Miniter gave directions for a walk too long for her to attempt, and I followed an ancient road—full of striking vistas—to the pleasant village of Hampden. The town lies at the bend of a stream, and all the houses are strung at length along a road winding up the side of a mountain from the valley. Here the traditional white-steepled church building shelters a thriving grocery store—one of those humour-fraught contrasts in which Mrs. Miniter always delighted. Here, also, stands a World War memorial in the most flamboyant taste (or lack of taste) of Civil War times—the gift of an aged local magnate who remembered the past and knew what he wanted!

The hours spent at Maplehurst among the old books and antiques, with Pettie and Tardee and the Prince weaving dexterously through the narrow lanes of navigation and venerable Printer often drowsing, purring, or sneezing in my lap, will not soon be forgotten. Mrs. Miniter and Miss Beebe formed unsurpassable hosts, and the impromptu course in folklore which they gave me was illustrated at every turn by volumes, pictures, and actual objects from the local past. The fireflies at evening—the distant, wind-borne strains of melodious Chauncey tramping homeward across the fields—the delightful agricultural-pedagogical household next door, whose kindly proffered Model T helped to solve many problems of distance—the tales of other days brought forth by Mrs. Miniter from her inexhaustible store of erudition—all these varied recollections spring up at mention of the name of Wilbraham.

During the final years Mrs. Miniter was harassed by illness—largely an increase of the asthmatic tendency which had long troubled her. Letters, though always cheerful and overflowing with wit, became fewer and fewer. It was hoped that she might attend the Boston convention of the National in 1930, but her health was unequal to the trip. Just after that conclave the brilliant young western amateur Helm C. Spink, who had been a leading delegate, paid her a memorable visit at Wilbraham; and I still treasure the jointly written sheet of humour which hostess and guest sent me—a mock-journal whose title, *The Dog-matic Cat-egory*, was based on my keen interest in Maplehurst's furry fauna.

After 1931 came the illness and ultimate invalidism of Miss Beebe, which placed upon Mrs. Miniter new burdens and responsibilities. There were likewise accidents—two falls involving fractures—affecting Mrs. Miniter herself. And always the anxieties and retrenchments attendant upon the depression hung in the offing. Work, however, went bravely if intermittently on; and the unpublished novels doubtless bear myriad touches made almost at the last.

Messages from the outside world shed many a heartening beam—and the familiar countryside itself, of which she was so wholly and innately a part, must have been a potent balm in its way. Never was she separated from the old things and ancestral influences that she loved so well. Her health gave way bit by bit; but the cherished books and favourite china and home-like confusion of andirons and crickets and warming-pans were always around her, while from her front windows age-old Wilbra'm Mountain always loomed up across the eerie marsh-meadows. She died on June 4, 1934—late enough, perhaps, to have seen the year's first fireflies dancing over the pasture grasses. And now she rests among the time-crumbled headstones of her forefathers in the old graveyard below the mountain—The Dell, with its trees, its shadows, and its spectral stream.

It is difficult to realise that Mrs. Miniter is no longer a living presence; for the sharp insight, subtle wit, rich scholarship, and vivid literary force so fresh in one's memory are things savouring of the eternal and the indestructible. Of her charm and kindliness many will write reminiscently and at length. Of her genius, skill, courage, and determination, her work and career eloquently speak. Though a lifelong antiquarian, she was not one to yearn vainly for the past or bewail the present and future—her staunch mood of acceptance being admirably summed up in one of her rather infrequent specimens of verse, a sonnet entitled "1921", appearing in the pages of the clever *Muffin Man.* There is no better way of closing this tribute than to quote that sonnet complete—for in it so much of its author stands revealed:

"Dear dreams of youth—could one seek your return,
Ask glamour of an earlier spring to glow,
Or clothe in verdure trees now lying low,
In ashes dull cause wonted fires to burn,
Still life's best lessons would be left to learn.
Of many brooks is made one river's flow;
From yesteryears tomorrows thrive and glow;
The future nothing of the past may spurn.

"Nor is aught forfeit. In its course the stream
Denotes accretion, gain for evermore;
So ripples life with joy beyond the dream,
When mellow hues of autumn tinge the shore.
I would not call you back, dear dreams of youth,
So much you're bettered by the present truth!"

Providence, R.I., October 16, 1934

SOME CURRENT MOTIVES AND PRACTICES

In the opening issue of *Causerie* Mr. Ernest A. Edkins touches ably and pointedly upon one case of an evil which, though always present in amateurdom, has formed a particularly offensive nuisance during the past year—the evil of personal malice as a major motive of activity. The time was ripe for such an editorial, and more in the same vein from other pens would be welcome. Good will and a rational attitude cannot be established by force or edict, but widespread pertinent comment can sometimes help to discourage their most senseless and persistent violations.

It is again appropriate, as on many past occasions, to ask whether the primary function of amateur journalism is to develop its members in the art of expression or to provide an outlet for crude egotism and quasi-juvenile spite. Genuine criticism of literary and editorial work, or of official policies and performances, is one thing. It is a legitimate and valuable feature of associational life, and can be recognised by its impersonal approach and tone. Its object is not the injury or denigration of any person, but the improvement of work considered faulty or the correction of policies considered bad. The zeal and emphasis of the real critic are directed solely toward the rectification of certain definite conditions, irrespective of the individuals connected with them. But it takes no very acute observer to perceive that the current floods of vitriol and billingsgate in the National Amateur Press Association have no conceivable relationship to such constructive processes.

The sabotage, non-coöperation, legalistic harrying, published abuse, partly circulated attacks, and kindred phenomena which have lately cheapened the association and hampered its work are of an all too evident nature. Surface inspection and close analysis alike reveal only one motive behind them—the primitive and puerile desire of one individual or another, under the influence of childish caprice or ruffled self-esteem, to inflict pain or humiliation or general harm upon some other individual.

It is impossible to discover any useful purpose behind any example of the recent bickering, notwithstanding the lofty and disinterested motives professed in certain cases. Those who invoke trivial and obsolescent technicalities against others for the noble purpose of 'saving the constitution' are careful to confine their austere crusading to persons whom they do not like; while those who thunder against fancied official blunders are equally careful to let their eagle-eyed alertness and civic virtue find such blunders only among their personal foes. Not in any instance can we trace these attacks and persecutions to an actual wish to help the association—for their authors ignore myriads of opportunities to serve and upbuild in other ways. All the zeal very plainly centres around the mere savage process of venting private dislike and vindictiveness, and making somebody else uncomfortable.

Unfortunately the evil is not confined to a riff-raff whom the National could readily repudiate. Like other bad habits, egotism and sadism spread to the useful as well as the useless, and form regrettable weaknesses in otherwise gifted and admirable persons. In the present epidemic we ruefully note a great deal of unmotivated savagery from prominent members who are not only capable of better things but who have accomplished and are accomplishing much for the association. Plainly, the needed campaign of reform must be one against *attitudes and practices* as distinguished from *individuals.*

That the N.A.P.A. can—or should—attempt to control the private ethics and individual taste of its various members is greatly to be doubted. It is the function of other social forces to do whatever can be done toward redeeming this or that person from the sway of paltry emotions, primitive perspectives, blunted group-consciousness, and a distorted sense of proportion. What amateurdom may well attempt is simply to oppose the use of its own facilities and mechanism—its papers, its address-lists, and its administrative organisation—as agents in the exercise of loutish personal rancour and gratuitous small-boy brutality. It does not pay to encourage practices which place the institution in a cheap and contemptible light, and tend to alienate the best type of members and prospective members.

Just what can be done about the matter remains to be seen—but the ampler the public discussion, the sooner a feasible avenue of effort can be found. The problem is not one in which absolute suppression can be aimed at. Rather must we work for the discouragement, restriction, and minimisation of the given evil. A good beginning would be the closing of the mailing bureau, critical columns, historian's and librarian's records, and all other departments of official recognition to a paper containing material manifestly unsuitable for publication. The mailing manager might well be required to secure the approval of the president or executive judges before releasing to the membership anything open to suspicion as personally scurrilous or non-constructively savage, while such officials might also be given the power to declare any offending journal—publicly or privately mailed—invalid and technically non-existent as an activity item or vehicle for laureateship entries. Parallel with such action the executive judges should double their alertness in detecting complaints brought to them in a spirit of personal malice, and should exercise a large measure of discretion in dealing with these efforts to use the association as a feudists' accessory.

The part of individual editors is to attack cheap personalism in their columns, and to ignore—except when giving proper refutation to certain specific lampoonings—such exchanges as habitually transcend good taste and fraternal harmony. For the membership at large there remains the duty of generally backing up the side of decency and reasonable decorum—of voting for remedial measures if given the chance; of going on record, when opportunities come, as friends of good conduct; and of withholding acknowledgment and approval from journals which persistently and consciously lapse below civilised standards. Naturally, it sometimes takes a developed analytical ability and fund of tolerant humour to distinguish really anti-social malevolence from the mere ignorant coarseness and harmless low buffoonery which can so closely resemble it. Mistakes will occur, as in other fields. But most of the offences are too manifest to demand hesitancy.

One special phase of the evil needs close consideration and possibly separate action—this being the circulation of derogatory material behind the backs of the victims. It seems to be a growing custom to attack or ridicule a person in print, yet to refrain from sending that person a copy of the attack. This is manifestly a double offence—indeed, it makes offensive many perhaps legitimate criticisms which would be above censure if sent openly to their objects. The effect of a lampoon sent to everyone but the victim is obvious. Instant reply is cut off, and the original hostile impression has an unfair chance to sink into public consciousness before it can be combated. A punctiliously honourable fighter gives his foe a chance to see hostile material even *before* publication. Comment on an opposite policy is almost needless. While the partial circulation of ordinary papers is hardly to be controlled by rule (although it should be obligatory to supply certain officers and recognised major workers), the practice of attacking in print without supplying a copy to the victim is so gross an injury that its legal punishment is at least a matter worthy of debate. It would pay amateurs to consider the adoption of some measure penalising editors guilty of this practice, even though such a measure would have to be drawn very carefully to prevent injustice and discourage retaliatory sharp practice (in the form of false denials of receipt) on the part of persons properly criticised and supplied by honourable editors.

So far as concrete instances go, the current evil reaches its grotesque apex in the absurd and fantastic persecution meted out during the past year to President Hyman Bradofsky—a persecution which, however, spreads much more ridicule upon its authors than upon its victim. Just what it is about, no one seems to be aware—indeed, nearly every commentator including Mr. Bradofsky assigns a different ostensible cause. The present executive is probably contributing more to the amateur cause, in effort and in publications, than any of his contemporaries. His *Californian*, with its unprecedented space opportunities, has been the greatest recent influence in stimulating amateur prose writing. His high qualitative ambitions for the National are responsible for Mr. Spencer's present critical chairmanship. His financial support—given at the cost of great personal hardship—has floated a sadly burdened official organ. His generosity and good will have been manifested in a dozen channels to the association's advantage. And most of all, he has been a faithful and conscientious president throughout his term; proving inadequate in no respect, and seeking the proper advice before making any move which might be challenged. His encouragement of a policy of high endeavour has won recruits, stimulated worthy writing, and evoked such brilliant new papers as *Causerie* and *The Dragon-Fly*.

Now Mr. Bradofsky may or may not be a superman. He may not combine in a single person the varied talents and aptitudes of a Morton, a Miniter, an Edkins, a Cook, a Spencer, a Loveman, and so on. His official messages may tend toward diffuseness rather than detail, and his prose rhythms may not compete with those of Flaubert or Dunsany. His fiction—still frankly experimental and pursued for the sake of development—may fall considerably short of Balzac's or Dostoievsky's. His response to criticism may shew a bit too much ethical sensitiveness and a bit too little tough combativeness . . . it is yet too early to give a complete report on this. His handling of sundry communications may or may not involve the tact of a diplomat and the self-effacement of a Trappist. There is no need to present an imposing brief for Mr. Bradofsky, or to become his particular partisan and defender. But granting all his possible variations from theoretical perfection, and comparing his record with that of each of his nearly seventy predecessors, can we find in his acts and policies any conceivable basis for a campaign of general heckling, hounding, and attempted ridicule even a tenth as virulent and systematic as that which certain individuals and groups in amateurdom have seen fit to conduct against him?

Here, indeed, is merely one more case of the prevailing vicious personalism. Mr. Bradofsky, a sterling amateur and dependable president, has offended a few egos; either through some of his maturely considered official acts—appointments, replacements, &c.—or through his outspoken partisanship of sincere literary striving as distinguished from the slapdash imitation of tenth-rate sensational journalism. Therefore, according to the mode, he becomes an object of personal spleen and infantile nose-thumbing among the select circle upon whose toes he has unintentionally trod. Such cases have occurred before; and we cannot, perhaps, blame the tongue-thrusting circle quite so much as the general tolerance of such tactics. Indeed, it is possible that we ought to be grateful to it for bringing such scurrilousness to a *reductio ad absurdum* and crystallising associational sentiment in favour of a cleanup.

The history of this case is amusingly typical. There may be a dozen points in President Bradofsky's official course—as in any president's—which could justify constructive criticism; but the present Thersitean chorus has, no doubt inadvertently, neglected to mention any of these. What, instead, do we find? Counting out mere spiteful digs at the victim's literary efforts and casual utterances, there remain only a series of completely absurd charges concerning administrative moves—the falsity of many of which must have been known even by the makers.

For a characteristic specimen we may take the shrill hue and cry over Mr. Bradofsky's treatment—as a member of the Constitution Committee—of certain amendments and suggestions for amendments submitted to him last January. Irresponsible editorials have shrieked of his "throwing out" this or that measure for reasons of partisanship. Actually, he did not even lay himself open to the suspicion of so doing. Intent on fairness, he referred every debatable point to the executive judges and acted strictly according to their unanimous decisions. He said as much at the time, and all attempts to make it appear that he tried to pass off the private letters of judges as their official rulings will be revealed as silly when the executive board's report appears in *The National Amateur*. Mr. Bradofsky "threw out" nothing whatever. In one case he *requested* the author of a proposed new constitution to resubmit its measures as separate amendments, and in another case he asked the authors of some unformulated suggestions to frame the latter as true amendments and send them in again . . . all on the advice of the judges. From this record of thoroughly proper official conduct the wild charges have grown—simply because certain individuals have ceased to hold a personal liking for Mr. Bradofsky.

The mere jeering demands less extensive notice, since it bespatters its sources more than it does its target. The ethics of publishing a sneer-annotated version of a story received for printing—before the circulation of the story itself, and without the sending of a copy to the victim—may justly excite indignation; but the indignation tends to be lost in amusement (and not at the intended victim's expense) when we note the misspelled words and crude solecisms with which the sneering comment abounds! So, too, do we smile (and not at Mr. Bradofsky) when a viciously meant (and absolutely unmotivated) lashing is headed by a phrase in ungrammatical Latin and riddled with the repeated misspelling of a well-known proper name. Most certainly, Mr. Bradofsky is the last person who needs to worry about such a campaign—and the votes which he will receive next month for major offices will doubtless shew how little this childish vituperation has affected the general membership's appreciation of his really notable services. It is the association as a whole which suffers—in dignity, prestige, ethical tone, and general efficiency—when it tolerates the use of its mechanism as an instrument of personal spleen.

Mr. Edkins started a long-needed movement when he spoke out frankly against the prevailing wave of abusive personalism. One hopes to see that movement grow and bear fruit. If amateurdom is to become a playground for private spite, it can scarcely hope to hold those who are seeking an environment favourable to literary development.

VIII
EPISTOLARIAN

It is now commonly known that Lovecraft was one of the most prolific letter-writers in the history of literature. Whether he actually wrote 100,000 letters—a sum arrived at somewhat speculatively by L. Sprague de Camp, and which is probably too high—it is the substance, not the number, of his letters that is important. Lovecraft wrote letters from a compulsive need to communicate with like-minded individuals, to argue his philosophical and literary theses, and to enlighten his scattered correspondents on his activities. But he also wrote to cheer the drab life of an invalid, to encourage the mental and emotional development of teenage fans, and to act as benevolent uncle to those needing guidance and reassurance. It is this Lovecraft, perhaps more than the weaver of cosmic horrors, that genuinely deserves our admiration.

Lovecraft's letters were, however, occasionally written for more public purposes, as when he sent letters to the editors of magazines or newspapers to voice his opinions or to correct errors. It is from the surprisingly ample body of such material that the letters in this section are drawn.

Given Lovecraft's early immersion in the sciences, it should not be surprising that his first appearance in print should have been a letter to the *Providence Journal* (published in the issue for June 3, 1906) debating a point of astronomy. Another early appearance is his celebrated letter to the *Scientific American* of July 16, 1906, recommending a concerted effort to find new planets in the solar system beyond Neptune. A quarter of a century later Lovecraft would utilize in fiction the new planet that had been discovered by means not entirely dissimilar to those outlined in this letter: Pluto becomes the dark planet Yuggoth in "The Whisperer in Darkness" (1930).

Other letters reveal Lovecraft the debunker of pseudoscience at his best: the hollow-earth theory is destroyed in another letter to the

Journal, while the hapless astrologer J. F. Hartmann is mercilessly dispensed with in a series of letters and parodies in the *Providence Evening News*, where Lovecraft conducted a monthly astronomy column. In truth, these letters are not so much triumphs of logical thinking as entertaining polemics, while the parodies (not included here), written under the pseudonym of Isaac Bickerstaffe, Jun., are obvious but amusing send-ups of astrological jargon.

At the same time that Lovecraft was absorbing science, he was consuming the early pulp magazines with great avidity. In his 1914 letter to the *All-Story Weekly* he announces that he has read "every number of your magazine since . . . January, 1905." The staggering amount of pulp fiction Lovecraft must have read in his teens and twenties should give us pause; and, as the letter indicates, he read not merely the weird contributions but apparently everything in the magazines, from humor to love stories: it was, we should remember, the romances of Fred Jackson that led to Lovecraft's entry into amateur journalism. This letter is one of the few instances where Lovecraft admits to unaffected enjoyment of Edgar Rice Burroughs; in later years he would find such enthusiasm a source of embarrassment and seek to conceal or diminish it.

This early reading of pulp fiction should make us less surprised at his discovery of *Weird Tales* in 1923 and his quick success there, in spite of his avowed amateur status. Lovecraft's cover letter to Edwin Baird accompanying his first submissions seems designed to ensure their rejection; indeed, when printing this letter, Baird appended the comment: "Despite the foregoing, or because of it, we are using some of Mr. Lovecraft's unusual stories. . . ." In later letters to Baird he unwinds, telling of the surprising influence of Sherwood Anderson's *Winesburg, Ohio* on "Arthur Jermyn" and uttering the core of his theory of weird fiction long before he did so in his famous letter to Farnsworth Wright of July 5, 1927. Just as in that letter he spoke of the need to escape convention by adopting an attitude of cosmic amoralism, he here lambastes the common run of weird tales and their "conventional values and motives and perspectives."

But for all Lovecraft's cosmic theorizing, in his own emotional makeup he always remained a Providence gentleman. It was because Lovecraft had a stable and familiar background that he was able to traverse the heavens in fiction; and it was the need to preserve that background that impelled his several-year quest—unsuccessful, as it happened—to save the quaint old warehouses on South Water Street in Providence called the Brick Row. The poem "The East India Brick Row" (1929) is well known, as is the letter of October 5, 1926, where he first takes up the defense of these venerable but decaying structures; his 1929 letter is virtually his final effort, and one can sense in it the desperation of defending a lost cause. (The letter was not published in full in the *Providence Journal*, and in its appearance here it has been restored by consultation of the surviving typescript.)

Lovecraft the grandfatherly tutor appears in his late letter to the young Canadian fan Nils H. Frome. This letter was not intended for publication, as were most of the others included here, but Frome published it in a fan magazine after Lovecraft's death. In steering Frome away from the fallacies of fortune-telling, numerology, and the like, and in recommending a whole shelf of up-to-date works on astronomy, physics, and biology for a proper understanding of man and the cosmos, Lovecraft comes full circle. Science was never far from his thoughts: his philosophy was founded upon it, his tales are infused with it, and his mind never functioned save by its tenets or within its parameters. And yet, as he writes to Frome, it is precisely because he does not believe in the supernatural that he gains such pleasure from it.

As an epistolarian Lovecraft was by turns friend, instructor, and wit. His letters reveal both his literary and his intellectual powers at their widest compass, and it may not be too bold a prediction to assert that one day his letters will equal, and perhaps surpass, his fiction as the quintessence of Lovecraft's literary expression.

TRANS-NEPTUNIAN PLANETS

To the Editor of the *Scientific American:*

In these days of large telescopes and modern astronomical methods, it seems strange that no vigorous efforts are being made to discover planets beyond the orbit of Neptune, which is now considered the outermost limit of the solar system. It has been noticed that seven comets have their aphelia at a point that would correspond to the orbit of a planet revolving around the sun at a distance of about 100 astronomical units (9,300,000,000 miles).

Now several have suggested that such a planet exists, and has captured the comets by attraction. This is probable, as Jupiter and others also mark the aphelia of many celestial wanderers. The writer has noticed that a great many comets cluster around a point 50 units out, where a large body might revolve. If the great mathematicians of the day should try to compute orbits from these aphelia, it is doubtful if they could succeed; but if all the observatories that possess celestial cameras should band together and minutely photograph the ecliptic, as is done in asteroid hunting, the bodies might be revealed on their plates. Even if no discoveries were made, the accurate star photographs would almost be worth the time and trouble.

H. P. LOVECRAFT.

Providence, R.I., July 16, 1906.

THE EARTH NOT HOLLOW

To the Editor of the *Sunday Journal:*

In the *Sunday Journal* for Aug. 5 appeared an article concerning a book which advances the doctrine that the earth is a hollow sphere, with openings at the poles. A few convincing arguments were brought up in support of the theory, but it seems to me that in most points it is contradictory to fact.

Among his arguments the author of the book, which is called *The Phantom of the Poles,* suggests that the compression at the ends of the earth is due to the apertures leading to the centre, but astronomy proves that a planet's polar compression is the result of centrifugal force, i.e. the power that causes the particles of a rotating body to retreat from the centre. All the members of the solar system are thus compressed, yet we see that they possess no polar apertures, which fact alone would almost prove by analogy that the earth is solid.

Another hypothesis introduced is that the Auroras of both hemispheres are burning volcanoes or fires, the "proof" being that they do not affect the magnetic needle. This is positively untrue, for the compass is not only disturbed but often deflected several degrees from the meridian during displays of the Northern and Southern lights. In fact, the general character of Auroral phenomena precludes the supposition that they are fires of any kind.

The rocks, gravel, wood, etc., often found in icebergs is also one of the facts with which he strengthens his theory; but they are, in all probability, the result of ocean currents.

"The open Polar seas" which are referred to as existing around both poles are likewise nearly proved to be figments of imagination, as the latest results of Arctic and Antarctic exploration seem to indicate that the North Pole is in the midst of a closely frozen ocean, while the southland is occupied by a great ice-bound continent the northern limits of which are already known to us as Graham, Victoria, and Wilkes Lands.

In regard to the surface gravity of the earth, which the new doctrine holds to be greatest at the "turning points" between the outer and inner worlds, it must simply be said that theory and experiment prove the attraction to be at its maximum on the equator, where, of course, is situated the largest amount of the earth's mass, owing to the polar compression before mentioned.

Again, the "hollow earth" theory at once becomes untenable when one reflects on the volcanic and seismic disturbances which so often convulse the crust of our planet and which, together with the fact that the heat of the ground increases with depth, tends to prove that the earth's centre is a mass of molten rock and fire.

From this we can easily see that the comparative warmth of the poles, which is emphasised most strongly, probably arises from the tenuity of the earth's crust in these localities.

In short, novel and attractive as the strange hypothesis may seem, it is certainly not possible, so we can still regard the earth as a solid body.

H. P. LOVECRAFT.

Providence, Aug. 6. [1906]

TO *THE ALL-STORY WEEKLY*

[c. February 1914]

Editor, *The All-Story Magazine.*
Sir:—

Having read every number of your magazine since its beginning in January, 1905, I feel in some measure privileged to write a few words of approbation and criticism concerning its contents.

In the present age of vulgar taste and sordid realism it is a relief to peruse a publication such as *The All-Story*, which has ever been and still remains under the influence of the imaginative school of Poe and Verne.

For such materialistic readers as your North-British correspondent, Mr. G. W. P., of Dundee, there are only too many periodicals containing "probable" stories; let *The All-Story* continue to hold its unique position as purveyor of literature to those whose minds cannot be confined within the narrow circle of probability, or dulled into a passive acceptance of the tedious round of things as they are.

If, in fact, man is unable to create living beings out of inorganic matter, to hypnotise beasts of the forest to do his will, to swing from tree to tree with the apes of the African jungle, to restore to life the mummified corpses of the Pharaohs and the Incas, or to explore the atmosphere of Venus and the deserts of Mars, permit us, at least, in fancy, to witness these miracles, and to satisfy that craving for the unknown, the weird, and the impossible which exists in every active human brain.

Particular professors and sober Scotchmen may denounce as childish the desire for imaginative fiction; nay, I am not sure but that such a desire is childish, and rightly so, for are not many of man's noblest attributes but the remnants of his younger nature? He who can retain in his older years the untainted mind, the lively imagination, and the artless curiosity of his infancy, is rather blessed than cursed; such men as these are our authors, scientists, and inventors.

At or near the head of your list of writers Edgar Rice Burroughs undoubtedly stands. I have read very few recent novels by others wherein is displayed an equal ingenuity in plot, and verisimilitude in treatment. His only fault seems to be a tendency toward scientific inaccuracy and slight inconsistencies.

For example, in that admirable story, "Tarzan of the Apes", we meet *Sabor*, the tiger, far from his native India, and we behold the hero, before he has learned the relation between vocal sounds and written letters, writing out his name, *Tarzan, which he has known only from the lips of his hairy associates*, as well as the names of *Kerchak, Tantor, Numa*, and *Terkoz*, all of which he could not possibly have seen written.

Also, in "The Gods of Mars", Mr. Burroughs refers to the year of the red planet as having 687 *Martian* days. This is, of course, absurd, for while Mars revolves about the sun in 687 *terrestrial* days, its own day or period of rotation is almost forty minutes longer than ours, thus giving to Mars a year which contains but 668$\frac{2}{3}$ *Martian* solar days. I note with regret that this error has been repeated in "Warlord of Mars".

William Patterson White, in writing "Sands o' Life", has shewn himself to be an author of the first order. The very spirit of the old Spanish Main pervades the pages of this remarkable novel. It is worthy of permanent publication as a book.

In the domain of the weird and bizarre, Lee Robinet has furnished us a masterpiece by writing "The Second Man". The atmosphere created and sustained throughout the story can be the work only of a gifted and polished artist. Very effective is the author's careful neglect to tell the exact location of his second Eden.

I strongly hope that you have added Perley Poore Sheehan permanently to your staff, for in him may be recognised an extremely powerful writer. I have seen Mr. Sheehan's work elsewhere, and was especially captivated by a grim short story of his entitled "His Ancestor's Head".

William Tillinghast Eldridge set such a standard for himself in "The Forest Reaper" that it seems almost a pity for him to be the author of "The Tormentor" and "Cowards All".

William Loren Curtiss tells a homely yet exciting sort of tale which exerts upon the reader a curious fascination. "Shanty House" seems to me the best of the two he has contributed to *The All-Story*.

Donald Francis McGrew is one of the "red-blooded" school of writers; he describes the Philippine Islands and the army there with an ease indicative of long residence or military service on the scene of his literary productions.

I hardly need mention the author of "A Columbus of Space" further than to say that I have read every published work of Garrett P. Serviss, own most of them, and await his future writings with eagerness. When a noted astronomer composes an astronomical novel, we need not fear such things as years of 687 Martian days upon the planet Mars.

As to your short stories, necessarily second in importance to the novels and serials, it may be said that some of them rise much above the middle level, while few of them fall beneath it. The merry crew of humorous writers, such as T. Bell, Jack Brant, Frank Condon, and Donald A. Kahn, are, though light and sometimes a trifle silly, nevertheless distinctly amusing. Kahn is especially clever in drawing the characters of callow college youths.

I hesitate to criticise adversely such an excellent magazine as this, but since my censure falls upon so small a part of it, I think I may express myself openly without giving offence.

I fear that a faint shadow from the black cloud of vileness now darkening our literature and drama has lately fallen upon a few pages of *The All-Story.*

"The Souls of Men", by Martha M. Stanley, was a distinctly disagreeable tale, but "Pilgrims in Love", by De Lysle Ferrée Cass, is contemptibly disgusting, unspeakably nauseating. Mr. G. W. S., of Chicago, has written that Cass "diplomatically handles a very difficult subject–Oriental love".

We do not care for subjects so near allied to vulgarity, however "diplomatically" they may be "handled". Of such "Oriental love" we may speak in the words of the lazy but ingenious schoolboy, who when asked by his tutor to describe the reign of Caligula, replied, "that the less said about it the better." We prefer a more idealised Orient to read about; let us have "Nature to advantage drest", as in the beautiful romance of "Prince Imbecile", by C. MacLean Savage, or "The Invisible Empire", by Stephen Chalmers.

Speaking of the last novel, is not the title somewhat misleading? In the United States the name "Invisible Empire" is forever associated with that noble but much maligned band of Southerners who protected their homes against the diabolical freed blacks and Northern adventurers in the years of misgovernment just after the Civil War–the dreaded Ku-Klux-Klan.

The broad editorial policy of *The All-Story* in making the magazine not merely a local American publication, but a bond of common interest between the United Kingdom, the United States, and the various British Colonies, cannot be too heartily commended.

Blood is thicker than water; we are all Englishmen, and need just such a leveler of political barriers as this to remind us of our common origin. Let the London reader reflect, that in Boston, Toronto, Cape

Town, Calcutta, Melbourne, Auckland, and nearly everywhere else, his racial kindred are perusing the same stirring stories that delight him.

America may have withdrawn from the British Empire of government, but thanks to such magazines as *The All-Story,* it must ever remain an integral and important part of the great universal empire of British thought and literature.

I cannot praise *The All-Story Magazine* by comparing it with others, since it stands alone in its class, but I think I have made it clear that I hold this publication in the highest esteem, and derive much pleasure from its pages. What I have said in criticism of some parts of it I have said only with friendly intent, believing that the humble opinions of one more reader may prove not unacceptable to you.

But ere I grow more tedious still, let me close this already protracted epistle, and, with the best wishes for the future of *The All-Story,* subscribe myself as

Your obedient servant,
H. P. L.

SCIENCE VERSUS CHARLATANRY

[c. September 5, 1914]

To the Editor of the *Evening News:*

It is an unfortunate fact that every man who seeks to disseminate knowledge must contend not only against ignorance itself, but against false instruction as well. No sooner do we deem ourselves free from a particularly gross superstition, than we are confronted by some enemy to learning who would set aside all the intellectual progress of years, and plunge us back into the darkness of mediaeval disbelief.

As a lover of Astronomy, and writer on that subject, I was the other day very much pained and shocked to see in the *Evening News* an article on the pseudo-science of Astrology, which has ever been the bane of the seeker after truth. While I entertain no doubt as to the sincerity of the author, a Mr. Hartmann, [it is difficult] for me to comprehend how any person of judgment and education can now give credence to the doctrines of a false and ridiculous system completely exploded over 200 years ago. In this age of enlightenment it ought not to be necessary to shew the utter absurdity of the idea that our daily affairs can be governed by the mere apparent motions of infinitely distant bodies whose seeming arrangements and configurations, on which the calculations of judicial astrology are based, arise only from perspective as seen from our particular place in the universe. It seems very provoking that astronomers and other men of sense should be obliged to waste their time and energy in proving Astrology to be false, when there exists not the slightest reason to believe any part of it true; yet the perverse sophistry of certain misguided individuals still raises up such a body of specious evidence in favour of it, that we must needs attack again what we had thought finally conquered. The fallacies of Astrology are like the many heads of the Lernean Hydra; chop off one, and two grow in its place.

Mr. Hartmann, in his recent article, seeks to defend Astrology by assertions that the astronomers and scientists who shew its falsity are unacquainted with its precepts. This statement loses force when we reflect that the whole mass of nonsense which constitutes this study is only a vague distortion and misuse of astronomical principles; indeed, the study of Astronomy absolutely proves the spurious nature of Astrology by elimination, or *reductio ad absurdum*. It is very amusing to read Mr. Hartmann's hostile allusions to Mr. Garrett P. Serviss and the late Richard A. Proctor. These two popular astronomical writers, similar in many ways, have by means of their double gifts of scientific and literary skill accomplished marvels in dissipating superstition and propagating truth; it is no wonder that they are hated and feared by the leaders of the hosts of ignorance.

Still more amusing is Mr. Hartmann's sober reference to the English astrological almanacks. These wretched pamphlets, though much perused by the vulgar and the ignorant, have been the laughing-stock of the intelligent British public since Queen Anne's time, when Dr. Swift destroyed with such exquisite humour the pretensions of the conceited astrologer and almanack-maker, John Partridge. In 1827 the Society for the Diffusion of Christian Knowledge severely attacked annuals of this sort and later caused most of them either to suspend publication or to discontinue their astrological predictions, so that today only two, *Zadkiel's* and *Raphael's*, are in existence. The prophecies of these almanacks are like the utterances of the Delphic Oracle; so vague and ambiguous that they can be made to suit any subsequent events. In many a time of peace have the mystics and seers given forth warnings fully as dire and dreadful as any that have preceded the present war.

The ravings of *Raphael* about lamentable losses to kings and emperors may be made to fit alike the loss of a handkerchief or of a throne. War in the Balkans, unrest in Russia, and revolutions in Central or South America are among the events most successfully predicted. Mr. Hartmann's mention of the predictions of Pope Pius' death reminds me that this same event was scheduled to occur in 1906 by a learned astrologer of Central Falls, R.I.

I should not like to take up your time nor seek to occupy your columns with this reply to Mr. Hartmann if I did not consider Astrology a dangerous as well as a silly subject. In the minds of the masses it tends to become confused with Astronomy, and thereby to injure the reputation of that science.

The *News* has ever been a friend to the improvement and instruction of the public, so that I am confident it will not begrudge me a little space besides that which I regularly occupy on the first of each month, in my humble efforts to diffuse truth and to expose fallacy regarding the heavens.

H. P. LOVECRAFT.

598 Angell Street, Providence, R.I.

THE FALL OF ASTROLOGY

To the Editor of the *Evening News:*

In perusing Mr. Hartmann's somewhat belated reply to my letter in the *Evening News* of October 10, I am impressed with the resentment the astrologer seems to harbour against me for what he deems my abusive treatment of him. It may be that contempt for the puerile fallacies of astrological lore has led me into a rather too caustic procedure with my opponent, yet I would assure him that I respect the sincerity of his opinions, and admire the spirit with which he defends his pseudo-science. In the present letter I shall strive to avoid the use of that denunciation and ridicule against which Mr. Hartmann so strongly protests; but shall instead try the novel experiment of suspending my attack, and of assuming a defensive attitude, endeavouring merely to justify the present universal rejection of astrology by the intelligent public.

Astrology was coeval with astronomy. It was indeed, as I pointed out in a previous article, the natural result of the contemplation of the celestial vault by a young and undeveloped race. In very ancient times it was of real value to science on account of the incentive which it offered to the precise observation and careful study of the heavenly bodies. The astronomical knowledge of the Chaldaeans was in fact wholly due to the zeal of their astrologers. Thus before the advent of modern scientific exactitude, the true and false studies of the sky were pursued side by side and in perfect harmony. If either one might be said to have precedence over the other, astrology was the one so favoured. Throughout the Middle Ages and the early Modern Period astrology enjoyed the condition of a respected branch of learning. Each monarch had his astrologer or astrologers, to whom he referred all projected affairs of state, both in war and in peace. Though at the time of the Renaissance some keener minds penetrated the specious exterior and discovered the fundamental unsoundness of the art, it was none the less very generally cultivated by all classes, foremost among them being the astronomers. Kepler, while discarding many of its more patently absurd notions, stoutly defended the underlying truth of astrology, and made known his views in a pamphlet entitled *De Fundamentis Astrologiae Certioribus* (1601). Lord Bacon and Sir Thomas Browne were likewise believers in the influence of the heavens. As late as Charles the Second's reign the public had scarce begun to doubt the genuineness of astrology, and the notorious William Lilly, though probably a conscious charlatan himself, was credited to a marvellous degree, even being summoned at one time by a committee of the House of Commons to predict the result of a certain piece of legislation.

Thus it may be perceived, that before the discovery of conclusive contrary evidence, astrology encountered no opposition either from the astronomers or from the people in general. So long as any man of science could find any reason to believe it true, it was accepted on a plane of equality with other serious studies. The only bigotry and blind prejudice which astrology ever aroused emanated from the early church; but this hostility did not extend to every department of the subject, and has no connexion with the later overthrow of the art on rational grounds.

The downfall of astrology was the inevitable result of intellectual progress; of new discoveries in science, improved methods of reasoning, more intelligent examination of history, and more discriminating investigation of the prophecies of astrologers. It became apparent that very few definite astrological predictions had ever been fulfilled even approximately, that almost all forecasts were couched in a vague style which might be interpreted in practically any way, that the most successful astrologers were obviously impostors who arrived at their conclusions only through shrewd guesses or profound knowledge of human nature, and that those who most honestly practiced astrology were the most conspicuous in their failures. At the same time, earnest students perfectly familiar with astrology and astrological methods commenced to realise the utter absurdity of the study. They saw that the very fundamental principle of casting horoscopes rests on mere allegory; the analogy of a man's birth to a star's rising. They saw that the various qualities attributed to the several planets and their positions in the Zodiac were derived wholly from the mythical gods and monsters after which the planets and stars were named. Not only was it shewn that astrological predictions were untrue, but also that every method employed to make them is false. Besides, no reason was found why the heavens should in any manner whatsoever influence or indicate the lives and destinies of mankind. What excuse, then, could any man have for adhering to a belief unsupported by the least particle of evidence, and possessing not the slightest shadow of probability? Even had there been no direct evidence against astrology, the complete absence of evidence for it would have been sufficient to justify its abandonment. Astrology died a natural and honourable death; and had the world been content to let it rest in peace, it would never have become an object of contempt and ridicule. But the greed of the charlatan and the vagaries of the eccentric kept it before the eyes of a public who had outgrown belief, and who could not but be intolerant of an art which they knew to be obsolete. The first opponents of astrology were perfectly conversant with its principles, and derived from their knowledge only the more material for use against it. But the study of the pseudo-science naturally disappeared amongst the intelligent as soon as its falsity was well demonstrated. It would of course be ridiculous for men to waste their lives in amassing information which is well known to be false, and which would seriously interfere with their acquisition of real learning. We cannot spend our precious years in repeating all the errors of our remote forefathers; we must rather profit by old blunders, and seek to avoid the false in favour of the true. Wherefore reputable authors, publishers, and institutions of learning have ceased to disseminate the fallacies of astrology, and the present generation have no hesitation in declaring their absolute unfamiliarity with that subject. It has been disproved so many times by those versed in its mysteries, that even were astronomy not enough to brand it false, we should not need to repeat such a redundant performance. Why does not Mr. Hartmann demand that we disprove the old, abandoned Ptolemaic theory of the universe once more?

Let me now consider some of my opponent's statements in greater detail. He declares quite gravely, that "when physicians say the moon's phases influence their patients, the astronomers call it truth." I hardly need answer that no astronomer of the present time would credit such an absurd assertion, nor would any rational physician make it.

Another paragraph of Mr. Hartmann's is truly amazing. He tells us that with but one exception the astronomical books in our public library leave the reader with the impression that planetary orbits are circular. I have read nearly all of the volumes in question, and can say with certainty that none of them could possibly convey such an idea to any intelligent person. The elliptical nature of orbits is too well known to be concealed even by the vaguest of books.

Mr. Hartmann inquires of me, in connexion with my denunciation of the "ordinary modern astrologer" as a mountebank, what I would consider an ancient or an extraordinary astrologer. Since the ancient astrologers believed to a greater or less extent their own predictions, I should call them somewhat misguided scientists; while as for the extraordinary modern prophets like Mr. Hartmann himself, I think I gave them sufficient credit for their fanatical sincerity in my previous letter.

Before concluding, I should like to comment on Mr. Hartmann's curious attempt at etymological derivation of the word "superstition". Surely he could not have obtained such a mass of nonsense from the authorities he quotes, for any man of education knows that the word comes directly from the Latin and not from the Greek. "Superstition" is from the Latin "superstare", in turn derived from "super", over, and "stare", to stand still; the implied meaning being a standing still over anything in dread amazement or reverence. All of this information can be obtained from Webster's Unabridged Dictionary, which should invariably be consulted on points of this sort. However, I fail to see how the origin of the word can interest Mr. Hartmann so much more than its present use, which is sufficiently well known to all.

I have here endeavoured to treat seriously a subject which can scarce be contemplated without a smile. This rather inappropriate method must find its justification in the sober and extremely zealous tone of my opponent's arguments.

H. P. LOVECRAFT.

Dec. 15, 1914.

TO EDWIN BAIRD

[c. May 1923]

My Dear Sir:—

Having a habit of writing weird, macabre, and fantastic stories for my own amusement, I have lately been simultaneously hounded by nearly a dozen well-meaning friends into deciding to submit a few of these Gothic horrors to your newly founded periodical. The decision is herewith carried out. Enclosed are five tales written between 1917 and 1923.

Of these the first two are probably the best. If they be unsatisfactory, the rest need not be read. . . . "The Statement of Randolph Carter" is, in the main, an actual dream experienced on the night of December 21–22, 1919; the characters being myself (Randolph Carter) and my friend, Samuel Loveman, the poet and editor of *Twenty-One Letters of Ambrose Bierce.*

I have no idea that these things will be found suitable, for I pay no attention to the demands of commercial writing. My object is such pleasure as I can obtain from the creation of certain bizarre pictures, situations, or atmospheric effects; and the only reader I hold in mind is myself.

My models are invariably the older writers, especially Poe, who has been my favourite literary figure since early childhood. Should any miracle impel you to consider the publication of my tales, I have but one condition to offer; and that is that no excisions be made. If the tale cannot be printed as written, down to the very last semicolon and comma, it must gracefully accept rejection. Excision by editors is probably one reason why no living American author has a real prose style. . . . But I am probably safe, for my MSS. are not likely to win your consideration. "Dagon" has been rejected by ———, to which I sent it under external compulsion—much as I am sending you the enclosed. This magazine sent me a beautifully tinted and commendably impersonal rejection slip. . . .

I like *Weird Tales* very much, though I have seen only the April number. Most of the stories, of course, are more or less commercial—or should I say conventional?—in technique, but they all have an enjoyable angle. "Beyond the Door", by Paul Suter, seems to me the most truly touched with the elusive quality of original genius—though "A Square of Canvas", by Anthony M. Rud, would be a close second if not so reminiscent in denouement of Balzac's "Le Chef d'Oeuvre Inconnu"—as I recall it across a lapse of years, without a copy at hand. However, one doesn't expect a very deep thrill in this sophisticated and tradesman-minded age. Arthur Machen is the only living man I know of who can stir truly profound and spiritual horror.

TO EDWIN BAIRD

[early November 1923]

My dear Baird:—

I was indeed glad to receive yours of the 14th, and to learn that your readers are taking kindly to my tenebrous effusions, as represented by "Dagon". I hope they'll like its successors as well—for I can certainly give them all you think they'll take! That "The Hound" merits your favour is pleasing news to me. I wrote it a year ago in New York, when I had been exploring an old Dutch cemetery in Flatbush, where the ancient gravestones are in the Dutch language, with such beginnings as "Hier Lydt" and "Hier leght begraaven". My companion was Rheinhart Kleiner (whose verse you may have seen in some of the popular magazines), and when we picked up some scaling red slate from one of the slabs as souvenirs, I wondered what *thing* might come to us some midnight to punish us for the wanton desecration.

And here is another horror for your approval or rejection. This thing—whose long title you can shorten to "The Late Arthur Jermyn" if the original presents typographical problems—was written about two years ago. Its origin is rather curious—and far removed from the atmosphere it suggests. Somebody had been harassing me into reading some work of the iconoclastic moderns—these young chaps who pry behind exteriors and unveil nasty hidden motives and secret stigmata—and I had nearly fallen asleep over the tame backstairs gossip of Anderson's *Winesburg, Ohio.* The sainted Sherwood, as you know, laid bare the dark area which many whited village lives concealed; and it occurred to me that I, in my weirder medium, could probably devise some secret behind a man's ancestry which would make the worst of Anderson's disclosures sound like the annual report of a Sabbath school. Hence Arthur Jermyn. Most of those who have seen the MS. profess themselves properly horrified—all, in fact, except one chap who has travelled to Rhodesia, and declares himself bound by ties of the purest and most undaunted affection to all the denizens, negro and simian alike, of the Dark Continent.

Popular authors do not and apparently cannot appreciate the fact that true art is obtainable only by rejecting normality and conventionality in toto, and approaching a theme purged utterly of any usual or preconceived point of view. Wild and "different" as they may consider their quasi-weird products, it remains a fact that the bizarrerie is on the surface alone; and that basically they reiterate the same old conventional values and motives and perspectives. Good and evil, teleological illusion, sugary sentiment, anthropocentric psychology—the usual superficial stock in trade, and all shot through with the eternal and inescapable commonplace. Take a werewolf story, for instance—who ever wrote a story from the point of view of the wolf, and sympathising strongly with the devil to whom he has sold himself? Who ever wrote a story from the point of view that man is a blemish on the cosmos, who ought to be eradicated? As an example—a young man I know lately told me that he means to write a story about a scientist who wishes to dominate the earth, and who to accomplish his ends trains and overdevelops germs (à la Anthony Rud's "Ooze"), and leads on armies of them in the manner of the Egyptian plagues. I told him that although this theme has promise, it is made utterly commonplace by assigning the scientist a normal motive. There is nothing outré about wanting to conquer the earth; Alexander, Napoleon, and Wilhelm II wanted to do that. Instead, I told my friend, he should conceive a man with a morbid, frantic, shuddering hatred of the life-principle itself, who wishes to extirpate from the planet every trace of biological organism, animal and vegetable alike, including himself. That would be tolerably original. But after all, originality lies within the author. One can't write a weird story of real power without perfect psychological detachment from the human scene, and a magic prism of imagination which suffuses theme and style alike with that grotesquerie and disquieting distortion characteristic of morbid vision. Only a cynic can create horror—for behind every masterpiece of the sort must reside a driving daemonic force that despises the human race and its illusions, and longs to pull them to pieces and mock them. This is true in even greater degree of pictorial artists—I wish you could get a staff of Clark Ashton Smiths to illustrate *Weird Tales!* The normal artist has conventional conceptions of line and detail, light and shade; but the macabre genius has the magic prism, and sees the world in that leeringly twisted, mockingly decorative light which gives rise to the achievements of an Aubrey Beardsley, Sidney Sime, John Martin, Gustave Doré, or—immortal of immortals—Francisco Goya y Lucientes. I wish you could get some illustrations and cover designs from Clark Ashton Smith himself—even though he isn't doing so much in that line lately as he used to do. He lacks technical assurance, but has the lurid vision to an abnormal degree.

I find Eddy rather a delight—I wish I had known him before. Next Sunday we are going on a trip which may bring you echoes in the form of horror-tales from both participants. In the northwestern part of Rhode Island there is a remote village called Chepachet, reached by a single car line with only a few cars a day. Last week Eddy was there for the first time, and at the post office overheard a conversation between two ancient rustic farmers which inspired our coming expedition. They were discussing hunting prospects, and spoke of the migration of all the rabbits and squirrels across the line into Connecticut; when one told the other that there were plenty left in the *Dark Swamp.* Then ensued a description to which Eddy listened with the utmost avidity, and which brought out the fact that in this, the smallest and most densely populated state of the Union, there exists a tract of 160 acres which has never been fully penetrated by any living man. It lies two miles from Chepachet—in a direction we do not now know, but which we will ascertain Sunday—and is reported to be the home of very strange animals—strange at least to this part of the world, and including the dreaded "bobcat", whose half-human cries in the night are often heard by neighbouring farmers. The reason it has never been fully penetrated is that there are many treacherous potholes, and that the archaic trees grow so thickly together that passage is well-nigh impossible. The undergrowth is very thick, and even midday the darkness is very deep because of the intertwined branches overhead. The description so impressed Eddy that he began writing a story about it—provisionally titled "Black Noon"—on the trolley ride home. And now we are both to see it . . . we are both to go to that swamp . . . and *perhaps* to come out of it. Probably the thing'll turn out to be a clump of ill-nourished bushes, a few rain-puddles, and a couple of sparrows—but until our disillusion we are at liberty to think of the place as the immemorial lair of nightmare and unknown evil ruled by that subterraneous horror that sometimes cranes its neck out of the deepest potholes . . . It.

THE OLD BRICK ROW

To the Editor of the *Sunday Journal:*

Discussion in these columns of the area between South Main and South Water Streets near Market Square, proposed either as a site for a Hall of Records or as a cleared plaza to enhance the effect of the new Court House, brings into very pertinent debate the future of the quaint, graceful old buildings now standing there. Behind it looms the far broader clash of city-planning ideals which it typifies; the eternal warfare, based on temperament and degree of sensitiveness to deep local currents of feeling, between those who cherish a landscape truly expressive of a town's individuality, and those who demand the uniformly modern, commercially efficient, and showily sumptuous at any cost.

Beyond doubt, the plans hitherto mentioned take a very superficial view in considering a permanent landscape for this focal, historic meeting-place of bay and hill. The side of tradition, which finds the soundest beauty in a retention of forms and proportions evolved from the continuous history of a proud old seaport, is well-nigh unrepresented; all the commentators apparently taking for granted the cruder, flashier ideal of a stridently modernised city of pompous vistas and spruce, mid-Western architectural luxury—not a haven to charm the connoisseur of richly mellow old-world lanes, but a tungsten-drenched Midway to lure the hard-boiled buyer from Detroit, or a scenic flourish in deference to Seattle and Los Angeles aesthetes attuned to a futuristic Chicago or the maltreated Paris of Haussmann and Viollet-le-Duc.

Amid such complacent "progressiveness" one feels almost timid in suggesting that the history and topography of Providence's older sections call for a decorative standard far removed from the expansive, the lavish, and the monumental. Suggest it one must, however, since the whole matter of a basic standard is evidently overlooked by those who glibly urge majestic spaces and imposing facades as fixed, absolute boons regardless of environment or atmosphere. To a chorus clamouring indiscriminately for lavishness and modernity in any and every place, the fact ought surely to be pointed out that what is appropriate in one type of locality is not necessarily so in another, and that the neighbourhood of our picturesque old "Market Parade" and head of navigation is distinctly unsuited to a formal, radical transformation upsetting its traditional character.

If Providence must have a sumptuous region of modern vistas like Boston's Back Bay, let it further emulate the latter by choosing an empty or unhistoric zone for the experiment. We have many sections topographically suited to this purpose; Exchange Place, Cathedral Square, and "Newmarket" (the confluence of Broad, Weybosset, Chestnut, and Empire Streets) being typical examples. These sections, ugly or Victorian in their dominant motif except for the Exchange Place park and mall, would have little to lose through a change; and their renovation would form a net addition to the city's beauty. How much more sensible to make monumental developments where they are fitting and where nothing of importance need be sacrificed, than to purchase a new and doubtfully appropriate splendour at the expense of an historic elder beauty which is absolutely irreplaceable and perhaps of greater worth!

Specifically, there can be little question but that the proper treatment of the Market Square region is a modest one preserving its colonial and maritime lines and maintaining an atmospheric harmony with the ancient Market House and the two exquisite Georgian steeples close by. There is space in abundance at present, with a promise of still more when the complete covering of the river is accomplished. The line of slant-roofed brick warehouses in South Water Street, built in the decade following the "Great Gale" of 1815, rounds out a satisfying picture and symbol of the old Yankee seaport spirit which ought to be precious to every native Providentian, and which surely would be if a greater sense of its historical significance were aroused. We are singularly lucky in possessing this quaint, characteristic waterfront at our advanced stage of civic growth, for very few ports of this size have been able to keep such links with the romantic days of brigs, privateers, and East-Indiamen. As it is, with a splendidly intact row instead of merely a few scattered examples, we can rival the choicest of New England's coast towns in colour; presenting the unusual synthesis of a busy and populous life against a bit of visible background comparable to anything in Portsmouth, Newburyport, or Newport. To lose such a generous, vivid fragment of the poetry of history at this late date, and for no valid reason, would be a tragedy peculiarly ironic.

But it is not merely as historic colour that this ancient brick row is worth cherishing. That indeed might be reason enough, for local fixity breeds a beauty of its own—a beauty of memories with very valid claims against the outward beauty of the eye. In this case, however, we have an actual visual beauty as well; for only a barbarian warped by garish standards could be blind to the intrinsic charm of these humbly harmonious structures. To call objects of such graceful simplicity and artlessly fine proportions "shabby, ramshackle old rookeries" is merely to display a stunted artistic feeling or ignorance of good design. They have been conspicuously praised by nearly every discriminating visitor who has seen them, especially Europeans of taste who know the magic of old-world towns and famous waterfronts. Offhand one recalls among these admirers the names of James Stephens, John Drinkwater, and Padraic Colum. Nor are the best-qualified local judges any different in their verdicts. Only a year ago the supreme architectural authority of all, Mr. Norman M. Isham, was quoted in the *Journal* as admiring the old brick row and wishing that it might be saved.

Just now the readers of that much-discussed novel *A Dead Man Dies* cannot fail to notice how the caustic author, blind though he is to nine-tenths of the city's good buildings and landscapes, is forced momentarily into a grudging appreciation by the sight of ancient Market Square. "There," he sourly concedes in somewhat laboured prose, "the old brick buildings facing the Providence River have a mellow redness that brings with it a glamour that neither the Italians vending garden truck nor the stench of the river can kill. Only a hundred yards away there is the harbour, and so long as there is salt water with a mast rising above it, there is romance."

The arguments for removing the old buildings are of two kinds, aesthetic and practical. Those who stress the first set are perhaps the more misled in their premises; for their one major plea, whether they wish a new Hall of Records or a wholly cleared plaza, is that the present brick row forms an inadequate environment for the massive new Court House now rising on the hillside behind it. To one who has studied the design of the Court House as it will ultimately look, or even to one who has carefully noted the part already reared, it ought to be obvious that such a plea is almost the sheerest nonsense.

The builders of this edifice, like the builders of many other recent local structures, have a truer instinct for Providence atmosphere than have the present destruction-advocates; and are creating something which not only does not clash with the old waterside warehouses, but which actually carries on their tradition and derives an additional grace and mellowness from their presence. Naturally, a neo-classic or Renaissance temple of gleaming white marble would be at variance with the quaint Yankee market-place which history has given us, and would demand a stilted new landscape to match it; but as it happens, the designers had too much sense and taste to rear such a thing. Instead, they have provided a marvellously adroit group of wings or units in the familiar red brick of the local tradition; so that in effect the spacious new pile will be not one continuous mass of incongruous and overawing vastness, but a graceful cluster of separate roof-lines and gables, many of them reproducing Providence colonial types, whose total impression will be that of the artistically irregular skyline of a terraced hillside town—just such a town as Old Providence.

The harmony with the old brick row facing the water will be complete, since these genuine survivors of the Georgian era will set the keynote for the soaring tiers of neo-Georgian gables above them; forming an ideal starting-point for the eye and the imagination, and bridging the years between the early maritime Providence and the modern metropolis. No other building or buildings, and no open landscape development, could compare with this old row as a frame for the tall, white-belfried newcomer. The glamorous loveliness of clustered roofs rising over roofs in an ancient town is something which artists have always appreciated abroad, and which they are beginning to appreciate here, as attested by Mr. Henry J. Peck's recent exhibition of captivating local drawings and etchings.

The practical arguments for removing the old buildings involve both the wish to widen South Main Street and the need for a Hall of Records. Regarding the first: this could of course be accomplished without disturbing the best group of structures concerned—the old brick row—since the latter fronts on South Water; yet it seems doubtful if even this programme of partial destruction is necessary in view of the continuous highway afforded by Canal and South Water Streets. The narrowness of South Main at this point is a quaint and not unbeautiful reminder of the old "Towne Street", as we may appreciate in the Duphinney painting reproduced on a calendar two years ago; and it would surely be a pity to destroy such a picturesque survival without adequate reason. Moreover, one of the buildings in South Main (Nos. 27–31) is the old Nicholas Brown house, erected about 1760 and used during the sojourn of Rochambeau's troops as the abode of three of his officers—de Vauban, de Dumas, and that appealing Swedish adventurer Count Axel de Fersen. It is one of only three surviving Providence houses in which French officers lodged during the Revolution.

Much better than street-widening would be a judicious reconstruction of the old-time atmosphere on the west side of South Main Street, involving the removal of the hopelessly decrepit and already mutilated houses, and the restoration of the remainder. The one desirable alteration of street lines may perhaps be the razing of the two buildings north of Leonard's Lane, which would open a larger area around the foot of College Street and give a broader spaciousness to Market Square. Of these buildings one is nondescript and Victorian, while its colonial companion is too much altered and defaced to be of architectural value. This removal, of course, gives South Water Street brick row an improved scenic position.

As for the need of a Hall of Records—it may reasonably be asked why no one has yet thought of using the old brick row itself for this purpose. By closing one or more of the alleys between South Main and South Water Streets—Wyeth, Hutchinson, and Mark Lane—as large a continuous structure as desired can be made of the venerable warehouses, linked where the gaps occur. The interiors, of course, would be totally removed and replaced by floors, partitions, and stacks of modern fireproof construction; but the grace of the ancient walls and roof-line would remain, and the ends of practicality prosper without loss to quaintness and tradition. There would, besides, be actual economy in such an arrangement; for the brickwork of Georgian times is as toughly solid as the Pyramids, and would form an admirable nucleus for the fresh interior. Successful experiments with modern fireproof construction inside old brick walls, as in the Municipal Museum Building of Paterson, N.J., proves that the notion is by no means extravagant or chimerical. The long, narrow dimensions of the composite building thus formed could hardly constitute a major objection.

Urban mellowness, picturesqueness, and historic colour are rare enough to America, and it is not unreasonable to hope that as much as possible will be spared in the few towns lucky enough to retain them. This could be made certain if appreciative persons would reflect maturely on the relative values of things; balancing the aesthetic against the baldly commercial, and recognising the need of discrimination and local feeling in landscape standards.

—H. P. L.

Providence, March 20, 1929.

TO NILS H. FROME

[February 8, 1937]

Regarding views of the universe and its phenomena—my ideas certainly do seem to differ quite diametrically from those which you have so far possessed. However, I can assure you that they are merely the normal ideas held by serious students of science and reflected in the majority of books by responsible authorities. You must realise that what the cheap pulp science-fiction magazines present is not real science. It is simply romance and day-dreaming based on thin scientific theories —the latter often badly twisted and strained. You will not find any real information about life and the universe in the circle of enthusiastic adolescent "fans" which has grown up around these magazines. These boys are all day-dreamers—who will forget all about science when they grow up. The place to get real facts about man and the world and the universe is in serious books written by the careful, thorough researchers and scientific scholars of today—men who do not try to write romance or invent fanciful ideas or keep alive the dead myths of the past; but who are interested only in setting down, so far as they know, the cold facts as they are. Virtually all serious students—biologists, physicists, chemists, astronomers—agree in their estimate of *life* as a very minor phenomenon. It is, of course, the most *highly organised* form of matter and energy which we know; but it is probably of very rare occurrence in the cosmos (since it requires special conditions involving what we must regard as an accident in order to produce the sort of planetary system adapted to its appearance and growth), and we have certain knowledge that its development to complex forms like man and other mammals depends wholly on an intricate chain of accidents extending over hundreds of thousands of years and so utterly peculiar to the one planet in question that nothing similar could possibly occur anywhere else. That is not to say that *some* highly complex form of life could not grow on some other planet in some other galaxy; but merely to say that it is impossible for such an alien form of life to be anything like *our* terrestrial higher forms.

Every feature of human life and appearance and thought that we know is determined solely by the chance environmental conditions peculiar to this one planet. Biologists can trace the origin of any phase of life, and see how it grew out of the accidents of terrestrial existence. There is no warrant for reading any such thing as "purpose" into the universe as a whole—indeed, the whole psychological attitude implied in the word "purpose" is merely a chance human characteristic. People who claim that the universe as a whole has "purpose" are merely perpetuating primitive man's crude myth-making process (called "animism") of imagining that abstract or inarticulate objects have the same thoughts and feelings as man. The "soul" is a purely mythical thing. Man's *consciousness* is a material reality—a definite electro-chemical process in a biological organism—and the concept of a "soul" is only a primitive and superstitious way of regarding this consciousness with its thoughts and feelings. The notion of anything "immortal" about man or any biological organism—that is, the notion of qualities not dependent upon the cells of the material body—is in the light of today's knowledge wholly untenable. But there is no need of getting depressed about man's insignificance. Who really *wants* to be cosmically important anyhow? What good would it do us if we actually were? There is plenty to keep us comfortably busy during the brief period of our individual existence—and when the momentary phenomenon called life vanishes from our planet we'll never know the difference. Instead of fretting about being insignificant, it's up to us to enjoy the faculties we have—exercising our intellectual curiosity in study and our aesthetic sense in imagination and artistic creation. And if our egos need a stimulus, we can at least reflect that we represent the most complex form of organisation within our radius of knowledge. We are only a momentary accident—but even so, we typify far subtler and more delicate energy-transformation processes than any other objects within our field of view. We may also conjecture that the basic principle of life exists (though sparingly) elsewhere, and that under the usual shifting of planetary conditions it probably evolves to considerable complexity—albeit a complexity wholly unlike ours—in many cases. Thus we may assume that life as a principle is perhaps eternal; although each local planetary manifestation of it is accidental and momentary, and will never know of any such manifestation elsewhere in the universe. Two or more planetary life-streams can never know of each other unless they occur on neighbouring bodies of the same solar system. The only life outside our earth of which we know is the primitive vegetation which probably exists on Mars—and it is very unlikely that (barring primitive life-forms in meteorites, if such are ever found) we shall ever know of any more. You can get an excellent idea of life, its development, place, nature, and psychological attributes, in H. G. Wells's large volume *The Science of Life.* Wells, like all sober men of science, has no illusions about man's importance in the universe; but believes that much can be made of man just as he is on this planet. We are temporary—but what of it? Let us live while we live—and there are probably hundreds of millions of years ahead for some form of life (perhaps ourselves, perhaps the descendants of some other terrestrial life-form which will supplant us) on this planet.

As to fortune-telling—all one can do is to urge you to use your common sense. You must be aware that every happening on this earth, or in all the universe for that matter, is the result of *an infinitely vast number of wholly unrelated causes.* If any one of these causes were different, the thing would not happen. If a man stubs his toe in a certain place on a certain day, it is because of an infinity of antecedent elements—hereditary factors, etc.—which have caused him to be in the given place when he is; which have caused the obstacle to exist where it does; and which have caused the man to react to the obstacle as he does. If the man had had another great-great-great-grandfather, or if a certain glacier had not been at a certain stage of plasticity when encountering a mountain 200 miles to the north 25,000 years ago, or if the man's great-great-grandmother in a wholly different line of heredity, then unknown to any other of his lines, had not died when she did instead of a year later, etc., etc.; this particular incident, involving as it does a particular conjunction of elements, could not possibly occur. And all happenings depend upon just as wide a conjunction of totally unrelated circumstances. Any event involving human beings depends on the *total heredity* of each one; and the average person has 4 grandparents, 8 great-grandparents, 16 great-great-grandparents, and so on. 200 years ago the ancestors of any one person were so scattered that only a minority are likely to have known of the others' existence; and even then, some who knew each other never knew their descendants would join in marriage. How do you suppose anybody in 1737 could predict what his descendants in 1937 would do? He didn't know when his great-great-grandchildren were going to marry, or what part of the globe they were going to move to. There is absolutely no clue to the future, because the events are compounded of so many *different* chains of past events, each of which may be taking place all unknown to the spectators of any other. In our present, which is the future's past, we can know of only one or two factors which will enter into any event of the future. There is no way of finding out the others, because *we don't know what to look for.* Indeed, no one can know that there *will* be any "event" until such a future time as the previously unknown factors shall, by combining, have caused it to occur.

There is no getting around this, and I can assure you that fortune-telling has no place in the belief of educated adults. As for fakes like "numerology"—these things are simply the products of infantile ignorance. I can scarcely believe that this chap Loeffler (from whom I've heard twice) accepts such hilarious nonsense, although I recall his bringing up some of the pedantic geometrical mysticism of Claude Bragdon. Any mental adult knows that people are named by chance, and long after the conjunction of hereditary factors which determine personality. But really—"numerology" is too silly for anybody over four years old to talk about.

There is no sense in invoking ideas of possible cosmic *recurrence* as a justification for fortune-telling—first, because all such ideas are improbable in the extreme; and second, because if such a recurrence cycle *did* occur in the universe, the successive reappearance-phases would be so infinitely far apart that no memories could ever hold over from one to the other. Indeed—no one planet with its resident organisms could ever hold over from one to the other . . . so that there wouldn't be any line of beings to remember! Let me advise you in all good faith to do a lot of serious reading in the sciences. You need it—and you are so keenly interested in the subject that you'll find it highly enjoyable and worth your while. You must get a lot of primitive myths and pseudo-scientific notions out of your head. For example—there is no such thing as "perpetual motion" (in the sense of anything producible on earth by machinery) *and never can be.* Telepathy is another very doubtful thing. The only apparent evidence in its favour is that of the recent Rhine experiments at the U. of N.C., and even these experiments are not universally accepted. (By the way—Hugo Gernsback is a notorious sharper who ought never to be trusted. He tries to sensationalise pseudo-science, and is so dishonest in his non-payment of contributors that reputable authors have virtually blacklisted his magazines.) Here's a list of really solid books on the sciences you should read:

Bartky	*Highlights of Astronomy*
Stokeley	*Stars and Telescopes*
Moulton	*Consider the Heavens*
Duncan	*Astronomy*
Eddington	*The Nature of the Physical World*
Jeans	*The Universe Around Us*
Swann	*Architecture of the Universe*
Darwin	*New Conception of Matter*

Jeans	*New Background of Science*
Reichenbach	*Atom and Cosmos*
Infeld	*World in Modern Science*
Foster	*Romance of Chemistry*
Findlay	*Spirit of Chemistry*
Longwell	*Foundations of Geology*
Norton	*Elements of Geology*
Moon	*Biology for Beginners*
Clendening	*The Human Body*
Dorsey	*Why We Behave Like Human Beings*
various volumes by	H. A. Overstreet and W. J. Fielding
Kroeber	*Anthropology*
Lewis	*Introduction to Cultural Anthropology*
Frazer	*The Golden Bough*

Also try to get the four-volume *Outline of Science* by Professor J. Arthur Thomson, and various volumes by Sir Arthur Keith, Sir G. Elliott Smith, Marcelin Boule, and W. K. Gregory. You may not be able to get hold of all of these, but even a few of them would prove an eye-opener. These are the solid products of real scholars, and would help to counteract the irresponsible day-dreaming which clusters around the pseudo-science-fiction magazines.

But don't think that I'm not interested in fantastic speculations about the universe and life, even if I don't believe them. Indeed, they are all the more interesting—like the shadowy dreams I write about in my weird stories—because I don't believe them.

IX
PERSONAL

Lovecraft's avowedly autobiographical writing is scanty and even a little disappointing; his letters are his true autobiography, and they make him one of the most voluminously documented figures in human history. The few brief autobiographical essays he wrote over his twenty-year literary career were all written for specific occasions; of the two included here, "The Brief Autobiography of an Inconsequential Scribbler" (1919) was commissioned by John Milton Samples, editor of *The Silver Clarion,* while "Some Notes on a Nonentity" (1933) was written for William L. Crawford's *Unusual Stories* but never appeared there. Lovecraft remarks in a letter to R. H. Barlow (December 17, 1933) that Crawford wished the sketch to be cut down to 900 words, which Lovecraft did, but even this version (now lost) was never published; Lovecraft handed over the original draft to Barlow, who later donated it to the John Hay Library. "Some Notes on a Nonentity" is certainly Lovecraft's most compact and expressive autobiographical piece, but even it provides only tantalizing hints where the letters supply copious detail.

The self-image that emerges from these articles is a miracle of conscious artistry: Lovecraft becomes his own greatest fictional character. This is not to say that he utters actual falsehoods about himself; but he practices extreme selectivity. Why does he never mention his marriage in "Some Notes on a Nonentity"? Why, in "The Brief Autobiography" (intended, let us recall, for an amateur audience and written before he had wholeheartedly embarked upon his career as weird fictionist), does he not allude to his voracious reading of the early pulp magazines? The fact is that Lovecraft is very deliberately fashioning an image of himself as classicist, scientist, and philosopher who "looked on man" (as he wrote in "A Confession of Unfaith") "as if from another planet." And in one detail there is actual falsehood: "A Confession of Unfaith" seems to suggest that his iconoclastic doubt of the existence of God caused him to be withdrawn from Sunday school at the age of about five or six, when in fact (as Kenneth W. Faig, Jr., has established) this event clearly occurred when Lovecraft was twelve. The "Confession" is a charming piece—who can forget the tableau of Lovecraft building altars to Pan, Apollo, and Diana?—and we have already remarked of its importance in delineating Lovecraft's early philosophical development; but it is also one more element in Lovecraft's grand self-portrait as the emotionless cosmic spectator.

Some of the other items in this section appear here for want of a better placement, and because their interest is frankly more biographical than intrinsic. "Within the Gates" is surely one of the strangest things Lovecraft ever wrote. Delivered at an amateur journalism convention in Boston on July 4, 1921, this short, humorous speech is startling for its mere existence: six weeks earlier Lovecraft was professing nearly suicidal depression at the death of his mother on May 24, 1921. And yet, the best thing that Lovecraft could have done after this traumatic event was to resume the normal course of his life, and this speech may indicate that he did just that. A few of the jokes are rather good—as when Lovecraft refers to Dante as his "fellow-poet"—and it would certainly have been an entertainment to see and hear Lovecraft deliver this light-hearted *jeu d'esprit*. One of those who may have done so was his future wife Sonia Greene, for the two appear to have met for the first time at this convention.

"Commercial Blurbs" (the title is R. H. Barlow's) is a testament to the depths of Lovecraft's despair as a jobless husband alone in New York in 1925. Can anyone imagine Lovecraft as a writer of advertising copy? These articles appear to have been written for a trade magazine in which Lovecraft's associate Arthur Leeds was involved. A passage in Lovecraft's letter to Mrs. F. C. Clark (May 28, 1925) seems to allude to them: "Leeds and I had talked very seriously about the Yesley writing venture; and when I rode down town with Leeds I continued the conversation, getting more and more workable details from his kindly and willing lips. . . . He agreed to shew me the ropes thoroughly, and see that my articles (which need not be signed) received proper sales treatment; and predicted that I ought to stand as good a chance at making money as himself or anybody else who has proved he can do it. And I told him I would tackle the thing—and he means to send me my first assignment in a week or two, when he can get together the leads best suited to me (real estate, largely) and find the right models for imitation among his old magazines." It is not known whether these sketches were actually published in any trade magazines or catalogues; but it is clear that they did not lead to a position for Lovecraft, as he endured another year of futile job-hunting before returning to Providence, without his wife, in April 1926.

That return, however, indirectly impelled one of Lovecraft's finest essays, "Cats and Dogs." His departure from New York caused his secession from the Blue Pencil Club, an amateur group in which James Ferdinand Morton was at the time a leading figure. This club was to have a debate on the relative merits of cats and dogs, and Lovecraft, unable to attend in person but unwilling to pass up an opportunity for registering his wholesale love of cats, wrote his response so that Morton could read it to the group. As pure rhetoric this essay is very fine—note its tongue-in-cheek humor, its skillful marshaling of facts, the dainty elegance of its style, so like the felidae it is extolling—but its real importance is its covert subject matter: the essay is not about cats, it is about Lovecraft. For Lovecraft claimed to see in cats all those traits he himself shared (or wished to share): emotional aloofness, aristocratic independence, philosophical calm. The essay is metaphysics ("The real lover of cats is one who demands a clearer adjustment to the universe than ordinary household platitudes provide"), it is politics ("The dog is a peasant and the cat is a gentleman"), it is aesthetics ("In [the cat's] flawless grace and superior self-sufficiency I have seen a symbol of the perfect beauty and bland impersonality of the universe itself"); in effect, Lovecraft utilizes every philosophical tool at his disposal to defend his love of cats, and conversely that love of cats is seen to entail and imply the whole of his cosmic philosophy. In no other essay did Lovecraft ever weave together the many and varied strands of his thought so seamlessly as here.

What essays like "Cats and Dogs," and to a lesser extent the rest of the essays in this section and in this entire volume, suggest is the degree to which Lovecraft infuses himself in all his work; in this sense everything he wrote is "personal" because it is the outgrowth of a keen mind reflecting upon the varied phenomena of the human and the cosmic realm. Mediocre, routine, or mechanical as many of his essays may be, they are all the distinctive product of a mind that continually and admirably grappled with the complex issues of human existence and strove to make sense of them as best it could. Let us repeat that Lovecraft will never be known purely as an essayist; but his essays are always surprising us by flashes of insight into the life of man or, at the very least, into his own life.

THE BRIEF AUTOBIOGRAPHY OF AN INCONSEQUENTIAL SCRIBBLER

Since the earthly career of a secluded and non-robust individual is seldom replete with exciting events, my readers must not expect the following chronicle to possess much which will hold their attention or awaken their interest. But for the mandate of a relentless editor, they would have been spared this affliction.

I was born in Providence, of unmixed English ancestry, on August 20, 1890. During the first few years of my existence, my mode of expression was more often oral than written; and my tastes much more modern than at present. It is indeed worthy of note, that my utterances prior to the summer of 1891 betray a marked kinship to the vers libre of today.

In the year 1892, from which my first genuine recollections proceed, my literary career began in earnest. Having mastered the art of connected speech, and assimilated the alphabet, I was an inveterate reciter of poesy, delivering such pieces as "Sheridan's Ride" and selections from "Mother Goose" with true declamatory finesse. I also dabbled in poetic imagism, with the aid of alphabetical blocks.

By the close of 1893, I had added another accomplishment to my catalogue—that of reading. My tastes ran to polysyllables, of whose pronunciation I was not always certain. About this period I began to supplement the fairy tales hitherto related to me, with individual research in the pictureful pages of Grimm, and developed a marked penchant for everything pertaining to myths and legends. The close of 1894 revealed still another accomplishment—that of writing.

The years 1895 and 1896 were uneventful, and although I was constantly scribbling both crude prose and crude rhymes, no specimen survives. The leading event of this era was my change of interest from Teutonic to Classical mythology, induced by perusal of Hawthorne's *Wonder Book* and *Tanglewood Tales.*

In 1897 I composed my earliest surviving attempt at authorship, a "poem" in forty-four lines of internally rhyming iambic heptameter, entitled "The Poem of Ulysses; or, the New Odyssey", whose opening four lines are as follows:

"The night was dark, O Reader, hark! and see Ulysses' fleet;
All homeward bound, with vict'ry crown'd, he hopes his spouse to greet;
Long hath he fought, put Troy to naught, and levell'd down its walls;
But Neptune's wrath obstructs his path, and into snares he falls."

In 1898 I commenced a school career, much interrupted by ill health, and supplemented by home reading and private instruction. It was my favourite diversion to spend hours in the midst of the family library, browsing chiefly over books over a century old, and insensibly forming a taste for eighteenth-century style and thought which will never leave me.

In 1899 I became interested in the sciences, and established my first enduring amateur publication, *The Scientific Gazette,* which ran continuously until 1904. It was published successively by pencil, pen, and hectograph, and afforded me infinite pleasure and pride.

In 1903 astronomy became my chief interest, and I established the hectographed magazine, *The Rhode Island Journal of Astronomy,* which survived until 1907. All this time I knew nothing of organised Amateurdom, and the reams of old-fashioned miscellany I had been evolving remained mercifully unpublished till 1906, when I made my debut in print by commencing a series of monthly astronomical articles in a local paper.

From 1906 to 1914 I was a contributor to sundry publications of no importance, veering about 1911 from pure science back to *belles lettres.* In March, 1914, I learned through Mr. Edward F. Daas of Amateurdom's existence, and soon joined the United; a connexion likely to subsist till my death, since it has furnished me with more enjoyment than any other I have experienced.

In the United it has been my privilege to become a frequent contributor to the press, and to hold several offices, including the Presidency and the Chairmanship of the Department of Public Criticism. I have endeavoured to support the most purely literary and progressive elements in the Association, and to aid in a revival of that conservatism and classicism which modern literature seems dangerously prone to reject. To this purpose is my individual publication, *The Conservative,* devoted. These various activities have doubtless gained for me the reputation of being an insufferable old pedant; yet I cannot wholly complain of my fate, since Editor Samples deems it fit to waste good white paper upon these overlong annals of Boeotian mediocrity.

Lovecraft holding "Felis,"
Frank Belknap Long's cat

WITHIN THE GATES

By "One Sent by Providence"

Mr. Toastmaster, Ladies, Gentlemen, and Politicians:—

Although not called upon by name, I have been informed that the reference to Providence is my cue; hence believe that this is the proper time to make myself ridiculous by attempted oratory. Providence is notable as a dispenser of both blessings and afflictions; the former to be hailed with gratitude, the latter to be borne with patience. I am one of the latter, and can but hope that your patience will prove adequate. Remember, at least, that this oration is not voluntary; and visit your wrath upon Providence—or the Toastmaster—rather than upon me!

The subject of my sermon is announced as "within the gates"—presumably referring to the presence of a strictly United man in the midst of the National's Babylonish revelry—more or less "alien and alone", as it were, to quote from a famous poem dear to the heart of the *Zenith*'s scholarly editor. Accordingly I have taken as my text that not unknown line about a gate which appears in the celebrated epic of my fellow-poet Dante—

"All hope abandon, ye who enter here."

I will omit the context—not only because I do not remember it, but because it would perhaps offend some loyal Nationalite by suggesting a certain comparison which I have with truly Heinsian delicacy suppressed.

Having thus introduced my remarks as artistically and verbosely as possible, let me dispense with further preliminaries and confess that I have not the slightest idea of what I should say this evening. This, however, is probably nothing unusual for a post-prandial Cicero or Demosthenes, hence it need cause me no anxiety. I may add, in ex-

Lovecraft in Boston with amateur colleague William J. Dowdell

tenuation, that this is only my second public oration. Having escaped alive after my first, in February, I may venture to hope for similar clemency now—in spite of the representation of the "Sun Group" on the jury.

Since I have nothing in particular to say, it behoves me to say it as tastefully as possible—allowing the appropriateness of my remarks to compensate for their vacuity. Within the gates of—the National, what could be more appropriate than a reference to that institution's chief interest—politics? I could say much of politics, but in a Puritanical city might not be able to say all that recent politics deserves; hence will confine myself to one point—a defence against a recent attack upon me, basely launched by an exceedingly eminent and heretofore respected amateur.

In *Views and Reviews* there appears an outrageous accusation, which although mentioning no names, affects me too obviously to permit of doubt. It is charged that I, as so-called Rhode Island Chairman of some "intensive recruiting drive", employed the backs of National application blanks to write "poetry" on. I take this opportunity to refute so unjust a charge, relying for absolute vindication on Mr. Dowdell; who will, as in the past, assure you all that I never could and never can write a line of genuine poetry! But I will go even further, and vow on my own responsibility that I did not even *attempt* to write verses on those blanks. My waste-basket contains the proof—for what I did write on them was a descriptive prose article for *Tryout*, which you may read for yourselves in the very next issue—if you are good at puzzles.

Mr. Houtain, noting my weight and elevation, once wrote in *The Zenith* that my voice is seemingly out of keeping with my size. This may or may not be true. If, however, I do not soon conclude, these remarks are likely to be sadly *in* keeping with my elephantine magnitude. I could say much of the honour and pleasure I feel at being present at this momentous conclave, but am reluctant merely to repeat the obvious.

As a text for this long and sonorous intellectual silence I quoted an epic. Let me, therefore, follow the example of the epic poets, and instead of tapering off with a grandiloquent peroration, cease abruptly and dramatically. I have held you within the gates of infernal dulness.

"Thence issuing, we again behold the stars!"

A CONFESSION OF UNFAITH

As a participant in *The Liberal*'s Experience Meeting, wherein amateurs are invited to state their theories of the universe, I must preface all remarks by the qualifying admission that they do not necessarily constitute a permanent view. The seeker of truth for its own sake is chained to no conventional system, but always shapes his philosophical opinions upon what seems to him the best evidence at hand. Changes, therefore, are constantly possible; and occur whenever new or revalued evidence makes them logical.

I am by nature a sceptic and analyst, hence settled early into my present general attitude of cynical materialism, subsequently changing in regard to details and degree rather than to basic ideals. The environment into which I was born was that of the average American Protestant of urban, civilised type—in theory quite orthodox, but in practice very liberal. Morals rather than faith formed the real keynote. I was instructed in the legends of the Bible and of Saint Nicholas at the age of about two, and gave to both a passive acceptance not especially distinguished either for its critical keenness or its enthusiastic comprehension. Within the next few years I added to my supernatural lore the fairy tales of Grimm and the Arabian Nights; and by the time I was five had small choice amongst these speculations so far as truth was concerned, though for attractiveness I favoured the Arabian Nights. At one time I formed a juvenile collection of Oriental pottery and *objets d'art*, announcing myself as a devout Mussulman and assuming the pseudonym of "Abdul Alhazred". My first positive utterance of a sceptical nature probably occurred before my fifth birthday, when I was told what I really knew before, that "Santa Claus" is a myth. This admission caused me to ask why "God" is not equally a myth. Not long afterwards I was placed in the "infant class" at the Sunday school of the venerable First Baptist Church, an ecclesiastical landmark dating from 1775; and there resigned all vestiges of Christian belief. The absurdity of the myths I was called upon to accept, and the sombre greyness of the whole faith as compared with the Eastern magnificence of Mahometanism, made me definitely an agnostic; and caused me to become so pestiferous a questioner that I was permitted to discontinue attendance. No statement of the kind-hearted and motherly preceptress had seemed to me to answer in any way the doubts I honestly and explicitly expressed, and I was fast becoming a marked "man" through my searching iconoclasm. No doubt I was regarded as a corrupter of the simple faith of the other "infants".

When I was six my philosophical evolution received its most aesthetically significant impetus—the dawn of Graeco-Roman thought. Always avid for fairy lore, I had chanced on Hawthorne's *Wonder Book* and *Tanglewood Tales*, and was enraptured by the Hellenic myths even in their Teutonised form. Then a tiny book in the private library of my elder aunt—the story of the Odyssey in "Harper's Half-Hour Series"—caught my attention. From the opening chapter I was electrified, and by the time I reached the end I was for evermore a Graeco-Roman. My Bagdad name and affiliations disappeared at once, for the magic of silks and colours faded before that of fragrant templed groves, faun-peopled meadows in the twilight, and the blue, beckoning Mediterranean that billowed mysteriously out from Hellas into the reaches of haunting wonder where dwelt Lotophagi and Laestrygonians, where Aeolus kept his winds and Circe her swine, and where in Thrinacian pastures roamed the oxen of radiant Helios. As soon as possible I procured an illustrated edition of Bulfinch's *Age of Fable*, and gave all my time to the reading of the text, in which the true spirit of Hellenism is delightfully preserved, and to the contemplation of the pictures, splendid designs and half-tones of the standard classical statues, and paintings of classical subjects. Before long I was fairly familiar with the principal Grecian myths, and had become a constant visitor at the classical art museums of Providence and Boston. I commenced a collection of small plaster casts of the Greek sculptural masterpieces, and learned the Greek alphabet and the rudiments of the Latin language. I adopted the pseudonym of "Lucius Valerius Messala"—Roman and not Greek, since Rome had a charm all its own for me. My grandfather had travelled observingly through Italy, and delighted me with long first-hand accounts of its beauties and memorials of ancient grandeur. I mention this aesthetic tendency in detail only to lead up to its philosophical result—my last flickering of religious belief. When about seven or eight I was a genuine pagan, so intoxicated with the beauty of Greece that I acquired a half-sincere belief in the old gods and nature-spirits. I have in literal truth built altars to Pan, Apollo, Diana, and Athena, and have watched for dryads and satyrs in the woods and fields at dusk. Once

I firmly thought I beheld some of these sylvan creatures dancing under autumnal oaks; a kind of "religious experience" as true in its way as the subjective ecstasies of any Christian. If a Christian tell me he has *felt* the reality of his Jesus or Jahveh, I can reply that I have *seen* the hoofed Pan and the sisters of the Hesperian Phaëthusa.

But in my ninth year, as I was reading the Grecian myths in their standard poetical translations and thus acquiring unconsciously my taste for Queen-Anne English, the real foundations of my scepticism were laid. Impelled by the fascinating pictures of scientific instruments in the back of Webster's Unabridged, I began to take an interest in natural philosophy and chemistry; and soon had a promising laboratory in my cellar, and a new stock of simple scientific text-books in my budding library. Ere long I was more of a scientific student than pagan dreamer. In 1897 my leading "literary" work was a "poem" entitled "The New Odyssey"; in 1899 it was a compendious treatise on chemistry in several pencil-scribbled "volumes". But mythology was by no means neglected. In this period I read much in Egyptian, Hindoo, and Teutonic mythology, and tried experiments in pretending to believe each one, to see which might contain the greatest truth. I had, it will be noted, immediately adopted the method and manner of science! Naturally, having an open and unemotional mind, I was soon a complete sceptic and materialist. My scientific studies had enlarged to include geographical, geological, biological, and astronomical rudiments, and I had acquired the habit of relentless analysis in all matters. My pompous "book" called *Poemata Minora*, written when I was eleven, was dedicated "To the Gods, Heroes, and Ideals of the Ancients", and harped in disillusioned, world-weary tones on the sorrow of the pagan robbed of his antique pantheon. Some of these very juvenile "poemata" were reprinted in *The Tryout* for April, 1919, under new titles and pseudonyms.

Hitherto my philosophy had been distinctly juvenile and empirical. It was a revolt from obvious falsities and ugliness, but involved no particular cosmic or ethical theory. In ethical questions I had no analytical interest because I did not realise that they were questions. I accepted Victorianism, with consciousness of many prevailing hypocrisies aside from Sabbatarian and supernatural matters, without dispute; never having heard of inquiries which reached "beyond good and evil". Though at times interested in reforms, notably prohibition (I have never tasted alcoholic liquor), I was inclined to be bored by ethical casuistry; since I believed conduct to be a matter of taste and breeding, with virtue, delicacy, and truthfulness as symbols of gentility. Of my word and honour I was inordinately proud, and would permit no reflections to be cast upon them. I thought ethics too obvious and commonplace to be scientifically discussed, and considered philosophy solely in its relation to truth and beauty. I was, and still am, pagan to the core. Regarding man's place in Nature, and the structure of the universe, I was as yet unawakened. This awakening was to come in the winter of 1902–3, when astronomy asserted its supremacy amongst my studies.

The most poignant sensations of my existence are those of 1896, when I discovered the Hellenic world, and of 1902, when I discovered the myriad suns and worlds of infinite space. Sometimes I think the latter event the greater, for the grandeur of that growing conception of the universe still excites a thrill hardly to be duplicated. I made of astronomy my principal scientific study, obtaining larger and larger telescopes, collecting astronomical books to the number of 61, and writing copiously on the subject in the form of special and monthly articles in the local daily press. By my thirteenth birthday I was thoroughly impressed with man's impermanence and insignificance, and by my seventeenth, about which time I did some particularly detailed writing on the subject, I had formed in all essential particulars my present pessimistic cosmic views. The futility of all existence began to impress and oppress me; and my references to human progress, formerly hopeful, began to decline in enthusiasm. Always partial to antiquity, I allowed myself to originate a sort of one-man cult of retrospective suspiration. Realistic analysis, favoured by history and by diffusive scientific leanings which now embraced Darwin, Haeckel, Huxley, and various other pioneers, was checked by my aversion for realistic literature. In fiction I was devoted to the phantasy of Poe; in poetry and essays to the elegant formalism and conventionality of the eighteenth century. I was not at all wedded to what illusions I retained. My attitude has always been cosmic, and I looked on man as if from another planet. He was merely an interesting species presented for study and classification. I had strong prejudices and partialities in many fields, but could not help seeing the race in its cosmic futility as well as in its terrestrial importance. By the time I was of age, I had scant faith in the world's betterment; and felt a decreasing interest in its cherished pomps and prides. When I entered amateurdom in my 24th year, I was well on the road to my present cynicism; a cynicism tempered with immeasurable pity for man's eternal tragedy of aspirations beyond the possibility of fulfilment.

The war confirmed all the views I had begun to hold. The cant of idealists sickened me increasingly, and I employed no more than was necessary for literary embellishment. With me democracy was a minor question, my anger being aroused primarily by the audacity of a challenge to Anglo-Saxon supremacy, and by the needless territorial greed and disgusting ruthlessness of the Huns. I was unvexed by the scruples which beset the average liberal. Blunders I expected; a German defeat was all I asked or hoped for. I am, I hardly need add, a warm partisan of Anglo-American reunion; my opinion being that the division of a single culture into two national units is wasteful and often dangerous. In this case my opinion is doubly strong because I believe that the entire existing civilisation depends on Saxon dominance.

About this time my philosophical thought received its greatest and latest stimulus through discussion with several amateurs; notably Maurice Winter Moe, an orthodox but tolerant Christian and inspiring opponent, and Alfred Galpin, Jr., a youth in approximate agreement with me, but with a mind so far in the lead that the comparison is impossible without humility on my part. Correspondence with these thinkers led to a recapitulation and codification of my views, revealing many flaws in my elaborated doctrines, and enabling me to secure greater clearness and consistency. The impetus also enlarged my philosophical reading and research, and broke down many hindering prejudices. I ceased my literal adherence to Epicurus and Lucretius, and reluctantly dismissed free-will forever in favour of determinism.

The Peace Conference, Friedrich Nietzsche, Samuel Butler (the modern), H. L. Mencken, and other influences have perfected my cynicism; a quality which grows more intense as the advent of middle life removes the blind prejudice whereby youth clings to the vapid "all's right with the world" hallucination from sheer force of desire to have it so. As I near thirty-two I have no particular wishes, save to perceive facts as they are. My objectivity, always marked, is now paramount and unopposed, so that there is nothing I am not *willing* to believe. I no longer really desire anything but oblivion, and am thus ready to discard any gilded illusion or accept any unpalatable fact with perfect equanimity. I can at last concede willingly that the wishes, hopes, and values of humanity are matters of total indifference to the blind cosmic mechanism. Happiness I recognise as an ethical phantom whose simulacrum comes fully to none and even partially to but few, and whose position as the goal of all human striving is a grotesque mixture of farce and tragedy.

COMMERCIAL BLURBS

Beauty in Crystal

In the leisurely days before the Revolution, when American craftsmanship and domestic life reached their greatest height in pure taste and subdued richness, there was no more notable product in the Colonies than the marvellously beautiful glassware of Heinrich Wilhelm Stiegel. The story of this brilliant immigrant, ironmaster, and glassblower, little known outside his chosen region of Pennsylvania, is itself a drama of the keenest interest; but today he is best remembered by the crystal perfections which he evolved in the great glass works founded in 1765 to supplement his already prodigious iron manufactures.

For this there is small wonder, since glassware is a prominent and carefully chosen item in every home of cultivation, and Stiegel was able to satisfy the most fastidious. The leading households of colonial America, demanding a variety of exquisite and classically moulded tableware and vases to suit every use, every type of interior decoration, and every choice of flowers and delicacies, soon recognised the supremacy of Stiegel's workmanship; and ordered in immense quantities the lovely and resoundingly bell-like pieces whose modelling and colouring so far surpassed anything previously available. These diamond-clear wineglasses, majestic opal vases in relief, superbly patterned tumblers, enamelled mugs and cordial bottles, jade-green and amethyst cruets and carafes, and above all the famous blue creations with their undertones of green and purple, form priceless heirlooms today for those fortunate enough to inherit them. Persons not so fortunate must rely upon the museums.

Luckily, however, the tradition of Stiegel is not without its upholder in the present age; and what his ware was to our forefathers, the celebrated "Steuben Glass" of the Corning Glass Works, Corning, N.Y., may be justly said to be for us. In this choice commodity we have a living source of the same rare beauty which a century and a half ago came only from the Stiegel furnaces; a beauty not a whit corroded by the haste and carelessness of our mechanical era, but shining as restfully and restrainedly as its colonial predecessor.

In Steuben Glass all the nicety and sense of fitness which characterised the best historical glasswares is retained unimpaired, yet not without permitting the creation of pieces adapted to the most modern uses. Here may one find vases of the exact shade and shape to blend with one's favourite blossoms, goblets to add sparkle to one's particular scheme of dining-room ornamentation, salad and iced-tea sets that fit each special occasion, and comports, sweetmeat-jars, and perfume and cigarette boxes that present the widest possibilities as gifts. The infinite diversity of blues, greens, ambers, and other tints vie with the crystal-clear models for intrinsic loveliness; and in all there resides that intangible and aristocratic charm which only artistically conceived and hand-executed glassware can attain.

Happily, these heirlooms of the future are obtainable at very sensible prices, and at most of the better-grade jewellers', glass and china shops, and department stores. To know their details and varieties in advance, though, it is best to send to Steuben Division, Corning Glass Works, Corning, N.Y., for the firm's free illustrated brochure. Therein one may behold the inmost spirit of the colonial Stiegel reincarnated in the twentieth century; and in the very region where a grateful congress voted a rural estate to that other mighty voyager from the Rhine valley—Baron Steuben.

The Charm of Fine Woodwork

In the recent renaissance of taste in domestic architecture and furnishing, nothing has figured more importantly than woodwork. We all know the superlative fascination of the colonial doorway, which seemingly took its place among the lost arts in the nineteenth century, nor can any beauty-lover remain unmoved by the matchless grace of the old-time interiors with their arches, mouldings, mantels, door-frames, wainscoting, window-seats, and china-cupboards. These things, for two or three generations banished by patterns of the most incredible heaviness, ugliness, and grotesqueness, are again coming into their own; and once more the wood-carver rises to prominence as a moulder of charm and atmosphere.

The standard source of fine and enduring woodwork in America today is the Curtis Companies, Inc., of Clifton, Iowa. Realising how completely we are surrounded by woodwork at every turn of our daily lives, and how essential it is to keep that woodwork at a high artistic level, this firm has recaptured the conscientious colonial standard of taste and beauty; and offers a variety of carefully evolved and architecturally sound designs for every conceivable purpose. With selected and seasoned woods and fastidious workmanship the antique level of sumptuous restfulness has been achieved anew, and no modern householder need worry lest his doors, staircases, panelling, and kindred accessories fall below the ideal of his entire scheme in artistic finish and historical correctness.

Curtis Woodwork embraces both the usual structural units and the cleverest contrivances of built-in or permanent furniture, such as bookcases, dressers, buffets, and cupboards. Every model is conceived and created with the purest art, ripest scholarship, and mellowest craftsmanship which energetic enterprise can command; and made to conform rigidly to the architecture of each particular type of home. The cost, considering the quality, is amazingly low; and a trademark on the individual pieces prevents any substitution by careless contractors.

It would pay those interested in fine woodwork to send for the free booklets of the firm—one on Interior Doors and Trim and another on Permanent Furniture—addressing The Curtis Companies Service Bureau, 281 Curtis Building, Clinton, Iowa. More elaborate plan books for all styles of dwellings are furnished at one dollar each, or free through certain dealers.

With woodwork always before one's eyes for better or worse, and comprising at least a sixth of the whole cost of a house, the contemporary homebuilder is fortunate in having so authoritative a service to depend on. Curtis taste and quality are a reliance which the years have tested and found adequate.

Personality in Clocks

If one were looking for an ideal symbol of that early American taste, enterprise, and craftsmanship which so strongly shaped our national character and gave our now treasured "antiques" the whole basis of their appeal, one could find no object more fitting than the Yankee pendulum clock.

The homes of our ancestors received much of their typical charm from the accurate and artistic timepieces of such master technicians as Simon and Aaron Willard of Massachusetts—the former of whom invented and first manufactured the celebrated "banjo" clock—while the whole life and industrial history of Connecticut were moulded by the famous group of clockmakers beginning with Thomas Harland and culminating in Eli Terry and Seth Thomas.

Today the tall "grandfather" clocks of makers like the Willards, Daniel Burnap, or Silas Hoadley, the Connecticut shelf clocks on the order of Terry's pillar and scroll-top model of 1814, or the various "banjo" designs of Simon Willard and Elnathan Taber, are among the most prized heirlooms and collectors' items in the country.

All this is not without reason, and would never have occurred in connexion with a carelessly stereotyped and wholly commercialised product. It is true that the early clockmakers were business men—often pedlars—but they were really much more than that. They put into their work all of the scrupulous thoroughness and honest zeal which marked their age, nor were they satisfied till they had furnished the maximum accuracy of works and most choicely quiet beauty of case for the least possible price. Eli Terry, for example, ceased to make a certain clock after a year's trial because he found he could do better, though at no greater profit.

But our own age is not without clockmakers to carry on the great tradition. The Colonial Manufacturing Company of 109 Washington Street, Zeeland, Michigan, has studied the clock needs of the modern home as Terry and the Willards studied those of another time; and has produced as a result a series of designs surpassed by none for beauty, accuracy, and appropriateness. We here find the same individual craftsmanship which distinguished the older colonial article, embodied in an exquisite variety of tall and other patterns, each perfect of its kind, impeccable in historic background, unequalled for mechanism by any clock in America or Europe, and made complete by the mellowest and most musical of chimes.

Colonial Clocks, about which the company will gladly send a free booklet on request, are created with a keen realisation of the permanence and strategic decorative importance of the great clock in an American home. Artistic insight and conscience enter into their building, for the makers acutely visualise the clock as a focus of domestic cheer and nucleus of household life. They understand that the face and voice of a clock must be such as will never pall or grate throughout the years, and that a family's best traditions must find an echo in its intimate furniture.

A Real Colonial Heritage

One of the first fruits of our modern revival of early Americana has been the welcome disappearance of ugly and nondescript household furniture, and the flooding of the market with patterns based on the classic colonial ideal. The horrors of mission and golden oak have gone to join those of haircloth and black walnut, and shop windows of today shew a very creditable array of rich woods and chaste designs in the manner of the Jacobean, Queen Anne, and Georgian designers.

Seldom, however, can our mechanical civilisation quite approach the elder spirit of thoroughness and individual craftsmanship. The bulk of the newer furniture is not offensive, but it is negative. Its vast quantity production forbids the loving attention to detail which marked the careful output of cabinet-makers like Duncan Phyfe, while widespread industrial conditions make harder and harder the achievement of such conscientious solidity as was possible to master-workmen who personally selected and seasoned their woods, created their own ornamental adaptations with mature original artistry, and thought less of intensive selling than of building something as perfect as possible of its kind. One cannot, for example, imagine the average frail, commercial "knock-down" furniture of our day as a potential heirloom to be bequeathed from generation to generation.

The exception which proves the rule is "Danersk" furniture, created in special New England factory-studios for the Erskine-Danforth Corporation, whose new and commodious Manhattan showrooms were opened a year and a half ago at 383 Madison Avenue, opposite the Ritz-Carlton. Here, if nowhere else, we have a genuine perpetuation of the old-time atmosphere; and a painstaking construction of classically derived pieces from tried walnuts, maples, and Cuban mahogany in a fashion likely to resist the wear and tear of coming centuries. Here, indeed, we have one remaining place where a person of taste may buy the future heirlooms of his great-grandchildren, and actually "found a household" in a sense which modernity has almost forgotten.

Free from the superficial and almost contemptuous attitude toward art and scholarship which many strictly commercial enterprises nowadays profess, the Erskine-Danforth Corporation has without sacrifice of surprisingly moderate prices adopted the highest standard of historic accuracy and exact beauty of detail in the choice of its models. American domestic life from the landing of the Pilgrims to the decadence of style in the eighteen-thirties has been minutely and appreciatively searched for inspirations, and all the country's leading collections have contributed their share toward the making of a wide and versatile body of designs authentically expressive of every phase and period of our lineal tradition. A consistently "Danersk" furnished home, besides enjoying the friendly and livable quality conferred by quiet attention to the most modern needs (and one Georgian "Danersk" desk offers even an unobtrusive compartment for the radio!), has meaning, repose, mellowness, and associations; nor is it likely to violate any aesthetic or historical convention, great or small.

Under this label we may rove at will through the colonial age, choosing a Queen Anne mirror, a chintz-upholstered wing rocker, a Plymouth cupboard, a six-leg highboy, a Chippendale secretary in the Salem manner, or a delicate Empire four-poster, with equal confidence in the faithfulness of the article to its type and antecedents. "Danersk" furniture, in short, is really less of a reproduction than a legitimate continuation of the good old Yankee spirit; and forms perhaps the only contemporary colonial ware which a trained connoisseur would be likely to mistake for the actual products of the seventeenth, eighteenth, and early nineteenth centuries.

A True Home of Literature

There are few persons, perhaps, who have not wondered at one time or another why the average bookstore does not more fully live up to its obvious possibilities. Necessarily frequented by every sort of literature-lover, it ought logically to become a vital meeting-place for the bookish and the scholarly—the definitely individualised nucleus and headquarters for many a group of wits or informal cultural circle. Yet in most actual cases such a place is provokingly content to remain a mere emporium without distinctiveness or personal appeal; an emporium so little different from any other that the unimpressed customer cares not a whit whether he buys his next book there or at the shop across the way.

It has remained for Paterson, New Jersey, to break ground so far as America is concerned for a newer and sounder custom. Misses Helen and Daisy Modeman, proprietors of the Alexander Hamilton Book Shop at 22 Hamilton St., have visualised the need and the opportunity; and in enlarging their popular establishment to twice its former size have adopted features not heretofore to be met with except at such rare European bookselling salons as Pergolan's near the Sorbonne in Paris.

In an addition measuring forty-five by fifteen feet, with commodious office balcony and space for a vast variety of desirable used books, will be installed a tasteful and hospitable reading-room designed to meet the uses and comfort of choice lettered spirits and societies of book-lovers. There, amidst friendly shelves, mellow woodwork, quaint recesses, and a delightful fireplace of antique brick bearing the appropriate inscription "Ye Ornament of Ye House is Ye Guest Thereof", the Misses Modeman will act as hostesses to literary Paterson; providing that reposeful background which is almost the inherent right of a great and all-embracing storehouse of written knowledge, tradition, and romance. Of business-like library formality and austerity there will be none. Instead, we shall find a cheerful home where all our favourite characters of the printed page will vie with one another to welcome us.

Paterson is singularly fortunate in possessing this novel and truly metropolitan enterprise; an enterprise which ably emancipates the city from literary dependence on any of the larger centres of population. The stock is as exceptional as the atmosphere, and competes on equal terms with that of the most esteemed Manhattan book marts. "Nothing too good for our clientele" is a well-fulfilled Modeman motto.

Besides the standard line there is a select department of rare and valuable books, soon to be increased to such proportions that the connoisseur in every branch may have a chance to indulge his bibliomania without seeking outside specialists. Truly, the Alexander Hamilton Book Shop holds an unique and indispensable place among the intellectual influences of its community; and is an achievement worthy of study and emulation in every corner of the nation.

CATS AND DOGS

Being told of the cat-and-dog fight about to occur in the Blue Pencil Club—a new thing for your circle, perhaps, though not unfamiliar to amateurdom as a whole—I cannot resist contributing a few Thomasic yowls and sibilants upon my side of the dispute, though conscious that the word of a venerable ex-member can scarcely have much weight against the brilliancy of such still active adherents as may bark upon the other side. Aware of my ineptitude at argument, my valued correspondent Curator James Ferdinand Morton of Paterson has sent me the records of a similar controversy in the *New York Tribune,* in which Mr. Carl Van Doren is on my side and Mr. Albert Payson Terhune on that of the canine tribe. From this I would be glad to plagiarise such data as I need; but Mr. Morton, with genuinely Machiavellian subtlety, has furnished me with only a part of the feline section whilst submitting the doggish brief in full. No doubt he imagines that this arrangement, in view of my own emphatic bias, makes for something like ultimate fairness; but for me it is exceedingly inconvenient, since it will force me to be more or less original in several parts of the ensuing remarks.

Between dogs and cats my degree of choice is so great that it would never occur to me to compare the two. I have no active dislike for dogs, any more than I have for monkeys, human beings, negroes, cows, sheep, or pterodactyls; but for the cat I have entertained a particular respect and affection ever since the earliest days of my infancy. In its flawless grace and superior self-sufficiency I have seen a symbol of the perfect beauty and bland impersonality of the universe itself, objectively considered; and in its air of silent mystery there resides for me all the wonder and fascination of the unknown. The dog appeals to cheap and facile emotions; the cat to the deepest founts of imagination and cosmic perception in the human mind. It is no accident that the contemplative Egyptians, together with such later poetic spirits as Poe,

Gautier, Baudelaire, and Swinburne, were all sincere worshippers of the supple grimalkin.

Naturally, one's preference in the matter of cats and dogs depends wholly upon one's temperament and point of view. The dog would appear to me to be the favourite of superficial, sentimental, emotional, and democratic people—people who feel rather than think, who attach importance to mankind and the popular conventional emotions of the simple, and who find their greatest consolation in the fawning and dependent attachments of a gregarious society. Such people live in a limited world of imagination; accepting uncritically the values of common folklore, and always preferring to have their naive beliefs, feelings, and prejudices tickled, rather than to enjoy a purely aesthetic and philosophic pleasure arising from discrimination, contemplation, and the recognition of austere absolute beauty. This is not to say that the cheaper emotions do not also reside in the average cat-lover's love of cats, but merely to point out that in ailurophily there exists a basis of true aestheticism which kynophily does not possess. The real lover of cats is one who demands a clearer adjustment to the universe than ordinary household platitudes provide; one who refuses to swallow the sentimental notion that all good people love dogs, children, and horses while all bad people dislike and are disliked by such. He is unwilling to set up himself and his cruder feelings as a measure of universal values, or to allow shallow ethical notions to warp his judgment. In a word, he had rather admire and respect than effuse and dote; and does not fall into the fallacy that pointless sociability and friendliness, or slavering devotion and obedience, constitute anything intrinsically admirable or exalted. Dog-lovers base their whole case on these commonplace, servile, and plebeian qualities, and amusingly judge the intelligence of a pet by its degree of conformity to their own wishes. Cat-lovers escape this delusion, repudiate the idea that cringing subservience and sidling companionship to man are supreme merits, and stand free to worship aristocratic independence, self-respect, and individual personality joined to extreme grace and beauty as typified by the cool, lithe, cynical, and unconquered lord of the housetops.

Persons of commonplace ideas—unimaginative worthy burghers who are satisfied with the daily round of things and who subscribe to the popular credo of sentimental values—will always be dog-lovers. To them nothing will ever be more important than themselves and their own more primitive feelings, and they will never cease to esteem and glorify the fellow-animal who best typifies these. Such persons are submerged in the vortex of Oriental idealism and abasement which ruined classic civilisation in the Dark Ages, and live in a bleak world of abstract sentimental values wherein the mawkish illusions of meekness, devotion, gentleness, brotherhood, and whining humility are magnified into supreme virtues, and a whole false ethic and philosophy erected on the timid reactions of the flexor system of muscles. This heritage, ironically foisted on us when Roman politics raised the faith of a whipped and broken people to supremacy in the later empire, has naturally kept a strong hold over the weak and the sentimentally thoughtless; and perhaps reached its culmination in the insipid nineteenth century, when people were wont to praise dogs "because they are so human" (as if humanity were any valid standard of merit!), and honest Edwin Landseer painted hundreds of smug Fidoes and Carlos and Rovers with all the anthropoid triviality, pettiness, and "cuteness" of eminent Victorians.

But amidst this chaos of intellectual and emotional grovelling a few free souls have always stood out for the old civilised realities which mediaevalism eclipsed—the stern classic loyalty to truth, strength, and beauty given by a clear mind and uncowed spirit to the full-living Western Aryan confronted by Nature's majesty, loveliness, and aloofness. This is the virile aesthetic and ethic of the extensor muscles—the bold, buoyant, assertive beliefs and preferences of proud, dominant, unbroken, and unterrified conquerors, hunters, and warriors—and it has small use for the shams and whimperings of the brotherly, affection-slobbering peacemaker and cringer and sentimentalist. Beauty and sufficiency—twin qualities of the cosmos itself—are the gods of this aristocratic and pagan type; to the worshipper of such eternal things the supreme virtue will not be found in lowliness, attachment, obedience, and emotional messiness. This sort of worshipper will look for that which best embodies the loveliness of the stars and the worlds and the forests and the seas and the sunsets, and which best acts out the blandness, lordliness, accuracy, self-sufficiency, cruelty, independence, and contemptuous and capricious impersonality of all-governing Nature. Beauty—coolness—aloofness—philosophic repose—self-sufficiency—untamed mastery—where else can we find these things incarnated with even half the perfection and completeness that mark their incarnation in the peerless and softly gliding cat, which performs its mysterious orbit with the relentless and unobtrusive certainty of a planet in infinity?

That dogs are dear to the unimaginative peasant-burgher whilst cats appeal to the sensitive poet-aristocrat-philosopher will be clear in a moment when we reflect on the matter of biological association. Practical plebeian folk judge a thing only by its immediate touch, taste, and smell; while more delicate types form their estimates from the linked images and ideas which the object calls up in their minds. Now when dogs and cats are considered, the stolid churl sees only the two animals before him, and bases his favour on their relative capacity to pander to his sloppy, unformed ideas of ethics and friendship and flattering subservience. On the other hand the gentleman and thinker sees each in all its natural affiliations, and cannot fail to notice that in the great symmetries of organic life dogs fall in with slovenly wolves and foxes and jackals and coyotes and dingoes and painted hyaenas, whilst cats walk proudly with the jungle's lords, and own the haughty lion, the sinuous leopard, the regal tiger, and the shapely panther and jaguar as their kin. Dogs are the hieroglyphs of blind emotion, inferiority, servile attachment, and gregariousness—the attributes of commonplace, stupidly passionate, and intellectually and imaginatively undeveloped men. Cats are the runes of beauty, invincibility, wonder, pride, freedom, coldness, self-sufficiency, and dainty individuality—the qualities of sensitive, enlightened, mentally developed, pagan, cynical, poetic, philosophic, dispassionate, reserved, independent, Nietzschean, unbroken, civilised, master-class men. The dog is a peasant and the cat is a gentleman.

We may, indeed, judge the tone and bias of a civilisation by its relative attitude toward dogs and cats. The proud Egypt wherein Pharaoh was Pharaoh and pyramids rose in beauty at the wish of him who dreamed them bowed down to the cat, and temples were builded to its goddess at Bubastis. In imperial Rome the graceful leopard adorned most homes of quality, lounging in insolent beauty in the atrium with golden collar and chain; while after the age of the Antonines the actual cat was imported from Egypt and cherished as a rare and costly luxury. So much for dominant and enlightened peoples. When, however, we come to the grovelling Middle Ages with their superstitions and ecstasies and monasticisms and maunderings over saints and their relics, we find the cool and impersonal loveliness of the felidae in very low esteem; and behold a sorry spectacle of hatred and cruelty shewn toward the beautiful little creature whose mousing virtues alone gained it sufferance amongst the ignorant churls who resented its self-respecting coolness and feared its cryptical and elusive independence as something akin to the dark powers of witchcraft. These boorish slaves of eastern darkness could not tolerate what did not serve their own cheap emotions and flimsy purposes. They wished a dog to fawn and hunt and fetch and carry, and had no use for the cat's gift of eternal and disinterested beauty to feed the spirit. One can imagine how they must have resented Pussy's magnificent reposefulness, unhurriedness, relaxation, and scorn for trivial human aims and concernments. Throw a stick, and the servile dog wheezes and pants and shambles to bring it to you. Do the same before a cat, and he will eye you with coolly polite and somewhat bored amusement. And just as inferior people prefer the inferior animal which scampers excitedly because somebody else wants something, so do superior people respect the superior animal which lives its own life and knows that the puerile stick-throwings of alien bipeds are none of its business and beneath its notice. The dog barks and begs and tumbles to amuse you when you crack the whip. That pleases a meekness-loving peasant who relishes a stimulus to his sense of importance. The cat, on the other hand, charms you into playing for its benefit when it wishes to be amused; making you rush about the room with a paper on a string when it feels like exercise, but refusing all your attempts to make it play when it is not in the humour. That is personality and individuality and self-respect—the calm mastery of a being whose life is its own and not yours—and the superior person recognises and appreciates this because he too is a free soul whose position is assured, and whose only law is his own heritage and aesthetic sense. Altogether, we may see that the dog appeals to those primitive emotional souls whose chief demands on the universe are for meaningless affection, aimless companionship, and flattering attention and subservience; whilst the cat reigns among those more contemplative and imaginative spirits who ask of the universe only the objective sight of poignant, ethereal beauty and the animate symbolisation of Nature's bland, relentless, reposeful, unhurried, and impersonal order and sufficiency. The dog *gives*, but the cat *is*.

Simple folk always overstress the ethical element in life, and it is quite natural that they should extend it to the realm of their pets. Accordingly we hear many inane dicta in favour of dogs on the ground that they are *faithful*, whilst cats are *treacherous*. Now just what does this really mean? Where are the points of reference? Certainly, the dog has so little imagination and individuality that it knows no motives but its master's; but what sophisticated mind can descry a positive virtue in this stupid abnegation of a birthright? Discrimination must surely award the palm to the superior cat, which has too much natural dignity to accept any scheme of things but its own, and which consequently cares not one whit what any clumsy human thinks or wishes or expects of it. It is not *treacherous*, because it has never acknowledged any allegiance to anything outside its own leisurely wishes; and *treachery* basically implies a departure from some covenant explicitly recognised. The cat is a realist, and no hypocrite. He takes what pleases him when he wants it, and makes no promises. He never leads you to expect more from him than he gives, and if you choose to be stupidly Victorian enough to mistake his purrs and rubbings of self-satisfaction for marks of transient affection toward you, that is no fault of his. He would not for a moment have you believe that he wants more of you than food and warmth and shelter and amusement—and he is certainly justified in criticising your aesthetic and imaginative development if you fail to find his grace, beauty, and cheerful decorative influence an aboundingly sufficient repayment for all that you give him. The cat-lover need not be amazed at another's love for dogs—indeed, he may also possess this quality himself; for dogs are often very comely, and as lovable in a condescending way as a faithful old servant or tenant in the eyes of a master—but he cannot help feeling astonishment at those who do not share his love for cats. The cat is such a perfect symbol of beauty and superiority that it seems scarcely possible for any true aesthete and civilised cynic to do other than worship it. We call ourselves a dog's "master"—but who ever dared to call himself the "master" of a cat? We *own* a dog—he is with us as a slave and inferior because we wish him to be. But we *entertain* a cat—he adorns our hearth as a guest, fellow-lodger, and equal because *he* wishes to be there. It is no compliment to be the stupidly idolised master of a dog whose instinct it is to idolise, but it is a very distinct tribute to be chosen as the friend and confidant of a philosophic cat who is wholly his own master and could easily choose another companion if he found such an one more agreeable and interesting. A trace, I think, of this great truth regarding the higher dignity of the cat has crept into folklore in the use of the names "cat" and "dog" as terms of opprobrium. Whilst "cat" has never been applied to any sort of offender more serious than the mildly spiteful and innocuously sly female gossip and commentator, the words "dog" and "cur" have always been linked with vileness, dishonour, and degradation of the gravest type. In the crystallisation of this nomenclature there has undoubtedly been present in the popular mind some dim, half-unconscious realisation that there are depths of slinking, whining, fawning, and servile ignobility which no kith of the lion and the leopard could ever attain. The cat may fall low, but he is always unbroken. He is, like the Nordic among men, one of those who govern their own lives or die.

We have but to glance analytically at the two animals to see the points pile up in favour of the cat. Beauty, which is probably the only thing of any basic significance in all the cosmos, ought to be our chief criterion; and here the cat excels so brilliantly that all comparisons collapse. Some dogs, it is true, have beauty in a very ample degree; but even the highest level of canine beauty falls far below the feline average. The cat is classic whilst the dog is Gothic—nowhere in the animal world can we discover such really Hellenic perfection of form, with anatomy adapted to function, as in the felidae. Puss is a Doric temple—an Ionic colonnade—in the utter classicism of its structural and decorative harmonies. And this is just as true kinetically as statically, for art has no parallel for the bewitching grace of the cat's slightest motion. The sheer, perfect aestheticism of kitty's lazy stretchings, industrious face-washings, playful rollings, and little involuntary shiftings in sleep is something as keen and vital as the best pastoral poetry or genre painting; whilst the unerring accuracy of his leaping and springing, running and hunting, has an art-value just as high in a more spirited way. But it is his capacity for leisure and repose which makes the cat preëminent. Mr. Carl Van Vechten, in *Peter Whiffle,* holds up the timeless restfulness of the cat as a model for a life's philosophy, and Prof. William Lyon Phelps has very effectively captured the secret of felinity when he says that the cat does not merely *lie down,* but *"pours his body out on the floor like a glass of water".* What other creature has thus merged the aestheticism of mechanics and hydraulics? Contrast with this the inept panting, wheezing, fumbling, drooling, scratching, and general clumsiness of the average dog with his myriad false and wasted motions. And in the detail of neatness the fastidious cat is of course immeasurably ahead. We always love to touch a cat, but only the insensitive can uniformly welcome the frantic and humid nuzzlings and pawings of a dusty and perhaps not inodorous canine which leaps and fusses and writhes about in awkward feverishness for no particular reason save that blind nerve-centres have been spurred by certain meaningless stimuli. There is a wearying excess of bad manners in all this doggish fury—well-bred people don't paw and maul one, and surely enough we invariably find the cat gentle and reserved in his advances, and delicate even when he glides gracefully into your lap with cultivated purrs, or leaps whimsically on the table where you are writing to play with your pen in modulated, serio-comic pats. I do not wonder that Mahomet, that sheik of perfect manners, loved cats for their urbanity and disliked dogs for their boorishness; or that cats are the favourites in the polite Latin countries whilst dogs take the lead in heavy, practical, and beer-drinking Central Europe. Watch a cat eat, and then watch a dog. The one is held in check by an inherent and inescapable daintiness, and lends a kind of grace to one of the most ungraceful of all processes. The dog, on the other hand, is wholly repulsive in his bestial and insatiate greediness; living up to his forest kinship by "wolfing" most openly and unashamedly. Returning to beauty of line—is it not significant that while many normal breeds of dogs are conspicuously and admittedly ugly, *no* healthy and well-developed feline of any species whatsoever is other than beautiful? There are, of course, many ugly cats; but these are always individual cases of mongrelism, malnutrition, deformity, or injury. No breed of cats in its proper condition can by any stretch of the imagination be thought of as even slightly ungraceful—a record against which must be pitted the depressing spectacle of impossibly flattened bulldogs, grotesquely elongated dachshunds, hideously shapeless and shaggy Airedales, and the like. Of course, it may be said that no aesthetic standard is other than relative—but we always work with such standards as we empirically have, and in comparing cats and dogs under the Western European aesthetic we cannot be unfair to either. If any undiscovered tribe in Thibet finds Airedales beautiful and Persian cats ugly, we will not dispute them on their own territory—but just now we are dealing with ourselves and our territory, and here the verdict would not admit of much doubt even from the most ardent kynophile. Such an one usually passes the problem off in an epigrammatic paradox, and says 'that Snookums is so homely, he's pretty!' This is the childish penchant for the grotesque and tawdrily "cute", which we see likewise embodied in popular cartoons, freak dolls, and all the malformed decorative trumpery of the "Billikin" or "Krazy Kat" order found in the "dens" and "cosy corners" of the would-be sophisticated cultural yokelry.

In the matter of intelligence we find the caninites making amusing claims—amusing because they so naively measure what they conceive to be an animal's intelligence by its degree of subservience to the human will. A dog will retrieve, a cat will not; *therefore* (sic!) the dog is the more intelligent. Dogs can be more elaborately trained for circus and vaudeville acts than cats, *therefore* (O Zeus, O Royal Mount!) they are cerebrally superior. Now of course this is all the sheerest nonsense. We would not call a weak-spirited man more intelligent than an independent citizen because we can make him vote as we wish whereas we can't influence the independent citizen, yet countless persons apply an exactly parallel argument in appraising the grey matter of dogs and cats. Competition in servility is something to which no self-respecting Thomas or Tabitha ever stooped, and it is plain that any really effective estimate of canine and feline intelligence must proceed from a careful observation of dogs and cats in a detached state—uninfluenced by human beings—as they formulate certain objectives of their own and use their own mental equipment in achieving them. When we do this, we arrive at a very wholesome respect for our purring hearthside friend who makes so little display and ado about his wishes and business methods; for in every conception and calculation he shews a steel-cold and deliberate union of intellect, will, and sense of proportion which puts utterly to shame the emotional sloppings-over and docilely acquired artificial tricks of the "clever" and "faithful" pointer or sheep-dog. Watch a cat decide to move through a door, and see how patiently he waits for his opportunity, never losing sight of his purpose even when he finds it expedient to feign other interests in the interim. Watch him in the thick of the chase, and compare his calculating patience and quiet study of his terrain with the noisy floundering and pawing of his canine rival. It is not often that he returns empty-handed. He knows what he wants, and means to get it in the most effective way, even at the sacrifice of time—which he philosophically recognises as unimportant in the aimless cosmos. There is no turning him aside or distracting his attention—and we know that among humans this very quality of mental tenacity, this ability to carry a single thread through complex distractions, is considered a pretty good sign of intellectual vigour and maturity. Children, old crones, peasants, and dogs ramble; cats and philosophers stick to their point. In resourcefulness, too, the cat attests his superiority. Dogs can be well trained to do a single thing, but psychologists tell us that these responses to an automatic memory instilled from outside are of little worth as indices of real intelligence. To judge the abstract development of a brain, confront it with new and unfamiliar conditions and see how well its own strength enables it to achieve its object by sheer reasoning without blazed trails. Here the cat can silently devise a dozen mysterious and successful alternatives whilst poor Fido is barking in bewilderment and wondering what it is all about. Granted that Rover the retriever may make a greater bid for popular sentimental regard by going into the burning house and saving the baby in traditional cinema fashion, it remains a fact that whiskered and purring Nig is a higher-grade biological organism—something physiologically and psychologically nearer a man because of his very freedom from man's orders, and as such entitled to a higher respect from those who judge by purely philosophic and aesthetic standards. We can respect a cat as we cannot respect a dog, no matter which personally appeals the more to our mere doting fancy; and if we be aesthetes and analysts rather than commonplace-lovers and emotionalists, the scales must inevitably turn completely in kitty's favour. It may be added, moreover, that even the aloof and sufficient cat is by no means devoid of sentimental appeal. Once we get rid of the uncivilised ethical bias—the 'treacherous' and 'horrid bird-catcher' prejudice—we find in the 'harmless, necessary cat' the very apex of happy domestic symbolism; whilst small kittens become objects to adore, idealise, and celebrate in the most rhapsodic of dactyls and anapaests, iambics and trochaics. I, in my own senescent mellowness, confess to an inordinate and wholly unphilosophic predilection for tiny coal-black kitties with large yellow eyes, and could no more pass one without petting him than Dr. Johnson could pass a sidewalk post without striking it. There is, likewise, in many cats something quite analogous to the reciprocal fondness so loudly extolled in dogs, human beings, horses, and the like. Cats come to associate certain persons with acts continuously contributing to their pleasure, and acquire for them a recognition and attachment which manifests itself in pleasant excitement at their approach—whether or not bearing food and drink—and a certain pensiveness at their protracted absence. The late "Tat" of Allston and Malden, grey companion of our fellow-amateur Mrs. Miniter, reached the point of accepting food from no other hand but hers, and would actually go hungry rather than touch the least morsel from a kindly Parker source. He also had distinct affections amongst the other cats of that idyllic household; voluntarily offering food to one of his whiskered friends, whilst disputing most savagely the least glance which his coal-black rival "Snowball" would bestow upon his plate. If it be argued that these feline fondnesses are essentially 'selfish' and 'practical' in their ultimate composition, let us inquire in return how many human fondnesses, apart from those springing directly upon primitive brute instinct, have any other basis. After the returning board has brought in the grand total of zero we shall be better able to refrain from ingenuous censure of the 'selfish' cat.

The superior imaginative inner life of the cat, resulting in superior self-possession, is well known. A dog is a pitiful thing, depending wholly on companionship, and utterly lost except in packs or by the side of his master. Leave him alone and he does not know what to do except bark and howl and trot about till sheer exhaustion forces him to sleep. A cat, however, is never without the potentialities of contentment. Like a superior man, he knows how to be alone and happy. Once he looks about and finds no one to amuse him, he settles down to the task of amusing himself; and no one really knows cats without having occasionally peeked stealthily at some lively and well-balanced kitten which believes itself to be alone. Only after such a glimpse of unaffected tail-chasing grace and unstudied purring can one fully understand the charm of those lines which Coleridge wrote with reference to the human rather than the feline young—

". . . a limber elf,
Singing, dancing to itself."

But whole volumes could be written on the playing of cats, since the varieties and aesthetic aspects of such sportiveness are infinite. Be it sufficient to say that in such pastimes many cats have exhibited traits and actions which psychologists authentically declare to be motivated by genuine humour and whimsicality in its purest sense; so that the task of 'making a cat laugh' may not be so impossible a thing even outside the borders of Cheshire. In short, a dog is an incomplete thing. Like an inferior man, he needs emotional stimuli from outside, and must set something artificial up as a god and motive. The cat, however, is perfect in himself. Like the human philosopher, he is a self-sufficient entity and microcosm. He is a real and integrated being because he thinks and feels himself to be such, whereas the dog can conceive of himself only in relation to something else. Whip a dog and he licks your hand—faugh! The beast has no idea of himself except as an inferior part of an organism whereof you are a superior part—he would no more think of striking back at you than you would think of pounding your own head when it punishes you with a headache. But whip a cat and watch it glare and move backward hissing in outraged dignity and self-respect! One more blow, and it strikes you in return; for it is a gentleman and your equal, and will accept no infringement on its personality and body of privileges. It is only in your house anyway because it wishes to be, or perhaps even as a condescending favour to yourself. It is the house, not you, it likes; for philosophers realise that human beings are at best only minor adjuncts to scenery. Go one step too far, and it leaves you altogether. You have mistaken your relationship to it and imagined you are its master, and no real cat can tolerate that breach of good manners. Henceforward it will seek companions of greater discrimination and clearer perspective. Let anaemic persons who believe in 'turning the other cheek' console themselves with cringing dogs—for the robust pagan with the blood of Nordic twilights in his veins there is no beast like the cat; intrepid steed of Freya, who can boldly look even Thor and Odin full in the face and stare contemplatively with great round eyes of undimmed yellow or green.

And so, Sir (I employ the singular since I cannot imagine that you, O Jacobe Ferdinande, would have the truly feline cruelty to spring all these ten-plus pages on a deserving club which has never done you any harm), I believe I have outlined for you with some fulness the divers reasons why, in my opinion and in the smartly timed title-phrase of Mr. Van Doren, "gentlemen prefer cats". The reply of Mr. Terhune in a subsequent issue of the *Tribune* appears to me beside the point; insomuch as it is less a refutation of facts than a mere personal affirmation of the author's membership in that conventional "very human" majority who take affection and companionship seriously, enjoy being important to something alive, measure merit by devotion to human purposes, hate a "parasite" on mere ethical grounds without consulting the right of beauty to exist for its own sake, and therefore love man's noblest and most faithful friend, the perennial dog. I suppose Mr. Terhune loves horses and babies also, for they go conventionally together in the great hundred-per-center's credo as highly essential likings for every good and lovable he-man of the Arrow Collar and Harold Bell Wright hero school, even though the motor car and dear Mrs. Sanger have done much to reduce the last two items.

Dogs, then, are peasants and the pets of peasants; cats are gentlemen and the pets of gentlemen. The dog is for him who places crude feeling and outgrown ethics and humanocentricity above austere and disinterested beauty; who just loves 'folks and folksiness' and doesn't mind sloppy clumsiness if only something will truly care for him. (Tableau of dog across master's grave—cf. Landseer, "The Old Shepherd's Chief Mourner".) The guy who isn't much for highbrow stuff, but is always on the square and don't (sic) often find the Saddypost or the N.Y. World too deep for him; who hadn't much use for Valentino, but thinks Doug Fairbanks is just about right for an evening's entertainment. Wholesome—constructive—non-morbid—civic-minded—domestic—(I forgot to mention the radio) normal—that's the sort of go-getter that had ought to go in for dogs.

The cat is for the aristocrat—whether by birth or inclinations or both—who admires his fellow-aristocrats (even if Little Belknap isn't especially fond of Felis). He is for the man who appreciates beauty as the one living force in a blind and purposeless universe, and who worships that beauty in all its forms without regard for the sentimental and ethical illusions of the moment. For the man who knows the hollowness of feeling and the emptiness of human objects and aspirations, and who therefore clings solely to what is real—as beauty is real because it pretends to no significance beyond the emotion which it excites and is. For the man who feels sufficient in the cosmos, and asks no false perspective of exaltation; who is moved by no mawkish scruples of conventional prejudice, but loves repose and strength and freedom and luxury and superiority and sufficiency and contemplation; who as a strong fearless soul wishes something to respect instead of something to lick his face and accept his alternate blows and strokings; who seeks a proud and beautiful equal in the peerage of individualism rather than a cowed and cringing satellite in the hierarchy of fear, subservience, and devotion. The cat is not for the brisk, self-important little worker with a "mission", but for the enlightened dreaming poet who knows that the world contains nothing really worth doing. The dilettante—the connoisseur—the decadent, if you will, though in a healthier age than this there were things for such men to do, so that they were the planners and leaders of those glorious pagan times. The cat is for him who does things not for empty duty but for power, pleasure, splendour, romance, and glamour—for the harpist who sings alone in the night of old battles, or the warrior who goes out to fight such battles for beauty, glory, fame, and the splendour of a kingly court athwart which no shadow of weakness or democracy falls. For him who will be lulled by no sops of prose and usefulness, but demands for his effort the ease and beauty and ascendancy and cultivation which alone make effort worth while. For the man who knows that play, not work, and leisure, not bustle, are the great things of life; and that the round of striving merely in order to strive some more is a bitter irony of which the civilised soul accepts as little as it can.

Beauty, sufficiency, ease, and good manners—what more can civilisation require? We have them all in the divine little monarch who lounges gloriously on his silken cushion before the hearth. Loveliness and joy for their own sake—pride and harmony and coördination—spirit, restfulness, and completeness—all here are present, and need but a sympathetic disillusionment for worship in full measure. What fully civilised soul but would eagerly serve as high-priest of Bast? The star of the cat, I think, is just now in the ascendant, as we emerge little by little from the dreams of ethics and democracy which clouded the nineteenth century and raised the grubbing and unlovely dog to the pinnacle of sentimental regard. Whether a renaissance of monarchy and beauty will restore our Western civilisation, or whether the forces of disintegration are already too powerful for even the fascist sentiment to check, none may yet say; but in the present moment of cynical world-unmasking between the pretence of the eighteen-hundreds and the ominous mystery of the decades ahead we have at least a flash of the old pagan perspective and the old pagan clearness and honesty.

And one idol lit up by that flash, seen fair and lovely on a dream-throne of silk and gold under a chryselephantine dome, is a shape of deathless grace not always given its due among groping mortals—the haughty, the unconquered, the mysterious, the luxurious, the Babylonian, the impersonal, the eternal companion of superiority and art—the type of perfect beauty and the brother of poetry—the bland, grave, competent, and patrician cat.

November 23, 1926

SOME NOTES ON A NONENTITY

For me, the chief difficulty of writing an autobiography is finding anything of importance to put in it. My existence has been a quiet, uneventful, and undistinguished one; and at best must sound woefully flat and tame on paper.

I was born in Providence, R.I.—where, but for two minor interruptions, I have ever since lived—on August 20, 1890; of old Rhode Island stock on my mother's side, and of a Devonshire paternal line domiciled in New York State since 1827.

The interests which have led me to fantastic fiction were very early in appearing, for as far back as I can clearly remember I was charmed by strange stories and ideas, and by ancient scenes and objects. Nothing has ever seemed to fascinate me so much as the thought of some curious interruption in the prosaic laws of Nature, or some monstrous intrusion on our familiar world by unknown things from the limitless abysses outside.

When I was three or less I listened avidly to the usual juvenile fairy lore, and Grimm's Tales were among the first things I ever read, at the age of four. When I was five the Arabian Nights claimed me, and I spent hours in playing Arab—calling myself "Abdul Alhazred", which some kindly elder had suggested to me as a typical Saracen name. It was many years later, however, that I thought of giving Abdul an eighth-century setting and attributing to him the dreaded and unmentionable *Necronomicon!*

But for me books and legends held no monopoly of fantasy. In the quaint hill streets of my native town, where fanlighted colonial doorways, small-paned windows, and graceful Georgian steeples still keep alive the glamour of the eighteenth century, I felt a magic then and now hard to explain. Sunsets over the city's outspread roofs, as seen from vantage-points on the great hill, affected me with especial poignancy. Before I knew it the eighteenth century had captured me more utterly than ever the hero of *Berkeley Square* was captured; so that I used to spend hours in the attic poring over the long-s'd books banished from the library downstairs and unconsciously absorbing the style of Pope and Dr. Johnson as a natural mode of expression. This absorption was doubly strong because of the ill-health which rendered school attendance rare and irregular. One effect of it was to make me feel subtly out of place in the modern period, and consequently to think of *time* as a mystical, portentous thing in which all sorts of unexpected wonders might be discovered.

Nature, too, keenly touched my sense of the fantastic. My home was not far from what was then the edge of the settled residence district, so that I was just as used to the rolling fields, stone walls, giant elms, squat farmhouses, and deep woods of rural New England as to the ancient urban scene. This brooding, primitive landscape seemed to me to hold some vast but unknown significance, and certain dark wooded hollows near the Seekonk River took on an aura of strangeness not unmixed with vague horror. They figured in my dreams—especially those nightmares containing the black, winged, rubbery entities which I called "night-gaunts".

When I was six years old I encountered the mythology of Greece and Rome through various popular juvenile media, and was profoundly influenced by it. I gave up being an Arab and became a Roman, incidentally acquiring for ancient Rome a queer feeling of familiarity and identification only less powerful than my corresponding feeling for the eighteenth century. In a way, the two feelings worked together; for when I sought out the original classics from which the childish tales were taken, I found them very largely in late seventeenth- and eighteenth-century translations. The imaginative stimulus was immense, and for a time I actually thought I glimpsed fauns and dryads in certain venerable groves. I used to build altars and offer sacrifices to Pan, Diana, Apollo, and Minerva.

About this period the weird illustrations of Gustave Doré— met in editions of Dante, Milton, and the *Ancient Mariner*—affected me powerfully. For the first time I began to attempt writing—the earliest piece I can recall being a tale of a hideous cave perpetrated at the age of seven and entitled "The Noble Eavesdropper". This does not survive, though I still possess two hilariously infantile efforts dating from the following year—"The Mysterious Ship" and "The Secret of the Grave", whose titles display sufficiently the direction of my tastes.

At the age of about eight I acquired a strong interest in the sciences, which undoubtedly arose from the mysterious-looking pictures of "Philosophical and Scientific Instruments" in the back of Webster's Unabridged Dictionary. Chemistry came first, and I soon had a very attractive little laboratory in the basement of my home. Next came geography—with a weird fascination centring in the antarctic continent and other pathless realms of remote wonder. Finally astronomy dawned on me—and the lure of other worlds and inconceivable cosmic gulfs eclipsed all other interests for a long period after my twelfth birthday. I published a small hectographed paper called *The Rhode Island Journal of Astronomy* and at last—when sixteen—broke into actual newspaper print with astronomical matter, contributing monthly articles on current phenomena to a local daily, and flooding the weekly rural press with more expansive miscellany.

It was while in high-school—which I was able to attend with some regularity—that I first produced weird stories of any degree of coherence and seriousness. They were largely trash, and I destroyed the bulk of them when eighteen; but one or two probably came up to the average pulp level. Of them all I have kept only "The Beast in the Cave" (1905) and "The Alchemist" (1908). At this stage most of my incessant, voluminous writing was scientific and classical, weird material taking a relatively minor place. Science had removed my belief in the supernatural, and truth for the moment captivated me more than dreams. I am still a mechanistic materialist in philosophy. As for reading—I mixed science, history, general literature, weird literature, and utter juvenile rubbish with the most complete unconventionality.

Parallel with all these reading and writing interests I had a very enjoyable childhood; the early years well enlivened with toys and with outdoor diversions, and the stretch after my tenth birthday dominated by a persistent though perforce short-distanced cycling which made me familiar with all the picturesque and fancy-exciting phases of the New England village and rural landscape. Nor was I by any means a hermit—more than one band of local boyhood having me on its rolls.

My health prevented college attendance; but informal studies at home, and the influence of a notably scholarly physician-uncle, helped to banish some of the worst effects of the lack. In the years which should have been collegiate I veered from science to literature, specialising in the products of that eighteenth century of which I felt myself so oddly a part. Weird writing was then in abeyance, although I read everything spectral that I could find—including the frequent bizarre items in such cheap magazines as *The All-Story* and *The Black Cat.* My own products were largely verse and essays—uniformly worthless and now relegated to eternal concealment.

In 1914 I discovered and joined the United Amateur Press Association, one of several nation-wide correspondence organisations of literary novices who publish papers of their own and form, collectively, a miniature world of helpful mutual criticism and encouragement. The benefit received from this affiliation can scarcely be overestimated, for contact with the various members and critics helped me infinitely in toning down the worst archaisms and ponderosities in my style. This world of "amateur journalism" is now best represented by the National Amateur Press Association, a society which I can strongly and conscientiously recommend to any beginner in authorship. (For information address the Secretary, George W. Trainer, Jun., 95 Stuyvesant Ave., Brooklyn, N.Y.) It was in the ranks of organised amateurdom that I was first advised to resume weird writing—a step which I took in July, 1917, with the production of "The Tomb" and "Dagon" (both since published in *Weird Tales*) in quick succession. Also through amateurdom were established the contacts leading to the first professional publication of my fiction—in 1922, when *Home Brew* printed a ghastly series entitled "Herbert West—Reanimator". The same circle, moreover, led to my acquaintance with Clark Ashton Smith, Frank Belknap Long, Jun., Wilfred B. Talman, and others since celebrated in the field of unusual stories.

About 1919 the discovery of Lord Dunsany—from whom I got the idea of the artificial pantheon and myth-background represented by "Cthulhu", "Yog-Sothoth", "Yuggoth", etc.—gave a vast impetus to my weird writing; and I turned out material in greater volume than ever before or since. At that time I had no thought or hope of professional publication; but the founding of *Weird Tales* in 1923 opened up an outlet of considerable steadiness. My stories of the 1920 period reflect a good deal of my two chief models, Poe and Dunsany, and are in general too strongly inclined to extravagance and overcolouring to be of much serious literary value.

Meanwhile my health had been radically improving since 1920, so that a rather static existence began to be diversified with modest travels giving my strong antiquarian interests a freer play. My chief delight outside literature became the past-reviving quest for ancient architectural and landscape effects in the old colonial towns and byways of America's longest-settled regions, and gradually I have managed to cover a considerable territory from glamorous Quebec on the north to tropical Key West on the south and colourful Natchez and New Orleans on the west. Among my favourite towns, aside from Providence, are Quebec; Portsmouth, New Hampshire; Salem and Marblehead in Massachusetts; Newport in my own state; Philadelphia; Annapolis; Richmond with its wealth of Poe memories; eighteenth-century Charleston; sixteenth-century St. Augustine; and drowsy Natchez on its dizzy bluff and with its gorgeous subtropical hinterland. The "Arkham" and "Kingsport" figuring in some of my tales are more or less adapted versions of Salem and Marblehead. My native New England

and its old, lingering lore have sunk deep into my imagination, and appear frequently in what I write. I dwell at present in a house 130 years old on the crest of Providence's ancient hill, with a haunting vista of venerable roofs and boughs from the window above my desk.

It is now clear to me that any actual literary merit I have is confined to tales of dream-life, strange shadow, and cosmic "outsideness", notwithstanding a keen interest in many other departments of life and a professional practice of general prose and verse revision. Why this is so, I have not the least idea. I have no illusions concerning the precarious status of my tales, and do not expect to become a serious competitor of my favourite weird authors—Poe, Arthur Machen, Dunsany, Algernon Blackwood, Walter de la Mare, and Montague Rhodes James. The only thing I can say in favour of my work is its sincerity. I refuse to follow the mechanical conventions of popular fiction or to fill my tales with stock characters and situations, but insist on reproducing real moods and impressions in the best way I can command. The result may be poor, but I had rather keep aiming at serious literary expression than accept the artificial standards of cheap romance.

I have tried to improve and subtilise my tales with the passing of years, but have not made the progress I wish. Some of my efforts have been cited in the O'Brien and O. Henry annuals, and a few have enjoyed reprinting in anthologies; but all proposals for a published collection have come to nothing. It is possible that one or two short tales may be issued as separate brochures before long. I never write when I cannot be spontaneous—expressing a mood already existing and demanding crystallisation. Some of my tales involve actual dreams I have experienced. My speed and manner of writing vary widely in different cases, but I always work best at night. Of my products, my favourites are "The Colour Out of Space" and "The Music of Erich Zann", in the order named. I doubt if I could ever succeed well in the ordinary kind of science fiction.

I believe that weird writing offers a serious field not unworthy of the best literary artists; though it is at most a very limited one, reflecting only a small section of man's infinitely composite moods. Spectral fiction should be realistic and atmospheric—confining its departure from Nature to the one supernatural channel chosen, and remembering that scene, mood, and phenomena are more important in conveying what is to be conveyed than are characters and plot. The "punch" of a truly weird tale is simply some violation or transcending of fixed cosmic law—an imaginative escape from palling reality—hence *phenomena* rather than *persons* are the logical "heroes". Horrors, I believe, should be *original*—the use of common myths and legends being a weakening influence. Current magazine fiction, with its incurable leanings toward conventional sentimental perspectives, brisk, cheerful style, and artificial "action" plots, does not rank high. The greatest weird tale ever written is probably Algernon Blackwood's "The Willows".

Nov. 23, 1933

BIBLIOGRAPHY

"The Little Glass Bottle," "The Secret Cave," "The Mystery of the Grave-Yard," "The Mysterious Ship." A.Mss., John Hay Library. In *The Shuttered Room and Other Pieces* (1959); rpt. in *Juvenilia: 1897–1905*, ed. S. T. Joshi (1984).

"A Reminiscence of Dr. Samuel Johnson." *The United Amateur* 17, No. 2 (November 1917): 21–24.

"Old Bugs." In *The Shuttered Room and Other Pieces* (1959).

"Memory." *The United Co-operative* 1, No. 2 (June 1919): 8. In *Beyond the Wall of Sleep* (1943).

"Nyarlathotep." *The United Amateur* 20, No. 2 (November 1920): 19–20. *The National Amateur* 43, No. 6 (July 1926): 53–54. In *Beyond the Wall of Sleep* (1943).

"Ex Oblivione." *The United Amateur* 20, No. 4 (March 1921): 59–60. In *Beyond the Wall of Sleep* (1943).

"What the Moon Brings." A.Ms., John Hay Library. *The National Amateur* 45, No. 5 (May 1923): 9. In *Beyond the Wall of Sleep* (1943).

"Sweet Ermengarde." A.Ms., John Hay Library. In *Beyond the Wall of Sleep* (1943).

"The Very Old Folk." A.Ms., John Hay Library. *Scienti-Snaps* 3, No. 3 (Summer 1940): 4–8.

"History of the *Necronomicon*." A.Ms., John Hay Library (reproduced in *Lovecraft at Last* [1975]). Oakman, AL: Rebel Press (Wilson H. Shepherd), 1938. In *Beyond the Wall of Sleep* (1943).

"Ibid." *The O-Wash-Ta-Nong* 3, No. 1 (January 1938): 11–13. In *Beyond the Wall of Sleep* (1943).

"Discarded Draft of 'The Shadow Over Innsmouth.'" A.Ms., John Hay Library. *The Acolyte* 2, No. 2 (Spring 1944): 3–7. In *Something about Cats and Other Pieces* (1949).

"The Battle That Ended the Century." T.Ms. (with A.Ms. revisions by Lovecraft), John Hay Library. [De Land, FL: R. H. Barlow, 1934.] In *Something about Cats and Other Pieces* (1949).

"Collapsing Cosmoses." A.Ms., John Hay Library. *Leaves* 2 (1938): 100–101.

"The Challenge from Beyond." A.Ms., John Hay Library. *Fantasy Magazine* 5, No. 4 (September 1935): 221–29. In *Beyond the Wall of Sleep* (1943).

"Commonplace Book." A.Ms., T.Mss., John Hay Library. Lakeport, CA: The Futile Press, 1938. In *Beyond the Wall of Sleep* (1943) and *The Shuttered Room and Other Pieces* (1959). West Warwick, RI: Necronomicon Press, 1987 (ed. David E. Schultz).

"Lord Dunsany and His Work." A.Ms., John Hay Library. In *Marginalia* (1944).

"Notes on Writing Weird Fiction." *Amateur Correspondent* 2, No. 1 (May–June 1937): 7–10. *Supramundane Stories* 1, No. 2 (Spring 1938): 11–13. In *Marginalia* (1944).

"Some Notes on Interplanetary Fiction." *The Californian* 3, No. 3 (Winter 1935): 39–42. In *Marginalia* (1944).

"In Memoriam: Robert Ervin Howard." T.Ms., John Hay Library. *Fantasy Magazine* No. 38 (September 1936): 29–31. In *Skull-Face and Others* by Robert E. Howard (1946).

"Idealism and Materialism—A Reflection." *The National Amateur* 41, No. 6 (July 1919): 278–81. In *The Shuttered Room and Other Pieces* (1959).

"Life for Humanity's Sake." *The American Amateur* 2, No. 1 (September 1920): 93–94.

In Defence of Dagon. A.Ms., John Hay Library. *Leaves* 2 (1938): 117–19 (excerpts). West Warwick, RI: Necronomicon Press, 1985 (ed. S. T. Joshi).

"Nietzscheism and Realism." *The Rainbow* No. 1 (October 1921): 9–11.

"The Materialist Today." T.Ms., John Hay Library. North Montpelier, VT: Driftwind Press, 1926. *The Drift-Wind* 1, No. 7 (October 1926): [6–9]. In *Something about Cats and Other Pieces* (1949).

"Some Causes of Self-Immolation." A.Ms., John Hay Library. In *Marginalia* (1944).

"Heritage or Modernism: Common Sense in Art Forms." *The Californian* 3, No. 1 (Summer 1935): 23–28. In *Marginalia* (1944).

"Metrical Regularity." *The Conservative* 1, No. 2 (July 1915): 2–4.

"The Vers Libre Epidemic." *The Conservative* 2, No. 4 (January 1917): [2–3].

"The Case for Classicism." *The United Co-operative* 1, No. 2 (June 1919): 3–5.

"Literary Composition." *The United Amateur* 19, No. 3 (January 1920): 56–60.

"Ars Gratia Artis." T.Ms., John Hay Library.

"The Poetry of Lilian Middleton." A.Ms., John Hay Library.
"Rudis Indigestaque Moles." *The Conservative* No. 12 (March 1923): 6–8.
"In the Editor's Study." *The Conservative* No. 13 (July 1923): 21–24.
"The Professional Incubus." *The National Amateur* 46, No. 4 (March 1924): 35–36.
"The Omnipresent Philistine." *The Oracle* 4, No. 3 (May 1924): 14–17.
"What Belongs in Verse." *The Perspective Review,* Spring 1935, pp. 10–11. In *The Dark Brotherhood and Other Pieces* (1966).
"The Crime of the Century." *The Conservative* 1, No. 1 (April 1915): [2–3].
"More *Chain Lightning.*" *The United Official Quarterly* 2, No. 1 (October 1915): [4–5].
"Old England and the 'Hyphen.'" *The Conservative* 2, No. 3 (October 1916): [1–2].
"Revolutionary Mythology." *The Conservative* 2, No. 3 (October 1916): [9–10].
"Americanism." *The United Amateur* 18, No. 6 (July 1919): 118–20.
"The League." *The Conservative* 5, No. 1 (July 1919): 9–10.
"Bolshevism." *The Conservative* 5, No. 1 (July 1919): 10–11.
"Some Repetitions on the Times." A.Ms., John Hay Library. *Lovecraft Studies* No. 12 (Spring 1986): 13–25.
"Vermont–A First Impression." T.Ms., John Hay Library. *Driftwind* 2, No. 5 (March 1928): [5–9]. In *Something about Cats and Other Pieces* (1949).
"Observations on Several Parts of America." T.Ms., John Hay Library. In *Marginalia* (1944).
"Travels in the Provinces of America." T.Ms., John Hay Library.
"An Account of Charleston." A.Ms., John Hay Library.
"Some Dutch Footprints in New England." *De Halve Maen* 9, No. 1 (18 October 1933): 2, 4.
"Homes and Shrines of Poe." *The Californian* 2, No. 3 (Winter 1934): 8–10.
"In a Major Key." *The Conservative* 1, No. 2 (July 1915): 9–11.
"The Dignity of Journalism." *Dowdell's Bearcat* 4, No. 4 (July 1915): [6–9].
"Symphony and Stress." *The Conservative* 1, No. 3 (October 1915): 12–14.
United Amateur Press Association: Exponent of Amateur Journalism. [Elroy, WI: E. E. Ericson, 1916.]
"A Reply to *The Lingerer.*" *The Tryout* 3, No. 7 (June 1917): [9–12].
"*Les Mouches Fantastiques.*" *The Conservative* 4, No. 1 (July 1918): 7–8.
"For What Does the United Stand?" *The United Amateur* 19, No. 5 (May 1920): 101.

"Amateur Journalism: Its Possible Needs and Betterment." T.Ms., John Hay Library. In *The Dark Brotherhood and Other Pieces* (1966).
"What Amateurdom and I Have Done for Each Other." *The Boys' Herald* 46, No. 1 (August 1937): 6–7.
"Lucubrations Lovecraftian." *The United Co-operative* 1, No. 3 (April 1921): 8–15.
"A Matter of Uniteds." *Bacon's Essays* 1, No. 1 (Summer 1927): 1–3.
"Mrs. Miniter—Estimates and Recollections." A.Ms., John Hay Library. *The Californian* 5, No. 4 (Spring 1938): 47–55.
Some Current Motives and Practices. [De Land, FL: R. H. Barlow, 1936.]
"Trans-Neptunian Planets." *Scientific American* 95, No. 8 (25 August 1906): 135.
"The Earth Not Hollow." *The Providence Sunday Journal* 22, No. 7 (12 August 1906), Sec. 2, p. 5.
To *The All-Story Weekly. The All-Story Weekly,* 7 March 1914, pp. 223–24.
"Science versus Charlatanry." *The* [Providence] *Evening News* 45, No. 95 (9 September 1914): 8.
"The Fall of Astrology." *The* [Providence] *Evening News* 46, No. 25 (17 December 1914): 8.
To Edwin Baird. *Weird Tales* 2, No. 2 (September 1923): 81–82.
To Edwin Baird. *Weird Tales* 3, No. 3 (March 1924): 89–92.
"The Old Brick Row." T.Ms., John Hay Library. *The Providence Sunday Journal* 44, No. 39 (24 March 1929), Sec. A, p. 5.
To Nils H. Frome. *Phantastique/The Science Fiction Critic* No. 13 (March 1938): 6–10.
"The Brief Autobiography of an Inconsequential Scribbler." *The Silver Clarion* 3, No. 1 (April 1919): 8–9.
"Within the Gates." T.Ms., John Hay Library. *Lovecraft Studies* No. 10 (Spring 1985): 29–30.
"A Confession of Unfaith." *The Liberal* 1, No. 2 (February 1922): 17–23.
"Commercial Blurbs." T.Ms., John Hay Library. *Lovecraft Studies* No. 16 (Spring 1988): 19–24.
"Cats and Dogs." A.Ms., John Hay Library. *Leaves* 1 (Summer 1937): 25–34. In *Something about Cats and Other Pieces* (1949).
"Some Notes on a Nonentity." A.Ms., John Hay Library. In *Beyond the Wall of Sleep* (1943).

The UNITED AMATEUR

Official Organ of the

United Amateur Press Association

Entered as second-class matter February 13, 1918, at the post office at Athol, Mass.

Published Bi-monthly for the Association by

W. Paul Cook, Official Publisher, 451 Main Street, Athol, Mass.

Vol. 18 **July, 1919** **No. 6**